Dr Ken Paige

BEHAVIORAL ACCOUNTING

GARY SIEGEL
Associate Professor
School of Accountancy
DePaul University

HELENE RAMANAUSKAS-MARCONI
Professor
School of Accountancy
DePaul University

A65
PUBLISHED BY
SOUTH-WESTERN PUBLISHING CO.
CINCINNATI   WEST CHICAGO, IL   CARROLLTON, TX   LIVERMORE, CA

Copyright ©1989
by South-Western Publishing Co.
Cincinnati, Ohio

ISBN: 0-538-01650-7

Library of Congress Catalog Card Number: 87-61569

1 2 3 4 5 6 7 D 4 3 2 1 0 9 8

Printed in the United States of America

Preface

This book describes the relationship between the accounting system, human behavior, and organizational efficiency. It is written for an audience of students and business people. The book is intentionally descriptive. There are no rigorous quantitative applications or complex statistical discussions.

Each substantive chapter begins with a business dilemma. After discussion of the relevant behavioral science concepts that bear on the dilemma, a diagnostic review of the dilemma pinpoints important concepts for consideration and offers solutions. This approach is intended to demonstrate the practical applications of behavioral accounting. The book includes examples, cases, discussion questions, references, and appendicies. A teacher's manual is also available.

BEHAVIORAL ACCOUNTING

Behavioral accounting is an area of accounting that has slowly but steadily grown over the past 25 years. An increasing number of journal articles deal with behavioral topics, and many textbooks include some mention of behavioral accounting. More and more schools offer courses in behavioral accounting, and a growing segment of accounting students and professors focus their research on the behavioral dimensions of accounting. Interested academicians have formed a Behavioral Accounting Section within the American Accounting Association and have established two journals, one devoted solely and one partially, to behavioral accounting topics.

While managerial accounting, cost accounting, and budgeting textbooks mention the behavioral aspects of accounting, and may even have one chapter that describes behavioral accounting, they do not provide interested readers with complete coverage. This book aims to fill that gap; it is the first comprehensive textbook/handbook in behavioral accounting to be published, and is a needed complement to the several monographs and books of readings on behavioral topics that are available. Each of the existing monographs and books of readings addresses a small portion of the broad scope of behavioral accounting; this book covers most major areas. Depending on the functional orientation of the instructor, business person, or other user, outside readings emphasizing specific topics in behavioral accounting may be used as supplementary sources.

AUDIENCE

The primary audience for this textbook is students enrolled in behavioral accounting courses that are offered at the advanced undergraduate and graduate levels of colleges and universities.

The book is also intended for decision makers and for managers responsible for leading and motivating. It could be used by practitioners who are members of such organizations as the National Association of Accountants (NAA), Financial Executives Institute (FEI), the Planning Forum (PF), etc. It applies to both profit-oriented and not-for-profit organizations.

The book can also be used as a supplementary text in accounting courses dealing with budgeting, international accounting, and decision theory, as well as in management, engineering, or other business courses concerned with operations, production controls, information theory, planning and control. In all these courses repeated reference is made to the importance of the human factor in business operations. A supplementary book like this one, that offers practical examples of the interrelationship between accounting control systems, human behavior, and productivity will benefit students, instructors, and practitioners.

People using the book should have an understanding of basic accounting and management concepts and principles, and have some exposure to the behavioral sciences.

ACKNOWLEDGEMENTS

We applaud the people at South-Western Publishing Company for their commitment to professional accountancy as evidenced by their decision to publish this book. We are also grateful to the pioneers in the field of behavioral accounting for contributing chapters to this text. A heartfelt "thank you" is offered to the DePaul MBA students who pretested this textbook in the Behavioral Accountancy course. Finally, we thank the School of Accountancy at DePaul University for the support they provided.

Helene Ramanauskas-Marconi
Gary Siegel

CONTRIBUTING AUTHORS

Shahid Ansari, California State University, Northridge; George A. Barnett, State University of New York at Buffalo; Robert Chatfield, Texas Tech University; Donald K. Clancy, Texas Tech University; Frank Collins, University of Miami; Eric Flamholtz, University of California at Los Angeles; Martin Freedman, State University of New York at Binghamton; William T. Geary, College of William and Mary; Kenneth Merchant, Harvard University Graduate School of Business Administration; Denise Nitterhouse, DePaul University; W. Peter Salzarulo, Miami University, Oxford, Ohio; Donald S. Shannon, DePaul University; William Thomas Stevens, Pace University.

CONTENTS

PART ONE

Foundations of
Behavioral Accounting

CHAPTER 1

Introduction to
Behavioral Accounting

A 1984 profile of New York Governor Mario M. Cuomo[1] described the behind-the-scene activities preceding the governor's first budget meeting. Taxes had to be raised to reduce a nearly $300 million excess of spending over revenues. Cuomo had promised voters that he would not raise any of the "big three" taxes: individual income, corporate, or sales tax. The governor's advisers presented about 40 revenue options but privately urged Cuomo to raise the sales tax. Mr. Cuomo later explained to a visitor that his advisers were "budgeteers; they don't understand psychology." While an increase in one or more of the big three taxes would be simpler to collect, it would retard the image of stability that Cuomo wanted to create and tarnish Cuomo's credibility with his constituency.

If Mr. Cuomo's meeting were to be held today—with a new generation of advisers trained in behavioral accounting—he would not make the statement that "they don't understand psychology." Behavioral accounting is the interface of accounting and social science. It is concerned with how human behavior influences accounting data and business decisions and with how accounting information affects business decisions and human behavior.

THE TRADITIONAL
ROLE OF ACCOUNTING

Accounting is a service discipline whose function is to provide relevant and timely information about the financial affairs of businesses and not-for-profit entities to assist internal and external users in making economic decisions. *Internal users* of accounting information are the organization's own line and staff personnel, who view accounting reports as the foundation on which financing, investing, and operating decisions are made. *External users* include such groups as stockholders, creditors, labor unions, financial analysts, and government agencies. These seemingly diverse groups have in common a keen interest in the financial affairs of business enterprises and not-for-profit organizations.

A distinction is made between financial accounting and management accounting. The emphasis in *financial accounting* is on reporting to external users. The information presented is governed by Generally Accepted Accounting Principles (GAAP)—the rules that prescribe the manner of presentation and the method of computation.

Management accounting (or managerial accounting) is concerned with internal reporting. The information presented to managers is not bound by GAAP. Rather, it is governed by the information needs of the decision maker.

Behavioral accounting is the third major branch of accounting. It is concerned with the relationship between human behavior and the accounting system. Its domain includes both financial and managerial accounting.

The Accounting Information System

Accounting is called the language of business because it measures and communicates financial and other information about people, organizations, social programs, government activities, and business ventures to decision makers.

Accounting can also be viewed as an information system. In most organizations, accounting is the major quantitative information system. The accounting system receives information from the environment (the firm, government agencies, suppliers, customers, etc.), measures the information, records it, processes it, and issues reports back to the environment. People act on the basis of the accounting reports. The results of some of these actions, in turn, are received, measured, recorded, and processed by the accounting system.

Accounting information systems are built around the particular structure and business activities of the organization. A well-designed system includes procedures for measuring, recording, and summarizing economic events; it provides internal controls designed to safeguard assets and promote operational efficiency; and it permits the retrieval of relevant data for internal or external reporting.

Where Accountants Work

Accountants work in business firms, not-for-profit organizations, or in public accounting firms.

Accountants who work in business or not-for-profit organizations are responsible for the design and maintenance of the accounting information system, financial planning and control, and the production of reports for both internal and external users. The reports to internal users provide information needed to maintain and improve operational efficiency and profitability, develop organizational policies and plans, and make nonroutine decisions.

Business and not-for-profit organizations engage public accounting firms to conduct an independent *audit* of their financial records. An audit involves the examination of information presented in financial statements. Based on the results of the examination, the public accounting firm issues an audit report, which expresses an opinion on the "fairness" of presentation of the financial statements. All states require that the report be signed by a *certified public accountant* (CPA). Public accounting firms also provide their business and not-for-profit clients with tax, accounting, and management consulting services.

CPAs who work in public accounting are considered to be "independent" of their clients. While they have a responsibility to their clients, CPAs also have a responsibility to the external users of publicly reported financial information. This responsibility is manifest in the *attest function*, whereby the CPA expresses an opinion on the fairness of presentation of publicly reported financial data. It is important to note that the opinion does not certify or guarantee the accuracy or reliability of the data.

The attest function is of paramount importance to external users because it lends credence to, and promotes public confidence in, published financial reports. Since publicly reported financial statements are used by outsiders as a basis for major economic decisions, and since these statements are usually the only financial and operating information available to outsiders, the need for the attest function is evident. Its importance to public confidence in reported financial data and to the smooth functioning of the economy can hardly be overstated.

THE BEHAVIORAL DIMENSION OF ACCOUNTING

Accounting has traditionally focused on the reporting of financial information only. Over the last several decades, however, managers and professional accountants have recognized the need for additional quantifiable economic information not presently generated by the accounting system or reported in the financial statements. It is believed that such additional quantifiable economic information, not necessarily financial in nature, would lend more meaning to the data presently reported and therefore allow for more-informed decision making. Part of the nonfinancial, quantifiable information meant to complement the financial data falls into the area of behavioral accounting: the subfield of accounting that integrates the human behavioral dimension with traditional accounting.

Definition and Scope

Behavioral accounting goes beyond the traditional accounting role of collecting, measuring, recording, and reporting financial information. It is that dimension of accounting concerned with human behavior and its relationship with the design, construction, and use of an efficient accounting information system. Behavioral accounting, by considering the relationship between human behavior and the accounting system, reflects the social dimension of an organization and becomes, thereby, a vital supplement to the financial information that accountants currently report.

The scope of behavioral accounting is quite broad. It includes: the application of behavioral science concepts to the design and construction of accounting systems; the study of human reaction to the format and content of accounting reports; the ways in which information is processed for decision making; the development of reporting techniques to communicate behavioral data to users; and the development of strategies to motivate and influence the behavior, aspirations, and goals of the people who run the organization. The scope of behavioral accounting can be broken down into three general areas:

1. *The effect of human behavior on the design, construction, and use of the accounting system.* This area of behavioral accounting is concerned with how the attitudes and philosophies of management affect the nature of accounting controls and the functioning of the organization. For example, managers who are averse to risk will demand different types of financial control systems than managers who are more inclined to take risks. Thus, the looseness or rigidity of accounting controls are influenced by human behavior.

   Similarly, interaction patterns within the firm lead to development of a group perspective toward the accounting system. This perspective is characterized by worker attitudes toward the control system, their behaviors in operating the system, and the consistency of enforcement.

2. *The effect of the accounting system on human behavior.* This area of behavioral accounting is concerned with how the accounting system affects motivation, productivity, decision making, job satisfaction, and cooperation. For example, a budget that is too "tight" may lead people to believe that the goals are not attainable and that there is no sense in trying to achieve them. A budget that is too "loose" may result in carelessness and inefficiencies in production.

3. *Methods to predict and strategies to change human behavior.* This third area of behavioral accounting is concerned with how the accounting system can be used to influence behavior. For example, the accounting control structure can be tightened or loosened, compensation plans can be altered, or performance evaluation reports can be modified.

Applications of Behavioral Accounting

The economic and human benefits of recognizing the behavioral aspects of accounting are numerous. The following decision situations delineate some of them.

Company X, after a careful cost-benefit analysis, concludes that a new accounting information system should be installed. How should that decision be implemented? Can the firm simply buy the hardware, develop the software, train its work force, and watch expenses dwindle? Or will the company, after buying the hardware, developing the software, and training its work force, later discover that the system does not work as anticipated because of employee resistance to change?

Research suggests that if the behavioral aspects of such decisions are not investigated thoroughly, and if immediate corrective action is not taken when dysfunctional attitudes are detected, the second alternative is the more likely outcome.

In such a case, managers who are aware of the behavioral aspects of accounting would call for an investigation of how people view the innovation, whether they favor or oppose it, and what their fears about it are. The investigation should also ascertain whether or not people have misinformation or misconceptions about the system, how they perceive their roles in operating it, and how they are likely to react if the system is installed. Further, the behavioral accountant should determine whether people's apprehensions about the system are based on real security issues (e.g., compensation or job security) or simply reflect fear of the unknown.

If people have no fear of the system and eagerly anticipate its installation, management may then proceed with its plan, relatively confident that human problems will not preclude expected results. If, however, people fear and resist the innovation, management must discover the basis of these attitudes and determine how people's outlooks can be changed so that the installation of the new system will be successful.

Consider the behavioral implications of the following situation.

A few years ago, Company Y adopted a new standard cost system and instituted a formal budgeting process. The objective was to increase productivity and improve cost control. Each year, however, actual operating results deviated widely from planned, or "budgeted," results. Are these problems due to unrealistic budgets? Or can the deviations be traced to the employees who are responsible for achieving budgeted goals?

If it is determined that employee attitudes and behavior are responsible for the budget problems, Company Y should investigate the behavioral aspects of this situation. Questions such as the following would have to be answered: How do people currently behave during the budget-making process? Are they constructively and harmoniously relating to each other? How do employees perceive the process as a whole, their roles in it, and their individual goals in relation to organizational goals? A behavioral accountant would also want to know the cause of the attitudes and behavior and the likelihood that the same behavior will be repeated in the future. Obviously, if the undesirable behavior is likely to be repeated, thus perpetuating inefficiencies in the budget-making process, the behavioral accountant would suggest strategies to change existing behavior to make it compatible with smooth organizational functioning.

The next situation highlights the incompleteness of the information contained in traditional external and internal accounting reports. Although the additional information called for in the following example is more likely to be reported internally to top management or to the board of directors of an organization, there have been suggestions to expand the scope of the auditor's attest function to include such information in financial reports to outside users.

> Companies Z-1 and Z-2 are similar in financial structure, earnings history, and relative market shares in their industry. Even the most careful scrutiny of their financial statements will not provide any clues as to which firm is the better investment alternative, because the financial statements themselves emphasize the similarities between the firms. How can a potential investor who is concerned with the future prospects of these companies make an informed investment decision?

In such a situation, additional information, nonfinancial in nature, about the firms may help prospective investors make rational choices. Part of this nonfinancial information might be behavioral and might indicate, for example, that Z-1's work force is enthusiastic and highly motivated and that absenteeism is very low. In firm Z-2, on the other hand, the work force is characterized by low morale, high absenteeism, and excessive turnover. The behavioral accountant might also provide information on the differences in management styles of the two companies. It could be useful for potential investors to know something about the risk perceptions, economic outlooks, experience, and backgrounds of the two management teams.

The behavioral accountant's tasks in this situation are to investigate how people currently behave and how they view their work, their firm, and their co-workers. It is then up to the users of this behavioral information to make their own assessments of how people are likely to behave in the future and how these behavior patterns will affect the relative potential future earnings of each company. For internal purposes, the behavioral accountant would provide management not only with information about how people behave, but also with the reasons why people behave as they do and recommendations for changing behavior that is dysfunctional.

The preceding three examples demonstrate that the goal of behavioral accounting is to measure and evaluate relevant behavioral factors and communicate the results to internal and external decision makers. Without such information, accounting reports are incomplete, and decision makers are not being provided with all relevant data. Information on the behavioral dimension of the firm complements the financial data and provides economic decision makers with a more well-rounded view of the organization.

Behavioral Accounting: A Logical Extension of Accounting's Traditional Role

Decision makers who use accounting reports are better informed when those reports contain as much relevant information as possible. Accountants acknowledge this fact through a time-honored accounting principle known as *full disclosure*. This principle requires not only supplementary explanations and additional details supporting the reported financial data, but also the reporting and explanation of critical nonfinancial organizational events. This additional information is reported either within the framework of the financial statements or in notes accompanying the statements.

To further sharpen the economic picture of a firm, a logical and necessary application of the full disclosure principle would require the inclusion of behavioral information to supplement the financial and other data presently reported. It would be difficult to argue convincingly that decision makers would not be interested in and benefit from access to such additional relevant information. In fact, behavioral information about major business organizations is standard fare in the business press. Business newspapers, newsletters, and magazines frequently report on existing managerial philosophies in particular firms, the morale of middle-level managers, the relative success of innovative approaches to management or operations, and the effects of managerial activities and outlooks on such topics as operations, earnings, labor negotiations, and work force attitudes. The business press also reports on the implications of these behavioral phenomena for future organizational success.

These reporting practices indicate an interest in and a demand for behavioral data. Unfortunately, the behavioral information reported in the business press is not yet presented in a way that allows for meaningful interfirm (i.e., Company X vs. Company Y) and intrafirm (i.e., Division A vs. Division B in Company Z) comparison. Advances in measurement techniques in the behavioral sciences now permit more accurate measurement of behavioral processes and allow accountants to expand the reporting function to include the behavioral dimension of organizations.

Few would argue with the assertion that information on the behavioral dimension of organizations is useful to a variety of internal and external decision makers. Open to discussion, however, is whether accountants should assume the task of such investigating and reporting. There are many other professions that may lay claim to the domain of measuring and reporting behavioral phenomena. Sociologists and industrial psychologists, for example, have worked in this area for decades. Market research firms and survey research methodologists regularly measure certain aspects of behavior and report the results to their clients. The list of professionals engaged in these activities could go on.

The accountant's claim to the investigation of behavioral phenomena is based on the nature of accounting; it always has been and still is an organization's major information system. The accounting information system reports on the organization's economic activities, of which the behavioral phenomenon is but one dimension. Accountants might claim that through centuries of experience they have become familiar with the information needs of both outside users and internal managers, the process of business decision making, and the kinds of financial data and reports that are relevant to various types of decision situations. Therefore, accountants would be most qualified to select behavioral phenomena for investigation because they know which behavioral data would most meaningfully supplement financial data. Further, accountants are the single group that could most logically incorporate the behavioral information into the existing business reports.

It should be emphasized, however, that accountants are not rigorously trained behavioral scientists. A course in behavioral accounting, along with three or four behavioral science courses, will provide accountants with a basic working knowledge of behavioral science concepts, an appreciation for the potential and limitations of behavioral science applications in accounting, and the ability to recognize quality research. A few behavioral science courses, however, do not make an accountant a behavioral scientist, just as three or four accounting courses do not make a person an accountant. Therefore, accountants who are interested in working in the behavioral area should consult with competent behavioral science researchers when designing behavioral research projects and analyzing their results.

HISTORICAL DEVELOPMENT OF BEHAVIORAL ACCOUNTING

The accounting profession's awareness of and interest in the behavioral aspects of the discipline began to develop in the early 1950s. In June 1951, the Controllership Foundation of America sponsored a research study that explored the impact of budgets on people. The study was carried out under the direction of the School of Business and Public Administration of Cornell University. Professor Schuyler Dean Holett was the project director and Professor Chris Argyris the research associate in charge of the field work. This exploratory research resulted in a number of tentative conclusions about the behavioral pitfalls in budgets and budgeting and in numerous thought-provoking suggestions for possible remedies.

The research was then used by Chris Argyris as the foundation for the 1953 landmark *Harvard Business Review* article, "Human Problems with Budgets"[2], which introduced the problem area, and with it accounting's behavioral dimension, to a broader business audience. Of considerable interest is the fact that both of these events preceded the works of Maslow[3], McGregor[4], and Likert[5], which many consider to be the pioneering studies of behavioral science applications in business.

Beginning in the late 1960s and continuing into the 1980s, increasing numbers of behavioral articles have appeared in professional accounting journals. These articles are quite diverse. Early articles attempted to define behavioral accounting; later articles discussed certain behavioral science concepts and theories in terms of their relevance to accounting and their implications for accounting principles and practices. Some articles dealt with the effects of the accounting system and accounting reports on decision making; still others reported the results of behavioral experiments in an effort to learn about the relationship between the accounting system and improvements to organizational effectiveness and efficiency.

The impetus to behavioral accounting has come chiefly from the academic branch of the accounting profession. Practically all of the behavioral studies have been published in academic journals and authored by academicians. These studies have produced interesting insights into the nature and causes of human behavior and may have influenced the way practicing accountants design their information systems. It is very likely that behavioral accounting research will have considerable impact on accounting theories and practices in the future.

Workshops, conferences, and symposiums on behavioral accounting are frequently held throughout the United States and Canada. Innovative courses in behavioral accounting are slowly being introduced into the curriculums of major universities. A bimonthly journal, *Accounting, Organizations, and Society*, was established in 1976 as an outlet for academic research for scholars engaged in the study of behavioral accounting. Within the past few years, a new special-interest subsection of accountants interested in behavioral accounting was established and officially recognized by the American Accounting Association. This special-interest section is sponsoring a second behavioral accounting journal to be called *Behavioral Research in Accounting*.

All of these events indicate that behavioral accounting is not a passing fad; the accounting profession's awareness of and interest in the behavioral dimension are here to stay. This development presents the potential for dramatic changes in the scope of accounting services and the future information content of accounting reports. These events also compelled the writing of this behavioral textbook.

FORMAT OF THE BOOK

The book is divided into three parts. The chapters in Part One, "Foundations of Behavioral Accounting," provide background material in the behavioral sciences and familiarize the reader with the historical and contemporary behavioral assumptions of accounting and related business disciplines. In Part One, the role and function of the behavioral aspects of accounting will be delineated.

Part Two, "Behavioral Implications of Management Accounting," concentrates on major operational activities, such as planning, controlling, and decision making. The chapters in Part Two highlight the applications and implications of behavioral accounting in such operational activities as budgeting, internal communications, centralized and decentralized performance measurement, internal control, and auditing. These chapters emphasize the importance of recognizing various behavioral considerations when designing and implementing a cost accumulation system, choosing a transfer price, setting performance standards, or trying to overcome employee resistance to change.

The chapters in Part Three, "Behavioral Aspects of Financial Accounting and Reporting," create an awareness of the behavioral aspects of generally accepted accounting concepts and principles and how they affect management decisions and behavior. The behavioral ramifications of accounting as an organization's information and communication system are discussed. The topics of human resource accounting and social accounting are also introduced.

The chapters themselves are built around the three elements that make up the scope of behavioral accounting: how people affect the accounting system, how the system affects people, and how dysfunctional behavior can be corrected. The chapters in Parts Two and Three begin with a hypothetical organizational dilemma, proceed with the introduction of the relevant behavioral concepts, and conclude with the application of those concepts to the resolution of the dilemma. Suggested readings, discussion questions, and cases are included at the end of each chapter. Technical terms are defined throughout the book in the chapters in which they appear.

REFERENCES

[1] *New Yorker*, April 16, 1984, pp. 53–56.

[2] Argyris, Chris. "Human Problems with Budgets." *Harvard Business Review*, January-February 1953.

[3] Maslow, Abraham H. *Motivation and Personality*. New York: Harper & Row, 1954.

[4] McGregor, Douglas. *The Human Side of Enterprise*. New York: McGraw-Hill, 1960.

[5] Likert, Rensis. *New Patterns in Management*. New York: McGraw-Hill, 1961.

SUGGESTED READINGS

Caplan, Edwin H. *Management Accounting and Behavioral Science*. Reading, Mass: Addison-Wesley, 1971.

Collins, Frank, Paul Munter, and Don W. Finn. "The Budgeting Games People Play." *Accounting Review*, January 1987, pp. 29–49.

Libby, Robert, and Barry L. Lewis. "Human Information Processing Research in Accounting: The State of the Art in 1982." *Accounting, Organizations, and Society*, 1982, pp. 231–285.

Schiff, Michael and Arie Y. Lewin. *Behavioral Aspects of Accounting*. Englewood Cliffs, N.J.: Prentice-Hall, 1974.

Young, Mark S., "The Organizational Context of Accounting." *Accounting, Organizations, and Society*, Q 1983, pp. 111–129.

DISCUSSION QUESTIONS

1. What behavioral information would be relevant to investment bankers? To bank loan officers? To mutual fund managers? To a chief negotiator for a labor union? How might this behavioral data be used?

2. Why should accountants concern themselves with reporting behavioral information, since it may already be reported by journalists, industrial psychologists, or survey researchers?

3. Given that accountants are not rigorously trained in the behavioral sciences, how much credence can be placed in behavioral information measured and reported by accountants?

4. Give some examples of behavioral information reported in a recent business newspaper or magazine.

5. How do you see behavioral accounting developing over the next five or ten years?

CHAPTER 2

A Survey
of Behavioral Science
Concepts and Perspectives

SCOPE AND OBJECTIVES OF
BEHAVIORAL SCIENCE

In their 1971 report, the American Accounting Association's Committee on the Behavioral Science Content of the Accounting Curriculum developed the following definition and scope of "behavioral science":

> The term behavioral science is of a relatively recent coinage. The concept is so broad that it is desirable at the outset to attempt to delineate its scope and content. Behavioral science encompasses any field of inquiry that studies, by experimental and observational methods, the behavior of man in the physical and social environment.
>
> To be considered a part of behavioral science, research must satisfy two basic criteria. First, it must ultimately deal with human behavior. The primary aim of behavioral science is to identify underlying regularities in human behavior—both similarities and differences—and to determine what consequences follow from them. Second, the research must be accomplished in a "scientific manner." This means there must be a systematic attempt to describe, interrelate, explain, and hence predict some set of phenomena; that is, the underlying regularities in human behavior must be observable or lead to observable effects.
>
> The objective of behavioral science is to understand, explain and predict human behavior . . . to establish generalizations about human behavior that are supported by empirical evidence collected in an impersonal way by procedures that are completely open to review and replication and capable of verification by other interested scholars. Behavioral science, thus, represents the systematic observation of man's behavior for the purpose of experimentally confirming specific hypotheses by reference to observable changes in behavior.[1]

A more concise definition of behavioral science was offered by Bernard Berelson and G.A. Steiner: "scientific research that deals directly with human behavior."[2] This definition captures the essence of the lengthier one above and describes the two most salient features of behavioral science: scientific research and human behavior.

Behavioral science is the "human side" of social science. Social science includes the disciplines of anthropology, economics, history, political science, psychology, and sociology. Behavioral science includes psychology and sociology, the behavioral aspects of economics and political science (e.g., consumer behavior and voter behavior), and the behavioral aspects of anthropology (areas such as archaeology, technical linguistics, and physical anthropology would be excluded).

While only a subset of social science, behavioral science is itself quite broad. Several journals publish articles on behavioral research methods, theory development, practical applications, and descriptions of human behavior in various settings. Thousands of research findings are added annually to the store of behavioral science knowledge. Consequently, professional behavioral scientists are able to keep abreast of current literature in only a few subareas in their disciplines. This has resulted in a high degree of specialization among behavioral scientists. Because behavioral science is so broad, this chapter can present only an overview of the discipline. The chapter does not contain a complete list of all behavioral concepts, nor are any of the concepts discussed here presented in all their completeness or complexity. The purpose of this chapter is to introduce the behavioral concepts that we believe to be most relevant to behavioral accounting. These concepts are presented concisely and in nontechnical terms so that their essence and their applications to behavioral accounting will become apparent.

SCOPE AND OBJECTIVES OF BEHAVIORAL ACCOUNTING

In the past, accountants were concerned solely with measuring revenue and cost and studying a firm's past performance in an effort to predict the future. They ignored the fact that past performance was the result of past human behavior and that past performance itself is a factor that will influence future behavior. They overlooked the fact that any meaningful control of an organization must begin with motivating and controlling the behavior, goals, and aspirations of the individuals who interact within the organization.

Behavioral accountants focus on the relationship between human behavior and the accounting system. They realize that the accounting process involves summarizing huge numbers of economic events that are the result of human behavior and that accounting measurements themselves are among the factors that affect behavior, which in turn determines the success of those economic events. Thus, some would describe accounting as, in essence, a behavioral process.

Behavioral accountants look beyond the technical reality of company sales and consider the behavior of clerks who record customer telephone orders; beyond construction costs to the structural engineers who review architectural plans; beyond manufacturing costs to the factory supervisors who explain the proper use of machine tools to new employees. Behavioral accountants must keep in mind that whether or not those performing the work are aware of it, their activities are necessary for organizational survival and their behavior at work is tied in several ways to the accounting system. The results of employees' actions are quantified and translated into monetary terms: Their salaries are considered costs of doing business, and their accomplishments are necessary steps in the process of earning revenue. Actual operating results are compared to predetermined standards for work performance. All of these events are duly recorded in the accounting system. If accounting reports indicate success in meeting the established goals, the work force is rewarded. If the reports indicate failure in meeting standards, the ultimate individual penalty is loss of one's job.

Behavioral accountants also realize that they can deliberately design information systems to influence employee motivation, morale, and productivity. Their responsibility goes beyond simple data measurement and data aggregation to include the perception and use of accounting reports by others. Behavioral accountants believe that a major purpose of accounting reports is to influence behavior in order to motivate desirable actions. For example, a firm may have been successful in meeting its budget because of good organizational teamwork, or it may have been unsuccessful because people were working toward conflicting goals. As a result, the format and content of the budget reports may have spurred employee productivity and caused people to work together, or they may have created internal conflict and stifled individual initiative. Recognition of the interrelationship between accounting measurements and behavior has resulted in a modification of conventional definitions of accounting. The most recent definitions of accounting in academic and professional circles include or imply the measurement and communication of economic data for various decision making and other behavioral objectives. For example, in his 1986 financial accounting textbook, Professor Belverd E. Needles, Jr. traces the evolution of accounting's definition from an early focus on recordkeeping to a modern definition that stresses the communication of economic information to decision makers. Needles concludes that "business activities are the input to the accounting system, and useful information for decision makers is the output."[3]

The introduction of behavioral science to accounting is an important in the development of the profession. It has opened a new body of knowledge with which accounting professionals should be familiar. In turn, the awareness of the relationship between human behavior and accounting has provided accountants with yet another tool for assessing and solving organizational problems.

BEHAVIORAL SCIENCE AND BEHAVIORAL ACCOUNTING: THEIR SIMILARITIES AND DIFFERENCES

Behavioral science is concerned with the explanation and prediction of human behavior. Behavioral accounting is concerned with the relationship between human behavior and accounting. Behavioral accountants ask: "What effect does the accounting process have upon individual and collective behavior, and what effect does human behavior have on the accounting process?" Behavioral accountants are also interested in how these effects can be altered by changes in the manner in which accounting is carried out and how accounting reports and procedures can be used most effectively to help individuals and organizations attain their goals.

While behavioral science is a subset of social science, behavioral accounting is a subset of both accounting and behavioral science. That is, *behavioral scientists* may engage in research on any aspect of motivation theory, social stratification, or attitude formation. *Behavioral accountants,* however, would apply only the specific elements of these theories or research results that are relevant to the accounting situation at hand. Behavioral accountants do not engage in theoretical speculation on interesting but unrelated behavioral issues. For example, a cultural anthropologist might study differential behavior patterns of people who live in primitive matriarchal or patriarchal societies. A behavioral accountant would not study such an issue, simply because it is beyond the boundaries of accounting. However, should any findings of the anthropological study prove relevant to explaining the relationship between people and the accounting system, they would surely be taken into consideration by behavioral accountants.

By its very nature, behavioral accounting, like its parent discipline—accounting—is applied and practical. It uses research results from its other parent—behavioral science—to explain and predict human behavior. Accounting has always used concepts, principles, and approaches from other disciplines to improve its utility. For example, accounting borrows freely from economics, mathematics, statistics, and information engineering. Therefore, it is not unusual that accounting also borrows from the behavioral sciences.

A reasonable question at this point would be: Is a behavioral accountant in reality an applied behavioral scientist? It is true that the work of behavioral accountants and applied behavioral scientists do overlap in some areas. Both groups use established sociological or psychological principles to assess and resolve organizational problems. Certain aspects of the sociology of organizations, industrial psychology, role theory, or learning theory would attract the attention of both behavioral accountants and applied behavioral scientists. However, there are significant distinctions between the two groups in terms of their objectives, focus, education, expertise, and functions.

The differences between behavioral accountants and applied behavioral scientists outweigh their surface similarities. Accounting is a profession, and those who aspire to become accountants are trained to think and act as professionals. This training is different from that experienced by those seeking to become scientists. Some specific differences between behavioral accountants and applied behavioral scientists that flow from their divergent educational backgrounds are shown in Table 2-1.

Using Table 2-1 as a guide, we can see that while behavioral accountants and applied behavioral scientists might be equally capable of approaching an accounting-related organizational dilemma, they would play different, yet complementary, roles in resolving it. The behavioral accountant would best understand the structure and function of the accounting system and peoples' relationship to it. The behavioral scientist would have greater insight into the overall organizational dynamics and the development of behavior patterns. Together, they can define the problem and develop a strategy to gather the necessary evidence. They could also cooperate in the choice of research methods, in the analysis of data, and in the writing of reports. The views of the behavioral scientist should dominate when it comes to research methods. In addition, the behavioral scientist would be more capable of analyzing technical social science data. The portion of the data that concerns the accounting system and the implications for operational efficiency would clearly be in the domain of the behavioral accountant. The report to management should generally be prepared by the accountant, because accountants are more familiar with the perspectives, needs, and jargon of the users of accounting information.

PERSPECTIVES ON HUMAN BEHAVIOR: PSYCHOLOGY, SOCIOLOGY, AND SOCIAL PSYCHOLOGY

The three major contributors to behavioral science knowledge are psychology, sociology, and social psychology. All seek to describe and explain human behavior, but they differ in their overall perspective on the human condition. *Psychology* is primarily interested in how the individual behaves. The focus is on the actions of people as they respond to stimuli in their environment,

TABLE 2-1

Some Differences between Behavioral Accountants and Applied Behavioral Scientists

Differences	Behavioral Accountants	Applied Behavioral Scientists
Area of expertise	Primarily accounting; basic knowledge of social science	Primarily social science; no knowledge of accounting
Ability to design and execute behavior research projects	Not a major element in training	Key element in training
Knowledge and understanding of the workings of business organizations in general and accounting systems in particular	Key element in training	Not a major element in training
Orientation	Professional	Scientific
Approach to problems	Practical	Theoretical and practical
Function	Serve clients; advise management	Advance science and solve problems
Interest in behavioral science	Limited to accounting-related areas	Limited to broad subdisciplines in behavioral science

and human behavior is explained in terms of individual traits, drives, and motives. The emphasis is on the person as an organism.

Sociology and *social psychology*, on the other hand, focus on group, or social, behavior. Their emphasis is on the interactions between people, not on physical stimuli. Behavior is explained in terms of social relations, social influences, and group dynamics. An attempt is made to understand how a person's thoughts, feelings, and actions are influenced by the actual, imagined, or implied presence of others. The emphasis is on the person as part of a social system.

There are many complex factors that influence human behavior, including individual needs and motivations, group pressures, organizational demands, the personal histories and unique backgrounds of individuals, conflicting messages from inside and outside the organization, time demands, personal and social responsibilities, and so on. These factors may be clustered into three major categories: character structure, social structure, and group dynamics.

Character structure refers to the personality traits, habits, and behavior patterns of individuals. Psychologists are generally associated with the study of character structure. *Social structure* refers to any system of relationships among people, including the economic, political, military, and religious institutional frameworks that define acceptable behavior, control behavior, and perpetuate social order. This is the domain of sociologists. *Group dynamics* can be viewed as a synthesis or combination of character structure and social structure: It refers to the development of human interaction patterns, the process of social interaction, and the results of that interaction. Social psychologists engage in the study of group dynamics.

Sociologists, social psychologists, and psychologists, despite their differences in perspective, study many of the same topics. For example, in explaining the behavior of the corporate controller, psychologists would focus on the individual's personality traits, pressures, anxiety, expectations, and motivations. In contrast, sociologists and social psychologists would focus on social structure, socialization, group memberships, roles, norms, and communication patterns.

Sociologists contend that people cannot be taken out of their social contexts. People learn the most basic skills—for example, language or eating—from other people. We respond to stimuli—for example, red or green traffic lights—based on social conditioning, and our responses to these stimuli are usually the same whether or not other people are present. All human knowledge is passed from one generation to the next through various social institutions such as the family, school, church, or peer group. People develop beliefs and opinions based on ideas and information passed along by others. There are myriad social forces that act on a person to create a truly social being.

Psychologists would counter that despite social influences, each individual is unique. Similar social backgrounds may produce people who differ in their personality traits, their level of conformity to social rules, their outlooks on life, or their value systems. Some psychologists might argue that the group is a mirage; actions of individuals create a group dynamic.

Thus, it is possible to explain human behavior by adopting either a psychological or sociological approach, or by some combination of the two. Within both psychology and sociology, there are additional competing frameworks with which to explain human behavior. For example, some sociologists are "symbolic interactionists" and explain behavior based on shared meanings that help people determine how they should act in different situations. Other sociologists are "structuralists" and look to social institutions and established rules of interaction for explaining behavior. Within psychology, there are "psychotherapists," who seek to understand behavior in order to change it, and "behaviorists," who are concerned with finding methods to change behavior without necessarily understanding the cause. Among the psychotherapists, one may adopt a Freudian, Jungian, Rogerian, or Adlerian perspective (these schools of thought are based on ideas of their founders). Further, there are orthodox Freudians and neo-Freudians.

One can also explain behavior in terms of heredity, social environment, tension reduction, or rational decision making. There are different opinions on the relative importance of ideas, economic conditions, or neurological impulses in shaping behavior. Each of these competing viewpoints has considerable scientific support.

In this text, we take the position that all of these frameworks contain an element of truth and that we can learn from each of them. We do not advocate any single framework, because each explains some aspect of human behavior but cannot explain everything. For this reason, and because behavioral accounting is an applied, practical science, we believe that behavioral accountants should be flexible. If practicing behavioral scientists cannot agree on a single framework with which to view the human condition, it would be highly presumptuous for accountants to argue for one best approach. Rather than adhere to a single model or framework for explaining behavior, behavioral accountants should use the framework that best explains the peculiarities of the behavior exhibited in a particular situation. This approach is most compatible with the function of behavioral accounting.

ORGANIZATIONAL INFLUENCES ON BEHAVIOR

People work within the confines of organizations. Their behavior is affected by many factors, including organizational size and structure. Management leadership styles or philosophies, authority/responsibility relationships, status relationships, and group norms also affect behavior and organizational functioning.

People in the organization exchange information through either "official" or "unofficial" channels. The information may be accurate, distorted, or false. Based on the information that people receive and process, decisions are made and attitudes are formed. For example, the "official" information channels may state that hard work and steady progress ensure job security and promotion. The "unofficial" information channels may indicate otherwise. Decisions based on distorted or false information may lead to the formation of work attitudes and attitudes toward the organization and its leadership that are not conducive to operational efficiency.

We will discuss some behavioral science concepts by examining a hypothetical business firm from the point of view of the vice-president of finance, who is in charge of all aspects of financial planning and control.

The partial organizational chart in Figure 2-1 indicates that the vice-president of finance occupies a particular position, or office, in the organization. A position in a social hierarchy is called a "status," which implies inferior and superior places on a vertical scale. The term "status" is often used with respect to other hierarchies, such as income, education, and prestige.

FIGURE 2–1
Organization Chart

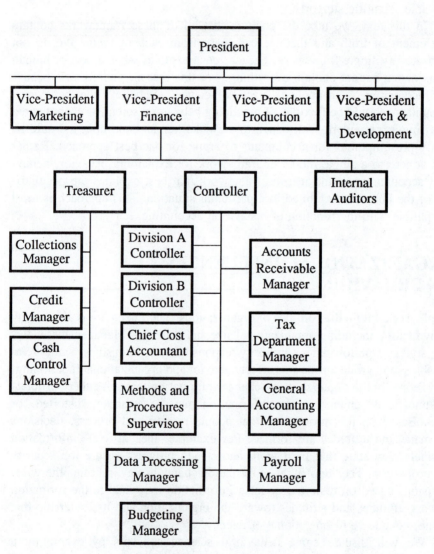

Each position in an organization is occupied by a person whose duties and responsibilities are clearly defined, usually in writing. As such, a clear-cut division of labor exists. Those who occupy the various organizational positions do not impinge upon the work of others. Every position can be viewed as a set of specialized duties and responsibilities. Individuals are hired to fill these positions and to execute the duties, and they are held accountable for meeting predetermined standards of performance.

The structure of the offices, or positions, in the organization follows the principle of hierarchy. Every subordinate position is under the direction or control of the one above it. Every lower position is controlled by a higher one. Social relations within organizations are based to a great extent on power and authority, or on superior-subordinate relationships. Thus, large business organizations, by their very nature, are not democratic institutions. They are authoritarian systems that distribute power and authority. The flow of power and authority is downward, from superior to subordinate offices, and the flow of responsibility and accountability is upward. The authority inherent in each position, or status, is clearly prescribed and limited to official operations. Insubordination, or refusal to be controlled by a higher office, cannot be tolerated because it would upset the system for achieving organization goals. Thus, based on the bureaucratic model that governs the structure of most business firms, we expect the people who occupy particular organizational positions to behave in particular ways.

This is not to say that the people who occupy high organizational positions are merciless despots who rule with an iron hand. The manner in which people exercise their authority varies. Several leadership styles have been identified, including the "democratic" leader who encourages participative decision making. The point is that authority is ultimately vested in a position, and even a democratic leader may have to overrule the group.

The vice-president of finance is a case in point. The duties of the office are clearly prescribed, and the vice-president's behavior toward others in the organization should be a rational means of fulfilling these responsibilities. We would not expect this vice-president to berate the advertising director for poor wording in a brochure or to hire a new factory supervisor. We would, however, expect behavior to be aimed at coordinating the marketing and production functions in terms of overall goals, budget limitations, and available staff.

ROLE THEORY

The set of behavior patterns or behavioral responses that we would expect and require the vice-president of finance to exhibit is referred to as a social role. *Roles* may be defined simply as the parts that people play in their interactions with others.

A *social role* defines the rights, duties, obligations, and appropriate behaviors of people who hold a particular position in a particular social context. In formal groups or organizations, roles are explicitly defined, usually in an organizational manual or set of bylaws. In informal groups, they are "understood."

Roles differentiate the behavior of people who occupy particular organizational positions and serve to unify the group by providing for specialization and coordination of functions. In business organizations, the division of labor, and thus role differentiation, is quite elaborate. The leadership of an organization must structure the various roles so that they complement each other. Leaders must also educate organization members about what behavior to expect from occupants of certain organizational positions.

The actual behavioral component of a role is called a norm. *Norms* are the expectations and requirements of behavior that are appropriate for a specific role. For example, the vice-president of finance, the vice-president's secretary, and the independent auditor are each expected to be on time for meetings, to be appropriately dressed, and to be relatively polite to each other. The vice-president has the additional normative responsibility for calling the meeting to order; this illustrates that there is a narrower, unique set of role expectations for each member of the group.

Every role has attached to it an *identity*, which defines for individuals who they are and how they should act in particular situations. In fact, we think of ourselves in terms of attitudes others hold towards us. If people think of us as knowledgeable and capable, we tend to believe it. If they think otherwise, we would tend to believe that also.

People have numerous roles and identities, depending on the situation in which they find themselves. The vice-president of finance may also be a parent, choir member, tennis player, or ham radio operator. Each of these activities carries with it a set of expected behavior patterns, or a role. The vice-president is not expected to take on the parent role at a meeting of corporate executives, nor to exercise executive behavior during choir practice.

Society will permit a certain amount of role discrepancy. For example, a person may be the boss at work, but only a relief player on the recreational softball team. Role conflict occurs when a person occupies several positions that are incompatible or when a single position has mutually incompatible behavioral expectations. One such situation would occur if a police officer were faced with the task of arresting a friend or a family member. Should the officer carry out this responsibility? One set of role expectations says yes; the other says no, friendship and family loyalty come first. Or, consider the following situation: the factory supervisor is expected to be close to the factory employees and to win their confidence, but also is expected to be a member of the management team. Whose side is the supervisor really on?

Failure to carry out the behavioral components of social roles is not tolerated. Sanctions, or punishments, are applied to those who violate expected behavior patterns. The sanctions could be mild, such as a friendly reminder to do what is expected, or more severe, ranging from "dirty" looks to total ostracism from a group. Thus, we can see the power of social forces that define behavior.

One significant aspect of role theory is that identity and behavior are socially bestowed and socially sustained. The position a person occupies within a formal organization or an informal group carries with it expected behavior patterns. The vice-president of finance, for example, acts like an executive because he or she occupies an executive position. It is very likely that the vice-president did not have an "executive" manner or attitude before being appointed to the office. It is also likely that, if fired, the individual's confidence in his or her identity as an executive will be severely shaken.

Another key notion is that expectations of behavior are both learned and shared. We learn what constitutes appropriate role behavior for gas station attendants, friends, or corporate executives from the groups into which we are born and those we join later. The consensus among people that those occupying a particular position will exhibit certain behavior reflects the shared social definition of social roles.

SOCIAL STRUCTURE

The systematic study of human behavior depends on two facts: first, that people act in regular and recurring patterns; second, that people are not isolated creatures, but that they interact with others. If people did not act in regular patterns, there would be no basis for behavioral science. People do engage in repetitive behavior. We arise at certain times, perform morning rituals, go to school or work, fulfill our responsibilities, and so on. We may lose sight of these regularities by focusing on either individual idiosyncracies or deviant behavior. But we can regain the proper perspective by comparing ourselves to others. For example, as Americans we shake hands with new acquaintances; in other cultures the form of greeting may be different. As New Yorkers, Texans, or Oregonians, we are aware of "how we do things." As members of a particular corporation or student body, we are aware of differences between "us and them." If we recorded or daily behaviors, we would have a vivid account of our behavioral rituals and routines.

To account for the regularities in human behavior, we will consider the concepts of society and culture. *Society* may be defined as the sum total of human relationships. The concept of society implies continuity and a complex of interpersonal and institutional relationships. Society is made up of the interconnected and overlapping groups, roles, and relationships that characterize human life. These overlapping groups include families, trade unions, political parties, business firms, bowling leagues, and others. People belong to several of these groups, have various roles to play, and are themselves links between the various groups.

The society or social system of primary interest to behavioral accountants is the business organization or business community. Within this social system are still more subsystems and interrelated human groups that would be of interest to behavioral accountants.

The concept of *system* is used in the behavioral sciences as it is used in other sciences. It refers to a configuration of interrelated and interdependent parts. Thus, we can speak of the solar system, a biological system, or a social system. The patterns with which the various parts and subsystems operate is referred to as the *structure* of the system. The term *social structure* refers to the patterned relationships between various social subsystems and individuals that make possible the functioning of a society, social organization, or social group.

CULTURE

Culture is the way of life of a society. Society cannot exist without a culture, and culture cannot exist outside of a society. The culture, or way of life, includes common belief systems, appropriate or expected modes of behavior or thinking, the store of technical knowledge, and established ways of doing things. Culture affects the regular patterns of human behavior because it defines behavior that is proper for particular situations.

The essential aspect of culture is that it ensures human survival, both physically and socially. Unlike other animals whose survival depends primarily on instinct, humans survive primarily on the basis of what they learn. A human is the only animal to possess culture, or an ongoing transmittal of the store of knowledge from one generation to the next. The culture is learned from others and shared with others. What we know and how we act is based on information we received from parents, peers, teachers, colleagues, and work supervisors.

To understand behavior in an organizational setting, a behavioral accountant should be aware of the idea of culture. In some instances, the culture of an organization is referred to as the "work environment," or the "organizational climate." The basic idea is that the elements of culture influence behavior. The *business culture* is the prevailing system of business ethics, business practices, technical knowledge, and hardware that influence behavior.

The Idealistic versus Materialistic Framework

What causes particular cultural norms to develop in the first place? The *idealistic framework* holds that cultural norms or behavior can be explained in terms of people's ideas and values. For example, a theological society will have values that differ from those in a secular society. These differences in values will create differences in people's motivations and in their ultimate behavior. In his major work, *The Protestant Ethic and the Spirit of Capitalism*, Max Weber argues that the values inherent in the Protestant reformation were necessary for the development of capitalism.[4] That is, the Protestant belief system emphasized the importance of hard work, explained why some people succeeded and others failed, justified the role of entrepreneurs, and placed poverty in a particular context. In short, ideas and values spurred the development of a political and economic system by justifying the structure of that system and the roles that people played in it.

In contrast to this idealistic framework, there is the *materialistic framework* espoused by Karl Marx and his followers that holds that ideas are not the prime cause of behavior. Instead, ideas are dependent on the economic base (i.e., property) and people's relationship to it. They contend that ideas do not cause the development of cultural norms, economic systems, or political systems. Rather, they hold that a particular type of economic system will create an ideology to justify it. For instance, a feudal economic structure will create a value system that justifies feudalism, and a capitalist economy will create an ideology to justify capitalism. Thus, a materialistic approach holds that ideas reflect the economic or material substructure and that the primary cause of behavior is that economic substructure. If it appears that ideas influence behavior, the Marxists would argue that the idea itself grows from the economic base.

The Interactionist Framework

The *symbolic interactionist framework* holds that meaning and "reality" are socially determined through the process of people interacting with each other, reaching mutual definitions of social situations, and collectively agreeing on "what is." The universe is assumed to be meaningless until people create a shared meaning. For example, a computer is a physical reality, and even a strong consensus cannot make it disappear. However, the "meaning" of that computer depends on the consensus of those who relate to it. Groups of computer programmers, grammar school students, business executives, or disgruntled credit card customers will define computers differently. And if their definitions of an object or a social situation differ, so too will their behavior toward that object or social situation.

In some ways, symbolic interaction may be viewed as an alternative to role theory. In fact, symbolic interactionist theorists see several weaknesses in role theory and claim that symbolic interaction corrects these weaknesses. The concept of role is usually tied to the concept of status. The former implies obligations, and the latter implies rights. Roles are the obligations to perform according to the norms expected of a particular status. But what is the norm? Symbolic interactionists say we do not know until people actually act in a situation. They say that one flaw or weakness of role theory is that the concepts of rights, obligations, and norms are ambiguous.

Role theorists cling to the "exterior model of man," which holds that society, which is outside of the individual, determines behavior. The individual is seen as passive rather than active. Behavior is mechanical in the sense that social structure places people in a particular status that assumes a particular role in behavior. Role theory, therefore, in the view of symbolic interactionists, does not allow for "minded" behavior. Humans are seen as automatons and society as static. Role theory does not allow for change and does not consider temporal situations.

In contrast, symbolic interactionist theorists hold to the "interior model of man," which assumes that people are motivated by needs, attitudes, and the expectations of others. In symbolic interaction, people engage in minded behavior. In this approach, behavior is the outcome of negotiation through interaction. Interaction is a process, and through it, identities are negotiated between interacting parties, and rights and obligations are mutually defined.

Other Frameworks

Behavior can also be explained in terms of attitudes, motivation, perceptions, learning, and personality. These concepts are discussed in Chapter 3.

REFERENCES

[1] "Report of the Committee on Behavioral Science Content of the Accounting Curriculum." *Accounting Review* (supplement to vol. XLVI), 1971, p. 248.

[2] Berelson, Bernard and G.A. Steiner. *Human Behavior: An Inventory of Scientific Findings*. New York: Harcourt Brace and World, 1964, p. 11.

[3] Needles, Belverd E., Jr. *Financial Accounting* (second ed.). Boston: Houghton Mifflin, 1986, p. 4.

[4] Weber, Max. *The Protestant Ethic and the Spirit of Capitalism*. New York: Charles Scribner's Sons, 1958.

SUGGESTED READINGS

Berger, Peter L. *Invitation to Sociology*. Garden City, N.Y.: Doubleday, 1963.
Bruns, W.J. and D.T. De Coster. *Accounting and Its Behavioral Implications*. New York: McGraw-Hill, 1969.

Durkheim, Emile. *The Division of Labor in Society*. New York: Free Press, 1933.

Goffman, Erving. *Behavior in Public Places*. New York: Free Press, 1963.

Gerth, Hans and C. Wright Mills. *Character and Social Structure*. New York: Harcourt Brace and World, 1964.

Gerth, Hands and C. Wright Mills (eds.). *From Max Weber: Essays in Sociology*. New York: Oxford University Press, 1964.

Levine, Donald N. (ed.). *George Simmel: On Individuality and Social Forms*. Chicago: University of Chicago Press, 1971.

Sieler, Robert E. and Robert W. Bartlett. "Personality Variables as Predictors of Budget System Characteristics." *Accounting, Organizations, and Society*. 1982, pp. 381–403.

DISCUSSION QUESTIONS

1. Discuss the following:

   a. For a system of social control to be effective, group members must accept as legitimate the authority of those empowered to administer sanctions.

   b. To be effective, both formal and informal groups must be supported by ˄up consensus.

2. In your opinion, what are the favorable aspects of status structures? What are the unfavorable aspects?

3. Describe some of the roles you play in both the formal and informal groups to which you belong.

4. Could a business organization function effectively without a clear definition of who has authority and how that authority is to be exercised? Could an informal group function effectively without such a definition of authority relationships?

5. Are bureaucracy and democracy compatible?

6. What are the functional and dysfunctional aspects of bureaucratic organizations?

7. Why do informal groups establish standards of behavior? What impact do these standards have on group members?

CHAPTER 3

Behavioral Concepts from Psychology and Social Psychology

In this chapter the focus shifts from the sociological to the psychological and social psychological factors that are most relevant to behavioral accountants. These factors include attitudes and attitude change, motivation, perception, learning, and personality.

ATTITUDES

Attitudes are learned tendencies to react in a consistently favorable or unfavorable manner toward people, objects, ideas, or situations. The term *attitude object* is used to incorporate all the objects toward which a person might react. For example, an attitude object might be a real person (Mr. Franklin, the corporate controller), an abstract person (the landlord), a company policy, an abstract concept, or a social group.

It is important to notice from the definition that an attitude is a tendency or predisposition to respond, not the response itself. Attitudes are not behaviors; rather, they represent a readiness for action or behavior. Thus, attitudes drive and guide behavior.

Attitudes are learned, well-established, and difficult to change. People acquire attitudes from personal experiences, parents, peers, and social groups. Once learned, the attitudes become an established part of an individual's personality and help account for behavioral consistency.

Behavioral accountants need to know about attitudes in order to understand and predict behavior. There are many ways in which behavioral accountants might use attitudes. Consider, for example, two firms, Y and Z, that are planning to merge. Their product lines, business methods, financial structures, and earnings histories are similar and compatible. In order to accomplish the merger as smoothly as possible, it would be beneficial if the two management teams shared the same business philosophies and attitude set. If the management teams of Firm Y and Firm Z perceive business events differently and have predispositions to respond to events based on these opposing perceptions, then conflict is likely to characterize the relations between managers in the new firm. If, however, the differences in attitude set are discovered early on, then strategies can be developed to reconcile the attitude sets of the two management teams. This will ameliorate the possibility of conflict and enhance the success of the new firm.

Behavioral accountants might also be interested in the attitudes of employees toward a proposed compensation package, the attitudes of internal auditors toward the introduction of a new software package, and customer attitudes toward a change in product packaging.

Components of Attitudes

Attitudes have cognitive, emotional, and behavioral components. The *cognitive component* is made up of the ideas, perceptions, and beliefs one has about the attitude object. It also refers to the information one has about the attitude object and to the stereotypes or generalizations (either accurate or inaccurate) one might make. For example, the cognitive component of attitudes toward computerization might be that "Our business is not large enough to take advantage of computers" or "The time saved in data processing is lost in training, data entry, and output bottlenecks."

The *emotional or "affective" component* refers to the feelings one has toward the attitude object. Positive feelings include liking, respect, or empathy. Negative feelings include dislike, fear, or disgust. For example: "I would enjoy working on computers" or "Computers make me feel clumsy and uncomfortable."

The *behavioral component* refers to how one might react to the attitude object. For example: "If this company computerizes, I am going to quit" or "As soon as that new software package is available, I want to learn how to use it."

Beliefs, Opinions, Values, and Habits

Closely related to attitudes are the concepts of beliefs, opinions, values, and habits. Broadly, *beliefs* may be defined as the cognitive components of attitudes. Beliefs may be based on sound scientific evidence, on prejudice, or on intuition. Whether or not a belief conforms to fact does not affect the potency of the belief for forming attitudes or inducing behavior. People will act just as single-mindedly and energetically toward superstitious beliefs as they will toward scientific beliefs.

An individual can have many unrelated beliefs about an attitude object. For example, a person might believe that a software handbook is "interesting," "poorly written," and "useful." There need not be congruence between beliefs, attitudes, and ultimate behavior. For example, the belief that a handbook is "interesting" does not imply that a person is predisposed toward "liking" the handbook or that he or she will act one way or another toward it.

Opinions are sometimes defined as synonyms for both attitudes and beliefs. Generally, however, opinions are viewed as narrower concepts than attitudes. Like beliefs, opinions are associated with the cognitive component of attitudes and are concerned with how a person judges or evaluates an object. As a judgment held to be true, opinions are arrived at through some intellectual process, though not necessarily based on strong proof or evidence.

Values are important life goals and behavioral standards. They are the deep-seated and basic sentiments by which people orient themselves toward higher goals and by which they differentiate what is worthwhile and beautiful from what is sordid and profane. For example, one may value prosperity, achievement, freedom, and self-respect as major goals. These values will influence attitudes and, subsequently, behavior. Values are the most important and central element in attitude formation.

Values are more general than attitudes. That is, while attitudes are related to specific objects such as company policies, people, or situations, values are not related to any single object. For example, consider a person who values achievement and equality but is confronted with a work situation in which the manager tends to reward and promote "favorite" subordinates over those who are clearly more competent. This person may have a "negative" attitude toward the work, exhibit poor work behavior, and begin to lag in productivity. These outward signs should not be interpreted as a dislike for work. The values at the core of the attitude are very positive toward work; however, conditions have led to the development of negative attitudes toward a specific job-related situation.

Habits are unconscious, automatic, and repeated patterns of behavioral response. They differ from attitudes in that attitudes are not behaviors.

Functions of Attitudes

Attitudes serve four major functions: understanding, need satisfaction, ego defense, and value expression. The *understanding, or knowledge, function* helps a person give meaning to, or "make sense" out of, new situations or events. Thus, attitudes allow a person to appraise a new situation quickly, without necessarily gathering all the relevant information about the situation. For example, the revelation of widespread fraud in a major corporation might be understood by some people in reference to their existing attitude that "corruption is rampant in high places." Other people may react to the same facts with the belief that "a few bad apples can spoil the bushel."

Attitudes also serve a utilitarian, or *need satisfying function.* For instance, people tend to form positive attitudes toward objects that meet their needs and negative attitudes toward objects that thwart their needs. An employee might form a positive or negative attitude toward a proposed company policy depending on whether that policy is seen as being in the employee's best interest.

Attitudes serve an *ego defensive function* by developing or changing to protect people from acknowledging basic truths about themselves or the world. For example, attitudes can enhance people's self-esteem and allow them to avoid thinking about their own shortcomings by blaming others. Employees who dismiss all negative reviews about their behavior with the statement that "the supervisor is really crabby" are using attitudes as an ego defense.

Finally, attitudes serve the function of *value expression*. People gain satisfaction by expressing themselves through their attitudes. Attitudes may tell the world who a person is and for what a person stands.

Attitude Formation and Change

Attitude formation refers to developing an attitude toward an object when none existed previously. *Attitude change* refers to substituting a new attitude for one that was held previously.

Attitudes are formed on the basis of physiological, personal, and social factors. Physiological and genetic factors may create a predisposition toward the development of certain attitudes. For example, genetic factors may influence a person's level of aggressiveness, which in turn could affect the formation of attitudes toward people, work, and cooperation.

The most fundamental way in which attitudes are formed is through direct personal experience with an object. Pleasant or unpleasant experiences with objects, traumatic experiences, frequent or repeated exposure to particular objects, and the development of stereotypes are examples of personal factors that affect the formation of attitudes.

Social forces affecting attitude formation include parental and peer influence, school and church influence, reference groups, and mass media. For example, friends, television commercials, or celebrity endorsements may influence the development of attitudes toward new movies, cars, or snacks.

Frequently, managers are interested in changing people's attitudes to elicit desirable behavior. In the following section, several theories of attitude change will be discussed briefly.

Theories of Attitude Change

Every day we are bombarded with messages designed to change our attitudes and behavior. Radio, television, billboards, newspaper advertisements, and personal appeals urge us to vote a certain way, buy a certain product, be more sympathetic toward particular causes, and so forth. Theories of attitude change should help us predict which appeals are most effective, which attitudes are likely to change as a result of the appeal, and the circumstances under which an appeal will not be effective.

We should keep in mind that attitudes may change without any outside prompting. For example, if people are exposed to new information about an object, attitude change may result. A loyal employee who learns that top financial officers of the company have been embezzling funds for the past several years may change his or her predisposition toward the firm, corporate executives in general, and the work itself.

Stimulus-Response and Reinforcement Theories

Stimulus-response and reinforcement theories of attitude change focus on how people respond to particular stimuli. Responses are likely to be repeated if they are rewarded or reinforced. These theories place more emphasis on the stimulus component than on the response. For example, persuasive messages are frequently used as the stimuli in efforts to change attitudes. The communicator must be aware that for the message to be effective, it must attract the attention of the target audience, it must be understood by the audience, and it must be accepted. It is necessary that the reward or incentive for responding to the stimulus be stronger than the incentive for not changing attitudes.

Social Judgment Theory

The *social judgment theory* of attitude change takes a perceptual approach. This theory considers attitude change as resulting from a change in how people perceive an object rather than a change in belief about the object. The theory holds that we can create small changes in an individual's attitude if we know about the current structure of that person's attitudes and if we make the appeal to change in the least threatening manner. An underlying assumption is that an attempt to cause a major change in attitude is likely to fail because the extent of the change would be too uncomfortable for the subject. But a small change in attitude is possible if we know the limits of acceptable change. For example, a member of a professional association might reject the request to attend meetings of the political action committee (PAC) because of a negative predisposition toward involvement in politics. However, that same member might be convinced to make a small contribution to the association's PAC.

A major factor affecting the success of a persuasive message is the discrepancy between the position advocated by the communicator (the external anchor or reference point) and the subject's current attitude (the internal anchor or reference point). If the communicator's position is too far from the internal anchor, contrast is the likely result, and attitudes will not change. If the communicator's position is closer to the internal anchor, assimilation may result because the subject does not perceive the persuasive communication as extreme or threatening, will evaluate the message positively, and might change his or her attitude.

Consistency and Dissonance Theories

Some theories of attitude change assume that people try to maintain a consistency, or congruence, between their attitudes and behaviors. These theories emphasize the importance of people's ideas and beliefs. The theories view attitude change as a rational and cognitive process whereby people, when made aware of inconsistencies between attitudes and behavior, will be motivated to correct the inconsistency by changing either the attitude or the behavior. An underlying assumption of such theories is that people cannot tolerate the inconsistencies.

Consistency theory holds that the relationship between attitudes and behavior is in balance when there is no cognitive stress in the system. For example, if Bob likes Jim, and both Bob and Jim like Henry, a state of harmony exists. The relationship is unbalanced, or inconsistent, if Bob dislikes Jim, and both Bob and Jim like Henry. In general, balance or consistency exists if all three relationships are positive, or if two are negative and one is positive. Unbalanced or inconsistent states exist when all three relationships are negative, or when two are positive and one is negative.

Using a business example, the theory holds that tension would result when the new company controller (P), an antinuclear activist, meets the vice-president of production (O), who advocates more research on nuclear power and nuclear weapons. Both P and O favor centralized decision making for the firm (X). An imbalance or inconsistency is caused by P's dislike for O, and the fact that P and O favor X. The theory holds that psychological forces would be generated to achieve a state of balance.

Dissonance theory is a variation of consistency theory. The theory is concerned with the relationship between cognitive elements (i.e., information, beliefs, and ideas that people have about themselves). *Cognitive dissonance* exists when a person possesses two contrary cognitions. For example, if Bob Larson thinks of himself as a responsible and dedicated employee, it would create dissonance if he missed a crucial sales meeting to take advantage of an end-of-year clothing sale.

The theory holds that dissonance motivates people to reduce or eliminate the dissonance. It is assumed that because dissonance is psychologically unpleasant, people seek ways to avoid it. Dissonance is reduced by decreasing the number, or importance, of the dissonant elements. For example, Bob Larson may downplay the importance of the sales meetings, convincing himself that he already had all the crucial information and that his presence was not really needed. Or, he may increase his level of participation in other areas by making special efforts to demonstrate his involvement in budgeting for sales. A third way to reduce dissonance is to change one of the dissonant elements so that there is no longer any inconsistency. In this case, Bob may change his self-perception so that he no longer defines himself as responsible and dedicated.

Self-Perception Theory

Self-perception theory holds that people develop attitudes based on how they observe and interpret their own behavior. In other words, the theory posits that attitudes do not determine behavior, but rather that attitudes are formed after the behavior occurs in order for the attitude to be consistent with the behavior. According to this theory, then, attitudes would change only after behaviors change. The behavioral accountant would first have to change behavior; attitude change would follow.

Functional theories of attitude change hold that attitudes serve to meet people's needs, as discussed earlier in the chapter. In order to change attitudes, we must discover what those needs are and develop stimuli based on those needs.

MOTIVATION

Motivation is the process of initiating conscious and purposeful action. It is the key to initiating, driving, sustaining, and directing behavior. Motivation is also concerned with the subjective reaction that occurs during this process.

Motivation is an important concept for behavioral accountants because organizational effectiveness depends on people performing as they are expected to perform. Managers and behavioral accountants must motivate people to this level of expected performance in order for the organization's goals to be met.

A *motive* is a single factor that sparks the motivation process. For example, some people want money, while others want power, fame, or security. A motive is personal in nature. Somebody from a wealthy family may seek work that provides a sense of achievement and self-worth. Another person from a poor family may seek work that offers freedom from financial worry.

Need Theories

A well-known theory of motivation is *Maslow's need hierarchy*. The theory holds that people are motivated by their desire to satisfy a hierarchically ordered set of needs: basic physiological needs (food, air, sex), safety needs (physical and psychological security), social and belongingness needs (friendship, love), esteem needs (self-respect, recognition, power, and status), and self-actualization needs (fulfillment of one's potential).

According to Maslow's theory, after a person fulfills a lower-order need, the next higher need becomes important in directing behavior. It is not necessary that lower order needs be completely satisfied before the next higher need becomes potent. The theory also holds that once satisfied, a need is no longer a motivator.

The need hierarchy concept has not been well supported by empirical research. This may be because in the United States, where most of the research was conducted, most people's basic needs are satisfied. Some researchers question the notion of separating a complex human need structure into a hierarchical order. Other critics contend that the theory does not allow for the prediction of behavior.

Despite its weaknesses, Maslow's need theory is important for managers and behavioral accountants to know because it does focus attention on individual needs and recognizes that the same incentive may not satisfy everybody's needs.

The ERG concept is a refinement of the need hierarchy. It proposes three need categories: existence (physical and material desires), relatedness (friendship, belonging), and growth (personal development and self-fulfillment). It differs from Maslow's need hierarchy in that there are not necessarily higher and lower order needs and that even though a need may have been satisfied, that same need may still remain the dominant motivator. For example, a well-paid executive who is frustrated by attempts to fulfill relatedness needs may be motivated by the desire for further salary increases.

A third need theory of motivation is *McClelland's need-for-achievement theory*, which holds that all motives, including the need for achievement, are learned. Therefore, the critical time to develop these motives is during childhood when it is possible to structure learning so that children will increase their expectations and develop the habit of working to actualize those expectations.

While the need for achievement is important for success in business, people in high executive positions also have a strong need for power. Thus, the need-for-achievement theory does not help us explain the motivation for all people and must be used in combination with other theories to fully understand motivation.

Herzberg's two-factor theory focuses on two sets of rewards that result from work: those related to job satisfaction (motivators) and those related to job dissatisfaction (hygiene factors). *Motivators*, related to the *content* of the job, include promotion, recognition, responsibility, the work itself, and the potential for self-actualization. *Hygiene factors*, related to the *context* of the job, or environment in which the job is performed, include job security, salary, company policy, working conditions, and personal relationships at work.

The theory holds that motivators are related to job satisfaction but not dissatisfaction. Hygiene factors are related to dissatisfaction but not to satisfaction. Thus, employees are motivated by things such as recognition and advancement in the firm. Salary increases will not motivate; they serve only to prevent job dissatisfaction.

Expectancy Theory

The *expectancy theory of motivation* assumes that the level of motivation to perform a task depends on the beliefs one has about the reward structure for the task. In other words, motivation exists when a person expects to receive a particular reward for performing a particular task.

In general, motivation is the product of expectancy, instrumentality, and valence. *Expectancy* refers to the perceived probability that a specific act will result in a specific outcome. For example, employees may believe that satisfactory performance will result in promotion. *Valence* is the strength of a person's desire for a particular outcome. For example, how important is the promotion to the employee? *Instrumentality* refers to the causal effect of one outcome on future outcomes. For example, a valence has a value because an expected outcome is believed to be instrumental in obtaining other outcomes. The employee's desire for a promotion may be seen as instrumental in obtaining a transfer to the firm's home office.

The theory distinguishes between intrinsic and extrinsic rewards. *Intrinsic rewards* are internally created and result from doing the work itself; they include the feeling of accomplishment one may get from doing a job well or the feeling of satisfaction gained when a project is successfully completed. *Extrinsic rewards* include pay, recognition, job security, and promotion; they represent the payment for performance. The theory holds that motivation is a function of both intrinsic and extrinsic rewards.

PERCEPTION _____

Perception is how people see or interpret events, objects, and people. People act on the basis of their perceptions regardless of whether those perceptions accurately or inaccurately reflect reality. In fact, "reality" is what each person perceives it to be. One person's description of reality may be far from another person's description. The formal definition of perception is the process by which we select, organize, and interpret stimuli into a meaningful and coherent picture of the world.

Managers and behavioral accountants must develop accurate perceptions of the people with whom they deal. The differences that they perceive between key groups of people may account for successful or unsuccessful operations. For example, a plant manager must develop perceptions of individual supervisors, major customers, union officers, sales representatives, and other managers. The plant manager must correctly perceive the strengths and weaknesses of each supervisor in particular areas. That is, it is insufficient to say that supervisors X and Y are top-notch and supervisor Z is average. The plant manager must perceive which supervisor is strongest in resolving employee conflict, correcting production bottlenecks, motivating the work force, and so on. An incorrect or incomplete perception of these individual differences may result in the wrong person being assigned to a critical task.

Behavioral accountants need to know about perception because the perceptions that people form develop into the ideas and attitudes that influence behavior. If a potential employee perceives a company's promotion and compensation policy as fair, that person is likely to join the firm and become a satisfied worker. If the policies are perceived as unfair, the prospective employee will join some other firm or be a less than totally productive worker. Some applications of perception are discussed below.

Physical Stimuli versus Individual Predispositions

People experience the world differently because perception depends on both physical stimuli and individual predispostions. *Physical stimuli* are raw sensory inputs such as sight, sound, and touch. *Individual predispositions* include motives, needs, attitudes, past learning, and expectations. Perception differs among people because individual sensory receptors may function differently, but primarily because predispositions differ. Thus, the same company policy will be perceived differently by production workers, middle managers, and the top management.

Four other factors associated with individual predispositions are familiarity, feeling, importance, and emotions. People generally perceive familiar objects faster than unfamiliar objects or people. For example, if we know that a new manager is a member of the Elks or Lions, our familiarity with these organizations may result in a quick—although not necessarily accurate—perception of the manager. If the manager is known to be a member of the Turtles or Tigers, our lack of familiarity with these organizations will result in a slower development of perceptions.

People's feelings toward an object or person also affect perception. There is a tendency for people to seek more information about objects toward which they hold strong positive or negative feelings. Similarly, the more important a person or object is, the more information is sought. In both cases, the more information available about an object, the more complete the perception of the object.

Finally, a person's emotional state can affect perception. Perception may differ depending on whether we are having a good day or bad day, whether we feel cheerful or depressed, and so on.

Selection, Organization, and Interpretation of Stimuli

Perception, as mentioned above, is the process by which we select, organize, and interpret stimuli. We are only able to perceive a small portion of all the stimuli to which we are exposed. Thus, consciously or unconsciously we *select* what we perceive. That is, we concentrate or pick up on some things and ignore others. Usually, we select for perception those things that we find most interesting and important.

What we select to perceive typically depends on the nature of the stimuli, our expectations, and our motives. The nature of the stimuli include such factors as physical attributes, design, the contrast with other stimuli, "buzz words," and brand names. Expectations are based on our previous experiences and conditioning. Frequently, we see what we expect to see and are motivated to perceive what we need or want. For example, depending on our needs or expectations, we may see only the "good" or "bad" in a particular situation.

People usually seek out sympathetic or pleasant stimuli and avoid painful or threatening stimuli. They may screen out the unimportant, may distort information that is not consistent with existing beliefs, or simply "turn off" to protect themselves from too great a bombardment of stimuli.

People *organize* stimuli into groups and perceive it as a unified whole. If given incomplete information, people will fill in the gaps and then behave as though they had complete information about the situation. Perceptual *interpretation* depends on past experience and social group membership. When stimuli are ambiguous, for example, people will interpret them in a manner that is consistent with their needs, interests, and attitudes.

Perceptions are distorted by accepting stereotypes, believing information received from respected sources, relying on first impressions, and jumping to conclusions. Perceptions may also be distorted by a "logical error" whereby an initial impression about a person is formed based on only one known characteristic. For example, if a person is known to hold a responsible position—such as a doctor—that individual also may be perceived to be conscientious, reliable, trustworthy, and honest in dealings outside work. This perception, however, may be inaccurate. It is "logical" to assume that certain characteristics appear together. But when they do not, our perceptions may be distorted.

Related to logical errors in perception is the halo effect, whereby we generalize from one set of qualities to a nonrelevant set of qualities. For example, firefighters who risk their lives to save others may be perceived as friendly, outgoing, and concerned, when in fact, they may possess none of these qualities.

Perceptual defenses arise because people do not want to be proven wrong in their perceptions. Thus, people may ignore, overlook, or distort information that calls existing perceptions into question.

Relevance of Perception for Accountants

Behavioral accountants can apply knowledge of perception to many organizational activities. For example, in performance evaluation, the manner in which a person is appraised may be affected by the accuracy of the supervisor's perception. Incorrect or biased ratings may result in good performers becoming discouraged, and dissatisfied and, ultimately, leaving the firm. Therefore, supervisors should recognize that their feelings about certain subordinates may affect their evaluations and should be on guard against this source of perceptual bias. In employee selection decisions, managers should be sensitive to the possibility that their decisions might be biased due to a favorable or unfavorable first impression, on factors not relevant to the work situation such as appearance or ethnic background, or on incomplete information.

There is always risk in making business decisions. The decisions managers make may depend on the risk they perceive and their tolerance for risk. People who perceive high risk tend to be "narrow categorizers." That is, they limit alternatives to safe alternatives. Those who perceive low risk tend to be "broad categorizers" who select from a wider range of alternatives.

Frequently, differential perceptions are the cause of communication problems in an organization. The sender perceives the message one way, and the receivers perceive it another way based on their frames of reference. For example, a manager may instruct the word processing supervisor to delete the file they discussed yesterday. But they discussed two files: the manager may be referring to one and the supervisor to the other.

Misperceptions may also lead to strained interpersonal relations at work. When interactions appear to be tense or strained, a supervisor should determine if the cause is a business event being perceived differently by different people.

LEARNING

The patterns of thinking and behaving that people bring with them to the work environment reflect their own experiences, perceptions, and motivations.

These behavioral patterns may not be optimal for the organization. Therefore, behavioral accountants must be familiar with the principles of learning theory in order to correct employee perceptions and modify dysfunctional behaviors.

Learning is the process by which new behaviors are acquired. It occurs as the result of motivation, experience, and repetition in response to particular stimuli or situations. This combination of motivation, experience, and repetition occurs in two forms: classical conditioning and operant conditioning.

Classical Conditioning (Pavlov's Dog)

Pavlov observed that dogs would salivate not only when food was placed in their mouths, but also when they observed food. The food is an unconditioned stimulus that causes a reflex (unconditioned) behavior to occur. Unconditioned behaviors are not learned.

In his experiments, Pavlov first rang a bell, then fed the dog. At first, the dog only salivated when the food was presented. But after repeated treatments, the dog eventually salivated at the sound of the bell. In this case, the bell (stimulus) was followed by a conditioned response. Conditioned responses are learned. The relationship between a stimulus and a conditioned response is called *classical conditioning*. If reinforcement (in this case, the meat after the sound of the bell) is withdrawn, the learned behavior will cease.

Operant Conditioning

In classical conditioning a neutral stimulus is followed by a reward, which produces a response. After many repetitions, the neutral stimulus by itself will result in the same response. In *operant conditioning*, the response brings on the reward. For example, when commanded with the stimulus "shake," a dog will respond by extending its paw. The animal responds in this manner because it has learned that this response will bring on a reward.

Learning principles have been applied to many organizational objectives. Positive reinforcement and feedback, in the form of recognition, bonuses, and other rewards, have been used to improve productivity, reduce turnover and absenteeism, and make employees more responsive to customer needs. Punishments, or negative sanctions, have been used toward similar ends.

Behavioral accountants and managers should examine company policy and procedures to determine whether rewards and punishment are properly used to encourage desired behavior. For example, they may discover that the firm has no specified penalty for tardiness or absenteeism. To minimize tardiness and absenteeism, company policy should reward the appropriate employee behavior and punish the inappropriate behavior. These policy changes should quickly extinguish personnel practices that harm the firm.

PERSONALITY

Personality refers to the inner psychological characteristics (e.g., traits, qualities, and mannerisms) that determine and reflect how a person responds to his or her environment. Personality is the essence of individual difference. No two people are alike in terms of personality, but they may be similar in terms of particular personality characteristics.

Personality tends to be consistent and enduring. A shy individual will likely remain shy and a domineering person will likely remain domineering for long periods of time. The concept of personality and knowledge of its components are important because they enable us to predict behavior. For example, an introverted person is likely to be withdrawn and shy and to exhibit nonassertive behavior. We would not expect that person to be a force for change in the organization. Personality, however, can change. A major life event, for instance, can cause a change in personality. Behavioral accountants can deal effectively with people if they understand how personality develops and how it can change.

The main application of personality theory in organizations is in predicting behavior. Personality tests might determine who would be most effective in stressful jobs, who would respond well to criticism, who first must be praised before being told of undesirable behavior, who is a potential leader, who is likely to work better in a participative work environment, who is likely to be a security risk, and so on.

SUMMARY

In this chapter we examined some of the major areas within psychology and social psychology and discussed major concepts including attitudes and attitude change, motivation, perception, learning, and personality. We then applied theoretical systems to behavioral accounting and to other behavioral considerations in organizations.

SUGGESTED READINGS

Berelson, Bernard and Gary A. Steiner. *Human Behavior: An Inventory of Scientific Findings*. New York: Harcourt Brace and World, 1964.

Cartwright, Dorwin and Alvin Zander. *Group Dynamics*. New York: Harper & Row, 1960.

Lindzey, Gardner and Elliot Aronson (eds.). *The Handbook of School Psychology* (third ed.) vols. 1 and 2. New York: Random House, 1985.

Lindzey, Gardner and Calvin S. Hall. *Theories of Personality*. New York: John Wiley, 1965.

Maslow, Abraham H. *Motivation and Personality*. New York: Harper & Row, 1954.

DISCUSSION QUESTIONS_____

1. Under what circumstances might people behave differently than their personality characteristics predict?
2. Why might the vice-president of marketing be very interested in personality theories?
3. Why might attitudes remain the same even if our behaviors and attitudes are unbalanced?
4. Describe three situations in which operant conditioning might be used in business.
5. Do attitudes determine behavior or does behavior determine attitudes?
6. How could learning theory be used in motivation?
7. How would theories of attitude change be applied to financial and production problems in an organization?
8. How would a manager motivate employees who are basically satisfied with their jobs and salaries?
9. Compare classical and operant conditioning from the point of view of a behavioral accountant who wants employees to be more careful with power tools.

CHAPTER 4

Assumptions About Human Behavior: A Historical Perspective

Chapters 2 and 3, which presented an overview of those areas of behavioral science relevant to accounting, demonstrated that human beings are complex, that their behavior is influenced by many different factors, that they have complicated and changing goal structures, and that their behavior is adaptive. In other words, people modify their behavior due to learning, peer pressure, and changes in attitude. Further, the behavioral sciences teach us that people are motivated by a number of diverse drives, including—but not limited to—the desire for economic rewards, social status, a sense of belonging, and security. This understanding of human behavior is a relatively new phenomenon. As recently as the early twentieth century, the assumptions about human behavior inherent in economic theory and business practice were that people were basically lazy and that they were motivated only by economic rewards.

In this chapter we present a historical overview of the perceptions of human behavior and assumptions about motivation. We will show how classical and modern assumptions about human behavior in organizations affect the accounting model.

FEUDALISM AND CAPITALISM

All economic systems are characterized by basic social relations between those who exercise authority and those who obey it and between those who own the means of production and those who do not. An examination of the historical development of these social relations will give us an idea of the underlying assumptions about human behavior that have characterized business, economics, and accounting.

We will begin by contrasting capitalism with the feudal order that it replaced. This is extremely relevant because the change from feudalism to capitalism has been the major change in modern times. All other revolutions pale by comparison. Then, we will contrast the assumptions about human behavior that characterized the early stages of capitalism with those of the advanced stages that characterize the United States and other Western countries in the 1980s.

The Feudal System

By the end of the fifteenth century, a political, social, and economic order was coming to a close in Europe. Known as feudalism, this socioeconomic order was defined by a series of social relations based on status derived from lineage and age. In medieval Europe, a man was a serf or a lord, a merchant or a guild member. His position in the social structure depended on the family into which he was born, rather than on merit.

Land and labor were not objects of commerce; both were communized in medieval Europe. Ownership of land passed from a lord to his heir, and trading in real estate was rare. Serfs were part of the estate; they had the right to live on the land and to work it.

Guilds were unions of artisans. The guild system—the center of "industrial" production—was also steeped in tradition. A man became a carpenter or a glassblower because that is the work his father did.

Masters elected their own guild government and set their own work rules. They set wage rates, output standards, and working conditions. They regulated social conduct and expected guild members to dress in an appropriate manner and to be involved in civic affairs. In short, guilds were concerned with both the economic and noneconomic dimensions of life.

The guilds of the Middle Ages wanted to preserve an orderly way of life, so they regulated behavior at work and in the community. To maintain the status quo, guilds shunned innovation and technological change. They worked to prevent the formation of monopolies by sharing techniques and technology. They avoided competition by limiting entry into the guild and regulating advancement from apprentice to journeyman to master. The guilds set the terms of sale and expected their members to adhere to those terms. Advertising was prohibited. Guild members, who owned the means of production, were expected to take pride in their work.

The idea was to maintain one's position in life, rather than to enhance it. There was not a clear-cut distinction between one's social and economic life. People did not "make a living"—the work was an end in itself.

The Rise of Industrial Society

The steam engine, invented by James Watt in 1776, could mark the beginning of the Industrial Revolution and the decline of the guilds. It allowed for the beginning of the factory system, as opposed to cottage industries where people worked at home. The steam engine freed people as a source of energy. That is, it enabled an energy source to be established *anywhere* because it used inanimate energy and could be moved. Before the steam engine, water, wind, and animals were used as power sources.

The factory used large numbers of workers who operated machines driven by inanimate power. Each worker had his or her specific role to play in the manufacturing process. This was much different than work done by guild members, who completed an entire job with their own tools in their own workshops.

The factory relied on the availability of wage laborers—a free labor class unknown in medieval Europe. The availability of this labor pool developed over time as the result of other economic events. One of the more important events was the *enclosure movement* in England.

The demand for wool led to the development of sheep farming, which resulted in the land being enclosed—or fenced off—for the grazing needs of the animals. These enclosures drove large numbers of serfs, who previously worked the land, off the estates into the cities. This movement created an impoverished working class with nothing to sell but their labor. The great migration to the cities also caused the standards in guilds—indeed, the entire guild system—to break down because there was too much labor competing with guilds.

Thus, the enclosure movement transformed the serfs who remained on the land into peasants and the serfs who left the land into a free, mobile, propertyless labor class that robbed the guilds of their former power. Moreover, the enclosure movement changed the perception of land use—with the advent of an industrial society, land became acceptable as an object of commerce. Up until the time of the French Revolution in 1789, landed estate (land, buildings, equipment, and serfs) was a source of social privilege. The process by which landed estate changed from common land to private land took a long time. It represented a new idea: that land, as property, could be *owned*. In medieval Europe, land was *held* but never owned.

Another major change was the development of a new middle class. Merchants now stood between producers and consumers. The rise of this entrepreneurial class was also necessary for the development of capitalism.

Capitalism versus Feudalism

Feudalism stressed tradition; capitalism was *not* traditional. Feudalism penalized innovation; capitalism encouraged it. In feudalism, economic activity was for the immediate satisfaction of wants. Capitalism put a premium on planning and the rational use of technology.

In feudalism, there was social equality *within* a social class but not across classes. Capitalism did not stress equality; the child of an innkeeper had the same opportunity as the child of a baron to be successful at work. Capitalism stressed equality of opportunity.

The notion of *social justice* was the basis of economic reward in medieval

Europe. In capitalism, there was no such notion. Instead, there was the idea of free wages—"we pay jobs, not people."

Factory life, and the discipline it demanded, was new for workers, who were used to a traditional society where they were more-or-less "their own boss." Workers intensely disliked the new system. Wages were low and working conditions poor. Whether they worked or not, they were considered lazy or no good and were ostracized from society.

There was also the notion of a *just price* in feudalism. Capitalism substituted *competitive wages*—the lowest wage that would maximize profit. Capitalism stressed compulsion and a duty to work hard. An important motive of capitalism was the duty to accumulate wealth.

Economists say the rise of the market brought all this about. They point to the increase in trade, to a whole new set of productive forces, to a change in the social relations of production, and to a free labor force that swept aside many of the old customs and laws that were in conflict with capitalism.

The behavioral view takes into account the rise of the *capitalist spirit*. This is the idea that a person should pursue gain for its own end and should rationalize everything in life. Adam Smith, David Hume, and Jeremy Bentham glorified this doctrine of enlightened self-interest.

The behaviorial view provides an important link: a value system that would be compatible with capitalism. The value system answers a question that has no rational explanation: Why do people work so hard when they have so much? Max Weber analyzed this tendency and concluded that capitalist ideology and values were rooted in Protestantism. The values inherent in early Calvinism shaped the world view of the entrepreneurial middle class that began capitalism.

The Protestant Ethic and the Values of Capitalism

All economic and social orders depend on congenial social relations and on a shared set of beliefs and sentiments. Thrift, self-discipline, and rationality constituted a set of values that were "virtuous" and that Weber called the ethos of capitalism. These values, missing in noncapitalist society, were especially characteristic of middle class entrepreneurs and were necessary for the development of capitalism.

The development of capitalism required enterprisers who were motivated to work hard, save, accumulate capital, and expand their businesses. Self-discipline was essential.

This self-discipline needed general cultural support, and it was important that it be extended to the working class. To this end, schools were established to prepare people for work. The schools stressed values such as respect for authority, discipline, punctuality, patriotism, and so on. These values were part of the "Protestant ethic."

By the "Protestant ethic" Weber meant the driving force that compelled people, on the basis of service to God, to work hard and diligently, be frugal, save, and invest. It was Weber's explanation for the psychological conditions (i.e., ideology, values, rationale, etc.) that made possible the development of capitalism. It includes those values, grounded in the theology of John Calvin and Martin Luther, that were adapted to the economic sphere by the rising class of English merchants. These applied ideas and beliefs led people to behave in a manner conducive to, and have the attitudes necessary for, the development of capitalism.

The interpretation of Protestant theology by the new class of capitalists contributed to the development of capitalism. This new "word," or theology, differed dramatically from the views of medieval Catholicism. Weber uses this difference as an explanation for the fact that Protestant countries (England, the lowlands, and the Protestant parts of Germany) were the most fertile areas for the development of capitalism.

The emphasis on self-discipline and hard work grew out of particular Protestant religious beliefs. In Protestantism individuals stood alone before God and therefore were responsible directly to God for their individual actions. Nor were they responsible to the holy representatives of God through the church. Further, early Calvinists believed in the doctrine of predestination. This doctrine held that an individual was, from birth, either among the "saved" or "unsaved"—among the elect or eternally damned. Nothing people did in their lives would change this condition. Only God knew the truth about a person's status. People were uncertain and lived in anxiety. However, one's behavior in this world, which *could be controlled*, was a "sign" as to one's fate. Those who were saved showed outward signs of their "elect" status in the form of industriousness, thrift, self-discipline, and accumulation of wealth.

Rejection of worldly pleasures and righteous success in this world— through hard work—were other signs of grace that indicated one might be among the elect. Thus, religious anxiety was relieved through honest and efficient toil.

The Protestant theology was applied to the economic sphere by making hard and diligent work "noble"; historically, work was considered to be denigrating. The concept of a "calling" (unique to Protestantism) developed. It was a favorable sign—indicating salvation—if one succeeded at his calling. Thus, work and prayer were synonymous: Hard work was form of prayer; it was one's calling. This calling from God required discipline in a job or profession; it required that one devote one's life to one's calling. Devotion implied that a person should not switch jobs—only a "ne'er-do-well" did that. The elect kept their noses to the grindstone. A highly valued calling was to be in business.

The emphasis in capitalism on the accumulation of wealth also had its roots in this religious doctrine. Only God could judge a person's behavior.

Since people had to do good works to serve God, and because people could succeed at their calling by working hard and living righteously, the idea of "rationality" came to the fore. Acting rationally meant that resources were utilized in the most efficient manner in pursuit of an end—to succeed in a calling. One had to save and be frugal. Wealth was not to be squandered or used to live ostentatiously. Material displays of wealth were forbidden. Because a person was supposed to engage in self-denial and avoid worldly pleasure, the money earned from consistent work had no use except for reinvestment in the business. Wise investment of savings was both rational and righteous. Thus, the early Calvinists used their capital to expand their businesses, establish new enterprises, and eventually to employ others. Providing work for others was considered pleasing to God; it was another favorable sign that one was virtuous and among the saved. Thus, having the virtues of an entrepreneur indicated success in both religious and secular life. But becoming a successful entrepreneur was not enough: the entrepreneur must *continue* to save, invest, and grow by any means necessary. The end and means were the maximization of profit, which required the attitudes of a "hard-nosed" person of business and competition with others through innovation, technology, and the taking of risks.

The notion of individual competition, inherent in capitalism, also developed from these religious beliefs. Because Calvinists emphasized that an individual stood alone before the Maker, they believed that individuals should not trust the friendship of others and should not establish close ties with others because they might be among the damned. Further, if one is judged by the company one keeps, then friendships with possible sinners might have negative consequences: the Grace of God might be withdrawn with dire consequences for one's business. The idea was that a person should be an "individual," work hard, save, and stand alone before God. Doing this, the individual would not be confused with others. Because individuals would enter heaven only on their own works, their only responsibility was to God. The thoughts of others did not matter.

The religious revolution influenced general attitudes toward work, poverty, and leisure. For example, poverty was a sign that a person was lazy or morally irresponsible. Poverty was not pleasing to God. It was a sign that a person was not among the saved.

The rising merchant class linked themselves to these new values and expanded on them. Protestantism made merchants acceptable and legitimate rather than pariahs.

In summary, the Protestant ethic contributed to the development of capitalism by providing the motivation toward work and entrepreneurship. It also provided the type of people needed for capitalism: honest, sober, impersonal, rational. As capitalism became more formal and institutionalized, it depended less on religious motivation and looked to utilitarian and pecuniary motivations.

Perspectives on Workers

Calvinists viewed work as noble, but workers as lacking virtue. If workers were virtuous, there would be outward signs of success. Early industrialists, espousing a philosophy of Social Darwinism, believed workers to be inferior because they were still struggling to survive. The scientific management movement, associated with the works of Frederick Taylor in the early 1900s, viewed workers as inherently lazy and interested only in economic rewards. By the 1920s workers were viewed as a bundle of traits that could be understood through extensive testing. The human relations movement of the 1930s, growing out of the work of Elton Mayo, regarded workers as human beings, but still treated them as a cost factor.

The ideology of the early industrialists, based on the traditionalism of feudal society, was that the rich and upper classes were responsible for the poor. Poverty was seen as an economic condition. The upper classes had an obligation to think for and provide for the poor. The poor (workers) only had to work and to be moral, humble, and religious.

In the later stages of English industrialization (circa 1800) the working class came to be viewed as a factor of production—still stupid and childlike, but now dependent on themselves. The old "traditionalism" interfered with discipline. Relations at work became less personal. Poverty was now seen as a result of indolence, laziness, and depravity. Poverty, economically useful in keeping wages low, could be overcome only by holding such Christian virtues as industriousness, subordination, and piety. To this end, charity schools and Sunday schools were established in England to promote religion and discipline.

The new ideology said the the upper classes were no longer responsible for the poor. The belief was justified by many, including Malthus, whose essay on population held that the natural order of things proved that the rich could not always care for the poor. After all, the poor were responsible for their own condition because they added to the population in a world where the food supply was fixed.

An ideology of self-help later arose that said anybody, even the poor, could become successful. This self-help doctrine, which stressed willpower and hard work, along with some Calvinist ideas, became the ideology of the early American industrialists.

During the late 1800s the concepts of self-help and Social Darwinism were popular in America because of the seemingly unlimited opportunity. Success and riches were signs of progress and reward. It was a world where only the most able and persevering survived. The "new thought" movement (1895-1915) said further that initiative, individual effort, and a positive attitude toward work were the keys to success for anybody who strived toward a goal. (By the time these ideas were disseminated, workers had already formed unions, and adopting this ideology would have undermined solidarity. Therefore, the "new thought" ideas were rejected by workers.)

The self-help idea was extended to the point where management viewed every worker as a potential capitalist. Hard work and vision were all that one needed. In this *laissez-faire* environment, workers were seen as free agents who always had the free choice to leave a bad job and find a better one.

The scientific management movement (1912) had a theme of labor-management cooperation. Taylor believed that the worth of a worker was determined by scientific testing and training rather than the worker's success in the struggle for survival. There was one best way of performing a job. If this best approach were followed, both labor and management would earn more and the labor-management conflict would be resolved.

During the 1920s, the ideology of American management stressed teamwork, or cooperation between labor and management. The success of managers was now seen as a consequence of ability and training rather than a sign of virtue. Workers, though viewed as human beings, still had to be led because they were unreasonable, lacking in initiative, and motivated only by economic incentives. The old Calvinist virtues that led to success were obsolete in twentieth-century bureaucratic organizations.

By the late 1920s and early 1930s, managers came to believe that it was more important to explain workers' attitudes and behavior than to engage in moral condemnation. Managers came to recognize that people worked for things other than money. Workers became a conglomerate of traits that could be measured and identified. There was a shift from looking at workers' actions to looking at their feelings and attitudes. Job classification systems and aptitude tests were developed during this period. Worker needs were recognized.

Elton Mayo and his co-workers discovered the existence of group norms among workers and demonstrated that people had other interests besides money. Mayo believed that workers should consider their work as socially necessary and the managers should provide the type of work environment where the spirit of cooperation would foster such a set of positive worker attitudes. If the work was not interesting, then management should show an interest in the worker. If the work did not provide contentment, then management should find other ways to make the workers feel a sense of contentment, because Mayo held the contented workers were more productive. This is the basis for the human relations movement: that getting along with other people and building a productive team is the most important skill.

Following the human relations movement of the 1930s, jobs were enlarged and rotated. When possible, work was made less routine and in some industries workers were asked to participate in some organizational decision making. These personnel policies often cost more, but management found that they enhanced worker satisfaction. Modern American industry is now characterized by this view of work and workers.

ASSUMPTIONS ABOUT HUMAN BEHAVIOR

Both classical economist and classical management theorists assumed that the primary goal of business activity was profit maximization and that organization members were motivated primarily by economic factors. Thus, these theorists assumed that managers would engage in behavior that would maximize revenue and minimize cost. They further assumed that work was essentially unpleasant and that people would avoid it whenever possible. People were assumed to be lazy and inefficient. Only economic incentives could motivate people to work.

Given these assumptions about business and human behavior, the accounting systems of that era were structured to help management maximize profit, measure and control performance, and rationally plan for the future. Thus, as the major providers of information to management, accountants would select the information they considered most useful to management. They would also decide how to present the information and who would receive it.

Modern organizational theory propounds a different set of assumptions about the goals of business firms and the behavior of organization members. First, there is no overriding goal, such as profit maximization. If such a primary goal does exist, it is probably organizational survival. In the view of modern organization theorists, business firms pursue many goals, which may change in response to the external environment and the changing goals of dominant organization members. Moreover, in some cases, certain organizational goals might conflict with other goals. In short, the objectives of a firm, according to modern theorists, are much more complex than the objectives that classical theorists ascribed to organizations.

Similarly, modern theorists see human behavior as more complex. Rather than being motivated by primarily economic incentives, people are now seen as motivated by a mix of social, psychological, and economic drives and needs. The relative strength of these drives differs among people depending on their backgrounds and current life situations. Modern theorists see work as possessing the potential for providing meaning and satisfaction in life. People will work, and enjoy it, if that work can satisfy some of their basic needs. Thus, instead of blindly pursuing greater profits, managers should be problem solvers, coordinators, and decision makers whose actions—on balance—are intended to ensure both the short-run and long-run survival of the firm.

In light of this set of assumptions, accounting is perceived as an information system that provides the appropriate, relevant data to the various levels of management for their use in decision making. Further, for the various planning, control, and financial reports to be of greatest use, the accounting system must be based on an awareness of the complexities of human behavior and an understanding of how people are likely to react to accounting information. This implies that for an accounting system to be useful to modern business organizations, it must report more than just financial data; it must be an all-inclusive management information system. The accountants who design the system must be aware of the complex nature of organizational goals and of the social, psychological, and economic factors that affect human behavior.

SUMMARY

In this chapter we presented a brief history of the development of capitalism, focusing on the values necessary for this new economic and social order to supplant feudalism and to evolve to where it is today. The value system of early capitalism grew out of the religious beliefs of the Calvinists. This "Protestant ethic" stressed hard work, self-discipline, thrift, and the avoidance of worldly pleasure. The possession of these virtues was the justification for managerial and entrepreneurial prerogatives. Those lacking these virtues, or those who did not show visible evidence of possessing them were considered lazy and immoral.

The values inherent in capitalism evolved over time. We traced the change, for example, from the organizational goal of profit maximization to the goal of organizational survival. We also described the changes in the assumptions about human behavior as they evolved from the view that workers were basically lazy and in need of managerial guidance to the eventual realization that workers were, in fact, human beings with needs that must be satisfied.

Finally, we presented some differences between the characteristics of accounting systems based on classical, profit-maximization assumptions and those of organizations held by modern theorists.

SUGGESTED READINGS

Bendix, Reinhard. *Work and Authority in Industry*. New York: John Wiley, 1956.
Caplan, Edwin H. *Management Accounting and Behavioral Science*. Reading, Mass: Addison-Wesley, 1971.

Likert, Rensis. *New Patterns of Management*. New York: McGraw-Hill, 1961.

Mayo, Elton. *The Human Problems of an Industrial Civilization* (second ed.). New York: Macmillan, 1946.

McGregor, Douglas. *The Human Side of Enterprise*. New York: McGraw-Hill, 1960.

Polanyi, Karl. *The Great Transformation*. Boston: Beacon Press, 1944.

Veblen, Thorsten. *The Theory of Business Enterprise*. New York: Charles Scribner's Sons, 1904.

Weber, Max. *The Protestant Ethic and the Spirit of Capitalism*. New York: Charles Scribners' Sons, 1958.

DISCUSSION QUESTIONS

1. How important are religious values in American business today?
2. Do any of the "classical" assumptions about workers linger today? Are those assumptions realistic?
3. What are some examples of financial and nonfinancial data that an accounting system might report to a personnel manager concerned with employee satisfaction?
4. What difference does it make to an accountant whether a firm's goal is to maximize profit or to engage in "satisfying" behavior?
5. Given the changes in management ideologies over the past three centuries, what do you think will be the dominant set of managerial values in 10 years? In 50 years?

CHAPTER 5

Research Methods

This chapter reviews the elements of behaviorial science research methods. The chapter covers a great deal of material in a very short space. It is not meant to be an exhaustive treatment of the topic; indeed, several chapters or entire books can be written on each topic. For more complete and detailed coverage, readers should consult methods textbooks or research handbooks.

We first describe what research is and what it is not. Then we discuss the major steps in behavioral research: project design, data collection, data analysis, and report production.

WHAT IS RESEARCH_____

Research is a systematic, organized effort to investigate problems and answer questions. Research begins with a question, requires a clearly stated description of the problem to be solved, and calls for a plan to answer the question. *Applied research* is intended to solve specific problems. *Basic* or *pure research* is intended to improve our understanding of particular phenomena. Research employs the scientific method, is unbiased, and has verifiable conclusions. Research should be distinguished from simple fact-finding. Looking up information in an encyclopedia and reporting the results does not employ the scientific method; it may contain bias, and its conclusions may not be verifiable.

Goals of Research

Five major goals of scientific research are: description of phenomena, discovery of relationships, explanation of phenomena, prediction of future events, and influence over events.

Events can be described by collecting and classifing information. This is usually the first step in a scientific investigation and the step on which subsequent steps in the research process are based. Sometimes, however, a research project will seek only descriptive information. For example, a behaviorial scientist may seek information on how people perceive their work, identify with their firms, or relate to co-workers.

The next level of scientific investigation is the search for the discovery of relationships. For example, the behavioral scientist may be interested in the relationship between social structure and human perceptions. Specifically, he or she may want to learn how people in production, clerical, or managerial positions perceive their work; how an employee's age, sex, or tenure with a firm affects the level of identification with the firm; and how management style affects the relationships between workers. The existence of these relationships does not imply causality. For instance, if it were found that women workers were more confident in their abilities than men, it would mean that there is an apparent relationship between self-confidence and gender. However, gender does not necessarily cause this relationship; rather, it may be due to other factors such as an association between gender and quality of relationships outside the workplace.

The explanation or understanding of phenomena usually implies that a causal relationship exists between events. Theories, which are based on causal relationships, provide insight into the causes or consequences of events predicted by the theory. For example, we might conclude that women workers are more confident in their abilities because they perceive themselves to be victims of discrimination and consequently try harder in company training programs than do their male co-workers.

It is important to distinguish descriptive and causal hypotheses. A descriptive statement proposes only a simple association between two or more variables. For example, a descriptive hypothesis might state: The greater a woman's level of education, the more confident she will be in her ability to meet the demands of the organization. In order to scientifically assess the hypothesized relationship between these variables, we must be sure that people can be accurately classified in terms of the variables (i.e., as women, according to educational level, and according to ability to meet demands) and that our sample is representative.

A *causal hypothesis* proposes, in addition to an association between variables, that one variable causes, or determines the outcome, of another. A causal hypothesis might state: Having parents with high socioeconomic status causes children to have high aspirations. To evaluate causal statements, it is necessary to demonstrate that the variables are statistically related, that they are properly sequenced (i.e., the assumed cause should not follow the effect), and that the association between the variables does not disappear when other causally prior variables are removed (i.e., the relationship is not spurious).

An association between two variables, X and Y, is spurious if, instead of a causal connection between X and Y, the relationship between the two depends on a third variable, causing the assumed relationship. In this case, Z influences both X and Y so that, in fact, X is not causing Y. Instead, the alleged relationship between X and Y is really due to the influence of Z.

Events are predicted based on established causal relationships. A behavioral researcher might be interested in knowing whether a new set of cost standards will have a favorable impact on employee motivation and company profits. The effects of the new standard on motivation and profits can be predicted with a well-designed research study.

Influence and control are the goals of much research. Companies want to control employee turnover, influence motivation and morale levels, and affect customer loyalty and buying behavior. Control strategies are developed based on what we know about the relationships between events.

PROJECT DESIGN

The first, and often the most crucial, step in behavioral research is problem definition. The nature of the information collected, the method of data collection selected, and the type of samples drawn depend on how the problem is perceived, the research questions framed, and the information the study designer decides to collect. Just as a physician diagnoses a case based on a patient's symptoms, a research director or study designer diagnoses an organization's problems based on available information.

It should be kept in mind that the term *research problem* does not necessarily imply that all behavioral research is designed to correct dysfunctions in the organization. In many cases, applied research is undertaken to improve already satisfactory situations, to expand established markets, to take advantage of various opportunities, or to prepare people for innovations in the organization.

The research director begins the process of problem definition by collecting information from the client. For independent behavioral researchers, the client may be the chief executive or another officer of a firm; for researchers employed in a corporate organization, the "client" may be a staff or line officer of the firm. In any event, the client presents the symptoms on which the project director acts.

For example, suppose XYZ Company is experiencing problems in customer satisfaction. In fact, the company, a consulting firm specializing in the financial aspects of human resource management has been experiencing a slow but consistent decline in clients and revenues over the past three years. After ten years of remarkable growth, averaging 20 percent per year in revenues, the firm began to exhibit 5 to 7 percent declines in revenues about three years ago. More worrisome to the partners has been the loss of valued clients. Concerned about the firm's future, the partners meet with the research director to discuss the firm's problems. The research director is given the symptoms: falling revenues, client attrition, and decreased profits.

After being briefed on the problem, the research director begins the task of problem definition by gathering background information, assessing key internal and external factors, and isolating potential areas of concern. Then the scope of the project is determined, and key research questions are delineated.

The background information tells the research director how long the problem has existed, the nature of business or interpersonal events that might have brought on the problem, how the client perceives the problem, and what variables the client associates with the problem. For example, in the case of XYZ Company, the research director may ask about changes that have occurred over the past several years in the organization, in the industry, and in the economy that might have affected the level of revenues. Have new staff members been properly trained? Do they possess the necessary knowledge, skills, and abilities to meet the established standards of performance? Are there standards of performance? How have deviations from the standards been communicated to the staff? How has performance been measured and evaluated? Have staff members been trained in customer relations and made aware of the importance of client service to the long-run success of the firm?

How has the industry changed? Are there more firms offering similar services? Has XYZ kept pace with technological and procedural changes? What are competitors doing that XYZ is not doing? Has government economic or tax policy caused clients to alter existing procedures so that they no longer require the services of consulting firms like XYZ?

Why does XYZ think that clients have been leaving the firm? Is it because of the quality of service, the delivery of the service, the fees, competition, or the client-consultant relationship? Has XYZ investigated any of the possibilities? Why has XYZ waited three years before seeking help?

Armed with answers to these questions, the research director will be in a position to define the problem. After the problem has been defined, the next step is to design the research project.

Determination of Project Scope

In many cases, all areas of potential concern cannot be investigated in a single behavioral research project. The project scope is usually limited to one or two major questions. For various reasons, it may be undesirable, impractical, or impossible to investigate every aspect of a problem. Frequently, a major limitation on project scope is the amount of funds available. Behavioral research can be expensive, and budgetary constraints often result in restricting the scope of the study to the most important issues.

Drawing on experience and on the results of the research into background and environmental information, the research director will often be able to determine the relative importance of various issues associated with the problem. If a few key issues are identified, the scope of the study is usually limited to these.

In some cases, there may be so many issues associated with a problem that they cannot be adequately addressed in a single study, simply because there is a limit to the number of questions that can be asked of potential respondents. Moreover, there is an inverse relationship between the length of a research instrument (i.e., a telephone interview or mail questionnaire) and the ultimate response rate. This factor would also induce a research director to limit the scope of the study to the issues that are deemed more important.

The nature of the problem may require that it be approached in steps. For instance, to determine how employees perceive themselves in relation to their jobs, their colleagues, and the firm, it may be necessary to conduct an initial study whose scope is limited to discovering the concepts or attributes that people associate with the variables in question. The next phase of the study would measure the perceived association, in the minds of the employees, between those concepts or attributes and the relevant variables.

Time is another factor that might limit the project scope. The study of certain processes might require a longer time frame than is reasonable to wait for results. For example, a firm might want to evaluate the effects of greater participation in the budget-making process on managers' identification with the goals of the firm. The anticipated effect of participation on identification may take several months or years to manifest itself. Thus, the firm might limit the scope of an initial research project to the measurement of managerial identification with the firm's goals. These benchmark measures would be compared to the results of future research that would measure managerial identification after a specified period of increased participation.

Finally, it may be impossible to investigate certain issues. For example, in an effort to attract a larger percentage of highly qualified college graduates to join its ranks, a firm might consider offering free lunch to all employees. Before making this decision, the corporate planners might want to know whether this policy (1) will be imitated by competing firms and (2) whether this benefit is attractive or important to potential recruits. The first concern is an example of an issue that probably cannot be investigated. Assuming that there is no literature that describes similar company histories with this same issue, the only effect of research into this area would be to inform the competition of your intentions. The second issue can be addressed in a research study.

Other Factors

Project design goes beyond determining scope. Other aspects of design include, defining the population, specifying information needs, selecting data collection methods, and budgeting.

The next step in the research process is to identify the type of information that must be collected. The research director must first consider the advantages and disadvantages of primary and secondary data sources.

Primary and Secondary Data

Some information, such as past financial data about a firm, can be obtained from available published records. Other information, including company policies, employment histories, and minutes of meetings, can be obtained from a firm's files. These are examples of *secondary data*. Secondary data sources are those that have been collected, summarized, and prepared by others. The existence of the secondary data is independent of the current research project.

Other types of information, including the measurement of attitudes and opinions and the observation of behavior, are obtained by collecting data directly from the target population. This is *primary data*, a term that refers to the collection of unpublished data.

The major advantage of primary data is that it lies closest to the source of the phenomenon and, therefore, is more likely to reflect the "truth" we are seeking. Primary data can be collected and ordered in a way that effectively answers the questions of the research director. Primary data, however, can be expensive and very time consuming to obtain. In some instances, primary data are not available; in these cases the researcher will have to use secondary data.

The advantages of secondary data include generating savings in cost and time, clarifying problems, creating benchmarks for evaluating primary data, and filling information gaps. Obviously, if information already exists, substantial dollar and time savings can be realized by using secondary data. Researchers should consult libraries, trade or industry associations, and government agencies for the existence of relevant information.

The search for, and examination of, secondary data can help the researcher clarify the problem. By determining what questions have already been asked, and how they were answered, the researcher's understanding of the problem may be enhanced. Also, the secondary data may be used as a benchmark against which primary data is compared. For example, a behavioral accountant might want to know if attitudes toward decentralization in his or her firm are the same as the attitudes held by others in that industry.

Another advantage of secondary data is that it may enable a researcher to obtain information that would otherwise be unavailable. For example, a firm may be reluctant to reveal specific product or employee information to a researcher. However, by consulting trade association statistics, the researcher may obtain the desired information.

VALIDITY AND RELIABILITY _____

The physical attributes of people can be measured in inches or pounds. There is little doubt about what is being measured when we refer to a person's height or weight. When we are interested in measuring the behavioral attributes of people, however, we encounter imposing obstacles. There are no ready rulers or scales to measure attitudes toward work, identification with an organization, or likelihood of success. A researcher has to develop instruments to measure such behavioral phenomena.

Two major risks associated with a behavioral research project are that we may measure the wrong thing and that the results may not be representative. These risks are assessed with tests of validity and reliability.

Validity refers to the extent to which what we measure is, in fact, that which we intended to measure and whether what we measure is related to our research problem. For example, a researcher interested in the degree to which middle-level managers identify with their firm may construct a test that measures the managers' knowledge of company policy. The test may be a reliable measure of managers' knowledge about specific company policies, but it is not a valid test of identification with the firm. The test did not measure what the researcher intended to measure.

Reliability concerns whether a particular technique, applied repeatedly, would yield the same result each time. Thus, it refers to the consistency of a measure. We can depend on reliable measures but cannot depend on unreliable measures.

Researchers who do not know about the validity and reliability of their measuring instruments can have little faith in the data collected or the conclusions drawn from the data.

Validity

There are several types of validity. *Content validity* refers to how well we have delineated the dimensions of the concept or issue we want to measure. Specifically, it concerns the degree to which a given measure covers the range of meanings included with a concept. For example, if we were interested in measuring employees' identification with their work groups, we would review the relevant literature to determine the definitions and dimensions of the concept, how the concept— employee identification—was measured in other studies, and how the concept might be further delineated in order to capture its more subtle meanings. Based on this analysis, we would develop a series of questions to measure the concept. Content validity is essentially judgmental. Each question we ask is judged in terms of its relevance to the concept being measured.

Criterion-related validity is determined by comparing the concepts we measure with an external criterion that is known or assumed to measure the concept we are investigating. There are two types of criterion-related validity, which differ on the basis of time and purpose: predictive and concurrent.

Predictive validity is concerned with whether a test or measure can accurately predict behavior. Predictive validity requires a criterion, or external indicator, of what is to be predicted. For example, a researcher may want to predict how well an applicant will perform on a particular job. An aptitude test might be used to predict performance. Predictive validity is based on the correlation between what the aptitude test predicts and the actual performance exhibited by the new employee. If the score on the aptitude test predicts success, and the employee does succeed on the job (i.e., performs all work-related tasks in conformity with firm standards), then we may conclude that the aptitude test has predictive validity. In this case, the external criterion—success at work—would be comprised of standard measures of performance in particular tasks.

Concurrent validity is concerned with the relationship between our measure and a past or present criterion. That is, it differs from predictive validity in that measures of predictive behavior are obtained at the same time as the actual measures of behavior. For example, concurrent validity would be established if supervisor ratings of individual typists (our measure of employee productivity) were highly correlated with the actual speed and accuracy of the individual typists (the criterion or predicted behavior). A test that has concurrent validity helps a researcher distinguish between individuals on some criteria—in this case, typing speed and typing accuracy.

Construct validity is based on a judgment as to whether the results of our measurements conform to theory. For example, we would expect there to be a positive relationship between employee morale, or overall level of satisfaction with a firm, and the length of tenure of that firm's employees. Construct validity is useful for measuring behavioral phenomena for which external criteria are not available.

Reliability

A reliable measuring instrument generates *stable measures* over time. For example, a wooden ruler used to measure a cereal box will consistently reveal that the box is 13 inches high. An elastic ruler might reveal, at one time, that the box is 11 inches high; at another time, 14 inches; at another, 12 inches. The wooden ruler is a reliable measuring device; the elastic ruler is not reliable. The stability or consistency of our measurement, however, does not guarantee the accuracy of our measurement. If the ruler is scaled improperly, then although the box repeatedly measures 13 inches, it would be wrong each time.

Thus, another aspect of reliability is the *accuracy* of our measuring instrument. Our ruler is reliable and its measurements can be depended on if the 13-inch mark on our ruler corresponds exactly to the 13-inch mark on all other rulers.

Validity versus Reliability

There is a tension between reliability and validity in that reliable measures are often simpler and cover fewer nuances of the concept we wish to measure. For example, counting the number of employees who remain with a firm for at least five years is undoubtedly a reliable measure of satisfaction. This measure, however, certainly misses many important aspects of satisfaction and, as such, is not a particularly valid measure. There is no single way to solve this problem of the trade-off between reliability and validity. However, using several different methods for measuring a concept, and measuring all the dimensions of a concept, generally does not compromise reliability, although it does enhance validity.

DATA COLLECTION METHODS_____

Primary data can be collected by observation of behavior, by surveys, or by laboratory experiments. Observation may or may not involve direct interaction with the people whose behavior is under study. *Unobstrusive observation* involves no interaction. For example, a researcher may watch people on a production line or customers examining merchandise. This technique is appropriate in situations where people are unwilling or unable to explain what they do and how they do it. There are two drawbacks to this method: (1) the observer may not understand what people are doing and why they are engaged in that behavior and (2) because sample size is small, it is risky to generalize results to an entire population. The advantage of such a method is that, by its unobstrusiveness, it cannot influence the behavior under observation in any way.

The observer may participate in the activities of the group whose behavior is being studied. *Participant observation* overcomes the limitation of not understanding the observed behavior, because the participant observer may ask questions. The participant observer, however, faces the risk of being obtrusive, in which case the subjects' behaviors may be staged or otherwise distorted. The problem of generalizing beyond the group to the population still exists.

Survey

With a survey, there is interaction between a researcher and respondent. The data could be collected by mail, telephone, or personal interview. There are advantages and disadvantages associated with each technique. Mail surveys are the least expensive, can provide anonymity, allow respondents to answer questions at a time most convenient for them, and may be best for asking long lists of repetitive questions. Mail questionnaires, however, are usually characterized by lower response rates than phone interviews and do not allow an interviewer to follow up immediately on a particular response.

Telephone interviews can collect data in the shortest period of time but are more costly then mail surveys. Personal interviews can probe for reasons underlying behavior and can explore both general and detailed questions. But personal interviews are the most costly and require the longest time for data collection. Both telephone and personal interview surveys also require a well-trained interviewing staff to ensure the absence of interviewer bias.

Selection of the appropriate data collection technique depends on the circumstances and nature of the research project. For example, if question wording is crucial, mail surveys should be used. If control over the ordering of questions, flexibility in that ordering, and an immediate response are desired, telephone interviews should be used. If the data collection requires a long period of time—say, 30 to 90 minutes—personal interviews may be best.

Experiments

Experiments are used when a researcher wants to manipulate or control certain variables in order to establish a cause and effect relationship. For example, if a researcher wants to determine the effect of feedback on productivity, an experiment could be designed to manipulate other variables that are known to effect productivity.

SELECTION OF RESPONDENTS

The *population* is the entire group of people or set of events that are relevant to the research project. The first step in selecting respondents is to define the population. Once the population is defined, the researcher must decide between a census or a sample. A *census* would seek to collect information from every element in the population. A *sample* collects information from a subset of the population.

A census would be appropriate when: (1) the population is small and data collection costs would not be significantly more than the costs of sampling, (2) it is important to know about every element in the population, and (3) the risks of improper generalization are very great.

In most cases, it is not necessary to take a census. In fact, sampling is often more advantageous to a researcher. Samples require less time and money for data collection, and they minimize the risk of inadvertently revealing a new idea to competitors by minimizing the number of people to be queried. Samples may also reduce total error.

Total error is made up of sampling error and nonsampling error.

Sampling error results from sample size and sample design. For example, bias may be introduced by a sample size that is too small or by a sample design that causes some segments of a population to have a different probability of being selected than other segments. For example, a sample of households selected from a telephone directory is biased because it omits from sample selection the segment of the population with unlisted telephone numbers and the segment of the population with no telephone. The sample drawn from the telephone directory is, therefore, not representative of the entire population of households.

Nonsampling errors are due to problems in project design and data collection, including misleading, poorly worded, or confusing questions; interviewer bias; and errors in recording, storing, and manipulating data.

With a census, there is no sampling error, but there may be a significant amount of nonsampling error due to problems of interview control, interviewer bias, data handling, nonresponse bias, and confusing questions. A well-designed sample would minimize both sampling and nonsampling error, so that total error could be less than the nonsampling error in a census.

Probability and Nonprobability Samples

The two main types of sampling designs are probability and nonprobability sampling. *Probability samples* use some form of random sampling; *nonprobability samples* do not use random sampling. In probability samples, each element in the population has a known probability of being selected. There are several types of probability samples: random, systematic, stratified, cluster, and so on. Nonprobability samples are those where the probability of selection is not known.

With probability samples, sampling error can be mathematically estimated because the probability of selection is known. This provides the researcher with an objective measure of the representativeness of the sample. The known probability of selection also enables a researcher to calculate the appropriate sample size. Probability samples are used when representativeness is important.

In some cases, researchers may not be interested in representativeness. For example, if we want to determine the traits of successful and unsuccessful managers, it may be better to use a nonprobability sample and select the 20 most successful and 20 least successful managers. In this case, a probability sample would not necessarily provide the researcher with the respondents who could best answer the questions at hand.

THE RESEARCH INSTRUMENT————————

The development of the questionnaire, or research instrument, is another crucial step in the research process. The questionnaire must encourage cooperation from the respondents and be designed to collect valid and reliable information.

Securing Respondent Cooperation

A well-designed questionnaire is useless if people do not cooperate with the researcher's request for information. Low levels of cooperation, or response rates, make it difficult for researchers to generalize from the sample to the population. If this happens, the question may arise as to whether the nonrespondents hold different attitudes and opinions than those who responded.

There are several techniques that could encourage higher response rates. First, in the case of personal interviews, respondents should be sent a well-composed letter explaining the general purpose of the project and that they will soon be contacted by phone to set up an appointment for the interview. When the call is made, the researcher should be courteous, impress upon the respondent the importance of the respondent's opinions, and thank the respondent for agreeing to cooperate. On the interview date, the researcher should arrive on time and again express gratitude for the respondent's cooperation.

Similarly, in the case of telephone interviews, it may be useful to send potential respondents a letter introducing the research team, explaining the nature of the project, and asking for cooperation when the call is made. It may be helpful to offer an incentive, in the form of cash, gift, charitable contribution, or merchandise discount. The letter may help overcome the dislike, or outright hostility, that people sometimes have for telephone solicitors or others whose phone calls intrude on their privacy. Once phone contact is made, the interviewer should be courteous and should not extend the interview beyond the promised time limit.

For all questionnaires—mail, telephone, or personal interview—a pretest is essential because it enables researchers to correct poorly worded or confusing questions. One major reason for low cooperation rates on mail surveys, for instance, is that a confusing question—even one at the end of a questionnaire—may prompt the respondent to set the questionnaire aside and never complete it. Obviously, the questionnaire should not be of excessive length. Questions should be easy to understand and should not require long and tedious responses. Response categories should be clear and include all options. On mail questionnaires, the questions should be easy to read and on good quality paper.

Securing Valid and Reliable Responses

Only essential information should be requested from respondents. The researcher should determine the nature of the desired information and select a question format that will provide that information with the least burden on respondents.

Questions can be open-ended or close-ended. An *open-ended question* asks for a free response. For example, we might ask: "What do you like most about your job?" or "What are the strengths and weaknesses of Joe Su as a foreman?" Respondents would be able to enter any answer, in their own words, without the researcher's suggestion introducing bias. Open-ended questions are generally used when the researcher cannot predict the nature of the answers to a question, if his or her suggestions will bias responses, or if the researcher is interested in exploring the range of possible answers.

Close-ended questions offer respondents a fixed set of response alternatives. Respondents are instructed to check one or more response alternatives. Advantages of this question format include ease of response for respondents and ease of tabulation and interpretation by the researcher. Disadvantages include suggestion bias and the chance that the response alternatives may not reflect the respondent's opinion. Regardless of the question format selected, the questions should be carefully worded, and instructions should be clear. Confusing questions, combined with a questionnaire layout that is poorly designed, can threaten reliability. Biased and leading questions are also a threat to reliability.

Double-barreled questions also should be avoided. A *double-barreled question* makes two statements and asks for one response. For example, respondents may be asked to provide a true of false answer to the following statements: "Our firm's product quality is high, and our on-time delivery record is the industry standard." Respondents may agree with the first statement but not the second, or with the second but not the first. If so, how is a response to be made? Double-barreled questions could frustrate respondents and cause them to discard the questionnaire, or, at best, to answer them inaccurately.

Researchers should avoid questions that ask for information beyond the respondent's knowledge or experience, that ask for too great an effort, that encourage lying, or whose response alternatives are not mutually exclusive. All questionnaires should be pretested in order to identify flaws in question wording and question ordering and to predict response rate to the main test.

A well-worded, well-designed questionnaire should provide information that is both valid and reliable.

DATA ANALYSIS AND REPORT PREPARATION————————————————

Before data can be analyzed, it must be edited and coded. Information collected from interviews or questionnaires should be examined for omissions or obvious errors. For example, a respondent may not have answered a question asking whether he or she reads the company newsletter. However, the respondent may have answered a set of five specific questions about newsletter content. The editor would then circle the "yes" response for the unanswered first question on reading habits. The editor would also check all written responses for legibility and scan all close-ended responses to be sure that where one response was solicited, only one response option was circled.

The most difficult and time-consuming aspect of data preparation is the coding of open-ended questions. All responses should be read and categorized. A numerical code is usually assigned to each category.

The final report should convey the conclusions drawn from analysis of the data. There is no single best report format; the way in which the report is organized depends to a great extent on the needs of the users. At a minimum, the report should provide a statement of purpose, specify the major research questions addressed, provide necessary background material, describe the research methods used, present findings and conclusions, and, if appropriate, give recommendations for action. An executive summary, which briefly presents an overview of the major findings, is usually included at the beginning of the report. This summary is particularly useful for busy executives who want to know the research results but do not have the time to read the entire report. Readers are referred to the communication chapter in Part Three for more detailed discussion of report content.

SUMMARY————————————————

In this chapter we reviewed the basic elements of research and the research process. We first defined research, then discussed the descriptive, explanatory, and predictive goals of research. Next, we discussed the difference between association and causation. Then we described the research process: research design, data collection, data analysis, and report presentation. During this discussion, we presented several important terms, including primary and secondary data and validity and reliability. We also provided a brief introduction to data collection methods and sampling and to the research instrument. We concluded the chapter with a brief discussion of preparing data for analysis and the content of the final report.

SUGGESTED READINGS

Campbell, Donald T. and Julian C. Stanley. *Experimental and Quasi-Experimental Designs for Research*. Chicago: Rand McNally, 1963.

Denzin, Norman K. *Sociological Methods*. Hawthorne, NY: Aldine, 1970.

Fink, Arlene and Jacqueline Kosecoff. *How to Conduct Surveys*, Beverly Hills: Sage Publications, 1985.

Kerlinger, F. *Foundation of Behavioral Research* (second ed.). New York: Holt, Rinehart and Winston, 1973.

Osgood, C. E., G. I. Suci, and P. H. Tannenbaum. *The Measurement of Meaning*. Urbana, Ill: University of Illinois Press, 1957.

Rosenberg, Morris. *The Logic of Survey Analysis*. New York: Basic Books, 1968.

Rossi, Peter H., James D. Wright, and Andy B. Anderson (eds.). *Handbook of Survey Research*. Orlando, FL: Academic Press, 1983.

Schuman, Howard and Stanly Presser. *Questions and Answers in Attitude Surveys: Experiments on Question Form, Wording and Context*. New York: Academic Press, 1981.

Selltiz, Claire, Lawrence S. Wrightsman, and Stuart W. Cook. *Research Methods in Social Relations* (third ed.). New York: Holt, Rinehart and Winston, 1976.

Sudman, Seymour. *Applied Sampling*. New York: Academic Press, 1976.

Sudman, Seymour and Norman N. Bradburn. *Asking Questions: A Practical Guide to Questionnaire Design*. San Francisco: Jossey-Bass, 1982.

DISCUSSION QUESTIONS

1. What are the ethical issues of doing behavioral research?
2. How is research design related to problem definition?
3. As a researcher, how would you handle an ill-defined problem?
4. Must a measure be valid to be reliable?
5. A large retail chain faced a decision as to whether purchasing should be centralized or decentralized. The decision would have a significant impact on company policy and on the organizational structure. Develop a problem definition, specify project scope, specify the information you would need to help reach a conclusion, and specify how you would collect the information.
6. Is primary or secondary data more likely to be valid?
7. A baseball bat manufacturer is considering the development of a new bat that is square on the bottom, pointed on the top, and flatter in the middle. The manufacturer wants you to assess demand. You recommend the use of mail and phone surveys and propose to scientifically select a sample. After receiving your proposal, the manufacturer complains that it is too expensive and would take too long to collect the data. The manufacturer asks why you can't just do interviews with some kids at a few playgrounds. How would you respond?

PART TWO

Behavioral Implications of Management Accounting

Management accounting is an action-oriented discipline that measures past actions and provides information to influence future actions. Statement No. 1A of the *Statements on Management Accounting* defines management accounting as "the process of identification, measurement, accumulation, analysis, preparation, interpretation, and communication of financial information used by management to plan, evaluate and control within an organization and to assure appropriate use of an accountability for its resources."

In this part of the book, we will study the impact of behavioral science on management accounting. We will discuss how people participate in creating accounting information, how they react to accounting information, and how the information or the system producing it can be modified to stimulate more efficient organizational performance. We will demonstrate how the behavioral aspects of management accounting help managers decide what to do and how to motivate people to do it more efficiently.

Our discussions are based on the assumptions that managers can best use the accounting system to maintain and improve operational performance if they have a clear understanding of the relationship between the elements of accounting control systems and the various factors that determine people's behavior. Our discussions also assume:

1. The accounting system is an organization's principal formal information and control system. This system is used to define and communicate organizational objectives, measure accomplishments, and identify the need for corrective actions. Accounting is primarily used for measuring profit and other relatively specific economic phenomena. But there is no inherent reason why accounting systems cannot be used for a broader set of organizational goals and objectives. A growing body of research indicates that accounting's contribution to efficient and effective business operation could be increased through sincere attention to behavioral considerations.

2. Organizational goals and objectives are complex and diverse. They represent a compromise of the conflicting demands articulated by the firm's subunits and influential participants. In business enterprises, profit is usually a significant goal, but it is seldom the exclusive one. There is often a broad range of other objectives. Many of these objectives are poorly defined and poorly communicated. Their relative importance to the organization may change over time.

3. Organizational participants have a variety of individual needs and goals, which are not always congruent with the organizational goals. Organizational survival and success requires individuals to sacrifice some degree of freedom of action and to cooperate with others in achieving organizational goals. Behavioral research has demonstrated that certain organizational and/or leadership policies and practices have a negative impact on goal congruence. A major problem facing top management of an organization is to develop congruence between the goals and objectives of the organization and the individual goals and needs of its employees.

4. Accounting techniques can be used either in a behaviorally positive and stimulating way or in a negative, punitive, and coercive fashion. Behaviorally naive accounting practices may act as a deterrent to goal congruence, motivation, and harmonious cooperation. Such practices may result in undesirable behavioral responses such as anxiety, frustration, conflict, and rigidity. Research has demonstrated that besides the accounting techniques, the attitudes of the people who design, operate, and use them also determine the behavioral consequences. Unfortunately, neither organization theory nor the behavioral sciences yet provide definitive answers to such behavioral problems. But it is possible to identify the causes of dysfunctional behavior and to suggest approaches to solve the problems.

CHAPTER 6

Financial Control

by
William T. Geary
Associate Professor
College of William and Mary

INTRODUCTION

The boundaries of accounting are extended because of new technologies and new demands on the part of clients seeking accounting support. Significant growth in the management advisory services provided by public accounting firms and the emergence of new departments for information systems within organizations offer ready evidence of this client demand. Clients require support for designing and implementing financial control systems. This chapter will focus on issues related to the topic of control in so far as these issues shape and influence the design and implementation of financial control systems.

The chapter begins with a control dilemma that illustrates the far-reaching consequences of financial accounting control. This dilemma is followed by an examination of objectives and definitions associated with the design of financial control systems. The consideration of objectives includes traditional concepts of control in accounting and auditing, which are reconciled with the behavioral objectives identified for financial control systems. Comprehensive financial control systems are then analyzed in terms of subsystems designed to support planning, operating, and feedback requirements. This analysis is followed by a consideration of the impact of contextual variables on the effectiveness of the design of subsystems. The chapter concludes with an analysis of the systematic thought process required for the successful design of control initiatives.

CONTROL DILEMMA

Four years ago Quality Products, Inc., a metal fabricating shop, was started by three owners to provide specialty products with computer-based production methods. The three owners have equal shares in the business and work together well. Their company specializes in precision metal fabricating, emphasizing both innovative design and high-quality production. Because of the emphasis on custom fabrication, it is not unusual to have production runs for fewer than 100 units. Customers come from many sources, including the automotive, telecommunications, defense, and computer industries. The majority of the items made in the shop are related to electronics.

The company has been very successful with its emphasis on flexibility, quality control, and customer service. Customers are often gained from the competition because a competitor's shop has failed to deliver the required quality or service. Because of the emphasis on service, quality production, quick turn-around, and follow-through after the sale, the company's prices may be higher than some of their competitors. But over the long-term, the advantages of higher quality and better service have attracted many loyal customers, and the shop is quickly approaching practical capacity.

The owners have been very intelligent and thoughtful in organizing and administering their firm, and they are justly proud of their success. They also recognize that there are many opportunities to expand their existing business or diversify into other areas. In assessing the competition, they have noted that no firm on either a national or a regional level controls a significant share of the market. Furthermore, the demand for what they do is increasing rapidly. Preoccupation with managing their existing business and its growth has kept the owners from making commitments to expansion. To overcome this short-term focus, the owners and key management personnel have scheduled a three-day planning retreat away from company facilities.

The company has been controlled primarily as an owner-operated enterprise. Given that the firm deals in highly nonstandard production activities, how can the owners keep their flexibility and maintain control over quality if they expand? Should they admit new partners and, in effect, continue with owner-managers assigned to an oversight role? Or should they pursue a diversification strategy and seek production work that is more standardized and therefore easier to control? Clearly, the number of different options and combinations of options can be increased at will.

Discussions during the course of the three days will center on the strategies for expansion that the company should pursue. What control issues should be on the agenda for the owners' meetings?

DEFINITION OF FINANCIAL CONTROL————

Mechanical Feedback versus Behavioral Responses

The primary focus in financial control subsystems is the behavior of an organization's people, not its machines. For this reason, financial control is best understood by emphasizing the importance of behavioral assumptions. Not all control designs are concerned with human behavior. Mechanical applications of control, such as the thermostat that controls room temperature, emphasize mechanical feedback rather than behavioral responses. Of course, mechanical and electrical devices and methods can also be used to influence human behavior. A warning alarm installed as a safety device to prevent injury or a password system designed to keep unauthorized persons from using a computer are ready examples. These examples employ mechanical and electrical means but the control objective is to affect a human rather than to induce a mechanical response. Because of the emphasis on a human response rather than a mechanical response, financial control subsystems are ultimately premised on behavioral assumptions.

The underlying behavioral objectives of financial control can be reconciled with a generalized definition of control. In general, *control* will be defined as: an initiative chosen because it is believed that the probability of obtaining a desired outcome will be increased. In financial control, the underlying desired outcomes are behavioral events and the application is to a financial problem.

The definition of control has been based on the concepts of "beliefs" and "probability." Managers have acquired beliefs about the way their world works and the responses that can be expected when an initiative is chosen. However, even the most self-assured manager is typically prepared to admit that few, if any, behavioral outcomes are 100 percent predictable. In the context of a real organization, well understood cause-and-effect relationships either do not exist or they are obscured by the complexity of the environment. Setting high standards in a cost accounting system, for example, does not guarantee that employees will be more productive. Similarly, the implementation of a responsibility accounting system cannot guarantee that managers will be more responsible and effective resource allocators. In selecting financial controls, managers will rely on their beliefs and their past experiences. The behavioral outcomes attributed to the control initiatives are more realistically and accurately understood in terms of these beliefs and probability assessments rather than naive causal relationships.

The mainstream of the accounting literature has only recently emphasized the underlying behavioral assumptions of financial control. This can be interpreted as both an evolution of thought and an extension of the sphere of influence of the accountant and the accounting discipline. There is much to be gained by reconciling a behavioral approach for control in managerial accounting with the traditional, non-behavioral concepts of control encountered in the accounting and auditing literature.

Extending Traditional Concepts

Traditional concepts of control in accounting have often presumed that the production of accounting information is the final step of the accountant's role. In the behavioral approach to the design and implementation of financial control subsystems, the production of information is not the end of the accountant's involvement. Instead, the production of information is viewed as an intermediate rather than a final step. The accounting information is employed as part of a signaling process designed to assist in managing the organization by influencing the behavior of its members. The control objective is rooted in the desire to select an initiative that will alter the probability of obtaining a desired behavioral outcome. And the production of accounting information is seen as a means rather than an end.

When designing control systems appropriate to the generation of accurate and reliable accounting information, emphasis is traditionally placed on the following seven factors.

1. Engaging personnel who will carry out their responsibilities competently and with integrity.
2. Avoiding incompatible functions by separating duties and responsibilities.
3. Defining the authority associated with a position so that the propriety of transactions that are executed can be evaluated.
4. Establishing a systematic method to assure that transactions are recorded accurately.
5. Insuring that documentation is adequate.
6. Safeguarding assets by designing procedures to limit access to assets.
7. Designing independent checks to promote accuracy.

The principles associated with sound internal control designs reflect many decades of experience on the part of auditing professionals. This invaluable experience can be extended to the design and implementation of financial control systems by expanding the set of objectives beyond the production of accounting information to encompass the administrative process. The term *accounting controls* has been associated with safeguarding assets and promoting accurate and reliable accounting information. The term *administrative controls* has been associated with promoting operating efficiency and adhering to management policies. Examples of accounting control include separation of duties concerned with record keeping and physical control over assets, whereas performance reports and quality controls are cited as examples of administrative controls. Both accounting and administrative controls, regardless of their classification, can be employed in the design and implementation of financial control systems intended to support the administrative process. The extension of traditional concepts of control requires an extension of scope beyond accounting controls and beyond the financial statements to include the administrative processes of the organization.

Extending the scope of the accountant's involvement to the administrative process does not deny the importance of accounting controls. Knowledge of traditional accounting controls and experience with accounting systems is powerful and can be readily extended to other control applications. However, to make the extension successfully, knowledge of accounting controls must be combined with many other sources of knowledge for the purpose of influencing the behavior of members of the organization through the use of accounting signals. In the following section, the relationship of accounting data and control to the administrative process will be considered in greater detail.

COMPREHENSIVE CONTROL

A formal, comprehensive control system is actually a configuration of integrated, formal subsystems that support the administrative process. To be formalized, a control subsystem must be structured in advance and designated as a process appropriate to the achievement of a specific objective. Informal approaches are ad hoc, highly personalized, and subject to considerable variability. Budgets, accounting reports, standard costs, and responsibility centers are examples of formalized approaches. Unspoken norms, seat-of-the-pants management, and control by intuition are examples of informal control approaches. To be comprehensive, a control system must encompass *planning* activities, *operating* activities, and the required *feedback* functions. These three phases of the administrative process and their control implications will be discussed in the following sections.

Planning

The planning process is characterized in terms of goal-setting behaviors. Formal planning efforts are much more than the statistics that ultimately fill the pages in the planning document. Important aspects of the goal-setting process are the basic concerns of organization and communication. If the organization structure is deficient, this should come to light during the planning process. The planning process will raise control questions such as: How are divisions to be identified? What use will be made of responsibility accounting? How will departments be structured and what accounting will be made for interdepartmental transfers?

It is readily apparent that planning is essential to effective control. Control can also be essential to effective planning. A plan that is technically or logistically brilliant may invite a control disaster for the unwary organization that is not attentive to the control implications of implementing the plan. In this sense, the control requirements can operate as a set of constraints for the planning function. This phenomenon is common in the high technology fields where technical feasibility has often exceeded our ability to protect the organization from threats such as security breaches, operating mishaps, fraud, and other control failures.

Operations

In structured organizations, operating functions presume the existence of a management plan, although the plan may be informal or unwritten. The term *operations* refers to the conduct of the operating activities of the organization, including the provision of services and the manufacture of products as well as the necessary support functions needed to sustain operations. *Operating control* is the process of monitoring and correcting operating activities during the implementation of the management plan. Examples of operating control subsystems include inventory and purchasing applications, standard costing, and housekeeping subsystems such as payroll administration and credit management. In some organizations, operating control is the responsibility of owner-managers who exert control through informal and personal means. Larger or more complex organizations must formalize operating control subsystems to assure a standard of effectiveness and to promote operating efficiency.

Feedback

Feedback in organizations comes from both formal and informal sources and ranges from nonverbal communication to routinely generated statistical tabulations. Feedback is sought as the basis for making evaluations that will influence the distribution of rewards, the assessment of penalties, and the alteration of the planning and operating processes that generated the feedback. A formal and systematic design for the collection and channeling of feedback requires that variables be identified, measures defined, and data collected. Measures can be generated internally, such as the feedback provided from an analysis of standard cost variances; measures can also be derived from sources external to the firm, such as industry marketshare or efficiency data. The feedback process in financial control subsystems is seldom as well understood as it is in mechanical applications that involve closed systems with well-defined cause-and-effect relationships. In a management application, the presence of the human factor and the complexity of human motivation suggest that the relationship between feedback and future actions is much more uncertain and complicated.

Control Interactions

Planning, operation, and feedback activities have been identified as the three aspects of the administrative process that must be supported in a comprehensive control design. While each of these dimensions has been discussed in turn, it is readily apparent that they are not independent activities. The design of planning subsystems for the near term and the long term, the creation of control support for operations, and the decisions to emphasize certain feedback measures to indicate success and failure are highly interrelated issues. These interrelationships can be managed to great advantage if an organization can successfully link the control subsystems designed to support the planning, operating, and feedback functions.

The interrelationships among control subsystems also hold the potential for highly unsatisfactory results. Logically, planning should precede operations and feedback measures should follow from stated objectives and operating plans. Also, if feedback measures are assumed to be neutral and unobtrusive, it would be expected that the act of collecting feedback measures would exert no significant influence over the planning and operating phases. This simple logic, however, is not suited to the complexities of empirical settings. Manipulating the feedback measures can become more compelling than the objectives being pursued, resulting in the feedback measures leading the operating phase rather than the reverse. For example, in a company with high fixed production costs, a production manager whose success is evaluated on the basis of lower average production costs can achieve the measure of success by extending production runs to produce more product. If this results in producing far more product than the company can sell, then the average cost per unit sold may actually increase. In this case, feedback is dominating operations and the measurement process is highly obtrusive.

A similar inversion can occur between planning and feedback. The planning process can be profoundly influenced by feedback effects. Planning goals that otherwise would not be very important can take on artificially high priorities because a plan's objectives emphasize statistical measures of performance based on predetermined feedback measures. Managers who know that they will be evaluated on the basis of the number of units sold may approach the planning process with a bias for products with a high unit sales potential rather than a high profitability potential. These and other aspects of the complex interrelationships in a comprehensive financial control system will be considered in greater depth in the chapters that follow. Another important determinant of the effectiveness of a control design, to be discussed in the section that follows, is the context in which a comprehensive control system is implemented.

CONTEXTUAL FACTORS

Context can be vitally important to success in the design and implementation of financial control systems. *Context*, as used in this sense, refers to the set of characteristics that determine the empirical setting in which the control system will be applied. The number of ways to describe a particular context is almost without limit. Further, the persuasive evidence relating contextual factors to a particular financial control application is very sparse. The challenge for managers is to understand which factors are the most critical to the success of a particular financial control application.

The process of identifying critical contextual factors is highly subjective and transitory. What is important in the opinion of one manager may appear less important to another manager. All listings of critical contextual factors are subject to revision over relatively brief intervals of time because of change. In this section, the contextual factors of size, environmental stability, profit motivation, and process factors will be discussed. The factors selected for discussion do not represent a complete set nor are they necessarily, in any given case, the most important factors to be considered; they do, however, clearly demonstrate the important role that context plays in the successful design and implementation of financial control subsystems.

Size

Size can be viewed alternately as both an opportunity and a constraint. Size can represent opportunities as the economies of scale make feasible control strategies that could not otherwise be entertained. Size can also become a constraint if growth causes the elimination of control strategies that were once efficient but cannot be formalized to fit the needs of the larger and more impersonal organization. Large scale control designs that are typically computer-based may begin as innovation, but they can quickly establish the economic standard that will determine competitive success in an industry. This phenomenon is applicable to heavy manufacturing as well as to financial institutions and service oriented companies. The planning, operating, and feedback activities in these large organizations require formal control strategies that should anticipate the risks of control failures as well as facilitate communications and promote operating efficiency.

While it is apparent that size can be an important factor in distinguishing between contexts, many other variables can also be associated with issues of size. This makes it impossible to isolate any one factor, such as size, as the dominant one. For example, the factors of environmental stability and process can often be associated with size. Nonetheless, the accountant should expect that size will be an important factor in assessing the feasibility and requirements of financial control designs.

Environmental Stability

Control design in a stable environment can differ greatly from control design in an environment characterized by continuous change. Stability in the exogenous environment can be assessed in terms of the number and strength of forces generated externally to the unit that requires a response. The degree of environmental stability can be gauged by selecting appropriate measures of environmental change such as the number of new products introduced over a specified time interval, competitor actions that render production methods obsolete or inefficient, or legislative initiative affecting units dependent on the results of these processes.

A stable exogenous environment is assumed in most introductory applications of standard cost systems and the related analysis of cost variance. This assumption persists despite the fact that many contemporary operating units must confront a business environment that requires continuous change in operating practices. By comparing costs actually incurred against a predetermined standard, these standard cost subsystems are necessarily retrospective. Such an analysis is not consistent with a control design that should sustain a forward-looking response. If responsiveness to a changed environment is essential, then meeting standards fixed last year is not a recipe for success. Several accountants have proposed forward-looking, ex-ante control designs to supplement the more common retrospective, ex-post designs. It can be expected that these innovative approaches will become more common when they are viewed as important to the success of the unit by management that must adapt to environmental change.

Profit Motive

The absence of a profit motive certainly does not preclude the use of accounting measurements and assessments of productivity. On the other hand, it is clear that control systems based on the motive and measure of profitability often cannot be transferred directly to the not-for-profit context. Profit measures are important, although overworked, indicators of success. While these profit-based measures suffer from many shortcomings, their preeminence in control design cannot be denied.

The greatest advantage associated with profit-based indicators is that they are highly visible summary statistics. These statistics are often interpreted as a summary of the overall success of the complex and intricate subsystems that comprise the total organization; they are also usually construed, rightly or wrongly, as a measure of the success of individual managers. When the profit motive is absent, other indicators of organizational and individual success must be relied upon. In these settings, the selection of alternative measures has proven to be a constant source of challenge to managers and consultants. Undoubtedly, meeting this challenge will continue to demand attention in our society as solutions are sought to common problems and social needs.

Process Factors

It is well known that the process subject to accounting controls can be a crucial determinant in control design. There are many ways to characterize organizational processes. Some of these characterizations can be important for control purposes, while others may be distinctions without differences. Simple/complex and variable cost/fixed cost processes will be briefly considered to illustrate the importance and meaning of process variables.

A *simple process* is one that is characterized by well understood cause-effect relationships; a *complex process* involves multiple relationships that are not well understood. A simple process is more readily controlled than a complex one. *Discretionary cost* is the term often used to describe a cost incurred by a unit where input-output relationships are not well understood. The unit could have a simple or complex process. Discretionary cost examples include units such as research and development, marketing, and personnel administration. It is often very difficult to design control initiatives for discretionary cost applications because of the uncertain effects of the control. (See Chapter 10 for a more complete discussion of cost control.)

A process factor important in controlling both discretionary and engineered costs is cost variability. Cost control strategies for variable cost processes are often substantially different from the cost control strategies suited to fixed cost applications. For example, variable cost processes suggest an emphasis on conservation; fixed cost processes are more likely to be associated with effective utilization.

Summary

The preceding discussion of the contextual variables of size, environmental stability, profit motivation, and process factors demonstrates that the assessment of contextual factors is a difficult and challenging process. The student of control must rely on informed judgment, experience, and sensitivity to identify the critical contextual variables that govern a particular setting. The chapters that follow provide many opportunities to gain further insights into the influence of context in assessing the adequacy of control designs.

DESIGN CONSIDERATIONS

A control has been defined as "an initiative chosen because it is believed that the probability of obtaining a desired outcome will be increased." To improve the probability of success, designers will seek to define cause-and-effect relationships believed to be present in the environment, thus enabling them to anticipate the logical consequences that can result from applying a control or set of controls. Since the focus is behavioral rather than mechanical, designers must think in terms of expectations and probability rather than certainties in describing outcomes. Developing the perfect or optimal design is not a realistic goal.

Control systems are designed to achieve satisfactory results. A pragmatic evaluation of success must collectively assess the benefits sought and weigh them against the penalties incurred. The Constitution of the United States is an excellent example of such a control design—it is widely acclaimed as a success on the pragmatic basis that it has established an interplay of forces that, while far from being perfect in the sense of efficiency, has served a nation exceptionally well. Controls intended for use in organizations must be designed with an understanding of the range of behavioral consequences likely to result and an appreciation for the need to accommodate change.

Anticipation of Logical Consequences

Anticipation of logical consequences is a key element in the design of controls. This emphasis is an important point of departure for financial managers who are accustomed to making judgments based on whether a result is correct or incorrect. A financial statement lends itself to a determination of whether the results are correct. A control, though, will be associated with results or consequences that are neither correct nor incorrect, but rather a reflection of the behavioral consequences of a particular control strategy. For example, a time and motion study engineer establishing a standard labor cost may seek to pad a labor standard by creating a more generous time allowance. In many circumstances, employees will take advantage of the built-in slack and actually work extra hours to complete a task. This employee behavior is rational, highly predictable, and logical. It is a logical consequence often associated with the introduction of a standard cost system.

Experienced managers are likely to anticipate most outcomes associated with control processes they are already familiar with and understand. However, a manager promoted to a new position or confronting a new technology or a different context will need to draw upon external resources to gain an understanding of the control environment. The business case literature has proven to be an especially fruitful source of understanding for students of control. Cases dealing with topics such as responsibility accounting and transfer pricing schemes increase the manager's understanding of possible logical outcomes without having to actually live through the experience. Similarly, theoretical approaches can be useful in predicting logical consequences associated with control initiatives. A theoretical approach of particular interest to students of control theory can be found in the application of agency theory to control design, which provides a good illustration of the contribution of theory to the solution of practical problems.

Relevance of Agency Theory

Agency theory facilitates the anticipation of logical consequences by providing a framework for understanding and subsequently predicting behavior. An agent is a person engaged by a principal to carry out tasks designated by the principal. The agent is allowed to have a set of objectives different from the principal. For example, an employee as an agent may prefer leisure to work, while the employer as a principal may prefer getting the job done to leisure. To motivate the agent to work rather than rest, the principal is expected to initiate a contractual arrangement to diminish the risk that the agent will be "out of control" and seek leisure. The principal can allocate resources to gain control in three ways: monitoring schemes, incentive/penalty plans, and insurance or risk-transferring options. Agents are assumed to be economically rational actors who ultimately can be counted on to find a way through any loophole left by an unsuspecting principal.

A particular strength of agency theory is the insight it provides for fashioning control designs that simultaneously advance the welfare of both parties. Because the principals and agents are allowed to have different utility functions, it may be possible to design a control strategy (i.e., monitoring scheme, incentive/penalty plan, or risk-transferring option) that will improve the well-being of all parties. This type of solution is sometimes referred to as a "plus sum" solution. To illustrate such a solution, let us assume that an agent can be enticed to perform a task for a low rate of pay if there is flexibility in selecting the work schedule. If the principal is not concerned about the time conditions under which the task is performed, this contract would provide the principal with the advantage of a low wage rate and the agent the advantage of flexible schedule. Another illustration could be drawn from the board rooms of the corporate world, where executive compensation contracts are sometimes designed based on the belief that executive behavior will be altered by establishing a contract that will bring shareholders more benefit than cost. This is accomplished through the successful management of the opposing self-interests present in the principal-agent relationship.

Agency theory is appealing in part because it can be invoked to explain happenings familiar to most people. Agency theory, however, has some major limitations. People assume many roles in organizations. The president may be your principal, at least indirectly, but the president in turn is the agent of the board of directors, who themselves are the agents of the share-holders. It is dangerously simplistic to presume that a particular principal-agent relationship can be extracted from context and singled out for indepen-dent consideration. Agency theory also assumes that a contractual view of human behavior will validly predict logical consequences. If this contractual worldview is further reduced to include only those rewards and costs that can be objectively measured in monetary terms, this theory leads to a concept of rational behavior for principals and agents based on unmitigated economic self-interest. This reduced application of agency theory omits rewards such as honor, achievement, loyalty, and other familiar intrinsic satisfactions. While such a purely economic view may sometimes be intended, it is also clear that agency theory can provide a seriously inaccurate assessment of the behavior a complex person can be expected to exhibit in a real world situation.

The preceding discussion of agency theory indicates the ways in which theoretical approaches can either clarify or obscure the understanding required to assess logical consequences. Individuals form a synthesis of their past experiences to enable them to predict the logical consequences associated with a control design. This process of intelligence gathering is essentially inductive and, like all inductive approaches, the individual is left vulnerable to changes in the environment that alter preexisting patterns. Thus, students of control design must draw on past experiences, but they must also make provision for and anticipate change.

Managing Change

Managing change is an important consideration in control designs. A man-ager employing controls to accomplish objectives is often confronted with a dilemma. The existing controls within the company may have ceased to function as well as they once did, but the manager may legitimately fear that a change in controls will cost more in terms of disruption of the status quo than the value of the potential benefits. A more challenging, and undoubt-edly a more frustrating, problem confronts the manager who concludes that new controls are cost-justified at a time when the organization is unable or unwilling to change. For these managers, it is appropriate to ask whether their organization can renew their control designs from within. Or must the organization experience a highly predictable and theoretically avoidable shock before responding by instituting a new set of controls?

Many organizations employ external consultants or internal auditors to stimulate the self-renewal of a control system. Even though the recommen-dations of the outside consultants or internal auditors may closely parallel the strategies advocated by the permanent staff, these advisors are often in a position to influence the course of events because of their special reporting relationship to top management. On the other hand, it is not difficult to cite examples of organizations that were able to effect the required control modifications through internal processes.

Over the long term, firms will maintain an in-control environment through a process of change and compensation. This will be true whether control designs are modified through a continuous process of internal regeneration or whether the change is caused by external factors that impact upon the organization, such as the loss of a major customer or the conspicuous financial failure of a major firm in a particular industry. Thus, a firm that has experienced severe penalties associated with the inflexibility of a highly centralized control approach will seek to decentralize; the same firm though, after some years with an emphasis on decentralization, will seek to compensate for the severe penalties associated with the inefficiencies of a decentralized approach by some degree of recentralization. In such a dynamic, there is a tendency to be critical of the organization because there appears to be confusion over the appropriate control objective. This criticism implicitly assumes that an organization must consistently seek a well-specified control equilibrium and, in many cases, this assumption is highly inappropriate. In a complex organization, equilibrium in the control environment will require constant change and compensation. The state of equilibrium is dynamic, not static. Only through change and compensation can most organizations seek a constant state of maintaining an in-control status within the organization.

SUMMARY

Control has been defined as an initiative chosen because it is believed that the probability of obtaining a desired outcome will be increased. A comprehensive system of control has been defined by reference to planning, operating, and feedback activities within organizations. In addition to being comprehensive, a successful control design must also be responsive to the organizational context. While the number of contextual factors affecting an organization is almost limitless, examples of factors often critically important in control designs were discussed. Control system designs quickly become complex and intricate; nonetheless, designers must strive to understand cause-and-effect relationships and to anticipate logical consequences. Very often, control designs must be dynamic and the objective of a constant state of "in-control" must be pursued through processes of continuous adaptation and change. Control design must be judged in terms of probability and cost-benefit comparisons rather than certainty and perfection.

In subsequent chapters, the topics of responsibility accounting subsystems, budgetary controls, cost accounting controls, performance evaluation models, and transfer pricing will be presented and discussed. These control strategies are commonly employed in practice and they represent important means of achieving organizational goals. As indicated in this chapter, the approach taken to these topics will emphasize an understanding of cause-and-effect relationships and the development of the ability to anticipate logical behavioral consequences.

SOLUTION TO CONTROL DILEMMA

In fixing the agenda, the owners of Quality Products, Inc., should certainly include among topics for discussion the factors of size, process complexity, and technological change. They should also assess the abilities and interests of the management team. The development and implementation of a successful control system to encompass the planning, operating, and feedback needs of the expanded organization will significantly affect the probability that the organization can meet its goals and generate the capital needed to finance the expansion.

The owners have a clear understanding of why there are no firms with a national market share in their industry. The methods of achieving control in a highly nonstandardized business such as theirs are not the methods that work well in a large organization. Just recently, a nearby competitor's failure to control the rapid growth of a business resulted in a significant loss of quality and severely damaged the company's reputation and its ability to attract new business. The owners are also aware that they can buy out shops roughly comparable to their own for a good value; on the other hand, this causes them concern over the resale value of what they might purchase. Apparently, value in their business is not as dependent on the assets acquired as it is on the quality of the personnel and the work that they perform.

The alternative of diversifying into related but more highly standard production activities is more consistent with the control methods that have been proven to work well in larger organizations. While this type of diversification may involve similar customers, its economic and control considerations are very dissimilar to the owners' current business. In standardized production, successful price competition and the realization of economies of scale are vital to profitability.

The owners have identified a plan that is a blend of their alternatives and aspirations. They have decided to add 5 additional shops, each with a capacity of approximately 80 employees, over the next 5 years. The shops will all be within 400 miles of their existing location and the thrust will be to establish a regional rather than a national reputation and market share. The owners believe that they can maintain control by instituting a reporting system and keying in on feedback measures such as "sales per labor hour" and "sales per labor dollar", as well as maintaining strict control over inventory. The new shops will be managed by people who have trained in the home shop with the owners, and the first two people expected to be named as managers are currently part of the management team. The new managers will be invited to participate in an employee stock ownership and profit sharing plan. After this phase of the plan has been implemented, the owners expect that they will have established a substantial presence in the marketplace, which will permit them to seek a partner for merger or even buy-out. By building on the goodwill established in phase one of the plan, they hope to expand into standardized production activities that necessitate a large investment base and a major infusion of working capital. The owners project that a complete reorganization and a divisionalized control system will then be needed to support the more complex business created by the business combination in phase two.

As the plans are implemented, no doubt changes will be made. Five may not be the right number of shops to add; five years may not be enough time to establish a solid regional reputation; the economy might not be right for a business combination at the end of phase one of the plan. Despite the risks, the owners believe that there are significant opportunities for prosperity and personal satisfaction in a high growth market. At the same time, they are aware that they can lose control over their formula for success. As expressed by one of the owners at the final meeting of the planning retreat, "The easiest way for a company like ours to lose control over everything that we have is to believe that our past success and our past ways make us invincible and that we can do no wrong."

DISCUSSION QUESTIONS

1. The definition of control emphasizes "beliefs" and "probability." How does this emphasis differ from an emphasis on "facts" and "certainty?"
2. Distinguish between controls that are behavioral and those that are not behavioral. Why is this distinction important to a manager?
3. How does the extension of the accountant's involvement beyond the production of accounting information to encompass the administrative process alter the auditor's traditional concept of control?
4. Distinguish between formal and informal approaches to control and give examples of each approach.
5. Measurements can be more than feedback; they can also be feedforward. That is, the act of taking a measure can cause significant future changes in the process being observed. Using the measure of "earnings per share," illustate how the decision to emphasize this measure of success can cause changes in behavior that are both productive and counterproductive.
6. Indicate how it is possible that the interaction between planning, operating, and

feedback activities in an organization can produce results that are not consistent with realizing the potential of the organization.

7. For an organization that you know well, indicate several important contextual factors that would need to be investigated and understood by an outside consultant brought in to design a financial control system.

8. To illustrate control challenge in the not-for-profit sector, indicate several key measures of performance evaluation that could be useful to central administration in achieving control in a large, private, urban university.

9. In predicting the logical consequences expected when a new control design is introduced, managers can sometimes be taken by surprise by the control failures that result. This has proven to be especially true in international settings when managers have taken control approaches from one culture into another. Explain why the risk of control failure associated with predicting logical consequences is an inherent risk present in the design of any behavorial control system.

10. Using agency theory, discuss the justifications for instituting an employee stock option plan designed to motivate managers. Your discussion should presume that the company's objective is to pursue the "maximization of shareholder wealth."

11. Cite several reasons why a much needed and overdue change in an organization's approach to control design may come as the result of an external factor beyond the control of the organization rather than an internally generated initiative.

12. Control design has been described as dynamic rather than static. How does this distinction influence your understanding of the control process over time in an organization?

CASE 6.1

The Company

Louis Schaefer, Inc., produces a diversified line of food products with operations in bakery products, refrigerated foods, frozen foods, and snack foods. In 1984, annual sales were approximately $800 million. Significant growth is expected in the short term because of the recent completion of a capital expenditure program undertaken to modernize facilities and increase productivity. This case will focus on control of the research and development program.

The Dilemma

The company has a large research and development group whose efforts are mainly devoted to new product development. Approximately 15% of sales each year is derived from products that were not produced the previous year. For example, this year the company introduced a new family of bread products adding varieties such as Honey Berry Wheat, Six Whole Grains, and Stone Ground Wheat to their basic bread offerings. In the refrigerated and frozen foods product groups in the past year, several major products were reformulated; new refrigerated dough products and a new line of frozen foods with an international emphasis were also introduced. Within the snack food group, twelve new products were added to their line of prime snack foods and nuts.

The company has a standing research committee that is responsible for controlling the entire research program. The committee meets monthly and includes the president, the executive vice-president, the marketing vice-president, and the director of research. The committee has full budgetary responsibilities, including allocating funds to new projects and reviewing on-going projects to amend as needed the annual operating budget for the project. Also, the committee has the responsibility for designing the reporting system and the budgetary documents used to collect information.

The committee has been supported by a group of very capable financial analysts who have pioneered the use of microcomputers within the company. Using microcomputers, the analysts have developed a reporting system that is tailored to the needs of the research committee. The following reports are routinely produced and distributed to committee members prior to the monthly meeting.

1. The Expense Report—all expenses are listed and accounted for according to the object of expenditure (e.g., salaries, supplies, allocated charges, and the like).
2. The Project Report—all expenses are listed and accounted for according to the project associated with the cost. Costs that are common to more than one project are allocated between projects.
3. The Departmental Report—all expenses are listed and accounted for according to the department or responsibility center associated with the cost. This departmental report shows costs classified both by object of expenditure within the departmental budget and by project classification. Costs that are common to more than one department are allocated among them.

Each of the reports reflects costs incurred to date, the annual budget, and the unexpended budget authority. The project report also includes an estimate of costs required to complete the project along with an analysis of cost variances based on the original project budget. All reports include relevant financial ratios, percentage relationships, and historical comparisons where appropriate.

To compile the annual budget, the director of research requires that each project submitted for approval show costs by object of expenditure, project, and departmental classifications. The director of research must then organize these submissions into a comprehensive budget to be presented to the research committee. The total budget request in the comprehensive budget should not exceed 5 percent of the projected sales level of the company for the coming year. To meet this target, the Director discusses budget submissions with managers, cutting costs in some instances, restricting project goals in other cases, and occasionally eliminating a project from consideration. While the research committee has the authority to alter the comprehensive budget submitted by the director of research, this does not occur very often. Once the budget has passed through the research committee, it becomes the basis for controlling actual expenditures.

At the monthly meetings, the committee members review the most recent financial reports, paying particular attention to the exceptions. In the case of projects with large variances, as well as for projects that are considered to be especially important to the company, the committee will schedule briefing sessions with members of the project team. These sessions typically involve formal presentations as well as a sometimes intense question and answer period. The members of the research committee are careful to stress the importance of the research and development program to the continued success of the company.

Required:

1. What aspects of the company's control system do you endorse?
2. What weaknesses do you find in the design of this control system?

CASE 6.2

The Company

Recently, the case of a faltering manufacturer of medical instruments was described in the financial press. Acme Medical Instruments had earned its glamorous reputation in the early 1980s by expanding more than fivefold in two years and by building sales and acquiring subsidiaries. However, in 1985 large losses were posted and the board of directors sought a new president and chief operating officer who could control bulging expenses and bring the manufacturing operations under control.

The chief executive officer and founder of the company is an entrepreneur who was the one to successfully pilot the company through its initial phase of dramatic growth. Since Acme has become a large company, it is now a matter of whether a charismatic but overly zealous chief executive officer can accept the necessary support of skilled managers as part of the management team. One new president and chief operating officer has already come and gone in the last year and this raises further questions about the ability of the company's founder to accept professional management in the company.

Because of the recent operating losses and the well-publicized leadership problems, the trading price of the company's stock has dropped significantly.

Required:

1. Identify the sources of feedback affecting the control process in the company that originate outside the company and exert pressure on top management.
2. Would it be appropriate to describe the investor risk associated with purchasing shares of stock in the company in 1985 as highly influenced by the probability that the board of directors can successfully solve the control problems confronting the organization?

CHAPTER 7

Behavioral Aspects of
Responsibility Accounting

BUSINESS DILEMMA

The Company

Star Packing Company is a multiplant cat and dog food manufacturer. The majority of its shares are owned by two brothers. The older, Ralph, is the company's president; the younger, Ronald, a mechanical engineer, is vice-president in charge of product development and procurement. The two brothers have built the company from scratch and have learned the business in the process. Ralph is the idea man who hates to be tied down by day-to-day responsibilities. Ronald, the engineer, developed the manufacturing process, designed and built the plants, and installed the machinery.

Because of the great demand for cat and dog food, the business grew rapidly and operations were very profitable. Both brothers now enjoy the fruits of their earlier labor. The president has joined the jet set and become a well-known figure in the various exclusive playgrounds of the world. His actual presence in the company has become rare and of short duration. However, he keeps in touch with the operations by telephone, even from such remote places as the center of Africa, the outback of Australia, and the trout-filled mountain rivers of Austria. Nothing of vital importance escapes his attention.

The day-to-day operations are run by four employees who have been with the company since its inception. Bill is in charge of production and rules his plant superintendents with an iron fist. Harry is vice-president in charge of sales. Before joining Star, he was general sales manager in two national food store chains, and his connections from those days account for the company's rapid growth. He is a super salesperson and his sales force admires and imitates him. The treasurer, John, is the president's brother-in-law. He is a quiet and withdrawn individual who rarely leaves his office, and very few employees outside of his staff have ever spoken with him. The controller, Ernest, is the typical old-time accountant. He passed his CPA exam nearly 30 years ago and does not think highly of new techniques and approaches.

Each of the four top executives is extremely loyal to the company and its president. Unfortunately, they do not like each other. Their frequent fights not only became the number one conversation topic throughout the organization but also resulted in interdepartmental bickering and decline in employee morale. At the last confrontation, the controller had enough, submitted his resignation, and walked out.

The president rushed back from the French Riviera to find out what caused the latest eruption and the break-up of his management "team." He hired Cynthia as the new controller. At her briefing interview, he gave her the special assignment of finding out what was causing the continuous bickering and of finding a solution that would reinstate peace and harmony in his company. The president promised to stay in the country until a solution was found.

Before joining Star Packing, Cynthia was assistant controller in a multi-plant flour company. The Star Packing Company job was her first opportunity to prove herself as controller. She was well educated, having earned an M.B.A. degree with a major in accounting from a leading university, and she had recently passed the CPA examination with distinction.

The Dilemma

In her first meetings with her new colleagues, Cynthia became aware that the animosity among them was not caused solely by personal dislikes, but it seemed to be fueled, at least in part, by perceived inequities in the company's accounting and performance evaluation methods.

Bill, the vice-president in charge of production, complained bitterly that the monthly income statements prepared for each plant and used for the evaluation of plant manager performance and bonus computation did not fairly represent their efforts. He claimed that his managers were held responsible for operating factors, standard cost variances, and environmental conditions over which they had no control. He also questioned the propriety of the bases used for allocating the cost of centrally supplied services such as the cost of material procurement, product development, and financial and accounting services.

John, the treasurer, when questioned as to the reason for the prior controller's abrupt departure, blamed the production and sales managers' inability to understand financial matters and their lack of comprehension of the accounting and performance evaluation system. John was convinced that his friend Ernest, the prior controller, had designed a highly sophisticated accounting and reporting system. He did not blame him for finally getting fed up with the continuous verbal attacks and challenges of his system's competence by people not qualified to judge.

Ronald, the president's brother, assisted by a chemical engineer, was in the midst of developing a new product during this time. He was therefore not interested, nor aware, of the war going on outside of his lab.

Harry, the sales manager, blamed Bill for hampering his sales efforts through incompetent production scheduling practices, frequent delays in deliveries, and his refusal to promptly process rush orders.

Cynthia reflected on the various claims made by the members of the management team. She came to the conclusion that they all pointed to weaknesses in the organizational structure and/or to improprieties in the accounting and performance evaluation practices. She decided to analyze these two areas carefully before drawing any further conclusions.

In the course of her investigation, she found that Star Packing had an unusual organizational structure (see Figure 7-1). Plant IV, despite being a separate corporation, had to report to the vice-president in charge of production, and the positions of vice-president of financial affairs and treasurer were held by the same individual. All accounting functions were centralized at the parent company office in Chicago. Several years ago, the prior controller had installed a standard cost system to control the various production costs. The controller's department prepared monthly income statements for each plant. The cost of the main office and of the various centralized functions were prorated to the individual plants. After eliminating intracompany and intercompany transactions, the individual income statements of the four plants were combined into a consolidated income statement, which was assumed to be a fair presentation of the results of companywide operations. The individual plant income statements were used to evaluate the performance of the plants and a quarterly bonus was paid to the plant managers based on plant net income.

Checking deeper into the data accumulation practices, Cynthia found that sales were accounted for on the basis of actual deliveries made by each plant and at prices negotiated by the central sales office. While this approach was as exact as possible from a financial accounting point of view, a quite different situation existed from a responsibility viewpoint. Despite the fact that the individual plant managers had no control over sales volume or sales prices, sales was the most significant item in the determination of each plant's net income, on which their bonus was based.

The second most significant item on the various plant income statements was the cost of raw material. Meat and flour were centrally purchased and charged to plants I, II, and III at actual cost. Since the company did not hedge, raw material cost could fluctuate considerably from purchase to purchase. Plant IV purchased its fish and shrimp requirements directly from a local fish wholesaler. The quantities available and the purchase price varied greatly from season to season. Despite the fact that the plant managers had absolutely

FIGURE 7-1
Star Parking Company Organizational Chart

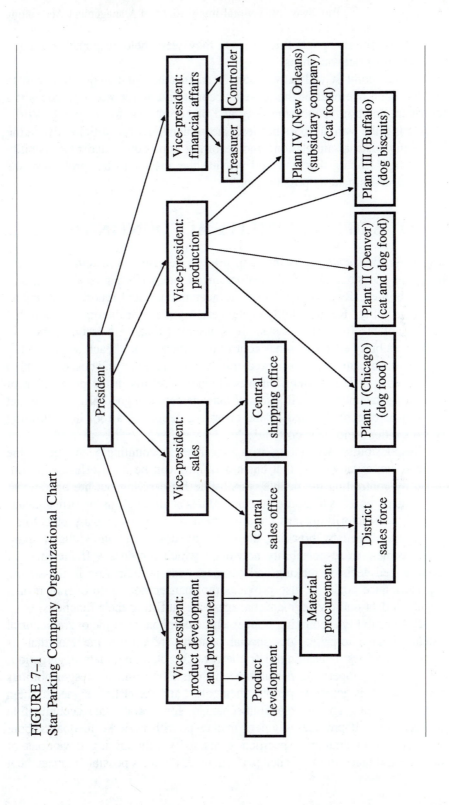

no control over the price fluctuations, they were held responsible for the standard cost price variances.

At that point, Cynthia was convinced that her first major task had to be a thorough overhaul of the present accounting and reporting practices if a permanent solution to the animosity and bickering was to be found. While considering the various possibilities, she remembered an article advocating a planning, data accumulation, and reporting approach called responsibility accounting. Hoping that it would provide the answer to her problems, she started to investigate its possibilities.

WHAT IS RESPONSIBILITY ACCOUNTING? _____

Responsibility accounting is the term used to describe an accounting system that plans, measures, and evaluates organizational performance along lines of responsibilities. Revenue and costs are accumulated and reported by centers of responsibility. Responsibility centers are segments of the organization that are accountable for certain tasks. It is assumed that there is one person in the responsibility center who has control over those tasks. Each responsibility center in the organization is charged only with the revenue and cost over which it has control. "This system," it was claimed, "results in the preparation of accounting statements for all levels of management designed primarily so that they can be effectively used by the operating people as a tool in controlling their operations and their costs." [1]

Responsibility accounting is management accounting's answer to the common sense knowledge that business affairs can be most effectively controlled by controlling the people responsible for carrying out the operations. One of its purposes is to assure that individuals at all levels in the firm are contributing satisfactorily toward the attainment of overall company objectives. It is accomplished by breaking the company down into individual responsibility centers (a responsibility network), which provides a framework for decentralized decision making and companywide participation in the setting of performance goals. It also provides top management with overall results as well as data on how segment managers are fulfilling their functions.

Responsibility accounting is an essential component of the overall control system of an enterprise. Its special benefits stem from the fact that its structure provides a meaningful framework for planning, data aggregation, and reporting of operating performance results along lines of responsibilities and control. It is geared to people, their roles, and the tasks assigned to them rather than being an impersonal mechanism for overall data accumulation and reporting. It provides segment managers with periodic feedback about their success in attaining specified goals. By highlighting deviations of actual performance from planned performance, it makes possible management by exception and by objective. (Management by exception [MBE] and management by objective [MBO] are discussed in detail in the section on "Behavioral Assumptions of Responsibility Accounting" in this chapter.) By making segment managers and their subordinates directly responsible for those operational factors over which they have control, this system encourages profit and/or cost consciousness. By tying goal attainment to a reward structure, it motivates individuals to perform more effectively and efficiently. By granting segment managers decision-making authority within their sphere of delegated responsibility, it boosts their self-esteem.

RESPONSIBILITY ACCOUNTING VERSUS CONVENTIONAL ACCOUNTING

Responsibility accounting does not involve any deviations from generally accepted accounting principles. It differs from conventional accounting in the way operations are planned and in the way accounting data are classified and accumulated. In conventional accounting, data are classified by their nature or function and are not delineated by individuals responsible for their occurrence and control. Conventional accounting data are therefore of limited value to managers in monitoring the efficiency of their day-to-day activities.

Responsibility accounting improves the relevance of accounting information by establishing a framework for planning, data accumulation, and reporting that is in accordance with each company's specific organizational structure and hierarchy of accountabilities. It adds a personal touch to the impersonal data accumulation mechanism of conventional accounting by addressing segment managers directly and by providing them with goals and actual performance results for the operational factors for which they are responsible and able to control. The various operational data are not only classified, accumulated, and reported by types (e.g., sales revenue, raw material and supplies consumed, salaries, rent, insurance, etc.), but also by individuals who have been assigned responsibility for them.

Responsibility accounting, therefore, does not allocate joint costs to the segments that benefit from them but charges them to the individual in the segment that initiates and controls their occurrence. For example, the manager of a repair and maintenance service department who is responsible for servicing the equipment in other departments should be held responsible for the costs associated with his assigned task. The repair and maintenance costs should not be allocated. Another example would be the salary of a person who works part-time as a salesperson and part-time as a purchasing agent. Conventional accounting would allocate this salary on the basis of the time devoted to each activity. Responsibility accounting, in contrast, would charge the total salary to the superior who is responsible for the person's activities.

Responsibility accounting reports both who spent the money and what the money purchased. It therefore adds a human dimension to planning, data accumulation, and reporting. Because costs are budgeted and accumulated along responsibility lines, the reports received by segment managers are ideally suited for performance evaluation and reward allocation. Furthermore, the performers are not likely to perceive the reports as unfair or to challenge them on the basis of arbitrary accounting allocation practices. Responsibility accounting instills cost and revenue consciousness throughout the organization and motivates segment managers to strive for goal attainment. It directs their attention to the factors that require their special attention and that they have power to change.

THE RESPONSIBILITY NETWORK

Responsibility accounting is based on the premise that all costs are controllable and that the problem is only establishing the point of their controllability.

For this purpose, the company's organizational structure is broken down into a network of individual responsibility centers or, as defined by the National Association of Accountants, into organizational units engaged in the performance of a single function or a group of closely related functions having a single head accountable for the activities of the unit.[2] In other words, each unit of this organizational network, or more specifically the individual in charge thereof, is responsible for performing some function (the output) and for using resources (inputs) as efficiently as possible in performing this function.

Most organizations have a hierarchy of such responsibility centers. At the top is the president or chief executive officer, who is responsible to the owners for the overall profitability of the enterprise. Those responsible to the president include the heads of the various operating and staff departments. Below them are other responsibility centers, each headed by a single individual who is accountable to a higher official for efficiency in performance.

To assure a smoothly functioning responsibility and accountability network, the company's organizational structure must be carefully analyzed and the true income and expense responsibilities determined. In practice, the delineation of responsibility centers is frequently the most difficult task in the construction and installation of the system.

To create an efficient responsibility network structure, responsibilities and scopes of authority for every individual, from the top executive down to the lowest level employees, must be logical and clearly defined.

There may not exist any overlapping of responsibilities at different hierarchical levels. The person charged with responsibility should be given sufficient authority for the work expected. Responsibility should not be shared by two or more individuals because division of responsibility invariably invites misunderstandings, confusion, duplication of efforts, or neglect in performance. It also makes it extremely difficult to determine who is at fault if something goes wrong.

In addition to the necessity of carefully assigning responsibility to only one individual, each individual in turn should report to only one manager. Supervisory positions have to be established over each logical grouping of activities at the various management levels.

In short, to create a well functioning responsibility network, there must be a perfect matching of responsibility and authority at all levels.

TYPES OF RESPONSIBILILTY CENTERS

Once delineated, individual responsibility centers function as the framework for measuring and evaluating the performance of segment managers. Managers' performance within a responsibility accounting framework is equated with their ability to manage certain controllable operational factors. The system is not able to measure and evaluate total performance, which in addition would include such factors as quality control, the level of subordinates' morale, and leadership qualities. Those factors must be measured and evaluated by other means.

Responsibility centers are grouped into four categories, each reflecting the range and discretion over revenues and/or expenses and the extent of control of the manager in charge. They could be cost, revenue, profit or investment centers. Their number and type will depend on the size of the company, its organizational structure, and top management's preference and leadership style.

Cost Centers

Cost centers are areas of responsibility that produce a product or render a service. Managers in charge of cost centers have discretion and control only over the use of the physical and human resources necessary to accomplish their assigned tasks. They have no control over revenues, since the marketing function is not their responsibility. Investment decisions, such as buying additional machinery or increasing the inventory of raw material and supplies, are made at a higher organizational level.

During the planning process, cost center managers are assigned production quotas and may participate in setting realistic and fair cost goals for the anticipated output level. Performance results are periodically reported to the managers in the form of reports that compare the actual costs incurred with the budgeted costs. These reports direct attention to problem areas that should be investigated. The frequency of feedback depends on the sensitivity and materiality of the operational factors under their control. Experience, however, has shown that performance reports should be prepared at least once a month.

Cost centers are a widely used form of responsibility centers. In manufacturing firms, both production and service departments are examples of cost centers. In merchandising firms, departments rendering support services would fall into this category. Typical examples would be shipping and receiving, credit, and customer service departments.

Revenue Centers

If the primary responsibility of segment managers is revenue generation, their segments should be treated as revenue centers. Examples of revenue centers include marketing departments, distribution centers, merchandise sections in department stores, or individual sales representatives.

Managers in revenue centers have no discretion or control over asset investment or the cost of the items or services to be sold. They have control only over direct marketing costs and their performance will be measured in terms of their ability to reach predetermined sales goals within specified expense restrictions. To receive optimal motivational and control benefits, revenue center managers should participate in the goal-setting process and should receive timely feedback of their performance results.

Profit Centers

Profit centers are segments where managers have control over both revenues and expenses; managers are evaluated on the basis of their efficiency in generating revenue and controlling costs. Their discretion over costs includes the expenses of producing the products or rendering the service. Their responsibilities are broader than those of cost or revenue center managers because they are responsible for both the distribution and manufacturing functions. Typical examples of profit centers are corporate divisions that manufacture and sell their products.

Because of the added prestige associated with profit center manager positions, many companies create artificial profit centers for manufacturing or service segments. This boosts the esteem of their segment managers and improves their motivation.

The conversion of a cost center into a profit center is accomplished by introducing transfer prices that act as internal selling prices and create artificial revenues and profits for the segments. The motivational benefits, however, depend upon the type of transfer price chosen. The choice of an unsuitable transfer price basis may create a host of undesirable behavioral responses and negate the motivational benefits. (For details, see Chapter 12, "A Behavioral Interpretation of Decentralization.")

The performance of profit center managers is evaluated on the basis of planned profit goals such as required minimum rates of return and hurdle amounts for residual income. To discourage dysfunctional actions dictated by strictly short-term profit orientation, profit center managers should also be expected to maintain and/or improve the morale of their subordinates, maintain buildings and production facilities, and contribute to product leadership and corporate citizenship. To encourage their concern for these aspects, the performance evaluation reward system should also include measures to evaluate their performance in regard to long-range aspects and their degree of success should affect the reward allocations. (See Chapter 11, "Behavioral Aspects of Performance Evaluation".)

Investment Centers

Managers of investment centers are responsible for investment in assets as well as control over revenue and expenses. They are responsible for attaining specific contribution margin and profit goals and for efficiency in asset utilization. They are expected to attain a healthy balance between profits achieved and the investment in resources used. The criteria used in measuring their performance and in determining their rewards include return on assets, turnover ratios, and residual income. Because they are responsible for every aspect of operations, managers of investment centers are evaluated in a manner similar to top executives.

Correlation with Organizational Structure

To function properly, responsibility centers must coincide as closely as possible with the organizational structure. Approaches used in designing the organizational structure and in assigning responsibilities vary from company to company depending on top management's choice and leadership style. The various approaches can be classified as vertical or horizontal structures.

Vertical Structure

In a vertical structure (see Figure 7-2), organizations are broken down by major function. The overall responsibility for the production, sales, and

FIGURE 7–2
Vertical Structure

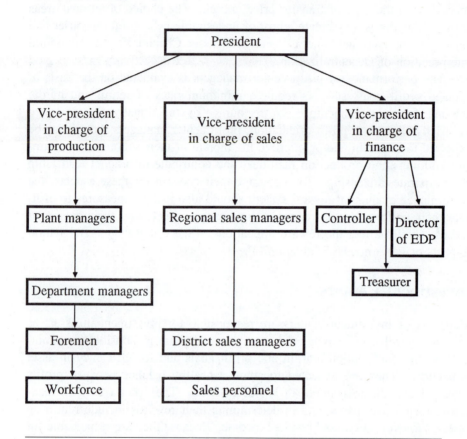

finance functions are assigned to vice-presidents, who delegate their responsibilities down the hierarchy. The final responsibility for each function,
however, ultimately rests with them.

From a responsibility center viewpoint, all production segments are cost
centers since revenues are only generated through the sales function. Sales
segments are revenue centers since the various managers are responsible
only for selling the products or services and have no control over the cost
of producing them. Only the president has control and discretion over all
activities and has the final say in accepting or rejecting investment proposals.

Horizontal Structure

If the intention is to assign profit and investment responsibility to several
vice-presidents, a horizontal structure for the delegation of responsibilities

is best suited (see Figure 7-3). The breakdown could be by product or geographical area. Each vice-president controls a profit or investment center rather than a functional cost or revenue center. They are responsible for production, sales, and financing, or, in other words, for all functional areas within their districts or for their product groups. From the plant level down, the segments are cost centers; the only difference to the vertical structure is that plant managers report to individuals concerned with both sales and production.

Choice of Structure

Neither type of structure is inherently superior. Their efficient use depends upon a variety of environmental factors. In small firms, the president may prefer to retain sole control over all activities and to delegate partial authority and responsibility by function. Firms that produce and sell a few highly differentiated products might use a horizontal breakdown. Firms that produce a great variety of products in each plant might also use a horizontal structure.

The type of structure chosen will influence the network of responsibility centers, which in turn serves as a framework for data flow and reporting requirements. If the responsibility center network coincides with the structure chosen, then the system should function effectively and induce managers to use it as a reference source in carrying out their assigned activities.

FIXING RESPONSIBILITY

After selecting the type of organizational structure, the next crucial task in constructing a behaviorally effective responsibility system is to delineate responsibilities.

Most people welcome responsibility and the challenges it represents. Being held responsible for something makes people feel competent and important. It implies decision-making authority and may motivate them to improve their performance. Responsibility is a job satisfier; without it, morale will suffer.

The favorable behavior effect of assigning responsibilities for specific functions to individuals is supported by empirical research. Unfortunately, the interdependencies of the various segments of an organization frequently make a clear-cut delineation of responsibilities difficult. A person charged with the responsibility for an activity or function might, in reality, share that responsibility with a superior. Segment managers with responsibility for specific tasks might not be independent from each other and their responsibilities may overlap. Individuals might have only limited discretion and

FIGURE 7–3
Horizontal Structure

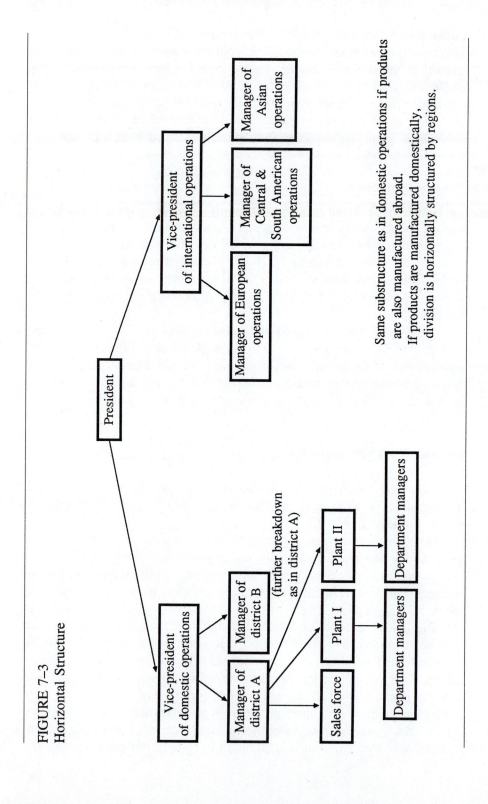

control over the resources necessary to carry out the tasks for which they are responsible. Staff people who are not links in the chain of command and who have no specifically assigned responsibilities do not fit readily into any responsibility structure.

Therefore, the construction of an equitable responsibility framework is extremely difficult and requires frequent compromise. The most crucial factor in the delineation of responsibilities is the degree of discretion and control over the resources required to carry out the delegated task or function. Segment managers should be only held responsible for those operating factors over which they exert control. Under no circumstances should arbitrary allocations devised for product costing be used in fixing responsibility. They are never equitable solutions and have no place in responsibility accounting.

In this context, control means that managers have ability to significantly change the amounts of the items. A marketing manager, for example, may control advertising and promotion expenses, but not the depreciation on the trucks used in delivering the merchandise. A production foreman controls the quantity of raw material and supplies used because he assigns work and supervises the workers; however, he has no control over the price of material used. The responsibility for deviations from usage goals should therefore rest with the foreman, while the responsibility for price deviations should be assigned to the purchasing department manager. If, however, the excess waste was clearly caused by faulty material, the responsibility for the additional cost incurred should be assumed by the person responsible for the procurement.

Another example of overlapping responsibility would be a rush order requiring overtime for a special customer. The production manager should not be held responsible for the cost of overtime for a job forced upon him. The overtime premium should be charged to the sales department since it clearly represents additional selling expenses.

Since control in a work environment is rarely complete, "significant influence" is frequently considered as sufficient to pinpoint responsibility. In 1956, the committee on cost concepts and standards of the American Accounting Association issued some guidelines but warned that their application must be tempered by good judgment and common sense. They recommended that:

1. The person *with authority over both the acquisition and the use* of goods or services *should* be charged with their cost.
2. The person who *can significantly influence* the amount of cost through his or her own actions *may* be charged with the cost.
3. Even the person *who cannot significantly influence* the amount of cost through direct action *may be charged* with elements with which management desires that person to be concerned, so that he or she will help to influence those who are responsible." [3]

The guidelines and the examples cited before demonstrate that the delineation of responsibilities for revenue generation and cost incurrence is quite difficult and fraught with behavioral pitfalls. It may well lead to interdepartmental dissention and animosity if not done with great care and a thorough understanding of the human factors involved in each situation.

The ultimate delineation of responsibility should be equitable and accepted by those involved. If done properly, it should be motivationally superior to the common practice of holding managers responsible for items they cannot change.

PLANNING, DATA ACCUMULATION, AND REPORTING BY RESPONSIBILITY CENTERS

Once a sound responsibility network structure is established, it becomes a vehicle for planning, data accumulation, and reporting. Each element of cost or revenue, both in the budget and in the accumulation of actual results, must be traced to the network segment in which its responsibility lies.

Responsibility Budgets

To proceed chronologically, we prepare budgets that assign cost and revenue goals to each network segment. This will be the basis for evaluating the performance of the person in charge of each organizational unit.

The characteristic of responsibility budgets is that responsibility center managers are assigned performance goals only for those revenue and cost items over which they have control. Although the heads of responsibility centers may not have complete control over certain elements of cost, if they have significant influence on the amount of cost incurred, then these costs may be considered "controllable" at their level and chargeable to their specific responsibility centers.

Controllable costs are not the same as direct costs. There are many direct costs—depreciation of equipment, for example—that are not controllable at the cost center level and for which the head of the cost center should not be held responsible. Depreciation or other similar costs that vary in accordance with the formula used for their computation are not affected by the supervisor's actions and therefore must be omitted from responsibility budgets. These costs should be included in the budget of the next higher responsibility level in which control resides.

By assigning only controllable costs to each cost center head, management will have a fair basis for comparing actual with expected performance, for judging the effectiveness of cost center supervisors at all organizational levels, and for identifying the causes of inefficiencies.

The budgetary process is most effectively started at the lowest organizational or network level for which budgets are to be prepared and then passed upward through the chain of command in a pyramid fashion. Each person in charge of a cost center is responsible for preparing budget estimates for the expense items over which he or she has control. At the next higher authority level, these estimates are reviewed, coordinated, and modified when necessary, until they are finally combined into an overall operating budget at the top-management level.

After approval of the overall budget by top management, all detail budgets acquire the status of agreed-upon plans. It then becomes the responsibilty of the various managers to put their parts of the plan into action. The degree of their success in executing the plans will be used later by their superiors as a basis for judging their performance. The evaluation is accomplished by periodic comparisons of planned and actual results.

Data Accumulation

To facilitate periodic comparisons with the various budgetary plans, the accumulation of actual income and expense items must necessarily follow the responsibility network pattern. This requires a three-dimensional classification of cost and revenues during the data accumulation process. Costs are classified first by responsibility center; secondly, within each center, by whether they are controllable or noncontrollable; and third, by cost types, or by line items, such as salaries, supplies, materials, and rents.

This type of data accumulation provides management with information pertinent to several dimensions of its operations. In the past, three-dimensional data accumulation was technically cumbersome because only manual and semi-automated systems were available for data accumulation. Today's electronic data processing equipment, though, makes possible the accumulation and breakdown of data in any desired fashion.

Responsibility Reporting

The end products of responsibility accounting systems are periodic responsibility or performance reports. These reports are the media through which costs are controlled, managerial efficiency is measured, and goal attainment is assessed.

This control device reports what happened both by account and by the functional responsibilities of individuals. The performance reports are distributed to top management and to lower level managers.

To enhance efficiency, responsibility reporting systems should be based on the so-called "pyramid reporting" or "telescoping" principle. This means that each responsibility manager receives only his or her own control report and that the lowest level detail reports are issued first. Only their totals are then carried to the next higher reporting level. The net result is that the higher the responsibility level, the more condensed the reporting becomes.

As already stated, all control reports include only those items which are controllable at the responsibility level to which the report relates. Costs controllable only at a superior management level are included in the condensed report for that level.

Responsibility accounting's major contribution is that it enables management to control cost and efficiency by assigning responsibility for the cost to the people who carry out the various tasks. By incorporating the human element into the accounting framework, responsibility accounting was a major event in the evolution of behavioral accounting.

BEHAVIORAL ASSUMPTIONS OF RESPONSIBILITY ACCOUNTING

Responsibility planning, data accumulation, and reporting systems are based on several assumptions concerning operational and human behavior, including:

1. Management by exception (MBE) is sufficient to control operations effectively.
2. Management by objective (MBO) will result in agreed upon budgets, standard costs, organizational goals, and workable plans for their achievement.
3. The responsibility and accountability structure coincides with the hierarchical structure of the organization.
4. Managers and subordinates are willing to accept the responsibility and accountability assigned to them through the organizational hierarchy.
5. Responsibility accounting systems induce cooperation rather than competition.

Management by Exception (MBE)

Management by exception assumes that to most effectively manage and control organizational activities, managers should concentrate their attention on areas where the actual results deviate substantially from budgeted or standard goals. Proponents of this approach claim that it results in the most efficient use of scarce management time, concentrates on correcting inefficiencies, and reinforces desired actions. Periodic reporting characteristic of responsibility accounting is ideally suited to draw management's attention to areas deviating from predetermined norms and to induce prompt remedial actions to reinforce or correct behavior.

Unfortunately, in many instances, only unfavorable variances or obvious trouble spots receive immediate attention. The recognition and attention given to favorable variances is either missing completely or is weaker than the response given to unfavorable ones. For this reason, responsibility center managers frequently perceive performance reports as tools that emphasize failure. Lower-level managers tend to see these reports as punitive rather than informative. Many managers feel that goal attainment, which represents successful performance, gets little or no recognition in performance reports. They try to defend their shortcomings by questioning the propriety and fairness of the performance norms and the techniques used in accumulating actual performance data. One defensive reaction is to manipulate the data to cover up unfavorable deviations. This approach may also result in managers becoming overly cautious and reluctant to try new approaches where the risk of failure is high. "Playing it safe" in the short run, however, may negatively affect the company's competitive position and profitability over the long run. It may also discourage and destroy employee creativity and innovation.

To rectify the punitive perception of variance reports, the company's reward system should equate goal attainment with successful performance. Managers at all levels should be induced to pay equal attention to both favorable and unfavorable variances from goals. (For more details on the behavioral impacts of variance analysis, see Chapters 8, 9,10, and 11). By emphasizing both the positive and negative aspects of responsibility center performance, the periodic reports will be perceived as important management information tools.

Management by Objective (MBO)

Responsibility accounting facilitates *management by objective* or *management by self-control*. This is a management approach designed to overcome the numerous dysfunctional human responses triggered by attempts to control operations by dominance. People resent cost constraints. They resent being dominated and being told what to do, and when and how to do it. They want to do tasks on their own because they believe they are capable of directing themselves and their work. History shows that many of our most significant achievements have been accomplished when individuals acted unrestrained, motivated and guided only by the worthiness of their objectives and goals.

As a management control technique, management by objective facilitates this desire for self-control by giving managers and their subordinates the opportunity to jointly formulate the goals and activities for their responsibility centers. These subunit goals must be congruent with overall company goals.

By delineating responsibility, responsibility accounting provides the ideal framework for the formulation of detailed goals and plans. Performance reports provide segment managers with effective tools for self-control and reinforce their awareness of accountability for the activities assigned to them.

To get optimum motivation and communication from both management by objective and the responsibility accounting system, certain favorable environmental conditions must exist or be perceived to exist. These include:

- In setting responsibility center goals, top management must provide overall direction by specifying the company's overall objectives and goals.
- In the joint formulation of detailed performance goals and action plans, top management and responsibility center managers must maximize the congruence between the personal needs and career aspirations of work groups and overall company goals.
- Motivation is enhanced if people believe that the achievement of company goals will simultaneously satisfy their personal needs.
- If people perceive organizational goals as compatible with their own, then they will internalize company goals and goal congruence is reached.

Responsibility center managers are crucial in this process. Their personal relationship with subordinates has an influence on whether company goals will be accepted or ejected. They will best succeed by educating the influential members of their various work groups about where their operations fit into the framework of overall organizational goals. Managers can also enhance cooperation by inviting staff members to participate in the formulation of realistic cost and revenue targets that will be presented to the next higher echelon level as responsibility center budgets.

After reviewing responsibility center budgets, it may become obvious to the supervising manager at the next higher level of the organizational hierarchy that specific responsibility managers should not be allowed all the resources their subordinates feel they need. In this case, the reasons should be explained thoroughly and employees' suggestions should be sought and considered when making reductions.

When evaluating the actual performance results in light of jointly formulated performance goals, responsibility center managers at all levels must refrain from using performance results as a means of assigning blame. Responsibility reports are not intended to be used in a blame-fixing or punitive fashion. They are tools for tracing favorable and unfavorable deviations in cost and revenue attainment to the individual who is in the best position to explain the reasons causing them and to initiate meaningful remedial actions. This approach emphasizes that responsibility center managers are only held accountable for those revenue and expense items that they have the power to change.

Periodic performance results should not be the only basis for immediate reward or punishment. To enhance motivation, reward and punishment should be based on consistency in performance and the quality of remedial actions taken by the person responsible. Managers must know that they will not be punished for occasional shortcomings. They should be rewarded based on the effectiveness of the changes they initiate and their ability of "self-control."

Coincidence Between Responsibility Network and Organizational Structure

Responsibility accounting assumes that organizational control is enhanced by creating a network of responsibility centers that coincide with the formal organizational structure.

Top management's intention to delegate and disperse is explained by the "authority hierarchy" or the "organizational structure," which assigns authority and responsibility for specific duties by hierarchy levels to accomplish meaningful division of work.

When authority is assigned to individual managers, they perceive it as the power to act officially within the scope of their delegation and to influence the behavior of their subordinates. However, authority by itself is meaningless if it is not accepted by those affected by it. Managers can redelegate part or all of the responsibility. They alone remain accountable to their superiors for the accomplishment of the assigned tasks and are expected to respond to deviations from negotiated performance goals.

Unfortunately, many organizations are plagued by severe weaknesses in delegation. This breakdown of the formal organization results in overlapping duties and responsibilities that invite "buck passing," interdepartmental bickering, and animosity. If responsibilities are assigned to a person who lacks the power to fulfill them, frustration and discouragement may result. Responsibility accounting assigns responsibilities to segment managers as if they were isolated individuals. It sometimes ignores the fact that they are leaders of formal and informal groups and that it is group performance that is being measured. Group dynamics, or the forces that affect the group's willingness to accept goals, should therefore be considered when designing responsibility accounting systems.

Because responsibility centers are the basis for the entire responsibility accounting system, the framework for them must be designed carefully. The organizational structure has to be analyzed for weaknesses in delegation and dispersion. If overlapping responsibilities cause unavoidable interdependencies, workable compromises have to be found. The responsibility center network is as effective for controlling an organization as the underlying organizational structure is rational.

Acceptance of Responsibility

The most crucial element in a successful responsibility accounting system is the responsibility center managers' acceptance of assigned responsibilities as equitable and their willingness to be held accountable.

Managers' willingness to accept responsibility depends on how they perceive their discretion and control over the human and physical resources necessary to accomplish their assigned tasks. They will react most favorably if the organizational culture grants them the freedom to perform their duties in their own way so long as they obtain the required results. To encourage responsibility acceptance, the organizational culture must also allow them to fail occasionally without fear of immediate punishment. Managers must always feel free to express their own views without fear of ridicule or retribution.

Since the performance evaluation phase of responsibility accounting discloses both successful and unsuccessful performance results, there is an implicit trust between those controlled and their superiors. The joint goal setting afforded by responsibility accounting will produce improvements in inter- and intra-segment communications only if all responsibility center managers are open and willing to reveal their expectations about realistic performance levels and the strategies for attaining them. Responsibility managers' dislike of the system may also be caused by their distaste for the disciplinary actions it calls for. They may feel demoted to the role of a "watch dog."

It seems obvious that there may be specific personality traits that lead to favorable attitudes toward responsibility acceptance. So far, research has only been able to demonstrate a definite correlation between the willingness of "disclosure" (or the capability of subjective cognitions and evaluation of oneself) and attitudes toward responsibility acceptance.

Capability of Inducing Cooperation

Responsibility accounting improves organizational cooperation by showing managers where their activities fit into the overall picture and that everybody is working toward common goals. It also enhances company loyalty, self-esteem, and feelings of importance by allowing people to formulate their own goals and make their own decisions within the framework of delegated responsibility. They will perceive their segment and themselves as important parts of the company as a whole and will be more willing to strive for goal attainment. They will accept performance reporting as a useful tool for mid-course corrections. Their cooperative spirit will improve since they will be convinced that they are working for the attainment of common goals. They will feel that they are a vital part of the organization and that their failure may seriously affect its future. They will associate failure with jeopardizing the fulfillment of their personal goals and aspirations.

Excessive pressure toward goal attainment, though, may destroy the benefits to be derived from harmonious cooperation. Instead, the result may be fierce competition among segments and exclusive emphasis on short-range goals.

DIAGNOSTIC REVIEW OF THE BUSINESS DILEMMA

After investigating the possibilities of responsibility accounting, Cynthia was convinced that it would provide a permanent solution to Star Packing Company's human problems and the widespread dysfunctional responses to the present accounting and performance evaluation system. She believed that it was possible to create an organizational climate conducive to the efficient functioning of a responsibility accounting system with only minor adjustments to the organizational structure.

Her first step in the design of a responsibility accounting system was to redefine responsibilities throughout the company based on the organization chart. Next she designed a network of responsibility centers. She saw that the present practice of treating the various plants as profit centers was misleading and was one of the major causes of Star's problem. Since plant managers had no control over sales, product development, and material procurement, it was understandable that they rebelled against the practice of having their performance evaluated on the basis of monthly income statements. They had discretion and control only over their own manufacturing activities and the resources required to perform them. From the viewpoints of responsibility and control, the various plants were clearly cost centers; therefore, managers should be responsible only for the use of the physical and human resources necessary to attain their assigned production quotas.

Cynthia also assigned cost center status to product development, material procurement, and the treasurer's and controller's departments. Since the sales department's primary responsibility was revenue generation, it was to be treated as a revenue center and the manager's performance was to be measured in terms of reaching the monthly sales quotas within the scope of predetermined expense restrictions. The central shipping office was to be handled as a cost center and cost compliance and timeliness of shipments were to be used as performance criteria. Cost and revenue center managers were to work with their respective vice-presidents to develop monthly and yearly activity goals and cost budgets for those costs over which they had sufficient control. Capacity costs (e.g., insurance and depreciation of building, machinery, and equipment) were the vice-presidents' responsibilities.

The New Orleans subsidiary (plant IV) was to be dissolved since its operations were of minor significance. There was no justifiable reason for its separate legal existence.

Other changes to be made were in the area of data accumulation and reporting practices. Monthly revenues and costs were to be accumulated by responsibility centers, combined into a single income statement, and supplemented by detailed reports for each responsibility area. The responsibility center performance reports would compare budget goals with actual results and highlight variation. Holding managers accountable only for the operating factors over which they had control would eliminate the necessity for cost allocations and the burdensome task of consolidating the present plant income statements. Similarly, plant managers were to be held responsible only for those standard cost variances that they had the power to change, such as material and labor usage and overhead budget variance. Material price variances were to be charged to material procurement. Labor rate variances were the responsibility of plant managers since they were responsible for hiring.

For the central sales office, Cynthia designed a supplementary report, which showed total contribution margins in relation to quantities sold and selling expenses incurred. This report was to be further broken down by territory, salespeople, and major customers (food chains) and was to give the general sales manager the basis for evaluating the profitability of territories, individual salespeople, and major customers.

Convinced that she had found a workable solution to the tense situation, Cynthia submitted her report to the president. After describing the inequities in the present accounting and performance evaluation system, she suggested the installation of a responsibility planning, data accumulation, and performance evaluation system. Such a system, she asserted, would allow the president to plan, measure, and evaluate the various activities throughout the organization along responsibility lines. It would enable him and his vice-presidents to control operations by controlling the individuals responsible for carrying out the functional activities at the various levels. Such a system would also provide them with monthly reports, which would not only tell them what happened overall, but would identify the results with the key individuals responsible for producing them. To assure optimal motivational benefits, Cynthia recommended the complete overhaul of the present reward system. She handed the completed report to the president's secretary and returned to her routine activities.

The following day, Cynthia was summoned by the president. He told her that he had studied her report and that he agreed with her about the reasons for the friction and animosity. The recommended new system and the benefits to be derived from it, he felt, sounded too good to be true, but if she was sure that it would work, he would be willing to give it a try. He scheduled a meeting with all his vice-presidents in which Cynthia was to present the new approach and answer all preliminary questions.

When presented with the proposed changes, the first reaction of the various vice-presidents was reluctance. But when Cynthia explained the new concept and pointed out the numerous inequities of the present approach, the logic and human benefits of the proposed changes became obvious to all. They agreed to sell the advantages of the responsibility and accountability planning and control approach to their segment managers and request their full cooperation for the conversion. They also willingly accepted the task of jointly reformulating the reward structure. They were obviously very convincing, since by the time Cynthia was ready to install the new system, there was considerable enthusiasm for the new approach throughout the company.

The first positive result from the new system was the notable improvement in interdepartmental communication and cooperation during the goal-setting and budget-making process. Another significant change occurred in the sales department. The emphasis was now placed on getting sales with minimum selling expenses. The sales manager, now responsible for overtime caused by rush orders, was more reluctant to give preferential treatment to quarrelsome customers. The individual salespeople became more cost conscious since their performance was no longer evaluated solely on the basis of quota attainment, but also on sales generated per selling expense dollar.

The plant managers' attitudes improved considerably since they were no longer held responsible for operating factors that they were powerless to control. They also felt that they had a fair chance of participating in the formulation of cost goals. Their production scheduling improved considerably since more effort went into sales planning and the monthly sales targets furnished to them were more dependable. But best of all, their self esteem and their motivation to attain the goals they had agreed to was at an all-time high. This condition was further reinforced by the new performance criteria, which rewarded them for goal attainment in production quotas and cost targets. They no longer perceived standard cost variance analysis and its reporting of deviations as punitive and threatening, but as vital informational tools that told them how their segment had performed and which areas or factors needed their immediate attention. The various vice-presidents were rewarded for their loyalty and enthusiasm through a bonus system based on residual income generated in excess of a predetermined minimum. Cynthia was given a substantial raise for her efforts and creativity.

With peace and harmony restored throughout his company, Ralph, the president, returned to the French Riviera to resume his normal activities.

REFERENCES

[1]Higgins, John A. "Responsibility Accounting," *The Arthur Andersen Chronical*, Vol. 12, no. 2, Arthur Andersen and Co., Chicago, April 1952, (p. 93-113).

[2]NAA Bulletin, August 1953, "The Analysis of Management Cost Variances," Research Series No. 2, *The National Association of Accountants*.

[3]American Accounting Association (AAA), Committee on Cost Concepts and Standards, "Tentative Statements on Cost Concepts Underlying Reports for Management Purposes," *The Accounting Review*, Vol. 31, no. 2, April 1956, p. 189.

SUGGESTED READINGS

American Accounting Association (AAA) Committee on Cost Concepts and Standards. "Tentative Statements on Cost Concepts Underlying Reports for Management Purposes." *The Accounting Review*, Vol. 31, no. 2, (April 1956): 189.

Anthony, Robert N. and James S. Reece. *Accounting: Text and Cases*, 7th ed., chs. 23 and 24. Homewood, Ill.: Richard D. Irwin, 1983.

Brady, Rodney H., "MBO Goes to Work in the Public Sector." *Harvard Business Review* 51, no. 2, 1973 65–74.

Belkaoui, Ahmed. "The Relationship Between Self-Disclosure Style and Attitudes to Responsibility Accounting," *Accounting, Organizations and Society* vol. 6, no. 4 (1981): 281–289.

Crowningshield, Gerald R. and Kenneth A. Gorman. *Cost Accounting*, ch. 16. Boston: Houghton Mifflin Company, 1979.

Ferrara, William. "Responsibility Accounting—A Basic Control Concept." *N.A.A. Bulletin* 46, sec. 1 (September 1964): 11–19.

Fremgen, J. M., and S. Liao, "The Allocation of Corporate Indirect Costs," *Management Accounting* (Sept. 1981): 66–67.

Higgins, John A. "Responsibility Accounting." *The Arthur Anderson Chronical* Arthur Anderson Co., Chicago, April 1952, 12, no. 2: 93–113.

Horngren, Charles T. *Introduction to Management Accounting* 7th ed., ch. 9. Englewood Cliffs, N.J.: Prentice-Hall, 1987.

Louderback, Joseph G. and Geraldine Dominiak. *Managerial Accounting*, ch. 10. Boston: Kent Publishing Co., 1982.

N.A.A. Research Series No. 22. "Report of Committee on Cost Concepts and Standards." *Accounting Review* (April 1956).

Odiorne, G. *Management Decisions by Objective*. Englewood Cliffs, N.J.: Prentice-Hall, 1970.

Pick, John. "Is Responsibility Accounting Irresponsible?" *The New York Certified Public Accountant* (July 1971): 487–494.

Rayburn, L. Gayle. *Principles of Cost Accounting with Managerial Applications*, ch. 20. Homewood, Ill.: Richard D. Irwin, 1979.

Shillinglaw, Gordon. *Managerial Accounting*, 5th ed., ch. 22. Homewood, Ill.: Richard D. Irwin, 1982.

DISCUSSION QUESTIONS

1. What is the purpose of responsibility accounting?
2. Why is responsibility accounting important in the overall control of an enterprise?
3. In what way does the responsibility accounting philosophy differ from conventional accounting?
4. On what premise is responsibility accounting based?
5. How are individual responsibility centers delineated?
6. What are the various categories of responsibility centers? What does the categorization depend on?
7. What do you understand by the Management by Exception (MBE) and Management by Objective (MBO) concepts?
8. How does responsibility accounting aid in the MBO concept?
9. We have mentioned that "The most crucial element in a successful responsibility accounting system is the responsibility managers' acceptance of assigned responsibilities as equitable and their willingness to be held accountable." How does this affect the overall performance of an enterprise?

CASE 7-1

The Company

Main Bank is a medium-sized bank in Chicago. It is part of a bank holding company with five banks in the group. Each bank within the group is full service, with some of its functions controlled by the holding company. One of these functions is loan operations. Loan operations is the area that handles the "booking" and monitoring of the loans.

During the past year, the holding company decided that all the banks would stop doing internal data processing and instead send it to an outside vendor. The outside vendor would be responsible for data entry, storage, and informational output. Each bank's budget was based on the estimated use of the new system. Every service that had previously been supplied by internal data personnel would be assumed by the external vendor. The holding company felt the level of service should improve.

The Dilemma

The commercial loan area generates the majority of input to the system. A management report that had previously been generated by the internal data group was not immediately available on the new system. This report had been distributed to customers as a token of gratitude. The outside vendor agreed to develop the report at a cost of $10,000 and would charge the bank a service charge each time the program was run. The holding company has determined that the report is necessary for all banks and that it should be developed by the external vendor. While all the banks would benefit from the new program, they are not willing to share the development costs. Main Bank is the primary bank that deals with customers who have expressed the desire to have this report back. Under the old internal system, the customer had not been charged for the report.

Required

1. Who should be responsible for the development and service costs associated with the new program?

CASE 7-2

The Company

Sellum Real Estate Company is an urban real estate sales and building management firm. The total number of employees is twenty-six. Sellum derives its revenues from real estate commissions, building management fees (a fixed percentage of gross total monthly rental revenues), and insurance commissions (mainly homeowners' policies).

The company is divided into four departments: (1) real estate sales, (2) building management, (3) insurance, and (4) administrative (which includes the accounting and data processing functions).

Although operating in the black, Sellum has had a difficult time meeting the minimum requirements of the employee profit-sharing plan for the past two years.

The Dilemma

The managers of the three revenue-producing departments receive commissions on their sales or fees. The manager of the administrative department receives a lower annual salary than the other managers and, unlike the other managers, no commission.

The size of the firm should indicate that transfer pricing for the accounting and data processing services rendered by the administive department would be too cumbersome given the dollars and number of people involved.

Turnover in the administrative manager's position has been extremely high. Managers left as a result of the inequity in the payscale. This managerial position is now vacant. In a brainstorming session, the department managers presented the following proposals.

Proposal 1

Do not hire an administrative manager. As best as possible, assign the accounting, administrative, and data processing functions to the real estate, building management, and insurance departments.

Proposal 2

Hire a new administrative manager. Offer a certain base salary and add to it a percentage of each of the other manager's commissions.

Proposal 3

Do not hire an administrative manager. Assign the administrative responsibilities to the remaining department managers and have accounting and data processing performed by an outside firm.

Required:

1. Which of the proposals has the greatest merit considering the various internal and external environmental factors?

CASE 7-3

The Company

ABC Co. is a telecommunications company that has been ordered to divest by the federal government. The company has been in existence for decades. All through its past, the company had no competitors and sold most of its computers and other hardware to divisions within the company. Now it faces a host of competitors for practically every service it renders and every product it manufactures.

The company is currently organized by product and other functional responsibilities, with many costs for centrally provided services allocated across the board.

The Dilemma

The company must now align its costs and expenses with that of the competition. Top management has agreed that a new accounting system must be developed to provide product line financial data. The product management will then be responsible for the product they control.

The responsibility of product managers in the computer division includes searching the market to ascertain the type of computer to be designed and the quantity to be produced. They are also responsible for the various sales activities and for product modification if necessitated by changes in customer needs.

Management must choose from among the following three proposals for type of accounting data to be provided to the product managers and the extent of their responsibility:

Proposal 1

Provide accounting data to the product managers regarding employees, expenses, sales, product mix, cost of sales, product levels, and so on. Although product managers will have direct control over only a portion of the expenses, they will be given the other data for information purposes.

Proposal 2

Provide accounting data to the product managers regarding employees, expenses, sales, sales mix, cost of sales, product levels, and so on. Assign all direct costs associated with a specific product to the product manager, but charge the indirect costs to the level that exercises control.

Proposal 3

Establish each product or group of products as a profit center and therefore hold each product manager accountable for hurdle rates of return on investment and minimum residual income.

Required:

1. Which proposal do you feel should be chosen? Elaborate on the reasons for your choice.

CHAPTER 8

Behavioral Aspects
of Profit Planning
and Budgeting—I

INTRODUCTION

Budget making is a technical task. Words like *financial, numbers,* and *estimation* come to mind when one thinks about "budgets." Behind all the technical images associated with budgets, however, are people. Human beings make the budget and have to live with it.

The behavioral aspects of budgeting refer to the human behavior that is brought out in the process of preparing the budget and the human behavior that is induced when people try to live with the budget. It refers to the anxiety caused by knowing that spending limits will not be increased this year, the dread of telling your staff that there will be no pay increases this year, and the jealousy that may develop when another department head receives the largest budget increase in recent years.

Budgets have a direct impact on human behavior. Budgets tell people what is expected of them and when it is due. They place limits on what may be purchased and how much may be spent. They restrain managerial action. They are the reason that managers' performance is continually monitored and the standard against which the performance results are compared. People feel pressure from tight budgets, anxiety from poor performance reports, and elation or relief from "making" the budget.

Managers often face the problem that something "is not in the budget," or that "you are already over budget." They are periodically reminded that "you have not reached the budgeted goals."

It should, therefore, be of no surprise that sentiments like "that budget is cramping my style" or "those budget people are only out to get you" are repeatedly voiced. Budgets are often viewed as bureaucratic impediments or threats to career advancement. The dislike of the whole budget process may even induce people to sabotage the budget.

If budgets, which are intended to motivate people, create personal fear and other human problems instead, why are they used? What benefits are derived? What are the unwanted side effects? What is the behavioral impact? What can be done to ensure their behaviorally most efficient and constructive use?

These are some of the questions we will attempt to answer in the next two chapters. We will start by presenting a behavioral dilemma in a budgeting situation. After we have portrayed some of the behavior, frustration, and human drama involved in profit planning and budgeting, we will give an overview of the budgeting process and its three distinct stages. Then we will discuss the relevant behavioral science concepts and their impact in the various stages of the planning process. Finally, at the end of Chapter 9 we will present a diagnostic evaluation of the business dilemma that opened this chapter and make suggestions for overcoming the behavioral problems that plagued the budget-making process of our hypothetical company.

THE BUSINESS DILEMMA

The Ramus Corporation manufactures electronic recording equipment that is sold throughout the United States. The firm's sales have grown steadily over its ten-year life. Its profits, however, have turned from promising to marginal to poor. In June, 1983, top management hired Paul Cooper as director of profit planning and assigned him the responsibility of installing a comprehensive profit planning and budgeting system. He was to start with a one-year budget to which a three-year profit plan was later to be added. Paul was given complete autonomy with budgeting approaches and techniques.

The new position was created because the Ramus Corporation's first quarter income statement for 1983 showed a loss. Roberta Powell, the controller, and Anthony Ramus, the founder and president, agreed that the informal budgeting approach adopted last year did not work and that the severity of the financial situation demanded the full-time attention of an experienced planning executive.

Profits began declining in 1980; the decline continued into 1981. To correct the unfavorable trend, Powell instituted a fully participative, loosely structured budget system in 1982. She asked the line managers to submit departmental budgets. She slightly modified these to achieve some degree of companywide compatibility and consolidated these into an overall organizational plan. The modified departmental budgets were then returned to the departmental managers. Powell's budget system did not provide formal implementation steps, nor did it attempt any periodic systematic follow-up.

The budgeting system instituted by Powell failed. Profits fell again in 1982. Powell attributed these results to her failure to effectively implement and monitor the budget. During 1982, she was occupied fighting off takeover attempts by two aggressive conglomerates. She did not have the time to carefully review or evaluate the budget plans submitted by the departmental managers, nor did she have time to work with the departmental managers in determining and correcting the causes for the operating inefficiencies that were indicated in the monthly performance reports.

Ramus, the president, is a research engineer who does not want to be bothered with financial details. When Cooper was hired, Ramus told him that the firm, because of its position as a technological leader in the industry, had the potential to achieve high levels of profits if waste and inefficiency were eliminated. Ramus explained that as president, he had certain functions to fulfill and that as chief research engineer, the balance of his time had to be spent in the lab where the future of the company is determined. He told Cooper to do a good job as budget director, to bring profits up to at least their 1979, predecline levels, and not to bother him with questions or details. Ramus said that the next time he wanted to hear about the budget was at the end of 1983 when Cooper would explain how he turned the company around.

Much of Powell's time was spent in meetings with lawyers, bankers, and financial consultants. The market position and profit potential of Ramus Corporation was especially attractive to firms interested in acquiring subsidiaries in high technology industries. The balance of the controller's time was spent in supervising the overall accounting function and working with the staff. Having Paul Cooper in the firm not only allowed her to deal with the takeover problems more thoroughly, but also filled a vital need in the profit planning area.

Cooper, 47, is an experienced planning executive. He began his professional career in public accounting, but was lured to private industry 18 years ago to become assistant controller of a large midwestern steel company. For the past 8 years, he has worked almost exclusively with the budget-making process. He views his new position at Ramus Corporation as an important personal challenge because he has to apply all his professional expertise to an especially complex organizational problem.

Cooper is an advocate of widespread management participation in the budget-making process. He believes that if people are involved in making the budget, they will have a better idea of the limitations facing the firm and the interdependencies of the departments. This generally results in people viewing the budget more positively because they experience firsthand the budget's role in allocating those limited resources to the areas of the firm that have the most pressing need. Moreover, Cooper is aware of the positive effects of budget participation on motivation, identification, and cohesiveness. Because managers participate in making the budget, they have a personal stake in trying to achieve the budget goals. They feel a unity of purpose with their counterparts in other departments. All of this makes for a work environment conducive to good personal relationships and efficiency in operations.

The dilemma facing Cooper is concerned primarily with participation and tangentially with top management's role in shaping the work environment. Were Cooper to follow his budget-making preference in developing the one-year budget and call for widespread managerial participation in the planning process, he would most likely fail in his goal of reestablishing Ramus' past profit levels in the near future. This is because last year, participation was ineffectively used; it resulted in padded budgets, departmental rivalries for funds, bruised egos, negative attitudes toward budgeting, some envy, and loss of control over quality standards. Last year, the budget-making process was not properly guided. Rather than inducing increased efficiency and cooperation, it resulted in various forms of hostility. Thus, the positive effects of participation were not realized. Without guidance by a chief executive, the intended democratic nature of managerial participation in decision making developed instead into confusion and anarchy. Some of the line managers told Cooper of the frustration and bitterness they felt when faced with the intrigues and power plays that took place during last year's planning activities and how those feelings linger. Cooper got the impression that to go ahead with widespread managerial participation this year might cause a repeat of last year's behavior.

In an effort to regain control, Cooper could go to the other extreme and adopt an authoritarian budget-making approach and give departmental managers an imposed set of production quotas and spending limits. However, some negative results may develop. When managers do not participate in setting the budget goals, they may view the budget as an unwanted intrusion into their managerial decision-making domain. They may reject the budget, attempt to undermine it, or see it as a pressure device. They may begin to consider Cooper as an enemy or a taskmaster. In short, hostility to the budgeting process might occur, both to Cooper as a person and to top management in general. If so, the cooperation necessary for budget success and the coordination necessary for operational efficiency would be lacking.

Thus, Cooper had to decide whether to try some type of participative budget-making approach and risk some negative results or use a more authoritarian approach and risk a different set of negative results. Compounding this was top management's apparent lack of interest in budgeting and profit planning. If the line managers perceive the budget to be given low priority by top management, the importance of the budget to the line managers will likewise be minimized. Thus, an additional dilemma confronting Cooper was whether to "bother" Ramus and Powell by asking them to give more visible support to the budget, or whether to try to gain budget acceptance without strong support from top managment.

In September, 1983, Cooper called a meeting of the departmental managers and outlined the anticipated planning procedures: "Within the next three weeks, each of you will receive a copy of my planning guidelines along with various revenue and expense budget forms. These are to be used for preparing your departmental budgets. The guidelines will contain procedural details for completing the budget forms, a summary of the company's major objectives, and the operational strategies chosen by top management for achieving them.

You will be given your profit goals and expected profit percentages. From then on you are on your own."

Cooper continued: "Your individual plans must be submitted to me by November 1. After I study and evaluate your plans, I will schedule meetings with each of you to discuss their merits. If they are not acceptable in their original form, you will have ten days to revise them. That will leave me with sufficient time to consolidate all your detailed plans, present the comprehensive plan to the president for approval, and return your portion of the comprehensive plan to you before Christmas."

Before finding out the degree of participation or authority Cooper decided on or how tight the profit goals and profit percentages actually were, we will first discuss the role of profit planning and budgeting and delineate the behavioral concepts that impact each phase of the process. We will then determine the nature of the dysfunctional behavior that took place and how that behavior affected profit, speculate as to factors that triggered the behavior, and suggest strategies to alter it.

THE MULTIPLE FUNCTIONS OF PROFIT PLANNING AND BUDGETING

Budgets are managerial plans for action expressed in financial terms. They are short-term comprehensive profit plans that put management's objectives and goals into operation. They are managerial tools that insure the attainment of organizational goals and provide the dollar-and-cent guidelines for day-to-day operations.

If a firm sets goals to capture a larger share of the market, increase profit, and enhance its image among consumers, then its budget should commit the resources necessary to achieve these goals. The budget should reflect the additional advertising and promotion costs necessary to spur sales and enhance the image. It should include estimated salary expenses necessary to sustain a larger sales force and the more generous commission structure that is meant to motivate greater sales efforts. It should include cash flow estimates that take into account the timing of cash collections from customers, the cash payments to suppliers, and anticipated increases in various expenses. In short, it should be a detailed, financial blueprint of how the firm expects to operate.

Budgets have several functions. First, they are the final result of a firm's planning process. As the outcome of negotiations among the dominant organizational members, they represent the organizational consensus about operating goals for the future.

Second, they are the firm's blueprint for action, reflecting management's priorities in the allocation of organizational resources. They indicate how the various organizational subunits are intended to work toward achieving the overall company goals.

Third, they act as an internal communication device that links the various organizational departments or divisions with each other and with top management. Message flows from top management to lower organizational levels contain performance expectation levels and standards; follow-up reports to top management contain results. Message flows from department to department serve to coordinate and facilitate overall organizational activity. Message flows from departments to top management contain operational explanations of budget attainment or deviation.

Fourth, by stating goals in terms of measurable performance criteria, budgets serve as standards against which actual operating results may be compared. This is the basis for evaluating the performance of cost and profit center managers.

Fifth, they serve as control devices that allow management to pinpoint the areas of the company that are strong or weak. This enables management to determine appropriate corrective actions.

Sixth, they attempt to influence and motivate managers and employees to continue to act in ways that are consistent with effective and efficient operations and in congruence with organizational goals.

Budgets have become accepted management tools for planning and controlling organizational activities. They are applied with various degrees of sophistication and success by most business and not-for-profit organizations.

A BEHAVIORAL OVERVIEW OF THE BUDGET-MAKING PROCESS

There are three major stages in the budget-making process: (1) goal setting, (2) implementation, and (3) control and performance evaluation. To develop a budget or profit plan, certain sequential steps have to be taken.

First, top management has to decide what the firm's short range objectives are and what strategies will be used to attain them. Objectives are desired results to be achieved. Strategies are the means to achieve the objectives.

Second, goals have to be set and resources allocated. Goals are the short-range quantification of the objectives. For example, the objective might be to capture a larger share of the market. The strategy calls for national television advertising and local newspaper coupons. One goal might be to increase sales this year by 10 percent.

Third, a comprehensive budget or profit plan has to be prepared, then approved by top management. After approval, it has to be communicated to the supervisors and employees whose performance it will control.

Finally, it is used to control cost and to pinpoint problem areas in the organization by periodically comparing actual performance results to the budgeted goals.

Human interaction is required at each step of the budget process. Thus, the behavioral aspects of budgeting should be fully understood in order to avoid the human-related dysfunctional side effects of budgeting.

Goal-Setting Stage

The planning activity begins with the translation of broad organizational objectives into specific activity goals. To develop realistic plans and create a workable budget, extensive interaction is required between the organization's line and staff managers. The controller and director of planning play key roles in this human process of budget making. As staff personnel, they are responsible for initiating and administering the budget-making process and for assisting line personnel, whenever necessary, in carrying out their various planning tasks. When formulating the organizational objectives and translating them into operating goals, care must be taken to establish a hierarchy of objectives and goals that are both realistic and, to the extent possible, in harmony with the personal goals and needs of managers and employees.

If compatible with both organizational structure and leadership styles, lower-level managers and employees should be given the opportunity to participate in the goal-setting process because they are more likely to identify with and accept goals that they have helped to formulate. Realistic goals established through meaningful participation will favorably affect the aspiration levels of managers and employees. Lack of participation, or mere lip service thereto, may result in a host of dysfunctional behavioral side effects.

The major behavioral concepts that impact the goal-setting phase of the planning process are participation, congruence, and commitment.

Implementation Stage

In the implementation stage, the formal plan is used to communicate organizational objectives and strategies and to positively motivate people in the organization. This is achieved by providing detailed performance goals to those responsible for action. For the plan to work, it must be effectively communicated; misunderstandings should be immediately detected and resolved. Only then is the formal plan likely to receive the full cooperation from the various groups it is meant to motivate.

The major behavioral science concepts that impact the implementation phase are communication, cooperation, and coordination.

Control and Performance Evaluation Stage

After the budget has been implemented, it functions as a key element in the control system. It becomes a yardstick against which actual performance is compared and it serves as the basis for management by exception. It should be pointed out that management by exception does not hold that only unfavorable variances need to be investigated. Rather, managers should concern themselves first with the unfavorable variances. Indeed, to maintain efficiency in operations, both above-standard and substandard performances are to be recognized and investigated. Favorable variances and above-standard performance will indicate how future periods may benefit by transferring knowledge and technology to similar operations. Alternatively, favorable variances may indicate the need for budget adjustments. Unfavorable variances and substandard performance should trigger immediate corrective actions in order to avoid costly recurrence. Management's policies, attitudes, and actions in performance evaluation and variance follow-up have a host of behavioral consequences, which, if not understood and controlled, can negate the success of the whole planning and controlling process. Some possible behavioral consequences include pressure, motivation, aspiration, and anxiety.

In later sections, we will discuss who should provide decision inputs during the planning stage, approve the plans, implement the budget, be responsible for the preparation of the performance reports, evaluate the variances, and be responsible for suggesting immediate remedial action. We will also discuss the behavior patterns of the people who interact in each planning phase. We will identify undesirable behavior and show its dysfunctional consequences. We hope to demonstrate that a thorough understanding of human behavior is a vital prerequisite for successful financial planning.

DYSFUNCTIONAL CONSEQUENCES OF THE BUDGET-MAKING PROCESS

The multiple functions of the budget as a goal setting, control, and performance evaluation mechanism may trigger numerous dysfunctional consequences such as distrust, resistance, internal conflict, and other unwanted side effects.

Distrust

A budget consists of a set of specific goals. Even though it may be adjusted for unanticipated events, it gives the appearance of inflexibility. It is a source of pressure that can create mistrust, hostility, and lead to declining performance.

Research has discovered a great deal of distrust of the entire budgetary process at the supervisory level. The reasons for this distrust are based on supervisors' beliefs that:

1. Budgets tend to oversimplify or distort the "real" situation and fail to allow for variations in external factors.
2. Budgets do not adequately reflect qualitative variables such as the know-how of the labor force, quality of materials, and efficiency of machinery.
3. Budgets simply confirm what supervisors already know.
4. Budgets are frequently used to manipulate supervisors so the indicated performance measures are suspect.
5. Budget reports emphasize results, not reasons.
6. Budgets interfere with supervisors' leadership styles.
7. Budgets tend to emphasize failure.[1]

Resistance

Although budgets are widely used and their benefits strongly supported, they are still resisted by many organizational participants. One major reason for this is that budgets foreshadow and bring about change, thereby threatening the status quo. The literature in the social sciences, management, and organizational behavior fields has described the phenomenon of employee resistance to change. Many people become accustomed to particular ways of doing things and to particular ways of viewing events and are simply not interested in changing. It is a challenge to management to overcome this resistance to change and to successfully introduce innovations that enhance organizational performance.

Another reason for budget resistance is that the budget process requires a great deal of time and attention. Managers or supervisors might feel overly burdened with extensive demands on their time and with other day-to-day responsibilities. Therefore, they do not want to become involved in the budget-making process.

Finally, many managers and supervisors simply do not understand the intricacies of budget making. They are often afraid to admit this or unwilling to learn enough about planning and the budget-making process to make meaningful contributions.

There are many excuses for this resistance. "Why should I budget? I am doing okay." "You cannot forecast the future with any degree of certainty, so why plan?" "Budgeting is too time consuming for me. I do not have the time, even if I wanted to do it." "I am in a cash squeeze and that is all I can think about." "It is too complicated. My business is simple and I know what the problems are." "My business is too small to need a budget. I can do all the planning I need in my head." Many of these excuses can be overcome by educating managers and supervisors about the benefits that can be derived from budgeting.

Internal Conflict

Budgets require interactions between people at different organizational levels. Internal conflict may develop as a result of these interactions, or as a result of performance reports that compare one department to another. The most common symptom of conflict is the inability to achieve interpersonal and intergroup cooperation during the budget-making process.

Internal conflict creates a competitive and hostile work environment. Conflict may cause people to focus exclusively on their own department's needs rather than the needs of the total organization. This situation renders goal congruence more difficult, if not impossible, to achieve. It breeds resentment toward management and, by extension, to the budget. To make things work, pressure will be increased downward and resisted by lower management, resulting in more pressure and greater conflict. Rivalry among subordinates may increase and the quality of work may decrease. In order to relieve the pressure, blame will be placed on particular individuals or groups. All of this will lead to greater conflict between the individual and the organization.

To end the cycle, management must identify and diagnose the cause. Then, actions to relieve the internal conflict and restore harmonious and productive working relationships may be initiated.

Other Unwanted Side Effects

Budgets may produce other undesirable side effects. One of these is the formation of small, informal groups that work against the objectives of the budget. These employee groups are usually formed to combat the internal conflict and the pressure that the budget creates. Their purpose is to reduce tension. However, their goals may conflict with the organization's goals, and the unintended effect of their activities may run counter to their intended purpose of reducing tension. These employee groups sometimes shift responsibility to other departments, question the validity of the budgeted data, and lobby for lower standards. Such situations make it difficult for the accounting staff functions to be effectively discharged, create a tension-filled organizational climate, and impair the usefulness of the budget.

Budgets are frequently perceived as managerial pressure devices. People feel pressure when top management attempts to improve efficiency by obtaining more output from given (or lower) levels of input. While some pressure is desirable, excessive pressure may be associated with frustration, short tempers, and the physical diseases brought on by stress.

Budget pressure is most acute for supervisors who are responsible for meeting particular goals. Because supervisors are often unable to pass this responsibility to subordinates, they resort to various dysfunctional actions, one of which is distorting the measurement process. This might be accomplished by overt manipulation of the data or by making operating decisions that improve immediate performance but harm the firm in the long run. For example, a foreman might delay needed maintenance, charge a particular expense to a different account, or build safety factors (slack) into the budget to increase the likelihood of meeting or exceeding performance standards.

Another undesirable side effect that may develop is the overemphasis on departmental performance and a deemphasis on overall organizational performance. By focusing attention exclusively on departmental performance, important interdepartmental dependencies and economies may be overlooked.

Budgets may also stifle individual initiative and cost-effective innovations because established business methods with known probabilities of success are preferred to new methods with unproven chances of success. Thus, individuals are often discouraged from innovating.

The problems associated with the budgeting process should not imply that the process should be scrapped, but rather that careful considerations are required in order to obtain the desired effect. To make a budget work, employees must be made aware of the budget's function as a positive vehicle for smooth organizational operation. Rather than viewing budgets as a heinous means of squeezing the last drop of sweat out of employees, people must learn to regard budgets as tools for establishing goal congruence and as performance standards which are meant to benefit all members of the firm.

An educated management and labor force are more likely to cooperate in the making of budgets and profit plans. Without budget education, such cooperation is less likely. No matter how sophisticated the budget techniques are, the budget process may be a drain on company funds unless the potential problems are addressed beforehand and dealt with appropriately.

RELEVANT BEHAVIORAL SCIENCE CONCEPTS IN THE PLANNING ENVIRONMENT

The Impact of the Planning Environment

Before we can meaningfully discuss the behavioral science concepts that impact the planning or budget-making process, it is necessary to introduce the factors that cause variation in the planning environment. The planning environment refers to the structure, process, and interaction patterns in the work setting. It is sometimes referred to as the organizational culture or the organizational climate. It includes the degree of formality in human inter-action, the receptivity of top management to new ideas, the procedures and hardware for getting work done, feelings of identification with the organiza-tion, the cohesiveness of the work force, and so on.

An organization's size and structure, leadership style, type of control systems, and environmental stability are some of the factors that influence the work environment in which planning occurs. The work environment or organizational culture affects behavior and therefore influences the planning process. Human behavior is adaptive and differs from one work environment to another. Thus, in one environment, a specific action by top management may induce favorable behavior and budget results, while the same action in a different environment may induce undesirable behavior and dysfunctional budget results.

Organizational Size and Structure

The size and structure of an organization influences human behavior and interaction patterns in the goal-setting, implementation, and control and evaluation stages of the planning process. Organizational size may be con-ceived of in terms of number of employees, dollar value of physical plant, sales volume, number of branch offices, or other quantitative measures that differentiate organizations. Organizational structure refers to the formal and informal relationships between organizational members. It includes the num-ber of layers of authority, the number of offices or positions at each layer, the responsibilities of each office, and the procedures for getting work done.

Organizational size affects the organizational structure. In small firms, the planning and control structure is relatively simple because organizational activities are carried out by only a few people. Activities can be more easily controlled and problems of goal congruence can be more readily addressed.

In contrast, large firms must develop complex bureaucratic structures to cope with the administration of the various organizational functions. Authority is delegated and widely dispersed from above. Jobs and tasks are reduced by necessity to small areas of responsibility, which creates a need for more stringent coordination and formal control along superior/subordinate lines. In such bureaucratic management structures, effective budget making is rendered much more difficult because of potential inefficiencies in intraorganizational communications, lack of goal congruence, and the inability of many to see the relationship between their work roles and the overall objectives of the organization. In large bureaucratic organizations, planning systems have to be designed to reduce the inherent ability of disgruntled managers to practice undetected insubordination. The planning systems must also strive to eliminate or reduce serious goal incongruence.

The sheer size and complexity of some organizations causes monumental problems in planning, implementation, and control. For example, the director of planning has to coordinate production, sales, and inventory levels with the vice-presidents of manufacturing, sales, finance, and marketing. These levels must correspond to proposed spending limits on market research and advertising. Each vice-president has his or her own ideas about what the target volume should be, based on personal or departmental considerations. The director of planning has to generate an organizational consensus by asking for compromise from all parties. The vice-presidents in turn must operate their own departments within the dollar constraints imposed by the budget and they must generate consensus within their own departments.

Organizational size confounds the budgeting process in other ways. For example, managers at various organizational levels may screen information and pass upward or downward only data that is favorable to them. Managers or supervisors may carry out only that portion of their responsibilities that is consistent with their own goals and interests.

The planning environment is also affected by the degree of autonomy, or decision-making prerogative, granted to subunits and/or lower-level managers. This aspect of organizational structure is usually expressed in terms of centralization versus decentralization. Centralized organizations are characterized by the concentration of decision making at higher managerial levels. Decentralized organizations are characterized by lower-level managers having relatively greater decision-making prerogatives. Since efficient profit plans have to be tailor-made for specific organizational environments, centralized firms need a system that provides for extremely close monitoring of all organizational activities. Decentralized firms will require a system that enhances companywide participation, cooperation, and coordination.

Leadership Styles

Leadership style also affects an organization's planning environment. McGregor's Theory X describes a tightly controlled, authoritarian leadership style in which need for efficiency and control dictates the managerial approach for dealing with subordinates. To monitor the performance of subordinates, these leaders assign their staff to collect information that allows for indirect supervision. The philosophy for inducing desired subordinate behavior is: pay them well and watch them closely.

Applied to the planning function, Theory X implies that the budget would be prepared by top management (the controller or director of planning) and imposed on lower-level management. Thus, under authoritarian leadership styles, budgets are viewed as managerial control devices designed to ensure employee conformity with the expectations of top management. In the follow-up phase, budget variances would be investigated by the controller or planning director rather than being handled as a line function. This allows top management to retain the responsibility for cost control.

Authoritarian leadership styles clearly facilitate coordination and control of activities, especially when the responsibility for tasks is unambiguous. They are relatively efficient in cases of language or cultural difference. However, they do not encourage participation and may cause excessive budget pressure, anxiety and motivation impairments.

In contrast, McGregor's Theory Y and Likert's democratic leadership style encourage employee involvement and participation in goal setting and decision making. Democratic leadership styles allow for flexibility in the budget-making process and give employees the opportunity to become involved in charting the course for the organization, to express their ideas about how the firm should be operating, and to use their talents effectively. With a participative approach, more time is required to complete the budget because of the back-and-forth communications and negotiations among departments. However, research has revealed that people identify more closely with the budget and make greater efforts to achieve the stated goals when they participate in setting those goals.

Hopwood [2] distinguished between budget-constrained and profit-conscious leadership styles. Budget-constrained leaders evaluate subordinates on the basis of how well short-term budget goals were met. In contrast, profit-conscious leaders are concerned with long-term success and place less emphasis on strict adherence to the current budget. Hopwood found that budget-constrained leadership styles were associated with poor service to customers, employee tension and mistrust, and lack of innovation.

Related to leadership style is leadership pattern. It was found that aggressive managers frequently use budgets and profit plans in a domineering manner and authoritarian leaders use budgets as weapons. Democratic leaders, in contrast, attempt to use them as motivational tools and communication devices.

Stability of Organizational Environments

Another factor affecting the planning environment is the external environment. This includes the existing political and economic climate, availability of supplies, structure of the industries that service the organization, the nature of competition, and so on. Stable environments pose limited risks and allow the goal-setting process to be democratic and participative. Rapidly changing environments result in high-risk situations. Dramatic changes in interest rates, foreign exchange rate fluctuations, and increasing competition from abroad are cases in point. To cope with such changes, decisions have to be made quickly and decisively. Frequent goal and/or strategy adjustments may be necessary. In these instances, authoritarian leadership styles have proven more efficient than democratic, participative styles.

REFERENCES

[1] Argyris, C. "The Impacts of Budgets on People," New York: *Financial Executives Foundation, 1952, 1–32.*

[2] *Anthony G. Hopwood* "An Empirical Study of the Role of Accounting Data in Performance Evaluation." *Empirical Research in Accounting: Selected Studies,* 1972, Supplement to *Journal of Accounting Research;* and "Leadership Climate and the Use of Accounting Data in Performance Evaluation," *The Accounting Review, 49:3 (July 1974),* 485-95.

DISCUSSION QUESTIONS

1. Why are budgets often viewed as bureaucratic impediments to career advancement?
2. Why are budgets important to an organization?
3. What are the three major stages in the budget-making process and why is human interaction important in the process?
4. What are the major behavioral concepts that impact the various stages of the budget planning process?
5. Why should favorable variances and above-standard performance be recognized and reported together with unfavorable variances and substandard performance? Will this affect the employees?
6. What are some dysfunctional consequences of the budget planning process? Why do they happen? Can they be avoided?
7. Define organizational culture. How does it affect behavior and influence the planning process?
8. How does organizational structure and size affect the goal-setting, implementation, control, and evaluation stages of the budget-making process?
9. What is the difference between McGregor's Theory X and Likert's democratic leadership style? What are the advantages of each and under what situations will one be chosen over the other?

CHAPTER 9

Behavioral Aspects
of Profit Planning
and Budgeting—II

RELEVANT BEHAVIORAL SCIENCE CONCEPTS IN THE BUDGETING PROCESS

The Goal-Setting Stage

Now we turn our attention from the factors that influence behavior in the planning environment to the concepts that affect behavior in the goal-setting stage. During the goal-setting stage, top management's broad objectives are translated into definite and measurable goals for the organization and for each of the major subunits (the responsibility centers).

It is important to keep in mind that people in the organization are responsible for determining objectives and setting goals. People in the organization are also responsible for achieving the objectives and goals. Thus, the goal-setting phase of planning is fraught with behavioral pitfalls.

Classical economic and management theories of the firm considered goals to be non-problematic. Whether it was economic theory's single goal of profit maximization or classical management theory's personal goals of the founders or entrepreneurs, goals were considered given facts with which the organization had to deal. The question of how goals were set was considered irrelevant and was of no interest to these early theorists.

These views were challenged in the early 1960s by modern organization theorists. Modern organization theory assumes that organizational goals are varied and reflect decisions to commit the organization to a particular course of action. The advocates of this new philosophy define goals as "a desired state of affairs which the organization attempts to realize," [1] or expressed differently, "future attainments to which present effort or commitments are made." [2] Both these definitions make it clear that to be "real" goals (rather than goals that are merely "stated" ones or "wishful thinking"), human effort and the commitment of sufficient organizational resources are required.

Organizational goals are strongly influenced by the goals of the dominant organizational members, who collectively have sufficient control of organizational resources to commit them in certain directions and to withhold them from others. Goals are seen as a complex compromise that reflect the sometimes conflicting individual needs and personal goals of the organization's dominant constituency. Organizational goals are determined through negotiation. The bargaining and influence trading are constraints imposed by the various participants and by the external and internal environment.

The weight of any individual's input into the budget-making process depends in many cases on that person's power in the firm. This is discussed more fully in the following sections.

Goal Congruence

A major problem encountered in the goal-setting stage is achieving a workable degree of goal congruence or compatability among the goals of the organization, its subunits (divisions and/or departments), and its participating members. Goal congruence or compatability occurs when individuals perceive that their personal needs can be best satisfied by achieving the organizational goals. If organizational goals are perceived as a means for attaining personal goals or for satisfying personal needs, it will motivate employees to complete the desired actions.

Projects that pose unusual challenges may be instrumental in fulfilling people's needs for self-actualization and self-esteem. People may feel honored to be entrusted with important and difficult tasks and may be stimulated to increase their efforts to ensure successful performance. Congruence between organizational and personal goals can also be enhanced by explaining to employees the rationale upon which the organizational goals are based. Since neither organizational nor individual goals are static, goal congruence has to be accomplished anew at each planning cycle. Thus, regular communication between top management and lower-level managers and employees concerned with organizational objectives is well advised. Similarly, congruence between organizational and subunit goals must be periodically reestablished.

If goal congruence is not established, a variety of problems may develop. Managers of different subunits may work to competing ends, a spirit of competition may replace one of cooperation, or a feeling of frustration may pervade the managerial ranks. People's identification with the organization may become weakened. This may be reflected in the quality of service rendered to customers or in the quality of merchandise produced.

Participation

Participation in the budget-making process is acclaimed by many as a panacea for meeting the esteem and self-actualization needs of organizational members. Participation is a "process of joint decision making by two or more parties in which the decisions have future effects on those making them."[3] In other words, workers and lower-level managers have a voice in the management process. When applied to planning, participation refers to the involvement of middle- and lower-level managers in the decisions leading to the determination of operational objectives and the setting of performance goals. The involvement may vary from mere attendance at budget meetings to participation in discussions concerning the reasonableness of sales quotas and production targets to the right to negotiate in setting one's own goals.

Almost all studies of participation in the management process conclude that participation benefits the organization. Participation has been shown to positively affect employee attitudes, increase the quantity and quality of production, and enhance cooperation among managers. However, Becker and Green [4] found that when applied in the wrong settings, participation may impair employee motivation and decrease efforts to attain the organizational goals.

The many studies on participative decision making do not agree on an exclusive desirable format for employee participation that would work for all organizations. There is relatively little discussion or agreement on the depth, scope, or weight of participation. That is, there is no uniform view on who should participate (depth), what kinds of decisions they should participate in (scope), or the degree of the participant's power in the final decision (weight). There is also a question concerning whether the benefits of participation increase proportionally to the number of participating employees.

The depth, scope, and weight of participation in goal setting depends on organizational leadership styles, organizational structure, the speed with which decisions have to be made, the expertise of the work force, and the type of contribution they can make. Thus, organizations have to decide whether to include middle managers, lower-level managers, supervisors, foremen, factory workers, or office workers in the budget-making process. Then the decision has to be made concerning the budget activities in which these organizational members are to participate. Finally, top management has to decide when to intervene to settle disputes, to prod stagnating budget discussions, or to announce that time is up and a decision must be made by the budget participants.

In its broadest sense, participation is the essence of the democratic process and is therefore unnatural when superimposed in an authoritarian organizational structure. Thus, in large, centrally managed bureaucractic organizations, participation in determining objectives and setting goals will by definition be limited to a handful of top executives. Top management will prepare the budget and pass it down the hierarchy as a set of orders to be obeyed. It will be used both as a mechanism to inform lower-level managers about what top management wants accomplished and as a tool for controlling people's spending and motivating optimum performance.

Firms with democratic leadership styles and/or decentralized organizational structures allow for greater management participation in budget-setting decisions. Many of these firms encourage both lower-level managers and employees to contribute to the planning process. However, participation is not always successful. One reason is that people react differently to the prospect of taking part in setting their own performance standards. Authoritarian and/or highly dependent employees may feel threatened by the prospect of becoming a part of the decision-making process. They would feel more comfortable if they received clear-cut instructions concerning spending limits and performance standards. On the other hand, people with strong independence and self-esteem needs will thrive when allowed to participate in formulating their own performance goals.

Another reason why participation may not succeed is that no serious attempts are made to insure the participation and cooperation of lower-level managers and employees. For participation to be effective, participants must have "real" input into decisions and their views must carry some weight in the final outcome. If people's budget suggestions are rejected at the next higher level with no explanation at all, or with a glib statement that the suggestions do not comply with top management objectives, then participation will be viewed as a sham. People will become disillusioned. If this occurs, negative or hostile attitudes toward management may develop, and it may signal coming declines in efficiency and output.

Research has demonstrated that if top management is strongly committed to participation, it can be successfully implemented even under authoritarian and highly structured conditions. If such managerial commitment is lacking, successful participation might be undermined even in the most decentralized and democratic organizations.

Benefits from Participation

One benefit of successful participation is that participants become ego-involved and not just task-involved in their work. It enhances morale and induces greater initiative at all management levels. Meaningful participation also increases the sense of group cohesiveness, which in turn tends to increase cooperation among group members in goal setting. The organizational goals that people help establish will then be perceived as being in congruence with their own personal goals. This process is called *goal internalization*. Lack of goal internalization may result in conflict between an individual's personal goals and employee-related goals. Because personal goals and needs usually dominate over organizational goals, lack of goal internalization may be associated with declines in morale and productivity. When people internalize and accept organizational goals, and when there are high levels of group cohesiveness, the prerequisites for maximal efficiency in goal achievement are present.

Meaningful participation is also credited with reducing budget-related pressure and anxiety. This is because the people who participated in the goal setting know that the goals are reasonable and achievable. Participation may also reduce perceived inequalities in the allocation of organizational resources among organizational subunits, as well as the negative reactions that result from such perceptions. Managers who are involved in goal setting will have a better understanding of why resources are allocated in a particular way. Through the process of negotiation and the many budget discussions that occur in meetings, managers will become aware of the problems of their counterparts in other organizational subunits and have a better understanding of the interdependencies between departments. Thus, many potential budget-related problems can be averted.

Limitations and Problems of Participation

Even under the most ideal conditions, participation in goal setting has its limitations. The process of participation gives managers power to establish the content of their budget. This power may be used in a manner that has dysfunctional consequences for the organization. For example, managers may build "organizational slack" into their budgets. *Slack* is the difference between the resources that are actually necessary to efficiently complete a task and the larger amount of resources that are earmarked for the task. In other words, slack is *budget padding*. Managers create slack by underestimating revenues, overestimating costs, or overstating the amount of inputs necessary to manufacture a unit of output. They do this to provide a margin of safety for meeting the budgeted goals. This cushion of extra resources relieves the budget-related pressure and frustration often induced by tight budgets. It gives managers more flexibility and greater certainty of achieving their personal and organizational goals. Some argue that a small amount of slack is desirable precisely because it relieves some pressure and permits a blending of personal and organizational goals, making goal congruence more likely to occur. However, excessive slack is clearly detrimental to the best interests of an organization. Excessive slack renders meaningless spending limits, production quotas, and performance standards. It undermines the drive for organizational efficiency by failing to impose meaningful organizational controls. The problem of excessive slack can be alleviated if top management establishes effective procedures for in-depth reviews during the budget-making process.

If the budget goals are extremely easy to attain because of slack or other factors resulting from participation in the budget-making process, then the motivational benefits are minimal or nonexistent. People may produce at less than their optimal level of capability. If, on the other hand, the budgeted goals are extremely difficult to reach and actual performance begins to deviate unfavorably from standard, people will initially try to improve their performance. If the budget deviation grows larger, however, people will eventually become discouraged and give up trying to improve the situation. Obviously, it is not in the organization's best interest to permit people to become so discouraged.

The point is that budgets that are too tight or too loose or are built with excessive slack or no slack at all can create behavioral responses that are not in the best interests of the firm. Care must be taken to ensure that the final budget document avoids the pitfalls associated with the extremes of tight or loose budgets. As in most things, organizations should aim for a middle course.

Several researchers and consultants have observed another problem associated with participative goal setting. Some firms profess to use participative budgeting but actually do not. Instead, they are involved in what has been termed "pseudoparticipation." As one consultant described it:

> The typical controller's insistence on others' participation sounded good to us when we first heard it in our interviews. But after a few minutes of discussion, it began to look as if the word "participation" had a rather strange meaning for the controller. One thing in particular happened in every interview, which led us to believe that we were not thinking of the same thing. After the controller had told us that he insisted on participation, he would then continue by describing his difficulty in getting the supervisors to speak freely.
>
> For example, "We bring them in, we tell them that we want their frank opinion, but most of them just sit there and nod their heads. We know they're not coming out with exactly how they feel. I guess budgets scare them; some of them don't have too much education.....Then we request the line supervisor to sign the new budget, so he can't tell us he didn't accept it. We've found a signature helps an awful lot. If anything goes wrong, they can't come to us, as they often do, and complain. We just show them their signature and remind them they were shown exactly what the budget was made up of."
>
> Such statements seem to indicate that only "pseudoparticipation" is desired by the controller. True participation means that the people can be spontaneous and free in their discussion. Participation, in the real sense of the word, also involves a group decision, which leads the group to accept or reject something new. Of course, organizations need to have their supervisors accept the new goals, not reject them; however, if the supervisors do not really accept the new changes but only say they do, then trouble is inevitable. Such half-hearted acceptance makes

it necessary for the person who initiated the budget or induced the change not only to request signatures of the "acceptors," so that they cannot later deny they "accepted," but to be always on the lookout and apply pressure constantly upon the "acceptors" (through informal talks, meetings, and "educational discussions of accounting").[5]

It is doubtful that pseudoparticipation provides any benefits to an organization. Rather, it may create serious morale and motivation problems. If a firm is unable to effectively use true participation, it may be wiser to follow authoritarian budget practices—and honestly admit it. To engage in the pretense of participation may cause employees to perceive the process as a "management trick."

Status and influence in an organization may also put a damper on effective participation. People who occupy higher organizational positions, have more dominant personalities, or have greater social status may have excessive influence on policy determination and the goal-setting process. Less dominant personalities, or people who are at lower levels in the organization, may feel threatened, intimidated, or inadequate when faced with more powerful colleagues. The result may be that the less dominant people defer on important issues to the more powerful. The less dominant may see participative budget making as a game where they are forced to play the role of "yes men."

Finally, firms have to realistically deal with the questions of participative depth, scope, and weight. Where should a firm draw the line and limit the amount of participation? Should all middle-level managers be included in the process? All lower-level managers? The foremen and first-line supervisors? How seriously should a lower-level manager's suggestions be taken if they are at odds with experienced top managers? How does the firm break a deadlocked situation? What should be done if decisions are needed quickly? Answers to these questions may determine the success or failure of participation.

The Implementation Stage

After the organizational goals have been set, the planning director consolidates them into the comprehensive formal budget. This companywide blueprint for action is then approved by the president or the board of directors. The budget is implemented through communication to key organizational personnel. This informs them of management's expectations, resource allocations, production quotas, and time limits.

To make a budget work, all employees must learn to see it as a positive vehicle for organizational action and as an improvement rather than a burden or management weapon. They must learn to consider budgets as managerial tools for planning and controlling organizational activities. Without such an understanding, even the most technically sophisticated budgeting processes may become a drain on company funds and fail to improve operational efficiency.

Communicating the Budget

The controller or director of planning is responsible for implementing the budget. This is accomplished by communicating the approved operational goals to people at lower organizational levels. This is sometimes referred to as "selling" the budget downward. Many complex communication problems may develop in this selling task because the messages must be understood by people who have diverse backgrounds and training and who work at different organizational levels. To alleviate some of the potential problems, the controller must translate overall organizational goals into understandable subgoals for each organizational subunit.

The subgoals can be communicated most effectively if they are personally explained and supplemented with written guidelines or informal follow-up discussions with subunit leaders. That is, the planning director should explain the basics of the budget-making process and the assumptions that resulted in the final budget amounts. If inflation rates, for example, had to be taken into consideration when the budget was being put together, then the director of planning should indicate why a particular rate was used. Likewise, people at lower levels should be told the assumptions regarding cost allocation, marketing priorities, economic expectations, and other problems anticipated by the firm.

In addition to its purpose of informing lower-level managers of their responsibilities, the communication of budget subgoals is also meant to win the confidence of lower-level personnel. For example, if top management has doubts about the feasibility of attaining the organizational goals, this perception may inadvertently be communicated to subordinates and induce undesirable behavior. Thus, top management should see to it that realistic goals are set. Then top management can exhibit the confidence in making the budget that will inspire the desired behavior in subordinates.

Cooperation and Coordination

Successful budget implementation requires the cooperation of people with widely diverse skills and talents. Each dimension of the plan should be carefully explained to those responsible for action to develop in them a sense of their own involvement and importance in the overall budget context. This will also demonstrate the interconnected tasks that comprise the whole of organizational activity and will reveal the role that each subunit plays. The planning director should be mindful that possible intragroup conflicts may impair cooperation among subunits. These problems should be dealt with as soon as detected to avoid more serious organizational consequences.

The planning director should also be aware of the attitudes of people toward the budget and the budget-making process. If the budget is held in low regard by nonfinancial management, it is less likely to be accepted. This poses potentially severe problems for overall organizational performance because key organizational subunits that are not cooperating in the overall plan will upset the expected interdepartmental coordination.

Coordination is the art of effectively combining all organizational resources. From a behavioral viewpoint, this means the merging of talents and strengths of the organizational participants and having them strive toward the same goal. To accomplish this, the implementer must successfully communicate how each person's work contributes to the achievement of organizational goals. More than that, the planning director should indicate which departments are responsible for particular aspects of the work to be done, which individuals in the departments are responsible, and where people could go for help.

Thus, employee knowledge of the organizational structure is important for successful communication and cooperation. To get things accomplished, people should know the roles that others play in both the formal and informal organizations. That is, some individuals who may not be "official" leaders will nevertheless be "informal" leaders and have the ability to expedite work. Others, although responsible for certain organizational functions, may be avoided if they are considered difficult to get along with. The planning director should be aware of the informal organizational structure, use it when necessary, and fight it when it appears to be threatening the goal-attainment process.

The planning director needs more than a technical understanding of the financial dimension of the organization. He or she must understand human behavior, group dynamics, organizational structures, and formal roles. Knowledge and understanding of factors affecting individual and group behavior are necessary in order to modify behavior. The planning director has to deal with people and usually cannot afford to offend anyone lest the budget be sabotaged. He or she must interact with groups and must assign rights and responsibilities. The planning director must demand performance, yet not be a taskmaster. In short, the planning director has the most difficult task of getting several self-centered, characteristically unique, power-seeking managers and supervisors to cooperate with a plan that is not 100 percent to their liking.

The Control and Performance Evaluation Stage

Budgeted goals are rarely attained without continuously monitoring employee progress toward achieving their goals. In the control and performance evaluation stage, actual performance is compared to the budgeted standards in order to pinpoint problem areas in the organization and to suggest appropriate actions to correct substandard performance. The comparison of actual and budgeted cost will also indicate above-standard performance.

Performance Reports

To maintain control over costs and to keep employees motivated toward goal achievement, performance reports should be prepared and distributed at least monthly. The importance of frequent communication of performance results has been repeatedly demonstrated in empirical studies. The timely issuance of performance reports has a reinforcing effect on employee morale. The lack of performance feedback, delays in feedback, and infrequent or sporadic feedback have an extinguishing effect on morale and performance. It was also found that increased feedback resulted in increased task accuracy and high confidence and amity. Lack of feedback was accompanied by low confidence and hostility.

Lack of performance feedback prevents people from knowing the actual level of achievement reached and may impair their subsequent aspiration levels. "Aspiration level" is the self-imposed standard that people shoot for. It is a goal that even when just barely achieved leads to subjective feelings of success and when not achieved, to subjective feelings of failure. Shifts in aspiration levels may be caused by changes in the employee's confidence about his or her ability to attain performance goals. It has been empirically demonstrated, for example, that success in one area usually leads to higher aspiration levels in related areas. Similarly, failure in one area results in lower aspiration levels in other areas.

If participation successfully increases goal internalization, and if people perceive the goals to be realistic and fair, then the achievement levels specified in the budget may become the aspiration levels of the work force. On the other hand, if the budget goals are not perceived as realistic and fair, then the aspiration levels of the work force are likely to be lower than the achievement levels specified in the budget.

Frequent performance evaluation and feedback enhances organizational efficiency by indicating which goals should be revised for the next planning cycle. Managers can infer this from what is known about aspiration levels. Since aspiration levels rise when actual performance meets or exceeds the budget, favorable performance may suggest that particular goals ought to be raised to conform to new aspiration levels. If actual performance is just slightly below expected performance levels, no immediate changes in budgetary goals are necessary because people will strive to reach the established goals. However, goal adjustments should be made when people feel that their efforts are futile and when it is apparent that they are discouraged.

If actual performance is well below expected levels, goals should be lowered so that aspiration levels do not decline to a dangerously low level. If goals are lowered to a level perceived to be attainable, then given a reasonable effort, people will again strive to attain the goals.

Thus, periodic performance feedback triggers subjective feelings of success or failure. Employees are confronted with biweekly or monthly reports that indicate whether they produced as much as they should have, in as short a time as possible, while spending as little as possible, and without sacrificing quality. It is not surprising then that when people "make the budget"— that is, meet all the goals—they "feel good." They deserve that feeling of accomplishment.

Performance reports can also induce employees to feel pressure, anxiety, envy, anger, disillusionment, remorse, elation, and so on. We know from the social sciences that people will act based on what they think or feel. Thus, planning directors should be especially sensitive to human reactions to performance reports.

It must be emphasized that the feelings of success or failure triggered by the performance reports are, in fact, "subjective." Success or failure is defined by the relation of actual performance this month with a standard established in the past. On the basis of these predetermined performance standards, employees are judged in a clear-cut, absolute manner: You made the budget or you did not; you succeeded or failed. However, the seemingly clear-cut categories of success and failure can be interchanged by simply redefining the predetermined performance standard. This implies that people's feelings of pride and pressure, their concerns, anxiety and aspiration levels, motivation, and general perspective on their work are not solely determined by their actual performance. The employee attitudes and behavior that are induced by the budget depend instead on the predetermined performance standards. That is, the same actual performance could be judged as success or failure and employees made to feel "good" or "bad," depending on the standard.

This points out the extreme relevance of goal setting, predetermined performance standards, and slack to human behavior and makes clear the importance of continuously updating standards. It also demonstrates the essential nature of performance reports as communication devices that trigger human reactions. It reveals the importance of setting standards for quality control as well as for spending and production limits. People's spending and production levels can appear favorable on a performance report if poor quality inputs are substituted for better quality inputs. Finally, it shows how modifications in the accounting system, through budget adjustments, and the information generated by the system, in the form of performance reports, can change human behavior.

DIAGNOSTIC EVALUATION OF THE BUSINESS DILEMMA _____

We now turn our attention back to the business dilemma described at the beginning of Chapter 8. Using the behavioral concepts that impact behavior in each phase of the planning process, we will discuss the dysfunctional behavior that occurred, explore the possible causes, and suggest strategies to avoid recurrence during Paul Cooper's attempt to restructure the budget-making system.

A vital prerequisite for successful budgeting is top management's whole-hearted commitment to planning as a way of doing business. Without such executive support and the favorable planning climate it creates, even the most sophisticated budget system is likely to fail. The Ramus Corporation president, who does not want to be bothered by financial matters, and the controller, who is totally occupied with other problems, certainly do not provide an atmosphere conducive to serious planning activities.

The preoccupation of the two chief executives with other matters suggests that the Ramus Corporation is run in a decentralized, laissez-faire fashion. Departmental managers apparently enjoy a great degree of decision-making autonomy because top management control appears to be loose or nonexistent. Up to 18 months ago, the company had neither a formal planning system nor any formal periodic evaluation of operational performance. The only tangible signs of success or failure were semiannual and annual income statements. Without a standard cost system, there was no way of evaluating the efficiency of production activities; the cost information generated by the company's accounting system only indicated whether per-unit cost had increased, decreased, or stayed the same since the last report. It should therefore be no surprise that the informal and poorly structured budgeting approach introduced by the controller did not succeed.

Thus, the task of Paul Cooper, the new director of planning, was quite involved. He had to develop from scratch a systematic approach to formulate the organization's operational objectives and goals, translate them into financial terms, and allocate the resources necessary to get the work done. He also had to educate the departmental managers about the purpose and benefits of planning, gain their confidence, and get from them a commitment to cooperate with a budget-making process that they already viewed with suspicion and distaste.

Before meeting with the departmental managers, Cooper had top management formulate their short-range (one-year) objectives, operational strategies, and profit goals. The case does not tell us who was involved besides the president and the controller. It would have been desirable if objectives, strategies, and desired rates of return were determined by a group composed of all functional executives (e.g., research and development, production, sales, etc.).

Cooper would have liked the goal-setting process to have been democratic and participative. The departmental managers were given top management's objectives, operational strategies, and desired profit goals. It was then their responsibility to translate these overall targets into operational goals for their departments. That is, departmental managers were responsible for setting sales and production levels and for determining the associated revenues and costs that would result in the expected profit levels and percentages.

To ensure uniformity of approach, the departmental managers were supplied with the required schedules and procedural guidelines. Thus, except for the lack of top management's visible commitment and support, the final decision on the extent of participation in the planning approach seems well thought out. We do not know, however, whether Cooper sufficiently explained the purpose of planning to the department managers and indicated what the budget could do *for* them, not *to* them. He should have convinced them that their own career goals were closely associated with their participation in goal setting and with their efforts to achieve the goals. That is, departmental managers had the power to directly influence the corporation's efficiency and profitability and thereby their own destinies as well. Cooper should also have pointed out to the managers how the budget could be used to motivate and evaluate their subordinates and how it is possible to minimize severe losses by discovering inefficiencies in operations before they become problematic.

The case does not mention the interactions that occurred between the department managers and their subordinates when they set the sales and production goals and formulated their initial plans. We do not know the extent to which the department managers permitted their subordinates to participate in the budget-making process. Since the organization appears to be decentralized and since we can expect that the different managers vary in leadership style and supervise people with diverse educational backgrounds and personality traits, it is likely that their approaches to participation differed as well. In those departments with broad participation, it is possible that the budgets contained considerable slack because everyone participating wanted to increase their chances of attaining the goals. Slack could also have occurred in authoritarian goal-setting situations. The departmental managers (without consultation with their subordinates) could have padded their budgets to improve their own chances for success, recognition, and possible promotion.

While Powell was insensitive to slack and was concerned only with obvious companywide planning inconsistencies, Cooper, in his restructuring attempt, showed a definite awareness of the possible dysfunctional side effects. He introduced the following formal review steps for the preliminary budget plans. He said: "After I have studied and evaluated your plans, I will schedule meetings with each of you and discuss their merits. If they are not satisfactory, you will have ten days to change them." The statement seems to indicate that Cooper wanted true participation. Rather than rejecting plans outright, he indicated a willingness to meet with all departmental managers and discuss each plan's merits. In his discussions with the department managers, Cooper probably instructed them to minimize slack and to adjust those portions of the plan that were not in congruence with companywide or other departments' objectives and goals. This discussion should have been on a friendly, constructive basis to thwart the development of the negative attitudes or hostile sentiments toward top management that sometimes occur when budgets are sold downward.

If the review discussions were productive, Cooper's task of implementing the budget after its approval by the president would have been made relatively easy. Again, we can only speculate on how the line managers were informed of the final expectations of top management or how the budget was "sold" down the line. For example, the human reaction would differ depending on whether the budget arrived through intercompany mail or was submitted at a departmental "pep" meeting. The point is that a person-to-person approach is the most effective way to introduce a budget to those people who will be held responsible; each manager should be spoken with individually. If we assume that the companywide objectives and goals were effectively delineated and that Ramus Corporation employees were told of their own importance in the context of overall company success, then it is likely that a willingness to cooperate and to strive toward the goal attainment would develop.

The control phase of the budgeting process at the Ramus Corporation exhibited the most dysfunctional behavior. The case mentions that monthly performance reports were prepared and that they all showed unfavorable variances between actual performance and budgeted goals. There was no mention of any search for the causes of the inefficiencies, nor of attempts by departmental managers to correct situations that apparently were out of control. By neglecting to investigate the variances and determine the causes, the management of Ramus Corporation lost the opportunity of using the budget system to limit the more severe dysfunctions that occurred later.

The ultimate responsibility for failing to investigate the variance lies with Roberta Powell, the controller. It was her responsibility to effectively use the overall profit planning system. She should have seen to it that the departmental managers made efforts to correct inefficiencies. She should have followed up the monthly delivery of performance reports with meetings to discuss corrective actions. There was no excuse for watching months of unfavorable performance occur without pressing the departmental managers for action.

People want to be periodically informed about their performance results and to know why their efforts to reach the stated goals succeeded or failed. With no investigation into the underlying causes of the variances, the Ramus Corporation employees could not know for certain how to modify their efforts to improve the chances of meeting the goals. As mentioned previously, the employees could have become so discouraged that they would stop trying to meet the goals. They would psychologically and/or physically withdraw from the budget environment, their aspiration levels and performance levels would deteriorate, and they may have resorted to various kinds of dysfunctional behavior to relieve the excessive budget pressure. This may also have stifled management's efforts to try new approaches, which would compound an already difficult situation.

Investigation of the variances would have revealed whether the budget had structural flaws and whether the employees perceived the budget goals as fair and attainable. Because last year was Ramus's first planning cycle, procedural and structural flaws could have existed. To become concerned about operational deviations and flaws in the budget system only when the annual income statement discloses a loss will not correct the damage already done.

It is too late to do anything about the inefficiencies in the first quarter of this year. Corrections instituted for the future will be quite costly, painful and time consuming.

From our diagnostic review of Ramus Corporation's attempt to institute a formal planning system, we conclude that the disappointing results of last year could be overcome if Cooper, the new planning director, corrects the several errors made last year and gains the confidence and commitment of the departmental managers. First, Cooper should create a healthy budget-making climate in which planning would be appreciated and perceived as a way of doing business. To do this, it is essential that he secure the wholehearted and active commitment of the president and controller. He has to impress upon the president that top management's attitude toward the budget has an important effect on its success. Cooper has to risk approaching the president even though he was told not to bother him with financial details. The ability of the firm to achieve its profit goals depends on it. Second, employees have to be re-educated on the purpose and process of budgeting so that the mistakes of last year would not be repeated, that the habits of last year be broken, and that participation in goal setting be perceived as being in their own career interests.

To correct the situation, the president will have to come out of his research lab and convince the functional managers and employees that he wants the budget system to succeed. He will have to make clear that the managers are personally responsible to him for attaining company goals. The departmental managers should certainly be given some degree of input into goal setting. However, the extent of participation that would be optimal cannot be determined with anywhere near absolute precision. Cooper would have to decide how much autonomy to give to departmental managers based on what the managers say or do not say during meetings that he holds with them. Cooper has to determine the departmental managers' attitudes toward the budget and assess whether those attitudes would be easy to change. An additional burden facing the new planning director is to bring all the departmental managers together to air and resolve the bitter differences that developed last year.

Finally, there must be more emphasis on the use of performance reports and the investigation of variances in the follow-up stage of the planning cycle. All variances, favorable as well as unfavorable, should be investigated, and immediate corrective actions should be taken where necessary. If structural and procedural flaws exist in the system, Cooper must correct them. Extreme care should be taken not to publicize the failure of one department or manager throughout the company. This may cause embarassment, stifle initiative, and further limit people's involvement in the budget process. By using the budget effectively as a planning, control, communication, and learning device, the company will be better able to achieve its goals.

It is a common misconception that budgets and budgeting are instant cures for overcoming organizational crises. This is simply not the case. Experienced planning directors realize that it takes two to three years for a budget to reach technical maturity and have a decided impact on company operations. The first time through, a budget will not work exactly as expected. This does not mean that Cooper cannot expect to see dramatic results this year; rather, the full potential of his contribution to Ramus Corporation will probably not be realized for a few years.

CONCLUSION

Several questions that were raised earlier in Chapter 8 may now be answered. We asked who should provide decision inputs during the planning stage, approve the plans, implement the budget, evaluate the variances, and be responsible for correcting inefficiencies. The answer depends on the many variables that impact the budget-making process. The organizational structure, organizational culture, leadership styles, degree of employee participation in decision making, amount of slack to be allowed and the degree of pressure the budget is to induce are some factors that will affect the answer.

While there are no definitive answers that apply to all organizations, there are certain general rules that do hold. Participation of the work force in decision making has been shown to have positive psychological effects on the work force and to enhance both the quantity and quality of worker output. This would suggest that wherever possible, as many people as possible be included in some aspect of the decision-making process. It must be kept in mind, however, that employee participation will not automatically solve all organizational problems. Further, while participation is desirable, there is still a need for authority in an organization. Somebody has to be the coordinator; somebody has to have the power to say "no" to a decision reached by a group of organizational participants. In short, participation within workable limits can greatly benefit organizations; anarchy or the complete lack of authority will surely result in the organization's collapse.

Approval of the budget is the responsibility of the president and/or the board of directors. Implementation of the budget is the responsibility of the budget director or controller; this is a staff function. Cost control is the responsibility of the line personnel. Thus, we suggest that departmental managers, responsibility center supervisors, or factory foremen be charged with evaluating the variances in their areas and with developing means to overcome the inefficiencies. This is not the responsibility of the planning director or his or her staff. The planning director is only secondarily responsible. If it is discovered that the departmental managers are not doing what they should be doing, the planning director should intervene. We might say that the immediate supervisor of each lower-level manager is contingently responsible for investigation and correction of variances. Their contingent responsibility would become real if their subordinates failed to do their work. This system of contingent responsibility would continue up the organizational ladder until it reaches the director of planning and the other top financial executives.

REFERENCES

[1] Etzioni, A., *Modern Organizations*, (Englewood Cliffs, N.J.: Prentice-Hall, Inc. 1964).

[2] Hall, F. S., "Organizational Goals: The Status of Theory and Research," paper presented at the Workshop in Behavioral Accounting, Annual Meeting of the American Institute for Decision Sciences, Atlanta, Georgia, October 30, 1974.

[3] J.R.P. French, Jr., J. Israel, and D. As, "An Experiment on Participation in a Norwegian Factory," *Human Relations*, vol. 13, p. 3, 1960.

[4] Selwyn W. Becker and David O. Green, Jr., "Budgeting and Employee Behavior," Journal of Business, 35:4 (October 1962), 392-402.

[5] Edwin H. Caplan, "Management Accounting and Behavioral Science," Addison-Wesley Publishing Company, Reading, Massachusetts, 1971, 87.

SUGGESTED READINGS

Argyris, C. "The Impact of Budgets on People." (New York: Financial Executives Research Foundation, 1952) 1–32.

Broconell, Peter. "A Field Study Examination of Budgetary Participation and Locus of Control." *The Accounting Review* 57, no. 4 (Oct. 1982).

Broconell, Peter. "Leadership Style, Budgetary Participation and Organizational Behavior." *Accounting Organizations and Society* 8, no.4 (1983): 307–321.

Bruns, William J. Jr., and John H. Waterhouse. "Budgetary Control and Organization Structure." *Journal of Accounting Research* (1975) 177–200

Flamholtz, Eric G., "Accounting, Budgeting and Control Systems in their Organizational Context: Theoretical and Empirical Perspectives." *Accounting, Organizations and Society* 8, no. 2/3 (1983): 153–169.

Hopwood, Anthony G. *Accounting and Human Behavior*. United Kingdom: Accountancy Age Books, 1973 and Englewood Cliffs, N.J.: Prentice-Hall, 1976.

Kerr, Steven. *Organizational Behavior*. Columbus, Ohio: Grid Publishing Co. 1979.

McGregor, D., The Human side of Enterprise, McGraw Hill, New York, 1960.

Merchant, Kenneth A., "The Design of the Corporate Budgeting System: Influences on Managerial Behavior and Performance." *The Accounting Review* 56, no. 4 (Oct. 1981).

Otley, David T., "Budget Use and Managerial Performance." *Journal of Accounting Research* 16, no. 1 (Spring 1978).

Robbins, Stephen P., *Organizational Behavior: Concepts, Controversies and Applications*. Englewood Cliffs, N.J.: Prentice-Hall, 1983.

DISCUSSION QUESTIONS

1. Define goal congruence. Why is goal congruence important in the goal-setting stage?
2. What do you understand by the depth, scope and weight of participation in goal setting? What do these depend on?
3. What is goal internalization? Why is it important?
4. What are some problems and limitations of participation in goal setting?
5. What are some of the instruments used to monitor performance in the control and evaluation stage of the budget planning process? What is the importance of this?
6. Explain and define the function of the budget planning director.
7. "A thorough understanding of human behavior is a prerequisite for successful planning." Discuss.

CASE 9-1

The Company

Denny Daniels is production manager of the Alumalloy Division of WRT Inc. Alumalloy has limited contact with outside customers and has no sales staff.

Most of its customers are other divisions of WRT. All sales and purchases with outside customers are handled by other corporate divisions. Therefore, Alumalloy is treated as a cost center for reporting and evaluation purposes rather than as a revenue or profit center.

Daniels perceives budgeting as an historical number-generating process that provides little useful information for conducting his job. Consequently, the entire fixed budgeting process is regarded as a negative motivational device that does not reflect how hard or how effectively he works as a production manager. Daniels tried to discuss these perceptions and concerns with John Scott, the controller for the Alumalloy Division. Daniels told Scott, "I think the performance report is misleading. I know I've had better production over a number of operating periods, but the performance report still says I have excessive costs. Look, I'm not an accountant; I'm a production manager. I know how to get a good quality product out. Over a number of years, I've even cut the raw materials used to do it. But the cost report doesn't show any of this. Basically, it's always negative, no matter what I do. There's no way you can win with accounting or the people at corporate headquarters who use those reports."

Scott gave Daniels little consolation. The budgeting system and the performance reports generated by headquarters, Scott stated, are just part of the corporate game and almost impossible for an individual to change. "Although these performance reports are pretty much the basis for evaluating the efficiency of your division and the means corporate management uses to determine whether you have done the job they want, you shouldn't worry too much. You haven't been fired yet! Besides, these performance reports have been used by WRT for the last 25 years."

The Dilemma

Daniels perceived from talking to the production manager of the Zinc Division that most of what Scott said was probably true. However, some minor performance reporting changes for Zinc had been agreed to by corporate headquarters. He also knew from the trade grapevine that the turnover of production managers was considered high at WRT, even though relatively few were fired. Most seemed to end up quitting, usually in disgust, because of beliefs that they were not being evaluated fairly. Typical comments of production managers who have left WRT are:

> "Corporate headquarters doesn't really listen to us. All they consider are those misleading performance reports. They don't want them changed, and they don't want any supplemental information."

"The accountants may be quick with numbers, but they don't know anything about production. As it was, I either had to ignore the performance reports entirely or pretend they are important even though they didn't tell how good a job I had done. No matter what they say about not firing people, negative reports mean negative evaluations. I'm better off working for another company."

A recent copy of the performance report prepared by corporate headquarters for the Alumalloy Division is shown below. Daniels does not like this report because he believes it fails to reflect the division's operations properly, thereby resulting in an unfair evaluation of performance.

Alumalloy Division
Performance Report
For the Month of April, 19 × 0

	Original Fixed Budget	Actual Cost	Excess Cost
Aluminum	400,000	437,000	37,000
Labor	560,000	540,000	
Overhead	100,000	134,000	34,000
Total:	$1,060,000	$1,111,000	$71,000

Required:

1. What caused the hostility with which the budget and performance reports are viewed?
2. What actions should be taken to restore user acceptance of the planning, performance reporting and evaluation process?

CASE 9-2

The Background

Sleepytime Hotels Corporation (SHC) owns 100 hotels located in the west and southwest regions of the United States. Sleepytime hotels average 200 rooms, with restaurant/bar and banquet facilities. SHC has been in the hotel business for over fifty years.

Two years ago, due to intense competition in some of the major markets where Sleepytime hotels are located, Mr. Harmon, president of SHC, decided to add gift shops to these hotels. He had observed that SHC's biggest competitor had gift shops in all of its hotels and that they seemed to draw business from the surrounding hotels.

The Dilemma

Annual budgets are reviewed and approved two months prior to the beginning of the fiscal year. Each hotel that houses a gift shop is required to include that shop in its budget. The operating results of the gift shop are included in the computation of the bonus for the hotel's general manager.

SHC employs a corporate supervisor for the twenty-five company-owned gift shops. This supervisor is responsible for purchasing merchandise for the shops as well as hiring and firing the gift shop managers.

Several of the hotel general managers have complained at budget meetings that they do not want the gift shops included in their budgets. The gift shops generally meet the budget in terms of gross sales but fail to meet their profit goals. The general managers stated that:

1. General managers are trained in hotel/restaurant management and are not familiar enough with retail operations to give adequate supervision to the gift shops.
2. The gift shop managers are selected by the corporate supervisor and report to that supervisor. For the most part, they operate independently of the hotel general manager.

Confronted with these issues, the corporate gift shop supervisor replied that there is no possible way he can be in twenty-five gift shops at the same time. He stressed his need for cooperation from the general managers because budget constraints do not allow him to hire seasoned gift shop managers.

Proposal 1

Keep the gift shops in the hotel budgets, but eliminate them as criteria in the computation of general manager's bonus.

Proposal 2

Set up separate budgets for each of the gift shops, and make the corporate supervisor responsible for the profit performance of each shop. There should be a bonus set up for the supervisor based on profit.

Required:

1. Discuss the merits of each proposal.

CASE 9-3———————————————————————

The Background

Vogue Cosmetics, a subsidiary of Cosmopolitan Enterprises, is a cosmetic company that is based in New York and owns five smaller cosmetic companies: Janice Field Cosmetics, Anne Yardly Co., Aphrodite Inc., Queen Cosmetics, and LeVonne Inc. Each of these companies has its own line of cosmetics. LeVonne and Janice Field are considered separate entities, whereas Queen Cosmetics, Anne Yardly, and Aphrodite Inc. are grouped together to form one entity, called Vogue Inc. The three entities are each headed by a general manager who reports to the president of Vogue Cosmetics. Each entity has its own advertising, marketing, sales, and finance departments.

Manufacturing for all companies takes place in a large plant in Itasca, NY, headed by the vice-president of manufacturing. The finance department of LeVonne, Janice Field, and Vogue Inc., are each headed by a controller who reports to the vice-president of finance, who in turn reports to the president of Vogue Cosmetics.

For the last few. years, sales and profits for each company have been considerably lower than budgeted amounts. While sales have remained relatively constant, overhead has increased considerably, reducing profits.

The budgeting process starts when the general manager meets with the controller. The general manager provides the controller with the sales number and a percentage of profit that he or she would like to achieve. The controller then works up a P & L Statement that achieves the desired bottom line. The department heads are then budgeted total amounts for their departments, which in the end will support the bottom-line profit number. They are then told to come up with detailed expenses to support their budgets. A detailed budget package is then put together by the controller, examined by the vice-president of finance, and brought to the president of Vogue Cosmetics for approval.

Required:

1. Comment on the budgeting process at Vogue.

CHAPTER 10

Behavioral Aspects of Accumulating and Controlling Costs

BEHAVIORAL DILEMMA

The Company

The American Concrete Company (ACC) is a manufacturing firm located in a southern suburb of Los Angeles. ACC produces much of the concrete used by home builders in the Los Angeles metropolitan area and along the west coast. In 1970, ACC expanded enormously by acquisition and consistently increased its capacity to meet the strong demand for concrete. The company began the 1980s with a 40 percent market share.

The recession in the housing industry in 1981–82 caught ACC in a very vulnerable position. At the onset, the company softened the drop in sales by courting government contracts. This effort was insufficient to turn the tide. Sales dropped 28 percent in 1981 and an additional 10 percent in 1982. ACC practices traditional absorption costing. Budgeted costs for each following year are based on management's best guess as to expected volume.

The Dilemma

In planning the 1982 costs, management relied heavily on predictions of a recovery in the housing industry. They counted on sales reaching 85 percent of their 1980 levels and planned material usage, labor costs, and the rate for overhead absorption accordingly. The result was disappointing and extremely confusing budget variances across the board.

In estimating the 1983 volume, top management was gun-shy. The recession seemed to be deepening rather than reversing. In planning their production volume, they anticipated sales to be 65 percent of the 1980 figure. Instead, sales for 1983 were 90 percent of the 1980 figure at the close of the third quarter.

Although this was welcome news on all fronts, it presented a problem in terms of the cost system. Budget allowances for material and labor had been based on a lower than actual production volume, resulting now in unfavorable variances in all parts of the production process. The budgeted costs per pound of concrete were now too high, since the fixed costs were assumed to be absorbed by a much lower output volume than appropriate under the actual conditions. This resulted in huge favorable overhead variances in all performance reports, a fact that made it nearly impossible to identify problem areas and inefficiencies. Tempers started to flare, and name-calling between operating and accounting personnel was an everyday occurrence.

In one of his weekly meetings with his management team, the president of ACC demanded an explanation for this dilemma and the serious frictions it had caused between financial and operations managers.

After an extended discussion, it became clear that the present cost accounting system seemed to be the cause of most of the budgeting, control, and performance evaluation problems. It was decided to contact the management advisory group of their CPA firm and assign them the task of modifying the present system, if at all possible, or designing a new one that would end the frictions and animosities.

TRADITIONAL VERSUS STANDARD COST SYSTEMS

Purpose and Uses of Cost Accounting Systems

Whether an organization produces and sells products or renders services, it needs to know what its costs are. Cost data must be accumulated for a variety of external and internal purposes.

Cost accounting identifies, quantifies, accumulates, and reports the various cost elements associated with the manufacture of goods or the rendering of services. It has a twofold purpose. Through accumulating costs for inventory valuations and income determination, it serves the needs of external users such as stockholders, the Internal Revenue Service, and creditors. By providing management with timely and relevant cost information, it assists in planning, controlling, and evaluating the day-to-day operational activities and the people responsible for them. Cost data also play a role in the analysis and appraisal of the relative profitability or desirability of decision alternatives.

Approaches and systems used in providing cost information differ widely. Each type has its own specific behavioral aspects. When these are neglected, unwanted human responses may result that range from mildly annoying to outright destructive.

We will first discuss the major cost accounting systems presently in use and their behavioral strengths and weaknesses. Then we will analyze the behavioral consequences of various cost accounting and reporting steps. Finally, we will use our findings to analyze the ACC business dilemma, render a diagnosis, and suggest remedial actions.

Traditional (Historical) Cost Systems

The term *traditional* (historical) refers to cost systems that limit the inputs to historical costs and attempt full absorption of fixed and variable costs by unit of product or service. Traditional or historical cost systems are primarily concerned with the identification and accumulation of unit costs of products or services. They are used to calculate inventory values and cost data of goods sold or services rendered for external financial reporting. However, traditional cost systems are inappropriate for effective managerial control since the mere accumulation of historical cost data without their comparison with predetermined cost goals does not satisfy the contemporary concepts of control. To satisfy contemporary concepts of control and to motivate managers and employees, performance objectives or cost goals per unit or for specific future periods must be established. Actual performance by responsibility centers must be periodically compared with desired performance levels; deviations must be noted and fed back to the individuals concerned, thereby encouraging immediate corrective actions. To avoid dysfunctional responses, it is generally advocated that segment managers should be charged only with those costs that can be influenced by their actions.

One of the major shortcomings of traditional cost systems is that the requirements of financial accounting demand that unit costs of a product or service include *all* costs: those traceable to a product or service and those incurred for a specific time period or for more than one cost objective. Period or capacity costs and those incurred for more than one product or segment cannot be traced directly to individual units of service, products, or specific departments. They are charged to products or services through more or less arbitrary allocations. These allocations may mislead management and adversely affect the quality of managerial decisions such as short-run pricing and make-or-buy decisions, which require incremental cost information. When using traditional cost reports for evaluating the performance of segment managers, they may in part be charged with costs over which they have no control. Performance reports that lump together direct and allocated indirect costs invariably produce bickering and frustration over the validity and amounts of the allocations. But even more important, their long-term consequences may include low employee morale and aspiration levels and even destructive responses.

Another major shortcoming associated with the use of traditional cost systems for control purposes is that the only basis for control is the comparison of current performance with performance in some prior period(s). Comparing current and prior period performance can be quite misleading since there is no way of knowing whether the costs of the prior period were too high, too low, or about right. Equally confusing are budget variances that result from comparing actual performance results with budget allowances set for an activity level that is different than the one actually attained. The ACC Company's dilemma is a case in point.

It is therefore quite clear that the information provided by traditional cost systems is incompatible with modern control objectives. They also provide little useful information for managerial planning and decision making. Their greatest weakness is the inherent danger of inducing unwanted and destructive behavioral responses when used in evaluating the performance of the individuals charged with carrying out the various activities within budgetary constraints.

Standard Cost Systems

Their Scope

Recognizing the shortcomings of the traditional cost systems, many organizations adopted "standard cost systems." Standard cost systems represent a potentially effective blending of accounting with the control concepts of modern organization theory. Standard costs are scientifically predetermined cost goals per unit of product or service which have been developed through engineering and accounting studies. They represent detailed and sophisticated estimates of what it should cost to carry out a particular task or to produce a certain product. The inherent control aspect of standard costing is its capability to compare, as part of the regular data flow, actual performance with predetermined standards and to highlight variances (favorable or unfavorable) between the two levels of costs. Standard cost systems are even capable of determining causes for the deviations. To produce optimum control benefits and to retain their relevancy, the standard costs must be continuously updated.

Their Compatibility with Modern Organization Theory Concepts

In developing a framework for a standard cost system that is compatible with modern organization theory concepts, the following control steps as discussed by Edwin Caplain [1] are essential:

1. The establishment of organizational objectives.
2. The designation of appropriate responsibility centers and the assignment of functions to each.
3. The staffing of responsibility centers with individuals who have sufficient ability, motivation, and knowledge for the performance of their functions.
4. The creation of channels of communication between the responsibility center and other units of the organization and, where necessary, the external environment.
5. The development of procedures that assure adequate, relevant, and timely information moves along the communication channels.

6. The design and implementation of control mechanisms that measure and evaluate performance in terms of organizational objectives and provide feedback concerning necessary adjustments in objectives and/or performance.

Standard cost systems are designed to serve simultaneously as a source of information, channels of communication, and control and performance evaluation devices. As a source of information for the responsibility centers, they inform the individuals in charge what is expected from them costwise. As a communication channel, they transmit cost expectations and attainment levels. The control over responsibility center operations is accomplished through periodic standard cost reports that provide the feedback about past performance results and their deviations from standard to the appropriate individuals. Predetermined tolerance limits can be designed to perform a filtering function, thereby permitting concentration in areas in which variances are significant and warrant immediate attention (management by exception). Because performance reports are programmed in advance with respect to when they will be prepared and what data they will contain, it is difficult to bury important information. A well-designed standard cost system also provides the assurance that the required information will, in fact, reach the accountable individual. Furthermore, the insight gained through developing and evaluating cost and performance standards has proven to be of valuable assistance to management in formulating, testing, and revising the objectives of the organization.

Standard cost systems have the potential to be used either as aids in increasing motivation and goal congruence or as devices to achieve high levels of autocratic and coercive control. To achieve their greatest possible control value, most systems in use will have to undergo certain modifications— modifications that affect not so much the techniques themselves as the attitudes and philosophies of the people who operate and use them.

DIRECT OR VARIABLE COSTING

Its Underlying Philosophy

All traditional cost accounting methods, in compliance with the cost concept, charge units of products or service with full costs. Direct material and direct labor is charged directly to product or service units, while fixed and variable overhead in most instances is absorbed on the basis of an estimated rate based on predetermined volume. Whenever the basis used for absorption differs from the predetermined capacity level, the absorption procedure will result in overabsorption or underabsorption of the manufacturing (or service) overhead. Supplementary analyses are required to identify the various components causing overabsorption or underabsorption.

The traditional cost accounting methods also disregard the fact that certain overhead costs will remain constant regardless of the quantity of units produced or service rendered, while others will fluctuate with volume. To overcome these shortcomings, devices such as flexible budgeting and cost-volume-profit analyses were introduced.

To facilitate decision making and cost control without the necessity of preparing time-consuming supplementary reports, a new costing philosophy was introduced in the 1930s. This method, called direct or variable costing, was credited with providing more meaningful results to management and those faced with day-to-day decisions on the basis of cost accounting results. One of its most acclaimed attributes is that it avoids the confusing accounting terminology explaining the cost-volume-profit relationship.

Direct or variable costing distinguishes between the costs of producing (direct material, direct labor, and the variable portion of overhead) and the costs of being ready and able to produce (fixed overhead or period costs). Only costs that result from current production or services rendered (the variable costs) are classified as product or service unit costs and capitalized until the items are sold or the service is rendered. According to John A. Bekett, costs that "result from the long-term preserving and availability of productive potential are said to be period costs"[2] and are charged against revenues in the period when their service potential expires.

Direct costing advocates consider the division of overhead according to their cost structure a basic necessity for effective cost control and meaningful decision making. They claim that the conventional practice of assigning the fixed portion of overhead to products confuses management by obscuring their true nature and behavior. By excluding capacity or fixed costs in valuing inventories and costs of goods sold, it places manufacturing and merchandising companies on a similar basis as far as the costs of products are concerned. Production volume, they argue, does not affect the procurement costs of either company. One manufactures its products at known variable costs; the other purchases its merchandise at definite purchase prices. The only difference is that manufacturing companies, when determining their monthly contribution margin or the spread between variable costs and selling prices, have to provide for the fixed manufacturing overhead as one of the costs of doing business along with administration, warehousing, and selling expenses.

Its Behavioral Inducements

Accounting concepts, principles, and practices influence the measurement of managerial performance and, consequently, management decisions. This does not always lead to desirable results since many performance measures have built-in biases that motivate managers to select action alternatives that may not be in the best operating and/or financial interest of the company.

Through its authoritative bodies, the accounting profession is presently reexamining accounting's basic concepts, principles, and practices in the light of their possible behavioral implications.

In the process of their reexamination, questions such as the ones asked by David Hawkins seem appropriate:

> What might this accounting concept, principle, or practice motivate managers to do in their own selfish interests?
>
> Could this possible action obscure actual managerial performance, give the illusion of performance where none exists, or lead to unsound economic actions? [3]

If any part of the second question calls for an affirmative answer, the use of such accounting concept, principle, or practice should be discouraged, although it might be sound from a technical viewpoint.

Hawkins maintains that accounting concepts, principles, and practices are behaviorally and technically sound if they:

> Inhibit managers from taking undesirable operating actions to justify the adoption of an acounting alternative [and if they]
>
> Inhibit the adoption of accounting practices by corporations which create [only] the illusion of performance. [3]

This leads us to the following questions: Is direct or variable costing truly superior in controlling costs and in providing information that will lead managers to more meaningful decisions? Is this practice technically and behaviorally better than generally accepted traditional approaches?

Cost Control

Dividing costs into variable and fixed components provides a better basis for cost control. It enables the preparation of contribution margin income statements, which emphasize cost behavior patterns and provide management with details as to engineered, committed, and discretionary costs. This distinction is important to management since each type of cost requires different control procedures.

Engineered costs include direct material, direct labor, and variable overhead costs such as fuel and electricity. According to Charles Horngren they have an "explicit, specified relationship with a selected measure of activity."[4] They are readily controllable at the lowest organizational level through the use of flexible budgets and standards; their feedback time is short and they are physically observable by the managers responsible for the activity that causes their occurrence.

Committed fixed costs or capacity costs "are all those organization and plant costs that continue to be incurred (regardless of the activity level) and which cannot be reduced without injuring the organization's competence to meet long-range goals."[5] Controlwise, they are the least responsive fixed costs and they can be controlled in the short run only by attempts to improve the utilization of the committed facilities.

Discretionary costs (also called managed or programmed costs) are those costs "(1) that arise from periodic (usually yearly) appropriation decisions regarding the maximum amounts to be incurred and (2) that do not have a demonstrable optimum relationship between inputs (as measured by costs) and outputs (as measured by revenues or other objectives.)"[6] They include costs such as advertising, auditing and management consulting services and human resource training. In contrast to committed fixed costs, they can be reduced or even entirely avoided in dire times and they are controlled by negotiated static budgets.

Decision Making

Besides stressing the distinction between variable and fixed costs and providing differential cost information, in certain decision situations, direct or variable costing provides managers with another important piece of information. We are referring to contribution margins of products, product lines, service activities, divisions, and the like. Knowledge of differential or variable costs and of contribution margins will influence the behavior of managers and will lead them to better decisions. Some typical decision situations follow.

Product Mix Decisions. When faced with product mix decisions, sales managers who know the contribution margins of their products will be better able to decide which product to push and which to deemphasize or to tolerate only because of its sales benefits to other products. In case of limited resources (e.g., machine time, materials, etc.), the contribution margin will provide management with information for choosing the desirable mix, which would result in the largest total contribution to profit. Knowledge of the desired contribution margin for a product line will enable management to price a certain product below full cost, as long as the complementary products can be priced to yield sufficient profit to keep all products in the product line.

New Product Pricing. New products are generally accepted in the market only after they are extensively tested by reputable firms in the industry. To encourage companies to use the product on a trial basis, management may sell it at variable costs. Once the product is sufficiently tested and accepted by the users, it will be priced at full cost plus a mark-up consistent with the company's overall profit goals.

Market Penetration.   Managers may use variable costs as a basis for pricing when they intend to enter a new market (i.e., an overseas market) with an existing product or when they are forced to meet increased competition during periods of declining demand.

Product Deletion.   Contributions margins will assist management in deciding whether to drop a product or whether to discontinue to sell in a specific market. Being familiar with the cost-volume-profit relationship, they will realize that as long as a product (line) or a specific market produces short-run revenues in excess of its variable costs, it makes a contribution to the absorption of the fixed costs, or to profits, if sales are already in excess of break-even. Traditional costing methods lack this kind of relevant information.

Special Order.   Companies can be faced with two types of special order situations; they may involve accommodations for a preferential customer or special requirements for size, delivery methods, or packaging. As long as special orders do not involve major changes in the production process and as long as the company has unused capacity, any selling price in excess of variable costs will improve overall profitability.

Advertising and Promotion Campaigns.   To increase its present sales volume, companies may launch special advertising and promotion campaigns. If the company uses a traditional cost system, the decision most likely will be based solely on a comparison of the added costs with the prospective increases in sales volume. Direct (variable) costing will provide them with additional information relevant in their appraisal of the various alternatives. The higher the contribution margin of the product (line) to be promoted or featured by advertising, the greater will be the potential net benefit; the lower the contribution margin, the more additional units will have to be sold to recover the additional costs.

Cost Reduction Decision.   If a company's selling price is firmly established by its competitors, management will know how much variable costs are allowable at their current operating volume if a certain profit goal must be reached. This knowledge will induce management to be extremely cost-conscious and to possibly introduce cost saving devices and procedures.

Summary

These discussions demonstrated that direct or variable costing is superior in providing relevant information for controlling the various types of costs and in leading management to better decisions in the light of overall profitability.

From a decision making viewpoint, its superiority was never questioned, since it is the only method that separates fixed and variable production costs. Direct or variable costing is also a technically and behaviorally sound method. Direct costing advocates belief that the method should be pronounced as an acceptable alternative for external reporting by the rule-making bodies of the accounting profession.

BEHAVIORAL ASPECTS OF SELECTED COST ACCOUNTING STEPS

We have discussed the various types of cost accumulation and reporting systems in view of their technical and behavioral soundness. In the remaining part of the chapter, we will analyze the behavioral aspects of selected cost accounting steps. We will examine whether they might trigger dysfunctional human responses and if they do, how they might be modified to be more effective in inducing desirable employee behavior.

Standard Setting

The most influential elements determining the success or failure of any standard cost system are the standards used as performance criteria. Standards have a dual function; they serve as goals to motivate cost control and they function as performance evaluation tools. Standards will generate efficient worker behavior only if they are accepted as aspiration levels by the individuals for whose control and performance evaluation they were designed. Acceptance or ego involvement will only occur if the standards are perceived by foremen and workers as valid performance goals. If they are perceived as unreasonable and unattainable, workers will attempt to refute or override them and thereby destroy their usefulness.

Raymond Miles and Roger Vergin spelled out four basic prerequisites for behaviorally sound control systems:

1. Standards must be established in such a way that people accept them as realistic rather than arbitrary;
2. People must feel that they have some influence in establishing their own goals;
3. People must believe that they will not be unfairly punished for normal, chance variations in performance; and
4. Feedback on performance must be aimed at correction as well as evaluation. [7]

Two of the recommended prerequisites pertain directly to standard setting. Standards are still quite frequently set by engineering and accounting methods that fail to provide opportunities for a meaningful participation of the individuals controlled by them. As already discussed, individuals will accept performance goals as realistic and attainable only if they were included in the standard-setting process. Without it, they will reject and sabotage them. If they truly believe that their participation has impact on the standards, they will no longer feel helpless in influencing their work environment and they will become more motivated to strive for goal attainment.

Participation in Standard Setting

The importance of participation in standard setting has been discussed extensively in the behavioral accounting literature. Michael Foran and Don DeCoster summarize the logic underlying all arguments in favor of participation as simply, "If a worker participates in the setting of his own performance standards, he will have made an overt commitment to the standards, and hence, will work hard to achieve them." [8]

In one of their empirical studies, they used the theory of cognitive dissonance to gain more insight into why participation is more effective in setting performance standards. Cognitive dissonance theory centers around three key concepts: volition, dissonance, and commitment.

In the context of standard setting, this theory implies that if management wants a definite commitment to the standards, the controlled individuals must have a choice (volition). Once they have chosen a certain set of performance standards, they will experience doubt (dissonance) as to the wisdom of their choice. Their doubt (dissonance) will only be reduced or eliminated when they receive feedback about the performance results. If the results are favorable, their doubts (dissonance) will be resolved and increased commitment will occur. Dissonance resolution or increased commitment will occur even in nonparticipative goal-setting situations. Unfavorable feedback in nonparticipative situations may result in rejection of the standards and lack of further commitment. The workers may become so discouraged that they stop trying to improve their performance. They will claim that the standards were unattainable from the start. If, however, the individuals are allowed to choose the standards by which they are to be controlled, they will be more committed to them. Instead of being immediately discouraged by negative feedback results, the workers will exert even greater effort to reach the goals they set for themselves.

How much participation is desirable? Should all operational personnel from foremen up participate, or is involvement of middle management sufficient? The ideal degree of participation depends upon production and human considerations and will vary from situation to situation. People might even be unwilling to be burdened with the responsibility of participation and the postdecision doubts about the wisdom of their choice. Surveys [9] have shown that in democratically organized firms, active participation in goal and standard setting is an important source of employee satisfaction. In autocratic organizations, however, employees frequently indicated that they liked their jobs because they knew where to get a decision. From these results, one could speculate that foremen and managers in democratic organizations prefer more independence and have a greater tolerance for ambiguity. Those in autocratic firms are satisfied with greater dependence upon authority and are bothered by ambiguity.

Tight versus Loose Standards

To function as motivational devices, the standards to be used should be neither too tight nor too loose. Tight standards will be missed more often than met. The resulting variances may be unfairly associated with poor performances and not identified as having been caused by extremely tight standards. They are useful challenges (intrinsic rewards) only for foremen or managers who are motivated by a need for outstanding achievement. For these individuals, accomplishment of difficult tasks produces a strong feeling of pride and self-reward. For most individuals, too-tight standards and the possibility of failure result in frustration and discouragement. Their performance will decline even further since they stop trying to improve. Loose standards do not provide any motivational benefits since they may be so easy to attain that foremen and managers will ignore them as meaningless.

The level of desirable tightness must be evaluated in each situation on the basis of the type of production process, the product or services to be rendered, and the personalities of the involved individuals.

Regardless of the degree of participation or their tightness, once the standards are set, they must be continuously updated so that they retain their relevancy. Neglect in updating will result in mispriced inventories and in misleading variances, which will hinder rather than assist management in controlling costs and evaluating performance.

Overhead Absorption

Another area full of dysfunctional inducements is overhead absorption. This common practice charges fixed and variable manufacturing overhead to the products at an estimated rate based on a predetermined capacity level. Whenever the basis used for absorption differs from the predetermined one, overapplied or underapplied variances will occur. The size of these variances is also affected by the capacity level chosen as denominator in the rate determination. A long-run capacity level (normal capacity) will produce different variances than a short-run capacity level (actual attainable capacity); switching from one to the other will cloud the picture even more. Since the fixed portion of overhead (period costs) is capitalized in the products and expensed only when the products are sold, managers can manipulate income by altering the actual production levels. A knowledgeable manager is able to meet a short-run profit goal merely by increasing production levels and thereby deferring part of the fixed overhead. Such manipulation should be suspected whenever inventory levels exceed the quantities justifiable to meet future sales.

The aspect of capitalization of fixed costs in inventories also affects the interpretation of income statements in seasonal businesses. Companies with seasonal fluctuations in sales frequently produce more in slack periods to build up sufficient inventory to last them during their high sales period. Their quarterly income statements will therefore most likely show higher profits in slow quarters than in those with high sales. This fact not only gives the illusion of a performance that does not exist, but it may also lead to unsound economic actions. Sales managers unaware of the cost-volume-profit relationship might become distrustful of the accounting system that reports declining profits in periods of rising sales and rising profits in periods of declining sales. They may lose their motivation to improve their performance and ignore the confusing information altogether.

Income tax law provides an inducement for using actual attainable capacity levels as the denominator in rate computation. Although companies are prevented from using direct or variable costing for determining taxable income, they are permitted to use currently attainable capacity as a (or the) basis for the rate used in absorbing fixed overhead in the products. The volume or capacity portion of any underapplied variance can be charged against income in the period when it occurs. Only budget and efficiency variances need to be capitalized. In periods of idle capacity (excess of currently attainable over actual capacity), this will result in reducing taxable income; in periods of excess capacity, it will increase it. By choosing a high currently attainable capacity level, companies are therefore able to reduce their tax liability in a specific year. What is surprising is that the law that prohibits the use of direct or variable costing induces the use of an approach that produces very similar results.

Allocation of Indirect Costs

One of the most controversial decisions facing each organization is whether or not to allocate indirect cost to products and/or responsibility centers and what allocation basis to use.

In a study sponsored by the National Association of Accountants (NAA), James Fremgen and Shu S. Liao found that the responding firms distinguished clearly between two types of indirect costs: corporate service costs and corporate administrative costs.

Corporate service costs are the costs of services performed centrally for the benefit of both corporate and the various responsibility centers. They include costs for accounting, data processing, WATS lines, research and development, and have some identifiable relationship with the activity levels of the various responsibility centers.

Corporate administrative costs are those costs that are necessary to operate the corporate office. They include corporate salaries, public relations, and all other costs incurred to maintain the corporation as a whole. There is no obvious relationship between these costs and the operating levels of the various cost and/or profit centers throughout the organization.

When asked about the purpose of indirect cost allocation, the survey respondents mentioned external financial reporting, internal performance evaluation, cost-based pricing, and decision making. As criteria for selecting an allocation basis, they mentioned most often "factors that cause the indirect costs to be incurred, benefits realized by profit centers, and fairness. The criterion of a profit center's ability to bear some portion of the indirect costs was mentioned by only a few. Yet, the allocation bases actually used by these companies often reflected the notion of ability to bear...rather than cause or benefit." [10]

The literature on indirect cost allocation deals mostly with the computational aspects of allocation. It ignores almost completely their behavioral sensitivities, which are greatest when used in performance evaluation and decision making. The recommendation almost exclusively offered by researchers and educators is that companies should avoid charging responsibility center managers with costs over which they have no direct or indirect control. If they have no power to change them, they should not be held responsible for them; otherwise they will respond in dysfunctional ways. (For more detail see Chapter 7 on Responsibility Accounting and Chapter 11 on Performance Evaluation.)

Despite all the theoretical arguments in favor of not allocating, the NAA research study discovered that 84 percent of the companies allocate their indirect costs for certain purposes. The most commonly mentioned one was performance evaluation. This brings us to the following interesting questions: Why do firms persist in allocating indirect costs in spite of the admonitions by educators against doing so? Why do they bother with time-consuming allocations that are arbitrary and, according to many accountants and most economists, serve no useful purpose? Is a firm's allocation of indirect costs *prima facie* evidence of irrational behavior? What are the reasons why rational, maximizing individuals would want to allocate indirect costs? Is it possible that some benefits derived from cost control were overlooked?

In the past, only a few accountants linked cost allocations to management behavior. Horngren [11] expressed this feeling as follows:

Whether to include uncontrollable or indirect costs is a difficult question, which must ultimately be resolved in terms of how the given alternatives influence management behavior in a particular organization. In one organization, allocation may be desirable because it induces the desired behavior. In another organization, the same allocation procedure may cause an opposite behavioral effect.

In his award winning article, Zimmerman [12] links agency theory with cost allocation and portrays various situations in which definite behavioral benefits are derived from allocation of indirect costs to subordinates and users. He found that one can control a superior's (manager's) discretionary spending by allocating such costs and charging them to subordinates. The subordinates will thereby be motivated to monitor these expenses since their welfare (goal attainment and/or future promotions) is affected by their superior's overconsumption.

Zimmerman further showed that corporate service costs are frequently allocated among the users. The allocated costs are used as proxy for the opportunity costs (e.g., degradation and delays in service, etc.) that arise when a common resource or limited capacity service is shared by a number of users. If the amount charged to a user is higher than that from an external provider, the responsibility center manager will bring the inefficiency to top management's attention by requesting permission to use outside sources. Zimmerman also came to the conclusion that cost allocation appears to proxy for certain hard-to-observe costs that arise when decision-making responsibilities are decentralized within the firm. [13]

When coupled with incentive schemes, cost allocations induce managers to pay attention to reported costs and help to solve some organizational control and coordination problems. [14] Cost allocation is not a perfect proxy for determining the cost arising from decentralization nor a tool for eliminating a superior's overconsumption or for measuring degradation or delay costs arising from shared resources or services. However, there is no doubt that it functions in specific situations as a mechanism for motivating and controlling managers.

Variance Analysis

The most essential ingredient of cost control is the periodic comparison of actual cost with predetermined cost goals, whether in the form of budgets or standards. The comparisons will result in numerous variances since it is very unlikely that the actual cost incurred will equal the standard or budgeted allowances for operational elements to be controlled. The variances may be the result of a variety of causes—some explainable and controllable, others inexplainable and uncontrollable. Only some are significant enough to warrant immediate investigation and possible remedial action. Since the behavioral aspects of variance reporting and interpretation are discussed in detail in other chapters (Chapter 11 on Performance Evaluation and Chapters 8 and 9, Profit Planning and Budgeting), we will limit our discussion to the investigation decision.

The Variance Investigation Decision

When facing the decision as to whether or not to investigate variances, management should ask the following crucial questions: What variance should I investigate? Will my results be worth the cost of the investigation? Will it reveal a controllable cause for all or part of the variance? What is the chance that my investigation will reveal nothing (since by that time the process—or the cost element—is back in control)? How do I know whether a variance is significant or not?

Management's decision depends solely on its assessment of the significance of the observed discrepancy. Variances have control significance only if they stem from assignable causes or, in other words, are of a nonrandom nature and susceptible to remedial action.

It would be pointless to investigate variances from cost goals only to find out that a machine operator had a hangover, was coming down with a cold, or was more concerned with his domestic difficulties than with his output quota or his machine setting. In such instances, the system is not at fault and the variance will, in due course, correct itself. If, however, defective production piles up because a machine is not functioning properly, the quality of material is substandard, or the operators have serious morale problems, the system is out of control. Such a situation calls for immediate suppressive action before more damage is done and serious losses are incurred.

The real complexity of the problem, however, lies in the fact that without investigation, management has no basis for determining whether a certain variance resulted from assignable and therefore controllable abuses, or whether it was of a random or uncontrollable nature. Even if the discrepancy is investigated, management has no guarantee that it will identify the cause of the variance with absolute certainty since the investigation may prove to be only partially successful or may even be a complete failure. The variance may even have disappeared completely and the cost element is back to normal without any interference.

To compound the problem even more, an investigation is only economically justifiable if the benefits from remedial action are at least equal to or greater than the cost of investigation and correction. Since management has no prior knowledge of the cause, the cost of investigation and corrections is rarely predictable with accuracy. It depends on the nature of the search dictated by the cause of the deviation.

If management decides not to investigate, it is again faced with two possibilities: the variance may disappear without interference in the next operating period or it may continue and the deviant condition will go unremedied.

To break this seemingly vicious cycle, accounting scholars designed variance investigation decisions (VID) models. Unfortunately, they are all cybernetically oriented; they are designed for automated manufacturing processes and completely ignore the reactions of the people affected by the control policy.

More specifically, most accounting VID models are applications of statistical quality control techniques where product quality is replaced by the cost to be controlled and where standard or budgeted costs act as the mean when the system is in control. Instead of tolerance limits for product quality, the VID models determine the span of variances within which investigation and corrective action is assumed to be either impossible (random variances) or unjustifiable from a cost-benefit standpoint (insignificant variances). Some of the models also incorporate the costs and benefits of investigation.[15]; others use statistical decision theory and apply Bayesian probability revisions[16] to deal with the possibility that the process is back in control at the time of the investigation.

Despite all of the efforts, neither of the recommended decision models is widely used in making investigation decisions; on the contrary, management still uses subjective judgment and rules of thumb when deciding whether or not an investigation and remedial action is desirable and economically justifiable.

The Behavioral Aspects

All accounting models for investigation of cost variances are based on the structural or cybernetic view of control. This view envisions control as "a homostatic machine for regulating itself."[17] Its advocates[18] see no difference between the mechanical regulator in a cybernetic system (such as a thermostat) and a human regulator (e.g., a worker, foreman, or manager). They believe that the responses of the regulator are predictable and solely determined by the content of the communicated information. They fail to recognize that humans do not respond mechanically for various reasons. Humans may perceive the information differently and their reactions may be affected by factors such as their personal goals rather than those of the organization. They can also be affected by social interactions such as group pressure to limit production at an agreed level. The cybernetic models at best regard human behavior as a random disturbance factor or a nuisance. They also ignore the fact that the behavioral climate within which performance information is perceived may reduce or destroy its usefulness.

The reaction of controlled individuals or groups is never completely predictable. Their response may be affected by the various components of the control policy in use. The response may be a true behavior modification or it may be only a reported change. The original Hawthorne experiments showed that highly efficient workers may be pressured by their peers not to report their actual output so they don't exceed the level set by a group norm.

The specific components of a control policy that may affect human response are factors such as the limits set by management, the type of feedback results, the strictness of enforcement, and the rewards and penalties attached to the control policy.

Control Limits.   The range of performance results considered acceptable by management are the control limits. They determine how easy or difficult it will be for the controlled individuals to perform within the acceptable range and how much leeway they have to fail occasionally. The perceived degree of tolerance may affect their actual performance. If individuals perceive the range of acceptable performance as very tight, fear of failure may lower their performance levels even further (aspiration level effect). If the range of acceptable performance is perceived as extremely generous, they may ignore it as not challenging.

Feedback Results.   Unlike with machines, feedback of human performance information will result in feelings of success or failure in the controlled individuals. Positive feedback will tell them that they are on the right track and will motivate them to repeat the same effort. Negative feedback will not automatically induce them to greater effort, but it may eventually lower their aspiration levels and erode their effort and performance levels.

In the control of certain cost centers (e.g., legal department, research and development, data processing, etc.), feedback of performance discrepancies may play only a minor role in behavior modification, or may not affect behavior at all. In such settings, it is the degree of participation allowed in the goal-setting process that will determine the degree of effort extended in reaching the performance goals.

Strictness of Enforcement.   Strict enforcement of the control policy will instill in the controlled individual the feeling of pressure. While pressure may be invigorating for some individuals, it may intimidate others and reduce their already poor performance even further. Over the long run, lax enforcement will deteriorate the motivation of individuals to strive for goal attainment.

Reward Structure.   People and groups will modify undesirable behavior and repeat desirable behavior when they perceive that the behavior change or repetition is coupled with intrinsic or extrinsic rewards. The type and degree of response to specific rewards differ from individual to individual and may vary over time. (For more details see Chapter 11 on Performance Evaluation.)

Since there is a psychological feedback effect between the various factors of the control policy and future performance, the ideal control policy will have to be tailor-made and will vary from situation to situation. The investigation's premise that cost variances are independent of the control policy is therefore untenable. It is no surprise that VID models are not applied more frequently in practice.

DIAGNOSTIC REVIEW OF THE AMERICAN CONCRETE COMPANY'S DILEMMA

On a Monday afternoon in early May, the phone in Mike Monelli's office rang. Monelli was the partner in charge of the management consulting group of the Prince and Whales CPA firm. On the line was the president of the American Concrete Company, a long-time audit client, who seemed very annoyed about the planning, control, and performance evaluation problems his company was experiencing and the behavioral turmoil they had caused. He told Monelli that his top management team believed that the present cost accounting system seemed to be the root of the problem. He requested that Monelli investigate the present system, modify it if at all possible, or design a new one that would end the frictions and animosities. ACC's president also requested early action so that by October, the start of their planning cycle, the new system would be in place.

Since Monelli had no expertise in these areas, he assigned the investigation to Aldona Iverson, the group's cost and systems specialist. Iverson holds a master's degree in management accounting from a leading university, and she is both a CPA and a CMA. She had held various upper-level management positions prior to joining Prince and Whales and was the director of the information system when her company merged with another company and her position disappeared.

The present assignment was tailor-made for her and she was looking forward to getting involved. When she arrived at ACC, she was briefed by the company's controller, Kurt Niessen, since the president was out of town. Niessen told her that he had been trying for a number of years to convince the president that their manufacturing process (mass production of a single product) was ideally suited for a standard cost system. He said that such a system would not only enable them to improve their cost control and performance evaluation, but would also provide the basis for more effective budgeting. His suggestions were ignored and the reasons given for the denial were that such a system would be too complicated, too time consuming, and too costly for their simple production process. The controller also complained that his role in the budget-making process was only clerical and involved only the consolidation of the submitted detailed budgets. He found it outrageous to be blamed for the inefficiencies of the budget when he played only a minor role in its preparation.

Iverson asked the vice-president in charge of sales, John Miller, why the sales budget was not adjusted as soon as he became aware that the chosen capacity assumptions were completely unrealistic. He told her that revisions were the controller's job and that he had to use his time to secure sufficient sales to keep the company alive. When asked how he could use the erroneous total cost (produced by the unrealistic capacity assumptions) as basis for pricing, John replied that even if he knew what the exact cost per pound was, he could not use it, because the price for the concrete was dictated by their competitors.

The vice-president in charge of production, Patrick O'Malley, was disgusted with both the sales manager and the controller. He blamed the sales manager for not undertaking any market research or using at least a more objective quantitative forecasting technique when deciding on the actually attainable capacity level for the planning cycle. He was convinced that the poor quality of the forecasted sales was the only cause of his serious problems in production scheduling. The difficulties in controlling the various manufacturing costs on the basis of erroneous performance reports bothered him very little since he was convinced that he could readily spot inefficiencies on his daily walks through the factory. He blamed the controller for not noticing the poor quality of the sales estimates and for not insisting that a more objective forecasting method be used.

When reflecting on the results of the various interviews and the animosities observed, Iverson decided to scrap the present system and design a new one. Since it was very unlikely that she would be able to convince the sales manager (who was the president's brother-in-law) to undertake either serious market research or to use a formal forecasting technique when determining the sales volume to be expected for the future year, she decided to introduce a standard cost system. Such a system, she reasoned, would provide more meaningful performance evaluation data for the manufacturing process. In its variance analysis step, it adjusts the budget allowances for material and labor costs, as well as the variable portion of factory overhead, to amounts allowable at actual capacity and standard capacity. The resulting variances are realistic indicators of the efficiencies or inefficiencies in the manufacturing process and provide a dependable basis for effective control. A standard cost system would also isolate the gains or losses incurred through overabsorption or underabsorption of fixed factory overhead cost caused by idle or excess capacity variances for which top management and not the production manager would be held responsible. This, she hoped, would remove the reasons for the production manager's frustrations and might even induce him to pay more serious attention to the performance variances in the future. The only costs that would be exclusively controlled through the budget would be the selling and administrative expenses, and for those she hoped to find a special solution.

After securing the president's permission for the new system and his commitment, Iverson met with the members of his management team and explained the reasons for her choice and the benefits it was to provide. She told them that she considered her role in the construction of the new system as that of an advisor and technical expert and that they, as the future users, had to make the various decisions that would determine the structure and the output of the system. She then assigned to the controller and the production manager the task of setting standards for direct material, direct labor, and factory overhead use per pound of cement produced. The overhead was to be broken down into fixed and variable components on the basis of historical data from the past five years. At that meeting, she also instructed the two managers to involve the foremen of the various production departments in the standard-setting process. The foremen were to make sure that the final control and performance evaluation standards were perceived by the controlled individuals as realistic and attainable. It was decided to use pounds of output as the basis for rate determination and absorption of the overhead in the product since ACC's production process was highly automated and people performed only minor supporting tasks.

At the meeting, it was further decided to charge the sales and production departments for all centrally provided services such as data processing, accounting, legal services, product development, and quality control. The fixed portion of the total service costs was to be allocated on the basis of assets employed. The variable portion was to be absorbed by the users on the basis of actual use. Through such allocations, it was hoped that the providers would exercise special care since declines in service quality or timeliness would undoubtedly cause immediate user complaints. People pay more attention to the quality and the timeliness of services for which they have to pay and that affect their own performance evaluations. The allocations were used as proxies for transfer prices since it was believed that the costs of a full-fledged transfer-price system would not be justifiable for a company of their size.

After a heated discussion, it was decided to zero-base all major selling and administrative expenses at least once every other year to insure more realistic budgeting. The sales department's efficiency was to be evaluated, in addition to the present budget variance analysis, on the basis of industry averages for sales generated per dollar of selling expenses.

All executives were to have their assigned tasks completed by mid-August, at which time a progress meeting was to be held. At this meeting,

Iverson hoped to receive the agreed upon cost standards and the various chosen allocation bases for corporate indirect costs so that she could start constructing the system.

Everything proceeded according to schedule. Iverson presented her report to the president and his management team and asked them to study the new system carefully and report any omissions or ambiguities to her within a week. She also insisted that all employees affected by the new cost accounting and reporting system were to be carefully educated on its objectives and structure and that training sessions were to be held to ensure proper use and maintenance. She offered her services in the education process and promised to be available at the budgeting time if any unforeseen implementation problems should surface.

Back in her office at PW, Iverson reflected on her completed assignment. She was convinced that she had performed well and that she had solved the problems that had caused such animosity within the top management team. By working together in the standard cost system design stage, they had learned to understand each other's needs. They realized that they all shared one goal—the growth and well-being of the organization that provided their livelihood.

SUMMARY

In this chapter, we demonstrated the behavioral aspects of accumulating and controlling costs. We showed that traditional (historical) cost systems are behaviorally unsound and may induce unwanted and destructive responses when used in controlling and evaluating individual performance. Although standard cost systems have the potential to increase motivation and goal congruence, they may also be used to achieve high levels of autocratic and coercive control. The behaviorally superior method is direct (variable) costing, which, by isolating product cost and period cost, provides the most relevant information for controlling the various types of costs and in leading management to more profitable decisions. We also analyzed the behavioral aspects of cost accounting steps and suggested approaches that could induce desirable employee behavior.

REFERENCES

[1] Edwin H. Caplan, *Management Accounting & Behavioral Science* (Reading, Mass.: Addison-Wesley Publishing Co., 1971), 60.

[2] John A. Bekett, "An Appraisal of Direct Costing," *NACA Bulletin* Sect.1 (December 1951): 407–415.

[3] David Hawkins, "Behavioral Implications of Generally Accepted Accounting Principles," *California Management Review* (Winter 1969), 13-21.

[4] Charles Horngren, *Cost Accounting*, 5th ed. (Englewood Cliffs, N.J.: Prentice-Hall, 1982), 325.

[5] Ibid., 324.

[6] Ibid., 325.

[7] Raymond E. Miles and Roger C. Vergin, "Behavioral Properties of Variance Controls," *California Management Review 2* (Spring 1966): 57–65.

[8] Michael F. Foran and Don T. DeCoster, "An Experimental Study of the Effects of Participation, Authoritarianism and Feedback on Cognitive Dissonance in a Standard Setting Situation," *Accounting Review* (Oct. 1974): 751–763.

[9] James M. Fremgen and Shu S. Liao, NAA Research Report, "The Allocation of Corporate Indirect Costs," *Management Accounting* (Sept. 1981): 66–67.

[10] Ibid.

[11] Charles Horngren, *Cost Accounting*, 5th Edition, 1982, Chapter 15 (Englewood Cliffs, N.J.: Prentice-Hall).

[12] Jerold L. Zimmerman, "The Cost and Benefits of Cost Allocations," *The Accounting Review* 54, no. 3 (July 1979): 504–521.

[13] Ibid., 519.

[14] Ibid., 505.

[15] A. J. Duncan, "The Economic Design of X Chart to Maintain Current Control of a Process," *Journal of the American Statistical Association*, vol.51, (June 1956), 228.

[16] H. Bierman, L. E. Fouraker and R. K. Jaedicke, "Use of Probability and Statistics in Performance Evaluation," *The Accounting Review* (July 1961): 408–17.

[17] Shahid L. Ansari and Masao Tsuji, "A Behavioral Extension to the Cost Variance Investigation Decision," *Journal of Business Finance and Accounting*, 8, no.4, (1981): 573–589.

[18] Shahid L. Ansari, "An Integrated Approach to Control System Design," *Accounting, Organization and Society*, no. 2, Pergamon Press, Great Britain, (1977): 101–112.

DISCUSSION QUESTIONS

1. What is the main purpose of cost accounting? What will happen if its behavioral aspects are neglected?
2. Why are traditional cost systems inappropriate for effective managerial control? What is required to satisfy contemporary concepts of control?
3. Name two major shortcomings of traditional cost systems. To what can these lead?
4. What do you understand by a standard cost system? What are the steps essential in the development of a standard cost system framework?
5. How is control over responsibility center operations accomplished in a standard cost system?
6. How are costs distinguished in direct or variable costing? What is the advantage of this cost system?

7. Define engineered costs, committed costs, and discretionary costs. Which of these is readily controllable at the lowest organizational level through use of flexible standards and budgets?
8. What is the importance of the contribution margin in decison making? Give an example of a situation where this concept is used.
9. How are standards established in a standard cost system? Why is it important that standards be perceived by workers as valid performance goals?
10. What are the four prerequisites for a behaviorally sound control system? Why are they important?
11. What are the two types of indirect costs distinguished by companies in the study by Fremgen and Liao?
12. Name some components of a control policy that may affect human responses. How will these affect workers?

CASE 10-1

The Company

The DEF Company is a large manufacturer of men's work and dress shoes and is located in New England. The company is a closely owned corporation with the owners holding most of the key management positions, including president and CEO, vice-president of finance, treasurer, and six other vice-presidential positions.

The sales volume for the last two years was $22 million in fiscal 1981 and $17 million in fiscal 1982.

The DEF Company has two different types of customers. The main customer (a large department store chain) accounted for about 76.6 percent of the volume and shoe stores the balance of 23.4 percent. The large department store production is privately branded and the small stores use the nationally known company brand name.

The company has a long-term "cost plus contract" with their main customer. This requires the total involvement of this customer in the semiannual budget meetings at which the dilemma was recognized but not initially handled.

The Dilemma

The foreign manufacturers of men's work shoes had become increasingly competitive in price, quality, and styling while the DEF Company was experiencing continuing cost increases caused by increasing labor rates. This resulted in idle capacity as more of the volume was transferred overseas by the main customer.

This trend was readily identifiable, but no action was taken by DEF management until it became obvious that there was no longer sufficient production to maintain the existing three factories. The large volume customer had been requesting that they consolidate from three to two factories to save capacity cost, but the DEF Company refused.

The dilemma was how to allocate the indirect fixed overhead costs (absorbed until now by the factory to be closed) between the large volume customer and the other customers.

The unabsorbed indirect fixed overhead costs resulting from the closing of the third factory amounted to about $2.50 per pair of shoes, which would increase the cost per pair produced at the other two factories by 10 percent. The required price increase would make all shoes produced in the future non-competitive and force their production overseas.

The controller insisted that the remaining two factories had to absorb this added cost increment regardless of the consequences. The sales manager argued that the closing of the factory was not the responsibility of the customers currently buying shoes from the two factories and they should not be penalized by this added cost.

Required:

1. Who do you think is right and why?
2. As the president of DEF Company, how would you solve the excess capacity and costing dilemma without permanently upsetting either the controller or the sales manager?

CASE 10-2

The Company

Ray Johnson, who manages the First National Bank's lockbox operation, has been looking to improve the profitability of his area. The lockbox department is very busy during the beginning and end of the month, but is very slow during the middle of the month.

A couple of weeks ago, he was approached by the new head of the cost accounting group, Jack Smith. Smith heard that Johnson was looking to improve the efficiency of his area, and Smith thought that a review of the area could provide some opportunities. Smith was very surprised when Johnson told him that he had approached the previous cost accounting manager a year ago and was told that the system could not accommodate the changes required.

The Dilemma

Smith did some investigating and found that the staffing of the lockbox area caused overtime during the peak periods, yet during the slow time of the month, the employees did not have nearly enough work to keep them busy. Johnson had someone come in to evaluate the staffing level of the lockbox area. The consultant told Johnson that the current staffing level was sufficient. If additional employees were hired, the overtime would be cut, but there would be more employees idle during the middle of the month. On the other hand, if the staff was reduced, there would be an increase in overtime during the busy period. There was also a concern that a staff cut would adversely affect quality of work.

In discussing the situation with the cost accountant assigned to lockbox, Smith found out what had happened between Johnson and the previous cost accounting manager. Johnson had approached cost accounting with the idea that he would like to charge customers less if they used his department's services during the "slow" time of the month. He felt that he could keep his employees busy and he was concerned about covering the overhead expenses. All Johnson was told was that the system could not handle it.

After reviewing the situation, Smith set up a meeting with Johnson. He told Johnson that he could appreciate his frustration in having overtime expenses eating at profits and then seeing employees idle during the middle of the month. Smith said he was concerned that lower customer charges during the slow period would cause a majority of the customers to conduct their business with lockbox during the slow period. This could result in the slow period actually becoming the peak period. If this happened, it could have a disastrous affect on lockbox profits.

Required:

1. Can this problem be solved?
2. How would you handle the situation?

CASE 10-3

The Company

The ABC Shoe Company is a medium-sized manufacturer of children's shoes and is located in the Midwest. The company is family owned and members of the family hold each of the three key management positions: president and CEO, vice-president of finance and treasurer, and vice-president of manufacturing.

Sales volume for the last two years was $12,825,000 in fiscal 1981 and $15,350,000 in fiscal 1982.

The ABC Shoe Company has two different types of customers. The main customer (a large department store chain) accounted for 70 percent of the volume and small "Ma and Pa" shoe stores for the balance of 30 percent. The large department store production is privately branded; the small stores market the company brand name.

The ABC Shoe Company has a long-term cost plus contract with their main customer which requires the total involvement of this customer in the production quantity and product cost budgeting process. It was during these semi-annual budget meetings that the dilemma was recognized although not initially handled.

The Dilemma

During the last two years, the ABC Shoe Company reported large favorable variances in two major accounts. This signified a possible lack of accurate budgeting procedures.

The following is a two-year history of these accounts and their effect on product cost:

Variances	1981	1982	Increase in Variance
Purchase Price Variance	$450,000	$675,000	
Material Usage Variance	$ 95,000	$125,000	
Total	$545,000	$800,000	+46.8%

Since the contract price is set on the basis of the budgeted amounts, these variances represent an overstatement of 4.2 percent in product cost for 1981 and 5.2 percent in 1982.

The company claimed that these favorable variances were unintentional and just reflected the differences between budgeted goals and actual performance. The main customer insisted that these variances were either deliberate or the result of less than "professional budgeting" procedures because these variances were significantly larger than those of other shoe companies.

The ABC Shoe Company uses a standard cost system to account for its product costs.

A review of the income statements of the past two years disclosed that there were substantial unfavorable variances in direct labor usage and loss on seconds and that factory overhead was grossly underabsorbed as presented below:

Variances	1981	1982	%Change
Direct Labor Usage	($ 46,100)	($ 11,000)	
Factory Overhead	($522,000)	($385,000)	
Loss on Seconds	($ 80,200)	($ 40,400)	
	($648,300)	($436,400)	−32.6%

Investigations disclosed that the unfavorable variance for factory overhead is the result of the main customer not placing contracts for the same quantities as submitted during the budget process. Loss on seconds and the direct labor usage variances represented true indications of inefficiencies.

When combined, these five variances resulted in a substantial addition to ABC Shoe Company profit:

	1981	1982
Total Favorable Variances (Per Performance Reports)	$545,000	$800,000
Total Unfavorable Variances (Per Income Statement)	($648,300)	($437,000)
Net Total	($103,300)	$363,000

After the 1982 final results were published, management of both companies held meetings to arrive at recommendations on the best approach to a more accurate budgeting process. It was mutually agreed that the factory standard cost system was realistic and acceptable, but that people—"The Human Factor"—were the obvious problem.

Required:

1. Despite the mutual agreement that the standard cost system was realistic, could it have behavorial flaws and if so, what kind?

2. What induced the ABC Shoe Company employees to overstate the production costs for their main customer?

3. How are the two sets of variances interrelated and how are they intended to control the performance of the labor force?

4. Why was the excess slack in the budget not discovered earlier?

5. What changes should be made in the budget-making process and in the cost accounting system to prevent the problem from recurring?

CASE 10-4

The Company

A large retail firm with thirty stores in the Chicago area evaluates its store supervisors once a year. Each supervisor is in charge of four stores and is responsible for their operating efficiency. Each supervisor visits the stores once a week to make sure that proper procedures are being followed. All stores are supported by an area office that has various functions. It controls inventory, repair and supply purchases, payroll processing, and distribution of payroll for the various stores. The supervisor receives monthly reports of the sales volume and manpower used in each store. These reports also rank the stores by performance in these two areas.

The stores' profitability is affected by revenues and a variety of expenses such as the costs for repairs to the stores as well as a portion of the area office repairs. The costs of all other support functions at the area office are also prorated to each store on the basis of its sales volume.

The year-end performance review is based on the overall profitability of the stores. The supervisors are ranked based on the total profitability of the four stores for which they are responsible. This ranking determines which supervisors get the highest raises and bonuses.

The Dilemma

In the past few years, there has been an unusually high turnover in the supervisor staff. They feel that the items used to determine the stores' profitability are not completely in their control and therefore should not be the sole factor in their evaluation. They also feel that the maintenance and other functions provided by the area office are not done properly and should not be reflected in their profitability figures.

Required:

1. Do you agree with the complaints raised by the supervisor staff?

2. What, if any, are the reasons why rational, maximizing individuals

would want to allocate indirect costs? What benefits does the company perceive from arbitrary allocations?

CASE 10-5

The Company

Lincoln National is a large midwestern bank. Until two years ago, the costs for the service products were absorbed by the various lending areas of Lincoln National. To improve the products and the caliber of employees, the service area was divided into profit centers.

The project was conducted very professionally. All of the employees were encouraged to take part in the various task forces. Even though all of their recommendations were not implemented, they were very open and enthusiastic about the changes that were going to take place because they did play a part in making the recommendations and influencing decisions. Many jobs were changed and enhanced. People were promoted from within and also hired from the outside for some of the key higher-level positions. Marketing, systems, and management positions were created. The area was divided by products such as lockbox, check processing, and securities processing.

In a year, many improvements in the operations area were implemented. Old products were enhanced and many new products were developed. The marketing area held seminars for the lending officers to assist them in understanding how all the products were marketed to various customer groups. There were product managers who would assist the lending officers on their customer calls. The products area developed a professional and competent image. Products were enhanced and service to customers improved. Employee morale had never been better and profits also reflected all the positive improvements.

Systems were redesigned and implemented to accommodate the profit center concept. Also, additional new systems were being considered to assist management in their day-to-day decision making.

The Dilemma

After a year and a half of operating with the reorganization, it was realized that the lending officers were not putting a great deal of effort into marketing the service products. The "sales" were not increasing and some were actually declining.

It was determined that the problem was with the accounting system. In most cases, the lending officers were charged the actual customer cost of the product. Also, some of the lending officers were losing money when they sold products that cost more than the customer paid. All in all, it was a no-win situation for the lending officers because these products were negatively affecting their bonuses.

Required:

1. What accounting system changes could be made to motivate lending officers to sell the products and have the product area receive their share of profits?

CASE 10-6

The Company

Through the foresight and marketing genius of its entrepreneurial founder, a fledgling direct mail marketer of collectibles had grown from nothing to a hundred million dollar organization within ten years. In addition to its marketing insights and satisfaction of customer needs, a good deal of the organization's success was attributable to the dissemination of the entrepreneurial spirit of the founder among the employees. In those early years, sales increased at an annual rate of nearly 100 percent and employees were motivated by universal pride and satisfaction in their work.

The organization's manufacturing process consisted of firing clay products with decorative stencils. The process was manually intensive and consisted of stencil preparation, adherence to a prepurchased clay product, manual decorating (where appropriate), and kiln firing. Rapidly increasing sales, high employee morale, and a generous profit-sharing plan precluded the necessity of a standardized cost system.

The Dilemma

As the growth curve tapered off, the owner brought in "professional management" to establish a cost accounting department that would determine, promulgate, and report on standard costs for the manufacturing process. As the science of accounting was applied by the prestigious MBAs, employee production and morale fell off. The cost accounting system regularly reported unfavorable variances that affected the bottom line.

Required:

1. What went wrong? Could it have been anticipated?
2. What should be done to turn the company around and restore employee morale?

CASE 10-7

The Company

The WFH Printing Company has six plants and sales of approximately $200 million. Three of the plants are in Chicago and three are in the southern United States. The southern plants have all been built in the past ten years.

The Dilemma

For the past ten years, the northern plants have become progressively less profitable. This loss in profitability has been due to increasing union labor costs and deterioration of plant and equipment. Many of the core customers have moved to the southern locations to take advantage of lower labor rates and faster equipment. This movement has left the northern plants with a tremendous amount of underutilized capacity. Because of the high labor rates and poor machine productivity, the excess capacity is very difficult to sell. The cost accounting department has historically used plantwide overhead rates to achieve full absorption. As more and more excess capacity appeared, the burden rates went higher and the profitability on the remaining jobs plummeted.

The management was not fully aware of the effects of the cost accounting system. Management only saw that the plants that used to be profitable were now drowning in red ink. The situation was made worse by the fact that selling prices were derived by marking up or marking down estimated total cost. Management began making plans to close the plants.

Required:

1. What specifically was wrong with the cost accounting system?
2. What should be done to turn the situation around and save the northern plants?

CHAPTER 11

Behavioral Aspects
of Performance Evaluation

BUSINESS DILEMMA_____

John Miller, a recent MBA graduate and brand new certified management accountant (CMA), has just been hired as administrative assistant to the corporate controller of a giant eastern multinational firm. His first assignment is to evaluate the effectiveness of the company's performance evaluation system. The controller, who is always extremely busy, was not able to spend sufficient time with the new assistant for a detailed briefing. Therefore, Miller had to use internal questioning and external investigations to understand the environmental conditions and the functioning of the present system. These are the results of his investigation.

The Company

Amex, Inc. is a Fortune 500 corporation with 25 subsidiaries, 17,000 employees, $2.5 billion in sales and $2.3 billion in assets. It manufactures products almost exclusively related to a single industry. New and replacement demand share the market on a two-to-one basis respectively. The company's earnings are highly dependent on the economic health of the countries in which it operates. Interest rates and population growth and movement have a very strong influence on the company's future and performance.

   After studying numerous articles about the company in the business press and talking to managers at various levels, Miller found that the company could be characterized as follows:

Characteristics of AMEX, Inc.

Internal	External
Conservative	Ultra-Conservative
Expert in Field	Single Market Oriented
Risk Conscious	Risk Adverse
Industry Leader	Industry Leader
Financially Solvent	Highly Liquid

The company is organized by divisions, and each profit center is responsible for marketing, manufacturing, and customer service functions. Centralized functions such as computer and legal services, accounting, insurance, research and development, advertising, acquisition, and engineering services are supplied by special departments at corporate headquarters.

Performance Evaluation

The performance evaluation system is designed to measure three basic elements: personal performance, attainment of operating goals, and return on investment. Subordinates are evaluated only on the basis of their personal performance; segment managers are judged on all three criteria. The relative weight assigned to each performance criteria or key result area for all profit centers is 20-70-10. At corporate headquarters, the breakdown is 40-40-20. The personal performance factor is highly subjective since it is guided by a results management system. This system rates individuals on their accountabilities and compliance with written objectives and performance rules. The personal rating is done by the employees' immediate supervisor and is approved one level higher. The attainment of goals and return on investment are accounting measures based on goals and standards set by the profit center or corporate unit head.

Goal Setting

The goal-setting process is the same for all units. Table 11-1 represents a simplified model of the company's structure and goal-setting elements. The following notes explain in more detail the various elements of the goal structure and performance reporting.

1. *Sales* are set and controlled by the profit center.
2. *Other income* represents net estimated corporate income from sales of assets, interest income, and the like, and is determined by corporate.
3. *Manufacturing costs* are set and controlled by a standard cost system. Unusual costs, such as major losses from insurance deductibles, are borne by corporate headquarters. The standards for direct material, direct labor, and overhead are determined by the manufacturing plants. Each plant manager's rating and bonus is *highly dependent* on the capability of not exceeding the standard allowances and the degree of cost absorption by the products.
4. *Selling and administrative expenses* are determined by a rigid fixed formula and format, with half of the elements zero-base budgeted. Items such as salary expenses are based on annualized December salaries plus an average increase factor for the next year. However, Miller was assured by a manager that if one is careful, this rigid formula proves to be quite flexible.
5. *Distribution center profits* are duplicate credits for distribution center profits given to the manufacturing divisions. Manufacturing division managers are

TABLE 11-1

AMEX Inc. Consolidated Goal Structure, 19-1 (in millions of dollars)

Elements*	Profit Center A	Profit Center B	Group Adjust-ment	Group	Corp.	Total
Sales	100	300	—	400	—	400
Other income	—	—	—	—	30	30
Manufacturing cost						
Standard	(75)	(170)	—	(245)	—	(245)
Nonrecurring	—	(25)	—	(25)	(10)	(35)
Selling and adminis-trative expense	(10)	(30)	(5)	(45)	(40)	(85)
Distribution center credit	—	14	(14)	—	—	—
Direct overhead-actual	(2)	(12)	(2)	(16)	(10)	(26)
Corporate direct overhead—allocated	(1)	(15)	—	(16)	16	—
Operating profit	12	(62)	21	53	(14)	39
Corporate indirect overhead—allocated	(1)	(18)	—	(19)	19	—
Earnings before tax	11	44	(21)	34	5	39
Tax	(5)	(22)	10	(17)	3	(14)
Net earnings	6	22	(11)	17	8	25
Capital employed (in millions of dollars)	75	163	(75)	163	20	183
Ratios:						
Return on capital employed	7%	14%	—	10.4	—	13.7
Receivable days outstanding	45	40	—	—	—	41
Inventory turnover	9	4	—	—	—	5

*For a detailed explanation of these elements, read the section in this chapter entitled "Goal Setting."

thereby induced to supply products to internal users even at times when demand exceeds supply and they could get higher prices externally.

6. *Direct overhead—actual* includes such items as bad debts and management incentive provisions, which are determined by the profit centers. For their computation, see the following section on bonus computations.

7. *Corporate direct overhead—allocated* includes items such as research and development, advertising, and direct corporate service charges. They are set by corporate, but allocated on the basis of a fixed formula to the profit centers and affect their operating profit.

8. *Operating profit* represents the net of items 1 through 7 and is used as an incentive measurement point for the profit centers (see the section on bonus computations for more detail).

9. *Corporate indirect overhead—allocated* consists basically of current cost whose benefits are long-term in nature. They include long-range advertising and research and development, as well as indirect corporate service charges set by corporate.

10. *Tax* is determined on the basis of a fixed formula, which uses the effective tax rate for the profit center after considering all permanent tax benefits.

11. *Net earnings* represent the basis for group and corporate incentive measurement.

12. *Capital employed* is composed of actual current assets and fixed assets of the profit center, less allocated current liabilities and deferred taxes. Profit centers that are legal subsidiaries use actual book values for ratable items.

13. *Return on capital employed* is computed by dividing capital employed into net earnings. No minimum required return level is yet established, since this measurement tool has been in use for only a short period of time.

14. *Receivable days outstanding* are intended to monitor cash flow from receivables and to induce minimization of capital employed.

15. *Inventory turnover* is used as an inventory control measure to prevent excessive inventory build-up.

Bonus Computations

Segment managers' bonuses are determined on the basis of the performance ratings achieved in each of the three key result areas. Using the relative weights noted earlier as base, a typical incentive payout for a profit center manager would be computed as shown at the top of page 194.

Since performance rating for attainment of operating goals receives the highest weight, it will benefit or hurt the unit by a factor of 2. There is an upper limit of 200 percent bonus or 150 percent attainment and a lower minimum of 50 percent bonus or 75 percent attainment.

Subordinates are not entitled to bonuses; however, their personal performance appraisal results are used by their superiors when deciding on raises and promotions.

	Base $	Percent	Performance rating	Weight factor	Actual
Personal					
Performance	$2,000	20	100%	1	$ 2,000
Attainment of					
Operating Goals	7,000	70	125%	2	17,500
Return on					
Investment	1,000	10	80%	1	800
	$10,000				$20,300

Performance Reporting

Actual performance of the profit centers and corporate units is reported monthly in the form of segmental statements of earnings and on the basis of various ratios.

1. *Statement of earnings.* Such a statement is prepared each month on a cumulative basis with variances from goals flagged. Return on capital employed is shown as a footnote to net earnings. The segmental statements of earnings inform the managers simultaneously of their success or failure in attaining their operational goals and of the return on investment accomplished during the period.
2. *Receivable days outstanding.* This ratio is presented on a comparative two-year monthly trend basis with the annual objective shown. Actual current-year results are flagged when performance is unfavorable, which permits a modified form of exception reporting.
3. *Inventory turnover.* This ratio is determined using the same format as for receivables.

Perceived Dilemma Areas

During the course of his investigation, Miller discovered various contradictions, which he perceived as dilemma situations requiring diagnostic attention and possible remedial actions. A discussion of the main areas of concern and the problems encountered follows.

Sales

When studying sales and market share trends, Miller noticed that the company's market share was slipping, a condition that would mandate increased market penetrations. To sell to a broader market, the sales force and advertising would need to be increased. Sales managers, however, are not motivated to such actions since administrative and selling budgets are fixed in the short-run and goal attainment receives the highest weight in the bonus computations. In the short run, increased sales would produce more profit for the profit centers and thus increase bonuses. However, the additional selling and administrative costs, while more than offset by increased revenue, would result in unfavorable budget variances. With personal performance ratings being highly subjective, the managers have no idea whether the negative performance in goal attainment would outweigh the benefit from increased profit attainment. The performance evaluation system seems to induce dysfunctional behavior by forcing the managers to sacrifice the long-range goal of market share increase and thus profit improvement in order to comply with short-term budget constraints. Miller wondered whether the budget limit is top management's way of deemphasizing the market share goal by reminding the performer to strive for improvement, but not at any cost.

Manufacturing Costs

When investigating manufacturing costs, Miller observed that variances from standard costs were always favorable. This made him suspect that the standard costs were "padded" or data was manipulated. From his experiences, he knows that under normal conditions, truly meaningful variances must be both favorable and unfavorable.

Miller speculated that this condition could be caused by errors in estimating the sales volume, with plant managers attempting to compensate for the problem. He reasoned that since the plant managers are heavily rated on their ability to meet standards, it would be normal behavior to "stack their decks." The review control feature, although it is supposed to exist, obviously did not work as intended. Standard padding by the plant manager also works to the division manager's benefit and will therefore not be questioned. Hence, the behavior is self-serving at the plant as well as at the division level.

Selling and Administrative Expenses

Miller was told by profit center managers that top management is very adamant that actual performance be at or below budget. In goal setting, limits are set on specific items and on the total increase from the prior year. Miller observed, however, that salary factors used in budget setting are in excess of the guidelines published annually by the company, thereby inflating the limits.

While interviewing the various managers, Miller got the feeling that the budget system is perceived as too rigid. People complained that it does not allow for realistic goal setting. They generally viewed it as a bureaucratic impediment or threat to their career advancement. Miller observed that the dislike of the whole budget process seems to induce people to sabotage it. The constrained budget style apparently triggered routine budget padding to assure performance attainment at goal level. Although this behavior is dysfunctional on the surface, Miller had to admit that it induced managers to stay within the budget limits as prescribed by top management. It became a question of whether the end justifies the means. Miller felt that in this case, there is a high degree of doubt that it does, since the excessive padding prevented using the budget system in a meaningful fashion. The distortions caused by behavioral reactions to the constrained style resulted in meeting the objective, but not necessarily in an optimal fashion. This unhealthy condition is caused by the fact that the objective itself is the result of dysfunctional behavior.

Direct Overhead—Actual

The two major components of this category, the provisions for doubtful receivables and management incentive bonuses, appeared on the surface to be directly related to current earnings.

Since the management incentive payment is the reward for performance, the budgeted amount for this item is based on 100 or par performance. If earnings contribution and goal attainment exceed par, actual bonuses paid exceed the budget provision. Since there was widespread padding of manufacturing cost and selling expenses, par performance is virtually assured. Since goals are easy to reach, the incentive payouts are always higher than if the goals were set realistically. Thus, Miller felt the performance evaluation system was dysfunctional. Not only was it unable to control the widespread budget padding practices, but it even encouraged them. This resulted in an unnecessary cash drain and overstated compensation cost for the company, which both reduce its possible return on investment.

In regard to the doubtful receivables, Miller felt that there could be a tendency to resist placing accounts in the suspense category because this adversely impacts on reserve needs. The incentive payout thus becomes an overriding factor in proper accounting practices, determination of the profit center capital employed, and determination of the rate of return on capital employed (ROCE).

Corporate Direct and Indirect Overhead—Allocated

As outlined in the goal-setting section, the components of these categories are both short-range and long-range in nature. They are composed of three classes of costs: service costs, marketing costs, and cost reduction or product improvement costs. Each centralized function is normal to the business, but can presumably be provided at lower cost on a centralized basis. The costs of the various service units are allocated to the profit centers. The service provider is held accountable for attainment of the cost goals. The recipients of the service, the profit centers, have no control over the cost allocation formula nor over the total amounts spent. They also have no way of effectively controlling cost occurrence; they feel helpless and mistrust the benefits of the services rendered. The provider has no incentive to assess its operational efficiency since all costs incurred are allocated to and absorbed by the users. As long as the service center stays within the assigned budget, its performance evaluation will not suffer. Thus, Miller observed, there was no effective way of measuring whether providing these services on a centralized basis is cost effective or wasteful. Under the present system, a given profit center manager might seek more usage of a given service area, which would enable it to produce more revenue. This request might be turned down because the additional cost would put the provider over budget and thus hurt its performance. The performance evaluation system of centrally supplied services also lacked routine measures to evaluate and control quality. Quality of service can be controlled by the providers only if they are driven by a self- or peer-motivating esteem or through complaints by the users.

Miller feels that corporate may be on the right track in controlling "corporate wide services," but that its efforts are incomplete. He feels that its intent is frequently counterproductive because it fails to recognize the interdependence between service departments and profit centers.

Return on Capital Employed

The elements of the formula used for computing the rate of return on capital employed are fixed, and the earning levels are highly dependent on current economic conditions. Short-term assets and liabilities partly offset each other, and thus little improvement in capital employed can be achieved by altering their makeup. Long-term assets represent mostly the net book value of productive facilities less associated deferred income taxes. Thus, the ROCE cannot be easily altered in the short run.

However, the performance evaluation system employed by Amex, Inc. is short-term oriented. There is little incentive to increase ROCE since all the possible methods are of a long-term nature. Hence, the philosophy throughout the organization: "If it is acceptable today, tomorrow I'll get promoted and then it's someone else's problem." The result is that neither the organization nor its profit and cost centers achieve profit maximization. Instead of planning properly for the future, they simply react to it.

The dysfunctional performance behavior of the various segments is understandable. It is based on the reasoning, "Why spend time on performance factors that don't help me today?". This results in less attention being paid to long-range performance elements, such as product improvement and market penetration, since they do not benefit segment managers in attaining the rewarded short-term criteria.

Accounts Receivable and Inventories

Accounts receivable are measured in terms of the number-of-days-sales outstanding (Accounts receivable/Daily sales). The inventory turnover ratio shows the number of times inventory turns over per year (Cost of sales/Average inventory).

Neither of the two measurements is a directly rewarded performance criterion. Miller found out that they are provided to the profit centers only as a health measure. While the profit centers are not required to maintain a certain level of performance in either area, truly abnormal performance is questioned by corporate. The abnormality is determined by comparing the results of the various divisions and by reference to past trends. Although the company has a very strict credit policy, the determination of economically justifiable inventory levels is generally left to the discretion of the profit center managers. Only in downside economic times does top management "hoot and holler" about these measurements.

One would expect the performers to interpret the sporadic attention as lack of interest by top management and thus to concentrate their efforts where a performance-reward linkage is perceived to exist. But Miller found, to his surprise, that much attention is given to receivable data. There appears to be a definite awareness in the profit centers that control of credit (a nonrated measure) assists in measured performance rating areas because of the relationships among credit, bad debts, and capital employed. The voluntary control of credit by the profit centers results in the unique situation that a nonperformance rated, unrewarded measure controls behavior and results in benefits to ratable items.

Interestingly enough, though, the same is not true for inventory turnover. Obviously, keeping inventory down and improving its turnover have an impact on profits. This is not understood by the profit center managers, though, since the only time improvement occurs is when it is mandated by corporate.

The key lies in the fact that no minimum turnover ratios have been set. Thus, as long as actual and planned inventory levels approximate each other, it is assumed that no problems exist. In fact, Miller found that two units have ratios that result in a significant drain on their ROCE measure, yet management has failed to correct the problem. The dichotomy of these two measures is that while they are both essentially the same kind of measures and affect the ROCE in similar fashion, the performers apparently perceive their benefits differently. The result is that the behavior, in this case as in all cases, is based on perception not reality.

DEFINITION AND PURPOSE OF PERFORMANCE EVALUATION

Performance evaluation is the periodic assessment of the operational effectiveness of an organization, its subunits, and its personnel in light of predetermined goals, standards, and criteria. Since organizations are run by people, performance evaluation is in reality the evaluation of people's behavior in the roles assigned to them in the organization.

The primary purpose of performance evaluation is to motivate employees to attain organizational goals and to comply with predetermined behavior standards to produce desired actions and outcomes. The behavior standards could be prescribed managerial policies or formal plans for desired integrated actions (e.g., budgets, profit plans, or standard costs).

Another aspect of performance evaluation is the discouragement of dysfunctional behavior and the encouragement and reinforcement of desired, or functional, behavior through timely feedback of performance results and intrinsic or extrinsic rewards. In this chapter, emphasis is placed on performance evaluation that uses data provided by the accounting system. Subjective appraisals of individual performance is an aspect of performance evaluation that does not use accounting data, and it is mentioned only briefly in our elaborations. This, however, does not mean that subjective employee appraisals and ratings are not a vital part of an effective performance appraisal system. Without them, many aspects of employee behavior would not be noticed and might then be considered unimportant by the employees.

USES OF PERFORMANCE EVALUATION

Managers use performance evaluation results in many ways. The greatest benefits are realized when they are used for the following purposes:

1. To manage the operations of the organization effectively and efficiently by maximizing employee motivation;
2. To assist in personnel decisions such as promotions, transfers, and terminations;
3. To identify specific training and development needs and to provide criteria for selection and evaluation of training programs;
4. To provide feedback to employees about how superiors perceive their performance; and
5. To provide a basis for reward allocations.

Performance evaluation affects every component of management responsibility. A thorough understanding of the behavorial aspects of this vital task is therefore necessary for its effective deployment.

In the next section of the chapter, we will define motivation and elaborate on its use as a tool for promoting operational efficiency. Since people expect rewards for complying with organizational rules, the impact of rewards on human behavior and the benefits derived from various types of rewards will be discussed. We will analyze the steps in performance evaluation procedures and point out their possible behavioral pitfalls. Finally, we will elaborate on the various factors that may induce undesirable subordinate reactions to performance evaluation data.

The chapter will conclude with the diagnostic review of the business dilemma presented at the beginning of the chapter, and suggestions for remedying the situation.

MOTIVATION AS A TOOL FOR PROMOTING OPERATIONAL EFFICIENCY_____

Motivation is concerned with what induces people to behave in particular ways. Motivation researchers have delineated hierarchies of needs, types of motivators (extrinsic versus intrinsic ones), and motivation hygiene factors. They have developed several motivation theories, including equity theory, goal-setting theory, reinforcement theory, and expectancy theory.

Expectancy theory is one of the best predictors of motivation and performance. According to this theory, behavior is influenced by the probabilities people assign to the following relationships:

1. *The effort necessary to achieve the goal.* Intrinsic motivation, or the pleasure people associate with the content of a job or task, is stimulated when the task is perceived as challenging but not overwhelming. Very difficult goals can motivate people only when they are perceived to be fair and realistic. Easy goals with high probabilities of success have less positive motivational impact because people may not consider their accomplishment worthwhile.
2. *Performance and reward.* The rewards could be in the form of raises, bonuses, profit sharing, stock options, praise, or just in experiencing the pleasure of accomplishment.
   If there is a low probability of getting rewards for outstanding performance, effort is reduced. The key factor is how people perceive the situation. The fact that past performance and rewards were closely correlated is irrelevant if people perceive otherwise; lower performance and decreased job satisfaction may result. Later consequences include lack of interest in the work, absenteeism, and turnover.
   Furthermore, rewards such as pay raises may cease to motivate if they are granted for reasons other than performance (e.g., effort, seniority, skills held, etc.)

3. *Rewards satisfying personal goals.* Since different employees have different goal priorities, uniform reward systems do not always motivate equally well. To achieve optimum motivation, rewards should be tailored to the needs of each individual.

EFFECT OF REWARDS ON BEHAVIOR

A typical reaction to a proposed business deal is: "What's in it for me?" Before people act, they generally look for the reward or payoff. This is also true for people working in organizations.

There are three ways to shape the behavior of the people who work in organizations:

1. The response to desirable behavior can be made something pleasant (a praise or a reward). This behavioral influence is called *positive reinforcement.*
2. Desirable behavior can be induced by the elimination of something unpleasant. This is called *negative reinforcement.* For example, the supervisor will stop watching an employee if he or she seems busy.
3. *Punishment* is a common remedy for undesirable behavior. For example, ballplayers may be suspended without pay for a certain length of time or fined because of gross infringement of game rules. Another example of punishment would be a profit center manager who is transferred to a less desirable division, or even fired, for not reaching predetermined profit goals.

In an organizational setting, the most effective tool for shaping desirable behavior of participants is positive reinforcement or rewards. Reinforcement generally increases the probability of repeating desired behavior. On the other hand, punishment may produce unwanted side effects. It may only temporarily suppress undesirable behavior and produce instead lower morale, anxiety, resentment, and increased absenteeism.

Regardless of what the organization "says" it rewards, people will shape and repeat the behavior they "perceive" to be rewarded. For example, suppose a multinational bank expected its loan officers to market noncredit services, but rewarded them only on the basis of the revenue generated from their lending activities. Despite the department head's strong encouragement to market the bank's noncredit services, the loan officers ignored the cues and concentrated exclusively on the lending — the activity they perceived as being rewarded.

TYPES OF REWARDS AND THEIR BENEFITS IN FUNCTIONAL BEHAVIOR INDUCEMENT AND REINFORCEMENT

Rewards can be grouped into intrinsic and extrinsic categories. *Intrinsic rewards* are personally satisfying feelings that people experience for jobs well done and for goals attained. Intrinsic rewards can be enhanced by techniques such as job enrichment, increased responsibility, participation in decision making, and other efforts that lead to increases in people's self-worth and drive to excel.

Extrinsic rewards include direct, indirect, and nonfinancial compensations given to employees. Direct compensations are payments for basic wages or salaries, overtime and holiday pay, profit sharing, stock options, and other types of performance-based bonuses. To have a positive motivational effect, direct compensation must be perceived by employees as a fair assessment of their contributions to the firm's success. It also must be in line with the direct compensation given to other employees with comparable abilities and performance records.

Indirect compensation provides employees with fringe benefits such as insurance, vacation pay, sick leave, pensions plans, and other benefits. Since most of the indirect compensation is given to all employees at particular organizational levels, they are no longer motivators, but hygiene factors (see Chapter Seven) that are taken for granted and which will affect behavior only when withdrawn. To be motivationally effective, indirect compensation must be controllable by top management and used to reward outstanding performance.

Nonfinancial rewards include desirable "extras" such as preferred office location, elaborate office furniture, assigned parking spaces, impressive titles, and private secretaries. If nonfinancial rewards satisfy personal needs, then they will be perceived as rewards and provide the stimulus for desired behavior.

BEHAVIORAL ASPECTS BY PERFORMANCE EVALUATION STEPS

The following steps are used to measure and evaluate performance. Each step has behavioral implications.

Preliminary Steps
1. Define the segments and activities to be controlled and the individuals associated with them.
2. Set performance criteria (policies, goals, and standards) for each organizational segment and activity.
3. Measure actual performance.

Performance Evaluation Steps
4. Compare actual performance with predetermined goals. Promptly report results to individuals responsible for segments and activities.
5. Determine operational and behavioral causes of unfavorable variances.
6. Reinforce desired behavior and act to prevent recurrence of undesired behavior.

Define Segments and Activities to be Controlled

If people are to be held accountable for their performance, their responsibilities first have to be clearly defined. If they are held accountable for activities over which they have no control, they may experience anxiety or frustration. Motivation may suffer and undesired behavior may result.

If an organization is not extremely careful in setting clear demarcation lines for responsibilities, no meaningful setting of performance goals or standards is possible. Performance evaluation is doomed to failure from the start.

To be effective in motivating employees, assigned responsibilities must conform to the following criteria:

1. Responsibility must be consistent with the authority that managers have over the revenues and/or expenses. Managers must have discretion over both revenues and expenses to be held accountable for profit. If managers have discretion only over costs, they should be judged only on their success or failure to operate within the budgetary constraints and standard cost goals.
2. The definition of responsibility must be accurate and fair. It should avoid overlapping responsibilities which often result in "buck-passing." The scope of each manager's responsibility and authority must be stated clearly.
3. To enhance operational control, the areas of responsibility assigned must be capable of measuring operational efficiency and effectiveness in the fulfillment of specific tasks. To evaluate actual performance, the system should use carefully developed current standards for predictable costs (e.g., product costs) and budget allowances for discretionary costs (e.g., advertising).
4. The performance evaluation criteria chosen must conform to the scope of assigned responsibilities. For example, cost center managers should be judged on their success in complying with the budget. Profit center managers should be evaluated on their success in reaching minimum rates of return on profits. Investment center managers should be evaluated on the outcome of their investment decisions in addition to their profits.

Set Performance Criteria

Top management must ensure that people are motivated to act in conformity with organizational goals. For this to occur, there must be congruence between individual goals and organizational goals. Goal congruence is affected by the procedures used to evaluate performance.

Most organizations no longer consider profit optimization as the single organizational goal. Today's enterprises strive for the attainment of multiple goals and establish performance criteria that are tailored to their multiple goal structure. Performance is evaluated in terms of "key result areas" such as profitability, market share, product leadership, utilization of human resources, and corporate citizenship.

Sometimes, the relative importance of these criteria (key result areas) is not clearly defined by top management. Any change in criteria must be communicated quickly and effectively. Sometimes, criteria compete against each other or may be incompatible, since the attainment of one precludes the attainment of the other. Managerial actions and decisions may result in positive contributions to the achievement of some criteria and negatively impact the achievement of others.

Measurability of Criteria

Profitability is a short-run criterion that is easily measured. Other criteria, such as product leadership, utilization of human resources, and corporate citizenship, are long-term and harder to quantify. Despite their measurement difficulties, they are likely to be as important as those criteria that are quantitative and easily measured.

It is likely that easily measured criteria will receive more attention from top management. If one criterion is perceived to receive more attention or weight in performance evaluation, managers will concentrate their efforts on the attainment of that goal and pay little attention to others. Concentration on short-run profitability may hinder the achievement of all other criteria and thereby seriously endanger future profitability.

Time Span on Resources and Expenses

Another problem inherent in multiple criteria performance evaluation concerns the different time spans involved in the flow of costs and benefits associated with each specific criterion. A long-range research project may be expensive in the short-run and provide little immediate benefit. Yet the long-range benefits, in the form of improved product leadership, operational efficiencies, and corporate citizenship, may favorably affect the operating results of the firm for many years. Because of the timing difference, performance measurement for particular periods may be seriously distorted.

Each of the difficulties mentioned above is significant in its own right. In combination, they pose a problem of enormous magnitude.

Companies frequently give mere lip service to their multiple goal structure and performance evaluation criteria and place undue emphasis on short-run profitability. As a result, they force managers to act against company interests. Thus, managers may favor projects that meet current-year profit goals and reject projects that would improve the company's technological leadership and utilization of human resources over the long-run. This tendency could, however, be counteracted by introducing trade-off rules that would attempt to reconcile long-range expenditures and benefits with the short-term goal of profit maximization without penalizing forward-planning managers.

Weights Assigned to Criteria

The assignment of relative weights and trade-off rules to the performance criteria is of crucial importance. They signal top management's preference and influence the behavior of lower-level managers.

If managers perceive, rightly or wrongly, that the emphasis is on the attainment of short-run criteria such as profitability and market share, they will restrain from actions and behavior that could jeopardize the possibility of reaching short-range sales quotas and other specific profit goals.

Performance Indices versus Performance Criteria

Performance criteria are companywide performance objectives based on the multiple goal structure of the firm. To evaluate the attainment of each performance objective by individuals and/or segments, quantitative measures or *indices of performance* must be established. Such indices include rates of return, residual income, earnings per share, asset utilization ratios, product profitability ratios, and others. Although such indices are extremely useful in performance evaluations, undesirable side effects may result if they are not carefully used.

Behavioral Aspects of Usage

Three different types of indices are used for measuring quantities. They are *single criterion* indices, which involves the measurement of only one quantity; *multiple criteria* indices, which simultaneously measure several quantities, and; *composite criteria* indices, which involve several separate quantities that are measured, weighted, and then averaged.

Single Criterion Measures (Indices).   Single criterion measures of performance may result in behavior that overemphasizes one single criterion to the exclusion of others that may be equally important to organizational success. If the single factor being measured is quantity of output, people will concentrate on that and neglect other major considerations such as quality, costs, maintenance of equipment, and human resources.

Many American corporations have established sophisticated overall performance objectives that reflect their multiple goal structures. Included as elements are profitability, market position, productivity, product leadership, personnel development, employee attitudes, public responsibility, and balance between short-range and long-range goals. Each of these areas represents a criterion by which the overall performance of divisional managers is evaluated.

It is possible that performance directed at one criterion (e.g., profitability) could conceivably have an unfavorable effect on other criteria (e.g., personnel development, employee attitudes, or public responsibility). This means that guidelines must be established for evaluating decisions that produce conflicting results.

Multiple Criteria Measures (Indices). The limitations inherent in single criteria indices have given way to increased use of multiple criteria measures that focus attention on several aspects of performance. However, multiple criteria measures also have behavorial weaknesses.

When using multiple criteria, people may commit their efforts, attention, and organizational resources to those activities that promise the greatest improvement in their overall standing when performance is evaluated. Firms must develop a composite measure that incorporates all the various performance criteria.

Without an overall composite measure of performance, people must rely on their own judgment to determine whether increased effort on one criterion will improve overall performance. It should be kept in mind that even with a composite measure, people may be working at cross-purposes because some criteria are contradictory to other criteria.

Composite Criteria Techniques. Since some goals are more important to the overall well-being of the organization than others, some firms have developed composite criteria techniques that place numerical ratings or different weights on each of the multiple measurement criteria.

Such weighting systems make it possible to combine the various criteria into a single composite measure of overall performance. This in turn raises a new set of human problems. When multiple criteria are used, pressure to improve one aspect of performance can be accommodated by reductions in efforts to attain other objectives. With a composite index, however, this is harder to accomplish since the reduction in any of the variables being measured will reduce the overall index. Increases in pressure in one area cannot be absorbed throughout the system, and the results of this increased pressure can trigger several unwanted behavioral reactions.

The behavioral impact of any quantitative performance measurement (whether it is single, multiple, or composite) depends upon the variables that it measures (its content) and the force with which it is applied (the rewards and/or punishments associated with it). Since the content of most indexes creates numerous complications, excessive force in applying any particular index has to be avoided. When using performance evaluation indexes, accountants must therefore continually reexamine their validity and appropriateness for the specific purpose. They must also be constantly aware of the possibility of unintended and undesirable behavioral responses by those evaluated.

Rate of Return on Investment. The most common index of profitability used by accountants in performance evaluation is return on investment. Although return on investment can be a worthwhile index of performance, the definition and calculation of this index involves numerous subjective accounting decisions that make the outcome much less precise than it appears to be at first glance.

Advantages.   Return on investment is determined by dividing net income by investment in assets. Conceptually, it is an ideal index because it relates accomplishments to resources. Because return on investment is a ratio measure, it can be used to compare the performance of different size firms. It induces managers to get the maximum sales out of each dollar invested or to reduce the investment. Attention is directed to profit margins, cost control, and efficiency in asset use.

Disadvantages.   There are many disadvantages. The definitions of *income* and *investment* can vary and will influence behavior. The investment figure can include all assets, assets available, or assets actually used. Further, assets can be valued using historical cost, standard costs, various calculations of net book value, or current cost. Some or all liabilities may be deducted from total assets. If long-term assets are included net of depreciation, then the depreciation method in use will affect the ratio.

Similarly, income could be defined in several ways. A shrewd manager whose objective is to maximize short-term return on investment can be expected to identify the specific set of variables used in the computation of the index and adjust his or her behavior accordingly.

Another problem associated with the use of the return-on-investment index is the tendency to place too much emphasis on it or to use it exclusively. This tendency may be caused by top management's failure to recognize the subjective nature of this index and by the difficulties associated with quantifying performance relative to other important goals. The return on investment figure for a given period highlights the accounting view of profitability for that single period.

Overemphasis on short-run profit maximization can lead to many dysfunctional consequences for the organization. For example, an expansion opportunity may be turned down because short-run incremental returns would not result in the arbitrary minimum rate of return set by top management. That the expansion would yield high returns in the future is ignored because of the index's short-run nature and emphasis.

The claim that this problem can be avoided by concentrating on long-range profits is a mere academic argument. A manager who dares to ignore the short-run profitability goals and justifies his or her actions in the light of long-run benefits will not be around long enough to experience the results of those long-range decisions.

If the rate of return on investment is used intelligently and its importance as a measure of performance is not overemphasized, the resulting influence on behavior need not create serious problems.

Residual Income.   Residual income is the excess of actual net income over desired net income, as measured by the imputed interest on capital employed. It has the same problems of income and investment measurement as does return on investment. Its use in measuring profitability of performance would not stifle expansion, but would induce segment managers to expand as long as the incremental returns from the expansion project exceed the charge for invested capital. Major companies, such as General Electric, favor this approach since they have observed that it induces their managers to concentrate on maximization of dollars of residual income rather than on a percentage of return. Maximization of dollar return in excess of the cost of invested capital has more meaning to managers; therefore it is a better motivator for inducing decisions of benefit for both the segments and the company as a whole.

Other Indices.   Other ratios may also produce counterproductive responses. The machinery/economy ratio, for example, is the relationship between maintenance cost and depreciation. The lower the ratio, the better. In order to reduce the ratio, people will be induced to retire machinery and equipment as early as possible since this would result in low maintenance costs. The fact that this action would at the same time result in high depreciation costs and lower profits is ignored.

Another example is the standard manufacturing cost/sales ratio. If the marketing department allows special discounts, manufacturing managers may complain that their cost control is jeopardized. One remedy for this situation would be to use list price rather than net price for the ratio. Another counterproductive inducement could result from the use of the factory efficiency ratio (production shipments/gross payroll) since it could obviously be improved by increasing order backlog, which might prove extremely costly and undesirable over the long run.

The key to the meaningful use of the indices and ratios in performance measurement and evaluation is to look at several of them to get a complete picture of performance and thus minimize undesirable side effects.

The impact that any particular performance measure may have on behavior is determined by the nature of the measurement and the strength with which it is applied. The more pressure is associated with a specific performance index, the more likely managers will concentrate on the index itself instead of making decisions that are in the best interest of the whole enterprise.

Short-run profitability measures such as the return-on-investment index are misused by many firms, especially when they adopt them without thoroughly understanding their potential behavioral consequences. When traditional accounting concepts are combined with autocratic styles of management in developing and applying short-run profitability measures, they focus too much attention on too few variables. Furthermore, the increasing use of computers and powerful data processing procedures has made it possible to apply dysfunctional measures with increasing efficiency.

Measurement Of Actual Performance

The next step in evaluating performance is measuring the actual results of the segments or activities. Although it appears on the surface to be an objective, repetitious, and routine activity, the measurement itself may trigger many dysfunctional responses. People will try to manipulate information to suit their own purposes. They do this by controlling the nature and timing of messages to produce favorable reactions from their superiors. In turn, superiors might enhance (highlight) or degrade (hide) certain aspects of the performance results received to suit their own needs. Some common types of such behavior are described in the paragraphs that follow.

Smoothing

Smoothing includes all activities used by managers to affect the flow of data. This may be done by accelerating or delaying messages. Managers may send messages in the current period concerning events that will occur in future periods or they may delay sending a message about current events until future periods. For example, expenses may be shifted between accounting periods. To avoid unfavorable budget or standard cost variances, managers may prematurely include revenue items that will be realized in a future period to reach a rewarded profit goal. The smoothing process may also operate in the opposite direction. To avoid huge, favorable budget variances in the current period, managers may include in the current period future expenses and defer current revenues to future periods where goal attainment seems doubtful. These types of manipulations may occur where performance above the stated goals is ignored when determining rewards. The widely published financial and reporting irregularities of the H. J. Heinz Company provided an excellent example of ongoing smoothing activities by division managers. To attain their budgeted performance goals, the managers induced their service suppliers to post-date their invoices at the end of the year. This practice remained undetected for quite some time since the suppliers' invoices were the only documentary evidence of the transactions.

Biasing

Another common data manipulation method is biasing, whereby managers select from a set of possible messages those likely to produce the most favorable picture of their performance. The variety of generally accepted accounting methods available provide ample opportunity for these types of activities.

Gaming

Manipulation of actual performance results can also be accomplished by exploiting various aspects of the superior-subordinate relationship. This activity is called gaming and refers to behavior where the sender acts to cause the desired message to be sent. If the superior sets the rules of the game (budget levels, cost standards, production quotas, rules for reward allocations), the subordinate chooses one of several possible actions that promise to maximize favorable impact. For example, at mid-month, a manager whose bonus is tied to quota attainment will be very concerned about reading the required output level; this may induce the manager to delay required maintenance to avoid production time losses and use overtime despite cost overruns. The inducement to gaming can be minimized by basing the rewards on more than one aspect of performance. To base the reward allocation on various aspects of performance will discourage overemphasis of one aspect to the detriment of all others.

Focusing and Illegal Acts

Other strategies through which senders can manipulate messages to suit their own selfish needs are focusing and illegal acts. Focusing occurs by highlighting favorable messages and hiding unfavorable ones. Performance evaluations based on multiple criteria are most susceptible to such practices. If segment managers perceive that goal attainment receives the highest weight by top management in performance evaluation and reward computations, they might resort to conspiracy. If a manager desperately needs certain services or equipment but has already exhausted the budgetary allowance, he or she might induce another manager who has available funds to get the needed service with the understanding of future reciprocation. The philosophy "I help you and you help me out of tight spots" is fairly common. Its practice may be undetected for quite some time. These practices would be illegal if they violate either organizational rules or public laws.

There are many cases of focusing. Workers may falsify data when quota fulfillment seems unattainable. Managers may restrict output to avoid higher future quotas. Very productive workers may be pressured by co-workers to slow down.

Illegal acts are not limited only to the production flow. Companies falsify cost and sales figures to increase net income to portray a more attractive impression to prospective investors. The fact that people are willing to take risks to violate organizational policies and/or public laws to "do their jobs" was the impetus for the Foreign Corrupt Practices Act.

The manipulations and distortions of performance measurement data can be discouraged through a behaviorally sophisticated internal control system, which can be reinforced through an effective operational auditing force (see Chapters Thirteen and Fourteen, "The Behavioral Dimensions of Internal Control" and "The Behavioral Patterns of Auditors" for more detail.) The chance of their occurrence will also be minimized through a well constructed accounting system capable of motivating desirable behavior and team spirit (see Chapter Seven on responsibility accounting).

Comparison of Actual and Expected Performance

The comparison of actual and expected performance is done through periodic performance reports. This feedback to managers is intended to pinpoint inefficiencies and efficiencies in performance.

For optimum impact, separate performance reports should be prepared for each segment, starting with those at the lowest hierarchy level. The relevant data should then be fed into summary reports at the next higher level. Performance reports should clearly distinguish between controllable and noncontrollable items. From a strictly motivational and performance evaluation viewpoint, only those cost and revenue items subject to the authority and responsibility of the specific segment manager should be considered. All costs and revenues not directly controllable at a specific level should be included in the performance report at the level at which they are controllable. If costs are included at the level at which they are charged to the products or services, but are not controllable, it should be only to make the segment managers aware of the full cost of operating their segments. The costs should not affect the evaluation of the manager's performance.

Performance reports should include all deviations or variances of actual performance from expectations. Both favorable and unfavorable variances signal to those in authority deviations from goal and suggest the need for investigation. To segment managers, they further pinpoint the areas in which they succeeded or failed in their attempts to comply with the predetermined goals. This will result in behavior reinforcements and/or modifications.

Performance reports showing all deviations or variances from expectation should be prepared at least monthly. Shorter time periods may be advisable in specific problem situations that require immediate attention and behavior modifications.

Performance reports should be geared to the needs and experiences of the users. Reports to top management should represent a readily comprehensible summary of the vital aspects of the operations. They should clearly identify major events and should be supported with sufficient detail to trace problem situations to their source. Reports to middle management or to individuals in charge of major divisions should include more detailed data, since these people are responsible for the day-to-day operations. Reports to lower level managers should be limited to those items over which they have direct authority. They must be simple, easily understandable, and perceived as relevant and useful in guiding day-to-day activities.

Since performance reports are prepared by accountants, they are predominantly tabulations of financial statistics. To make the reports understandable to users with no accounting background, many companies have found it beneficial to use charts and graphs in their presentation. The reported variances are more meaningful if they are expressed in both absolute amounts and in percentages of actual or budgeted goals.

Percentages and ratios give the evaluated managers a more common frame of reference and avoid possible misinterpretation of materiality and relativity of the variances. Behavorial research has also discovered that the order of variance presentation can affect user perception of the efficiency of the evaluated segment. In the minds of the users, listing the unfavorable variances first might "highlight" the negative aspects. Listing favorable variances first will "highlight" the positive and diffuse the negative.

Finally, variances should be reported for past and current periods (months or quarters) and on a cumulative basis to date. Footnotes should be used to explain known causes for specific deviations and to direct attention to conditions that require attention.

Analysis of Variances

Causes of variances must be found so that corrective and/or commendatory actions can be taken.

Both unsatisfactory and satisfactory conditions deserve management's attention and should be analyzed and interpreted. Unfavorable variances signal danger and require further investigation to discover their precise cause.

Favorable variances should receive similar attention, since they also have high informational content. They can be used to identify and reward exceptional performance or specific "know-how" and to indicate whether the goals were realistic. They might also explain inefficiencies in other areas.

One problem in determining the causes of variances is that managers and subordinates may not cooperate in the investigation. This may be caused by their perception that the evaluation process is a way to fix blame. Managers may feel threatened, act defensively, deny the shortcomings, or attempt to blame others. To avoid this type of reaction, managers have to be convinced that the evaluation process is searching for causes and is concerned with solving future problems and not with fixing blame for past unfavorable results.

To make the process of variance interpretation and cause detection behaviorally effective, individual and group conferences should be held at various management levels. The conferences should be used as joint problem solving sessions and active participation should be encouraged. Properly handled, these feedback conferences can be an effective control and management development tool. To have optimum impact, superiors should at all times exhibit a supportive and constructive attitude and refrain from publicizing and punishing failures.

Corrective Actions

The final step in the performance evaluation process is taking corrective actions to reinforce desirable behavior and modify undesirable behavior. Behaviors are the actions of people who produce results. Results are indicators of effectiveness, such as profit, quality of output, and sales levels. Organizations should evaluate both behavior and results simultaneously.

For example, sales personnel should not only be evaluated on their ability to reach sales quotas, but also on their persistence on tough accounts, their use of new sales techniques, and their successful cultivation of new clients.

Future results can be affected by reinforcing desired behavior and by modifying or discouraging undesired behavior through a performance-based reward system. To effectively motivate, the rewards must be perceived as closely linked to the attainment of organizational goals and task-oriented behavior. Motivation can be ex-ante, or based on the expectation of receiving the reward. It can be ex-post, based on giving a reward to reinforce or improve past performance.

The performance evaluation function of the accounting system provides most of the quantitative data for determining how, to whom, and for what rewards should be distributed or withheld. It also indicates the areas in which behavior modifications have to take place to enhance future health and growth.

BEHAVIORAL ASPECTS OF PERFORMANCE EVALUATION USING ACCOUNTING INFORMATION

Firms use accounting information alone or in conjunction with other information as the basis for evaluating segment and subordinate performance. The reasons for this are that accounting data are "hard" or objective rather than "soft" or subjective. They are one of the few objective measures of performance available.

People may react unfavorably to the performance data supplied by the accounting system for a number of reasons. The following sections outline such reasons.

The Relationship of the Organizational Structure to the Financial Reporting Structure

If organizational structure and reporting structure correspond, there is harmony between the managers' responsibilities and control over revenues and/or expenses. Performance evaluations will be perceived as fair and meaningful and will guide future behavior and aspirations. If managers are held responsible by the organizational structure for factors over which they have no control, they will ignore the performance reports and may even sabotage their preparation through manipulations and/or falsification of information.

These responses may also occur if the information provided by the accounting system does not adequately reflect the complexity of the underlying organizational and environmental conditions affecting performance.

To improve the motivational appeal of performance measurement and evaluation, performance reports should contain "need-to-know" information. They should only cover areas that the manager addressed is able and expected to control; those that cannot be controlled should be excluded from the report.

Unfavorable reactions are also caused by overlapping responsibilities. If two or more managers are responsible for the same factor, "buck passing," animosity, deterioration of cooperation, and inefficiency may result.

All those dysfunctional conditions could be minimized through a carefully constructed responsibility accounting system. (See Chapter Seven).

Degree of Participation in Standard Setting

People rarely object to performance evaluation per se. Hostile reactions are often triggered by unsuitable criteria used in performance evaluation or if the goal-setting and report formats are considered weak. For example, a manager may complain that: "This criteria tells only part of the story. If I strive to attain this goal, I will jeopardize my short-run profit performance and will not be around long enough to see the long-range profit benefits resulting from my efforts. Nobody ever asks us what goals are realizable. The budget allowances and cost standards were set by top management, who are not close enough to operations to understand our environmental and human resource limitations or the day-to-day tribulations I have to deal with. Why should I try to attain those goals when I know from the start that they are unattainable?"

To minimize these complaints and to encourage acceptance of budget goals and cost standards as realistic and fair, segment managers should participate in setting the measures used in their performance evaluation. If they have sufficient voice in determining budget goals and cost standards, they will perceive them to be reasonable, will accept them as legitimate, and will try to attain them (for more details, see Chapter Eight and Nine, "The Behavioral Aspects of Profit Planning and Budgeting," and Chapter Ten, "The Behavioral Aspects of Accumulating and Controlling Costs").

Level of Understanding of the Accounting System

Since performance data supplied by accounting entail every phase of organizational activity, the people controlled by them should have a good understanding of the methods used in their accumulation: budgeting, standard cost setting, and the process of setting performance goals.

The more managers understand the system, the greater the likelihood of effective functioning. Ignorance of the composition and objectives of the accounting control and performance evaluation system may result in mistrust, anxiety, and excess tension. People feel threatened by things they do not understand, and may fight back in unreasonable and destructive ways.

DIAGNOSTIC REVIEW OF
BUSINESS DILEMMA

Amex, Inc. has a complex and sophisticated performance evaluation system. It uses both subjective ratings and accounting data to motivate employees to act in ways beneficial to and compatible with organizational objectives and corporate characteristics such as those listed on page 190.   Through its reward linkage, the performance system emphasizes top management's concern for the quality of personal performance, goal attainment, and short-term profitability. The weight assigned to each performance criterion in the reward computations communicates clearly top management's priorities for the various levels of managers. Since goal attainment receives the heaviest weight at the profit center level, the company intends to induce strict adherence to budgeted cost and revenue goals. It obviously envisions the goal-setting or budgeting process as the core of operational control and the major tool for inducing desirable behavior.

Unfortunately, it appears that the goal-setting or budgeting phase is precisely where many of the problems occur. The company adheres to participative management practices and gives its center managers great freedom in setting their performance goals. The weakness of the review process observed by Miller, however, induces excessive padding in standard and budgetary goal setting. Since no serious effort seems to be made to detect or discourage these practices, segment managers perceive them as tolerated. This perception is further supported by the fact that goal attainment is heavily rewarded, while non-attainment is punished. That it would be very difficult, if not impossible, for division managers to review the large number of line items and standard cost goals thoroughly is no excuse. A periodic review on a sample basis would have the same deterring effect. Segment managers would refrain from excessive budget padding if there was the possibility that they would have to justify the goals in a review interview with their superiors. Extreme care should, however, be taken in such review sessions to arrive at goals that give segment managers the chance to fail once in a while without the threat of instant punishment (a reduction in their bonus payments).

Group and corporate management should also investigate the propriety of the standard cost goals in use for manufacturing costs per output unit. If Miller's suspicion that they are also highly overstated is correct, the whole standard cost system could be rendered impotent. It would no longer be of practical value in operational control and performance evaluation and would represent only a waste of funds and energy. If all the reported favorable variances from standard costs had been periodically analyzed for detailed causes, the standard cost overstatements would have been discovered automatically and could have been corrected.

There is no indication that the material unfavorable budget variances were analyzed as to specific causes. Miller did not mention any such procedure, nor any remedial actions taken to rectify operational deficiencies or to modify present behavior patterns if they are identified as the cause of inefficiencies. If in reality such follow-up does not exist, management is deprived of the most important benefit of performance measurement and evaluation. Managers will not know what actually went wrong or how they can avoid future recurrence of the same problem through operational changes and behavior modifications.

Furthermore, it seems advisable to review the behavioral benefits of the relative weights assigned to the various performance criteria. To diffuse somewhat the widespread perception at the profit center level that goal achievement is an absolute necessity and has to be attained at all costs, the weight assigned to this criterion should be lowered. The weight assigned to goal attainment at the divisional level should probably also be reevaluated. At its present level, it clearly induces divisional managers to tolerate excessive budget padding and possibly even manipulation of input data by plant managers. These are practices that should be discouraged in the interest of improving efficiency and profitability.

Miller discovered various other apparent contradictions and dysfunctional behavior patterns in his review of the performance evaluation system. For those that were perceived as dilemma situations requiring analytical attention, we offer the following diagnosis and suggestions for remedial actions.

Miller's main concern in regard to sales and market share trends was that the performance evaluation system appeared dysfunctional because it forced sales managers to sacrifice the long-range goal of market share increase, and thus profit improvement, to comply with short-term budget constraints. It is true that long-range criteria, such as industrial leadership, and long-range profitability are not part of the short-run performance evaluation process and go unrewarded at the plant and division level. This, however, does not mean that coporate is ignoring them. The company's position as an industry leader and expert in the field, as well as its reputation for training conservative but well-rounded managers, attests to the contrary. However, all long-range performance goals seem to be determined strictly by corporate. The services necessary for their attainment, such as advertising and research and development, are offered in a centralized fashion at the corporate level and at quantities and costs determined by top management during the budgeting process. Another example of this practice would be acquisitions for expansion, for which the short-term allowances are also filtered down through the budgeting process. That great attention is given to determining short-run allowances for the attainment of long-range goals is evidenced by the fact that in various areas zero-base budgeting is in use. Compliance with short-run allowances for long-range goals is monitored and rewarded at segment levels. Top management's philosophy is obviously: "We determine the scope of the short-term activities necessary to implement our long-range goals; you, segment managers, comply with our instructions!"

Miller also observed among segment managers widespread hesitancy to place doubtful accounts in the suspense category. As a reason for this unconservative behavior, they cited the adverse impact on short-term profitability and goal attainment caused by the reserve needs. Here, the incentive payout clearly becomes the overriding factor to proper accounting valuation, which in turn affects the determination of capital employed and its rate of return. To rectify this dysfunctional situation, it may be advisable for corporate to selectively assume responsibility for collection of unusual bad debts or those of a material size. Such an approach would recognize that some credit problems are not controllable by the profit center and are detrimental to a center's ability to function in a "normal" environment. Because profit center managers would no longer need to protect themselves by misrepresenting data, they could concentrate on improving performance by "legitimate" means.

If there is really widespread mistrust of the benefits of the various centrally provided services and if segment managers are bickering about the fairness of the cost allocations, Amex is faced with a very serious dysfunctional situation that calls for a thorough investigation. Judging from the consolidated goal structure (see Table 11-1), corporate overhead is grouped into direct and indirect. Only the allocated-direct overhead portion adds to the costs used in determining profit center operating profit, which represents their incentive measurement point. The allocated-indirect is used in determining earnings before tax and does not affect the rewarded profitability of the profit centers. Miller does not tell us what basis is used for the allocation of the direct portion. To be behaviorally satisfactory, the formula should be based on some measure of usage. Profit center managers should be consulted in the choice and convinced of its fairness to everybody concerned. If no satisfactory allocation formula can be found, Amex might charge a transfer price for the services consumed based on competitive bids by outside providers. Before such drastic changes are made, it should be kept in mind that such steps would alter the status of the provider unit from a cost center to a profit center. Further, the practice of billing for the services, instead of merely allocating their cost, would result in substantial increases in clerical and accounting costs.

Of the three ratios in use, only return on capital employed is rewarded. The two others are treated as supplementary measures to monitor liquidity and inventory turnover, as well as to control bad debts and capital employed, a procedure that seems quite logical. The only substantial weakness in ratio use is the obvious ignorance of segment managers about the impact of inventory turnover on their ROCE.

Management would not need to "hoot and holler" if all managers understood the importance of this ratio. That no minimums for segmental ROCE are set is immaterial from a motivational viewpoint, since the budgeted ROCE, determined on the basis of short-range cost and revenue goals, serves as such.

Conclusions

Despite various minor flaws, the performance evaluation system of Amex, Inc. is well thought-out, technically quite sophisticated, and behaviorally sound. It communicates management's priorities well and effectively reinforces cost consciousness, compliance with predetermined goals, and behavior rules.

The overall strength of the company proves that the system, despite its minor faults, works well. Cash flow is excellent in good economic times and thus capable of accumulating sufficient funds for the down times. While the average cycle ROCE is not as strong as it could be, there is evidence that the inclusion of ROCE as a performance criterion has a positive impact on profit center awareness of the need to generate an acceptable return.

By discouraging the dysfunctional practice of excessive padding in the goal setting stage, people will be motivated to improve the efficiency of their operations, which in turn will result in increased operational profits and ROCE.

SUGGESTED READINGS

Hopwood, Anthony G. "Problems with Using Accounting Information in Performance Evaluation." *Management International Review*, 1973, Nos. 2-3. pp. 83-91.

Hopwood, Anthony G. "Leadership Climate and the Use of Accounting Data in Performance Evaluation." *The Accounting Review* (July 1974): pp. 485-495.

Hopwood, Anthony G. "The Role of Accounting Data in the Evaluation of Performance." *Accounting and Human Behavior*, Englewood Cliffs, N.J.: Prentice-Hall, 1976, pp. 95-119.

Hopwood, Anthony G. "An Empirical Study of the Role of Accounting Data in Performance Evaluation." *Empirical Research in Accounting: Selected Studies*. 1982. Supplement to *Journal of Accounting Research*. Institute of Professional Accounting, University of Chicago.

Kerr, Steven. *Organizational Behavior*. Columbus, Ohio: Grid Publishing Co., Second Edition, 1983.

Kida, Thomas E. "Performance Evaluations and Review Meetings: Characteristics in Public Accounting Firms." *Accounting, Organizations and Society,* Pergamon Press Ltd., Great Britain, 9, no.2, 1984.

Podsakoff, Philip H. "Determinants of a Superior's Use of Rewards and Punishments: A Literature Review and Suggestions for Further Research." *Organizational Behavior and Human Performance* 29, 1983.

Ridgeway, V. F. "Dysfunctional Consequences of Performance Measurements." *Administrative Science Quarterly* 1, no. 2 (Sept. 1956).

Robbins, Stephen P. *Organizational Behavior: Concepts, Controversies and Applications*. Prentice-Hall, Inc., Englewood Cliffs, N.J. 1983.

Sauser, William I. "Evaluating Employee Performance: Needs, Problems and Possible Solutions." *Public Personnel Management* (Jan./Feb. 1980).

Wexler, Kenneth N. "Performance Appraisal and Feedback." *Organizational Behavior*, ch. 10, edited by Stephen Kerr. Columbus, Ohio: Grid Publishing Co., 1979.

DISCUSSION QUESTIONS

1. Why is it important to have performance evaluation, and in what ways is it beneficial to an organization?
2. How can motivation be used as a tool for promoting operational efficiency?
3. What are the basic premises on which the expectancy theory of motivation is built? In what ways does it affect behavior?
4. Define positive reinforcement, negative reinforcement, and punishment. Which of these is most effective in an organizational setting?
5. What is the difference between intrinsic and extrinsic rewards? How are they used for effective motivation?

6. What are the steps involved in the measurement and evaluation of performance? Why are these important?

7. What are some "key result areas" other than profitability upon which performance is evaluated? What would result if the relative importance of these criteria is not clearly defined by top management?

8. What are some of the factors that have to be taken into consideration when performance is evaluated in terms of "key result areas"?

9. How do multiple criteria measures differ from composite criteria measures? What must be considered when they are used to evaluate performance?

10. Define rate of return on investment. What are some of the disadvantages when this index is used for performance evaluation?

11. What do you understand about smoothing? How is it used to manipulate performance?

12. What are some of the factors that result in unfavorable reactions to the performance data supplied by the accounting system? Why do these result?

CASE 11-1

The Company

A large commercial bank follows the philosophy of maintaining close customer relationships through its credit officers. These officers are trained in all areas of banking but are specialists in commercial lending. In recent years, the bank's customers have increasingly sought additional assistance on non-credit services: cash management, trade financing, and capital markets. To serve these needs, the bank developed specialists in these areas to work with the credit officers. Thus, the bank expects its credit officers to serve customers' credit or lending needs and also to market the noncredit services by providing necessary introductions and follow-up with the specialists until consulting fees are received by the bank.

The bank's upper management requires a detailed quarterly review of each functional area based on performance reports prepared by the management accounting group. The performance reports contain basic balance sheet and income statement data by area and highlight that area's contribution to the bank's overall earnings.

The Dilemma

In recent months, the credit officers have been reluctant to spend any time or effort on marketing noncredit services. They feel that since the revenue resulting from these services does not appear in their quarterly performance reports, they get no recognition for their marketing efforts. With the end of the year approaching, they are putting all of their efforts into credit services since these are included in their year-end results and will receive attention from upper management.

As a result, the noncredit areas are introduced to fewer business prospects and generate less fee revenue. The noncredit areas, also concerned with their performance, use their management accounting performance reports to review their contribution to earnings. Management obviously must find more realistic means to evaluate both types of areas through the management accounting reports so that both groups will be motivated to work harmoniously together.

Required:

1. What steps would you take to resolve the dilemma?

CASE 11-2

The Company

ABC Company is a large advertising agency located in Chicago. All clients are furnished monthly estimates for the various advertising services to be rendered and some of them record them on their books on that basis to facilitate timely monthly reporting. An accounting manager assigned to each client is responsible for accounts receivable and payable, as well as for the estimates and billings to the client.

One client, a large consumer goods manufacturer, has nine different agencies representing various products. Since the client deals with so many agencies, it gives out "report cards" to the agencies twice a year, indicating their performance against other agencies. They are ranked from 1 to 9 with 1 being the best. The agency's performance on these report cards is based entirely on the accuracy of the estimates that are sent out every month. In a perfect world, the estimates would exactly match the billings sent to the client, but this is rarely the case.

The Dilemma

The accounting manager in the advertising agency is becoming very frustrated by these "report cards" because the client uses the estimates as some sort of "bible," even though many things may have changed by the time the billing is sent out. Last month, for example, many T.V. spots were missed because of special reports dealing with earthquakes in Mexico and a hostage situation.

Those spots will not be billed to the client, even though they are on the estimate. Also, stations will often send the invoice to the wrong agency. Last month, a newspaper sent an invoice for $40,000 to the wrong agency, who held onto it for a while before sending it back. By the time the invoice got to ABC, the billing date had passed and the client called and asked why the invoice for the $40,000 was not included.

Even though these situations are not the manager's fault, the agency's "grade" suffers because of these unavoidable events.

Required:

1. The accounting manager is a friend of yours and she takes your advice. What would you tell her to help her avoid such frustrating experiences in the future?

CASE 11-3

The Company

The Zillicom Company is organizationally divided into three major product groups. Each product group is headed by a vice-president and is further subdivided into several product divisions. Each division is headed by a division general manager and is a semi-autonomous business.

To achieve goal congruence, the company president defines divisional operating goals in terms of overall corporate goals. Division performance is regularly evaluated in terms of short-range and long-range criteria as follows: profitability, market share, product leadership, utilization of human resources, and corporate citizenship.

Each division set its own sales targets and develops its own requests for operating funds and capital. Sales targets and budget requests are reviewed by the divisions' respective vice-presidents. The vice-presidents do not have authority to change the division's proposals, but since they can change division personnel, they can and do exert pressure. The divisions are formally reviewed by their respective group vice-presidents each quarter and by the corporate review board once a year. The review board also has final say on budget requests.

The Dilemma

One division head, manager M, has been with the company for fourteen years and in charge of the division for five years. His performance during the first three years was regarded as excellent. However, for the last two years, M's division fell short of realizing its profit goals.

In developing next year's profit plan, M is faced with three proposals for capital investments. Because of the size of the outlay, he can choose only one investment (assume the outlays are approximately the same).

Proposal 1

The proposal recommends the introduction of a new production process that will reduce manufacturing costs over a three-year period. However, the original outlay required will be treated as a period expense, creating the distinct possibility that the division's profit goals for the next year will again not be met.

Proposal 2

This proposal recommends the purchase of a new machine that will reduce manufacturing costs over a five-year period, but the total reduction will be less than in Proposal 1. The capital outlay involved will be amortized over five years, thus reducing the burden of expense for the next period.

Proposal 3

This investment involves research into an area that, if successful, will benefit not only M's division, but other firms in the industry and other divisions of the company as well. No return is expected on this project until the fourth year. Profit is not projected until the sixth year.

Required:

1. Which proposal should M choose to satisfy as many performance evaluation criteria as possible?

CASE 11-4

The Company

Henry Harrison is the research analyst in the personnel development and training department of the J.L.D. Corporation. This corporation has 9,000 employees and is headquartered in Chicago. There are eight divisions in various sections of the country with sales offices in many of the large cities. The director of the personnel development and training department requested that Harrison review the performance evaluation system and recommend any improvements or changes.

The Dilemma

Harrison was aware that all employees were appraised once a year by their superiors and that these evaluations were then reviewed by the next higher-ranking supervisor. The evaluation procedure occurs up to the level of senior vice-president. At the department/division level, appraisal begins with the director being evaluated by the vice-president. All of the director's subordinates are evaluated and the process continues through the lowest-ranking employee of the department/division.

Each appraisal begins with a review of the goals established in the prior year's session to determine goal attainment. The goals are mutually agreed upon between the employee and supervisor. Each goal is required to flow directly from the duties and responsibilities contained in the employee's job description.

Performance expectations are established for each goal. These expectations should answer the questions: "What specific work results are expected?" "How will we recognize that the goal has been accomplished effectively?" These standards establish criteria for subsequent evaluations.

A mutually agreed-upon index value is attached to each goal to reflect its priority and importance relative to the employee's duties. At the yearly appraisal, the supervisor determines the extent to which the goal has been accomplished based on the performance expectation. Points are awarded for the percentage of goal accomplishment.

In this meeting, the supervisor evaluates the employee's general work activities, which are based on general criteria established by headquarters to standardize evaluation procedures throughout the company. Not all activities in any one category apply to a particular position. The activities are grouped under the following categories: *customer service, sales, rate, and market analysis; revenue collections; accounting and information management; office services, planning, and budget management; personnel management; and material management*. These activities are rated on a scale of 1 (rarely meets expectations) to 7 (rare level of expertise that far exceeds expectations).

Finally, the new goals and standards for the following year are established. Completed forms are delivered to the reviewing officer and a subsequent meeting between the subordinate and immediate supervisor is scheduled. After this conference, the immediate supervisor retains one copy of the goals for the following year, one copy of the goals is given to the employee, and the evaluation form is placed in the individual's personnel file at headquarters.

Salary review can occur twice a year and merit increases are determined by the supervisor as long as the increase does not violate salary administration guidelines established by headquarters. Individual personnel files are not available for review by supervisors. When a vacancy occurs, the human resource information system from headquarters provides a list of candidates to supervisors. This listing shows present job status, results on standard tests, education, and other qualifications. Performance evaluations are not entered in the human resource system.

An executive bonus plan has been implemented with the participants determined by top management. The main criterion for participation is present job title, which also determines the division of the bonus, with higher job status receiving a large percentage of the bonus. The total bonus is based on the profits of the corporation for the year. Once an individual becomes a member of the plan, he or she is rarely removed.

Required:

1. What changes might Harrison recommend to his superior?

CASE 11-5

The Company

A large electronics firm has a sales force located throughout the United States. Salespeople are evaluated annually on their overall performance by their individual supervisors, the regional sales managers (RSMs). Informal reviews are also given to these salespeople quarterly. Because these progress sessions are informal, they give the salesperson a chance to discuss any problems or possible opportunities with the RSM.

The yearly evaluation is divided into two parts—one subjective and the other objective. The subjective portion evaluates personal qualities such as leadership and organizational skills. The objective portion is divided into planned sales projections and budgeted expenses. Planned sales shows where the sales dollars are generated by account and the percentage change from the previous year. The budgeted expense section contains the actual dollars that each salesperson is allocated for entertainment and travel in assigned territory.

The planned sales percentages are determined from a corporate forecast and sent to the RSMs for their sales personnel. The RSM then sits down with the salesperson at the beginning of the year to determine which portion of the forecasted plan will fit into the salesperson's accounts. The bonuses and raises that the salespeople and RSMs receive are determined by the success of meeting the sales quotas while keeping expenses within budget.

The Dilemma

Unattainable sales volumes are sometimes forced upon the RSMs and their salespeople by management's demand for a percentage increase across the board with no flexibility. The salespeople become very "unmotivated" when such an increase is unrealistic and practically impossible to obtain within their business environment, especially since they affect many of the criteria upon which they are evaluated. In addition to this, the salespersons' willingness to look for new sales is gone because they are spending all of their time just trying to increase sales from their existing accounts.

Required:

1. What are the behavioral weaknesses of the company's performance evaluation system?

CASE 11-6_____

The Company

Main Bank is a medium-size bank in St. Louis with $220 million in assets. Its loan portfolio is $135 million, with $125 million concentrated in commercial loans. Sixty-six percent of the bank's total income is derived from interest and fees on loans. The commercial division has four calling officers that report to the vice-president of commercial banking. The lending officers' primary responsibilities are maintaining the loan portfolio and developing new commercial loan business. In addition to this, each officer is expected to cross-sell other bank services such as cash management, trust accounts, investment, and discount brokerage services.

The Dilemma

The officers are reviewed annually by the vice-president of lending. Their performance evaluation is a subjective appraisal of each individual's performance. Each officer is rated on a scale of 1 to 5 (5 being the highest) based on the following criteria: communication, leadership, decision making, administration, and working relationships. Promotions and raises are based on these factors.

Because the performance criteria is subjective, the feedback the officer is given on his or her evaluation is subjective. Individual motivation to change behavior is difficult because of the subjectiveness of the criteria. Responsibilities do not match performance criteria.

Required:

1. How should the performance evaluation be changed to better define the criteria and standards by which an officer is appraised?

CASE 11-7

The Company

The Second Bank and Trust is a large regional bank headquartered in Los Angeles. With assets of nearly $7 billion, Second ranks as one of the 50 largest banks in the country. Highly regarded in the banking industry, Second has always prided itself on attracting and keeping highly qualified people at the officer level and above.

In recent years, as banking has become more competitive, Second has instituted a new performance evaluation system for officers of the bank.

All personnel at the officer level and above are given an annual performance review at the June 30 close of the fiscal year. At the review session, usually held in August, individuals meet one-on-one with their immediate supervisors to discuss actual performance versus the goals set for the previous fiscal year.

Criteria used to judge quantitative performance include:

- Loan commitments, outstanding
- Deposits
- Fee income
- Calls, call mix
- Cross-selling of other bank services
- Maintenance of account relationships
- Average profitability (ROE) of portfolio

In addition, communication skills, job knowledge, organizational abilities, and other subjective factors are also reviewed.

Prior to the review session, each individual is given an evaluation form identical to the one the manager uses to record the actual evaluation. The individual details actual versus budgeted goals on the form and submits it to the manager. The manager has meanwhile done the same with input received from his or her superior.

At the review session, the results are compared, but differences between the forms are rarely noted on the manager's form. Each performance category is assigned a rating (exceeded, met, not met), weighted, and combined with the subjective factors to yield an overall rating of 5 (outstanding) to 1 (poor).

For salary administration purposes, the rating is then entered into a matrix to determine the individual's pay increase (see Table 11-2).

The salary range maximum represent a premium salary for a position and also the maximum amount that will be paid for a particular position. Therefore, individual employee salaries may not be increased beyond the salary range maximum.

As noted in Table 11-2, total salary increases are limited to an overall percentage increases over the previous year's salary levels. Individual loan groups are also presented with a total salary increase limit.

The Dilemma

Second Bank and Trust has experienced a large amount of employee turnover, concentrated at the vital first two officer levels. As a result, a large and growing number of its revenue-generating staff is composed of young,

---

TABLE 11-2
Individual Adjustment Guidelines

| Current rating | POSITION ON SALARY RANGE | | | |
	1st quartile and below	2nd quartile	3rd quartile	4th quartile
(within 12 months prior to increase date)				
5	9–15%	7–13%	5–11%	4–10%*
4	7–11%	6–10%	5–9%	4–8%*
3	5–9%	4–8%	3–7%	2–6%*
2	0–4%	0–4%	0%	0%
1	0%	0%	0%	0%
Missing	0%	0%	0%	0%

*Limited to range maximum

To assist departments in determining individual salary increases and to ensure salary administration equity throughout the organization, this matrix is provided for 19-1. Departments will be given a specific dollar budget figure for their merit and market adjustments. This figure is determined by applying the overall 8 percent approved by the board to the department's year-end salary base.

relatively inexperienced people, which is a definite disadvantage in the highly competitive markets Second has targeted as desirable.

Required:

1. Did the evaluation system cause the high turnover? If so, what modifications would you suggest?
2. Is the performance evaluation system behaviorally sound?

CASE 11-8

The Company

XYZ is a telecommunications company that has recently been ordered to divest by the federal government. The company has since undergone many reorganizations. Currently, there are various divisions of XYZ. Within the divisions are lines of businesses (LOBs) and sublines of businesses (sub-LOBs). The sub-LOBs are controlled and administered by product managers.

The product managers are responsible for overseeing many functions associated with their products, such as production, distribution, sales, accounting, billing, and repair. Although they do not have direct control over any of these functional areas, they can at times make requests or apply enough pressure for their needs to be met.

The Dilemma

The product managers' performance is evaluated on a very subjective basis. Based on their performance results, they are grouped on a numerical scale from the highest to the lowest in the group. For example, if 20 individuals were evaluated, they will be ranked from 1 (the lowest) to 20 (the highest performer). Goals and objectives are established at the beginning of the performance evaluation period to produce a high-quality product, to increase sales, to lower the cost of manufacturing, and to provide timely repair services.

The product managers are very unhappy with this evaluation method. As mentioned, the product managers have no direct control over many of the functional areas. They can make specific requests for what they require to meet their goals and objectives, but they have no guarantee that their requests will be granted. Accurate, detailed data are not available. For example, the product manager may never know what the true sales of his or her product are for a specified period of time. There are many organizations working to resolve the problem, but it is a very long process.

The result is that the product managers are evaluated on a very subjective basis. Many factors enter into their evaluation, but these factors do not necessarily indicate how well or poorly they managed their product. They are very unhappy with this process and would like a more equitable evaluation method to be established.

Required:

1. What steps would you take to overcome the motivational deficiencies of the present performance evaluation system?

CASE 11-9

The Company

Marconi, Inc. is an engineering firm that employes about 350 people. The company is run by 25 partners (engineers) and is divided into three divisions: mechanical, electrical, and structural. Each division has about 50 engineers and 65 support personnel. Marconi is mainly involved in the development of computers and other communication equipment.

The employees are evaluated at the end of every year to determine raises and promotions. The support personnel are evaluated using standardized forms, which are filled out by their immediate supervisors. These forms request ratings of job performance and attitude. The forms have a scale that goes from 1 (outstanding performance) to 5 (poor performance), and the supervisors check the rating that they feel is appropriate. Once the forms are filled out, they are passed on to the division heads, who are responsible for all raises and promotion decisions. The engineers, on the other hand, meet with and are evaluated by one of the partners. The meetings are informal and unstructured. Generally, these meetings wind up being more of a social event than a discussion of job performance. After this meeting, the partner decides upon the amount of the raise and/or the promotion.

Morale at the firm is low and office politicking is prevalent. Support personnel do not know, except through gossip, about how their performance was evaluated by their supervisors. Certain engineers have adopted a "cut-throat" attitude and camaraderie among the engineers has almost disappeared.

The Dilemma

The partners have noticed the deteriorating morale. To correct this, they have decided to concentrate on making the work atmosphere a pleasant one. The partners have come up with several ideas to improve the situation. Among these are an across-the-board pay increase, an employee newsletter to highlight individual and firm achievements, and a variety of social activities (e.g., a golf outing and a company picnic) to promote company unity.

They have hired a personnel manager, Pat Sloan, to take care of the details of their plans. After spending time talking with some of the employees, Sloan feels that none of the plans suggested by the partners will provide a permanent or long-term solution to the problem.

Sloan is scheduled to meet with the partners and fill them in on the details of the plans but is not sure how they will feel if given this view of the situation. Sloan's dilemma is deciding whether to rock the boat and risk losing her job or to say nothing to the partners and follow through with their suggestions.

Required:

1. If you were the personnel manager, how would you proceed? Elaborate on your reasons for whatever action you advocate.

CHAPTER 12

A Behavioral Interpretation of Decentralization

by
Shahid Ansari
Professor of Accounting
California State University, Northridge

BUSINESS DILEMMA

Please don't misunderstand. It is nice to be out of the office and back in the field. Also, Sharjah is a nice change of scenery from Lahore. However, I am afraid that I will be held accountable by Mr. Z. for all the problems that will accrue during my absence from Lahore. The head office in Karachi does not understand that Lahore is seriously short of trained managerial staff. With me in Sharjah, there is no one who can take charge effectively.

The speaker was Mr. K., a senior executive of the POLKA group of companies. The listener was Mr. A., senior director and founding member of the POLKA group. POLKA initially started in 1972 as an ice cream manufacturing company in Lahore—a city in northern Pakistan. This plant was capable of supplying ice cream from Lahore (near the Indian border) to the Khyber Pass (near the Afghanistan border)—a radius of nearly 500 miles. The idea for an ice cream plant was the brainchild of Mr. A., who was actively assisted by his brother, Mr. Z., in getting it off the ground. The plant was an immediate success because of a creative marketing and distribution effort. In 1975, the group set up its second ice cream plant in Karachi to cover the southern half of Pakistan. The Karachi plant made POLKA the largest manufacturer of ice cream in Pakistan.

By 1978, the POLKA group had expanded in two different directions. They set up a plant to produce packaging materials for use in ice cream, cereals, cigarettes, and other products. Only a small fraction of the packaging capacity was needed for ice cream and the rest was planned for external sales. They also set up an ice cream plant in the oil-rich sheikdom of Sharjah—a part of the United Arab Emirates. By early 1980, both the packaging plant and the Sharjah ice cream plant were scheduled to start production. Mr. Z was responsible for Pakistan's operations while Mr. A moved to Sharjah to look after the operations there.

The conversation described above took place in early 1980 between Mr. A and Mr. K. The latter, a dairy engineer by training, had been brought in from Lahore (where he was senior manager of operations) to help with the installation of the ice cream plant in Sharjah. Mr. K went on to add the following to his earlier reported comments:

> While you are in the process of explaining my predicament to Mr. Z, will you also ask him why the packaging plant recently sent us such poor quality packaging material. We are paying market prices for their materials and yet the quality is far inferior to what we can buy locally at much lower prices. I understand they are part of the group, but their poor quality and delivery have had an adverse affect on our operations in Lahore and now in Sharjah.

Shortly after this conversation, Mr. A sat down with the case writer to describe some of the problems of the POLKA group.

> You see, we have enjoyed a phenomenal rate of growth in the past few years. In the process, we have not had time to think through the organizational ramifications. The result is that we find ourselves operating as a functional organization—We borrow functional specialists such as Mr. K where needed, and yet require them to have line responsibilities in the interim. The family organization has resulted in a failure to draw up a clear charter so that key top personnel are confused about the lines of communication and reporting and too much authority is still vested in the family members. The transactions between the packaging and ice-cream plants are a constant source of friction and I am somewhat at a loss about what to do. Having functional specialists like Mr. K or Mr. H, our sales manager, available for trouble-shooting when needed, saves us the cost of having people in the organization perform the same function. Similarly, I know that once the packaging plant is off the ground, it will be able to produce the requisite quality at less than market prices. In the meantime, we have to find a way of resolving these disputes so the packaging plant is not killed before it gets a chance to stabilize. We also need a system for measuring performance of the various units to evaluate how they are doing. In short, some form of reorganization is clearly called for.

TO DECENTRALIZE OR NOT

The problem described above is not unique to the POLKA group. More than one growing company has faced the problem of having to reorganize in the face of growth, contraction, or change. One dimension of organizational restructuring which has received considerable attention is the centralization/decentralization dichotomy. In most circumstances, this is understood as the hierarchical level at which decisions are made in an organization.

The purpose of this chapter is to examine the behavioral prerequisites for successful decentralization in organizations. Two main themes are developed in this chapter. First, decentralization is a philosophical attitude and a behavioral response to the needs of an environment. Second, effective decentralization requires setting up an appropriate organizational structure devising a charter which lays down operating rules for participants and following up periodically with appropriate performance measures. A set of normative guidelines will be developed to aid organizations such as the POLKA group in moving toward decentralization.

Some specific questions addressed in this chapter are: What does decentralization mean in the context of business organization? What are the conditions that create a need for decentralization? How does decentralization enable organizations to reach desired ends? What are the different types of decentralized structures from which one can choose? How does one develop the appropriate charter within which decentralized sub-units will operate? In what ways does headquarters control the operations of decentralized units? How does one measure the performance of decentralized units?

The remainder of this chapter is divided into six sections. The first section examines the many ways in which the term decentralization is used and offers a definition of the term. The next section presents a model explaining the conditions that lead to the need for decentralization. The three sections that follow discuss the three key steps in decentralizing—choosing structures, charters, and measures. The main conclusions and some guidelines that organizations can use for effective decentralization are offered and applied to POLKA in the final section.

THE MEANING OF DECENTRALIZATION

The term decentralization is used in a large and diverse body of literature. As such, it has come to mean different things to different people. To restrict the scope of this chapter, decentralization is discussed only in the context of business firms. Even here, decentralization assumes several meanings. The most popular definition of decentralization is the one provided by H.A. Simon:

> An administrative organization is centralized to the extent that decisions are made at relatively high levels in the organization; decentralized to the extent that decisions are delegated by top management to lower levels of executive authority.[1]

While in theory the above definition is straightforward, in practice, it is difficult to implement. This is primarily because the concept of an identifiable decision is a nebulous one. For instance, it may be difficult to identify a particular hierarchic level at which a decision is made because formal authority does not correspond to the reality of who makes decisions. As March and Simon[2] point out, decisions are not made; they simply filter up to a manager after being adapted, changed, or added to in different stages. Mintzberg et al.[3] present a similar view of decisions, while March and Olsen[4] question the central concept of decision making by characterizing organizational decision making as solutions in search of problems. A related viewpoint asserts that in many instances the ability to define a problem is more important than formal decision-making authority since the agenda dictates the choice of solutions. Finally, the use of standard operating procedures, search routines, professionalization, socialization, and the like in organizations can influence decisions by controlling the premises on which they are made.[2]

Even if we were to accept decision-making locus as the key aspect of decentralization, there still remains the problem of which decisions to decentralize. Simon et al. use the term "important" to characterize decisions that are to be delegated if a firm is to decentralize. This is not very helpful, since an argument can be made that important decisions should be centralized and unimportant ones delegated. Importance also does not explain why production and sales decisions tend to be delegated lower in the organization than financial decisions. Clearly, the former are just as important (maybe more so) than the latter.

A more useful distinction is used by A.D. Chandler[3], who separates strategic from operating decisions. The former are concerned with the broad, long-range issues of acquiring and using resources, while the latter are concerned with routine, day-to-day operations. In practice, however, it may be difficult to draw a sharp distinction between strategic and operating decisions. Generally, the former cover a longer time period and are one-shot type decisions, while the latter are short-run and recurring. Thus, capital budgeting decisions are one-shot, considered strategic, and usually centralized; production and sales decisions are recurring, considered operating, and are usually decentralized.

Given these difficulties, it is not surprising that L.P. Jennergen's 1980 survey of the field shows that decentralization may mean: (1) the hierarchic level at which a decision is made; (2) the relative influence of a hierarchical level in decision making; and (3) participation in decision making without reference to hierarchic levels.[4] In addition, the term is also used to denote delegation of authority to carry out specific tasks. Accountants tend to equate decentralization with certain financial structures such as profit centers[5]. Economists speak of the M-form (multidivisional) as equivalent to a decentralized structure and a U-form (functional) as a centralized structure. In practice, many divisional firms may be centralized while functional organizations may provide considerable authority to managers over their areas. As the POLKA case shows, geographical dispersal in no way reduced the highly centralized operations of that company. Thus, an organization that considers itself highly decentralized may appear centralized when viewed with a different definition of the term.

Since there is little agreement on the meaning of the term decentralization, it may be more useful to focus on what an organization wants to accomplish through decentralization. That is, the issue should be what *behaviors* an organization desires of its managers. Accordingly, this chapter employs a behavioral definition of *decentralization as a system that encourages various managers in a hierarchy to think and act independently while being part of a team*. It is a management philosophy that attempts to encourage independent managerial thought and actions without sacrificing organizational needs. Decentralization thus requires balancing independence of managers with team player needs; it is also a philosophical commitment on the part of an organization. R.F. Vancil captures this spirit when he states that the purpose of decentralization is to develop a manager "who has the confidence to act alone on some occasions, the wisdom to seek counsel on other occasions, and the common sense to distinguish one occasion from another."[6]

ENVIRONMENT AS A DETERMINANT OF DECENTRALIZATION

This section examines the antecedent conditions that create the need for the kinds of managerial behaviors described by Vancil. Only by understanding why such behaviors are needed is it possible to understand the need for decentralization. A typical discussion of the reasons for decentralization will include the following:

(1) Decentralization frees top management to focus on long-range strategic decisions rather than being involved in operating decisions. This is a better use of valuable managerial time.

(2) It allows organizations to respond quickly and effectively to problems because those closest to a problem (local managers) have the best information and therefore can respond better to local needs.

(3) A centralized system is unable to handle all of the complex information needed to make optimal decisions. Centralized decisions may be inferior to locally-made decisions in a decentralized system.

(4) It provides a good training ground for future top management.

(5) It fulfills the need for autonomy and is thus a powerful motivational tool for managers.[7]

While most of the statements above are basically correct, they are more in the nature of consequences rather than antecedents of decentralization. For example, while decentralization may allow firms to respond more rapidly or train future managers, it does not explain what creates the need for decentralization in the first place. Traditional management theory is of no help in this regard since it merely posits that decentralization is a consequence of size—that is, a necessity forced by a firm's growth. Several empirical studies showing a correlation between size and decentralization tend to confirm this view.[8] The inadequacy of this explanation is obvious when one considers that a number of single owners delegate considerable decision-making autonomy to property agents, both for reasons of geography (property not located near the owner) and reasons of expertise. Size may thus be correlated to decentralization, but does not always lead to or explain decentralization.

The most comprehensive theoretical and empirical foundation for understanding decentralization has been provided by Chandler in two major works. The first, *Strategy and Structure* (1962), argues that a firm's structure is a response to its strategy. The latter depends upon two key elements—the market environment and technology. The second study, *The Visible Hand* (1977), provides a historical survey supporting this proposition. In this study, Chandler relates the development of the decentralized divisional firm to changes in the environment (development of railroads and telegraphs) and changes in technology (development of mass production techniques). The availability of expanded communications and production capacity allowed firms to pursue a strategy of forward and backward vertical integration. For example, many manufacturers acquired wholesalers to market their products directly, while others acquired suppliers of parts used as raw materials in their production process. The resulting expansion and diversification caused firms to change from functional to multidivisional structures.[9] Several later studies have verified this move from functional to divisional structures as stated by Chandler.[10]

A key feature of the divisional organizational structure for Chandler is decentralization. It is decentralization that allowed firms to overcome coordination problems by delegating operational decisions down the line. Two studies, one by Jesse Markham in 1973 and Vancil's 1979 study, provide support for the proposition that a strategy of diversification leads to divisionalization, which is in turn usually accompanied by greater decentralization.[11] However, a general problem in establishing the empirical validity of this proposition is the difficulty of obtaining a satisfactory measure of decentralization. As Jennergen points out, obtaining a measure of decentralization is difficult and prior attempts have resulted in conflicting measures and conclusions about the extent of a firm's decentralization. Also, a great deal of this empirical evidence is correlational, suggesting only that divisionalization is generally associated with decentralization.[12]

Chandler's basic thesis of environment to strategy to structure is widely accepted as an explanation of decentralization and has been the basis for much later research. R.N. Anthony's framework of management control systems uses Chandler's analysis as its main theoretical base.[13] O.E. Williamson has expanded Chandler's work to argue that divisionally decentralized structures reduce transaction costs for market exchanges that involve repeated contracting under uncertainty among a small number of parties and are supported by investments in specific assets.[14] Thus, they provide a more suitable governance structure, explaining why such exchanges are removed from markets and conducted within hierarchical organizations. More recently, the "population ecology" approach to organizations also uses Chandler's evidence to argue that divisional forms emerge in response to changes in the availability, stability, and concentration of resources in the environment.[15]

Unlike Anthony's work on management control,[16] both the transactions cost approach and the population ecology approach give environment a prominent role in explaining a firm's structure. A key difference between the two approaches is in respect to strategic choice. Williamson, like Chandler, uses strategy as an intervening link between environment and structure. Population ecology, using a natural selection perspective, reflects a more deterministic view and leaves little room for strategic choice. It is also not concerned with individual organizations but with populations of organizational forms.[17] However, in both approaches, the environment either directly or through strategic choice leads to decentralization.

A difficulty in modeling the effect of the environment on decentralization is the lack of an agreement of what constitutes an organization's environment. Many competing notions are available and new ones are rapidly evolving, so what is written here may become dated fairly quickly. Following the approach used by J. Pfeffer and G.R. Salancik, an organization's environment may be split into two subgroups. The first is the "task environment", which defines the set of exchange relationships between the focal organization and other social actors. Examples are suppliers, customers, creditors, unions, and other resource providers. The other group consists of the larger "community" of political, cultural, and social actors that legitimate the activities of an organization.[18]

Task environment is typically described along three dimensions: munificence or the availability of scarce resources, interconnectedness or the number and pattern of interorganizational linkages, and concentration or the extent to which power, authority, and resources are dispersed in the environment.[19] These characteristics determine the degree of conflict and change that confront a focal organization. The larger "community", consisting of political, social, and cultural factors, determines the freedom with which an organization can pursue various courses of action. Thus, the set of responses available to an organization is determined by the interaction of the change, conflict, and constraints posed by its environment.

In general, the higher the degree of conflict and change in the task environment, the greater the need for an organization to develop specialized information processing capability, develop an ability to respond quickly, and encourage risk taking and innovative behavior on the part of its members. The method of pursuing these ends must be consistent with the values of the larger community so the organization does not jeopardize its legitimacy. Viewed from this perspective, it is now possible to see that decentralization allows organizations faced with greater conflict and change to develop specialized information, respond speedily, and encourage risk taking and innovation. Also, as J.W. Meyer and B. Rowan point out, decentralization in Western societies serves a symbolic function since it is consistent with the values of the larger community.[20] The various reasons for decentralization cited at the beginning of this section can thus be incorporated within an environmentally-based model of the type shown in Figure 12-1.

The figure shows that the key characteristics of the task environment are resource munificence, interconnection of social actors, and concentration of power. A key feature of the community is the set of values and beliefs it holds. The environment determines the context of an organization; resource providers determine the degree of conflict and change, and the value systems define a set of constraints. The context in turn specifies the required behaviors for organizational viability. For instance, speed of response is likely to be a function of the degree of conflict and change in the environment, while the mode of governance (democratic or autocratic) will be shaped by preferences of the larger community. Viewed from the perspective in Figure 12-1, decentralization becomes a response by organizations to cope with the demands of their environment. This response can be mediated by strategic choice as suggested by Chandler[21] or may impact directly as suggested by Aldrich and Mueller.[22]

CHOOSING A STRUCTURE

To implement decentralization, an organization must choose an appropriate structure, develop a charter, and measure the performance of decentralized subunits. No one structure is necessarily the best suited for decentralization. How to select one that enhances decentralization is the subject of this section.

The choice of an appropriate decentralized structure requires two key decisions: (1) how to divide the task/decisions in an organization, and (2)

FIGURE 12-1
An Environmental Response Model of Decentralization

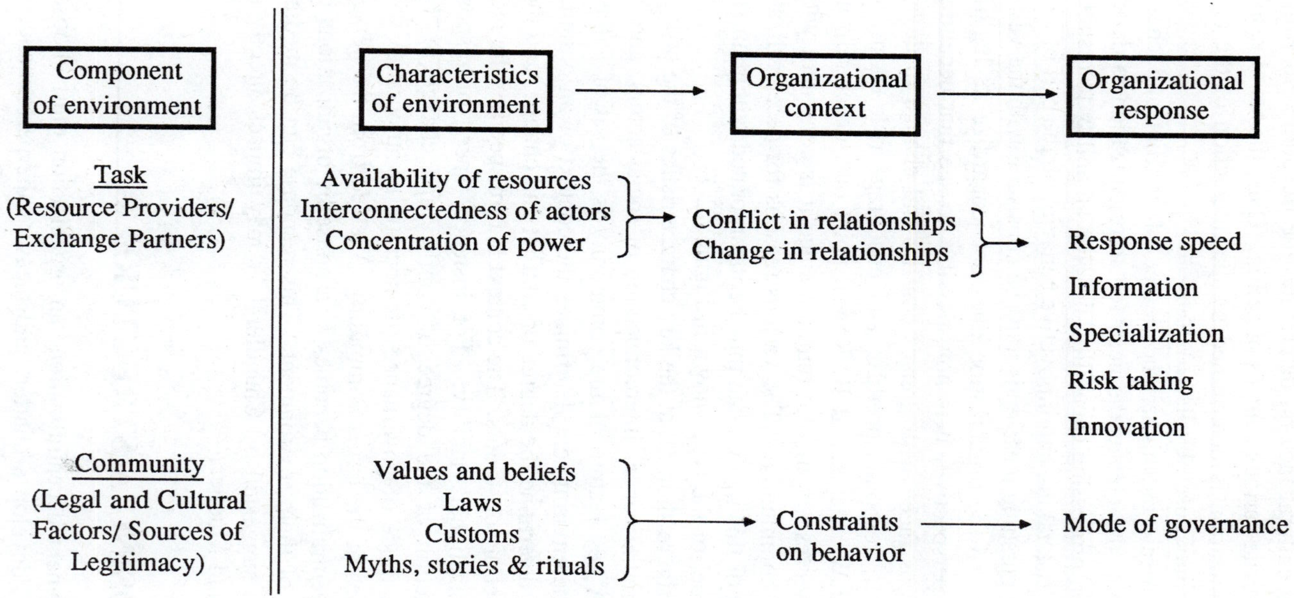

Component of environment	Characteristics of environment	Organizational context	Organizational response
Task (Resource Providers/ Exchange Partners)	Availability of resources / Interconnectedness of actors / Concentration of power	Conflict in relationships / Change in relationships	Response speed / Information / Specialization / Risk taking / Innovation
Community (Legal and Cultural Factors/ Sources of Legitimacy)	Values and beliefs / Laws / Customs / Myths, stories & rituals	Constraints on behavior	Mode of governance

what system of accountability to impose for resources expended in carrying out the various task/decisions.

Division of Task/Decisions

The functional-divisional types of organization structures represent two different ways of dividing the task/decisions in an organization. A functional structure divides an organization along the lines of its main functions such as production, marketing, finance, and so on. It is suited for exploiting economies of scale since people specialize in particular functions.[23] Such structures are particularly suited to organizations that require in-depth skill development in a technical area and/or have few and similar products. Computer manufacturers and airlines are good examples of large companies that are functionally organized.

The divisional structure usually divides an organization along product lines. It is particularly suited for multiproduct or highly diversified companies. In the case of multiproduct firms, the savings in coordination costs offset the costs of functional duplication created by divisionalization. The highly diversified conglomerate, on the other hand, is a collection of diverse businesses, each of which may have a very distinct production and marketing technology. The divisional form is thus a natural structure for such organizations.

An added complication in dividing task/decision in most large organizations is the geographical dispersal of their units. Geography adds to the coordination problem, especially when units cross national boundaries. Firms must now be organized by territories, with each territory having a further functional or product organization. A difficult problem arises when only a few products of a multiproduct firm are sold in the various territories. In such situations, organizations are faced with the difficult choice of duplicating product divisions in all territories or using geographical divisions for all their products.

For example, in the 1950s and 1960s, EMI, a major British multinational, found itself facing this problem. Its major product division was in the music industry and it was well represented worldwide by a network of subsidiaries. However, its other electrical products such as refrigerators, electric irons, and toasters, were separate divisions in Britain. Those divisions found it difficult to market their products through EMI - Music division's worldwide subsidiaries. The problem was the highly specialized marketing skills needed for the music industry, which made these skills nontransferable to other products. The result was a failure to sell many successful domestic products in what was then a huge and captive commonwealth market. Geography thus creates the need for duplication of facilities or creation of mixed structures where ordinarily a simple functional or divisional structure would have sufficed.

Devising Resource Accountability

The second step in choosing a structure is devising an appropriate system of resource accountability on the various functional, product or territorial sub-units. Typically, a resource accountability structure follows the logic of the physical distribution of activities and decisions achieved by the creation of subunits. Four types of resource accounting units are identified in the literature: cost centers, revenue centers, profit centers, and investment centers.[24] For more detail, see Chapter Seven on Responsibility Accounting.

Because of the correspondence between activities/decisions and resources expended, functional organizations primarily use revenue and cost centers. Also, because divisions typically combine both marketing and production under one manager, they are organized as profit or investment centers. This is probably why the terms divisions, profit centers, and decentralization are sometimes used interchangeably in the literature.

Decentralization, however, should not be treated as synonymous with divisionalization or with profit or investment centers. The latter two are the basic economic units in any business and management is therefore interested in assessing their economic viability. The resources identified with a unit thus do not correspond to a manager's ability to make decisions about them. This is particularly true of common facilities, which are always present no matter how much separation of activities exists in the organization structure. Also, profit centers are structural properties of an organization. They assist the process of decentralization by eliciting desired behaviors from managers. This means that profit centers do not have to correspond to the physical activities; they can be designed to exceed or be less than the bounds set by a unit manager's formal jurisdiction, authority, or control. The creation of such "artificial" profit centers should be guided by the ability of managers to *influence* an activity rather than by whether they have *formal control* over it. Behaviors, not formal organization charts, should determine what structure of resource accountability to superimpose on the various subunits in an organization.

It is important to recognize that the behavioral criterion for designing organization structures proposed here is too often ignored or confused in practice and theory. Many standard texts on the subject typically warn against holding managers responsible for so-called "noncontrollable costs." These noncontrollable costs are typically defined as costs that arise from activities over which a manager has no direct jurisdiction or line responsibility. While this may be a good practice, our criterion suggests that in some cases, violating this dictum may be beneficial since it may result in desirable rather than dysfunctional behaviors. Because a decentralized organizational structure is designed to elicit desired managerial behaviors, the creation of physical and financial subunits should facilitate this end. This means that a strict correspondence between task/decision accountability and financial accountability is not necessary in all situations.

Before concluding this section, it is appropriate to comment on the recent evolution of matrix structures. Such structures are usually common in many high technology firms because they enable firms to maintain functional decentralization and still overcome the problem of coordination created by a functional structure.[25] Matrix structures typically involve production of a large discrete project or a set of activities in a program. The responsibility for carrying out the project or program is usually assigned to a manager, while the control of resources remains in the hands of the functional managers. Matrix structures thus seek to combine functional and divisional decentralization.[26] This duality is also reflected in the financial structure, which accumulates costs by functional departments (typically cost centers) and by projects and programs. Since project or program managers are typically drawn from the third echelon, it tends to promote decentralization by giving more autonomy and influence to lower-level managers of an organization.[27]

DEVELOPING A CHARTER

The choice of an appropriate structure is the first step on the road to decentralization. An equally important task is the development of a charter—that is, a set of operating rules and principles that will govern the relationship of subunits with headquarters (HQ) and with each other. The subunits' relationship with headquarters requires delineating the activities over which a subunit has primary authority and responsibility, and the manner in which headquarters expects subunit managers to carry out the activities assigned to their units. The relationship among the units requires the establishment of guidelines to govern exchanges from one subunit to another.

Delegation of Activities

An important prerequisite for decentralization is the determination of which activities should be delegated to subunits and which activities should be controlled centrally. In theory, a completely decentralized system would assign all separable activities to subunits, with little or no role for central management. The theory of atomistic producers in a perfectly competitive market economy comes close to this model. If such markets existed in practice, which they rarely do, the role of central authority would be reduced to that of an umpire or an umbrella. Most businesses never come close to this level of decentralization. This is because central management of certain activities is typically more efficient than their separate execution by subunits. For example, legal services may be more economical if performed centrally rather than by separate business subunits.

A closer examination suggests *six* guides that may explain current practice and may be useful for organizations in the process of decentralizing. These are: (1) utilization of specialized talent; (2) economies of scale; (3) uniformity; (4) lasting consequences; (5) time frame; and (6) encouragement of experimentation.

The need for fully *utilizing specialized talent* probably accounts for activities such as legal, computing, and accounting being centralized. In economics, the concept of "economies of scope" captures this idea of expanding into activities that utilize existing capacity better. These activities typically require highly trained personnel who are in short supply and are usually available as "indivisible" assets. To avoid underutilization of trained personnel, which is likely if activities are duplicated, most organizations tend to centralize such activities.

Another familiar notion for capacity utilization is the idea of *economies of scale*. Where scale economies are available, activities tend to be grouped and centralized to exploit them. Activities such as cash management and purchasing are centralized because better interest rates and purchase prices are available when organizations deal in larger quantities. Subunits pooling their cash or purchase needs and having them managed centrally makes good economic sense in these circumstances. However, scale economies are counterbalanced by the increased administrative costs of a slower central authority. This is primarily what keeps many activities from being centralized.

The need for corporate *uniformity* in certain activities is another important reason for centralizing them. A good example is union negotiations because wage policy and benefits for the entire organization have to be uniform. Accounting systems, which have to conform to both internal and external reporting requirements, tend to be uniform for the same reason.

Another factor that determines the degree of decentralization is whether a decision has *lasting consequences* for an organization. A key consideration in delegating decisions is the extent to which an organization can tolerate mistakes by its managers. The freedom to fail is a necessary prerequisite for effective decentralization—especially if an organization desires risk taking on the part of subunit managers. This probably explains why operating decisions in the areas of production and sales tend to be decentralized. Mistakes in these areas are localized and generally do not have long lasting effects. Capital budgeting decisions, on the other hand, commit an organization to projects and expenditures that, because of their size, have long lasting and material consequences for an organization. These decisions are thus centralized.[27]

A popular reason for decentralization is the *time frame* within which decisions have to be made. This is the popular complaint against a central foot-dragging bureaucracy that does not make decisions in a timely fashion. Indeed, where time is of the essence, decisions cannot be centralized because of the delay caused by the need to communicate and process relevant information. While modern communications technology has removed some of the communications delay, the processing problems still remain. This is because information communication by its very nature requires aggregation and summarization in which *inferences* rather than *data* are communicated. The typical receiver is therefore operating on only a part of the data and reality that a sender may possess. One consequence is that a receiver may have to go back for more information, thus slowing the decision. Hence the move to decentralize.

Finally, some organizations decentralize to *encourage experimentation* at the local level. By creating subunits that have loose couplings with each other, experiments can be undertaken with results limited to a small segment of the organization. In this way, harmful effects from an experiment are contained while beneficial effects can be adopted later by the remaining organization. New products, new production methods, and new purchasing sources are typically introduced in most organizations after successful adoption in some part of an organization. The same is true of the relationship between state and federal governments in the U.S. A number of laws or standards have been enacted at the Federal level after successful experimentation at the state level.

Establishing Behavioral Norms

A charter must follow the division of activities by spelling out the behavioral norms headquarters expects of its subunit managers in carrying out these activities. For instance, while units may be free to make all product decisions, headquarters may expect such decisions to be guided by considerations of long-run profitability. Several options for communicating desired norms of behavior are available. The most important ones are: *socialization*, *specialization*, *standardization* and *formalization*. All of these methods provide a means by which headquarters can communicate its desires or structure situations so that subunit decisions and actions conform to acceptable norms of behavior.

Before examining how these methods can be used to set up norms of behavior, it is important to recognize that their use poses a real danger of moving an organization from decentralization to centralization. Controlling behavior directly or through control of the premises on which decisions are made defeats the philosophy of encouraging independent and autonomous managers.[29] In reviewing empirical evidence on this subject, Jennergen came to the conclusion that specialization, standardization, and formalization are indirect means of controlling behavior and thus introducing centralization.[30] It is therefore important that HQ should use these techniques to communicate norms and not dictate or control behaviors of sub-units.

Socialization is the process of orienting new members into the norms of an organization. It is perhaps the most important technique used in communicating what is acceptable behavior. Companies use elaborate orientation and training programs, create myths and stories, and use other such techniques to induct individuals into their value systems. Recently, much emphasis has been placed on these techniques as a way of creating a "corporate culture."

The basic idea behind the notion of corporate culture is that it is an effective way to instill in managers a value system that will guide their actions. Socialization is most effective in communicating an organization's values such as quality and service. It can be of great assistance in decentralization if freedom to make mistakes and take risks are among the values encouraged by an organization.

Specialization refers to the number of specialties and the extent of professionalization in an organization. The latter is particularly important since the use of professionals by an organization means socialization in the norms of their professions before joining an organization. Professionals also tend to be fairly autonomous and independent in their orientation. As long as the values of an organization do not conflict with professional values, increased professionalization will ensure that organizational behavior is governed by acceptable norms within the decentralized units.

Standardization denotes the degree to which standard rules are in place. A distinction must be made between *standards of behavior*, such as a code of ethics, and *standardized behavior*, such as producing products to a standard of quality. While the former is consistent with decentralization, the latter may not be. Use of standards to communicate norms of behavior is consistent only if such standards are broad and fall short of specifying actual outcomes. For example, standards of personnel selection, which have to be consistent with affirmative action guidelines, are consistent with decentralization; standards dictating the qualifications, experience, or sex of a prospective employee are not.

Formalization, or the extent to which there are written rules, procedures, and routines, is another technique of communicating norms. Extensive reliance on formalization is likely to inhibit decentralization because broad guides are generally difficult to reduce to crisp routines. Like standardization, decentralization can be preserved only if the written guides are broad and do not attempt to control specific behaviors. When combined with the assignment of activities, the processes of socialization, specialization, standardization, and formalization tell subunit managers what their sphere of action is and how much latitude they have in acting.

Clarifying Interunit Relationships

A good charter also provides the ground rules for managing inter-unit exchanges. These exchanges are necessary when sub-units are dependent on each other for inputs or outputs. The degree of dependence varies from high in vertically integrated companies to low in diversified conglomerates. Some interdependence is typically present in most organizations. This creates a need to manage these inter-relationships in a way in which both individual units and organizations can achieve their objectives. Decentralization increases the danger of subunits maximizing their goals at the expense of the organization by allowing subunit managers to act independently.

Competitive versus Collabortive Approach

A charter for decentralization attempts to prevent this chance of suboptimization. It can use two extreme approaches to do so. The first, a *competitive* approach, relies on a market mechanism and substitutes a fictitious internal market for the external market. Competition among subunits is encouraged and internal transfer prices perform the resource allocation role of the external price system. The other, a *collaborative* approach, emphasizes organizational membership and encourages individuals to work as a team by using appropriate rules, rewards, and values. In practice, it is not possible for most organizations to use either of these two approaches in its *pure* form. Hence, their choice is how to combine appropriate features of the two approaches.

The proposition that neither pure competition nor pure collaboration is feasible has ample support from the literature on organizations. The need for coordinated collective action has always been cited by organization theory as the primary reason for organizations. Markets fail to provide the needed coordination because agents can act autonomously. More recently, the literature on the economics of internal organization has formalized this argument by stating that markets and organizations are *alternative* ways of organizing economic activity.[31] Organizations exist because markets fail. They overcome market failures by reducing transactions cost incurred in market exchanges with contracts based on trust and collaboration. However, complete substitution of collaboration is not possible since it requires organizational members to completely subordinate their self-interests in favor of organizational goals. This is highly unlikely in utilitarian organizations such as business firms. Their challenge is to align self-interests of individuals with organizational interests.[32]

If pure competition is not possible, why is it that many decentralized firms create internal markets and encourage units to maximize their profits? The answer may be that the choice reflects an *ideological* rather than a *pragmatic* bias to the subject. The competitive approach is embedded in the values of free enterprise and the beneficial influence of the invisible hand.

These are important and cherished values in a market economy. It is therefore tempting to believe that the benefits of the market will be equally applicable to an internal market. Indeed, ideology may have played an important, if not a decisive, role in the decision by General Motors to opt for a competitive approach in regulating interunit exchanges.[33] It is not surprising that many decentralized companies, following GM's lead, have experienced difficulties in reconciling the ideology of the market place with realities of running an organization. The large body of literature on the still unresolved issue of transfer pricing attests to some of the difficulties of applying a pure competitive model.

Factors Influencing The Choice

A pragmatic approach to developing a decentralized charter attempts to mix the two approaches. Its task is to locate the organization on a continuum whose end points are competition and collaboration (bearing in mind that neither end point is generally feasible). There are four important factors that should be considered by an organization in deciding what point to choose on this competition-collaboration continuum. These are: (1) availability of external markets; (2) strategic independence; (3) incompleteness of price; and (4) availability of the exit option.

Availability of External Markets. The competitive posture among subunits is possible only when there is an external market for the product or service being traded internally. For example, spark plugs may be purchased by an automobile assembly division from an internal supplier or from an external producer. The availability of viable competition in the external markets makes the use of internal competition more feasible and practical. The internal supplier in these instances can be compared to the external supplier and can be expected to conform to the same standards.

There are two reasons why this type of comparable external market is difficult to find in practice. First, a number of internal units are created for administrative ease. This results in units that are *technologically inseparable* but are administratively separate. The product being traded in such situations may have no external market since it is the result of "administrative gerrymandering." Second, an external market cannot be considered viable if it involves exchanges among a small number of parties.[34] Here, the decision to internalize is made to avoid possible dependence on single source buyers or sellers. The presence of small numbers creates an external market that is not a comparable reference point for governing internal exchanges. Thus, the competitive approach must be modified whenever units have technological dependence or there is a small numbers exchange present.

Strategic Interdependence. A key factor in choosing between competition and collaboration is the strategy of an organization. Even when products are technically independent, an organization's strategy can make them interdependent. For example, a typical Las Vegas hotel offers four technologically separate products: lodging, meals, gambling, and entertainment. Strategically, it can choose to create four independent units and have transfers at market price or it can create four interdependent centers in which one product, say gambling, becomes the profit maker while the other three support it. This latter strategy requires the other three units to collaborate with the casino. Many organizations make the mistake of creating independent units on a technological or administrative criterion and then expecting them to collaborate on strategic matters.

Incompleteness of Price.   The competitive approach requires a price mechanism as the basic signal for regulating exchanges. To the extent that prices capture all relevant decision variables, the competitive approach will be successful. Internal transfer prices, however, rarely capture all relevant decision variables in an exchange. Of particular importance are quality differences, uncertainty, and externalities.

When quality differences between products are present, it is difficult to compare prices of an internal supplier to a referent external market. Uncertainty about sources of supply, which may lead an organization to internalize a supplier who has special knowledge, is another situation in which prices will fail to capture the full value of an internal supplier's contribution.[35] This is because the internal transfer price is a payment for *both* the product and the reduction in uncertainty. Finally, when the parties to an exchange do not bear the entire cost of an exchange, externalities are said to be present. Prices again fail to reflect the full dimensions of exchanges because other parties have to pay a part of the cost. For example, in a multistage integrated production process, such as carton making, failure of two units in a later stage in the process may hurt the paper mills (stage 1) more than the later units. The incompleteness of price as a signal means that competition between units must be moderated and supplemented with collaborative mechanisms that can recognize all important variables in an internal exchange.

Availability of the Exit Option.   An important requirement for the success of the competitive approach is the availability of the exit option.[36] The exit option allows an inefficient internal producer to be penalized by allowing the buyer to refuse to buy internally. The discipline of the market place, however, does not always stop or arrest internal inefficiencies. As A.O. Hirschmann argues, exit may increase inefficiencies by allowing quality conscious buyers to move, making it easier in the short run for an inefficient producer to focus on nondiscriminating buyers.[37] From the standpoint of a single firm, exit may solve the problem of the buying unit but may do nothing to arrest further declines in the quality of the seller. In such situations, the competitive approach has to be tempered to force both buyers and sellers to improve internal quality.

To summarize, the charter decides whether subunits within a firm will be primarily competitive or cooperative with each other. The factors that determine the relative balance between those two extremes are the extent to which: external markets are available; strategic independence or interdependence between units is desired; prices capture quality differentials, uncertainty of supply, and externalities; and exit is a viable option for arresting deterioration.

Decentralization and Transfer Pricing

A key mechanism used by organizations to regulate exchanges between subunits is the transfer pricing mechanism. Transfer prices encourage and promote certain types of behaviors in organizations. Since the charter for decentralization attempts to do the same, there is an intimate linkage between the two. The transfer pricing system can be used as a tool for reinforcing the behaviors desired by a charter. To understand how this may be possible, a brief digression on the various types of transfer prices is needed. Readers familiar with the transfer pricing literature may want to skip this next section.

Types of Transfer Prices

Organizations typically employ five types of transfer prices. These are: (1) market prices; (2) cost-plus prices; (3) variable costs; (4) negotiated prices; and (5) arbitrated or dictated prices.

Market prices are used when some type of external market for the product exists. It encourages competitive behaviors between subunits and may discourage commitment to an organization since it frees both buying and selling divisions to deal externally.

Cost plus may be *full* cost or *variable* cost plus profit margin. Both these rules may encourage internal suppliers to become inefficient by allowing them to pass costs on to buying divisions. Transfer prices based on cost plus a percentage mark-up are even worse because the manager of the selling division not only has no motivation to keep his costs down, but is actually encouraged to raise them since the larger his costs, the greater his profit. If cost plus is to be used, then, from a behavioral standpoint, the most desirable alternative is "standard cost" increased by an acceptable profit margin for the selling division. The use of standard costs for this purpose can be expected to encourage the manager of the selling division to minimize his actual costs since his control efforts will show up as favorable variances in his performance report. If costs exceed standard, he will not only be unable to recover the additional amounts from the buying division, but his inefficiency in controlling cost will manifest itself in poor performance reports.

Variable costs may be economically optimal because they approximate marginal costs of production in the short run. However, they are motivationally discouraging for a selling unit because they do not allow such units to show any profits.

Negotiated transfer prices encourage negotiating skills at the expense of productivity because the best negotiator can charge a higher price. According to N. Dopuch and R. Drake, negotiated transfer prices are "an unsatisfactory basis for the evaluation of subunit performance since they imply in fact an evaluation of power to negotiate rather than of performance itself."[38]

Arbitrated or dictated prices are used when two sub-units cannot agree on a mutually satisfactory transfer price or if one division refuses to deal with another. In such cases, it is common practice for top management to dictate an appropriate solution to resolve the dispute. When this is done, the managers involved no longer have complete responsibility for the activities of their divisions. This raises immediate behavioral problems with respect to morale and motivation; it also means that when divisional performance is evaluated, the managers will be held responsible for the results of decisions they did not make. Therefore, each time a corporate officer forces a particular course of action on a subunit, a breakdown in the entire fabric of decentralized profit responsibility has occurred and the organization has, in effect, reverted to a centralized decision-making structure.

Transfer Prices and Decentralization Charters

The behavioral impact of transfer prices suggests a possible reinterpretation of transfer prices as behavioral mechanisms to support the degree of competition or collaboration desired by an organization among its subunits. Table 12-1 shows a possible match among five possible locations on the competition-collaboration continuum and the type of transfer price best suited to support this decision. The five locations are purely suggestive and simply reflect a move along this continuum.

The left-hand side of Table 12-1 shows the behavior desired by a firm. The charter is a way to spell out these desired behaviors. For instance, it can choose a strongly competitive system (#1) or a strongly collaborative system (#5) or something in the middle (#3). Matched to each one of the desired behaviors is a transfer pricing system to govern internal exchanges (shown on the right side of Table 12-1). The strongly competitive posture among units requires a market-based transfer price as a measure of efficiency. It will probably require prohibitions against subsidizing internal units if they fail to meet the market price. The moderate degree of competition recognizes that the market price may capture some but not all variables. Market-based transfer prices are simply used as constraints and as a way of generating signals of how much the nonmeasured variables such as quality and uncertainty are costing.

TABLE 12-1

Matching Transfer Prices with Charter for Decentralization

Type of Behavior Desired	Type of Transfer Pricing Needed
1. High degree of competition and independence among units.	1. Market-based competitive prices to be used as measures of economic efficiency.
2. Moderate degree of competition between units. Collaboration needed on variables not captured by prices.	2. Market-based prices to be used as constraints to measure the common elements between internal and external prices. Difference between internal and external price to be used as a "variance" signal for further investigation.
3. Equal requirements for both competition and collaboration.	3. Negotiated transfer prices to provide units with a way to do some joint problem solving.
4. Greater collaboration than competition between units.	4. Arbitrated transfer prices to bring parties together and show them the need to collaborate.
5. Close collaboration and little competition.	5. Dictated transfer prices to join the separate units together.

Negotiated transfer prices allow voluntary collaboration to develop around market prices and are consistent with a charter that desires both. Arbitrated transfer prices move the units closer to collaboration by creating an umpire who can ultimately bring them together. On the other hand, dictated transfer prices force collaboration by removing them as a bone of contention between units. Table 12-1 thus shows how an appropriate transfer pricing system can be an effective aid in supporting and encouraging behaviors desired by a decentralized charter.

To summarize, this section argues that a key element of decentralization is the need to develop an appropriate charter. Such a charter must: decide what activities and decisions headquarters will make and which ones will be delegated to individual units; provide appropriate norms of behavior for units to follow in carrying out the activities assigned; and establish whether exchanges among units will be governed primarily by rules of competition or collaboration. A possible interpretation of transfer prices as a way of governing interunit exchanges was also offered.

MEASURING AND EVALUATING PERFORMANCE

The final step in decentralization is the setting up of a system for evaluating and rewarding performance. There is considerable debate about the merits of using specific measures of decentralized performance such as return on investment, residual income, budgeted income, and the like. There is, however, general agreement on the purpose and attributes such measures should possess.

Most writers regard "goal congruence" between top management and decentralized management as the major purpose of decentralized performance evaluation.[39] Attributes of performance measures most likely to lead to goal congruence are: (1) controllability, (2) completeness, and (3) separation of activity and managerial evaluation.[40]

Controllability is considered desirable because it excludes from measurement those aspects of performance that a manager cannot control. Control is defined as equivalent to formal authority. Thus, it is argued that it is inappropriate for manufacturing units to be held accountable for actions originating in sales and vice versa.

Completeness refers to the degree to which a measure can capture all relevant dimensions of performance. For example, a measure such as standard cost or profits may not capture a unit's efforts to increase market share.

Separation of activities and managerial evaluation is designed to distinguish the economic attractiveness of an activity from the way it is managed. For example, a bank branch or a department store's profitability may be primarily a function of its location rather than its management.

It is difficult to argue with the concept of goal congruence or with any of the three attributes discussed above. However, a close examination shows that in practical situations, these normative guides may be of limited use in establishing evaluation criteria in a decentralized organization. For example, the concept of goal congruence assumes that an organization has a well-specified goal on which congruence is desired. The notion of goal has been challenged in the organization literature by a number of different writers who have stated that organizations do not have well-formulated goals.[41] Also, A.L. Wilkins and W.G. Ouchi assert that goal sharing is not necesary for effective organizational control. If goals are not needed for collective structures, then goal congruence can not be regarded as a central concept for designing performance measurement systems.[42]

A similar situation prevails with respect to the three attributes of good performance measures—controllability, completeness, and separation of activity and managers. The ability to find measures that possess these attributes is severely limited in practice because of two problems—*jointness* of performance and *uncertainty* about outcomes. *Jointness* refers to the fact that organizational performance is the joint and synergistic effort of team work. *Uncertainty* refers to the inability to assess the impact of the external environment on a subunit's performance. The way in which these factors affect performance evaluation is discussed below.

Organizations are created largely to exploit the synergies of coordinated team efforts. They make possible outcomes that individuals alone cannot produce because of their biological limitations or indivisibilities[44] or transactional difficulties.[45] The advantages of organizations over other forms of cooperation is that they create a stable pattern of interdependencies between individuals and subunits. Outcomes or results are the joint products of closely coordinated actions between participants. Separating outcomes so they can be identified with actions of particular individuals or subunits requires disaggregation of this joint product. Since these efforts are synergistic, any disaggregation becomes arbitrary and artificial. For instance, if individuals A and B alone can each produce one unit of a product, but together they can produce three units, then it is not meaningful to say that each has a contribution of 1.5 units.

Accounting literature has long recognized that it is impossible to separate joint costs or joint revenues.[46] Yet in the area of decentralized performance measurement, the ideal of controllability requires precisely such a disaggregation of performance. Controllability requires separating the various components of performance, assigning them to individual subunits, and giving the subunit complete authority over the inputs that result in a particular output. However, when team efforts are required, or when an activity is internalized because it minimizes transactions cost, it creates a dependence among subunits.[47] Actions of a subunit therefore affect other subunits. For example, plants need sales people to generate adequate demand, which makes their scale of operations efficient; sales needs plants to accommodate rush orders to generate sales. The final profit results from the cooperation of sales and manufacturing. It is impossible in this situation to completely separate those aspects that are controllable by a subunit. This type of dependence or jointness is what economists recognize as *externalities*. Their presence makes it difficult to separate and control all factors affecting a subunit's performance.

Similarly, completeness of performance measures is problematic in a joint product situation. In addition to the disaggregation of joint efforts, completeness requires that all aspects of performance be measurable. In general, end products are easier to measure than "team player" contributions. This holds true for both individual and subunit performance. Thus, it is easier to use a measure for the basketball player who makes the shots than for the player who sets up the shot for his teammate.[48] Similarly, it is easy to measure the output of a unit that makes final sales, but more difficult to measure the performance of support units such as maintenance and engineering who make the final sale possible.

Uncertainty poses another difficult, albeit different, hurdle in measuring decentralized performance. Uncertainty about the impact of the environment on a subunit creates what economists refer to as "information asymmetries" between top management and managers of decentralized units. Thus, a subunit manager possesses private information, which decentralization encourages, but which is unavailable to top management. Separation of activity and management become problematic in such circumstances. Lacking information, top management does not have the ability to separate those results, good or bad, caused by random variables in the environment and those caused by management actions. This also impacts on controllability since, faced with poor performance, a subunit manager can blame it on random "noncontrollable" factors in the environment. To use controllability as a criterion under such circumstances requires that top management distinguish environmental effects from management action—that is, decide what was noncontrollable. Economists refer to this as the "moral hazard" problem and recognize the general difficulty of making such separations.[49] The experience of the Accounting Principles Board with Opinions 9 and 30 also shows how difficult it is in practice to legislate or define events which are "extraordinary" (i.e., environmentally caused) from events which are "operational" (i.e., managerially caused).

Thus far, we have argued that the presence of joint efforts and environmental uncertainty make it difficult to find decentralized performance measures that possess the attributes considered desirable by most existing writers. A more important question, however, is whether it is fruitful to continue the quest for these attributes to the extent possible within the constraints of jointness and uncertainty. Our answer, elaborated in the following pages, is that it may be more useful to abandon these attributes or at least supplement them with others that give prominent recognition to the jointness and uncertainty inherent in the process.

We suggest that for effective decentralization, performance measures must encourage both independent action and team work. For this to happen, the following three attributes should be present in such measures. They must: *focus attention* of managers on critical variables; provide specific *action guides* that generate desired outcomes; and enhance the perception of *fairness* for shared risks. Further elaboration on each of these attributes follows.

An important function of performance measures is that they galvanize actions in areas otherwise neglected by *focusing attention* on them. As E.G.

Flamholtz has pointed out, what gets measured, gets recognized. He uses the example of human resource accounting to show that the greatest contribution of such measures is not their "accuracy"; rather, it is that they make managers aware of the use of scarce human assets in organizations.[50] This ability of measures to focus attention on important variables is perhaps the most important argument against the use of single performance measures such as return on assets. The popularity of such measures tends to promote dysfunctional behaviors by promoting independent, self-centered actions by subunits. Even under the best of circumstances, they fail to capture the many areas that a manager should attend to. Multiple measures, even if some of them lack some ideal measurement properties, may be more useful in focusing attention on the right variables. A possible danger is mistaking them for accurate measures of the underlying constructs. They are signposts for moving in the right direction and should not be mistaken for the destination itself.

Guiding behaviors in desired directions can be accomplished if performance measures can link actions to outcomes. Organizations represent desired outcomes in the form of measures, which then become the focus of organizational action. For example, return on assets (ROA) represents the desired outcome of increasing corporate wealth, which in turn represents the desired outcome of improving "as-well-offness."[51] Organizational actions focus on improving ROA, which is a surrogate for the ultimate outcomes. However, many actions to improve ROA can actually decrease corporate wealth or "as-well-offness." In recent years, a large body of literature has criticized the ROA measure for encouraging dysfunctional actions that do precisely the opposite of what is desired.[52]

In general, the more complex the relationship between actions and measures—that is, the lower the correlation between a measure and the outcome it represents—the more difficult it is to link desired actions and outcomes. For example, consider the relationships in Figures 12-2a and 12-2b. Figure 12-2a shows a many-one relationship between actions and measures and low correlation between measures and outcomes in a simple situation. Several different actions (two in Figure 12-2a) can lead, with some probability, to both high and low scores on a measure; the high or low score can in turn be associated with some probability with a good or bad outcome. Assume that in Figure 12-2a the probability of action a_1 leading to a high score is .90 while that of a_2 is .60. Clearly, a manager will prefer a_1 to a_2. Now, however, suppose that a high score with a_1 has only a .20 probability of leading to a good outcome, while with a_2 this probability is 1.00. The measure has reduced the chances of a good outcome from 60 percent (.6 x 1) to 18 percent (.9 x .2) and thus provides a poor guide for selecting actions.

FIGURE 12–2(a and b)
Actions and Probabilities of Outcome

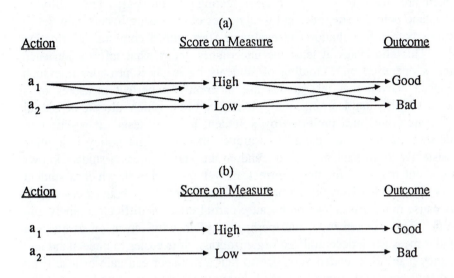

(a)

Action	Score on Measure	Outcome
a₁	High	Good
a₂	Low	Bad

(b)

Action	Score on Measure	Outcome
a₁	High	Good
a₂	Low	Bad

Contrast this with the situation in Figure 12-2b, where each action is uniquely associated with a measure, which in turn is associated with only one outcome. Here the action-outcome path is very clear. ROA was cited earlier as an example of the situation depicted in Figure 12-2a. An example of Figure 12-2b is a measure such as quantity of materials purchased. For instance, a leading manufacturer of paper products evaluates the performance of its converting division on the basis of tons of linerboard purchased from company-owned mills. Quantity purchased and converted is easy and unequivocal to measure; it is also associated directly with a desired outcome: "keep mill volume high." It thus serves as a good measure for guiding actions of managers of converting divisions.

Enhancing perceived fairness is perhaps one of the most important and most difficult attributes of performance measures. It is, however, a necessity if decentralization is to succeed. This is because effective decentralization requires rewards not so much for carrying out specific actions, but for sharing risks. Given uncertainty and information asymmetries, it is not possible to separate controllable from noncontrollable events. The only possibility is to devise an equitable risk-sharing scheme between top management and decentralized management.

Performance measures therefore need to capture and reflect these risks so that rewards are equitably distributed in the long run.

In general, measures that are easier to understand and are consistently applied are likely to generate greater feelings of fairness. The ability to understand both the strengths and weaknesses of a measure fosters confidence because both the evaluator and evaluatee start with a common information base. This eliminates at least the uncertainty about what information each party is operating on. Grading of students by teachers provides one such instance. Given that test grades are inherently imperfect measures of a student's ability and learning, multiple choice tests, which allocate no partial credit, are sometimes preferred by a student to essay tests. It is easier to understand a grade and there is assurance that the same policy is applied consistently to all students. Also, random answers in areas a student knows little about make up for the incorrect answer in an area in which a student is knowledgeable. Essay questions, which may provide a better assessment, may cause more dissatisfaction because partial credit is difficult to apply and justify. This phenomenon may perhaps explain why return on assets is a popular measure in decentralized organizations. It is easier to understand and captures many risk-related variables so that a manager can gain or lose from good environmental circumstances. Like multiple choices, it builds a gaming situation that may appeal to decentralized managers.

The three attributes discussed previously provide a concrete mechanism by which to address the three typical operational questions in performance evaluation. These are whether to: (1) use single or multiple measures of performance; (2) use financial or nonfinancial measures; and (3) measure outputs (results) or behaviors. Our criteria suggest that multiple measures using both financial and nonfinancial measurements are better at focusing attention on the many variables that should be attended to. However, they may diffuse actions by pointing in too many directions and are more complex to understand. Also, outputs or results are both appropriate and relatively easier to measure in decentralized units; however, outputs are end products and they may not provide adequate guidance for concrete actions, particularly if the action-outcome path is complicated. In the final analysis, the measurement system must balance these various attributes in choosing measures of decentralized performance.

To summarize, we have argued that for effective decentralization, the traditional notion of goal congruence may be inadequate. Similarly, the attributes of completeness, controllability, and separation of activity and manager evaluation may be difficult to achieve because of the joint product nature of organizational performance and uncertainty. Three alternative attributes—focusing attention, guiding actions and enhancing fairness—were suggested as alternative bases for choosing measures of decentralized performance.

A FINAL NOTE—POLKA REVISITED _____

The three steps in effective decentralization— choice of a structure, charter, and performance measures—can be illustrated with reference to the POLKA organization described earlier. Recall that the POLKA organization was geographically dispersed and diversifying in the direction of vertical integration. Decentralization seems necessary given its environment and size. A divisional structure based on geography or products also seems feasible. While more costly than the existing functional organization, it avoids the current problem of dual responsibility faced by technical specialists. Since the units are independent, it seems appropriate that they be treated as profit centers. This would reinforce the line obligations of all managers and will force each unit to acquire its own technical specialists. Since ice cream is not a high technology industry, the price for such duplication is likely to be minimal. The profit center concept should also help to push the organization toward a results orientation rather than a family orientation.

The choice of a charter for POLKA poses two questions: the role of headquarters and the relationship of the ice cream plants to the packaging materials plant. Given the environment in Pakistan, capital equipment and raw material purchases require a close coordination with banks because of general foreign exchange and import restrictions. These two subjects are clearly those which offer scale economies and require specialization and quick decisions. Centralizing them at headquarters seems logical. The remaining decisions can be safely delegated to local managers. The relationship between the packaging and ice cream plants seems to require more collaboration than competition. Packaging materials is a relatively oligopolistic industry in Pakistan. The key reason for this integration was an assured source of supply for ice cream. Competitive market prices may not be suitable in this situation and some sort of negotiated or arbitrated transfer prices may be more appropriate to encourage mutual problem-solving efforts.

Finally, given the increasing competition in Pakistan for both ice cream and packaging materials, performance measures must focus on five key variables: profits, market share, product reputation, product leadership, and cost effectiveness. It is clear that multiple measures (financial and nonfinancial) focusing on results as well as behaviors (particularly in the area of reputation and leadership) are needed to assess performance. Return on assets is not a meaningful measure since foreign exchange restrictions reduce the freedom with which capital equipment can be acquired or the sources from which it can be acquired. Residual income or budgeted profits seem more appropriate as overall measures of profitability. These measures, along with the other steps suggested above, provide a broad outline for POLKA to create an effective decentralized organization.

REFERENCES

[1] H.A. Simon, H. Guetzkow, G. Kozmetsky, and G. Tyndall, *Centralization vs. Decentralization in Organizing the Controller's Department* (New York, NY: Controllership Foundation, 1954), 1.

[2] J.G. March and H.A. Simon, *Organizations* (New York: John Wiley and Sons, 1958.)

[3] H. Mitzberg, D. Raisinghani, and A. Theoret, "The Structure of 'Unstructured' Decision Processes," *Administrative Science Quarterly* 21 (1976): 246-275.

[4] J.G. March and J.P. Olsen, *Ambiguity and Choice in Organizations* (Bergen, Norway: Universitats Porlaget, 1976).

[5] C. Perrow, *Complex Organizations*, 2d ed. (Glenview, Ill.: Scott, Foresman, 1979), 150.

[6] A.D. Chandler, Jr., *Strategy and Structure* (Cambridge, Mass.: MIT Press, 1962). See also *The Visible Hand: The Managerial Revolution in American Business* (Cambridge, Mass.: Harvard University Press, Belknap Press, 1977).

[7] L.P. Jennergren, "Decentralization in Organizations," *Handbook of Organizational Design*, Vol. 2, ed. P.C. Nystrom and W. H. Starbuck (London: Oxford University Press, 1981).

[8] R.F. Vancil, "Managing the Decentralized Firm," *Financial Executive* (March 1980).

[9] *Ibid.*

[10] See, for example: R.N. Anthony, J. Deanden and N. Bedford, *Management Control Systems*, 5th ed. (Homewood, Ill.: Irwin Dorsey, 1984); R.N. Kaplan, *Management Accounting* (Englewood Cliffs, N.J.: Prentice-Hall, 1982); and D. Solomons, *Divisional Performance: Measurement and Control* (New York, N.Y.: Markus Wiener Publishing, Inc., 1965).

[11] Jennergren, *Ibid.*

[12] Chandler, *Ibid.*

[13] For comprehensive reviews of these studies, see P.E. Caves, "Industrial Organization, Corporate Strategy and Structure," *Journal of Economic Literature* (March 1980): 18:64-92.

[14] Jesse W. Markham, *Conglomerate Enterprise and Public Policy* (Boston, Mass.: Harvard University, 1974); and Vancil, *Ibid.*

[15] Jennergren, *Ibid.*

[16] R.N. Anthony, *Planning and Control Systems* (Cambridge, Mass.: Harvard University Press, 1965).

[17] O.E. Williamson, *Markets and Hierarchies: Analysis of Anti-Trust Implications* (New York, N.Y.: Free Press, 1975). See also O.E. Williamson, "Emergence of the Visible Hand: Implications for Industrial Organization," in *Managerial Hierarchies*, ed. A. D. Chandler, Jr. (Cambridge, Mass.: Harvard University Press, 1980), 182-202.

[18] H. Aldrich, *Organizations and Environments*. Englewood Cliffs, N.J.: Prentice-Hall, 1979.

[19] Anthony, Dearden, and Bedford, *Ibid.*

[20] M. Hannan and J. Freeman, "The Population Ecology of Organizations," *American Journal of Sociology* 82, no. 3: 929-964.

[21] G. Pfeffer and G.R. Salancik, *The External Control of Organizations; A Resource Dependence Perspective* (New York, N.Y.: Harper & Row, 1978).

[22] *Ibid.*, p. 68.

[23] J.W. Meyer and B. Rowan, "Institutionalized Organizations: Formal Structure as Myth and Ceremony," *American Journal of Sociology* 83 (1977): 340-363.

[24] Chandler, *Strategy and Structure*, *Ibid.*

[25] Aldrich and Mueller, *Ibid.*

[26] Vancil, *Ibid.*

[27] See Anthony, Dearden, and Bedford; Kaplan; and Solomons, *Ibid.*

[28] S.M. Davis and P.R. Lawrence, *Matrix* (Reading, Mass.: Addison-Wesley, 1977).

[29] Jennergen, *Ibid.*

[30] *Ibid.*, p. 43.

[31] *Ibid.*

[32] Perrow, *Ibid.*

[33] Jennergen, *Ibid.*

[34] Williamson, *Markets and Hierarchies* and *Management Hierarchies*, *Ibid.*

[35] S.A. Culbert and J.J. McDonough, *The Invisible War: Pursuing Self-Interests at Work* (New York, N.Y.: John Wiley and Sons, 1980).

[36] A.P. Sloan, *My Years with General Motors* (New York, N.Y.: Doubleday, 1964).

[37] Williamson, *Markets and Hierarchies*.

[38] *Ibid.*

[39] A.O. Hirschman, *Exit, Voice, and Loyalty: Responses to Decline in Firms, Organizations, and States* (Cambridge, Mass.: Harvard University Press, 1970).

[40] *Ibid.*

[41] N. Dopuch and D. Drake, "Accounting Implications of a Mathematical Programming Approach to the Transfer Pricing Problem," *Journal of Accounting Research* (Spring 1964): 13.

[42] See Anthony, Dearden, and Bedford, *Ibid.*; and Horngren, *Ibid.* Also, G. Shillinglaw, *Managerial Cost Accounting*, 4th ed. (Homewood, Ill.: Richard D. Irwin, Inc., 1977).

[43] See Anthony, Dearden, and Bedford, *Ibid.*; and Solomons, *Ibid.* Also, E. E. Lawler III and J. R. Rhode, *Information and Control in Organizations* (Pacific Palisades, Calif.: Goodyear Publication, 1976).

[44] March and Olsen, *Ambiguity and Choice in Organizations*. H.A. Simon, "On the Concept of Organizational Goal," *Administrative Science Quarterly* 9, no. 1 (June 1964): 1-22. K.E. Weick, *The Social Psychology of Organizations*, 2d ed. (Reading, Mass.: Addison-Wesley, 1979).

[45] A.L. Wilkins and W.G. Ouchi, "Efficient Cultures: Exploring the Relationship Between Culture and Organizational Performance," *Administrative Science Quarterly* 28 (1983): 468-481.

[46] C.I. Barnard, *The Functions of an Executive* (Cambridge, Mass.: Harvard University Press, 1938).

[47] A.A. Alchain and H. Demsetz, "Production, Information Costs, and Economic Organization," *American Economic Review* 62, no. 5 (December 1972): 777-795.

[48] Williamson, *Markets and Hierarchies, Ibid.*

[49] A.L. Thomas, *The Allocation Problem in Financial Accounting Theory* (Evanston, Ill.: American Accounting Association, 1969).

[50] Williamson, *Markets and Hierarchies, Ibid.*

[51] S. Kerr, "On the Folly of Rewarding A, While Hoping for B," *Academy of Management Journal* 18, no. 4 (December 1975): 769–783.

[52] R.N. Kaplan, *Management Accounting* (Englewood Cliffs, N.J.: Prentice-Hall, 1982).

[53] K.J. Arrow, *Essays in Theory of Risk Bearing* (Chicago, Ill.: Markham, 1971).

[54] E.G. Flamholtz, *Accounting, Organizations and Society* 5, no. 1 (1980): 31-42.

[55] J.R. Hicks, "Income," in *Value and Capital*, 2d ed. (Oxford: Clarendon Press, 1964): 171-181.

SUGGESTED READINGS

Horngren, C.T. *Managerial Cost Accounting.* Englewood Cliffs, N.J.: Prentice-Hall, 1982.

Meyer, M.W. "'Bureaucratic' versus 'Profit' Organization.'" *Research in Organizational Behavior.* edited by B.M. Straw and L.L. Cummings, 89-126. Greenwich, Conn.: JAI Press, Inc., 1982.

Pfeffer, J. "Size and Composition of Corporate Boards of Directors: The Organization and Its Environment." *Administrative Science Quarterly* 17, no. 2. (June 1972): 218-228.

DISCUSSION QUESTIONS

1. What do you understand about decentralization in the context of a business organization?
2. What are the conditions that create a need for decentralization?
3. How is divisionalization/diversification related to decentralization?
4. What constitutes an organization's environment? What effect does it have on organizational structure?
5. What are some key decisions that have to be considered in choosing an appropriate organization structure?
6. What are some factors influencing the delegation of activities as specified in the charter?
7. What do you understand by the term *matrix structure*? How is this related to decentralization?

8. How do we determine to what extent an organization should be centralized or decentralized? What are some factors that may be helpful in arriving at such a decision?
9. What are some ways through which a charter can establish behavioral norms?
10. What are the different types of transfer prices employed by most organizations? How is this related to the decentralized charter?

CASE 12-1

The Company

Main Bank, a $220 million institution, is part of a $1 billion five-bank holding company. Located on the near northwest side of Chicago, Main is the founding member of the holding company. In August of 1984, the group purchased the Wheeling Trust and Savings Bank. If the Wheeling Bank had not been purchased by another holding company, the FDIC would have closed it down. To induce the holding company to purchase the Bank, the FDIC allowed the holding company to merge the Chicago Bank with the new acquisition in Wheeling. As a result of the merger, both the president and senior commercial lender moved their offices from Chicago to Wheeling. The Wheeling office is located 25 miles from the Chicago location.

The Dilemma

The holding company wanted the president and senior lender to implement and oversee the management and operations at the "new" bank. The bank in Chicago became a full-service branch facility. The commercial lending department remained intact with the three lending officers at Chicago continuing to report to the senior lender at Wheeling. The problems that began to develop could be blamed on logistics as well as the organizational structure. One example would be the problem in getting credit approvals in excess of $150,000. Since the authority for approvals remained with the senior lender and president, the loan officers' reaction time to customers increased. The officers at Main-Chicago also became frustrated by their inability to reach the two senior lenders. Obviously, these officers' performance in their day-to-day responsibilities were affected by this organizational structure.

Required:

1. How could decentralization be used to help with this dilemma?
2. Did the decentralization of the bank cause this problem?

CASE 12-2

The Company

TJM Company is a chain of off-price retail stores. There are 115 stores, all located east of the Mississippi, but anywhere from Maine to Florida. The home office is located in Boston, where all decisions are made and purchasing is done.

At the store level, there is a manager and usually two or three assistant managers. A very formalized structure exists. There is a 500-page manual at each store that explains all rules and procedures. This manual is used as part of the training and managers must read it in the first three months they are there. Supposedly, for any possible problem at a store, the solution would be in the manual.

The manager is in charge of store operations. This basically includes responsibilities for hiring and firing, opening and closing of the store, and store cleanliness. The home office controls all purchasing and shipment of merchandise, as well as all utility and cleaning/maintenance bills. The home office also provides each store with a payroll budget from which the manager must make up the work schedule. Directives are also sent to the stores about what merchandise should be displayed and what signs should be in the windows.

The Dilemma

The store manager is becoming very frustrated by the lack of control she has. Everything must go through home office first. The payroll budget allotted to her store is inadequate because she is in an older store and the average wage is higher than it is in a new store; therefore, her payroll dollars don't go very far. She spends a lot of time every week making up a schedule because she knows that overtime and requests for more money are looked down upon by the home office.

Another problem concerns the merchandise being sent to her store. She has tried to call the home office to tell them what items she needs and what items she has too many of, but they keep sending out the same items. She has spoken with other managers in her area and found that they were experiencing the same problem. As a result, the managers have set up a trading system where they transfer goods they have too much of to other stores.

Also, unlike the other stores, this manager's store has a very large front window. As a result, items placed near the window, especially sweaters, start fading from the sun. The manager has called many times about this and has even sent the damaged sweaters to the home office, but nothing has been done. It frustrates the manager that she must ask permission to put up blinds or shades to save merchandise.

Required:

1. What organizational weaknesses are causing the store manager's frustrations?
2. What remedial steps would you take to correct the situation and why?

CASE 12-3

The Company

The Chip Company is a large national corporation with locations in almost every state in the United States. Until recently, billing and ordering was centralized at seven regional centers. There has been a reorganization to consolidate almost all of the billing into two regional centers. There is some billing from other locations, but it is a small amount.

The Dilemma

Prior to the reorganization, the seven regional centers had problems correctly processing the billing. The reasons varied, but the most important ones were that the Chip Company was now selling to many different types of customers, at different price levels (including transfer price), and by different billing systems. This caused much confusion for the clerical workforce, and it took months to even get close to resolving the problem.

As previously mentioned, the seven regional centers are now consolidated into two regional centers. Many new people have been hired and old employees have been transferred. There have also been many promotions to manage the growth in personnel. The result is that there is much confusion at the regional centers. Although ordering and billing are processed more smoothly as employees become more familiar with their jobs, there are still many problems.

There are many divisional organizations that insist that they should have the capability to process billing. They say that the regional centers work much too slowly, do not adapt well to change, do not react to problems quickly, and do not handle "special cases" efficiently. They believe that their divisions can handle the billing process much more effectively.

The managers of these divisions have presented their needs to upper management of the regional centers and throughout the company. The consensus of upper management is that the regional centers are undergoing many changes to make them more efficient, timely, and adaptive to change. They claim that the cost of establishing decentralized billing systems will far outweigh the benefits. The divisional management is now uncertain about what course of action they should pursue.

Required:

1. What would you recommend?

CASE 12-4

The Company

A large electronics firm has expanded rapidly throughout the United States and overseas during the past ten years. With this growth, the organization divided its operation into six different units based on the industries they serve. The structure of this organization is diagrammed in Figure 12-3.

As indicated on the organization chart, there is an opening for a salesperson in the high tech unit. To fill this opening, there is a two-step process that the management of this organization must go through. First, the regional sales manager (RSM), who will be the direct boss for the new person, will initiate a proposal to fill this opening to the high tech marketing manager, who in turn will take the proposal to the high tech unit manager. From this point, the proposal goes to the electronics business manager (See Figure 12-3). At this point, no individuals are being discussed to fill the position; the question is whether or not to fill the position at all. The final decision is made by the business manager, who receives input from the general sales manager and the vice-president of marketing and sales.

Once a decision is made to fill the opening, the second step is finding the right person. To accomplish this, the RSM goes to personnel to obtain a computer printout of all available people who fit the criteria necessary for the sales positions. The RSM adds and deletes people and submits his initial list up through the same channel of managers. Each manager who sees the list is allowed to make additions or deletions. The outcome is generally a condensed list that goes back to the RSM, who then conducts informal interviews with the remaining candidates. From the interviews, the RSM recommends a few candidates, in order of priority, to the manager for approval. In most cases,

FIGURE 12-3
Organizational Structure

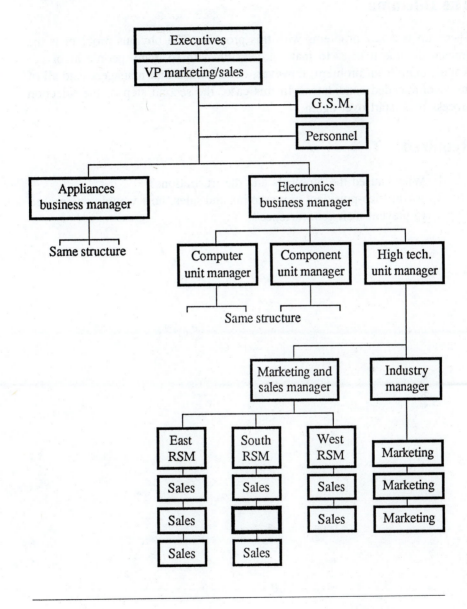

the manager will agree with the RSM on the top choice, but in cases of conflict, the final decision is made by the unit manager.

The Dilemma

There are two key problems with this process. The obvious problem is the amount of time it takes to make a decision with so many people involved. A more significant problem, however, occurs when unit managers veto all of the recommended candidates. In this case, the second step of the selection process must start over again.

Required:

1. What caused the problems and the frustrations?
2. As the vice-president of marketing and sales, how would you proceed to prevent their reoccurrence?

CHAPTER 13

The Behavioral Dimensions
of Internal Control

by
Kenneth Merchant
Associate Professor of Business Administration
Harvard University Graduate School of Business Administration

INTERNAL CONTROL PROBLEMS————————————

Case 1: Theft of Inventory

At the end of the 1982 fiscal year, auditors of a large U.S. office products manufacturer conducted physical counts of the inventories in the company's distribution warehouses. In one of the warehouses they discovered that the actual quantity of copier paper on hand was approximately $120,000 less than that shown on the company's perpetual inventory records. Since the missing inventory could not be found, the company was forced to take an unexpected write-off on its 1982 income statement.

The company's internal audit staff was called in to investigate the problem. The internal auditors determined that the missing inventory was apparently stolen and they were able to narrow down the list of personnel who were in a position to steal the paper supply. The case was finally solved when one of the production foreman confessed after being confronted with the evidence. He admitted that he stole the inventory with the cooperation of one of the company's regular truckers. The theft had been accomplished by loading extra boxes of paper to each load the trucker picked up. The trucker then sold the paper at a fraction of its value and shared the proceeds with the foreman. The foreman admitted that the scheme had been going on for several years but that it had been done on a much larger scale in 1982 because of his increased personal financial needs.

Case 2: Manipulation of Data

In 1979, a company that had been very proud of its steady and consistent rate of growth in earnings over a ten-year period disclosed that managers in several of the firm's divisions had conspired to transfer income between fiscal years. The income transferral scheme started in 1974 when some managers sought to reduce their profits to avoid exceeding the profit ratio limits of the wage and price controls in effect at that time. But the scheme continued even after the wage and price controls expired because managers found they could "save" profits and use them as a cushion to help ensure that they would be able to meet their annual profit targets.

The managers accomplished the income transferring, totaling many millions of dollars, through a number of procedures, including:

- Overpaying vendors and receiving rebates in the next year
- Soliciting and expensing invoices for services that would not be rendered until a future period
- Inflating accruals of the costs of sales incentive programs and shipping
- Writing down materials inventories in anticipation of price declines
- Postdating shipping documents
- Failing to record vendor credits on a timely basis

An outside team of investigators concluded that several specific working conditions in the company probably contributed to the existence and continuation of the income transferral practices. One was that there seemed to be a communications gap between corporate headquarters and the operating divisions. The company was highly decentralized and, importantly, the financial and accounting officers of the divisions were solely responsible to the chief executive officer of their respective divisions. This meant there was relatively little personal contact between financial staff in the divisions and those in corporate headquarters. A second factor was that the organization was operated under a meritocractic philosophy; that is, it was felt strongly that those who produced the desired results were those who merited rewards. But corporate headquarters sometimes issued orders and set financial standards without regard to whether complete attainment was possible. This often put operating management under considerable pressure. A third factor was the company's management incentive plan. This plan was very generous, promising rewards of up to 40 percent of salary, but it emphasized short-term (one year) operating results. There was also a very restrictive upper-level cutoff—no bonuses were paid for annual income greater than the preestablished target. The investigators felt that each of these factors increased the managers' motivations to transfer income between periods.

These two seemingly disparate management problems—one involving a loss of company assets and the other involving a distortion of the company's vital information resources—both resulted from failures in what is known as the *internal control* systems of the companies involved. This chapter describes what the term "internal control" means, how effective internal control systems provide benefits to organizations, and why internal control systems must be adapted to the different characteristics of different organizations.

DEFINITION AND SCOPE OF INTERNAL CONTROL

Establishing and maintaining an effective system of internal control is an important responsibility of management, but the term "internal control" was actually invented and defined by auditors. Auditors focused their attention on the controls in use in the organizations being audited because they realized that the type and extent of tests they need to perform in conjunction with audits should vary with the efficacy of the controls the organizations use to ensure the accuracy of their accounting data. This realization has been codified in generally accepted auditing practice as the second standard of field work:

> There is to be a proper study and evaluation of the existing internal control as a basis for reliance thereon and for determination of the resultant extent of the tests to which auditing procedures are to be restricted.[1]

The basic principle auditors follow is that the stronger the system of controls in place, the less extensive the tests of details that are needed.

Interestingly, however, there has never been unanimous agreement among auditors as to what should be included as part of an internal control system and how broad the study of controls should be. Much of the disagreement can be illustrated by tracking the evolution in the official definition of internal control in the United States over the years. Internal control was first defined in 1949 by a committee of the American Institute of Accountants as follows:

> Internal control comprises the plan of organization and all of the coordinate methods and measures adopted within a business to safeguard its assets, check the accuracy and reliability of its accounting data, promote operational efficiency, and encourage adherence to prescribed managerial policies. This definition possibly is broader than the meaning sometimes attributed to the term. It recognizes that a "system" of internal control extends beyond those matters which relate directly to the functions of the accounting and financial departments. Such a system might include budgetary control, standard costs, periodic operating reports, statistical analyses and the dissemination thereof, a training program designed to aid personnel in meeting their responsibilities, and an internal audit staff to provide additional assurance to management as to the adequacy of its outlined procedures and the extent to which they are being effectively carried out. It properly comprehends activities in other fields as, for example, time and motion studies which are of an engineering nature, and use of quality controls through a system of inspection which fundamentally is a production function.[2]

This is a broad definition that portrays internal control as having considerable overlap with the topics of concern identified in most definitions of management control. It did not, however, really help the practicing auditors for whom it was written to formulate operational tests of internal control. In fact, instead of allaying auditors' anxieties, as it was intended to do, this definition actually increased these anxieties because it raised concerns about legal liabilities.

In 1958, a new committee of the American Institute of Certified Public Accountants (AICPA) attempted to clarify the definition of internal control and the scope of study contemplated under generally accepted auditing standards. It held that:

> Internal control in the broad sense includes...controls which may be characterized as either accounting or administrative as follows:
>
> a. Accounting controls comprise the plan of organization and all methods and procedures that are concerned mainly with, and related directly to, the safeguarding of assets and the reliability of the financial records. They generally include such controls as the systems of authorization and approval, separation of duties concerned with operations or asset custody, physical controls over assets, and internal auditing.
>
> b. Administrative controls comprise the plan of organization and all methods and procedures that are concerned mainly with operational efficiency and adherence to managerial policies and usually related only indirectly to the financial records. They generally include such controls as statistical analyses, time and motion studies, performance reports, employee training programs, and quality controls.[3]

This distinction between accounting and administrative controls was made to clarify the scope of study contemplated under generally accepted accounting standards. The committee's conclusions in that regard were as follows:

> The independent auditor is primarily concerned with the accounting controls. Accounting controls...generally bear directly and importantly on the reliability of financial records and require evaluation by the auditor. Administrative controls...ordinarily relate only indirectly to the financial records and thus would not require evaluation. If the independent auditor believes, however, that certain administrative controls may have an important bearing on the reliability of the financial records, he should consider the need for evaluating such controls.[4]

The 1958 revision and clarification of the definition of internal control thus limited the auditor's scope of concern primarily to accounting controls. Another interpretation, issued in 1972, limited it even further.

Even after the 1958 revision, there was concern that within the definition of accounting controls, it was possible to interpret "safeguarding of assets and reliability of financial records" broadly, and this would then require auditors to examine any or all procedures or records entering into management's decision-making processes. Many auditors felt that an examination of such a broad scope was logically outside their responsibility. As a consequence, a 1972 AICPA committee issued an interpretation that limited the auditors' concerns to: (1) the safeguarding of assets "against loss arising from unintentional or intentional errors in processing transactions and handling the related assets," such as through incorrect computations, overpayments to vendors or employees, and physical losses of cash or inventory, and (2) "to the reliability of financial records for external reporting purposes."[5]

The combined effect of the 1958 and 1972 interpretations was to narrow the auditors' concern with internal control significantly from that of 1949. The currently operative definition of accounting control is quoted frequently in places such as the U.S. Foreign Corrupt Practices Act, which makes an effective system of accounting control a legal obligation of all firms that have a continuous reporting requirement with the Securities and Exchange Commission. The definition is as follows:

> Accounting control comprises the plan of organization and the procedures and records that are concerned with the safeguarding of assets and the reliability of financial records and consequently are designed to provide reasonable assurance that:
>
> a. Transactions are executed in accordance with management's general or specific authorization.
>
> b. Transactions are recorded as necessary (1) to permit preparation of financial statements in conformity with generally accepted accounting principles or any other criteria applicable to such statements, and (2) to maintain accountability for assets.
>
> c. Access to assets is permitted only in accordance with management's authorization.
>
> d. The recorded accountability for assets is compared with the existing assets at reasonable intervals and appropriate action is taken with respect to any differences.[6]

The first phrase of this definition describes what are now taken to be the main goals of an internal control system—safeguarding of assets and maintenance of the reliability of financial records. The phrases following the first phrase highlight some of the major devices that can be used to accomplish these goals. The devices are known individually as "internal controls" and collectively as an "internal control system."

It should be noted that while this definition of internal control is the official version used by public accountants in the United States, other parties often use the term in slightly different ways. For example, the International Federation of Accountants (IFAC), which in 1981 represented 80 accountancy bodies from 59 different countries[7] chose a much broader definition:

> The system of internal control is the plan of organization and all the co-ordinate systems, financial and otherwise, established by the management of an entity to assist in achieving management's objective of ensuring, as far as practical, the orderly and efficient conduct of its business, including adherence to management policies, the safeguarding of assets, the prevention or detection of fraud and error, the accuracy and completeness of the accounting records, and the timely preparation of reliable financial information.[8]

This definition is more similar to the broad 1949 U.S. definition of internal control than it is to the current U.S. definition. Conversely, the U.S. Institute of Internal Auditors describes internal controls much more narrowly, as "procedures that ensure the accuracy and completeness of manual and automated transactions, records, and reports, and the avoidance, detection and correction of errors."[9] There is obviously considerable overlap among all of these definitions—each of which encompasses the two problems described at the beginning of this chapter. Because some important differences do exist, care must be taken to understand what is intended when the term "internal control" is used.

THE BENEFITS OF INTERNAL CONTROLS

It is evident from these above definitions that internal control problems are really behavioral problems. That is, internal control problems are caused by risks that the personnel on whom the organization must rely may cause harm because they perform undesired actions or because they fail to perform desired actions. Thus, internal controls are beneficial to organizations because of their ability to (1) prevent, or at least reduce, the incidence of the undesired or omitted behaviors that can occur and (2) lower the costs of the unwanted or omitted behaviors that do occur.

Since internal control problems are behavioral problems, an understanding of how and why internal controls work should be done in behavioral terms; psychology, not accounting or economics, is perhaps the most important basic discipline underlying the theory and practice of internal control. This important fact about internal control is often unstated in the many writings about internal control, most of which are technically and procedurally oriented.[10]

The behavioral problems against which internal controls guard are derived from limitations present to a greater or lesser extent in all individuals. These limitations can be classified into three main categories: motivation, ability, and knowledge. It is widely recognized that individual motivations and organizational motivations do not naturally coincide; in the terminology that is used in many textbooks, there is lack of goal congruence. These *motivational limitations* manifest themselves in, for example, employee theft, sabotage, or merely carelessness.

But some people who are highly motivated to perform as the organization wishes are unable to perform some duties properly. They may be unable to perform appropriately because of *ability limitations*. For example, the tasks they are assigned may be so physically demanding that fatigue causes errors, or so complex that they forget important information or get confused with the details. People may also be unable to perform properly because of *knowledge limitations*, which occur when people do not know what to do or how to do it. For example, assigning an untrained person to prepare financial reports, or even to perform a bank reconciliation, will provide a very low probability of success.

All three of these limitations are present, to a greater or lesser degree, in all the people on whom all organizations must rely at virtually all times. As a consequence, it is essential that managers have a strong, effective set of internal controls in place; if opportunities for errors and irregularities exist, sooner or later the errors and irregularities will occur and their cost can be significant. Furthermore, the types of controls to be used should depend on knowledge or assumptions about the types of undesired or omitted behaviors that might occur, their likelihood of occurrence, and how the particular types of controls will affect the behaviors of those involved.

TYPES OF INTERNAL CONTROLS

Managers can use many different devices to guard against the undesired behaviors and/or lower the costs of the undesired behaviors that do occur. All of these devices can be called internal controls. There are many ways to classify the many kinds of internal controls. One way is to classify them according to their purpose—that is, whether the controls serve to *prevent* or to *detect* undesirable behaviors. This distinction is important because controls that prevent the undesired errors and irregularities from occurring are, when they are effective, the most powerful form of control because none of the costs of undesirable behaviors will be incurred. Detection-type internal controls differ from prevention-type controls in that they are applied *after* the occurrence of the behavior. Still, they can be effective if the detection is made in a timely manner and if it results in a cessation of the behavior and a correction of the effects of the harmful actions. This prompt detection of harmful actions will discourage individuals from engaging in such behaviors purposefully.

Another way to classify the controls is according to the specificity of their intent. Some internal controls are designed to achieve specific control objectives. Here, this form of internal controls will be called *specific* controls, but they have also been called primary controls[11] and application controls.[12] Specific controls are generally applied at those points in the processing of transactions and handling of assets where one or more types of errors or irregularities can occur.

Other internal controls are broader in their intent. They will be called *general* controls here, following the terminology used by John Willingham and Douglas Carmichael;[13] Gary Holstrum[14] called them secondary controls. General controls are intended to provide an environment conducive to good internal control and to support and assure the functioning of the specific controls. The distinction between specific and general controls is important because, except in unusual circumstances, auditors look for specific controls over all critical tasks (e.g., billings transactions) before they certify an internal control system as being effective.

These two ways of classifying internal controls can be portrayed in a 2 × 2 matrix. Some common examples of each of the four forms of controls shown in the matrix can be seen in Figure 13-1.

Cell 1: Specific/Prevention

1. *Restriction of access to areas where valuable assets or sensitive records are kept*. Restriction of access may be accomplished physically (e.g., bank vault) or administratively (e.g., computer passwords guarding access to sensitive data).
2. *Separation of duties*. This involves dividing up the tasks necessary for the accomplishment of certain sensitive tasks. For example, it is generally recognized that the person who makes the payment entries in the accounts receivable ledger should not also receive the checks. If these duties were not separated, this person could deposit the checks in a personal account and cover the action by making fictitious entries of returns of goods or price adjustments.
3. *Validation of data before entry*. Any of a number of checks can be performed on entries before the transactions are completed. These can include comparisons with a preestablished list of acceptable items (e.g., approved list of vendors), checks to see if the proper authorizations have been given, or simply checks to make sure that the entry balances.

FIGURE 13-1
Internal Control Classification Scheme

Purpose

		Prevention	Detection
	Specific	1	2
Specificity of intent			
	General	3	4

Cell 2: Specific/Detection

1. *Reconciliation of periodic inventory counts with inventory records.* Most inventory theft problems and many transaction-recording problems are not detected until this reconciliation is made.
2. *Prenumbered forms.* Many organizations put unique numbers on valuable documents, such as movie tickets, checks, and purchase orders, and then account for them to help ensure that none are lost and none are used for purposes other than that intended by the organization.
3. *Reconciliation of batch balance reports with logs maintained in originating departments.* If, for example, 80 invoices were processed in the sales department but the computer report shows only 79, someone will know to look for and enter the missing document.

Cell 3: General/Prevention

1. *Effective hiring and training policies.* If the organization can take steps to ensure that the personnel on whom it must rely are competent, well-trained and have high integrity, then errors and irregularities are less likely.
2. *Effective plan of organization.* A well-designed organization with clear definitions of every individual's duties and responsibilities, such as thorough job descriptions, organizational charts, and procedures manuals, helps ensure that critical tasks are not performed by unauthorized personnel.
3. *Code of conduct.* Most firms make it clear to all employees, usually in

written corporate policies and codes of conduct, that ethical goals are more important than financial goals in all cases where they conflict, and that deviations will be dealt with severely.

Cell 4: General/Detection

1. *Close supervision of personnel.* Effective supervisors can observe the behaviors or documentation about the behaviors of those for whom they are responsible and detect problems on a timely basis.
2. *Use of an internal audit staff.* Internal auditors can be valuable in identifying and investigating a broad range of potential problems.
3. *Scrutiny of financial reports.* Regular comparisons of financial transactions and reports with budgets, standards, and prior experience can lead to the identification of problems, particularly if they are material.

SITUATIONAL INFLUENCES ON THE CHOICE OF INTERNAL CONTROLS

In designing internal control systems, managers must choose combinations of devices (controls) such as those described previously. Since organizations' internal control needs differ, it is natural that the solutions chosen (the internal control systems) also differ. The diversity of internal control systems was documented in a recent survey by Mautz et al.[15]

The choice of the controls to use seems to depend on four factors:

1. *The types of errors and irregularities that may be faced.* This varies widely with the types of assets the firm has and the types of transactions in which it engages. For example, inventory loss is not a significant area of risk for service firms, which usually have only minimal inventories. Computerization of an accounting system causes major changes in the number and types of people who have, or might gain, access to the financial records, and this changes the points of risk.
2. *The cost to the organization if one or more of the errors or irregularities occurs.* Obviously, tighter control has to be exercised over critical transactions, such as billings and credit and collections, and high-value assets.
3. *The likelihood of occurrence of each type of error and irregularity.* Whether a problem is likely to occur varies with, for example:
   a. The types of people in the operation being controlled. The risk of errors in firms that hire only well-trained, experienced personnel is lower than that in firms that hire inexperienced personnel.
   b. The salability of the asset in the case of an asset loss problem. Businesses that deal with cash (e.g., banks and casinos) have the highest risk.

c. The complexity of the operation being controlled. Very complex processes may lead to lack of understanding on the part of the people doing the work.

d. The organizational structure. It is more difficult for top management to stay informed about all of the operations taking place in a diverse, highly decentralized organization.

e. The management philosophy. A working environment in which considerable pressure is placed on employees to perform will tend to encourage employees to manipulate data to meet targets. It can also produce alienation, which can lead to such dysfunctional behaviors as theft and sabotage.

4. *The cost and potential effectiveness of each of the types of controls that can be used.* Internal controls, like all economic goods, should not be implemented unless the potential benefits are greater than the costs.

SOLUTIONS TO THE CASE EXAMPLES

At the beginning of this chapter, two examples of problems caused by internal control deficiencies were described. Now that the internal control concept, problems, and solutions have been discussed, it is useful to refer back to these case examples and to discuss the responses the companies made after the deficiencies were uncovered.

The first case involved a theft of inventory. Absolute prevention of this type of problem is not feasible unless access to the inventory can be restricted to a single, trustworthy employee. In this case, further restricting access to inventory areas was not considered desirable, as certain employees needed to have access to the inventory area for delivery and shipping purposes. But the company did take the following steps to improve control over its inventories:

1. The production foreman who admitted to the theft was replaced with a more reliable employee.

2. A new procedure was instituted that required the shipping foreman to count the quantities of inventory loaded onto each truck and to sign the shipping document indicating agreement between the quantities on the document and his count. This procedure was designed to provide a prompt detection of any schemes that might be perpetrated to remove inventory from the warehouse on trucks picking up authorized shipments. The shipping foremen were also reminded that unauthorized truckers should not be allowed to pull up to the loading dock.

3. Inventory counts were scheduled more frequently. Counts of some of the most valuable and liquid forms of inventory were scheduled quarterly so that problems, if any, would be detected more promptly. The other forms of inventory were still counted only annually, but the internal audit staff

was instructed to do some spot checking on a surprise basis to see if the quantities on hand matched the quantities shown on the perpetual inventory records.

This case illustrates a fairly common control problem and a typical solution. The inventory itself was not valuable to the thief, but the theft was attempted because the inventory could be converted into cash. The problem was detected when the quantities of inventories on hand were reconciled with the amounts shown in the accounting records. A much more serious problem would have resulted if the foreman doing the stealing also had access to the accounting records; in that case, detection would have been much more difficult.

The second case did not involve a loss of company assets, but it did involve a fairly large-scale data manipulation in which managers conspired to transfer income between periods. This was a very serious problem because it caused a distortion in the company's information system. Strong steps had to be taken to ensure that the problem was stopped and that it would not recur. Some of the steps taken were designed to strengthen the internal control system; others were designed to change the working environment to reduce the managers' motivations to manipulate data. These steps included:

1. The company's code of conduct was revised and strengthened, and it was emphasized to all employees that deliberate violations of this code would not be tolerated.
2. A new corporate officer was hired and given responsibility for all company functions related to financial accounting, controls, and external reporting.
3. All existing policies, practices, procedures, and controls were evaluated in light of the requirements of the Foreign Corrupt Practices Act and good business practice. Steps were taken to rectify the deficiencies found.
4. An accounting policy manual was developed as a vehicle for establishing, documenting, and updating uniform accounting policies and procedures. The manual included a uniform chart of accounts with account descriptions; a set of accounting policies defining the criteria for timing, valuation, and recording of transactions; a list of the timing and formats for required disclosures of financial information; a set of policies specifying the minimum standards for accounting systems and procedures; and a list of the authority limits of personnel in authorizing transactions. The manual was intended to ensure that all divisions would have an accounting system that met at least minimum standards and, because of the common formats and definitions of data items, that users of financial reports would have a clear understanding of the nature of the data presented.
5. An ongoing program was established to monitor compliance with required policies and procedures and to ensure that the policies and procedures maintained their effectiveness over time.

6. A new policy to encourage transfers of personnel between finance departments at headquarters and the divisions was instituted. This policy was intended to increase the personal contacts between the two groups and reduce the communication gaps and adversarial feelings that had built up.

7. The internal audit function of the company was strengthened, and the lines of reporting were changed so that the function was responsible directly to the audit committee of the board of directors instead of the finance and accounting functions as before.

8. A review of the management incentive plan was conducted to determine how to maintain the basic incentives while reducing the motivations for the income transferral practices. Several alternatives were considered, including assigning awards based on corporate (not divisional) performance, long-term (multiyear) performance, or performance measured in terms of nonfinancial indicators.

These examples of internal control problems are by no means unique. Many firms have faced and are facing similar problems.

INTERNAL CONTROL-RELATED RESEARCH

Anyone who goes to the library and looks up references to internal control will quickly see that much has been written about it. Prominent in the internal control literature are a number of excellent books and pamphlets that document the wisdom public accountants have accumulated over the years in what can be called normative form; that is, these works describe how auditors should (and presumably do) evaluate internal control systems.[16] There are also many articles in practitioner-oriented journals that describe some of the internal control problems companies have faced and share insights that auditors and managers have reached about how to solve them.[17]

Academic research on topics related to internal control has been relatively sparce, however. The studies that do exist can be divided into three classes. The first class includes papers that use models of organizational systems to describe how different types of internal control weaknesses relate to numerical errors in reported balances.[18] This is a potentially fruitful line of research, but thus far these modeling efforts do not seem to have had much impact on practice, probably because of the lack of realism of the models and/or a lack of understanding of them by practitioners.

A second class of studies are of auditor judgments about the adequacy of internal controls in a controlled laboratory setting.[19] These studies have provided insight into the cues auditors use in making such judgments and the weights they give the cues. They have also provided the useful finding that auditors' internal control–evaluation judgments are generally highly consistent with each other and are consistent over time, particularly if the auditors are experienced. This is support for the idea that the knowledge contained in the "how-to" books has been well communicated.

The third class of studies suggests improvements in the ways auditors use the information they collect about internal controls to affect the substantive tests they perform.[20] This line of thought, backed up by statistical arguments, has probably influenced auditors to think about their sample selection policies.

It is obvious that there is much more research that can be done in areas related to internal control. All of the lines of inquiry described above are in their early stages and can be expanded in several directions.

There are also several research questions that have attracted no attention from researchers but would seem to be at least as promising to study as those described above. One example is studies of internal controls conducted with managers' perspectives in mind. It is true that internal control was invented by auditors, but it is managers who must implement and operate the systems of internal controls. Still, researchers have not studied the cost-benefit trade-offs faced by managers who are considering implementing particular types of internal controls or the judgment processes managers use in designing and evaluating internal control systems. Since managers' perspectives are quite different from those of auditors, who are primarily concerned with how the evaluations of internal controls should affect their audit processes, management-oriented studies would likely lead to some quite different conclusions.

Another fruitful area of research would be behavioral studies of the people who are being influenced by the internal controls. Researchers could study the causes of the unwanted behaviors, the behavioral effects of various types and combinations of controls, and the side effects that might be produced (e.g., operating delays, negative attitudes toward the organization). Much related research does exist in the fields of psychology and organizational behavior, but the findings from these fields have not been tied back into the internal control literature.

The main point about internal control and research is that there is much that can and should be done. Most of the knowledge about internal control has been developed by practitioners; an organized program of research could provide even more useful findings.

SUMMARY

The focus of this chapter was internal control. This is an important subject; it is important for auditors because they must evaluate systems of internal control to determine the auditing procedures they will use; it is also important for managers because it is their responsibility to establish and maintain effective internal control systems. The importance of internal control was reemphasized in 1977 when the U.S. Congress passed the Foreign Corrupt Practices Act, which makes good internal control a legal responsibility of the management of publicly held corporations.

This chapter provided only an overview of the subject of internal control. The major points discussed follow.

First, unanimous agreement on the boundaries of internal control does not exist, but it is generally agreed that internal control involves safeguarding assets and ensuring the reliability of financial records. Thus, good internal control is necessary but not sufficient to ensure good management control; the latter is concerned with many activities that do not affect the financial statements directly, at least in the short run.

Second, the problems that internal controls are intended to solve are best conceptualized in behavioral terms. Internal controls provide benefits to organizations because they prevent, or at least reduce, the impact of undesired or omitted behaviors that can result in loss of assets and/or distortion of financial records.

Third, internal controls come in many different forms. The controls can be distinguished according to their intent—that is, whether they are designed to prevent or to detect undesired or omitted behaviors. They can also be distinguished by their specificity—that is, whether they are designed to control a single type of activity or a broader set.

Fourth, it is natural that internal control systems differ significantly in different types of organizations. The controls must vary according to the types of undesired behaviors that may occur, the cost to the organization if the undesired behavior occurs, the likelihood of the behavior's occurrence, and the cost and probability of success of implementing each particular type of control. Each of these factors must be evaluated in light of the circumstances each organization faces.

Finally, there is much research that needs to be done in areas related to internal control. Most of the current knowledge about the functioning of internal controls in organizations comes from practitioners, and most is written from the perspective of the auditor rather than that of the manager.

REFERENCES

[1] American Institute of Certified Public Accountants, *Codification of Statements on Auditing Standards: Numbers 1 to 33*, Section 320.01 (Chicago, Illinois: Commerce Clearing House, 1981).

[2] American Institute of Accountants, *Internal Control: Elements of a Coordinated System and its Importance to Management and the Independent Public Accountant* (New York: AIA, 1949), 6.

[3] AICPA. Section 320.10.

[4] *Ibid.*, Section 320.11.

[5] *Ibid.*, Section 320.19.

[6] *Ibid.*, Section 320.28.

[7] F. D. S. Choi and G. G. Mueller, *International Accounting* (Englewood Cliffs, N.J.: Prentice-Hall, 1984), 492.

[8] International Federation of Accountants, *Study and Evaluation of the Accounting System and Internal Conflict in Connection with an Audit* (New York: IFAC, 1980) 1.

[9] Institute of Internal Auditing, (Altamonte Springs, Florida, IIA, 1977), 19.

[10] A notable exception in D. R. Carmichael, "Behavioral Hypotheses of Internal Control," *The Accounting Review* (April 1970): 235–245.

[11] G. L. Holstrum, *Auditscope: The Deloitte, Haskins and Sells Audit Approach* unpublished manuscript, March 1984).

[12] J. J. Willington and D. R. Carmichael, *Auditing Concepts and Methods* (New York: McGraw-Hill, 1979).

[13] *Ibid.*

[14] Holstrum, 1984.

[15] P. K. Mautz, W. G. Kell, M. W. Maher, A. G. Merten, R. R. Reilly, D. G. Severance, and B. J. White, *Internal Control in U.S. Corporations: The State of the Art* (New York: Financial Executives Research Foundation, 1980).

[16] See K. P. Johnson and K. R. Jaenicke, *Evaluating Internal Control* (New York: John Wiley & Sons, 1980); and Arthur Andersen & Company,, *A Guide for Studying and Evaluating Internal Accounting Controls* (Chicago: Arthur Andersen & Co., 1978).

[17] See R. Gevirtzman, "Controls in Automated Information Systems," *Journal of Systems Management* (January 1983): 34–41; P. Hooper and J. Page, "Internal Control Problems of Computer Systems," *Journal of Systems Management* (December 1982): 22–24; and W. J. Jhlanfeldt, "Shell Oil Company's Approach," *Financial Executive* (July 1979): 42–48.

[18] See W. O. Stratton, "Accounting Systems: The Reliability Approach to Internal Control Evaluation," *Decision Sciences* (January 1981): 51–67; B. E. Cushing, "A Mathematical Approach to the Analysis and Design of Internal Control Systems," *The Accounting Review* (January 1974) 24–41; and S. Yu and J. Neter, "A Stochastic Model of the Internal Control System," *Journal of Accounting Research* (Autumn 1973): 273–95.

[19] See R. H. Ashton, "An Experimental Study of Internal Control Judgments," *Journal of Accounting Research* (Spring 1974): 143–187; R. Weber, "Auditor Decision Making on Overall System Reliability: Accuracy, Consensus and the Usefulness of a Decision Aid," *Journal of Accounting Research* (Autumn 1978): 368–388; and R. H. Ashton and P. R. Brown, "Descriptive Modeling of Auditors' Internal Control Judgments: Replication and Extension," *Journal of Accounting Research* (Spring 1984): 269–277.

[20] K. A. Smith, "The Relationship of Internal Control Evaluation and Audit Sample Size," *The Accounting Review* (April 1972): 260–269; and D. Hatherly, "Linking

Internal Control and Substantive Tests: A Note," *Accounting and Business Research* (Winter 1975): 63–66.

DISCUSSION QUESTIONS

1. What is the distinction between accounting and administrative controls? Why does this distinction exist?
2. What are the main goals of an internal control system? What are some major devices that can be used to accomplish these goals?
3. Why are internal controls beneficial to organizations? What is the most important basic discipline underlying the theory and practice of internal control?
4. What are the limitations that bring about the behavioral problems against which internal controls guard?
5. Define internal controls. How can internal controls be classified?
6. What is the distinction between specific and general controls? Why is this distinction important?
7. Give an example for each of the four forms of controls shown in the matrix in this chapter.
8. What are the factors that affect the choice of controls to be used in an organization?
9. Why are internal controls important to auditors? Why are they important to managers?

CASE 13-1

The Company

WXYZ is a small but growing television station. WXYZ first went on the air 20 years ago, and its management believes it can still get a much larger share of the viewing audience.

Floyd Brown, the business manager of the television station, is responsible for all financial matters. Brown's finance department consists of an accounting supervisor, who supervises an accounts payable clerk, billing clerk, and credit and collections clerk.

Brown has been with the television station for 15 years. He has been the business manager for the last 5 years after having gained extensive experience in all areas of the financial department. Brown has a good business relationship with all department heads and feels his department is responsible for providing relevant business information for all departments of WXYZ. He feels that as long as he is providing timely and accurate information, he is doing a good job.

Bruno Faldi, the general sales manager of WXYZ, heads a force of seven local sales representatives. Faldi has increased sales substantially over the last three years and eventually wants to become general manager of WXYZ. Faldi's management skills have been recognized. He is viewed as the number two man at WXYZ below the station's general manager. The sales department is viewed solely as a profit center at WXYZ.

Bonuses are only paid to department heads at WXYZ. Because of the growth of the last few years, managers have received high yearly bonuses.

The Dilemma

While sales have increased, yearly entertainment expenses within the sales department have also increased. Tim Conley, the accounts payable clerk, has enjoyed a good relationship with all sales representatives of WXYZ. The local sales representatives take Conley out to lunch once or twice a week knowing they can pass the expense off on the station. At lunch, the fact that managers only get a bonus at WXYZ is often discussed by Conley and the local sales representatives. Conley and the representatives feel they deserve these lunches since they are not getting their fair share.

Conley gets the expense reports after they have been signed by the general sales manager. There is no cumulative yearly expense total kept by Conley for each sales representative nor is there any limit placed on the sales representatives so Faldi does not consider this information. An expense report signed by Faldi is then checked by Conley for accuracy and coded to the correct accounts. A check is then made by Conley and signed by Brown, the business manager. Brown feels these expenses are the responsibility of the sales department, and as long as Faldi signs the expense reports and the accuracy and expense distribution is correct, he signs the checks.

Conley knows the sales representatives take other liberties with their expense accounts, but feels that they take care of him and that the station can afford it, so it is okay.

Required:

1. Discuss the internal control in this organization. What recommendations would you make?

CASE 13-2

The Company

A large commercial bank with loan principal balances of $33 billion has one centralized loan operations area to maintain the records of all commercial loans. This operations area is divided into the following groups:

1. Loan Processing, which handles establishing loans on the loan system, maintaining proper accruals, billing customers, applying payments to the appropriate accounts, and making any needed adjustments to the loan records.
2. Loan Support, which is responsible for maintaining needed information regarding collateral and documentation for all loans.
3. Production and Operations, which provide support for the loan operations area in the form of printing and distributing computer reports and preparing specialized reports.

During the past several months, the bank's internal and external auditors have been studying the entire loan operations area to be sure adequate controls are in place. This review is in response to the growing number of problem loans the bank is encountering and complaints from lending officers that they are receiving bad information from loan operations. The Loan Processing group was cited for several "exceptions" in this review. These were:

1. Excessive amounts and duration of holdover items. These items represent transactions that cannot be completely recorded because of insufficient information at the time of the transaction. Entries are made to holdover accounts toward the end of the day to include these balances in the general ledger for the day. All holdover items should be properly identified and removed from these accounts within a few days. Loan Processing has had too many holdovers and has not cleared them in a timely manner.
2. Excessive amount and duration of unapplied payments. These amounts represent payments on loans that are received but cannot be properly identified to the customer's account because of insufficient information at the time of receipt. Entries are made to the unapplied payments accounts to include these balances in the day's general ledger. Loan Processing has had too many unapplied payments and has not cleared them in a timely manner.
3. Insufficient education and training of loan tellers. Further training on the loan system is needed to ensure that tellers understand their role. Tellers should pursue college-level courses in business at night school to further their understanding of accounting and finance. Most tellers have at most a few college-level courses.
4. Inadequate supervision of transactions requiring more technical expertise.

The Dilemma

Susan is a supervisor in the Loan Processing area. She has been with the bank for five years and has recently completed her college degree. Her manager has recently discussed the auditor's review with her and has stressed the need to deal with the exception items as quickly as possible. Susan is to tell her staff to reduce holdover and unapplied payment entries and to begin plans for taking college courses at night using the bank's reimbursement program. Susan is also expected to evaluate her section and formally propose any other changes she feels are needed. Her manager pointed out that if these proposals are especially good, her chances for a promotion in the next six months would be improved.

Terri is a loan teller in Susan's section. Susan's section handles customers whose names begin with the letters L through S and Terri handles the letter N. Terri is considered to be a hard worker who requests little guidance in performing her duties. In accordance with management's requests, she is taking a general accounting course at a local university one night a week. She is also trying to be more careful in handling holdover and unapplied payment entries.

One day, Terri received a large number of payments without sufficient information to completely process the transactions. Since she did not want to process the items as unapplied payments, she tried to get Susan's help in further identifying the entries. Susan had been very busy preparing her proposals, which were due in three days, so she was unable to help Terri that afternoon. Normally Terri would stay late to complete the transactions, but on this night, she had a mid-term exam in her accounting class. Terri decided to misapply the payments and correct the entries the next morning. A misapplied payment is normally the result of posting a payment to the wrong customer's account—it often remains undiscovered until the customer's bill is identified as past due. After incorrectly posting the entries, Terri wrote out all the entries on notepaper so she could correct them the next day.

The next two mornings, two of Susan's tellers called in sick. This required Susan to divide their workload among the other tellers. As a result, all the tellers were extremely busy both days and worked some overtime to keep up. Terri was unable to correct her misapplied payments during this time, but she came to work early the next day to work on them. When she got to her desk, she realized that she had misplaced the notepaper containing the details for these entries. She spent some time looking for the notepaper but was unable to locate it. In a staff meeting later that day, Susan commended Terri for working so hard during the week while maintaining low holdover and unapplied payment entries and getting through her mid-term exam. Terri realized that the misapplied payments were unlikely to be noticed. Over the next several weeks, Terri again misapplied payments several times to get out of tight situations.

Required:

1. Discuss internal control shortcomings and recommend action for correction.

CASE 13-3

The Company

Produce City is a family-owned and operated produce market. The owner, Joe Smith, is also the store's chief decision maker, buyer, advertising salesman, and bookkeeper. Smith runs the store in a centralized fashion; any decision or plan of action must be cleared through him first. However, because of his many roles, he is outside of the store much of the day and cannot be reached.

The Dilemma

Produce City has a number of business problems, including:

1. Incoming C.O.D. deliveries, in many cases, cannot be accepted because Joe Smith is the only person with the ability to pay for these deliveries.
2. Other suppliers have agreed to credit terms, yet Smith's failure to pay these bills has resulted in several weeks' worth of past due bills. This causes suppliers to refuse to ship further items until payments are made.
3. Produce picked up by Smith himself is usually an amount in excess of the store's current need. Smith purchases the excess amount because of the better price for high volume. The result, though, is that a substantial portion goes to waste and must be discarded.
4. The store has no set mark-up rate. Cost is determined by product only, with no consideration for transportation or delivery labor costs. An arbitrary selling price that "sounds good" is established. Labor, utility, building, and maintenance costs are not included in the calculation of product costs, and a desired profit margin is not included in determining the selling price.
5. Employees are paid weekly by a check processing company, yet all employees are virtually required to cash their checks while at work because the company's checking account usually cannot cover the checks.
6. There is no set performance standard and subsequent periodic pay raise system. Employees have to ask for their own pay raises, so those who have more reserved natures often go for longer periods of time between pay raises than the more outspoken employees.

Required:

1. What are the weaknesses in internal control and what dysfunctional employee behavior could result from them?
2. How would you redesign the various activities to avoid tempting your employees to engage in fraudulent behavior?

CASE 13-4

The Company

Mr. John Hall is the president and owner of A.B. Hall and Sons Company, a small leather tannery in Chicago. The business, which is family owned and operated, has been run by Hall for the last 50 years; prior to this, his father controlled the company.

The Dilemma

The company found itself a small niche in the leather market, producing softball leather and golf grips. This niche, largely ignored by the huge overseas tanneries, allowed Hall and Sons to survive on a profitable basis while many other domestic tanneries fell by the wayside. Hall ran the company with an iron fist, controlling almost all production and financial matters himself. Although he employed two capable individuals—Mr. Kent and Mr. Stern—for nearly 15 years each, Hall refused to give them any responsibility other than general supervisory reign in the plant.

In the summer of 1983, Hall's wife became seriously ill. As a result, Hall found his attention focused less and less on the running of the company. His wife began to put pressure on him to get out of the business and enjoy what little time they had left together (Hall was 77, his wife, 74).

In the fall of that year, Hall agreed to a sale of 10 percent of the company's stock to Mr. Stern for a total price of $644,000. At the closing, Hall signed an affidavit representing and warranting that the financial condition of the firm was as it was depicted in the unaudited October interim financial statements. Prior to making the final commitment for the sale, Stern approached Hall and Sons' bank to make sure that the company's current credit arrangements would not be affected by the change in ownership. The bank agreed to a continuation of the current financing parameters, as long as the company's financial health was not adversely affected by the accounting for the stock sale.

In the spring of 1984, Stern discovered that he had been suckered. The 1984 audited statements revealed a large discrepancy between what Hall had portrayed the company's condition to be and what its actual condition was. The firm had incurred a loss of over $250,000 on sales of roughly $3.3 million in the previous year; Stern had been expecting a loss of approximately $100,000. Upon investigation, it was revealed that Hall, who had ultimate control over the books and controlled the firm's cash disbursements, had somehow failed to expense certain items—including his generous salary, insurance payments, and inventory write-downs—on the October interim statements that were provided to Stern at the time the sale of the company was consummated.

As a result, Stern filed suit against his former employer for the $150,000 misstatement. To date, he has incurred substantial legal expenses related to the litigation. In addition, his bank has demanded that all loans be secured by the company's assets and that Stern provide a personal guarantee for any borrowings. The bank also increased the rate charged on borrowings by an additional 1 percent over the previous prime rate plus 1/4 percent.

Required:

1. What caused the problem?

CHAPTER 14

The Behavioral Patterns
of Auditors

by
Donald S. Shannon
Professor
School of Accountancy, De Paul University
William T. Stevens
Pace University

AUDITING AND AUDITORS

Introduction

Auditors exhibit most of the behaviors of other humans, but the nature of auditing raises some unique behavioral issues. Before these can be studied effectively, it is necessary to review the nature of auditing—what it is and, perhaps more importantly, what it is not.

The Nature of Auditing

The term "auditing" comes from the Latin verb *audire,* meaning to hear. Originally, auditing meant listening—the auditor heard evidence and, based on his or her judgment, formed a conclusion. Today, court proceedings are often referred to as hearings, with the judge as the principal listener. The idea of auditing as listening still persists. For example, a student attending an academic course and listening, but performing little or no work and receiving no formal credit, is said to be auditing the course.

In commerce, auditing became, in time, the act of verifying financial records. In this context, a body of investigative techniques for examining accounts developed, some of which found application in other inquiries, and the word "audit" came to refer to any investigation.

The Scope of Auditing

Auditing is a pervasive activity. It touches almost everyone, especially in a mature society such as ours. From birth to death, each of us experiences a variety of audits. So too, is every institution subjected to the audit. The following will illustrate this pervasiveness: The hospital where we were born undergoes constant auditing. An official verifies the precise time and place of our birth, sex, measurements, lineage, attending physician, and other data to be embedded in permanent records, not only at the hospital but in other places as well. A host of federal, state, and local government agencies examine the hospital to ensure that records are maintained according to rules; others seek assurance of institutional compliance with applicable regulations; and government auditors determine if government payments from support programs, such as Medicare, meet legal requirements. Insurance firms dispatch auditors to the hospital to delve into records and operations to determine whether billed services are proper and have been performed. Concerned citizens investigate various aspects of the institution's policies or operations, especially if the hospital is tax supported. Physicians undertake audits to oversee the quality of the facility in terms of both support and professional medical services.

Auditing pervades almost every institution and organization. Government units are audited endlessly for accountability for public funds and compliance with a bewildering host of statutes, regulations, and administrative fiats (some of which may be in direct conflict with others). Schools fall under the constant and often skeptical scrutiny of diverse audit groups armed with a variety of missions. Investments, bank accounts, and other financial instruments and institutions experience regular examinations for a smorgasbord of compliance and substantive purposes.

Our employers are audited for compliance with estate, excise, pay-roll, property, use, franchise, sales, employment, unemployment, retirement, income, and other taxes. Personnel practices and staff turnovers, disabilities, workmen's compensation, pension plan fundings, and insurance coverages are reviewed by streams of auditors. Records and activities are examined for conformity with health and safety standards, minimum wage constraints, and other workplace regulations. Teams of certified public accountants dig into all facets of business operations to ascertain financial health.

Our personal lives are constantly audited as we seek work, wish to attend school, want to borrow money and, unhappily, when we die. Private habits, appetites, and even our opinions are bared, examined in detail, and used to form the basis of a report. Many audits are open, known reviews, but many are covert, leaving us unaware that we have been audited.

The audit is a fact of life. It covers the entire spectrum of public and private activities of individuals and organizations from cradle to grave. There is no escape.

The Auditor Stereotype

The audit is performed by an auditor who is a person, not a robot. The auditor is a human being capable of emotions and subject to human frailties. However, auditors have been the subject of commonly held misconceptions that have led to a stereotype that encompasses a certain mystique. This is most evident in laypersons as they seek to capture the essence of the auditor's character. Perhaps the most biting, yet typical, of lay viewpoints was expressed by Elbert Hubbard, an early twentieth-century philosopher and something of an iconoclast:

> The typical auditor is a man past middle age, spare, wrinkled, intelligent, cold, passive, non-committal; with eyes like a codfish, polite in contact, but at the same time unresponsive, cold; calm and damnably composed as a concrete post or a plaster-of-Paris cast; a human petrification with a heart of feldspar and without charm of the friendly germ, minus bowels, passion, or a sense of humor. Happily, they never reproduce and all of them finally go to hell.[1]

There is some evidence that Hubbard's view represented the common perception of the auditor, and it was natural for the layman to look on the auditing process as matching the auditor in coldness and lack of personal emotion. Auditor detachment soon became associated with perceptions of perfection and infallibility. William Andrew Paton, often regarded as the father of modern American accounting, graphically expressed the public's perception of the process by commenting:

> Impressed by the neatly ruled lines and the array of equal footings exhibited by the typical system of accounts and financial statements, the layman is likely to conclude that...[auditing]...deals with certainties, with data capable of exact and precise statement; that accounts are either accurate or inaccurate; that the principles and procedures...if applied without clerical error, will always lead to correct conclusions.[2]

It is understandable that the public might transfer this perception of auditing omniscience to the doer of audits—the auditor. If auditing were 100 percent accurate, as often believed, it seemed reasonable to conclude that the impersonal individual who audits is also perfect.

Paton also observed that the auditor, having internalized the idea of supreme auditing accuracy, "at times may be found slipping, somewhat unconsciously, into the same misapprehensions" about himself.

But auditing is far from being perfect. Some critics assert that it is a nonscientific process that is far from being accurate, that adherence to generally accepted accounting principles (GAAP) deviates from economic reality, and that the auditing process is incomplete (for example, auditing processes will not effectively detect collusion). Likewise, auditors are imperfect. Like us, they are subject to psychological factors that may color judgment and alter action, sometimes with undesirable consequences.

At the outset, we noted that auditors as human beings exhibit most of the common human behaviors. However, the nature of auditing adds additional behavioral dimensions. To introduce some of these, we have created a typical audit situation leading to a behavioral dilemma.

AN AUDITOR DILEMMA

Introduction

Sara is a junior auditor completing her second year with Kantor and Company, a national public accounting firm. Sara works out of the firm's home office where her progress has been tracked by the managing partner and several senior audit managers. Sara hopes her upcoming annual performance appraisal will merit promotion to senior auditor. Sara believes she is ready and she would enjoy the recognition promotion brings as well as the increase in salary. However, Sara must complete her current audit assignment—a small job that she is running as a senior—well enough to convince her immediate superior of her readiness for advancement. This means meeting, or preferably underrunning, the time allocated for the job.

The Current Audit

One of the firm's long-standing clients is the Triple F Co. (FFF), which was one of Kantor's first clients. The two firms have more or less grown up together to the point where each now represents a significant force in its field. It has been a long, mutually pleasant, and profitable association. Two years ago, FFF purchased the Sub Company, a small but potentially significant acquisition. At FFF's request, Sub became a Kantor client.

Sara has been assigned to perform the field work on Kantor's second annual audit of Sub. Sara quickly discovers several problems with the assignment. FFF, on whose audit she had worked earlier, has extremely efficient accounting procedures and a well-trained, highly skilled accounting staff, which is not the case with Sub.

Before the acquisition, Sub had been a family-owned and family-managed firm with antiquated procedures and indifferent personnel, particularly in the accounting department. The staff were few, and their accounting education came largely through haphazard, on-the-job training. There had been little automation; many records were still prepared manually. Reports were frequently inaccurate and almost always tardy in reaching Sub's unconcerned management. This, however, annoyed FFF's anxious executives.

Sub's old guard accounting people continue to resist any introduction or implementation of FFF's modern, highly computerized systems. After reviewing the prior year's audit working papers, it is evident to Sara that any proposals for system changes would be viewed by Sub's staff as job-threatening.

Sub's Controller

The chief roadblock is Hiram F. Krenshaw, Sub's long-time controller. Krenshaw, who had close ties to Sub's founding family, joined the company in 1939. During World War II, he passed the certified public accountant's examination. Never thereafter did he allow anyone to forget that singular accomplishment. Even more irritating was the fact that he never let anyone forget that he was Sub's man in charge.

For 44 years, Sub survived annual audits with little strain. These had been performed by a local CPA, Will Doityourway. When Will died, his son, Les Doityourway—a Krenshaw boyhood chum and long-standing golf partner—took over. A Doityourway audit never presented Krenshaw with difficulties. The Doityourways, father and son, were generally happy to tailor their audit report to Sub's reporting desires.

When FFF took over, this comfortable situation began to crumble. The first blow was FFF's insistence that Doityourway be replaced with Kantor. Next came the changes demanded by the new owners and, after the first Kantor audit, a barrage of system "recommendations" from the auditors.

The Previous Audit

The site senior on Kanton's initial Sub audit was young, arrogant, well educated, and highly skilled Tony Travolta. Travolta hammered Krenshaw endlessly about Sub's antiquated accounting methods. The general lack of capabilities of Krenshaw and his staff were never spared the auditor's acerbic comments, much to Krenshaw's chagrin. The insensitive Travolta managed, without intent, to earn the controller's dislike by keeping him constantly apprehensive and uncomfortable.

Shortly after completing the Sub audit field work, Travolta, upset over what he regarded as Kantor's slow promotion policy, resigned. Although his tormentor had gone, Krenshaw remained bitter and convinced that the difficulties with the audit and the subsequent uncomfortable feedback were not due to his shortcomings. Kantor and Company, with their use of an auditor of Travolta's relative inexperience, was the culprit. Krenshaw knew that no one as green as Travolta could possible comprehend Sub's accounting. After all, Krenshaw was a CPA himself with over 40 years of experience in designing, operating, and fine-tuning Sub's accounting system. No book learning could ever duplicate that.

As Kantor's second Sub audit began, the air was charged with hostility. Krenshaw openly expressed his view that Kantor was not a good auditor choice. Sub's situation required a local CPA, someone who understood Sub and its peculiarities—someone like Les Doityourway. But FFF was satisfied with Kantor's work, and they remained deaf to Krenshaw's begging for Doityourway's reinstatement. With politeness but unmistakable firmness, FFF rejected the pleadings. They saw Krenshaw, not the auditors, as Sub's principal accounting problem.

The Audit Begins

It is this charged environment that Sara enters. To make matters worse, the manager assigned to the FFF consolidated audit is James Johnson Dummont, who has established a reputation as the most ruthlessly ambitious of Kantor's managers. As Sara prepares to start the assignment, she learns that Dummont has altered the audit's time budget, imposing an impossibly tight schedule. The new time constraints will make the audit heavily dependent upon client-generated data in which Sara, based on the previous year's audit working papers, has little confidence. Moreover, the budget is so tight that Sara is certain she will be unable to perform audit tests to the extent planned and will have to rely extensively on the previous work done by the brilliant but erratic Travolta.

The evening before starting the audit, Sara arrives at the site hotel and meets Dummont. To her dismay, the audit manager is unwilling to discuss time allocations, vapidly asserting his confidence in Sara. The next morning, after the introductory formalities, Sara and her junior auditors find themselves beginning the audit alone in Krenshaw's bailiwick; Dummont has already departed for another audit site.

Even before the morning coffee break, Sara and her staff discover that Krenshaw is the only individual connected with the accounting department who can answer most of their inquiries. But he is often not immediately available, delaying the work and consuming precious time. Worse yet, Krenshaw interprets the questions as a combination of Sara's inexperience and as evidence of Kantor's extravagant and unnecessary audit procedures, which are aimed only at running up Kantor's already outrageous audit fee. "Remember the good old days," he reminds his staff at every opportunity, "Les Doityourway never bothered with all this fancy, repetitive stuff year after year. He didn't have to; he knew Sub and what was going on—something Kantor would never know, especially if they kept changing audit personnel and assigning inexperienced people."

The Confrontation

After a week, the work is far behind schedule, even though Sara has worked extra hours, which she has not logged in order to appear on track. Driving to the site one morning, she runs into a massive traffic snarl. By the time she clears the congestion and reaches Sub, she is an hour late. She spies Krenshaw standing stiffly in his office doorway and bids him a forced but pleasant good morning. In front of Sub's entire accounting staff and Sara's juniors, the controller makes an exhibition of consulting his watch and exclaiming sarcastically, "And just how much will Kantor and Company, Certified Public Accountants, charge us for this time?"

Sara is shaken but hides it and does not respond. As she settles at her desk and begins a point sheet review, she reflects on why she ever got into auditing in the first place and wonders what she should do next.

BEHAVIORAL ASPECTS OF AUDITING

Introduction

The above situation is not uncommon; it is representative of the kinds of problems auditors face constantly. In order to understand the factors that tend to color the auditor's behavioral patterns and put them into proper perspective, it is first necessary to delimit the domain of auditing.

The Domain of Auditing

We have seen that auditing, broadly speaking, is any examination. It is now necessary to reduce that global concept to a limited working environment and then to an operational frame of reference useful for evaluating and perhaps predicting probable auditor behavior. To this end, we will restrict our focus to accounting-based investigations. It now remains only to contrast the two types of accounting-based audits—external or independent financial audits as opposed to internal or operational audits—and adopt one as a reference frame.

As our society matured and became more complex, the scope of financial auditing narrowed, coming to a focus on assertions about the "fairness" of financial statements. While this required skill, training, education, experience, and solid judgment, the severely constrained scope of the financial audit made the work, at its roots, mundane and a cut-and-dried, almost routine exercise. It was therefore to be expected that over time, emphasis would fall more on who performed the audit—the somewhat glamorized certified public accountant (CPA) in the case of the financial audit—than on the work itself. There is little real difference between CPAs and non-CPAs as people and, because the public tends to identify with the CPA in terms of caliber and, moreover, since our focus is on auditor behavior rather than job processes, we will adopt the CPA and financial auditing as our frame of reference.

There are, however, three additional reasons justifying the adoption of CPA financial auditing as our work environment reference frame:

1. The unique purpose of a CPA is the attestation of the fairness of financial statements. The attest function is the only operational factor distinguishing the CPA from other auditors and it is the only auditing function requiring a license. CPAs now perform most other kinds of audit work as well, but the licensing sanction has made the CPA an auditor with which the layman— even with the stereotyping—can identify and understand.
2. CPA auditing, while narrower than operational auditing, includes all of the basic audit functions and, accordingly, comprehends all of the behavioral patterns that form the subject of our study.
3. We contend that all accounting-based audits are similar and auditors, consequently, are pretty much the same in terms of personalities and skill levels. Success as an auditor will generally be measured in the same way for the CPA as the non-CPA—that is, not based on audits performed or results obtained, but on the basis of promotions awarded. This seems true of most auditors regardless of the type of audit employment.

Eliminating Personality Factors

We must now eliminate personality factors from our consideration of generalized auditor behaviors, because these lie outside the audit environment and are essentially extraneous. Let us see why this is so.

Personality can be most closely linked to the issue of failure as an auditor. A heavy majority of people who begin careers in auditing either do not last or do not truly succeed if they remain in the field. There are almost as many reasons for this as there are unsuccessful auditors. However, one thing seems clear: in almost no instance is the failure of an auditor in the profession due to a lack of competence in performing audit work. There are five principal reasons for this:

1. Today's beginning auditor is highly prepared academically (noncollege graduates are usually excluded from entry into the profession).
2. Intense prescreening before employment and multiple interviews tend to make the newly hired auditor one of a highly select group.
3. New auditors are extensively retrained by their employers.
4. Junior auditors are very closely supervised and rarely put into a situation where a possible lack of competence or experience might put the audit or the audit firm at risk. Experience is heavily stressed in the auditor's maturation.
5. Contrary to the profession's public pronouncements, there really isn't much decision making involved in auditing. Individuals might or might not perceive it as dull, tedious work, but it does seem to be routine. This is not intended to belittle the academic teaching of accounting. There is a tremen-

dous amount of material to be assimilated by students; not only is the breadth of such material expanding exponentially, but accountants are also delving deeper and deeper into issues. Nevertheless, we stand by our assertion that, once learned, auditing is essentially a routine exercise, always tempered, of course, by judgment.

The Two Classes of Situations Affecting Auditor Behavior

There appear to be only two basic types of behaviorally charged situations that present common dilemmas to the auditor.

1. Auditors are deeply affected—often subconsciously—by their perception of the audit environment of the moment (it is always changing) and by their opinions of the people involved. The cast of characters are in a constant state of flux, however far removed they may be from the immediate situation.
2. Auditors must constantly resolve for themselves many sets of interpersonal relationships, such as between colleagues, with subordinates or superiors, and with client personnel. Some of these overlap and some may be totally independent.

Using the foregoing as a foundation, let us begin our study of auditor behavior by considering the first behavioral situation—perceptions of the audit environment and the people involved. As we proceed, we will relate conclusions on probable auditor behavior to that of Sara from our auditor dilemma.

Audit Influence—The Impact on Auditees

Much study has been devoted to the ways and to what degree an audit affects the behavior of others, especially those undergoing audits (auditees). While our concern in this chapter is with auditor behavior, it is appropriate to address this issue briefly.

It is generally concluded that the audit has a definite effect on auditee behavior. There are several variants involved in this, which, although beyond the scope of this chapter, are listed as further readings for interested students. However, it can be noted that an audit generally results in auditee conformance—that is, auditee behavior moves toward a performance perceived as being what the auditor desires.

In another area, accountants have for years promoted the proposition that their audit reports had great influence on the behavior of financial statement readers such as investors and creditors. The evidence is incomplete, but recent research indicates that audit reports carry little influence, although the readers may share the auditor's perception of the financial data. How they will react, however, seems unpredictable.

In summary, it appears that auditing has some impact on auditee behavior but less, if any, on parties external to the organization being audited.

Auditor Perceptions and Behavior

Auditor judgment depends heavily on perceptions of a situation. Judgment, the cornerstone of the professional, is the product of several factors such as education, culture, and so on, but the most significant and controlling element appears to be experience—the auditor's sense of recollection of having previously dealt successfully with a similar situation. Judgment is the behavior most influenced by situation perceptions, of which the main factors of influence are materiality and what we will refer to as faith.

Materiality

In auditing, materiality refers to that which is important, significant, or essential, but the concept has no rules for its measurement. It is judgmental. A substantial amount of research has been devoted to identifying factors that may predictably influence auditor assessments of materiality. This research has focused on two broad areas: (1) what influence the degree of materiality has on ultimate judgments of what is material and what is not and (2) answering the interrelated questions, how and to what extent is the influence of materiality on auditor behavior strengthened or weakened? The studies have generated several generalized and somewhat interlocking conclusions.

A common conclusion is that auditor behavior will usually depend upon the auditor's willingness to accept the risk of being wrong on an issue of materiality. To a large extent, this depends upon past results.

Other researchers reached somewhat different conclusions since they approached the materiality-judgment problem with different ends in view. Generally, the concern was more with the auditor's decision-making process than with specific factors of influence. Some attacked the materiality issue as though it lay on an ordinal rather than nominal scale and measured results conjointly—that is, addressing scaling and structural matters simultaneously. Still others sought solutions by quantifying judgment thresholds or, in some instances, by establishing minimum-maximums.

Another tack was taken by those who reasoned that auditor behavior is primarily a function of individual judgment and thus the issue is judgment per se, regardless of how it might be influenced. Generally, these studies conclude that auditor behavior, as manifested by using judgment, is idiosyncratic. Accordingly, there is little knowledge on how to control such varied behavior, but proper communication between auditors, both laterally and vertically, tends to produce consensus views on appropriate audit actions. In turn, it is argued, this should lead to auditor homogeneity of thought and, hence, of behavior, at least within the audit organization.

In a broader context, several scholars used statistical analyses to assign probabilities to possible auditor behaviors as responses to specific situations. These researchers appear to have learned much about possible audit issues; but the results to date have not been very productive in terms of predictability and, thus, controlling auditor behavior. The general conclusion is that auditors, as people, are not probability-oriented; usually they rely on judgmental heuristics, which largely flow from experience. While probabilities of a certain behavior can be calculated, they provide only very general guidelines as to likely individual behavior.

We will conclude this brief excursion into the judgmental aspects of auditor behavior by noting that it seems impossible to predict specific behavior with much precision or confidence. The dominant controlling factor seems to be individual experience. While this may not be a very satisfying answer to a problem we have made considerable effort to identify, there are some useful, general conclusions to be reached.

We may be unable to predict actual behavior with assurance, but studies indicate that we may be able to obviate undesirable auditor actions. In our opinion, if this is so, this will prove more useful than knowing the undesirable ways an auditor may behave. A capability of negating unwanted actions can foster control—to paraphrase an old cliche: an ounce of prevention ability is worth a ton of uncontrollable prediction. Two elements are of considerable assistance in this regard: (1) communication between auditors concerning the work to be done and (2) reducing, as much as possible, auditor tendencies toward short-cutting necessary audit work through inappropriate rationalizations. For example, if the audit time allocation is too tight, auditors may compensate by rationalizing their perceptions of the audit issues and altering their judgment of what to do or how much to do to the detriment of the audit.

These considerations will become clear as we turn to the auditor perception issue that we referred to as faith (for reasons which will soon become apparent), but which is known in the literature as the halo effect.

The Faith Syndrome

One perception condition that may lead to altered behavior is the so-called halo effect, a highly positive but sometimes erroneous perception of other people. In auditing, the halo effect occurs when the auditor's perceptions are colored and lead to a belief that certain audit conditions exist, which may or may not be the case.

Let us assume that an auditor concludes that a client's system of internal control is strong and therefore reliable. Accordingly, the auditor's procedures and testing need not be as extensive as would be required if internal controls were weak. But the auditor may have no actual first-hand experience with the client's internal control system and thus no basis for a conclusion of its strength or weakness; the auditor's perception of system worthiness may be based on prior audit work and a simple assumption that what existed in the past continues to exist. More commonly, however, the audit conclusion is likely to be based on who performed the prior audit work. If the auditor has confidence in those people, a halo effect is applied to them and their work. Current status becomes strongly influenced by the auditor's faith in one or more fellow auditors. This response seems especially true on audits being carried out under tight time constraints. Perceptions of prior activities tend to influence current audit judgment, but the degree of influence is not known.

RESOLVING THE AUDITOR SARA'S DILEMMA THROUGH PERCEPTIONS_____

Introduction

As pointed out in the earlier description of the Sub audit dilemma, Sara was not only being harassed by the client's controller, Krenshaw, but was under heavy internal pressure to meet a tight time budget imposed by an ambitious audit manager—a set of problems complicated by Sara's impending evaluation for promotion. Sara tried to alleviate the time difficulty by working additional, unlogged hours to comply with the budget and to make her work appear efficient.

What is Sara likely to do now to ease the time pressure? In the absence of guiding responses by her fellow auditors, she will most probably take compensating action. Halo effect theory suggests she will search the prior audit working papers for shortcut opportunities, which she will justify using on the basis of a high perception of her predecessor, Travolta, and his skills (Travolta's halo). If time pressures increase, Sara's perceptions of Travolta will increase and she will rely more and more on Travolta's work, often much more than circumstances warrant. Sara's audit behavior will differ from what she would normally do without the time pressure.

Sara's actions may be further altered by her perceptions of materiality, risk, and other variables and her experience with similar audit issues. However, the degree to which Sara will color and follow her perceptions is neither known nor predictable. This is not encouraging, but there is some hope of exercising prior control through full communications between Sara and her juniors, her audit manager, and the engagement partner. Undesirable halo effects may be mitigated as communication makes clear what is to be done.

In addition, careful audit planning shared by superior and subordinate can do much to reduce tendencies toward short-circuiting necessary audit procedures. But without communication and participation, a supervisor who sets too tight a time constraint will discover his or her staff adjusting professional judgment and rationalizing their adjustments, frequently to the detriment of the job.

Summarizing Auditor Perceptions

It is essentially impossible to predetermine auditor perceptions and, more often than not, the behavioral patterns that will flow from those perceptions. Accordingly, specific behavior cannot be predicted. Favorable perceptions—the halo effect—will often cause behavioral changes, although how and to what degree is not known. Communication across all auditor levels and participation in audit planning can be effective methods of overcoming tendencies to undesirable or inappropriate responses.

Auditor Interpersonal Relationships

It is not possible to predict audit behavior arising from environmental perceptions. Neither can we predict the behavior emerging from the auditor's interpersonal job relationships, whether with other auditors or with client personnel. But in the latter case of interpersonal relationships, it may be controllable. More importantly, as we shall see, it can be self-controllable with full and rational consciousness.

One might suspect from this assertion that we are about to propose that auditors have a psychiatrist at the ready on every audit engagement. This might prove helpful, but the cost would be prohibitive. Not only is it impractical, but professional psychiatrists and psychologists have little more success in predicting specific auditor behavior than anyone else. Clearly, something else is needed.

We are convinced that self-understanding is the needed factor. If auditors can know themselves and exercise rational self-control of their responses, many of the seemingly insurmountable problems of reliable prediction of behavior vanish. If unpredictable and undesirable auditor responses can be avoided by communications, planning, and auditor self-understanding, it remains only to help auditors help themselves systematically.

Several paths are available to individuals for self-analysis and self-help. We will limit our discussion to two methodologies. One is adopted from psychiatry, which will supply a theoretical foundation, and the other, erected on that theoretical base, follows a psychologist-developed program. Let us begin with the psychiatric technique popularized by Eric Berne.

Transactional Analysis

Transactional analysis is a group therapy; it is not intended to be self-applied. By itself, it is of little practical value for auditor behavioral self-control, but its underlying concepts are applicable to a program of individual therapy.

Eric Berne is generally acknowledged as the founder of transactional analysis.[3] He was the great synthesizer who drew together the landmark works of others (principally Wilder Penfield and Harry Stack Sullivan), molded them into a coherent whole, and popularized the result. Penfield's significant contribution was the discovery that the details of past events and their accompanying emotions are recorded inseparably in the brain—one cannot be recalled without the other. Sullivan contributed the idea of interpersonal relationships, which he saw as transactions. People see transactions (interpersonal relationships and the accompanying emotions) as reflected appraisals—perceptions of an event and the associated feelings.

The "oneness" perception of event and emotion could be distorted and cause neurosis. Berne, linking Penfield's and Sullivan's work, demonstrated that because perception details are also emotionally charged, problems can be treated therapeutically if all the elements of the transaction are brought to light and examined rationally. Berne saw the group as the element necessary to make this operational. Only through shared involvement can relevant transactions be identified and their mixed pieces analyzed, ordered, and understood. But laypersons require two additional components before they can engage in effective group therapy.

The first need is to simplify the language of psychiatry—to strip it of complex professional jargon and make it comprehensible to all. The second need is more significant. To Berne, group therapy is a form of interaction involving role playing. To facilitate this, it is vital that the roles be well identified and understood by all. Berne found it helpful to relate transactions to three basic roles—child, parent, and adult. These provide the guidance for group therapy sessions. A detailed discussion of these roles is beyond the scope of this chapter. Interested readers are directed to the works cited at the end of the chapter.

The transactional analysis approach appears to have considerable merit for solving behavioral problems, but we must stress that it is specifically a group process, deriving much of its power from the group situation itself. This lacks practicality for audit assignments. The need is for effective self-analysis by the auditor functioning as an individual.

Rational-Emotive Therapy

We believe this need can be satisfied through the well-developed and established approach to self-analysis known as rational-emotive therapy, or the RET technique, the therapeutic offspring of psychologist Albert Ellis.[4] Before turning to the details of how RET may be used in audit situations, especially those involving interpersonal relationships, it is appropriate to present our justification for adopting the RET method over other approaches to the problem, some of which are excellent and, quite possibly, could serve as well or even better than RET. The practical aspects of our preference for the RET technique will become quite apparent when we apply it to Sara's audit dilemma. In addition, there are four basic reasons underlying our favoritism for the RET system:

1. RET is fundamentally designed to be self-applied. After a relatively brief introduction to the system, no external therapist is needed. This not only makes RET much less expensive than other therapy techniques, but also allows it to form the subject matter of the internal training sessions which can, over time, move from group education to individual applications.
2. RET is lay-oriented and does not employ complex jargon.
3. The RET method is one of the few therapeutic techniques that is, to some extent, embraced by both psychologists and psychiatrists.
4. Auditors pride themselves on their deductive logic and rationality, and RET is a totally rational technique.

Employing Sara's audit dilemma as the framework, we will demonstrate how RET can be used by individual auditors to resolve problems.

The Dilemma Reviewed

Auditor Sara, anxious to make a good showing on her final assignment before being evaluated for promotion, has encountered two major difficulties—a tight time budget and a poor relationship with the client's controller, Krenshaw. We saw that Sara may resolve, in part, the time problem by relying more than is warranted on the halo effect of her predecessor.

More pressing, however, is Sara's difficulty with Krenshaw. She must establish a working relationship with the controller if the audit—upon which Sara's promotion appears to depend—is to be concluded satisfactorily. Krenshaw sees Sara as lacking the maturity and experience necessary to comprehend his accounting operations and, through sarcastic comments, has made his distaste of Sara and her employer clear. What is Sara to do?

RESOLVING THE DILEMMA THROUGH RET

The RET Scheme

The RET objective is to achieve an emotional state of neutrality—to eliminate as much as possible unwarranted negative feelings. This rests on the idea that one can probably come much closer to solving a problem in a calm frame of mind rather than when one approaches a problem in a state of anger, anxiety, or depression.

RET emphasizes sequencing: (1) a triggering event occurs; (2) thought is given to the event; and (3) feelings about the event result. Often, as we mature, the thought process is omitted, and we react emotionally almost automatically. For example, if someone "tailgates" you in traffic or cuts ahead of you in line, anger may result without conscious thought. These examples may not arouse you but there are many events that irritate. RET seeks first to have you consider carefully your thoughts about the event—what thoughts are creating what emotions? Next, the thoughts are evaluated by asking yourself:

1. Is the thought based on objective fact and not subjective opinion? FACT?
2. If acted upon, will it produce my goals most quickly? GOALS?
3. If acted upon, will it prevent undesirable conflict with others? CONFLICT?
4. If acted upon, does it aid in my self-preservation? SELF-PRESERVING?
5. Is it causing me to feel the way I prefer to feel? PREFERRED FEELINGS?

After this evaluative screening has been completed, the feelings one has about the event should be neutral rather than negative.

For Sara, a triggering event occurred with her late arrival and Krenshaw's sour inquiry about who was to pay for the lost time. Let's fit this into the RET model by laying out Sara's transaction with Krenshaw, her thoughts and accompanying emotions (a sort of "self-talk" we will call mental reaction) and the rational screening used to neutralize emotions.

Applying RET

The RET process begins, as we have seen, with a triggering event: Krenshaw says: "And just how much will Kantor and Company, Certified Public Accountants, charge us for this time?"

Sara might have experienced a number of mental reactions to the event. These usually take the form of a series of thoughts, such as:

- That stupid idiot has gone far enough!
- Krenshaw should have more respect for me.
- Krenshaw should not talk to me like that—embarrassing me in front of my staff and his people as well.
- I'm going to tell him off.

What kind of emotions would this sort of thought sequence lead to?

Alternatively, in response to the controller's sour comment, Sara could have experienced something like the following series of thoughts:

- I just can't win.

- Krenshaw is never going to give me a break.
- I'll *never* get promoted (and that is just awful).

What kinds of feelings do you suppose might result from these thoughts?

Each of these mental reaction sequences leads to negative feelings. The first set of thoughts probably culminates in feelings of anger and the second in anxiousness, dejection, or depression.

These emotions must be neutralized. Sara now screens each mental reaction by challenging it—mentally debating its rationality or relevance in terms of the five questions described earlier. A thought that does not generate two or more positive answers is not a rational reaction.

Before we apply this process to Sara's dilemma, we must stress that this process requires much practice before one achieves a proficiency that will make the operation become almost automatic. We will address each of Sara's posited mental reactions, recognizing that these are two conjectural sets of an almost infinite range of possible reactions.

If the procedure is successful, Sara's feelings about each thought in the thought sequence and the series as a whole should become neutral. We must again stress that the process does not generate solutions as such. It only clears the mind, neutralizing emotions so that rational solution alternatives can be generated. The original event took place in a matter of seconds, but examining it is like a slow-motion replay allowing for scrutinization in minute detail. As an aid, the following format will prove helpful.

First, restate the event that triggered the negative feelings.

Second, establish two mental columns, which, for new practitioners, is best done on paper. On the left, restate the mental reactions that elicit negative emotions. We refer to these as self-talk. On the right, list each of the five questions posed earlier, allowing space for answers.

Third, fill in the responses generated for each of the five questions. With experience, the RET challenges will be done mentally. The following shows how Sara might document it:

Self-talk #1

That idiot has gone far enough!

Rational Challenge of Debate

(FACT?) Krenshaw is not mentally incompetent; he is a fallible human being and he hasn't gone anywhere, much less "far enough." This statement is not based on objective reality.

(GOALS?) If I call Krenshaw an idiot, it surely will not contribute to the efficient completion of the audit or to my promotion. This statement will not help me achieve my goals.

(CONFLICT?) If I call Krenshaw an idiot, his reaction might be quite severe. Who knows what might result? Later, it will be just that much more difficult to cement relations with him. This statement will not prevent undesirable conflict.

(SELF-PRESERVING?) This question is irrelevant, except in the extreme case. If I persist in calling clients or my employers idiots, I could eventually become very hungry.

(FEELINGS?) Thinking of calling Krenshaw an idiot and telling him what he can or cannot do tends to promote my anger. This statement does not cause me to feel the way I prefer to feel.

   Next, to neutralize negative emotions, a rational alternative to the mental reaction or self-talk is developed:

Rational Alternative

I don't like Krenshaw's comment. Is something special bothering him today? I'm going to try to think of positive ways to deal with him, perhaps even turn this episode into a "plus." If I put my coat and briefcase away before responding to him, maybe I can come up with something.

   The RET practitioner now proceeds to the next thought in the series:

Self-talk #1 cont'd.

Krenshaw should have more respect for me.

Rational Challenge or Debate

(FACT?) Not true. He is entitled to his opinion. His lack of respect may be ill-founded and I may not like it, but there is no rule that says any par-

ticular individual *must* respect or approve of *me*. This statement is not based on objective reality.

(GOALS? CONFLICT?) Thinking he SHOULD have more respect for me constrains *my* thinking in a foolish way—like pounding on an elevator door and yelling that it *should* be there when I want it while not thinking of other possibilities, like using the stairs. Rather than thinking of alternative ways to deal with the situation, my insistence on thinking that he *should* respect me could result in my responding negatively to his comments, thus increasing the potential for conflict and carrying me further away from my promotion goal. This statement will neither help me achieve my goal nor will it help prevent undesirable conflict.

(SELF-PRESERVING?) Irrelevant.

(FEELINGS?) Thinking he *should* have more respect for me than he seems to have tends to make me feel angry. This statement does not cause me to feel the way I prefer to feel.

Rational Alternative

I realize I am fallible and that I make mistakes. (Who doesn't?) Krenshaw seems to think it is in his best interests to emphasize my shortcomings and constantly criticize Kantor and Company. If I could better understand why he believes this, maybe I could persuade him that we don't have to be adversaries. On the other hand, it may not be worth trying to change his attitude. Perhaps I will be better off not dealing directly with this problem. Instead, maybe I should just prepare Dummont, my audit manager, for a possible barrage of criticism from Krenshaw. Perhaps Krenshaw needs a "higher authority" figure, like Dummont.

Self-talk #1 cont'd

He should not talk to me like that, embarrassing me in front of my staff and his people.

Rational Challenge of Debate

(FACT?) This is not true. He *did* talk to me like that. Again, there is no rule that states individuals must conduct themselves as I dictate. He may have made a mistake, but there is no reason why he shouldn't. Also, I can't know or assume what the others are thinking. There is a good chance that he actually embarrassed himself more than me. This statement is not based on objective reality.

(GOALS? CONFLICT?) Thinking Krenshaw *should not* talk to me in a particular manner won't make it happen. Indeed, the more I think this thought, the more restricted is my thinking and the less able I will be to come up with alternative responses. This will make it less likely that I will be able to avoid conflict or achieve my career goals. Also, speculating that others might be in agreement with my imagined negative implications of his comments only serves to increase my desire to tell him to knock it off. This statement will not help me achieve my goals nor will it help prevent undesirable conflict.

(SELF-PRESERVING?) Irrelevant.

(FEELINGS?) This thought tends only to make me feel even more angry. This statement does not cause me to feel the way I prefer to feel.

Rational Alternative

Krenshaw can say whatever he likes, when he likes, and where he likes, but I suspect most people would not find it easy to accept his comment if it were addressed to them. If I keep calm and respond in a confident way, I probably will score a few points with his people and with my staff. I am, at least, going to let him know I prefer to discuss this sort of thing privately.

Self-talk #1 cont'd	Rational Challenge of Debate
I'm going to tell him off.	*(FACT? SELF-PRESERVING?)* Irrelevant.
	(GOALS? CONFLICT? FEELINGS?) Obviously, this statement will not help me achieve my goals or prevent undesirable conflict. Neither does it cause me to feel the way I prefer to feel.

Rational Alternative

If I can think of a tactful way, I am going to let Krenshaw know I want to finish this audit efficiently and without friction. There are a lot of ways I might approach him. For starters, I can assure him that Sub will not be charged for our late arrival this morning. Maybe I'll invite him to lunch, get him talking about the "old days," how he got started, and so on. This will give him some understanding and recall of where I am now. Maybe I can empathize with him about dealing with a corporate structure like FFF and with new auditors. I've much to think about.

Initial Emotive Response	Desired Ending Emotive Response
Anger, resentment, frustration.	Calm, motivated to respond constructively.

This first hypothesized situation is thus emotionally resolved. Sara is left feeling calm and ready to tackle the problem. The second or one of many possible alternative courses of thought might be challenged as follows:

Self-talk #2	Rational Challenge or Debate
I just can't win.	*(FACT?)* If I mean I *never* accomplish what I set out to do, that's nonsense. I wanted to get dressed this morning, and I did. I wanted

to graduate from college, and I did. I wanted to work for Kantor, and I do. But if I mean I won't accomplish what I want to in this particular situation, then the statement is false. I don't know what will happen tomorrow or the next day so I can't be certain of what I will or will not be able to do. This statement is not based on objective reality.

(GOALS?) My immediate goals are to complete a good audit and get promoted. If I tell myself I can't do it often enough, the statement is likely to become self-fulfilling. This statement will not help me achieve my goals.

(CONFLICT?) Irrelevant.

(SELF-PRESERVING?) If I continue saying this to myself, I could wind up in bad straits. This statement will not aid my self-preservation.

(FEELINGS?) The hopelessness of this statement makes me feel depressed. This statement does not cause me to feel the way I prefer to feel.

Rational Alternative

I am a fallible human being and I make mistakes. Krenshaw apparently thinks I made a major one by being late this morning and expecting I'll charge for the time. His conclusions seem to be hasty since he probably has no knowledge of the traffic jam and especially since I have no intention of charging for that lost hour.

Self-talk #2 cont'd	Rational Challenge or Debate
Krenshaw is never going to give me a break.	*(FACT?)* First, this statement is vague. What does "give me a break"

mean? I am probably trying to say that Krenshaw will never approve of me. If so, then the statement can be challenged in several ways. Surely I can imagine at least one thing I could do that would solicit Krenshaw's approval, like alluding to how much I have learned about accounting through my exposure to him and his staff. Second, I really don't know—and can never know—what is going on in his mind. There is a reasonably good chance that he does approve of some of the things I do. This statement is not based on objective reality.

(GOALS?) My first goal is promotion. Winning Krenshaw's overall approval might be helpful to that end. Thinking he will never respond precludes my making further attempts to work with him. Therefore, this statement will not help me achieve my goals.

(CONFLICT? SELF-PRESERVING?) Irrelevant.

(FEELINGS?) This thought makes me feel anxious and depressed. This statement does not cause me to feel the way I prefer to feel.

Rational Alternative

Krenshaw seems to think he gains something by expressing his disapproval of me at every opportunity. Gaining his overall approval would, without doubt, be helpful. However, I had best think very carefully about how far I want to go with this. What are the costs? Would I have to let him control all my behavior on this job? Do I want this? Is it in my best interest? Most likely not. Perhaps I should simply try to gain his favor about certain carefully selected things, or perhaps I should just ignore him altogether.

Self-talk #2 cont'd	Rational Challenge or Debate
I'll *never* get promoted (and that is just *awful*).	*(FACT?)* I have no idea what might happen. This incident probably wouldn't block my promotion. If it would, I'm not sure I want to work for Kantor. Moreover, even if it did stop or delay my promotion, would it be *awful*? I do have my CPA license; I'm willing to work hard. Surely I can get another position. Changing jobs wouldn't be a disaster and probably wouldn't amount to more than a temporary inconvenience. This statement is not based on objective reality.
	(GOALS?) My goal is my promotion. Saying it will never happen does not help. This statement will not help me achieve my goals.
	(CONFLICT? SELF-PRESERVING?) Irrelevant.
	(FEELINGS?) This statement tends to make me anxious. This statement does not cause me to feel the way I prefer to feel.

Rational Alternative

This has been a delicate audit assignment. I am going to make sure that my manager or the engagement partner or both understand just how difficult it is for anyone to satisfy Krenshaw. Thus, if he complains to them, they will be expecting it. Meanwhile, I'm going to see if I can think of some new approaches for coping with Krenshaw. How can I respond about being late in a way he will likely find acceptable?

Self-talk #2 cont'd	Rational Challenge of Debate
I might as well quit.	*(FACT?)* This is nonsense. It implies I am a nebbish who can't do anything right . . . Hogwash! This

statement is not based on objective reality.

(GOALS?) This statement will not help me achieve my goals.

(CONFLICT?) Irrelevant.

(SELF-PRESERVING?) Making this statement or carrying it out will not aid in my self-preservation.

(FEELING?) Saying this makes me feel resigned to fate, dejected, and depressed. This statement does not cause me to feel the way I prefer to feel.

Rational Alternative

I have been in tough, awkward situations before, and I survived. I'm not going to let Krenshaw convince me that I am not competent. Somehow, I am going to come out on top of this. . .

Initial Emotive Response	Desired Ending Emotive Response
Anxious, dejected, and depressed.	Calm, confident, and determined.

Using self-operated and self-controlled RET, Sara continues to explore her original emotional reactions to the transaction, sorting them into rationalities and irrationalities and screening them for challenges and alternatives that will neutralize her original feelings. In the end Sara should: (1) fully understand the event, or be convinced that she does; (2) have converted her initial negative emotions into a truly rational neutrality; and (3) after achieving neutrality, be ready to take whatever rational course of action she has concluded is best.

We must again emphasize that the mental reactions or self-talks described are not the only possible reactions to the situation nor is there only one way to examine them. They are, however, typical. You can probably think of people (if not yourself) who would initially react to Krenshaw in the manner described. Again, Sara's actions may not lead to material success, but emotional success should arise from dealing rationally with alternatives, including failure if such is indicated. Specific behavioral actions are not predictable, but through RET, they can be controlled in the sense that whatever action is taken, it will be rational.

Finally, the RET system does not produce actual solutions to problems, but helps a person maintain an attitude conducive to allowing an efficient search for solutions.

Other Applications

In Sara's case, we hypothesized her rationalization of only one of several potentially disturbing situations. The same mental processes would be employed to prepare her for dealing rationally with the others, such as the problems with Dummont, her audit manager, and so on. We leave it to the reader to experiment with her situation as a practice exercise.

A similar exercise can be performed from the conjectural point of view of how Krenshaw, the controller and auditee, might react, keeping in mind the general reactions of auditees described earlier. We do not wish to leave the impression that RET is limited to use by auditors or in the auditing environment. It is applicable to all human activity. In such an exercise, one should conjecturally create the events that led to Krenshaw's eventual outburst when Sara arrived late. We believe this will be an interesting and enlightening process. Readers might also wish to reflect on the last time they felt significant negative emotions and how, given a basic understanding of RET, they might have reacted differently.

RET—A Concluding Overview

RET builds on linking events and their accompanying emotions, with a goal of altering original, perhaps destructive, emotions to a state of neutrality. Once neutrality exists, the event and responses to it (a transaction) can be treated rationally. After training, this process can be carried out by individuals without the assistance or physical presence of therapists.

We have perhaps made RET seem almost childishly simplistic and easy to use. It is easy to use but it does require initial guidance and a lot of practice before it can be used to its full potential. To be fully effective, RET needs frequent repetition—that is, practiced, so one's analytical process and responses become almost automatic.

Most importantly for auditing, however, RET is adaptable to group training sessions. Auditing firms, because of the independent, judgmental character of the work coupled with a heavy orientation and commitment to on-going training of their professional staff, appear to be especially strong candidates for adoption of the methodology. This seems even more beneficial when one considers the work environment of auditing—the frequent change of work sites and the constant change of both audit and client personnel.

This is not to imply that outcomes will always be positive, either for the auditor, for his employing firm, or for the client. It does, however, put control where it seems to belong for professionals—with the auditor himself. Auditors are human beings capable of emotion. As humans, they are subject to weaknesses, but there is reason to believe that good outcomes emerging from careful RET applications by competent and devoted professional auditors will outnumber undesirable results.

SUMMARY AND CONCLUSION

There is an obvious advantage in being able to predict behavior. This is equally true in the case of auditors. If we knew how they would behave in a specific audit situation, such situations could be avoided or altered and, thus, auditor behavior controlled. Predictability would also provide the auditor's employer with an improved sense of confidence in the auditor's work and it would be advantageous to clients (the auditees).

Auditing and auditors, while often misunderstood by the laity, are not set apart from the rest of the world to any degree. Auditors are neither more nor less human than others, but there are conditions with behavioral potential that are common to auditing, although perhaps not unique to it. Auditor difficulties fall into two broad categories: (1) auditor perceptions of the particular audit environment and the people and task at hand; and (2) interpersonal relationships with fellow auditors, superior and subordinate, and with client personnel.

The first category has been extensively studied; attempts have been made to quantify the probabilities of a particular course of auditor behavior in response to the stimuli of a particular type of audit situation. It was found that: (1) very little is really known or understood about the auditor's actual mental decision-making processes. Accordingly, it is difficult—probably impossible—to predict specific auditor behavior with any degree of assurance; (2) auditors may base their course of action on the quality of their perceptions of their fellows or other individuals. These perceptions, known as the halo effect, may color auditor judgment and action.[5] The difficulty is that it is, again, virtually impossible to predict how or to what degree the halo effect may influence behavior. Most often, it appears that auditor behavior depends on specific auditor experience, which itself exists in a myriad of varieties; and (3) communications between the auditor and others— his or her fellow professionals and client personnel—coupled with careful, adequate, and realistic audit planning could go a long way to forestalling undesirable auditor behavior on the job, even though that behavior cannot be predicted.

With respect to the second category—interpersonal relationships—it was found that the auditor could, with appropriate training and practice, develop skill at rational thinking and behavior. Again, while the specific behavior might not be predictable by others, predictability would become essentially irrelevant since the auditor would more often than not behave appropriately. Thus, through the self-applied process of Rational-Emotive Therapy (RET), auditor behavior could become broadly anticipated in that whatever the behavior exhibited, it would be rational.

The advantage of focusing on rationality is that the technique can be taught and, once taught, be self-applied. For those who demand quantification of every aspect of life—personal as well as professional—this is probably not a very satisfying conclusion. Rationality, however, is a definitive measure of behavior; an alterative measure does not appear to exist at this time in any consistent form.

REFERENCES

[1] Hubbard, Elbert, as quoted in Horngren, Charles T., *Cost Accounting: A Managerial Emphasis*, Fifth edition (Englewood Cliffs, N.J.: Prentice-Hall), 1982. pp. 350.

[2] Paton, W.A., *Accounting Theory* (New York: Ronald Press), 1922. pp. 471.

[3] See Berne, Eric, *Games People Play: The Psychology of Human Relationships* (New York: Grove Press), 1964.

[4] See Ellis, Albert, *Executive Leadership* (New York: Institute for Rational Living), 1976.

————, and Harper, Robert A., *A New Guide to Rational Living*, 1976 Ed. (North Hollywood, California: Wilshire Book Co.), 1975.

SUGGESTED READINGS

Ashton, Robert H. "An Experimental Study of Internal Control Judgments." *Journal of Accounting Research* (Spring 1974).

Berne, Eric. *Games People Play: The Psychology of Human Relationships.* New York: Grove Press, 1964.

————. Transactional *Analysis in Psychotherapy: A Systematic Individual and Social Psychiatry.* New York: Castle Books, 1961.

Biggs, Stanley F., and Theodore J. Mock. "An Investigation of Auditor Decision Processes in the Evaluation of Internal Controls and Audit Scope Decisions." *Journal of Accounting Research* (Spring 1983).

Blair, J. F. "Changing Concepts in the Last Decade." *Internal Auditor* (March 1954).

Blum, G. S. *Psychoanalytic Theories of Personality.* New York: McGraw-Hill, 1953.

Boatsman, James R., and Jack C. Robertson. "Policy-Capturing on Selected Materiality Judgments." *Accounting Review* (April 1974).

Burns, Thomas J. (ed.). *Behavioral Experiments in Accounting—II.* Columbus, Ohio: The Ohio State University, 1979.

Butler, John J. "Human Relations in Auditing." *Accountant's Digest* (September 1979): 3-5.

Churchill, Neil C., William W. Cooper and Trevor Sainsbury. "Laboratory and Field Studies of the Behavioral Effects of Audits." In William J. Burns, Jr. and Don T. DeCoster (eds.), *Accounting and Its Behavioral Implications*. New York: McGraw-Hill, 1969.

Crosby, Michael A. "Implications of Prior Probability Elicitation on Auditor Sample Size Decisions." *Journal of Accounting Research* (Spring 1981).

Einhorn, Hillel J., and Robin M. Hogarth. "Unit Weighing Schemes for Decision Making." *Organizational Behavior and Human Performance* 13 (1975).

Ellis, Albert. *Executive Leadership* New York: Institute for Rational Living, 1976.

———— and Robert A. Harper. *A New Guide to Rational Living, 1976 Ed.* North Hollywood, California: Wilshire Book Co., 1975.

Estes, Ralph. *The Auditor's Report and Investor Behavior*. Lexington, Massachusetts: D.C. Heath, 1982.

Felix, William L. Jr. "Evidence on Alternative Means of Assessing Prior Probability Distributions for Audit Decision Making." *Accounting Review* (October 1976).

Gibbins, Michael. "Propositions about the Psychology of Professional Judgment in Public Accounting." *Journal of Accounting Research* (Spring 1984).

Gul, Ferdinand A., "The Joint and Moderating Role of Personality and Cognitive Style on Decision Making." *Accounting Review* (April 1984).

Harris, Thomas A. *I'm OK—You're OK*. New York: Harper & Row, 1969.

Heyl, Carl (Ed). *The Encyclopedia of Management Vol 1*. New York: Reinhold Publishing, 1968.

Joyce, Edward J., and Gary C. Biddle. "Anchoring and Adjustment in Probabilistic Inference in Auditing." *Journal of Accounting Research* (Spring 1981).

————, "Are Auditors' Judgments Sufficiently Regressive?" *Journal of Accounting Research* (Autumn 1981).

Lewis, Barry L. "Expert Judgment in Auditing: An Expected Utility Approach." *Journal of Accounting Research* (Autumn 1980).

Libby, Robert. "Bankers' and Auditors' Perceptions of the Message Communicated by the Audit Report." *Journal of Accounting Research* (Spring 1979).

Maultsby, Maxie C. *Help Yourself to Happiness Through Rational Self-Counseling*. Boston: Marlborough House, 1975.

Milburn, Michael A. "Sources of Bias in the Prediction of Future Events." *Organizational Behavior and Human Performance* 13 (1975).

Miller, James G. "Information Input Overloads." In *Self-Organizing Systems*. Ann Arbor, Michigan: University of Michigan Press, 1962.

Mints, Frederick E. "Cooperative Auditing—The Key to the Future." *Internal Auditor* (November/December 1973): 32-45.

Moriarity, Shane, and F. Hutton Barron. "Modeling the Materiality Judgments of Audit Partners." *Journal of Accounting Research* (Autumn 1976).

Nelson, Jeanne H. "Behavioral Implications of Internal Auditing." *Management Accounting* (October 1973): 52-56.

Newton, Lauren K. "The Risk Factor in Materiality Decisions." *Accounting Review*. (January 1977).

Paton, W. A. *Accounting Theory*. New York: Ronald Press, 1922.

Penfield, W. "Memory Mechanisms." *American Medical Association Archives of Neurology and Psychiatry* 67 (1952).

Schultz, Joseph J. and Sandra G. Gustavson. "Actuaries' Perceptions of Variables Affecting the Independent Auditor's Legal Liability." *Accounting Review* (July 1978).

Senatra, Phillip T. "Role Conflict, Role Ambiguity, and Organizational Climate in a Public Accounting Firm," *Accounting Review* (October 1980).

Sullivan, Harry Stack. *The Interpersonal Theory of Psychiatry*. New York: W. W. Norton, 1953.

Swieringa, Robert J. "Discussion of a Judgment-Based Definition of Materiality," *Journal of Accounting Research* 17 (Supplement) (1979).

Thompson, William E. "Internal Auditing: A Survey of Its Past, Present, and Future." *Georgia Journal of Accounting* (Spring 1982): 24-38.

Ward, Bart H. "An Investigation of the Materiality Construct in Auditing." *Journal of Accounting Research* (Spring 1976).

DISCUSSION QUESTIONS

1. What does an audit involve? Why is auditing a pervasive activity?
2. Does auditing have any impact on auditee behavior? If so, how? Give an example.
3. What are the two classes of situations that affect auditor behavior?
4. It has been mentioned in the chapter that it is essentially impossible to predict specific auditor behavior. Explain why this is so.
5. List some of the common stereotypes of auditors.
6. Which frame of reference is used to study auditor behavior?
7. What factor is most closely linked to the failure of an auditor? Explain.
8. Explain transactional analysis.
9. Explain the halo effect and how it can affect the audit. How can this be minimized?
10. What are the advantages of using the Rational-Emotive Therapy (RET) technique in audit situations? What is the major objective of RET?
11. Dummont says to Sara: "Any 'competent' auditor should be able to meet this budget schedule." Identify some negative reactions which Sara might have to this comment. Use the Rational-Emotive Therapy to resolve these reactions.
12. Think back to the most recent time you experienced anger, anxiety, depression, or some other negative feeling. (If you are not comfortable analyzing this situation, pick another from recent memory that you might feel comfortable about.) (a) Identify the triggering event. (b) State the thought you had about this event. (c) Show how these thoughts are related to your feelings. (d) Use the five Rational-Emotive Therapy evaluative screens to challenge your thoughts and develop alternative, self-talk which leads to neutral feelings about the same event.

CASE 14-1_____

The Company

Wehaulit Corporation is a transportation company in a major urban area. It is divided functionally into six divisions. A subsection of the Accounting and Information Systems Division is the Control Group, which includes the Auditing Department. The company does not have any cost accounting system or any profit centers, and its departmental budgets are not closely monitored. It is therefore the responsibility of the Auditing Department to monitor accounting and procedural controls, to evaluate the efficiency of departments and systems, and to recommend improvements wherever weaknesses are found.

In recent years, management has attempted to upgrade the audit staff. New staff members have excellent scholastic records; many are CPAs, and several have attended or are attending graduate school. The audit director is a young, aggressive "up and comer." The two audit managers are seasoned company veterans with many years of audit experience. The six audit seniors all have many years in the Auditing Department.

Morale is, at best, poor, in the Auditing Department. Old-timers complain because they have spent so many years in the same department. Younger members complain because they do not feel they are being trained properly. They also complain because they do not feel the work they are given is challenging enough. They consistently request transfers within two to three years after being hired.

The Dilemma

Upper management has not been pleased with the output of the audit staff. Audit endeavors have produced very few substantial results. Top management has assigned a task force to evaluate the audit function and to make recommendations for improving the effectiveness of the audit function.

Required:

1. As the chair of the task force, write your report to the president.

CASE 14-2_____

The Company

In 1981, ABC Hotels Corporation owned and operated eight gift shops in eight of its hotels. Like the hotels, the gift shops generated a financial statement (including profit and loss statement plus balance sheet) each month. The treasurer of ABC noted to one of his accountants, Maria Lopez, that it appeared that one of the gift shops was showing unusually high inventories on its monthly financial statement. Lopez was instructed to investigate the situation.

The Dilemma

In the course of her investigation, Lopez discovered the following:

1. The bookkeeper and the manager of the gift shop didn't understand their monthly financial statement. Though the bookkeeper supplied most of the information for the financial statement, the hotel controller actually prepared the monthly journal entries and keypunched them into the computer.
2. Because the bookkeeper didn't understand the financial statement, several key accounts were never reconciled. One of these accounts was inventories. Though physical inventories had been taken every six months, journal entries were never made to reflect the shrinkage in inventories.
3. Merchandise purchasing for this shop was done by the gift shop manager as well as a corporate supervisor. The supervisor admitted that she never looked at the financial statement inventory figures when buying for the store because she felt that the financial statement was a report prepared by accountants for themselves.

Required:

1. What recommendations for improvement should Lopez include in her report?

CHAPTER 15

The Behavioral Aspects of
Decision Making and Decision Makers

INTRODUCTION_____

The chapter starts with a behavioral dilemma encountered in a decision situation. To familiarize the reader with the aspects of organizational decision making, we will discuss the various sequential activities of the decision-making process and how they are affected by accounting information. We will evaluate the strengths and weaknesses of individual and group decisions in organizational settings. Attention will also be given to specific psychological factors and personality traits that have been shown to affect decision behavior. We will discuss accounting's role in the decision process and demonstrate under which circumstances it is used as a source of information, a goal to be attained, and a feedback mechanism in human or organizational control. How the theories and concepts of information theory should be used in improving the impact of accounting information on the user is demonstrated in Chapter 18 on "Communication of Accounting Information." We also will analyze the decision dilemma and apply the various relevant concepts and findings of behavioral decision theory and its related disciplines in reaching a solution.

DECISION DILEMMA_____

The Company

Anthony Aliprandi, the newly appointed chief executive officer of Quality Food Stores Inc., sat behind the huge desk in his attractive new office. It was his first day on the job, and he was contemplating the steps and approaches to take to enable Quality Food to cope effectively with the numerous problems it faced.

Prior to this position, Aliprandi was the corporate controller of a midwestern department store chain. This new assignment represented the fulfillment of a dream that he couldn't have hoped to realize in less than ten to fifteen years had he stayed with the department store chain. He was a highly competent financial executive who possessed superior analytical ability and administrative qualities. He had a pleasant personality and was generally liked by the people who had contact with him. This was especially surprising since he was known to demand top performance from all employees reporting to him and to be aggressive in reaching goals that had been set.

Before starting at Quality Food, Aliprandi studied and assessed the environmental and financial condition of the company he was to be heading. He found that Quality Food currently has a 40 percent share of the Chicago area food market, a posture gained through its "people-oriented" organizational culture. Its major segments include food stores as well as some food and drug store combination units. He noticed that the company is continuing to invest in high-margin inner city stores, while its competitors are abandoning this market by closing their inner city stores.

Labor is currently the single largest increasing cost for the company. To control this cost, time-saving devices such as technological checkout, automated pricing, and other labor efficiency improvements were initiated.

In addition to its midwestern stores, the company owns a controlling interest in a highly profitable chain of food stores in Mexico.

Realizing that energy costs are currently high and that future costs are uncertain, Quality Food is contemplating various moves to control this factor. Quality Food's earnings and recent investment trends are documented in Table 15-1.

When reviewing the selected financial information, Aliprandi noticed that while the supermarket business currently accounts for 71 percent of the total sales volume of the company, it produces only 60 percent of operating

TABLE 15-1
Quality Food Stores, Inc. Selected Financial Information

Business segment	Sales ($000)	%	Operating earnings	%	Increase (Decrease) square ft. change (000 ft.)
Supermarkets	$3,021,989	71%	$ 55,447	60%	(359)
Drugstores	859,903	20%	31,459	34%	3,000
Other Operations	386,030	9%	4,710	6%	602
TOTAL	$4,267,922	100%	$ 91,616	100%	3,243

earnings. In contrast, the drugstore business segment represents only 20 percent of total sales but produces 34 percent of operating earnings. Aliprandi's reaction was that the company should continue diversification into higher-margin nonfood areas such as drug stores, liquor stores, and the like. The combination food/drug/liquor store appeared to him to provide maximum results since one provides customers for the other.

In his preliminary briefing by the board of directors, Aliprandi was informed that inflation had been a major factor in the company's inability to hold the line on food store gross margins during the past decade. The board members also felt that the thrift stores would pose a substantial threat to Quality Food Stores for the balance of the 1980s.

At the meeting, Aliprandi was also introduced to his management team. John Miller, a distinguished-looking gentleman in his fifties, is the vice-president in charge of finance. Aliprandi had met him before at various professional meetings and had worked with him on committees of the Financial Executives Institute. Miller impressed him as a highly competent but reserved individual. Reporting to Miller are the corporate controller, the treasurer, and the director of data processing; all had been with the company for several years. Gail Solomon is the vice-president in charge of merchandising. Her responsibilities include procurement, merchandising, and advertising. She is in her early forties, holds a master's degree from the University of Chicago, and is overflowing with futuristic ideas. The third member of the top management team is John Adams, the vice-president of operations. He is in charge of transportation, warehousing, general operations (store and warehouse construction and maintenance), and communications. Adams is an electrical engineer who started out in communications. Aliprandi could picture him in his shirt sleeves, dealing directly with traffic managers, construction crew foremen, and communication experts.

At this meeting, the board of directors also informed Aliprandi that the company was about to embark on facility and capital expansion programs in an effort to gain control of the markets in which they are currently participating. He was told that the board hoped that he would make the decisions in regard to the capital expansions in the near future.

The Dilemma

Aliprandi is aware that the decisions he is expected to make will affect the destiny of the organization for at least the next decade and he wonders how he should proceed. Should he use committees to obtain the necessary information and then formulate his own strategies and make his own decisions? Should he sample the ideas and suggestions of his management team without bringing them together as a group and proceed from there? Or should he involve as many individuals as possible, have them discuss the pros and cons of each possible course of action, and let them attempt to reach a consensus?

Mr. Aliprandi admits to himself that the participating decision-making approaches run counter to his perfectionist nature. He intends to study their feasibility, though, especially since he was informed that they were used extensively throughout the organization in the past.

THE DECISION-MAKING PROCESS

Definition

Decision making has been likened to the processes of thinking, managing, and problem solving. Therefore, several definitions exist, each one used for a particular purpose. In organizational settings, decision making is usually defined as the process of choosing from among alternative courses of action that affect the future.

Sequence of Decision-Making Steps

Like most social activities, the organizational decision-making process can be broken down into a series of sequential steps.

Recognition and Definition of a Problem or an Opportunity

This step may be a response to a problematic event, a perceived threat, or an envisioned opportunity.

To recognize and define problems and opportunities, decision makers need environmental, financial, and operating information. Information about external environmental conditions may reveal new product or market opportunities or threats to the status quo. Financial or operational information might alert management to problems that require their immediate attention. Budget overruns, for example, will highlight discrepancies between actual and expected performance in specific responsibility centers. The decision makers' education, experience, temperament, personality traits, and other behavioral factors determine whether problems will be considered critical, opportunities promising, or decision processes initiated. Some managers enjoy the status quo and will only react to major unanticipated events. Others are aroused by even minor discrepancies and will not rest before a satisfactory solution is found and implemented.

Once a problem or an opportunity has been singled out for attention, it must be carefully defined. In complex situations, this activity is best performed by a team whose members have different educational backgrounds and areas of expertise. This approach helps overcome the limitations inherent in one person's perception of a problem. For example, in explaining a problem, a marketing manager might perceive it to be caused by sales or sales-related factors. Accountants might blame excessive costs or weaknesses in control. Production people might point to defects in raw material, excessively short production runs, or organizational deficiencies.

Search for Alternate Courses of Action and Quantification of Their Consequences

When the definition of the problem or opportunity is completed, the search for alternate courses of action and the quantification of their consequences begins. In this step, as many practical alternatives as possible are identified and evaluated. The search often starts by looking at similar problems that occurred in the past and the course of action chosen at that time. If the selected course of action worked well, it probably will be repeated. If not, the search for additional alternatives will be extended.

Features that can be quantified will be in the form of monetary estimates of the benefits and costs associated with each alternative. These estimates will be refined and rechecked if the alternative is considered feasible and worthy of further attention. Nonfinancial quantifications will be translated into revenue and cost terms if at all possible.

Not all features of an alternative can be quantified. In these cases, relevant benefits and sacrifices are listed.

The alternatives are evaluated in terms of their ability to accomplish certain predetermined organizational objectives. The objectives or decision criteria vary from one decision situation to another. In situations where the consequences are readily quantifiable and predictable with reasonable certainty, decision criteria such as minimum internal rates of return or target profit levels might be used as selection tools. If the consequences of the alternatives are uncertain, compromise and judgment may replace strict quantitative decision criteria.

Choosing the Optimum or Satisficing Alternative

The most crucial step in the decision-making process is choosing one of the alternatives. Although this step may appear rational, the final choice is frequently based on political and psychological considerations rather than on economic facts.

The managers making the final choice may face several feasible alternatives, each of which has certain advantages over others in terms of the decision criteria chosen. Managers are also aware of the "political" benefits and costs of each alternative. For example, some alternatives might be associated with special interests or aspirations of "important" corporate executives. In other cases, rejection of an alternative might result in personal embarrassment for the sponsors.

Implementation and Follow-Up

The success or failure of the final choice depends upon the efficiency of its implementation. The implementation will only be successful if the individuals who have control over the organizational resources necessary to implement the decision (e.g., money, people, and information) are totally committed to make it work. The ideal situation exists if this resource power is exercised by the sponsor(s) of the decision choice. To assure efficiency in implementation, periodic feedback of results and immediate correction of undesirable deviations are necessary.

Cognitive Motive

The cognitive motive is crucial in decision making because it energizes the thinking process. The two most relevant components of the cognitive motive in the decision-making context are: (1) the need for balance or certainty and (2) the need for complexity and variety.

The balance need underlies our desire for predictability, familiarity, and order. It fuels our desire to make the parts of a concept fit each other consistently. This motive activates both conscious and unconscious thought to make sense out of imbalanced, ambiguous, or uncertain information.

The complexity motive causes our desire for stimulation and exploration. It activates the conscious and the unconscious thought to seek new data from memory or the environment, which the balance motive then organizes.

Two important dimensions of the decision-making process are its complexity and its predictability (certainty or uncertainty).

When considering predictability, one can make a distinction between programmed and unprogrammed decisions. Programmed decisions are those where precise decision rules can be developed and used. Unprogrammed decisions deal with situations where unpredictability is the inherent feature. Decision rules or criteria are not fixed, but rather emerge as the decision develops. In an unprogrammed decision situation, one learns through trial and error.

Closely related to predictability are the distinctions in mathematical decision theory between certainty, risk, and uncertainty. Certainty occurs when all outcomes of a decision alternative are known. Risk occurs when one can assign probabilities of occurrence to the various possible outcomes. Uncertainty exists when one has no idea of the probabilities of alternate courses of action.

Certainty enables programmed decisions; uncertainty results in trial-and-error approaches. Risky outcomes most frequently result in programmed piecemeal decisions, since once probabilities are known, precise decision rules can be developed for each segment.

Using the dimensions of complexity and predictability, behavioral scientists have developed four distinctive types of decision models:

1. Simple programmed decision models
2. Simple nonprogrammed decision models
3. Complex programmed decision models
4. Complex nonprogrammed decision models

The *simple programmed decision model* is characterized by uncomplicated prediction rules that are set by someone other than the decision maker. They are supplemented by clear rules establishing priorities. The information search focuses on the most relevant data from past experience; the data are to be used as an example of a previously useful action alternative. The first satisfactory alternative found is chosen (satisficing). Alternatives are evaluated on the basis of short-run criteria, with risk held to a minimum. Implementation is autocratic.

In *simple nonprogrammed decision models,* whatever looks good at the moment to the decision maker is chosen (satisficing). Problems and opportunities are dealt with when they occur or are intuitively sensed. Urgency determines the priorities. Information comes from within (as a hunch) through reliance on socially valued views. In an organizational setting, information can also come from the management information system, of which accounting is the major component. The first alternative able to meet the short-run profit goal is implemented regardless of the risk involved.

Complex programmed decisions involve detailed emergency planning. Problems and opportunities are anticipated through carefully established priority rules. The information search is extensive and frequently employs statistical sampling or other sophisticated quantitative search tools. Data are fed into mathematical decision models. Alternatives are evaluated on the basis of long-run utility maximization. Decision outcomes are periodically evaluated to improve the decision process whenever possible.

The *complex nonprogrammed model* features continuous participation by all involved individuals to maximize information gathering and coordination. Goals are set by all and the environment is actively searched for problems and opportunities. New criteria are developed for each new situation. Information is sought externally and internally and rationally analyzed. Alternatives are developed by trial and error or by simulation. The decision choice is made by group consensus, thereby integrating the various views and values of the involved individuals. Implementation is participative.

Types of Process Models

The motives behind decisions are complex. Three main decision-making models attempt to identify the motives of a decision maker within an organizational setting. These are the economic model, the social model, and Simon's satisficing model.

Economic model

This traditional model assumes that all human actions and decisions are perfectly rational and that within an organization, there is consistency among the various motives and goals. It is assumed that all possible alternatives are known and that the probabilities associated with alternatives can be calculated with certainty. Decisions do not depend on personal preferences, but rather are dictated by the consistent goals of the organization.

Social model

This model is at the opposite extreme of the economic model. It assumes that humans are basically irrational and that decisions are based primarily upon social interaction. It is felt that peer pressure and expectations are the primary motivating forces.

Satisficing model

This is a more useful and practical model. It is based on Simon's concept of the administrative man,[1] in which humans are viewed as rational because they have the capacity to think, process information, make choices, and learn. However, there is a limit to their rationality. They are bound by their ability to process information sequentially. They never possess full information and have a limited capacity to evaluate large quantities of data. Thus, human behavior under these conditions is one of satisficing rather than optimizing. People consider a problem solved as soon as a feasible, "acceptable" solution is found.

ORGANIZATIONAL DECISION MAKING

In this section, we discuss the behavioral assumptions underlying a firm's decision-making process. First, we will look at the firm as a decision-making unit and then at the individuals and groups acting as decision makers and problem solvers.

The Firm as a Decision-Making Unit

A firm can be thought of as a decision-making unit that is similar in many ways to an individual. The decision problems facing a firm are numerous and complex. They often involve more than one department or activity. Recurring or routine decisions arise on a regular basis; other decisions are unique and nonrecurring.

To cope with its decision overload, organizations develop formal or informal "standard operating procedures" for recurring problems, which will lead to solutions compatible with overall goals and expectations. These standard operating procedures become "decision rules" for routine decisions in areas such as inventory management, costing, pricing, and order processing. Decisions made on the basis of preestablished decision rules are called programmed decisions.

Standard operating procedures remain in use as long as the situation for which they were created continues to recur regularly and as long as they are perceived, rightly or wrongly, as performing satisfactorily. If this is no longer the case, a search for a better solution is undertaken and the new solution becomes the standard operating procedure.

Cybert and March[2] delineated four basic relational concepts as the heart of business decision making: (1) quasi resolution of conflict, (2) uncertainty avoidance, (3) problemistic search, and (4) organizational learning.

Quasi Resolution of Conflict

An organization is a coalition of individuals with different goals that frequently conflict. Since decision making involves choosing an alternative compatible with overall goals and expectations, procedures for resolving goal conflict are required. Classical decision theory assumed that conflict could be resolved by using local rationality, acceptable sublevel decision rules, and sequential attention to goals. Local rationality is accomplished by dividing decision problems into subproblems and by assigning them to subunits within the organization for resolution. Complex and interrelated problems are thereby reduced to a number of simple problems. If the decisions generated by this delegation and specialization process are consistent with each other and in compliance with the demands of the external environment, conflict will be resolved. In the theoretical sense, consistency requires that the decisions will also result in overall optimization. To resolve any conflict among sublevel goals, the subproblems are attended to at different times.

Uncertainty Avoidance

When making decisions, organizations are continually plagued by uncertainty in their internal and external environment. Therefore, it is no surprise that modern decision theory has devoted much of its efforts to the problems of decision making under risk and uncertainty. The solutions offered are mostly of a quantitative nature and involve statistical decision procedures for finding certainty equivalents (e.g., expected values, etc.), as well as tools for living with the uncertainties (e.g., game theory, simulation, and other probabilistic decision models). In their studies, Cybert and March found, however, that organizational decision makers frequently use less sophisticated strategies when dealing with risk and uncertainty. They describe the decision maker's behavior as follows:[3]

(1) They avoid the requirement that they correctly anticipate events in the distant future by using decision rules emphasizing short-run reaction to short-run feedback rather than anticipation of long-run uncertain events.

(2) They avoid the requirement that they anticipate future reactions of other parts of their environment by arranging a negotiated environment. They impose plans, standard operating procedures, industry tradition, and uncertainty-absorbing contracts on that environment. In short, they achieve a reasonably manageable decision situation by avoiding planning where plans depend on predictions or uncertain future events and by emphasizing planning where the plans can be made self-confirming through some control device.

Schiff and Lewin[4] add organizational slack to the means used to avoid uncertainty. Slack is created during the resource allocation process by underestimating the revenues expected and overestimating the cost to be incurred for the decision situation, thereby increasing the probability of success when the decision is implemented. They further observed that when firms are faced with a new, not previously encountered decision situation, or when the risk associated with a specific situation is considered extremely significant, they will develop and implement the solution through a series of short-term decisions, each one followed by immediate feedback of the results.

Problemistic Search

The most vital element of the decision-making process is the search for alternate courses of action and the quantification of their consequences. Cybert and March[5] developed a theory of organizational search to supplement the concepts of decision making. They used the term "problemistic search" and defined it as the process of finding a solution to a specific problem or a way to react to an opportunity. The search is directed toward a specific goal; it is neither random curiosity nor a mere search for understanding.

Organizational search has four characteristics. First, it is motivated by the existence of a problem or an opportunity and will not cease until the problem is solved or the opportunity is acted upon. Second, search is simpleminded since it originally concentrates only in the neighborhood of the problem symptoms and the most obvious alternative(s). Only if the original search proves unsuccessful will organizations widen their search and even extend it to organizationally vulnerable areas (e.g., research and development, human resource accounting, public relations and the like). Third, any search is biased. The bias may be the result of the decision maker's special training or experience in specific areas of the organization. Search bias may also reflect the interaction of hopes and expectations of the involved individual(s). Finally, search may be impaired by communication bias that reflects unresolved conflict somewhere within the organization and which by itself calls for immediate attention.

Organizational Learning

Although organizations do not go through a learning process like that of individuals, they do exhibit adaptive behavior through their employees. They learn to attend to some part of the environment and not to another, to use some criteria and to ignore others. When a particular search approach discovers a feasible solution to a problem, organizations will most likely repeat the same approach in solving similar problems in the future. When a specific approach fails, it will be avoided in future searches. The same applies to the order in which alternatives are considered; it, too, will change if the organization experiences failure with a specific preference.

People—The Organizational Decision Makers

It is important to keep in mind that people, and not organizations, recognize and define problems or opportunities and search for alternate courses of action. People select decision criteria, choose the optimum or satisficing alternatives, and implement them.

The organizational setting in which people are used depends upon the type of decision problem or opportunity encountered. Decision problems range from simple to complex. Problems are considered complex if they are ill-defined and unstructured and if the search process for a solution is in itself complex.

Simple, everyday problems are most likely to be solved by single individuals who, through their positions, possess special training and experience in the problem area. For recurring, routine decisions, they will probably use preestablished decision rules or standard operating procedures.

Interdepartmental or interdisciplinary committees or sub-groups are most likely used to solve complex problems because their definitions and solutions will reflect some type of consensus (departmental or interdisciplinary) and therefore will have broader support when implemented.

Instead of ad hoc committee approaches, some organizations maintain specialized in-house teams capable of solving complex problems. Examples of such in-house capabilities would be operation research specialists, value analysis teams, and various other highly specialized troubleshooting groups.

Strengths and Weaknesses of Individuals as Decision Makers

Humans are rational because they have the capacity to think, to make choices, and to learn. However, their rationality is severely limited since they almost never possess full information and are capable only of sequential processing of the available information.

The rational decision-making limits of individuals vary according to:

1. The scope of knowledge available with respect to all possible alternatives and their consequences
2. Their cognitive styles (e.g., the ability to think critically and analytically, dependence on others, associative ability, etc.), with the assumption that no one style is necessarily superior because in specific problem situations, more than one approach can lead to acceptable results
3. Their changing value structure
4. Their tendency to "satisfice" rather than to optimize

Rational behavior of individuals in decision situations therefore consists of search among limited alternatives for a reasonable solution under conditions in which the consequences of action are uncertain. Problems with any degree of complexity must be approached strategically. To be successful, search strategies, decision rules, and information storing must be carefully structured in order to overcome the limited problem-solving capacity of individual decision makers.

The Role of Groups as Decision Makers and Problem Solvers

"A camel is a racehorse designed by a committee." Who has not heard this or any similar joke about the inadequacies of committee or group decisions? But in spite of all the sarcasm, groups or committees are used as decision makers in almost all organizations.

Why are decision-making groups (committees) so popular in organizations? What are their advantages? Committees bring together people with heterogeneous characteristics. In decision-making situations, they offer the advantages of diversity in experience, knowledge, and expertise as well as breadth of ideas and mutual support. Sharing of knowledge, ideas, and expertise may result in better dialogue, comprehension of problems, and more creative alternative courses of action. Despite the fact that committees are more conflict-laden and less expedient than individuals, they perform well. Groups are also credited with investigating ideas more rigorously and with increasing the likelihood that decisions will be effectively implemented. The committee members will exert the extra effort to see that "the fruits of their labor" work.

The group's ability to analyze problems critically, define and appraise alternatives, and to reach valid decisions may be weakened by two behavioral phenomena: groupthink and the risky-shift or group discussion effect.

The Groupthink Phenomenon

Groupthink describes situations where pressure for conformity discourages individual group members from presenting unpopular ideas or views. This prevents the group from objectively appraising unusual or minority views. Individuals who hold views that differ from the dominant majority are under pressure to suppress or modify their true beliefs and feelings. They will bend to group pressure since they want to be a positive part of the group and not a disruptive force. They may not have the courage to oppose the popular view, although their opposition and disruption would improve group deliberations.

Groupthink diminishes a committee's effectiveness. Most of us have at one time or another been its victims. Irvin L. Janis[6] describes groupthink as the "deterioration in an individual's mental efficiency, reality testing, and moral judgment as a result of group pressure."

Janis articulates the symptoms of this phenomenon as follows:

1. Group members rationalize any resistance to the assumptions they have made. No matter how strongly the evidence may contradict their basic assumptions, members behave so as to continually reinforce those assumptions.
2. Members apply direct pressures on those who momentarily express doubts about any of the group's shared views or who question the validity of arguments supporting the alternative favored by the majority.
3. Those members who have doubts or hold differing points of view seek to avoid deviating from what appears to be group consensus by keeping silent about misgivings and even minimizing to themselves the importance of their doubts.
4. There appears to be an illusion of unanimity. If someone does not speak, it is assumed that he or she is in full accord. In other words, abstention becomes viewed as a "yes" vote.

There are several possible ways to prevent or correct groupthink, although no one remedy will work in every situation. Each tries to break up the tight-knit fabric of the group to allow dissident opinions to be expressed and evaluated. To avoid or correct groupthink, one should:

1. Assign different members of the team the role of devil's advocate at each meeting.
2. Include different outside experts at each meeting.
3. Divide the group into two or more subgroups and have them separately investigate the various alternatives.
4. Avoid stating a preferential solution at the beginning of the discussions, but allow the group to proceed without preconceived solutions in mind.

Another effective remedy is the use of heterogeneous groups. Experience has shown that decision teams composed of individuals of dissimilar characteristics perform better, as long as the dissimilarities do not negatively affect their cohesiveness.

The Risky-Shift Phenomenon (Group Discussion Effect)

The risky-shift phenomenon, or the effect of group discussion, is another by-product of human interaction. It is characterized by groups choosing more aggressive and risky alternatives than individuals would have if they were acting alone. J.P. Campbell, et al. [7] describes the phenomenon as follows:

> Caution, which the members feel privately, may not be communicated in a group setting and there emerges the impression that other participants are more daring. Once again we have a group situation in which participation may lead to a leveling rather than a sharpening of the differences among members.

What causes risky-shift? Clark[8] offers four explanations: the familiarization hypothesis, the leadership hypothesis, the risk-as-value hypothesis, and the diffusion of responsibility hypothesis.

The *familiarization hypothesis* contends that group discussions start with a "feeling out" or "go slow" period, but once the individuals become more familiar with the situation discussed and with each other, they become bolder and more willing to assume more risk.

According to the *leadership hypothesis,* risk takers are admired and perceived by groups as leaders. Since they are usually also dominant in the group discussion, they influence the other participants to choose more risky alternatives.

The risk-as-value hypothesis observes that in today's society, moderate risk has a stronger cultural value than conservatism and that people willing to take risks are admired.

According to the *diffusion-of-responsibility hypothesis,* groups' decisions free the individual from direct accountability for the final choice of the group. If the decision fails, no one individual can be held wholly responsible.

Although none of the four hypotheses fully explains the occurrence of risky-shift, when combined they have some credibility in predicting decision behavior of groups in risk situations.

Risky-shift, like groupthink, has to be checked to avoid an adverse impact on the quality of the decision choices. One approach is the careful selection of the team members on the basis of their attitudes in regard to risk taking. Preference (utility) theory and observation in prior decision-making situations are such selection tools. A decision-making group should always be composed of a mixture of conservative and moderate risk takers to control the risk content of decision outcomes.

Group Cohesiveness

Group cohesiveness is defined as the degree to which group members are attracted to each other and share the group's goals. Groups with high cohesiveness are generally more effective in decision-making situations than groups where there exists a lot of internal conflict and lack of cooperative spirit among its members. The degree of group cohesiveness is influenced by the amount of time the members spend together, the severity of initiation to the group, the group size, possible external threats, and the group's past record of success or failure. The greater the opportunity for the group members to meet and interact with each other, the greater the chance that the members will discover common interests and become attracted to each other. The more difficult it is to join the group, the more its members will treasure their membership. The feeling of "us, the selected ones" creates a strong bond among them. Generally, cohesiveness will decrease as group size increases, since member interaction in larger groups becomes more difficult and the adherence to a common group goal is less likely. There is also the danger of the formation of cliques (groups within the group), which are primarily loyal to their own and not the common group goal(s).

Another factor which favorably affects cohesiveness is the track record of the group. A history of successful decision making unites its members (esprit de corps) and increases cohesiveness, while failures have a deteriorating impact. A group's cohesiveness will also increase when the group is attacked from an external source such as their superior or another group[9]. Such threats can even unite disarrayed groups if their members perceive that their common goals are in jeopardy. The reaction to threat, however, is not universal. According to Alvin Zander[10]:

> If group members perceive that their group may not meet an attack well, then the group becomes less important as a source of security, and cohesiveness will not necessarily increase. Addi-

tionally, if members believe the attack is directed at the group merely because of its existence and that it will cease if the group is abandoned or broken up, there is likely to be a decrease in cohesiveness.

This brings us to the following questions: Are highly cohesive groups more effective in decision-making situations than groups with low cohesiveness? Is high cohesiveness always desirable? Does it result in greater efficiency in the decision-making process?

High cohesiveness increases satisfaction and reduces absenteeism and turnover. Its impact on effectiveness and efficiency in the decision-making process depends, however, on the alignment of the group's attitude with its formal goals and the goals of the organization of which it is a part. If the attitudes are favorable and cohesiveness is high, decision-making effectiveness and efficiency will be high. If the attitudes are unfavorable but cohesiveness remains high, the degree of efficiency and effectiveness will deteriorate. In groups with low or deteriorating cohesiveness but favorable attitudes, decision-making efficiency and effectiveness will still be high, but lower than in a high-cohesive (high-support) situation. Low cohesiveness and unfavorable attitudes will always impair decision-making quality.[11]

Decision Making by Consensus versus Majority Rule

Another controversial topic is whether decisions should be based on consensus or be the result of majority rule. Consensus in a decision-making context is defined by Holder[12] as "agreement by all group members in the decision choice." In most situations, consensus can be reached only after lengthy deliberations and critical evaluation of all pros and cons. Besides implying accuracy, consensus is credited with inducing individuals to share more freely their knowledge and expertise and inspiring them to communicate all relevant information. Some claim that it motivates the team members to do their best in the implementation stage in order to assure the achievement of the group's goals.

Decision making by consensus takes more time than decision making by majority rule. Therefore, it is less suitable when time is critical. Although it definitely has its proven advantages, decision making by majority rule (with opposing views and their justifications expressed in writing) has to be substituted and accepted in many decision-making situations as the only feasible alternative.

Controversy Caused by Superior/Subordinate Relationship

When decision-making groups are composed of superiors and subordinates, controversy is unavoidable. Superiors have access to different information and therefore form different opinions than their subordinates. The quality of the decision choice will depend to a large degree on how the superior handles the controversy. The existence of controversy in a decision situation is not necessarily detrimental to the functioning of the group. It is quite healthy and, when handled wisely and constructively by the superior, may lead to improved decision making.

According to Vroom and Yetton[13], superiors as leaders have the following behavioral choices:

1. Solve the problem or make the decision by him(her)self using information available at that time;
2. Obtain the necessary information from subordinates, then decide on a solution to the problem. (S)he may or may not tell the subordinates for which problem they are collecting the information. The role played by subordinates is to provide the necessary information; they are excluded from generating or evaluating alternative solutions.
3. Share the problem with relevant subordinates individually, get their ideas and suggestions without ever bringing them together as a group. Then make the decision which may or may not be influenced by subordinate ideas.
4. Share the problem with subordinates as a group, obtain their ideas and suggestions. Then make the decision which may or may not be influenced by the subordinates' opinions.
5. Share the problem with subordinates as a group, discuss the pros and cons and attempt to reach an agreement (by consensus or majority rule) on a solution.

Each behavior choice can lead to satisfactory decisions, but research[14] testing their validity found that participatory methods are superior when the quality of the decision is important and acceptance and forceful implementation are doubtful. A division controller, when questioned as to her behavioral preference, replied: "Upward decisions, which affect my superiors and the organization, I make myself or in cooperation with my peers. In downward decisions, which will have consequences for my people, I involve them in every step of the decision process and insist on consensus in the final choice."

Applying the possible behavior choices to conflict resolution, it was found that supervisors who avoid open confrontation (decision behaviors 1, 2, and 3) do nothing to resolve conflict since they either ignore their subordinates completely or consider them as mere information providers.[15] Merely sampling the opinions of relevant subordinates (decision behavior 4) also has very little direct impact on conflict solution. When the supervisor shares the problem with subordinates and elicits their opinions but makes the decision without allowing them to participate, he or she may or may not attempt conflict resolution by integrating their views into his or her own. Only if the problem is shared with the subordinates (decision situation 5), pros and cons are thoroughly discussed, and the feasible alternatives carefully evaluated is conflict resolution seriously attempted. The degree of success will depend on whether the group climate is cooperative or competitive.

Influence of Power Bases

In decision-making situations, an individual is able to influence the decision outcome because of the authority or power bestowed by the organization.

The most frequently mentioned components of power are position power, expert power, resource power, and political power. An individual may possess more than one power and exercise them to different degrees in any specific decision situation.

Position power exists when an individual's influence is the result of the person's position in the organization, the authority it bestows, and the responsibilities, duties, and functions it entails. Although authority to make decisions is generally considered to be legitimate and the most common basis of power used to influence decisions, it cannot be automatically equated with effective leadership. In technically and organizationally complex issues, personal qualities and expertise rather than position power promote effective leadership.[16]

The influence of position power is felt in every decision situation. Its intensity is inversely correlated with the degree of technical and environmental uncertainty. The lower the uncertainty, the greater is its impact and vice versa.

Expert power influences decisions when the outcome is the result of an individual's knowledge of the situation under investigation, special technical skills or expertise, experience in dealing with similar situations, and demonstrated expert judgment. Another component frequently mentioned is the power for information, which may be the deciding factor in dealing with risk and uncertainty in proposed courses of action. *Information power* can be viewed either as part of expert power or as an element of resource power, since lower-level employees can and frequently do control and manipulate the information the experts use in their decisions[17].

Like that of position power, the influence of expert power is also present in each decision situation, but increases with decision uncertainty. The more complex and uncertain the decision situation, the more decision makers must depend on experts to analyze the problem and to provide the information that will lead them to a feasible solution.

Resource power exists when an individual exerts control over organizational resources or the resources necessary to implement a decision and uses them as a tool to influence the decision outcome. Resources in this context are money, people, and information. Control over them can be exercised at various hierarchical levels and is usually distributed among individuals who depend on each other in implementing a decision. This interdependence is probably the reason for the low influence of resource power. Individuals with resource power will only have major impact if they control scarce resources. They will usually be more influential in the implementation stage than in the decision process.

Political power can be described as an individual's personal leadership superiority and skills in persuasion, negotiation, coalition formation, side payments, and other political "arm-twisting" strategies. Its impact is most noticeable in complex and uncertain decision situations where there is ambiguity about the decision choices of the participants. It is also present when a final choice has to be made between equally feasible alternatives.

Impact of Time Pressure

One of the most frequent excuses for poor performance is time pressure. Therefore, it is not surprising that we strive to ascertain how individuals, groups, and organizations respond to time pressure and how it affects decision accuracy and efficiency. The experimental findings can be grouped into the effects of time pressure on group processes and on group efficiency.

Time pressure causes group members to acquiesce more to achieve group consensus[18]; to be less demanding and more conciliatory in bargaining situations[19]; to restrict participation in the decision-making process to relatively few members; and to favor majority rule. Time pressure also induces autocratic decision-making behavior. Groups trying to integrate opposing views will achieve fewer joint payoffs in time pressure situations than will groups that are free of time pressure. Isenberg[20] found a curvilinear effect of time pressure on accuracy but not on decision-making efficiency. It was also observed that there was an increasing gap in the frequency of communication between the most and the least communicative members. In other words, in time pressure situations, the dominant members of the group will take over.

NOVICE VERSUS EXPERT DECISION MAKING

The decision-making process is further affected by the degree of prior experience in decision making of the involved individuals. A recent study by Bouwman[21] disclosed a number of interesting differences in strategies and approaches used and specific data selected by experts and novices when making decisions on the basis of accounting or other financial information.

The study used protocol analysis and involved only five MBA students (the novice group) and three certified public accountants (the expert group).

It also dealt with a comparatively simple decision task. Even with these limitations, though, the study produced very interesting findings of broad applicability.

Although both groups used similar evaluation processes, great differences appeared in their specific approaches. The study of overall decision-making attitudes showed that novices collect data indiscriminately and wait to see what happens. In contrast, experts collect data discriminately to follow up on specific observations; they regularly summarize the data and formulate hypotheses. Although more complex, their approach lacks the repetitious character of that of novices.

To delineate the differences in data use, the research[22] divided the financial analysis task into three components: (1) examination of information; (2) integration of observations and findings; and (3) reasoning.

The components do not occur in a static sequence, but can be executed simultaneously or in any order.

Examination of Information

Examination was defined as the activity of analyzing the presented information and selecting for further consideration only those facts which seem particularly relevant for the decision task at hand.

The study showed that both experts and novices translate the financial information into qualitative terms and use similar methods (e.g., computation of ratios, development trends, flow statements). What differs is the mix of methods used. Experts rely more heavily on rules of thumb than novices and they examine more years of data. Their analysis is guided by a "feeling for the company," which provides them with a framework for a structured checklist to guide their discriminating data search.

Integration of Observations and Findings

In this context, integration involves grouping the observations either on a "cause and effect relationship" basis or by functional components of the firm. When integrating observations and findings, novices link together those that explain each other and ignore those that do not. In contrast, experts place special emphasis on the potential contradictions in observations and findings as a means of detecting underlying problems.

Reasoning

Reasoning, used throughout the decision-making process, is most evident in formulating hypotheses, developing leads in formulating the final decision, and in summarizing findings. Novices seem to equate reasoning with deciding "*when* to select *what* observed facts as the main problems"[23]. For experts, reasoning is the attempt at developing in their minds "a picture of what is going on." They accomplish this by systematic use of techniques that result in shortcuts without sacrificing the logical sequence in their analysis. Experts do not keep track of individual findings but summarize them into related groups and formulate hypotheses to be tested. They use a list of typical problems encountered in the past as reference points in recognizing the current problem and in developing solutions.

THE ROLE OF PERSONALITY AND COGNITIVE STYLE IN DECISION MAKING

Since people make decisions, much research has been directed at how psychological differences affect decisions.

Individual psychological differences can be divided into two categories: personality and cognitive style. Personality refers to attitudes or beliefs of individuals, while cognitive style refers to the ways or methods by which an individual receives, stores, processes, and transmits information. Individuals of the same personality type may have different cognitive styles and use very different methods when receiving, storing, and processing information. By the same token, individuals with greatly different attitudes and beliefs may demonstrate the same cognitive style[24]. In a decision situation, personality and cognitive styles interact and influence (increase or decrease) the impact of accounting information.

Communication of accounting information will be discussed in greater detail in Chapter 18. In this chapter, we will limit our discussion of the interaction and modifying impact of personality traits and cognitive style to the impact of tolerance of ambiguity (a personal variable) and field dependence (a cognitive style).

Tolerance for ambiguity measures the degree to which individuals feel threatened by ambiguity in decision situations and how ambiguity affects their confidence in the decisions. Some writers feel that people who are intolerant of ambiguity are expected to be less confident in their decisions. They will seek more information in ambiguous situations than their tolerant counterparts[25]. Others suggest that intolerants may reduce their perception of uncertainty[26], causing them to ignore uncertainty[27] and ultimately act as if there were certainty[28]. They may therefore show greater confidence and seek even less information than tolerants.

Field independence is the ability of an individual to arrive at a correct perception by ignoring interfering context. *Field dependence* is the inability to exclude irrelevant and misleading information when attempting to form an opinion. Field-dependent individuals are more receptive than field-independent individuals to ambiguous information and problem situations. Once they have reached a decision, however, they are more confident in their judgments than are their field-independent counterparts. The conclusions reached so far suggest that "field dependence may in its own right be a useful dimension for predicting behavior"[29] in problem-solving and decision-making situations and may well allow us "to tap a particular dimension of individual cognitive differences that is sensitive to accounting information."[30]

In regard to the interaction impact of tolerance for ambiguity and field dependence, it was found that field-dependent individuals are more confident in their decision choices than are field-independent ones, regardless of their level of tolerance for ambiguity. The difference, however, is more pronounced for individuals with low tolerance than for those with high tolerance[31].

THE ROLE OF ACCOUNTING INFORMATION IN DECISION MAKING

To improve the relevance of accounting information, accountants have become increasingly interested in understanding the role accounting plays in the entire organizational decision process[32].

By definition, management decisions affect future events or actions. They may affect a single future event or they may affect all events or actions subsequent to the decision. No event or action can be altered by a decision once it has been completed. Accounting information that focuses on past events only cannot by itself change events or their effects unless it is through the decision process by which future events and their consequences are determined. Since decision making and strict accounting scorekeeping information focus on different time periods, they are related only by the fact that the decision process employs certain modified accounting data in addition to nonfinancial information. An important question is then, "When is accounting information relevant for decision making?"

According to Hopwood, accounting information can "provide some of the stimuli by which problems (and opportunities) are both recognized and defined and the alternative courses of actions are isolated and their consequences elaborated" and "plays a role in the analysis and appraisal of the alternatives."[33]

Accounting Data as Stimuli in Problem Recognition

Accounting can function as stimuli in problem recognition by reporting deviations of actual performance from standard or budgetary goals or by informing managers that they failed to reach predetermined output or profit goals.

A declining inventory turnover ratio will direct management's attention to inventory levels and sales. A weakening accounts receivable turnover may point to deficiencies in credit granting and/or collection practices. The extent to which the periodic accounting ratios, performance reports, and other attention-directing accounting data actually stimulate solutions depends on a number of factors. First, it will depend on how quickly the external and internal environmental conditions allow a reaction. A typical retailer, for example, has considerable flexibility in reacting to changing conditions in demand and costs. He can mark down part or all of the inventory and conduct closeout sales; he can use loss-leaders and special advertising to increase traffic and sales. In contrast, manufacturing firms will find their reaction time constrained by factors such as a given capacity, a commitment to specific operating facilities, and/or production runs. Manufacturing managers will be able to react immediately to deviations from budgets or standards, but their reaction to increasing reorders, changes in production runs, and changing demand for a specific product or product line will be delayed. This delay will occur because the company is committed to a certain capacity, specific manufacturing facilities, and a particular complement of products. Changes in any one component will require fundamental rethinking of long-range investment commitments.

The degree of stimuli also depends on the capability of management (the decision maker) to organize and use accounting information and on their personal preference for qualitative or quantitative information. Managers who are inclined to follow their hunches (rather than use quantitative documentation when observing symptoms of deficiencies) will rarely give much credence to accounting information. Managers who are quantitatively inclined will most likely perceive accounting information as a vital attention-directing tool. The extent of beneficial use will vary considerably. Ratio analysis and the meaningful use of performance reports or of other comparative data require specific skills and an understanding of accounting principles and approaches. When used incorrectly, they will lead to wrong inferences and costly misinterpretation of the problem at hand. To function as stimuli in problem recognition and resolution, the attention-directing accounting data must be geared to the manager's educational background and specific expertise. Any change in attention-direction tools and approaches must be proceeded by a careful education of the users on the benefits and possible pitfalls.

Of equal importance is the size of the firm and the degree of decentralization. In small firms, the manager (owner) not only makes the decisions, but also implements them. In most instances, on-the-spot observations and intuition will provide a stronger stimuli than periodic accounting data. In large, centralized organizations where planning, controlling, and performance evaluations are done from a central or corporate office, accounting information will be a strong stimulus, since it is the only routine attention-directing tool available. In highly decentralized organizations, the stimuli impact will depend largely upon the performance evaluation system in use. If standard and budget compliance, as well as rate of return attainment, are perceived by the managers as the most important performance criteria, periodic accounting data will be watched very carefully and will stimulate immediate reaction.

Another element of impact is readily available industry data. Where relevant external data (e.g., price information, turnover ratios, average rates of return) are readily available, managers may consider them extremely important and use them as primary attention-direction sources. Internal accounting data will be used only to show where the firm is in comparison to its competitors and industry averages.

Whenever accounting information is used as a problem recognition device, it will also be used as the basis for determining the quantifiable consequences of the alternate courses of action worthy of future consideration.

Impact of Accounting Data in the Decision Choice

Not all managers use accounting data in analyzing the relative profitability or desirability of alternate courses of action. The weight given to accounting information in the final choice varies greatly. It may depend on the extent to which it is perceived to reduce some of the uncertainties surrounding the decision process. Past sales and cost data will, for example, be used as the first approximation of future demand for items sold in the past. For new items to be added, managers cannot rely on accounting information, but will most likely search for external information, such as their competitors' experience with similar products or the possibility of creating customer demand for revolutionary new items (personal computers, video recorders, car telephones, etc.). If the new product involves the same or similar production methods as the existing products, modified accounting data will be used. If the production characteristics vary greatly, internal accounting information will be of little use. If the degree of uncertainty is extremely high and relevant nonaccounting and external information is scarce and costly, the firm might use accounting information as a substitute, simply because it is available and provides a means of circumventing uncertainty.

Two other elements that affect the credence given to accounting information are demand and competition. Firms that face little competition and have inelastic demand will depend more on cost data supplied by their accounting system when making pricing and product line decisions than will firms operating in competitive markets. The weight given to accounting information in the final decision choice also depends on the degree of accuracy that management attaches to accounting data. It has been found that the more urgent the need for a decision, the more emphasis is placed on readily available accounting data. Accounting information also plays a more important role in short-run decisions than in those entailing long-run consequences, since it only reflects costs and revenue pertaining to current operations. Furthermore, decision makers seem to favor external information whenever it is readily available and less costly than internally developed accounting data. Another fact that diminishes the impact of accounting information is its inability to measure opportunity costs. Accounting reports past costs, while opportunity costs are sacrifices. At best, accounting data can provide a starting point for estimating opportunity cost. Therefore, it is not surprising that in situations where opportunity costs are extremely important, accounting information will play a minor role in the final decision choice.

Behavioral Hypotheses of Accounting Data Impact

Over the past two decades, researchers have hypothesized the conditions under which accounting information affects decision making.

As already stated, accounting information is only one of the inputs into the decision model. The inputs can be of financial, nonfinancial, or even a nonquantifiable nature. It is up to the decision maker to decide whether a certain input is relevant or not. Only if the decision maker perceives accounting information to be relevant for the type of decision to be made will it affect the decision outcome.

Whether decision makers consider accounting information to be relevant depends upon their perception of accounting. Decision makers may be aware that accounting's aura of authenticity is unjustified and that accounting is, at best, a process by which the effects of economic events are reported as accurately as possible, but without the pretense of being perfect. They may perceive accounting as an "imperfect measure" with a strong possibility that the true value will differ from the reported one, since errors and inaccuracies in the process of measuring and reporting are inevitable. In some cases, this notion may affect the weight given to accounting information in input selection. If, however, accounting information becomes a goal to be attained, the difference in perception becomes irrelevant. Accounting information becomes a goal when rewards or penalties are tied to its results. If a manager, for example, hopes to be promoted if he or she can reduce costs, then the manager will look at accounting information as the basis for determining whether he or she has succeeded; it will thus be used extensively whenever a decision is to be made. The same holds true when management is rewarded by stockholders with salary increases or bonuses on the basis of reported earnings or growth. The reports that result in these rewards may become the short-range goals of the decision makers and more important than long-run earnings or healthy growth, which the stockholders intended to reward.

The degree of influence of accounting information also varies by types of decision makers. Bruns[34] classifies decision makers into three groups: (1) decision makers within the firm who make decisions about operations and the accounting system used to prepare reports (top management); (2) decision makers within the firm who can make operating decisions only (operations managers); and (3) those outside the firm who make decisions about the firm that may affect its environment and operations, but who have no direct control over the operation of the firm or any activities in which it is engaged.

The distinction between top management who may affect accounting information and other internal decision makers who cannot is most critical where accounting information is conceived as a goal. The decision function for top management may require important choices between operating decisions and decisions to change the methods by which the accounting information is prepared. Requirements for independent audits and certification of consistency in methods employed from period to period somewhat reduces the significance of the two levels of management.

A recent study[35] confirmed the notion that external use of reported accounting information can affect internal managerial decision making.

> The more management perceives external decision makers as using reported financial accounting information in their decision processes, the more such information will tend to influence the decision process of management.

Bruns[36] summarized his various hypotheses in the following impact model:

  I. Accounting information will either affect decisions or affect decisions about the accounting system if
  (a) accounting information is relevant to decisions,
    (b) the decision-maker conceives accounting as a goal,
      (c) the decision-maker is a member of a firm who can control the selection and operation of the accounting system.

 II. Accounting information will affect decisions if
  (a) accounting information is relevant to decision,
    (b_1) the decision-maker conceives accounting as a goal, and
      (c_1) the decision-maker is a member of the firm who cannot control the selection and operation of the accounting system, or
      (c_2) the decision-maker is external to the firm; or
    (b_2) the decision-maker conceives accounting as a perfect measure,
      (c) non-accounting information is not relevant to the decision.

III. Accounting information may affect decisions if
  (a) accounting information is relevant to the decision,
    (b_1) the decision-maker conceives accounting as a perfect measure and
      (c_1) non-accounting information is relevant to the decision;

(b$_2$) the decision-maker conceives accounting as an imperfect measure, but
    (c$_2$)   non-accounting information is not relevant to the decision.

IV. Accounting information will not affect decision if
  (a$_1$) accounting information is not relevant to decisions; or
  (a$_2$) accounting information is relevant to the decision, but
    (b) the decision-maker conceives accounting information as an imperfect measure and
    (c) non-accounting information is relevant to the decision.

Other researchers[37] studied the question of how decision makers adjust to changes in accounting methods and terminology. They found that there are two factors that determine the degree of adjustment: feedback and functional fixation.

Feedback

In order to understand the change in an accounting method or term and to adjust the decision rule accordingly, the decision maker must be either informed of the change or must have some indirect feedback about the change. The use of internal and external auditing to check any significant change in the accounting methods or terminology is one way to discover that the accounting system performs differently from the way it is supposed or assumed to be performing.

To have a situation where a decision maker has absolutely no feedback about a change is almost inconceivable. If one excludes a possible short-run effect due to lag between the change and its indication, it is highly unlikely that there will be a complete lack of feedback.

Functional Fixation

This is a behavioral phenomenon that implies the inability on the part of the users of accounting information to look behind the labels attached to certain numbers. Once they accept an accounting term or measurement approach as the means of organizing their decision process, their behavior can rarely be influenced by a change in the accounting method or terminology used. If outputs from a different accounting method have the same names (e.g., profits, costs, etc.), people who do not understand accounting will tend to neglect the fact that alternate methods were used in preparing the output.

A more specific example would be the consulting firm in which it was standard practice to charge clients 300 percent of the direct cost of each project. Through a change in the cost accounting system, total costs of a project now include certain allocated overhead, which amounts to 100 percent of direct cost. Under the new costing method, clients should be charged only 150 percent of the new total costs of each project. However, during the next operational audit, it was found that managers kept using the old rule because they either were unable to see the alternate meaning of costs (endogenous functional fixation) or because they were afraid their supervisor would be unable to adjust to the change and might blame them for not charging clients enough (exogenous functional fixation).

As an attribute of decision making, functional fixation varies in degree from situation to situation but is never completely absent. A recent study [38] investigated the response of individuals and groups to a fully disclosed, cosmetic change in depreciation methods in a product-pricing decision. It was found that both individuals and groups failed to adjust adequately for the difference in the depreciation methods but that the group exhibited a greater degree of functional fixation than did the individual decision makers.

DIAGNOSIS OF THE DECISION DILEMMA AND SUGGESTIONS FOR A BEHAVIORALLY SOUND APPROACH

Aliprandi's hesitation in deciding what decision-making style to choose is well-founded. He is obviously well aware that his first move will be watched very carefully by managers throughout the organization and interpreted as an indication of the new organizational climate, which will affect not only their decision making but also all other phases of their activities. The behavior mode he chooses will be equated with his leadership style, especially since only Miller, the vice-president in charge of finance, and possibly the corporate controller have any prior working experience with him.

Aliprandi's behavior mode as chief executive would immediately influence only nonrecurring decision situations such as the expansion decisions to be made in the near future. For recurring, routine decisions, standard operating procedures (rules) are very likely in use, which are perceived to yield results compatible with corporate goals and expectations. If Aliprandi's behavior mode should prove to be radically different from the one demonstrated by his predecessor, the present standard operating rules might be replaced by more compatible procedures.

The decision-making styles of the various managers in nonrecurring decision situations probably vary considerably. Each individual has a unique style and knows quite well whom to include, to what degree, and in which organizational setting. At this stage, attempting to initiate any radical changes in their behavior would be very unwise and could cause a host of dysfunctional responses.

The group of Aliprandi's immediate concern is his top management team. Before deciding on any specific steps, he should conduct informal interviews with his vice-presidents and the various managers reporting to them. He should attempt to find out as much as possible about their leadership styles, risk attitudes, and other personality traits that may affect their decision-making behavior. He should try to assess the degree to which the group, or the subgroups they might be used to working with, might be susceptible to the groupthink or the risky-shift phenomena. Based on the available information, his management team seems quite well balanced. His vice-president of finance seems to be a conservative risk averter; his vice president in charge of procurement and merchandising is definitely a risk seeker; and his vice-president of operations is an individual whose major goal is to keep things running smoothly without radical changes.

Aliprandi will also have to assess the degree of cohesiveness of his executive management team. To do this, he should keep in mind that its members are presently threatened by the uncertainty of his initial moves and therefore are more united than usual.

As the next step, Aliprandi should try to evaluate his own personality traits and his cognitive style and how they affect his decision-making behavior. Being an accountant, he probably will be intolerant of ambiguity and will be confident in decisions only if they are sufficiently backed by quantifiable information. Under his leadership, accounting information will provide a major stimulus in recognizing and defining problems and opportunities. He will expect it to be used whenever feasible by his management in isolating alternative courses of action and in portraying their consequences. His success as a financial executive would indicate that he is quite capable in arriving at a correct perception by ignoring interfering context. Without the ability to exclude irrelevant and misleading information when forming opinions, he would not have reached his present position.

His greatest handicaps in creating a harmonious and cooperative climate throughout the organization are his perfectionist nature and his skepticism as to the feasibility of truly participative decision making. He will have to be very careful not to overemphasize his position power and thereby create excessive controversy. In a top management team as diverse as his, controversy cannot be avoided and is, by itself, quite healthy if handled wisely and constructively. If he honestly attempts to share the problems facing Quality Food with his management team, discusses openly and thoroughly all the pros and cons, and evaluates all feasible alternatives with them, the decision reached should prove satisfactory and in the best long-range interest of the organization.

REFERENCES

[1] Herbert A. Simon, *Administrative Behavior* (Macmillian 1961), 20–79.

[2] Richard M. Cybert and James G. March, *A Behavioral Theory of the Firm* (Englewood Cliffs, N.J.: Prentice-Hall, 1963), 114–127.

[3] *Ibid.*, 254.

[4] Michael Schiff and Arie Y. Lewin, *Behavioral Aspects of Accounting,* (Englewood Cliffs, N.J.: Prentice-Hall, 1974), 10–12.

[5] *Ibid.*, Cybert & March.

[6] Irwin L. Janis, *Victims of Groupthink* (Boston: Houghton Mifflin, 1972).

[7] J.P. Campbell, et al., *Managerial Behavior, Performance and Effectiveness* (New York: McGraw-Hill, 1970).

[8] Russell D. Clark, III, "Group-Induced Shift Toward Risk: A Critical Appraisal," *Psychological Bulletin* (Oct. 1971): 251–70.

[9] Stanley E. Seashore, *Group Cohesiveness in the Industrial Work Group* (Ann Arbor: University of Michigan, Survey Research Center, 1954).

[10] Alvin Zander, "The Psychology of Group Process," in *Annual Review of Psychology*, M.R. Rosenweig and Lyman W. Porter, eds. (Palo Alto, Cal.: Annual Reviews, 1979), 436.

[11] A. Stein, "Conflict and Cohesion: A Review of the Literature," *Journal of Conflict Resolution* (March 1976): 143–72.

[12] Jack J. Holder, Jr., "Decision Making by Consensus," *Business Horizons* (April 1972): 47–54.

[13] Victor H. Vroom and Phillip Yetton, *Leadership and Decision-Making* (Pittsburgh: University of Pittsburgh Press, 1973).

[14] Victor H. Vroom and Arthur G. Jago, "On the Validity of the Vroom-Yetton Model," *Journal of Applied Psychology* (April 1978): 151–62; and Charles Margerison and Richard Glube, "Leadership Decision Making: An Empirical Test of the Vroom and Yetton Model," *Journal of Management Studies* (Feb. 1979): 45–55.

[15] Dean Tjosvold, "Effects of Approach to Controversy on Superiors' Incorporation of Subordinates' Information in Decision Making," *Journal of Applied Psychology,* 67, 2, (1982): 189–193.

[16] Ramesh K. Shukla, "Influence of Power Bases in Organizational Decision Making," *Decision Sciences* (July 1982): 450–70.

[17] J.D. Thompson, *Organizations in Action* (New York: McGraw-Hill, 1967), 136.

[18] R. Fry and T. Stritch, "Effect of Timed vs. Non-timed Discussion Upon Measure of Influence and Change in Small Groups," *Journal of Social Psychology,* 60(1) (1964): 139–43.

[19] D. Pruitt and J. Drews, "The Effect of Time Pressure, Time Elapsed and the Opponent's Concession Rate on Behavior in Negotiation," *Journal of Social Psychology,* 5 (1969): 43–62.

[20] Daniel J. Isenberg, "Some Effects of Time-Pressure on Vertical Structure and Decision-Making Accuracy in Small Groups," *Organizational Behavior and Human Performance,* 27 (1981): 119–34.

[21] Marinus J. Bouwman, "Expert Vs. Novice Decision-Making in Accounting: A Summary," *Accounting, Organizations and Society,* 9, 3/4, (1984): 325–27.

[22] *Ibid.*

[23] *Ibid.*

[24] J. Pratt, "The Effects of Personality on Subject's Information Processing: A Comment," *The Accounting Review* (July 1980): 501–06.

[25] W.M. Shields McGhee and J. Birnberg, "The Effects of Personality on a Subject's Information Processing," *The Accounting Review* (July 1978): 681–97.

[26] M.D. Dunnette, (ed.), *The Handbook of Industrial & Organizational Psychology* (Chicago: Rand McNally, 1976).

[27] Robert William Kates, *Hazard and Choice Perceptions in Flood Plain Management* (University of Chicago, Department of Geography, 1962). Research Paper No. 78.

[28] Cybert and March, *A Behavioral Theory of the Firm*. 119–27.

[29] Gilbert Fowler White, *Choice of Adjustment to Floods* (University of Chicago, Department of Geography, 1964). Research Paper No. 93.

[30] Ferdinand A. Gul, "The Joint and Moderating Role of Personality and Cognitive Style on Decision Making," *The Accounting Review*, 59, 2 (April 1984) 264–75.

[31] *Ibid*.

[32] James L. Gibson, "Accounting in the Decision-Making Process: Some Empirical Evidence," *Accounting Review*, 38, 3 (July 1963): 492-500.

[33] Anthony Hopwood, *Accounting and Human Behavior* (Englewood Cliffs, N.J.: Prentice-Hall, 1974).

[34] William J. Bruns, Jr., "Accounting Information and Decision Making: Some Behavioral Hypotheses," *Accounting Review*, 43, 3 (July 1968): 469-80.

[35] Mark W. Dirsmith and Barry L. Lewis, "The Effect of External Reporting on Managerial Decision Making: Some Antecedent Conditions," *Accounting, Organizations and Society*, 7, 4 (1982): 322.

[36] William J. Bruns, Jr., *Accounting Review*, 43, 3 (July 1968): 469-78.

[37] Yuii Ijirig, Robert K. Jaedicke and Kenneth E. Knight, "The Effects of Accounting Alternatives on Management Decisions," *Research in Accounting Measurement* (Sarasota, Fla.: American Accounting Association, 1966).

[38] Robert Bloom, Pieter T. Elgers, and Dennis Murray, "Functional Fixation in Product Pricing: A Comparison of Individuals and Groups," *Accounting, Organizations and Society* 9, 11 (1984): 1–11.

SUGGESTED READINGS

American Accounting Association. *Statement of Basic Accounting Theory*. Sarasota, Fla.: American Accounting Association, 1966.

J. Bower, "Managing the Resource Allocation Process." Division of Research, Graduate School of Business Research, Harvard University, 1970.

J.D. Thompson and A. Tuden, "Strategies, Structures and Processes of Organizational Decision," In Thompson, J.D., et al., (eds), *Comparative Studies in Administration*. University of Pittsburgh Press, 1959. Some supporting findings are present in: Conrath, D.W., "Organizational Decision Making Behaviour Under Varying Conditions of Uncertainty," *Management Science*, 13, 3, (April 1967): pp. B487-B500.

R.L. Hoffman, "Homogeneity of Member Personality and Its Effect on Group Problem Solving." *Journal of Abnormal and Social Psychology* (Jan. 1959).

Allison Hubbard Ashton, "Does Consensus Imply Accuracy in Accounting Studies of Decision Making?" *Accounting Review,* 60, 2 (April 1985).

D. Tjosvold and D.K. Deemer, "Effects of Controversy Within a Cooperative of Competitive Context on Organizational Decision-Making." *Journal of Applied Psychology* 65, 5 (October 1980). 590–595.

DISCUSSION QUESTIONS

1. Define decision making in an organizational setting. What are the steps involved in this process?

2. What information is required for the recognition and definition of a problem or an opportunity?

3. How are alternatives evaluated in the search for alternate courses of action? Why must nonfinancial quantifications be translated into revenue and cost terms?

4. What is the most crucial step in the decision-making process? What are some factors that may affect this?

5. What are the two most relevant components of the cognitive motive in the decision-making context? Why is this motive crucial?

6. What are programmed decisions? How do these differ from nonprogrammed decisions?

7. Define certainty, risk, and uncertainty. How do these affect the decision-making process?

8. Distinguish among the four types of decision models. In which of the models is the decision choice made by group consensus?

9. What are the various types of process models used to identify the motives of a decision maker within an organizational setting? Which is the more useful and practical model?

10. What are the four basic relational concepts that form the heart of business decision-making (Cybert & March)?

11. What do you understand by the term "slack"? Why is "slack" created?

12. Define problemistic search. What are its characteristics?

13. What are the strengths and weaknesses of individuals as decision makers? According to what do their rational decision-making limits vary?

14. What are the advantages of having decision-making groups in organizations? What behavioral phenomena can weaken this decision-making process?

15. Explain the groupthink phenomenon. What are some possible remedies that can prevent or correct this phenomenon?

16. What is the risky-shift phenomenon? What are the four explanations offered by Clark to explain the causes of risky-shift?

17. Define group cohesiveness. What factors influence the degree of group cohesiveness?

18. Define position power, expert power, resource power, and political power.

19. Give an example of an instance where accounting data can be used as stimuli in problem recognition.

20. What factors influence the role played by accounting information in the decision choice?

CASE 15-1

The Company

The company is a fairly large insurance company with approximately $2.5 billion in assets and over 2,700 employees. It sells all types of insurance protection.

The company decided to implement a new life insurance system. This system was to far exceed in capacity and technology the present system. Because of the system's $5 million price tag, the decision to implement it was made by the EDP steering committee composed of vice-presidents of the various divisions. However, once that decision was made, a whole new concept of system implementation was formulated.

An environment known as "model office" was established. It consisted of representatives from the various departments involved in the life insurance company. These representatives were to act as go-betweens or liaisons between their own departments or divisions and the programming staff. Decisions as to what to implement, how to implement, methodologies, and so forth were made by this staff.

The Dilemma

Most decisions were made within the group more or less democratically unless the weight factor involved in the decision at hand favored a policy decision that crossed all aspects of the business. As such, all of the staff was pertinently involved. Research was conducted and brought to the group for further input and discussion. Difficulty in implementing it within the system was also discussed and democratically determined. Because this decision had far-reaching implications, this method of decision making was extremely valuable to both the customer base and departments involved. All of the staff involved in the decision-making process were chosen based on their ability to reason and think things through prior to making a decision. Therefore, quite a bit of autonomy and trust was given to this group.

Required:

1. Discuss the behavioral strengths and weaknesses of the decision-making structure of the insurance company.

CASE 15-2

The Company

LBC Company is a large "in-house" advertising agency, which means it not only creates the advertising but also films and produces the ads.

Fast Food, Inc. is one of the larger clients of LBC. At this time, LBC is in the midst of creating some radio commercials for Fast Food. To make the best commercials possible with the best musicians, it has been decided that the ads will be produced in Nashville.

Kevin Smith, the creative director at LBC, and Larry Jones, the marketing executive at Fast Food, were to go to Nashville to supervise production. The agreed-upon budget was set at $30,000 and they were to produce three or four ads.

The Dilemma

Smith and Jones met in Nashville and they immediately hit it off. It turned out that both men were musicians. Smith had studied music most of his life, and Jones had played with a band that was popular back in the 1960s.

They began arranging and rearranging all the music and jingles for the ads. After hearing one track, Jones thought that a string section should be added, so one was brought in. At one point, they heard that trumpeter Herb Alpert was in the building, so they asked him to come in and play on one track.

This resulted in some outstanding radio commercials. LBC was happy with them and everyone at the home office of Fast Food in Willowbrook was extremely happy with their quality.

The problem was that instead of producing three or four ads at the budgeted $30,000, they produced eight ads at a cost of $140,000.

Smith did not think that this would be a problem since Fast Food's Jones was with him the whole time and Smith assumed that this was automatic authorization for the added expense. When he tried to explain this to the accounting manager at Fast Food, he was told that Jones was a marketing executive and had no control or authorization over budget matters. He then told Smith that they would pay only the $30,000 that was budgeted and that LBC should pick up the rest since they were not authorized to spend more than that.

Required:

1. What went wrong in the decision making structure?
2. How could a recurrence be avoided?

CASE 15-3

The Company

Paul Collins is a recent college graduate with a master's degree in hospital administration. He was recently appointed assistant to the president at Franklin Memorial Hospital. The president and chief executive officer of the hospital is George Bobbins, who has been with Franklin for over 20 years. He is a competent executive with a primary emphasis in the area of finance.

Because of drastic changes in the health care industry over the past five years, Franklin has been forced to increase its use of advertising and marketing. The hospital executive staff has very little experience in this area. The board of directors consists of three lawyers, two bankers, four doctors, and Bobbins. In February, at Bobbins's insistence, the board hired Jones & Associates, an advertising and marketing firm known for its expertise in the area of hospital marketing. The board has set the hospital's annual marketing and advertising budget at $250,000, a 350 percent increase over last year. Jones & Associates will be charging Franklin a $12,000 per month retainer. Because of Collins's one marketing class in graduate school, Bobbins has made him the main contact person to work with Jodi Olson, the account executive at Jones & Associates.

The Dilemma

The hospital's first major marketing program is for its ambulatory care unit. Olson had several meetings with Collins and the director of emergency to put together the informational background on the type of advertising program Jones & Associates would develop for the hospital. Olson consulted with the experts in her firm (artists, copywriters, media people, and the creative director) to put together the advertising plan.

Olson planned to present the plan to Collins and the hospital's newly appointed marketing committee, which includes Collins; Gail Heusiner, the director of nursing; John Meyer, chief of medicine and member of the board of directors; and Jim Turk, the hospital's corporate counsel. Before the meeting, Bobbins directed Collins to get the advertising program accepted and running so he can report some progress on the program to the board next week.

Collins began the meeting by introducing Olson to the rest of the committee. Before Olson could start her presentation, John Meyer interrupted by saying "only used car salesmen advertise—certainly not doctors or hospitals."

Required:

1. How could this blunt rejection have been prevented?

2. Were the "right" parties involved in the decision-making process?
3. How would you have handled the situation?

CASE 15-4

The Company

The ABC Toy Company is a medium-sized manufacturer of children's bicycles and outdoor gym sets. Located in the Southeast, the company is part of a large conglomerate which has sales of $1.25 billion.

The company's sales volume for the last two years was $30 million in fiscal 1986 and $41 million in fiscal 1987. The company has two different types of customers. The main customer, a large department store chain, accounts for about 50 percent of the volume and all other customers, both large and small, the balance. The merchandise for the large department store customer is built to exclusive specifications and is privately branded. The balance of the production uses the company's nationally known brand name.

The company has a long-term "cost plus contract" with its main customer. The contract requires the total involvement of this customer in the production and product cost budgeting process. It was during a semiannual budget meeting with the customer that the dilemma was recognized, but it was not initially handled there.

The Dilemma

The ABC Toy Company is allowed an 8 percent profit factor. During the last two years, the company was reporting large and ever increasing "over formula profits," which were shared equally with the customer. This appeared to indicate the lack of an accurate budgeting procedure. Table 15-2 is a two-

TABLE 15-2
ABC Toy Company Sales and Profits

Year	Cost plus contract sales	Formula profit*	Actual profit	% Actual profit	Amount shared with the customer
1986	$15,000,000	$1,200,000	$1,600,000	10.7%	$400,000
1987	$21,000,000	$1,680,000	$2,500,000	11.9%	$820,000

*8% of sales

year history of the sales and profits and their effect on product cost. These "over formula profits" caused overstatements of 2.7 percent for product cost in 1986 and 3.9 percent in 1987.

The ABC Toy Company stated that these "over formula profits" were unintentional and just reflected the difference between budget and actual. The customer contended that these results were either deliberate or the result of less than "professional budgeting."

A review of the ABC Toy Company's consolidated financial statements highlighted substantial variances in the volume of the national branded merchandise. These were reflected in reduced production costs by efficiency at the steel rolling mill.

An in-depth study of the budgeted national volume showed that management had consistently underestimated this business so they could achieve a higher profit factor that would be acceptable to their parent company, the conglomerate.

When the 1987 final results were published, management of both companies held meetings to develop recommendations for a more accurate budgeting process. It was at these meetings that the real problem surfaced, which was the misunderstanding of the 8 percent profit factor. The management of ABC and its conglomerate interpreted the 8 percent profit factor as the "floor"; they were prepared to share any profits above that figure with the customer. They saw "over formula profits" as a bonus to the customer and used whatever acceptable methods were available to achieve these results.

The management of the large department store chain believed that the 8 percent profit factor was the "ceiling" and that sharing of "over formula profits" was to be strongly discouraged since it was reflected in higher product cost.

Required:

1. How would you solve the pricing problem without jeopardizing the pleasant business relationship between the two companies?

CHAPTER 16

The Behavioral Factors
of Capital Budgeting

by
Donald K. Clancy
Associate Professor of Accounting
Texas Tech University
Frank Collins
Professor
University of Miami
and Robert Chatfield
Associate Professor of Finance
Texas Tech University

THE DILEMMA[1]

The XIN, Inc. board of directors was considering a set of project proposals in their quarterly meeting. The company has several subsidiaries, operates world-wide, and is one of the Fortune 500 industrial corporations. There are four proposals ranging from $2 million up to $10.8 million with a total projected investment of $21 million. The proposals promise after-tax rates of return from 26 percent up to 48 percent. Projects below $2 million have to be approved by the chairman of the board and those below $100,000 are approved by division managers. The board is composed of the chairman, the chief financial officer, and five outside directors.

The chairman is paid a salary of $220,000 per year plus a substantial bonus (up to $300,000 depending upon the net income for the year). The directors are paid a fee of $40,000 per year for their services.

Chairman John Chelsey (chairman and chief executive officer of XIN, Inc.): Ladies and gentlemen, let's get started. There are five items on today's agenda. The first item concerns the project proposals from the divisions. I trust you have all had a chance to carefully consider the proposals.

Director Alexia Henderson (outside director, bank president): I have and, like always, they look very good. Of the boards that I sit on, this company has the best sounding proposals. I wish we could loan money at these rates.

Director Joel Lischwitz (outside director, retail chain president): Same here. With the proposals I've seen here during the past three years, XIN should be among the most profitable names in electronics. But it's not. XIN's overall rates of return are low—only about 10 percent. Why?

Chairman Chelsey: As to the quality of the proposals, I only bring the absolute best proposals to you for consideration. I must admit, though, that relatively few proposals are ever submitted that have less than a 25 percent promised rate of return. As to the state of our current earnings, the entire electronics industry has had some problems with a downswing in volume recently. We have been doing about average for the industry, which I feel is extremely good considering that we are much smaller than General Electric or Westinghouse. Our defense contracting and construction divisions are doing very well. Consumer products is off a little, though. Overall, we are doing much better than just surviving. Now I would like to consider the projects. As in the past, we will have the various vice-presidents and division managers available to present their proposals and answer questions. I might add that since our average cost of capital is currently only about 10 percent after-tax, all these proposals are appealing.

(There follows a two-hour session in which the board calls in all proposers individually and questions them. After this, the board returns to closed session).

Director Andrea Logan (attorney): I trust this acquisition of Brogan Financial Services has been adequately reviewed. The state of California has very recently passed some restrictive legislation that will bear on this acquisition. The proposal looks very appealing otherwise. That price looks very favorable.

James Watt (corporate counsel): The proposal reflects those recent changes.

Chairman Chelsey: We had to sweeten that deal a little because of the new stock restrictions.

Director John Searight (outside director and independent oil producer): Remember the Jacobsen deal that we approved three years ago? How did that work out? I remember that it promised a very good return also. What happened with that deal?

Chairman Chelsey: John, you have a way with questions. That project was started under Wozniak (the previous chairman) and went very well until a competitor raided the engineering staff and took half our people. We just had to defer it. We lost several good people trying to make that work out. When we got back to the project, the momentum was gone and we had to get out. A British company has agreed to take it.

Director Searight: What about the other projects we accepted during the past two years?

Chairman Chelsey: As you well know, they are all associated with specific divisions or subsidiaries. Our performance evaluation system is more associated with people and divisions rather than with every project that we approve. Once a project is completed, there is no way to trace results to a specific project— only to the performance of divisions and people. Besides, we have high

turnover in our company, like yours. As our people change, there is no way
to hold a person responsible for the mess of a previous person. Is there?

Director Searight: I don't know about that, but we sure make it a practice to evaluate
the success of each oil well we drill. We know the difference between
whether we struck oil or not.

Director Jason Ankley (outside director, investor): John, there are some differences
between oil and electronics.

Director Searight: I know. Everything seems so safe and sound here that it's disgust-
ingly tame. I just don't like fishing in a barrel. Besides, after we approve a
project, it seems to disappear. What does XIN need directors for?

Director Henderson: Uh. We seem to be getting out of order here. I would move that
we accept these four projects as proposed.

Chairman Chelsey: Do we have a second?

Director Lischwitz: I'll second, but I am still concerned about the overall rate of
return for XIN.

Chairman Chelsey: I know. All in favor? Good. The motion passes unanimously.
Now we'll consider the second agenda item...

THE BEHAVIORAL FACTORS

Financial managers and managerial accountants are deeply involved in operational budgeting, both in developing the budget and in reporting subsequent
performance. Examples of operational budgets include sales budgets, labor
cost budgets, manufacturing cost budgets, and the like, where the emphasis
is on comparing actual results with budget for control, planning, and coordinating purposes, all on a short-term basis.

Financial managers and managerial accountants are also involved in
another type of budgeting process—capital budgeting. Because of this involvement, it is important that they be aware of factors—particularly the behavioral
factors—that greatly affect both capital budgeting and decision making. The
purpose of this chapter is to discuss these seldom-recognized factors.

Definition of Capital Budgeting

Capital budgeting may be defined as the process of allocating funds for long-
term projects or purchases. Capital budgeting decisions are made as the need
arises and involve relatively large sums of money,[2] long periods of funds
commitment, and uncertainty caused by the length of time involved and the
difficulties in estimating decision variables (cash flow amounts, timing, etc.).
Some examples of capital budgeting projects would include the purchase of
expensive and long-lived production equipment, the building of a new plant
facility, or the creation and staffing of a new and large company segment
(such as a division intended to produce and market a new product line).

Because of the usually large sums involved, faulty capital budgeting decisions may result in bankruptcy, difficult cash flow problems, or, at the very least, failure to optimize the operations of the firm. Consequently, most firms approach these decisions with gravity and constantly seek ways of improving the capital budgeting process.

To aide in this search, consultants, researchers, and those directly concerned with making such decisions have developed a number of techniques, most of which are concerned with improving the economic interpretation of data related to the decision. Some of these techniques are discounted payback, estimated net present value, sensitivity analysis, simulation, and mathematical programming.[3] While the literature is replete with discussions of these techniques, very little attention has been paid to important behavioral factors involved in the process.

Importance and Types of Behavioral Factors of Capital Budgeting

One might wonder what these behavioral factors are since the selection techniques mentioned earlier seem to require only an identification of potential projects, estimation of cash flows for each project, use of an analysis technique, selection decision, and then implementation of the project—a seemingly straightforward process. Yet the entire process involves a number of behavioral considerations of far-reaching impact.

The identification and specification of potential projects require creativity and the ability to turn a good idea into a practical project. Conceivably, the selection decision could be totally objective, but that is highly unlikely. Uncertainty inherent in the data describing a project (such as estimating the timing of cash flows or residual salvage values) prevents the selection technique application from being completely objective. Because the results of analysis techniques must be interpreted carefully, the human ability to consider and judge is an important factor.

As another example of the presence of behavioral factors, the a priori success or failure of a project depends upon the performance of the personnel implementing the project. Consequently, it would be unwise to evaluate and implement capital projects without taking into account the behavioral context of the process. Some of the behavioral factors are discussed in more detail below.

Problems In Identifying Potential Projects

As we have seen, persons involved in the budgeting process must have the creative ability to seek and scan the array of potential capital projects available to the organization. Once the projects have been identified (which is not easy task in itself), they must be adequately specified or defined so that the consideration process may take place. Unless the important decision variables have been described, decision making regarding the adoption of potential projects should not be attempted.

It is worthwhile to note that there is almost always great interest in evaluating the success of selected projects. (Indeed, we will later recommend that post-implementation reviews of on-going projects be conducted.) Yet projects forgone, either because of nonidentification or nonselection, are almost never considered on a post hoc basis. It could be that the opportunity costs of these forgone projects are greater than the benefit of selected and implemented projects.

Prediction Problems Caused by Human Behavior

While inputs to the mathematical decision models mentioned earlier seem to be fairly straightforward, the underlying uncertainty should be recognized. It should be realized that some of these inputs (such as timing and size of cash flows) depend on the ability to predict the behavior of those charged with implementing the project.[4]

Projecting the smoothness and compatibility of individual and group activities over a period of five to 20 years is a perilous undertaking. For example, while the budgeting decision might be predicated on a particular individual's project management, that person may leave the organization or be transferred and replaced by a very different person, thus affecting the accuracy of data estimates. Similarly, the possibility of labor and political unrest arising in capital projects that involve the automation of clerical and unskilled tasks should be considered in predicting the data for the selection of projects.

It is also commonly known that people learn over time as they operate a particular procedure. Therefore, the changing success of a project over time should be taken into account in predicting decision data by considering the improving performance of personnel involved in the project. This process of learning can be depicted in a graph of improving performance, often called a "learning curve."[5] These curves are different for different situations, so it is important that those engaged in capital budgeting carefully estimate the learning curve of the personnel involved in a project. Potential personnel turnover must also be considered when developing an accurate estimate of the costs associated with the project.

Problem of Short-Term Manager and Short-Term Performance Measures

Another behavioral aspect of the project selection procedure is that performance review methods are inconsistent with the methods of project selection.

Performance valuation and compensation tend to be short range in nature — usually for the past year, quarter, or month. Thus, the focus of lower-level management — and, to some extent, mid-level management — will naturally be on short-range performance, often measured by the accounting rate of return. Projects with performance that does not begin for several periods will be of little interest to lower-level managers. Top management should be aware of this natural bias caused by the performance review process.

Since there is seldom a one-to-one correspondence between managers and projects, individual managers will take over projects from their predecessors and start several of their own. Very few projects will be started and finished under the same manager because of the fairly rapid turnover (e.g., promotions, transfers, etc.) that occurs in most organizations. Managers tend to favor projects they have initiated themselves and will work on these to the exclusion of projects started by predecessors. If manager turnover is moderately rapid, no one can be held responsible for the success or failure of any particular project.

Capital will be wasted if new managers periodically scrap the projects of the previous manager and start new projects, only to be followed by yet another new manager who continues the cycle. Top management must consider this cycle in the project selection procedure and should evaluate to what degree the problem is occurring and how it will affect a particular proposal.

Problems Caused by Self-identification With Projects

In some cases, however, managers might stay in their positions without being promoted or transferred. This might cause difficulties if managers become self-identified with projects they conceived and started. Since projects are normally identified with specific persons or divisions, such persons tend to become self-involved with past projects they selected and may try to make the projects successful or appear to be successful after the projects are funded.[6]

Top management should be aware that the process of trying to make poor projects look good can strain even the best managers. There should be a graceful mechanism for "bailing out" of projects before otherwise outstanding managers leave the company or act dysfunctionally to avoid admitting that a project they proposed will not work.

Personnel Development and Capital Projects

In the process of project selection, top management should consider whether the proposed project is good for the development of the proposer at this time. The project may well be too large for the person or division to absorb without pushing managers beyond their limits.

On the other hand, top management may encourage divisions to engage in projects that are not economically attractive in themselves, but offer potential future personnel training benefits that cannot be quantified. For example, such projects could provide potential improvement of personnel skills, both in the selection and implementation phases of capital budgeting.

Thus, a company may undertake a project that has little or no profit involved just for the benefit of the personnel training. The consideration of personnel development may far outweigh a negative net present value of the individual capital project, particularly for smaller projects.

Capital Budgeting as a Ritual

Some behavioral scientists (notably, Anthony Hopwood)[7] have suggested that the entire capital budgeting process is a ritual. They suggest that few projects are submitted by lower-level managers unless they stand an excellent chance of being approved. Too much embarrassment and "loss of face" come with being identified with a rejected project.

Once a project receives initial approval at a lower organizational level, it typically must proceed through a series of reviews and approvals up the organizational hierarchy. As it proceeds, it gains a momentum that is difficult to stop. Indeed, after a project has received approval (or, one might say, blessing) at several lower levels, upper-level decision makers are usually loathe to reject it. Provided that funds are available, it will usually be approved since by this time, numerous lower-level managers and analysts have indicated their personal approval and commitment to the project. A rejection at this point would be taken as a "slap in the face" by those who had previously endorsed the project.

Thus, upper-level managers will usually reject a project only if there are overwhelming reasons for doing so. And as the project ascends even further up the hierarchy, the momentum continues to grow so that the final decision indeed resembles more of a blessing than a rational approval decision.

Risk-seeking and Risk-aversive Behavior

Individuals react differently to risk. Some persons seem to enjoy making risky decisions and being in risky situations while others go to great lengths to avoid doing so. The particular state of risk-averseness of a capital budgeting decision maker will affect how he or she reacts to projects. On the basis of the same set of data, two different decision makers are quite likely to make opposite decisions depending on their feelings about risk.

Sharing the Poverty

The phenomenon of "sharing the poverty" often has an important effect on the capital budgeting process.[8] This occurs when there are more potentially profitable capital budgeting projects available than there are funds to finance them—a condition called *capital rationing*.

Facing these circumstances, top management sometimes chooses to allocate the available funds to as many managers as possible, even though it might mean forgoing more profitable projects. For example, this might occur when Manager A has three projects of great potential while Managers B and C have projects of only fair potential. If only three projects can be funded, management might decide to fund only one of A's projects in order to fund B and C's projects also.

In a sense, top management is reacting to internal political pressures and is not making approval decisions based on the economics involved, even though the result may be nonoptimal from an economic perspective.

A RATIONAL FACADE

Human factors are very much involved in the capital budgeting process, even though very little attention has been paid to them in the literature.

In reviewing these factors, we have noted the problems caused by difficulty in identifying and selecting capital projects and the need for human creativity and judgment. We have noted the problems caused by difficulty in predicting human behavior and how these are exacerbated by the long-run nature of capital projects. We have also observed that many managers will tend to have a short-run perspective since their performance evaluations are usually based on short-run measures. This can be detrimental to the selection and management of capital projects that require a long-run perspective.

We have pointed out that there are managers who will make capital budgeting decisions and then be transferred or promoted before projects can be developed, utilized, and ended. As a result, these mangers are not present to receive praise or blame for the project's success or failure. Problems also exist when managers remain in their positions throughout the project's life; in this case, managers might engage in dysfunctional behavior in order to ensure the project's success.

We have observed that marginal capital projects are sometimes implemented to provide a mechanism for training management personnel. Capital budgeting may also become a ritual and thus fail to take advantage of rational decision techniques. We noted that the acceptance or rejection of a capital project might depend on the decision maker's personal risk-averseness. The risk-seeking or aversive behavior of individuals might also influence the process and should be monitored. Finally, we noted that political pressures may greatly affect the capital budgeting decision.

In conclusion, one might say that capital budgeting has a facade of rationality, particularly when elaborate, mathematical models are used. They convey an atmosphere of certainty, logic, and science. Yet underlying the decision process are the behavioral factors mentioned in this chapter. Unfortunately, decision makers may not want to admit that irrational human factors might have been foremost in the acceptance or rejection of a particular project.

SUGGESTIONS FOR IMPROVEMENT _____

What can be done to alleviate the adverse effects of human behavioral factors on the capital budgeting process? First of all, it is essential that those involved in capital budgeting be aware of the behavioral factors inherent in the process. Where possible, these factors should not be allowed to obscure relevant decision data of a more rational nature. While it would be impossible to totally eliminate the human factors, a fruitful approach would stress awareness of them and efforts to control their dysfunctional effects.

Furthermore, we suggest that post implementation audits be conducted for capital budgeting projects. By so doing, one may observe not only the suitability of a decision model (payback, net present value, etc.) and the accuracy of the data estimates that were used, but can also attempt to identify the various behavioral factors that affected the selection and project management process in a particular company. Here, one may attempt to determine which of the behavioral factors were detrimental to the proper decision and subsequent implementation. Once this is done, a capital budgeting decision maker can take steps to allow for these factors in the selection and implementation processes. In developing this awareness of detrimental factors, management should be particularly attuned to finding cases of ritualism in the capital budgeting process and noting whether the risk-averseness or risk-propensity of the individual managers are consistent with the overall goals of the firm.

The post implementation audits being suggested here should be conducted prior to the ending of the capital project's life and should take into account changed conditions. If done in this way, it would be possible to objectively determine new standards of performance for each of the managers who are managing capital projects—an approach quite similar to the concept of using flexible rather than static budgets in operational budgeting. This contrasts with the tendency to continue measuring capital budgeting performance against the original data used in making the budgeting decision. Thus, the concept of flexibility can be introduced into the management of capital projects.

Since the post implementation audits could be conducted from time to time and new performance objectives determined periodically, it would be possible to set short-term performance measures for the capital projects that are consistent with the long-range performance of the projects. This would have the effect of eliminating problems associated with the short-term manager—

managers would be evaluated strictly with short-term performance measures rather than a mixture of short-term measures for normal operations and long-term measures for capital projects.

At this point, one might wonder if it would be possible to assign continuing responsibility to managers (even if they have been transferred) for capital budgeting projects they initiated. Probably not, for managers must have control over activities for which they are held accountable. If continuing responsibility is assigned to a transferred manager, then that person would have to share the responsibility for a capital project associated with the original job assignment. It is axiomatic that if all have the responsibility, then no one has the responsibility. Accordingly, it is our recommendation that realistic short-term performance measures for capital budgeting projects be developed.

In conclusion, we suggest that those involved in capital budgeting processes and in capital project management should at the very least be aware of the behavioral factors involved. At best, they should take active steps to ensure that the behavioral factors of capital budgeting do not cause suboptimal decisions.

DIAGNOSTIC REVIEW OF THE CAPITAL PROJECTS SELECTION PROCESS AT XIN, INC.

There are several important behavioral factors influencing the project selection process at XIN, Inc. Generally, the directors (with some exceptions) are not taking an active enough role in the project generation and selection process. The specific behavioral factors will now be considered and recommendations for improving the circumstances will be suggested.

Problem Factor A

The first factor concerns the board's passive reaction to forgone opportunities. If Chairman Chelsey only brings projects with high rates of return (25 percent or higher) to the board, opportunities that promise only a 22 percent return are not considered. These projects are not brought to the board and are not even proposed to the chairman by the divisions. This circumstance should seem odd to the board. Further, a quarterly capital expenditure of only $21 million seems relatively low for a Fortune 500 company.

The chairman must have a history of not supporting projects unless they have a very high promised rate of return. However, projects with lower than 25 percent return could potentially increase the overall profitability of

XIN because the current achieved rate of return is low. The company is not achieving growth and increases in profitability because of this problem.

Recommendation A

The board should take a more active role in questioning the chairman on projects avoided because they fall below the 25 percent apparent required return of the chairman. If growth and profitability are important to the board, then they must persuade the chairman to look for more opportunities.

Problem Factor B

XIN, Inc. has personnel turnover that is common to most organizations. However, the company does not appear to connect the relationship between turnover and project success. This is demonstrated in the Jacobsen deal referred to by Director John Searight and the response of the chairman. The project was allegedly unsuccessful because a competitor hired half of the engineering staff. Further, several good people were lost trying to make the project work.

Recommendation B

Part of the project consideration process by the board should explicitly concern the correspondence between people and project success. They should request an analysis of the sensitivity of projected returns to various scenarios in personnel turnover.

Problem Factor C

There is an inconsistency between the way that projects are selected (projected returns for the project) and the way division managers are evaluated (divisional returns). Since the projects are merged into the division, there is a loss in identity. Except for the Jacobsen project referred to in the case, project accountability appears to be lost for most projects.

Recommendation C

The board should insist on a program of post implementation reviews. These are very useful devices for connecting the promises by proposers to their actual performance on projects.

Problem Factor D

The approval of projects by the board appears to be ritualistic. The board blesses or "rubber stamps" the proposals by accepting the statements of the chairman. Only directors Lischwitz and Searight appear to have any serious reservations about the process; Lischwitz is questioning the overall return rate and Searight is expressing concerns about the apparent riskless nature of the proposals and the fact that projects disappear into divisions and oblivion. The chairman is personally associating himself with the projects by the statement that ". . . I only bring the absolute best proposals to you for consideration." After such a statement, the board would hesitate to be critical of a project for fear of being critical of the chairman's judgment. To seriously pursue the particulars of a project, much less vote negatively on it, would be similar to saying to Chelsey: "Your judgment of what is best for the company is not good enough." It may also appear to be disloyal to the company. Finally, the current board is considering proposals primarily on the basis of their rates of return without going deeper.

Recommendation D

The board needs to be more aggressive in questioning proposals while at the same time letting the chairman know that he is all right. The board seems very passive, except for Searight, and could use some more determined personalities. Thus, some additions to the board would be appropriate.

Problem Factor E

The chairman seems to be risk-averse because the projects brought to the board are referred to as "tame" by Searight and only extremely attractive projects are presented. To grow and be more profitable, the company must seek out projects with potential, and be willing to take on some risk in doing so.

Recommendation E

The company should tie the personal interests of the chairman more closely with the interests of owners. The compensation package rewards the chairman for current earnings only and not for future benefits to the company. The compensation approach should be examined carefully to reward the chairman for efforts that may not show up in growth or earnings improvements for years. This can be accomplished by awarding shares in future profits (or increase in profits) as compensation for current performance.

REFERENCES————————————————————

[1] Adapted from D. K. Clancy, F. Collins, and R. Chatfield, "Capital Budgeting: The Behavioral Factors," *Cost and Management* (September 1982): 28–32.

[2] Charles T. Horngren, *Cost Accounting: A Managerial Emphasis*, 4th ed. (Englewood Cliffs, N. J.: Prentice-Hall, 1977), 377.

[3] Frank S. Budnich, Richard Mojena, and Thomas Vollman, *Principles of Operations Research for Management* (Homewood, Ill.: Richard D. Irwin, Inc., 1977), 322–25.

[4] Lawrence D. Schall and Charles W. Haley, *Introduction to Financial Management* (New York: McGraw-Hill, 1977), 278.

[5] Frank J. Abernathy and Kenneth Wayne, "Limits of the Learning Curve," *Harvard Business Review* (September–October 1974): 45–57; Frank J. Andress, "The Learning Curve as a Production Tool," *Harvard Business Review* (January–February 1954); Winfred B. Hirschman, "Profit From the Learning Curve," *Harvard Business Review* (January–February 1964).

[6] Robert W. Scofield and Donald R. Domm, *Human Behavior and Administration*, Revised pre-publication edition (Houston, Texas: University of Houston, 1970).

[7] See Anthony Hopwood, *Accounting and Human Behavior* (Englewood Cliffs, N.J.: Prentice-Hall, 1976).

[8] James H. Lorie and Leonard J. Savage, "Three Problems in Rationing Capital," *Journal of Business* 28 (October 1955): 229–39.

SUGGESTED READINGS————————————————

Burkert, R. L. "Recognizing Inflation in the Capital Budgeting Decision." *Management Accounting* (November 1971): 40–46.

Ferrara, W. L. and J. C. Hayya. "Toward Probabilistic Profit Budgets." *Management Accounting* (October 1970): 23–28.

Fleischer, Gerald A. *Capital Allocation Theory: The Study of Investment Decision.* East Norwich, Conn.: Appleton-Century-Crofts, 1969.

Fogler, H. R. "Overkill in Capital Budgeting Technique." *Financial Management* (Spring 1972): 92–96.

Fremgen, J. M. "Capital Budgeting Practices: A Survey." *Management Accounting* (May 1973): 19–25.

Gold, B. "The Shaky Foundations of Capital Budgeting." *California Management Review* (Winter 1976): 51–60.

Hendricks, J. A. "Analysis of Risk in Capital Projects." *Management Accounting* (April 1977): 41–44.

McGurgen, James R. and R. Charles Moyer. *Managerial Economics.* 2nd ed. St. Paul, Minn.: West, 1979.

Mehler, E. W. "Capital Budgeting: Theory and Practice." *Management Accounting* (September 1976): 32–38.

Ryan, W. G. "Management Practices and Research—Poles Apart." *Business Horizons* (June 1977): 23–29.

Tinker, A. M. "A Short Note on 'Is Emphasis of Capital Budgeting Misplaced?'" *Journal of Business, Finance, and Accounting* (Spring 1976): 23–25.

DISCUSSION QUESTIONS

1. Define capital budgeting; distinguish between capital budgeting and operational budgeting.
2. List four quantitative techniques used for capital budgeting. What are the behavioral consequences of each?
3. List five steps in the selection of projects. What sixth step was recommended by this chapter?
4. What is the relationship between learning and cash flow estimates made for project selection?
5. What is a common measure of performance of managers?
6. Why will very few capital projects be started and completed under the same manager?
7. Of what relationship is personnel development and project selection? What is the relationship among project size, personnel development, and project selection?
8. Hopwood hypothesized that capital project selection is often ritualistic. What is the relationship between ritualism and "loss of face?"
9. What is meant by "momentum" in the project selection process?
10. What is risk-seeking selection? Risk-averse selection?
11. Define "sharing the poverty" as a rule for the selection of capital projects. Under what circumstances will a "sharing the poverty" capital allocation rule be used by senior management?
12. What is facade? Why was capital budgeting attributed with a rational facade?
13. What is a post implementation audit?
14. Should managers be held responsible for the projects started by predecessors?
15. Should projects be evaluated on the basis of the original proposal or should allowances be made for changes?
16. What are the plausible relationships between the estimation of cash flows and the personalities of the estimators? Use the pessimistic versus optimistic person as a starting point.
17. Why is it unlikely that project selection processes are entirely objective? In your discussion, use the relationship between performance evaluation and project selection.
18. In what ways might the personnel implementing a project influence its success?
19. What opportunities might be foregone as a result of not entering a new market? Use the example of the robotics market for an electronics company.
20. Why is it easier to evaluate the success and desirability of projects undertaken than to evaluate projects turned down? Use the example of the university that you chose over another university that you considered.
21. Of what importance is projecting the compatibility of work groups to the future success of a project? Use the example of a new automobile assembly plant in your discussion.

22. Discuss the relationships among personnel turnover, learning, and project success. Use for discussion a hypothetical company that is considering a new customer billing system that involves some complexity. The current system takes two weeks to learn and there is turnover of about 20 percent of the workforce per year. The proposed system will take four weeks to learn and will likely increase clerical turnover because of the frustration.

23. Why has performance evaluation in the United States tended to be short term in nature, focusing on a month, quarter, or year?

24. Discuss the nature of habits and rituals in the performance evaluation of managers. Of what importance is the need for habitual good results to the selection of managers for promotion?

25. Why would a project that does not start for several years be of little interest to lower-level managers?

26. What natural motivations would there be to encourage managers to favor projects that they start rather than those of their predecessors? Use as an example a university president favoring a basketball arena that was completed recently and that he heavily supported versus an architecture building that was recently completed, but was started under a predecessor.

27. Sometimes a manager attempts to make a poor capital project look good. This is called a "white wash." Use as an example a new piece of equipment, such as a computer system, that was a poor purchase. What might the manager encourage subordinates to do and say to others?

28. What graceful mechanisms might senior managers use to help good managers "bail out" of poor capital projects?

29. What types of projects might senior managers encourage lower managers to undertake, even though the projects might have a small, but negative net present value? Give some specific examples.

30. Why have some companies developed what appears to be more a project "blessing" process rather than a project selection process?

31. Lower managers are often more risk-averse than senior managers because they have fewer opportunities and a shorter track record. Senior managers are often more risk-averse than owners because they cannot as easily diversify. What are the implications of these statements for the generation and selection of projects?

32. As noted in the chapter, there is a facade of rationality over the capital project selection process. Under this facade, there are behavioral and political processes. Why might senior mangers support this facade of rationality and even compete on the basis of appearing to be the most rational and scientific in project selection? After all, they are very bright people and are unlikely to be fooled by the facade.

33. What behavioral aspects of project selection can be examined in a post implementation review? Which ones cannot?

34. Short-term performance measures for long-term projects are needed for the evaluation of managers. Can you suggest plausible short-term measures for this context? Use as an example a project involving fighter jets, which normally have several years of development followed by three to ten years of production. Minor improvements are made in the fighter jet from year to year, but the basic design stays the same.

CASE 16-1

Locked In

Lois Layne, president of Supercapes, Inc., was talking to Dudley Bland, her administrative assistant.

Lois: Dudley, our new line of waterproof capes doesn't seem to be selling like it should. It worries me.

Dudley: Yes, you're right and I'm worried, too. I just knew we had over-invested in the Gothamville plant. Whew!!! A $6,000,000 investment for an untried product!

Tim Pennypaker (overhearing as he walks in): Right Dudley . . . as controller, I ought to know. For a $20 million net asset firm, we're way overextended.

Lois (speaking heatedly): Enough, enough. I'm tired of hearing negative talk. Don't either of you forget for a moment that I built this company almost single-handedly. (Lois pauses and speaks slower.) Judgment. Yes, my judgment and sense of timing have built us . . . not your project analyses, Tim. After all, you can't make a decision with an analysis. People make decisions. (Dudley and Tim leave the room; Lois returns to her desk.)

Lois: Klark, firing Dudley and Tim is tough, but at last I won't have to listen to their negative talk. Morale is the key! (Pausing and then speaking) Klark, you know if I could find some more right-thinking people like you, I'm convinced we could get the Supercape line moving. That guy we have modeling the cape seemed to have some good ideas. I wonder . . .

Klark (responding rapidly): I don't think so Lois. He has other commitments, but I think we need a radio advertising blitz—$100,000 worth of 30-second advertisements is what we need.

Lois: Right Klark. It takes money to make money. I'm convinced the Supercapes will be profitable. It's a good idea and we've got to hang tough . . . besides, we've spent too much already to stop now.

Klark: Right.

Required:

1. Identify the behavioral issues and problems suggested in this case and develop recommendations for solving them.

CASE 16-2

An Argument

Gene Johnson, personnel director, and Gary McGill, controller, were in Sherrie Mills' office arguing about replacing the manager of the Capital

Projects analysis section (annual capital budget, $2,500,000). Mrs. Mills, president of Hitek, Ltd., was trying to calm Gene and Gary down as they argued about the replacement.

Sherrie: Now boys . . . calm down. (pausing) Gene, let me hear your recommendation one more time. And Gary, let me do the talking for a while.

Gene: We achieved an annual growth in sales of 10 percent with an average R.O.I. of 12 percent for the past five years because of one thing . . . people! Yes, people. Hitek has succeeded in an uncertain and rapidly changing marketplace because we have had skilled and knowledgeable employees in key positions. We've been lucky to hire them from outside the firm. We need to start training inside and that's why I suggest promoting Terry Crane into the Capital Projects job. I know he's young and inexperienced, but that MBA degree of his must mean something. Besides, Gary, I know you watch our capital project analyses and selections pretty close. And after all, those projects analysis reports don't matter anyhow. Sherrie and you select the projects you want regardless of their R.O.I.'s, present values and . . . (Gary abruptly interrupts).

Gary: What do you mean regardless? Capital projects analyses are always carefully considered. After all, we usually agree with their recommendations. (pausing) And about that replacement manager—we don't have anyone in the firm with the experience as well as the training for the job. I still say we need to hire Richard Ott. While he may not have an MBA, he's been in the game for years. I hear that Molt, Inc. (a major competitor) will be promoting him to controller soon. Bet we can hire him away. (Gene starts to respond and Mrs. Mills interrupts).

Sherrie: Well, I can see you'll not agree. I'll announce my decision Monday. (She walks out of the room, muttering to herself) . . . analyses that don't matter . . . MBA's . . . experience . . . hmmm . . .

Required:

1. Identify the behavioral issues and problems suggested in this case and develop recommendations for solving them.

CASE 16-3

The Correct Target

Dave Krockett, chairman of the board, and Roy Been, chief executive officer of Texas Ordinance, Inc., were discussing the firm's profitability and selection of new projects. They both agreed firm profitability was a bit lower than some competitors, but this was a reasonable sacrifice to achieve sound, stable growth despite the objections of a couple of the outside directors.

Sam Houston, the manager of the rifles division, submitted two projects for approval as did John Slaughter of the pistols division. The rifle projects promised rates of return of 18 percent and 20 percent whereas the pistol projects promised 30 percent and 35 percent.

Since the board of directors always approved projects recommended by both Dave and Roy with little question, they were comparing one another's decisions to be sure they could present the board with a united front.

Dave: He's done it once again. John's always coming up with great ideas for a new product. If we could just clone him and have a John in every division, we could be number one in the country.

Roy: I have to agree, but let's get down to the business of picking two projects to recommend. As you know, we can't afford to fund all four projects or, for that matter, even three.

Dave: Even if we had the funds, a firm our size can't expand that fast. The personnel and logistical problems our organization would run into if we proceeded on all four projects would be incredible.

Roy: As usual, John's got a couple of humdingers, but he'll have to be happy with just the best one. Imagine the riot we'd have on our hands if Sam's division heard pistols has two new projects and they have none!

Dave: Besides, John's division couldn't handle the strain if it took on both projects.

Roy: Then we're agreed. Let's recommend one project each for John and Sam.

A couple of weeks later, the board of directors met and approved Dave's and Roy's recommendations on the two new capital projects. But a short time later, a key manager resigned.

Dave: Southwest Armaments!! They don't pay their managers any better than us!

Roy: That's true, but they offered John a nice package of stock options on top of the $150,000 a year. They're also giving him a free hand to proceed with production on several of those pistols—you know, the ones we turned down earlier.

Required:

1. Identify the behavioral issues and problems suggested in this case and develop recommendations for solving them.

CASE 16-4

Locked Out

Wall Climbers, Inc., an industrial cleaning company concentrating on skyscraper window washing, recently purchased state-of-the-art washing equipment. John Smith, the CEO, was just informed by the owners of the George Hancock building that the cleaning they had contracted for was nowhere near completion. Immediately, John rushed to the office of one of the executive vice-presidents to uncover the problem.

John: The Hancock building people are not at all happy with our progress. What's the problem here?

Mary Jane: We don't have anyone in our organization with the capability to manage a cleaning crew on that new equipment. Peter Parker was running the show over there, but he's in the hospital. Doctors said he had some kind of reaction to a spider bite. They don't know when he'll be back on his feet.

John: What about York or Hopkins? Didn't they attend the training sessions when we bought that state-of-the-art equipment?

Mary Jane: As you know, at the time, we were under severe pressure from Citybank to finish up their downtown headquarters. Consequently, York and Hopkins both missed the training sessions. Parker was the only one free at the time.

John: We still have the old equipment around here somewhere, don't we? Let's get it out and pay the crew to work overtime if we have to. If we don't finish their windows soon, our reputation won't be too clean.

Mary Jane: And I'll send Hopkins over for some training on that new equipment as soon as possible.

Required:

1. Identify the behavioral issues and problems suggested in this case and develop recommendations for solving them.

PART THREE

BEHAVIORAL ASPECTS OF FINANCIAL ACCOUNTING AND REPORTING

In Part Two we focused on the behavioral aspects of management accounting and how they affect the decisions of managers at various levels *within* an organization — the internal users. The chapters in that section demonstrated how the accounting system can be used to reinforce desireable behavior or to change or prevent undesireable behavior. The chapters in Part Three reveal the behavioral aspects of financial accounting.

Financial accounting, in contrast to managerial accounting, is concerned with the measurement, accumulation, summarization, and reporting of economic events to decision makers *inside and outside* the organization. Outside users of accounting information include stockholders, government agencies, creditors, potential investors, trade unions, insurance companies, etc. This diverse group of users relies on published financial statements for their decision making. For most business decisions the published financial statements of a firm — audited by independent accountants — are the primary and critical data upon which the decision rests. In fact, in the case of major corporations, financial information obtained from sources other than published financial statements may be considered "insider information" and may be illegal to use. The decisions made on the basis of information contained in published financial statements are the very decisions that influence our social and economic well-being and are reflected eventually in GNP and other national income statistics.

The centrality of accounting information to business decision making demands that standards be applied to the treatment and reporting of accounting data. These standards, known as generally accepted accounting principles (GAAP), when applied to financial data provide assurance to outside users that the information contained in one firm's financial statements is comparable to the information in the published financial reports of other firms. Without this assurance people would be unable to make meaningful business decisions. Yet, there are behavioral implications associated with the accounting principles.

Because of the extensive impact of accounting reports on the actions and decisions of internal and external users, on society, and the economy, behavioral accountants have an ethical obligation to communicate accounting information as effectively as possible. Behavioral accountants must understand how the structure of financial reports influences business decisions, and how the perspectives of people involved in the process of preparing information affect the structure of the published reports. Behavioral accountants must analyze accounting concepts, principles and methods of presentation in order to find any built-in biases that might induce a person to make an unsound decision. Chapter 17 discusses issues such as these.

The great variety of decisions to be made by outside users, as well as the divergent interests of outside users, result in different degrees of emphasis placed on certain parts of the financial statements. For example, short-term creditors would find the current asset and current liability sections of the balance sheet most useful because they reflect the degree of liquidity of the organization. In contrast, potential long-term investors may focus more on profitability as reflected in income statement data, and on those aspects of the statement of financial position that reflect a firm's long-term viability. Behavioral accountants must be aware of differences in user needs in order to more effectively present information and design report formats. Behavioral accountants must also be aware of how the presentation (tone, style, format, redundancy, etc.) of technical information affects decision makers. Chapter 18 applies some basic principles of communication and information theory to the accumulation and meaningful presentation of accounting reports and demonstrates their effect on human behavior.

Accounting information not only affects the decisions of people outside the firm, but the actions of people outside the firm also affect people inside the firm — board members, executives, accounting personnel, etc. People inside an organization are affected by the activities of rule-making bodies such as the Securities and Exchange Commission, Internal Revenue Service, state regulatory agencies, etc. Chapter 19 demonstrates how federal income tax laws affect decisions and actions of managers.

To provide as much relevant information as possible, behavioral accountants must report on economic events, sometimes *nonfinancial* in nature, that have not traditionally been included in accounting reports. Chapter 20 introduces readers to the valuation of and accounting for the firm's most important asset: human resources. This information, nonfinancial in nature, is critical to an array of business decisions and should be available to decision makers. Chapter 21 describes the measurement of, and accounting for, the social costs and revenues of a firm's operations.

CHAPTER 17

The Behavioral Effects of Reporting Requirements

by
Denise Nitterhouse
Assistant Professor
School of Accountancy, DePaul University

REPORTING DILEMMA _____

Sue Cranston was concerned. She had just reviewed the memo about the new report that headquarters would require beginning next month and the related preliminary data gathered by her personnel office. She was not at all sure she liked the implications. The preliminary data related to the past six months, while the data to be reported would begin with next month.

Cranston was manager of one plant of a large manufacturing company. The company had long been subject to government equal employment opportunity (EEO) reporting requirements on the sex and ethnic mix of its employees, but the new report asked for the race and sex of all job applicants, whether they were hired or not. Cranston had always sent the data necessary to comply with the government EEO reporting requirements. She had never received any feedback, though, except to clear up obvious clerical errors or omissions. Of course, there were occasional blanket memos from headquarters to all plant managers about being an equal employment opportunity employer and not discriminating on the basis of race or sex. There were also memos about the company not having a high enough minority or female representation in most job categories.

However, this reporting requirement appeared as if it might have originated within the company rather than from the government. It came from the same department in the personnel office that collected the usual EEO reports. The instructions were fairly clear about how the form was to be filled out but said nothing about why it was being required or to whom the information would eventually go. Cranston had spoken to a few other plant managers about it, but none of them or her immediate boss knew any more about it than she did. When she called the headquarters personnel office, ostensibly to get clarification on the instructions, she was told that "the data are needed for a study that's being done."

The problem was that the data she had now spelled potential trouble. When the applicant numbers were compared to the data on hires, promotions, and number of employees, it was clear that there was a higher proportion of minority and female applicants than selections. When Cranston asked her line personnel about this, they expressed surprise at the statistics but said that the chosen applicants must have been better qualified for the position. The preliminary data were admittedly questionable, since they had not been used or checked very closely before; it was just what the personnel office could pull together on short notice. However, beginning next month, the current month's data would be routinely reported to headquarters.

What should her next move be? Who would get the data and what would they use them for? Should she, or perhaps her personnel officer, start monitoring the hiring and promotion decisions more closely? How effective were their policy guidelines in this area? Not only would this take time, but Cranston's managers would probably perceive it as an encroachment on their jobs. If the data this month showed the same pattern as the preliminary data she now had, Cranston could write a justification to accompany the report, but that was asking for trouble. It was entirely possible that she would never hear any more about this report than she had about the others—as long as she did not call attention to it. On the other hand, if the report was sent to the government without careful review by headquarters, and if there were problems, she could easily see herself becoming a sacrificial lamb. But even if no one else ever noticed it, she had a nagging question in the back of her mind about what *had* caused those statistics.

REPORTING REQUIREMENTS

Today's world is full of requirements to report information to others about who or what we are, how we run our lives, how we do our jobs, how people and things we have responsibility for are doing, and so on. These are generally referred to as reporting "requirements," although some may not be strictly enforceable. Most behavioral accounting research on information effects has focused on how recipients use reported information to make judgments and/or decisions. This chapter is about the other side of the coin—that is, the effects of reporting requirements on the behavior of those required to report the information. The terms "reporters" and "senders" will be used interchangeably to refer to the individuals, organizations, or other groups required to report information.

The essence of the accounting process is the communication of information with financial or management implications. Since gathering and reporting information consumes resources, it is usually not done voluntarily unless the reporter believes it will influence the receiver to behave as the reporter would like. Advertising is an example of information most companies "report" voluntarily to influence people receiving their advertising information to buy their products. Most accounting information is communicated only because someone in a position of power, usually the person receiving the information, requires the sender to report it.

Reported information is a vital part of the process of managing and controlling organizations. Without information, managers, lenders, and owners cannot tell whether things are going as planned or if corrective action is needed. Although alternatives such as direct observation and surprise audits are sometimes used, reported information is the most common way of obtaining the information used for control. It is important to understand the effects of reporting requirements because of both their prevalence and cost.

Reporting requirements are imposed and enforced by a variety of persons and organizations in a variety of ways. Within organizations, managers usually have the right to require subordinates to report on any aspect of their work performance. Whether they can enforce such a requirement effectively is much less clear and depends on a number of organizational, and perhaps personal, factors. Publicly owned corporations are required to report extensively to the SEC and the general public on their financial status and operations. Numerous federal, state, and local government agencies also require organizations and individuals to report on a wide variety of financial and nonfinancial matters, with various sanctions imposed for noncompliance. Everyone involved in designing or using information systems needs to understand the possible effects of reporting requirements on the information senders, as well as how to predict and identify such effects.

HOW REPORTING REQUIREMENTS AFFECT BEHAVIOR

The idea that reporting requirements may affect reporters' behavior is not new, nor is it unique to management and accounting. Psychologists are well aware that people may respond to the "demands" of an experimental situation by behaving differently than they would in other situations. Whereas experimental psychologists try to avoid this because of their research orientation, managers and regulatory agencies actively try to place demands on others to cause them to behave in certain ways. Managers and regulatory agencies use reporting requirements both to impose such demands and to provide the information needed to evaluate behavior or performance.

It is recognized that senders may deliberately report false information—that is, they may lie. Inaccurate information may also be reported inadvertently because of inadequate information systems. Ensuring the reliability of reported information is an important function of audits of financial statements by independent certified public accountants, of internal auditing by a staff that answers only to top management, for spot checking of subordinates by superiors, and of "site visits" by funders of social service agencies. A mechanism for ensuring the integrity of the reported information is an important part of the design of any reporting requirement. The remainder of this chapter will assume that there is a means of ensuring reasonable accuracy, so references to changes in behavior will concern the behavior being reported on, not merely changes in the reported data.

Reporting requirements can affect reporters' behavior in several ways. Other forms of measurement used in organizations, such as audits and direct observation, also have many of the same effects of reporting requirements, as well as their own specific effects.

Anticipation of Information Use

When a reporting requirement is imposed, it is common for the sender to at least think, if not ask, "Why do they want this information? How will they use it?" The sender wants to know if the recipients will take some action related to, or hold some opinion about, the sender because of the reported information. Since recipients use reported information as a basis for performance evaluation and other judgments, the senders' consideration of likely use is well founded.

The sender uses the reporting requirement itself, along with other information, to anticipate how the recipient will react to the reported information. Since people generally act in ways they believe will lead to outcomes they want, the information sender tries to infer how the information recipient will use and react to the provided information. If senders anticipate an unpleasant reaction to information about their current behavior, they may modify their behavior so that the reported information will cause more desirable reactions.

Reporting requirements are most likely to affect the sender's behavior when the reported information is a description of the sender's behavior or of something that the sender influences or is responsible for. How reported information is related to the sender's behavior is important. The more directly the reported information reflects something the sender can control, the more likely it is that the sender's behavior will be modified; the sender can be relatively sure that a change in behavior will lead to the desired change in reported information.

In management contexts, the sender is often held responsible for controlling things that are also influenced by a number of other factors that the sender cannot control. For example, the economy can significantly affect a division's sales and is certainly not controllable by the division manager. Although a basic tenet of management accounting is to hold managers responsible only for things they have the authority and ability to control, it is usually not easy to know exactly how much of a given outcome was due to the actions of the sender as opposed to other factors. When many factors other than the sender's behavior influence an outcome, the sender is less likely to change behavior in order to generate different reported information for two reasons. First, the sender may not know how to behave to achieve the desired results and information. Second, it is often possible to blame the outcome on other factors if the sender is questioned about it.

Senders' Predictions of Recipients' Use

Sometimes recipients make it very clear how they would like senders to behave. Often though, they do not or they may want many different things that are difficult to accomplish simultaneously, such as high short-run profits, good long-run growth, or a good community image. If the sender is responsible to the recipient, the sender wants to behave in ways that will result in reported information that will please the recipient. What the sender is required to report on is a signal to the sender, before action is taken, as to what actions and outcomes are important to the recipient.

Sometimes one is certain how the recipient will use information, while at other times one is unsure of how it might be used. If everyone was always completely clear and honest about how they were going to use the reported information, there would be less of a problem, but there would still be the possibility that information would later be used in ways that were not intended when it was first requested. Frequently, the person requesting the information is not explicit about how it will be used or with whom it will be shared. In these cases, reporters may have a very difficult job of guessing if and how it will be used. They are likely to base their predictions on how reported information was used in similar situations in their experience, or how they would use it if they were in the requester's position, as well as on any information available about how this report will be used.

Sometimes, even when people state quite clearly how they plan to use reported information, they actually use it in ways that they indicated, or even promised, that they would not. You may have been placed in this position by someone who extracted information from you with the promise that it would not be repeated or used against you later, only to find that they did indeed repeat it or that they bring it up in every subsequent argument you have with them. In fact, such potential for misuse of certain information has led to elaborate security and privacy rulings with respect to personnel and medical records.

In other cases, it is obvious from the recipients' response, or lack thereof, that they did not use the reported information as they said they would. The classic anecdote about this is the student who types up the Gettysburg address and buries it in the middle of a paper to add weight; the paper is returned with a grade, but without any indication that the teacher noticed the filler.

While this example seems a bit extreme, many managers will admit that they do not have time to use all the information they receive about their subordinates' behavior. In many cases, their subordinates seem to be well aware of their superiors' not using certain reported information, and they act accordingly. If the recipient's credibility is low, senders will probably not place much weight on how the recipient says the information will be used. If the intended use is not stated clearly, the sender also has to guess how it will be used. In these situations, senders will use their past experience in similar situations and other beliefs about the recipient and the situation to make their own best estimate of how the reported information will actually be used.

Incentives/Sanctions

Once the sender has made his or her best estimate of whether—and if so, how—the recipient will use the information, the sender's next question is, "What will the recipient do about it?" In some cases, one knows that the recipient will not be pleased with the information, but nothing can be done about it. In fact, sometimes the person desiring the information cannot even enforce the reporting requirement, in which case the "sender" probably never sends it. However, when the recipient has at least enough direct or indirect power over the sender to enforce the reporting requirement, he also probably has at least some power over other actions of the sender.

The strength and nature of the recipient's power over the sender is an important determinant of how likely the sender is to change behavior. The more potential there is for the recipient to reward or punish the sender, the more concerned the sender will be with making sure the reported information is acceptable to the recipient. For instance, students are much more likely to do homework when it is collected and graded than when it is not, even though the learning benefits from doing the homework should be the same in both cases.

Timing

Timing is a critical factor in whether or not the reporting requirement will cause a change in the sender's behavior. In order for the reporting requirement to cause a sender to change his behavior, he must know of the reporting requirement before he acts. If the reporting requirement occurs only after the sender has already acted, there is no opportunity to change past behavior. However, most reporting requirements are repetitive in management contexts, so even if the first reporting requirement is imposed after the behavior to be reported on has already taken place, the reporter will know in advance that subsequent reports will have to be made. Since data usually are not gathered unless one intends to use it, new reporting requirements frequently require that new data be gathered, which provides the opportunity to change behavior before reporting.

Iterative Response Strategies

Changing behavior is usually costly. People are subject to many competing demands, constraints, and desires. Any change in behavior usually affects more than one of these dimensions and not always in predictable or desired directions. At the very least, spending more time on one task leaves less time available to devote to others.

When a new reporting requirement is imposed, the least costly strategy may be to continue to behave as usual, report truthfully on that behavior, and wait for a response from the recipient. If there is none, that strategy can be continued. Negative feedback from the recipient, indicating that the reported behavior is not desirable, improves the sender's estimate of what behavior the recipient desires and how he or she will respond. The sender then has better information on which to base the decision of whether or not to make the effort necessary to change behavior. On the first round, "we're working on it—these things take time to change" is probably an adequate response. Robert Ackerman[1] showed that even a combination of reporting requirements, clear statements of desired behavior, and feedback may not be sufficient to induce the desired behavior in certain situations. Rewards or punishment tied to the behavior are required in some, if not all, circumstances.

Therefore, the likelihood of a reporter changing his behavior in response to a reporting requirement alone depends at least partly on:

- how clear it is what the recipient wants to happen
- how clear it is what the recipient will use the reported information for
- what rewards or punishments the recipient could give the sender
- which of the possible rewards or punishments the recipient is likely to use
- how much a change in behavior on one dimension would affect performance on other important dimensions

Attention Directing

A reporting requirement may cause the sender to change his behavior even if he does not expect the recipient to react to the reported information. That is possible because information has a way of directing attention to the areas it relates to, which may lead to a behavior change. Although attention-directing effects are probably less powerful and less susceptible to prediction than anticipation effects, they can affect behavior in some circumstances. They are most likely to occur in situations where the behavior being reported on is important to the sender for some reason, and where there is enough slack in the system to allow the sender to change his behavior without having a negative effect on other aspects of his performance. These are generally weaker than anticipation effects.

Attention-directing effects might be considered effects of recording rather than of reporting information since they arise from the sender's own concerns and are not dependent on the information being reported to anyone else. However, they are considered here because they can occur in response to outside reporting requirements, even though they can also occur without them.

Many "time management" programs use attention-directing effects to produce behavior change. Participants are required to keep a detailed log of how they spend their time, but they are not required to report the information to anyone else. They then use that information to decide whether they are spending their time in ways that support their stated priorities or whether much of it is "wasted."

EFFECTS OF REPORTING REQUIREMENTS

Reporting requirements can affect behavior in all areas of accounting: financial, tax, managerial, and social. The complexity of the accounting environment is an impediment to assessing the effects of reporting requirements; there are so many things happening at once that it is hard to say with certainty which one(s) caused the observed behavior. Evidence about the effects of reporting requirements is still inconclusive, but more substantive knowledge and better research methodologies are being developed (see this chapter's "Suggested Readings" section for a partial list of research on the effects of reporting requirements). The following sections discuss the current thinking in the various areas.

Financial Accounting

Powerful bodies in financial accounting, including the Securities Exchange Commission (SEC), the Financial Accounting Standards Board (FASB), and the Financial Executives Research Foundation (FERF), have recognized the potential effects reporting requirements have on corporate conduct. The FASB and FERF have recently begun to encourage and support investigation of such effects and to consider them explicitly in the standard-setting process.

As early as 1969, it was proposed that "generally accepted accounting principles" (GAAP) can affect corporate behavior. Hawkins[2] discussed the likely effects on managers' operating policies of accounting principles for deferred taxes, investment tax credits, foreign currency translation, earnings per share, consolidations, extraordinary income and losses, common stock equivalents, and leases. He states that behaviorally sound GAAP would "inhibit managers from taking undesirable operating actions to justify the adoption of an accounting alternative and inhibit the adoption of accounting practices by corporations which create the illusion of performance." Unfortunately, he did not investigate whether the effects he argues for occurred or not, nor did he discuss the "attendant circumstances" that might influence the strength of the effects. However, changes have since been made in many of the areas of GAAP that he discussed.

Several accounting principles implemented since then have been argued to have detrimental effects on corporate behavior. Among the most controversial of these is *FASB Statement No. 8* (Accounting for the Translation of Foreign Currency Transactions and Foreign Currency Financial Statements, October 1975). It was argued that *Statement 8* would affect corporate behavior because it had two provisions that significantly affected reported earnings. These were the requirements (1) to use only the "temporal method" of translating to dollars the financial statements of foreign affiliates and (2) that *all* foreign currency adjustments must be shown in the income statement each quarter, whether realized or not. Only companies that had to change their accounting principles because of *Statement 8* were expected to also change other behaviors. Among the behavioral effects posited were changes in debt policy regarding currency denominations and term structure; in liquidity, inventory and receivables management; in exposure hedging; and in geographic investment patterns. These are quite far-reaching consequences of a reporting requirement.

Other controversial principles include the requirement to expense research and development costs (see Case 17-1) and the requirement to report inflation-adjusted accounting reports. GAAP for leasing is argued to influence companies to structure leases in such a way that they can be classified as operating leases instead of being capitalized. It is suggested that the methods of calculating earnings per share influence the nature of the stock and stock-related transactions because a company can use them to report the desired levels in their financial statements. The reporting requirements for debt retirement can lead to the manipulation of earnings by retiring old debt in times of changing interest rates. It is argued that these reporting requirements may influence management to make decisions that are economically suboptimal for the firm; because these decisions may present management in a better light to the external users of the financial statements, they can have a positive influence on stock prices. It is also likely that management can be influenced to make suboptimal decisions when debt covenants are tied to various financial statement numbers or ratios.

Tax Accounting

Behavioral tax accounting is a relatively unexplored area. However, it is certainly a sensitive area with respect to reporting requirements. Some people even believe that the current tax reporting requirements violate constitutional rights. It is commonly accepted that tax reporting requirements are complicated and difficult for many taxpayers. Case 17-2 explores the effects of one tax simplification proposal. (The behavioral dimensions of income tax are discussed in Chapter 19.)

Several reporting requirements have been imposed not only on taxpayers themselves, but on other parties, such as employers, with the intent of making tax laws more enforceable. The knowledge that the information will be reported to the Internal Revenue Service by someone else is expected to make taxpayers less likely to try to avoid taxes. Note that the tax law does not change; the reporting requirement essentially decreases the opportunity to cheat without getting caught.

The 1985 attempt to require detailed contemporaneous records for business expense deductions is perhaps the most recent and controversial example of the behavioral effects of a tax reporting requirements. It has been argued that business people would spend less and thus claim fewer expense deductions than under the current recordkeeping requirements. In fact, the more detailed records themselves would not have had to be reported, but the taxpayer and preparer would be required to report that they had been kept and were available for examination.

Social Accounting

There is very little known about the effects of social accounting on information sender(s). There is still relatively little social accounting to the public, and most of the research on it has related to the effects on recipients of the reported information. Since external social accounting is still voluntary, there can be no effects of reporting *requirements*, although there may still be effects of reporting voluntarily. Because social accounting is a relatively new area of concern and is often in conflict with better established performance criteria, it is especially important to combine reporting requirements with very explicit behavioral guidelines and punishments for noncompliance. The reporting dilemma posed at the beginning of this chapter is a social accounting case. Pollution and product safety are other particularly sensitive areas of social accounting. (Social accounting is discussed in Chapter 21.)

Management Accounting

Management can impose virtually whatever internal reporting requirements it wishes on subordinates. Internally reported items can be financial, operational, social, or a combination. However, there is little publicly available management accounting data because it is seldom reported outside the organization. It is also very difficult to generalize about because each organization has a unique management accounting system, set of reporting requirements, and organizational relationships.

The combined results of the research in this area point to a very complex process in which reporting requirements interact with a number of other organizational variables and processes. The most reasonable conclusion to draw from the available research results is that sometimes reporting requirements produce observable effects on the reporters' behavior and sometimes they do not. The variety of possible factors that must be considered makes it very difficult to predict when and what effects will occur.

V.T. Ridgeway[3] was among the first to call attention to what he called the "dysfunctional consequences of performance measurements." His warning that single numerical measurements usually cannot capture everything important about an operation is as relevant now as it was then. He discusses a public employment agency that used the number of interviews conducted as a measure of interviewer success rather than a measure of job placements actually made. Under this reporting system, the interviewers attempted to maximize the number of interviews they conducted instead of locating jobs, even though the stated goal of the agency was to place clients in jobs. This example is expanded in Case 17-4.

ASSESSING THE EFFECTS ON SENDERS

There are many ways to assess the effects of reporting requirements on information senders. The most readily available is deductive reasoning, which involves thinking carefully about how the reporting requirement will interact with other motivational forces to shape managers' behavior. This technique should always be used before imposing a reporting requirement. Try to put yourself in the sender's place and ask, "What would I do if I was in his or her position and had to report this information?" It is worthwhile to ask others with different backgrounds and perspectives to do the same, since they may see things in ways that would not occur to you. This is a simple, inexpensive, and quick way to try to predict the effects of reporting requirements before they are implemented.

Another method is to ask reporters about their behavior. A formal way to do this is a survey, which can be composed of narrow questions with specified response possibilities or broad, open-ended questions or a combination of both. It can ask directly, "Did this reporting requirement cause you to change your behavior?", or more indirectly try to get at the same thing. It can be administered in person, by phone, or by a mailed questionnaire. This method provides only what the reporters are willing and able to tell you about their own perceptions of their behavior and reactions to the reporting requirements. Unfortunately, these responses do not always accurately represent their behavior. Reporters might deliberately lie, but they might also have inaccurate perceptions of their behavior. This possible error can work both ways; the reporters may think they have changed their behavior in ways or amounts they actually have not, or vice versa.

The way to be most certain about whether a reporting requirement changes reporters' behavior is to observe the behavior with and without the reporting requirement. This should be done in a controlled experiment where the only thing that changes is the reporting requirement. However, if the results are to be useful, it is crucial that the experimental setting be sufficiently similar to the natural setting in which the reporting requirement would exist. This is not always easy to accomplish.

A variety of approaches can be taken to measure behavior in the natural setting itself. When there is direct access to reporters and at least some of the relevant variables can be controlled or manipulated, use a "quasi-experimental field study," which is a compromise between certainty and relevance. It is the method closest to the laboratory experiment in terms of control and it therefore provides a test of causality. When the sender can only be observed (i.e., none of the relevant variables can be controlled or manipulated), it is a "case study." In some accounting contexts, especially financial, no control is available, so one must use whatever data happen to be available about the behavior of the sender. We call this "post-hoc analysis of secondary data."

The problem in the natural setting is that many other things are likely to be changing at about the same time as the reporting requirement. This makes it difficult to attribute the cause of any observed behavior to the reporting requirement instead of one or more of the other factors. Also, particularly when post-hoc analysis of secondary data is used, direct measures of the behavior of interest may not be available.

In spite of these difficulties, it is important to attempt to determine how a reporting requirement has affected reporters' behavior in favorable or unfavorable and predicted or unanticipated ways. As with most performance evaluation tasks, a combination of several assessment methods is likely to provide the most reliable results.

DIAGNOSTIC REVIEW OF
THE REPORTING DILEMMA

At this point, Cranston must decide whether to devote time and energy to more closely monitoring the hiring process and trying to understand the causes of the resulting data. She must then decide whether to take actions to achieve different outcomes if that appears appropriate and feasible. She has already attempted to get clarification on what, if any, action is expected of her, but to no avail. Her line personnel may have been correct when they told her that the cause of the previously observed data was that the minority and female applicants were not as well qualified as those actually hired. Even so, it might be worth Cranston's time to devote energy to better documenting this fact to avoid future problems.

Cranston is obviously caught in a classic reporting dilemma. It is not clear what behavior her superiors would like her to take with respect to equal employment opportunity and affirmative action. (This is an area of many perils, with fine lines between affirmative action and reverse discrimination.) In general, employers see little benefit in spending resources for these areas, although most employers at least claim to be making efforts. This leads to conflicting signals to managers so it is not clear what is the "right thing to do" in many cases.

While Cranston might be able to predict the likely reaction if she knew who would get the reported information, she does not know who that will be. Even if the information initially will go only to her superiors at headquarters, this is no assurance that it will not be sent elsewhere later. Investigating the cause of the statistics will obviously require time and could have additional organizational repercussions if her managers feel she or her personnel office is "interfering with" their jobs. At the very least, it is one more report to be filled out.

If there are slack resources in the organization, or if Cranston happens to be personally concerned with women's and/or minorities' rights, she may make the effort to investigate what is causing the current statistical patterns. If she finds that there is indeed discrimination in the hiring and promotion processes, she may take action to correct this. However, since most managers in today's competitive environment are already under pressure, Cranston is unlikely to even investigate the causes of the observed data patterns unless she gets a clear signal from above that it is in her best interests to do so.

REFERENCES

[1] R.W. Ackerman, "How Companies Respond to Social Demands," *Harvard Business Review* (July-August 1973).

[2] D.F. Hawkins, "Behavioral Implications of Generally Accepted Accounting Principles," *California Management Review* 12, no. 2 (Winter 1969): 13–21.

[3] V.F. Ridgeway, "Dysfunctional Consequences of Performance Measurements," *Administrative Science Quarterly*, 1, no. 2 (September 1956): 240–47.

[4] Adapted from M.A. Miller, *Comprehensive GAAP Guide* (New York: Harcourt, Brace, Jovanovich, 1982).

[5] Adapted from W.A. Raabe, *Income Tax Simplicity: An Examination of an Elective Filing System,* unpublished Ph.D. dissertation, University of Illinois, 1979.

[6] Adapted from Ridgeway, 1956.

SUGGESTED READINGS

Bahr, Mary S., Lawrence A. Gordon, and V.K. Narayanan. "Information Inductance: A Contingency Perspective." Presented at the American Accounting Association's Annual Meeting, Boston, Mass., 1980.

Collins, James F. *Financial Reporting Methods and Management Decisions: An Empirical Examination of Information Inductance.* Ph.D. diss., Northwestern University, August 1978.

Cooper, W.W., N. Dopuch, and T. Keller. "Budgetary Disclosure and Other Suggestions for Improving Accounting Reports." *The Accounting Review* (October 1968).

Evans, Thomas G., Wm. R. Folks, Jr., and Michael Jilling, *The Impact of Statement of Financial Accounting Standards No. 8 on the Foreign Exchange Risk Management Practices of American Multinationals: An Economic Impact Study.* Financial Accounting Standards Board, 1978. Stamford, CT.

Financial Accounting Standards Board. *Economic Consequences of Financial Accounting Standards* (selected papers). 1978.

Flamholtz, E.G. and A. Tsui. "Toward an Integrative Theory of Organizational Control." Pacific Basin Economic Study Center, Working Paper Series no. 14, 1980.

Nitterhouse, D. *Effects of Reporting Requirements on the Behavior of Information Senders,* unpublished Ph.D. diss., Harvard Graduate School of Business, 1981.

Prakash, P. and A. Rappoport. "Information Inductance and Its Significance for Accounting." *Accounting, Organizations and Society* 2, no. 1. (1977): 29–38.

Shank, John K., Jesse F. Dillard, and Richard J. Murdock. *Assessing the Economic Impact of FASB No. 8.* Financial Executives Research Foundation, 1979. NY, NY.

Wilner, Neil A., "SFAS 8 and Information Inductance: An Experiment." *Accounting, Organizations and Society* 7, no. 1 (1982): 43–52.

DISCUSSION QUESTIONS

1. What is a "reporting requirement"? What types of reported information are typically *not* responses to reporting requirements?
2. List three reporting requirements that you personally are subject to. List three reporting requirements that a manager is likely to be subject to as part of the job.

3. What are alternatives to reporting requirements for management control? Discuss the advantages and disadvantages of each, relative to reporting requirements.

4. Discuss the mechanisms by which reporting requirements can affect the behavior of the information sender.

5. What are the characteristics of a reporting requirement that make it most likely to cause the sender to modify behavior?

6. How do reporters determine the purposes for which reported information will be used?

7. How do feedback, incentives, and sanctions interact with effects of reporting requirements?

8. How does the timing of a reporting requirement influence its effects?

9. What are reporters' possible responses to reporting requirements? What are the likely effects of each type of response?

10. Think of a reporting requirement (one that is not discussed in the chapter or cases) that is likely to cause a change in senders' behavior in each of the areas of financial, managerial, tax, and social accounting. Discuss how it is likely to influence senders' behavior. How might dysfunctional behavior changes be avoided by changing the reporting requirement or some other aspect of the situation?

11. How would you determine the actual effects of the reporting requirement discussed in question 10 above?

CASE 17-1

Financial Accounting for Research and Development Costs[4]

Much of the United States' economic power stems from the creativity and ingenuity of the people. Most large corporations conduct research, some of it fairly basic. Research and development projects are undertaken in the hope and belief that they will lead to the invention or discovery of new materials, products, services, processes, or techniques of value to the company. The costs of conducting research and development are incurred in one period in the hope and belief that they will produce increased revenue or lower expenses in future periods.

In 1974, the FASB issued *Statement No. 2*, which requires that essentially all research and development costs be reported as expenses in the period they are incurred. Conservatism was the dominant basic accounting principle used in arriving at this reporting requirement because of the high degree of uncertainty of resulting future benefits. Prior to the issuance of *Statement No. 2*, companies had the choice of capitalizing or expensing research and development costs.

Required:

1. What other accounting principles are relevant to this situation?
2. Discuss the possible effects on corporate behavior of the requirement to expense research and development costs.

CASE 17-2

Simplified Tax Reporting: A Proposal[5]

Many taxpayers have great difficulty complying with current tax reporting requirements. There have been a variety of proposals for tax reporting simplification. (Note that this is separate from tax law simplification, which has also received a great deal of attention.) In 1979, the following elective filing system was proposed, without any changes in the laws for tax liability:

> Each year, the taxpayer would submit choices concerning filing status, exemptions, and other elections to the IRS. Before February 28 of the following year, the IRS would compile and process all available relevant information (i.e., taxpayer elections, W-2, 1099, and other forms) to compute the individual's income tax liability and the balance or refund due. This would be sent to the taxpayer as a "tentative return". If it is complete and correct, all the taxpayer needs to do is sign and return it with the balance due, if any. If the return lacks any information that affects the proper determination of the income tax liability, the taxpayer must override the IRS' tentative computation and file a complete and correct return by April 15.

> Under this system, if the return is complete, the IRS computers have performed all the necessary calculations and completed the tax forms themselves. This would ease the tax filing burden for many individual taxpayers, especially in the lower income and educational brackets that are most adversely affected by the complexity of the current reporting requirements or the cost of hiring an outside preparer. The IRS would have taken responsibility for many of the taxpayer's computational duties, but not for his compliance. The taxpayer is still responsible for filing a complete and correct return under existing tax laws.[5]

Required:

1. Discuss the possible effects of this proposal on taxpayer's behavior.
2. How might the government test for behavioral effects?

CASE 17-3

Quality Control in a Manufacturing Department

Sam Scott is the manager of a manufacturing department that uses a three-step manufacturing process. In the past, the department has assessed quality control only at the end of the total process. Sam had been quite content with the department's average 95 percent acceptable product rate until he read an article stating that comparable Japanese firms had rates of over 99 percent.

Required:

1. How might Sam use reporting requirements to help improve the percentage of good units produced?
2. Design a set of reports and discuss how they would be used and what behavioral changes they are likely to produce.
3. What factors other than a new reporting requirement should Sam consider?

CASE 17-4

The Employment Office[6]

The typical goal of a public employment agency is to help workers find jobs and to help businesses find workers. This is accomplished primarily by interviewers who talk to potential workers and advise them which jobs they should apply for. The effects of using number of interviews as a single performance measure was discussed in the chapter.

Required:

1. What are other possible relevant measures of interviewer performance and what are the likely behavioral effects of using each?
2. How would you evaluate performance? What other measures would you take if you were in charge of the office?

CHAPTER 18

Communication of
Accounting Information

by
George A. Barnett
Associate Professor, Department of Communications
State University of New York at Buffalo

COMMUNICATION DILEMMA

David Anderson was a junior partner at Arnold, Fenner and Winston (AF&W), a large multinational accounting firm. He had an MBA with a specialty in behavioral accounting and had been working at the firm's Midland City office for five years. His performance evaluations had been outstanding and recently, he was made a junior partner. As a member of the corporate consulting group, he had two superiors, Emily Smith, the managing partner at Midland City, and Dawn Jones from corporate consulting in the firm's New York City office. Anderson received a memo from Jones directing Anderson to prepare a financial analysis for a high-tech division of a multinational conglomerate, MEGA. The division was located in Midland City. According to the memo, the division was planning to reorganize by adopting a matrix management structure and Japanese-style quality circles for production personnel. Members of top management at MEGA's corporate headquarters in New York City wanted to know what these structural changes would cost in the first year and what savings the company would realize over a five-year period, as well as the implications of these programs for management policy. A copy of the memo was sent to Smith at AF&W in Midland City. Since MEGA was an important AF&W client, Anderson proceeded immediately with the project.

Over the next month, Anderson and a staff of three performed the analysis. The keys of his personal computer clicked late into the night. He submitted his report to MEGA's corporate headquarters and to the manager of MEGA's Midland City division on Friday morning and spent a well-deserved weekend resting with his wife at a country inn. Monday morning, he was called into Smith's office. Expecting praise for a job well done, Anderson was devastated when Smith lambasted him for sending a copy of the report to the local MEGA division manager. It seems the reorganization was being planned at corporate headquarters without local knowledge. Later, Jones from corporate consulting in New York City called Anderson and screamed, "MEGA is furious because your report is unintelligible and not at all what they wanted. MEGA is changing auditors. We just lost an important client because of you!!" Anderson was crushed. He felt his career was ruined and asked to be transferred to auditing, where he would not do any harm.

What happened? Let's see what communication theory tells us. Simply, there were a number of communication breakdowns. The information that Anderson needed to successfully complete the assignment as MEGA expected never reached him. The memo was in error. Jones, who wrote the memo, never told Anderson that the report was confidential and should be sent only to MEGA's corporate headquarters. Further, Jones did not communicate with him during the project. Anderson was such an outstanding employee, Jones assumed there was no need to check on his progress. Anderson had no contact with MEGA's corporate management. Therefore, he had no specific information about their expectations for the analysis. All communication was through the division manager's secretary. As usual, when Anderson from AF&W, "the auditor," asked for information, it was readily provided. As a result, he had no idea that the local division staff was uninformed. Solutions to these and other communication problems will be discussed in greater detail at the end of the chapter in a diagnostic review. The theoretical material presented will facilitate the understanding of these recommendations.

COMMUNICATION THEORY

This chapter is about the communication of technical materials, such as financial reports. It reviews what is known about communication so that tasks that accountants perform—such as financial reporting, auditing, and management consulting—will meet clients' expectations. Further, since communication does not occur in a vacuum but rather in and among organizations, the area of organizational communication will also be discussed.

The essence of the accounting process is the communication of information with financial or management implications. Therefore, to be an effective accountant, one must be an effective communicator. Business information must be presented by accountants to meet user needs. It must be stated clearly, concisely, and, above all, accurately. It is hoped that when you complete this chapter, you will avoid the problems of David Anderson.

Communication is the process by which information is exchanged between two or more systems that exist within a common environment. These systems may be individuals, social organizations, animals, or machines. *Information* is generally defined as patterned matter or energy, which reduces the uncertainty in the future behavior of the interacting systems. Where the system includes people, meaning may be attributed to the information. In terms of accounting, individuals engaged in business generally exchange financial information, which, when interpreted, allows for the reasonable prediction of an organization's future operations and assists in day-to-day decision making and control.

This chapter reviews the theories and research about communication that have particular relevance to the transmission of accounting information. It focuses on those notions that concern the fidelity of information exchange or communication effectiveness. As a result, it deals with its subject matter in a prescriptive manner. That is, general recommendations will be made about how to proceed to maximize the likelihood of effective communication or effective reporting of accounting data.

MODELS OF COMMUNICATIONS

As a field of inquiry, communication has evolved from a variety of academic disciplines in both the humanities and sciences (natural and social). They range from rhetoric, speech, English, journalism, law, and linguistics at the humanistic end of the spectrum through the social sciences (anthropology, political science, sociology, economics, psychology) and management, to electrical engineering and computer and systems science at the scientific end. Communication cuts across all these fields. While its focus is the process and effects of information exchange, all these orientations have provided perspectives for analyzing the process of communication. Because of the variety of perspectives from which communication may be studied, there is no single comprehensive theory or set of theories to explain communication. Thus, to organize the large variety of communication theories, we will begin with a discussion of a number of models of the communication process. This will identify categories of variables and the relationships among them. After we review the models, the variables and how they influence effective communication will be discussed.

Models are abstract representations of some aspects of theories. They are classification systems that enable one to abstract and to categorize potentially relevant parts of processes. They help establish the boundaries to the question, "What does communication entail?" and to provide structure for the components of the process.

LASSWELL'S MODEL

One of the earliest models of communication was developed by Harold Lasswell[1]:

Who

Says What

In Which Channel

To Whom and

With What Effect?

It is simple and graphic, but lacks a number of elements necessary for an understanding of the communication process. In an accounting context, the accountant (who) presents financial information (says what), generally in written reports (which channel), to internal and external users (to whom), with the goal of providing reliable, relevant, and timely data for making informed business decisions (the effect).

The Shannon-Weaver Model

Claude Shannon and Warren Weaver[2] developed the mathematical model of communication presented in Figure 18-1. The model was developed to describe communication through an intermediary device such as a telephone or written correspondence. It represents an advance over Lasswell's model because it differentiates among the information source, the transmitter, the receiver, and destination. In an accounting situation, the source may be a bookkeeper or clerk; the transmitter, a controller; the receiver, the person who obtains the documents, an accountant; and the destination, the ultimate user, the client.

Shannon and Weaver also add noise into the communication process. *Noise* is any stimulus that contributes to the distortion of the information

FIGURE 18-1
Shannon-Weaver Model

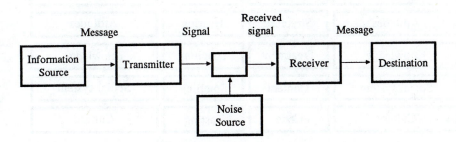

Source: C. Shannon and W. Weaver, *The Mathematical Theory of Communication* (Urbana, Ill.: University of Illinois Press, 1949).

transfer. It may lead to a breakdown in communication. Static in a telephone line is noise. Imagine the problems that could result from hearing the wrong client name because of static. The Shannon-Weaver model lacks the critical notion of *feedback*—the exchange of information rather than the one-way transfer of information—and the context or environment in which the process takes place.

Berlo's SMCR Model

The SMCR model of communication proposed by David Berlo,[3] shown in Figure 18-2, has some of the same faults as the earlier models. It suggests a one-way flow of information from a source to a receiver without feedback and it excludes the concept of noise. However, Berlo specifies the factors that influence the fidelity of communication and at which stage in the process those factors operate. For example, when considering the *message*, he suggests that the elements of the message—its content, structure, code, and treatment— will influence its understanding by the receiver. Further, while not explicitly including the context in which the process occurs, the model indicates that the social systems and cultures of the source and receiver, as

---

FIGURE 18-2
Berlo's SMCR Model

S Source	**M** Message	**C** Channel	**R** Receiver
Communication skills	Elements	Seeing	Communication skills
Attitudes	Structure	Hearing	Attitudes
Knowledge	Treatment	Touching	Knowledge
Social system	Content	Smelling	Social system
Culture	Code	Tasting	Culture

Source: David Berlo, *The Process of Communication* (New York: Holt, Rinehart and Winston, 1960).

---

well as the code system in which the message in constructed, do affect the fidelity of the communication process. These notions are especially important for multinational firms, which must consider the cultures and social systems of clients and customers. Further, as described in previous chapters, accountants possess a unique professional culture. Terms such as "debit," "credit," "assets," and "earnings per share" make up the language or code system of accountants. Communicating with individuals from outside the culture (lay people) who do not have a frame of reference for these symbols will often cause a breakdown of understanding.

The Westley-MacLean Model

Bruce Westley and Malcolm MacLean developed a model for communication research,[4] presented in Figure 18-3, which has a number of important implications. The model describes the ways in which individuals and organizations decide which messages are communicated and how they are modified or deleted in the process. Person *A* receives information or stimuli (X_i) from the environment. For example, in Figure 18-3, A receives stimuli X_1, X_2, and X_3. The process by which A reports the information received is imperfect. There are omissions and additions in what A reports caused by selective

FIGURE 18-3
Westley-MacLean Model

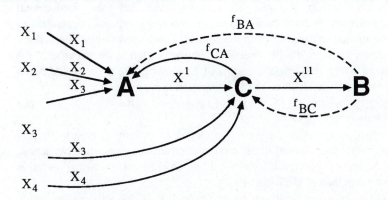

Source: Reprinted by permission of Bruce Westley and Malcolm MacLean, "A Conceptual Model for Communication Research," *Journalism Quarterly*. 34 (1957): 35.

perception and distortion resulting from A's bias. A then produces a message (X^1) and communicates it to C, who is an editor or "gatekeeper." C selects the message (X^1) to communicate to the eventual audience, B. C's message is based on the information received from A (X^1) and from the environment (in Figure 18-3, C receives stimuli X_3 and X_4). As illustrated in Figure 18-3, some of the same stimuli from the environment may be received by both A and C (e.g., X_3 in the example). Another important aspect of the Westley-MacLean model is feedback. Figure 18-3 shows feedback from B to A (f_{BA}), from C to A (f_{CA}), and from B to C (f_{BC}).

In the dilemma at the beginning of the chapter, MEGA's corporate management is A and Jones is C. Jones selected the message (X^{11}) to communicate to Anderson, who represents B. The message Jones selected was based on the information received from MEGA (X^1) and stimuli from the environment (X_i), modified by Jones' own perceptions and bias. The resulting message did not accurately convey to Anderson the client's (A's) expectations, and Anderson commenced working on the project without any follow-up communication, or feedback, to clarify the message in Jones' memo.

The Convergence Model of Communication

Everett Rogers and D. Lawrence Kincaid have criticized the preceding models because they lead to seven biases. These are:[5]

1. A view of communication as a linear, one-way act rather than a cyclical, two-way process in which information is exchanged over time.
2. A source bias resulting from an emphasis on dependency rather than on the relationship of those who communicate and their fundamental interdependency. In traditional models, the receiver is typically dependent on the information transferred from the source. There need not be interaction.
3. A tendency to focus on the objects of communication at the expense of the context in which they exist. In terms of accounting, the focus would be on the report itself rather than on the interaction that produced it.
4. A tendency to focus on the messages themselves at the expense of silence and timing of messages.
5. A tendency to consider the primary function of communication to be persuasion rather than mutual understanding, consensus, and collective action. In the business context, the focus would be on policy implementation rather than on participatory decision making.
6. A tendency to concentrate on the psychological effects of communication on separate individuals rather than on the social effects and the relationships among individuals within networks.
7. A belief in one-way mechanistic causation rather than mutual causation that characterizes human information systems, which are fundamentally cybernetic.

As an alternative to the biased models, Rogers and Kincaid propose the Convergence Model of Communication. They stress the unity of information and action. All information is a consequence of action; through information processing, action may result in additional information. The model has no beginning or end. Only the mutually defining relationship among the parts gives meaning to the whole. When information is shared by two or more participants, information processing may lead to mutual understanding, agreement, and collective action, such as solving business problems.

One consequence of this model is that communication always implies a relationship—a mutual process of information-sharing among two or more people. Consequently, the analysis of communication must take into account the participants' differences and similarities and, for our purposes, changes in the relations between the accountant and the user of the information— both with one another and with the other individuals they interact with about financial topics. It is worth noting that the client or line manager may not be the eventual user of the communication product: instead, the public may be the main users, as in the case of annual reports. Thus, the notion of context or environment in which communication takes place becomes increasingly important because it includes the interpersonal element.

VARIABLES OF IMPACT IN ACCOUNTING COMMUNICATION

One purpose of the discussion of models was to help organize those factors that impact on the communication of accounting information. The following review discusses the variables and their relationship to the fidelity of information exchange. Based on the models presented, the discussion is organized into sections dealing with sources, messages, channels, receivers, feedback, and the context or environment in which the preparation and communication of accounting information take place. The effects of communication will not be discussed explicitly. It is assumed throughout that understanding, which leads to appropriate behavior, is the result of the communication process. While these factors will be presented as separate categories, remember that communication is a complex process with interacting components. Thus, while the variables have been categorized for presentation, the organization is somewhat arbitrary.

Sources

Two aspects of sources and the way they affect the communication process will be discussed. These aspects are source credibility and the similarity between source and receiver.

Source Credibility

It is generally recognized that the more credible the source of a message, the greater its effectiveness. Effectiveness is usually understood to be attitude change in the direction advocated by the source. Source credibility, however, is a characteristic of the source as perceived by the receiver. It is part of the source's image and may vary among different communication situations. Usually, it is formed before the source and receiver enter the communication event.

Source credibility is a multidimensional construct. Empirical research indicates that it is made up of three factors. Recent research, however, suggests that the number of factors affecting credibility may be equal to the number of attributes used by receivers in evaluating the source. The three factors are:

1. *Authoritativeness*—how reliable, informed, qualified (through title or profession), intelligent, or expert the source is perceived to be.
2. *Trustworthiness*—how safe, honest, friendly, pleasant, and attractive the source is perceived to be.
3. *Dynamism*—how aggressive, forceful, bold, and energetic the source is perceived to be.

Accountants are generally taken to be credible. They are authoritative and professional. Many have the title of CPA. They are perceived as trustworthy—honest and safe. But to the public at large, accountants are anything but dynamic. It is perhaps worth noting how future accountants perceive themselves and practicing CPAs. G. Siegel reports that in one study, accounting students viewed themselves as honest, competent, hardworking, and intelligent but not as independent, respected, creative, or boring. The students did, however, see the latter attributes in CPAs as a professional group.[6]

The evidence suggests that although source credibility may be important in attitude change, it may detract from the fidelity of information exchange. W.J. McGuire writes:

> There is evidence that the source credibility factors affect attitude change via the yielding mediator rather than the attention and comprehension steps. While source credibility effects tend to show up in ultimate change, the source variables tend not to be manifested in detectable differences in the extent of learning of the message contents, . . . (Messages) from unknown sources may be better learned than messages from sources known to be high or low in credibility.[7]

Source-Receiver Similarity

Effective communication occurs more easily when source and receiver are similar. The degree of similarity or difference is determined by two factors: (1) objective or demographic similarity—similarity by age, sex, race, occupation, education, nationality, and the like; and, (2) cognitive similarity—similarity in attitudes, values, beliefs, culture, or knowledge.

Individuals who share common experiences, language, culture, and expertise tend to communicate with each other effectively because a person can empathize with another person in a similar role or position in society. E.M. Rogers cites a number of empirical studies indicating that success in getting people to adopt innovations is a function of an agent's similarity with his or her clients. Further, receivers prefer a source who is perceived as similar, especially in attitude and lifestyle.[8] Thus, it appears that the effectiveness of a message may be enhanced by using a "strategy of identification." Accountants should strive to be sensitive to the users of accounting information at least in terms of objective criterion. In this way, they will tend to be more effective.

This implies that effective communication results from source-receiver similarity. However, the reverse may be true. Initially, a source and receiver may have little in common. By interacting, the source and receiver converge on a common cognitive framework of mutual understanding. For example, the audience for a financial report may know little or nothing about the issue before they begin to read. Further, while it may be ideal to make the accountant as similar as possible to the users of a document, similarity may not be possible. Significant differences generally exist, at least to the extent that the accountant has extensive knowledge about what is being communicated and the user does not.

Messages

Berlo identifies five elements of messages that should be considered when analyzing communication: (1) content; (2) organization or structure; (3) code; (4) treatment; and (5) the elements of the message. Only organization and treatment will be discussed. It is assumed that content is financial material or information related to management policy and that the code system is the language of the source and receiver. The elements of the message are words, sentences, paragraphs, numbers, statistics, tables, and other graphics. They vary, of course, with different channels.[9]

Message Organization

The best way to organize a message depends on the culture in which the information is used. In Western societies, our patterns of thinking and reasoning are linear or sequential. Linear processing characterizes all linguistic processing (reading and listening) and also many sorts of problem-solving and reasoning activities. Since English has become the primary language of international business, it can be assumed that business reports will be organized in a linear fashion with a beginning, a middle, and an end. But just because two people use the same language does not necessarily guarantee effective communication. H.M. McLuhan has argued that this linear word-by-word arrangement of messages is true only for print media.[10] Thus, if accounting changes to make greater use of video and computer-based technologies, this manner of organization may prove less effective.

The optimal way to structure a message also depends on the audience's background. Factors such as their prior attitudes, education, commitment, skill in refutation, expectations of subsequent counterarguments, their attention, and their level of arousal associated with the material all help dictate how best to organize a message. For example, should you present both sides of a financial issue—such as evidence in support of and against a commercial decision? Research indicates that, for highly educated audiences (typical for financial information), two-sided messages are more effective than one-sided messages. However, for less educated audiences, the opposite is true.

Before presenting the specific content of a message, a source should determine the audience's level of attention and the level of their anxiety or arousal associated with the material and the context in which it is presented. An intermediate level of anxiety is optimal for effectiveness. The client should be looking at and listening to the accountant, but sitting still. If there is too little or too much anxiety, comprehension will be lower. Other sorts of motivations—for example, self-interest or curiosity—might function as well as anxiety. Thus, the first thing one should do is to structure the message to catch the audience's attention and manipulate their level of motivation or attention to the optimal level.

Research on the effects of order also has implications for financial communication. The theoretical assumption underlying this research is that message effectiveness depends upon the placement of arguments or material in a presentation. Three order strategies have been investigated: (1) *climax*, where the most important information is presented first; (2) *anticlimax*, where it is presented last; and (3) the *pyramidal pattern*, where it is placed in the middle. The climactic or anticlimactic orders are more effective than the pyramidal arrangement and most evidence suggests that the climax strategy is more effective than the anticlimax. Thus, it may be a good idea to begin business reports with an executive summary. This will guarantee that the report is organized in an effective manner—the climax structure.

Research on serial learning indicates that the relationship between order of presentation and learning is U-shaped. Audiences tend to learn the initial material and the material presented at the end better than they learn the material in the middle. This would suggest an organizational schema where the important information—the conclusion—is presented initially in the form of an abstract or executive summary and at the end in a summary. The body of the report is less important and may be filled with detail.

Recommendations about whether to present the conclusions first or last depend on when the information will be used. If it is to be used immediately after it is presented, the critical material should come at the end to take advantage of short-term memory. The longer after presentation the material is to be used, the less the effectiveness of this strategy. Learning diminishes rapidly over time. Over longer periods, material presented first has at least as good a chance of being remembered as does information presented last.

Researchers conclude that order of presentation affects such factors as attention, interest, comprehension, and recall. The most effective order in producing attitude change was: (1) *introduction*; (2) *transition*; and (3) *concluding information*. Schemas that employ a logical deductive order are more effective at securing retention than orders where the thesis sentence is placed in the middle, but there is no difference in reader interest. Generally, research on learning and mnemonic processes indicates that comprehension and retention depend undeniably on organization. That is, well-structured material is always understood and remembered better than unstructured material. On the other hand, research is somewhat equivocal about the exact way to structure the material.

How should topics be organized with respect to the relative desirability of the material? Research indicates that there is greater total agreement over a whole range of topics if the desirable ones are presented first. The explanation depends on a stimulus-response learning theory. The early contents of a message reward and habituate the person for paying attention to the material. When negative information is presented first, it tends to punish the receiver for paying attention in the beginning; this may cause the audience to stop paying attention to the later material. The communicator should determine the audience's attitudes and present material they will agree with or find pleasant prior to the material they may find offensive. Positive business information should precede the negative. For example, put difficult material after easy material or put the positive financial news prior to the negative. It may also be a good idea to begin a report or presentation with a bit of humor. On the other hand, there is little empirical research relating humor to effectiveness; it might be that while enhancing attention to the communication situation, humor may deter comprehension.

Message Treatment

Accounting information should be redundant. Repetition increases comprehension of the material. Retention increases with repetition of important facts and ideas. Summaries that pick out, highlight, and orient readers to the important facts also improve reader comprehension and retention. Redundancy across channels also improves retention. Reader's retention improves when facts in the verbal presentation are highlighted by attention-getters such as underlining, capitalization, charts, and colors.

How much redundancy is optimal for achieving an effective message? J. Woelfel and J. Saltiel argue that the relationship between repetition and effectiveness is linear. The more information one receives, the greater its effect.'[11] However, McGuire argues that while repetition has an effect, "an increase in impact usually appears for one or two repetitions but quickly reaches an asymptote beyond which further repetitions have little effect."[12]

There has been considerable research on how evidence affects message effectiveness. It indicates that the use of authoritative evidence produces significantly more attitude change than was obtained without citing authorities. However, evidence does interact with other factors in the communication situation, particularly the credibility of the source. Evidence may increase the effectiveness of a message when the source is only minimally or moderately credible.

Correct style makes a difference in message effectiveness. Faulty grammar, poor organization, pauses, and other nonfluencies do produce poor ratings of speakers, but their effect on message effectiveness is unclear. While they do not reduce the persuasive impact of a message, delivery is related to attitude change. For written technical materials, faulty grammar reduces comprehension, increases reading time, and reduces reader judgment of the author's competence as a writer as well as his credibility.

Accountants should strive to get the audience actively involved and committed to the presented information because active participation is more effective than passive reading for permanently adding material to a person's cognitive repertory. Given this conclusion, one would expect that if the audience were to draw its own conclusions from the material, the communication would be more effective. This view suggests that accountants should simply report and not make recommendations. The reason is that drawing the conclusions requires more active participation by the receiver. However, explicitly stating the conclusions has sometimes been shown to be more effective. For very complex analyses, the accountant should perhaps make specific recommendations.

There is considerable research about how to present effective technical materials. G.R. Klare describes how to make theses materials more readable. Readable materials are more comprehensible. Readability is a function of the characteristics of words and sentences, but Klare further specifies rules for producing readable documents:

1. Words of high frequency and familiarity increase readability.
2. Shorter words make reading easier and faster.
3. Words which have associative value (psychologically) calling up other words which appear later in the text should be used.
4. Concrete words, rather than abstract words, make documents more readable.
5. Active verbs, instead of nominalized forms, improve readability.
6. The use of pronouns and anaphora (words or phrases that refer back to a previous word or unit of text) should be limited.

7. Sentences should be short. If the writer is going to use conjunctions, he or she should use and, instead of but, for, or because.
8. Clauses should be short and sentence structure simple.
9. Active voice is more readable than passive voice.
10. Affirmative constructions are more readable than negative ones.
11. Statements produce better recall than questions.
12. Sentences with a great deal of word depth, which require a great deal of commitment by the reader, should be avoided.
13. Sentences with embedded words are less readable than embedded sentences.[13]

There is contradictory evidence on some of these rules of thumb. For example, shorter words may not increase reading speed or comprehension. The psychological research on commitment suggests that audiences committed to learning a set of materials comprehend the material better than do noncommitted audiences. Perhaps the accountant should strive to produce, rather than limit, reader commitment and involvement through a more technical vocabulary and complex sentence structure.

U.F. Anderson suggests that factors such as the idea-chain in the text, its structure, and the concepts should be used to determine how hard it will be to comprehend the material.[14] Future research based on empirical measurement is needed to determine the factors that predict comprehension in technical materials such as financial reports. The following parameters should be investigated specifically for financial materials:

1. Complexity of the structure and materials
2. Abstractness
3. New concepts
4. Need for background knowledge
5. Work load during reading
6. Time used
7. Sensitivity to outside noise
8. Long-term memory content

A great deal of material on message variables and their impact on communication effectiveness has been presented. The conclusions are often contradictory because communication is a complex process involving the interaction of all the components described in the models. When research is conducted on any single component, such as messages, these other factors may not consistently be taken into account. However, these external factors continue to affect the communication situation. This results in inconclusive findings, so any prescriptions should be viewed somewhat skeptically. Production of an effective message is contingent on the unique circumstances for which it is produced. Future research is needed to better determine these interactions so that guidelines can be established to help accountants effectively communicate with their clients, colleagues and non-accounting managers.

Channels

Dimensions of Differences in Communication Channels

A communication channel is a means of transmitting information. W. Schramm categorizes or differentiates channels along six dimensions:[15]

The Senses That Are Affected.   Face-to-face communication makes possible the use of all senses, while the different media use a subset of these in combination to produce differential impacts on receivers. For example, print media uses only the visual channel; video and film use both the auditory and visual channels; and radio and sound recording use only the audio channel.

The Opportunity for Feedback.   The chance of two-way exchange of information is maximal in face-to-face communication. Generally, interposing mass media restricts both the speed and amount of feedback. For example, the telephone restricts nonverbal feedback. The impersonality of mass media organizations further discourages feedback from audiences of television, radio, newspapers, and magazines. Feedback is required, however, to ensure effective communication and for the understanding of transmitted information. Through feedback, receivers may secure clarification or additional information, thus allowing them to overcome social and psychological barriers of selective exposure, attention, and retention. In our example, Jones should have requested feedback from Anderson about the exact specifications of his assignment. Thus, when media, such as teleconferences, are used for technical financial reporting, alternative feedback methods should be built in.

The Amount of Receiver Control.   There is a great deal of control in interpersonal interaction. When using print, receivers can read at their own pace and reread important or detailed sections. Receivers have little control over the broadcast media unless they record the program on tape or disk. The greater the user's control, the greater the learning.

The Type of Message Coding.   Face-to-face interaction allows for the use of nonverbal cues. This is less true for video, film, and especially print. However, print seems to be better for conveying abstract ideas such as management policies. The audiovisual media are better for presenting concrete information.

H.M. McLuhan argued that the code system used in communication is in great measure determined by the channel.[16] Print imposes a particular logic upon the organization of visual experience. It breaks down reality into discrete units that are logically and causally related; linearly perceived; and abstracted from the wholeness, disorder, and multisensory quality of life.

The Multiplicative Power.   Mass communication systems can efficiently and rapidly reach large, physically dispersed audiences. Interpersonal channels can reach these audiences only with great effort and over relatively long periods of time.

Preservation of Messages.   An advantage of mass media is a permanent record, which is absent in face-to-face interaction. Traditionally, this advantage has been restricted to print. However, with video and audio tape and disk and computer-based management information systems, this capacity has now been expanded to the electronic media.

Social Effects of the Media

There has been a great deal of research on the differential effects of channels. The social effects are summarized here.

Media Have the Power to Focus Attention and thus Direct Interpersonal Discussion.   For example, when the news media report labor statistics or other economic news, the public's attention is drawn to that topic. This may lead to discussions about those issues. M.E. McCombs and D. Shaw label this then "agenda-setting function" of the media.[17]

Media Confers Status.   People who appear in the media are viewed as important and highly credible. For example, those who appear on *Wall Street Week* or serve as editors for the *Wall Street Journal* or *Business Week* are considered as credible in the business community.

Face-to-face Communication Is More Effective for Persuasion Than Are the Audiovisual Media.   E.M. Rogers concludes from a number of studies that interpersonal communication is generally more effective but that the mass media are more effective in creating knowledge and changing weak attitudes. Further, he concludes that diverse information channels are far more effective in disseminating knowledge, while local media channels are more effective for persuading audiences. Among the media, the electronic ones are more effective than print for persuasion.[18] However, as J.J. Klapper points out, "The relative power of the several media is thus, in real-life situations, likely to vary from one topic to another."[19]

S.H. Chaffee has called the conflict over relative effectiveness of mediated and interpersonal channels a "synthetic competition." He notes a number of intervening influences related to accessibility of the different channels and perceived credibility of sources. In other words, the relative effectiveness of interpersonal channels depends more on receivers' needs and perceptions than on channel effects per se.[20]

A Combination of Face-to-Face and Mediated Communication Is Likely to Be More Effective Than Either Alone.   For example, when instructional media are used in combination with study groups or radio forums (groups that discuss what they have heard on radio), they tend to be more effective in producing learning and facilitating the adoption of new ideas. The reasons for this are that interest in attendance and participation is encouraged by group pressure and social expectations. Thus, the channel becomes more credible because the group believes the material is involving and important. Also, the media's message is reinforced by the group. Thus, it is a good idea for accountants to supplement written reports with oral presentations.

A Great Deal of Any Social Effect Depends on the Specific Audiences at a Particular Point in Time.   To produce effective reports, accountants must look at the receiver's social network and at the demographic characteristics that mediate the effects of the information from the media. For example, channel use depends on socioeconomic status. Highly educated, wealthy individuals use print to a greater degree than do less educated, poorer individuals, who tend to use the broadcast media.

Audiences Use the Media Differentially.   People use handy information sources. Further, they use print media and the serious parts of audiovisual media—news documentaries and educational programming—for information. People perceive print primarily as an information source and use the electronic media primarily for entertainment. This may change, however, as new technologies are used for information purposes. For now, financial and management reporting should use print.

What are the implications of this research on channel effects for accounting? The professional has traditionally relied on the print media because they allow a great deal of receiver control. Print is effective for communicating abstract ideas, and it can be efficiently disseminated to large, dispersed audiences. It allows for physical preservation of the message. In addition, audiences have learned to rely on print for information. However, print inhibits feedback, which is essential for ensuring comprehension. Print presents information using only the visual channel, which limits access to technical information for members of less educated groups. This may be important for financial reporting to community and other public organizations whose constituencies are made up of members of various social strata.

Comprehension of certain materials may be improved by using channels other than print. Further, one way to increase comprehension is through the redundant presentation of material simultaneously over different channels. This requires the receiver to use more than one sense at a time. H.M. McLuhan points out that this results in greater involvement and thus greater comprehension.[21] However, F.R. Hartman provides a warning against the use of multiple channels:

> Pictorial illustrations in many cases may distract rather than illustrate...The tradition in the television message is to place the majority of the information in the verbal audio channel and to attract attention and illustrate it in the pictorial. Too often the

picture is not properly related to the sound and a real barrier to effective communication is created by a tendency to focus attention on the picture when the message to be learned has been coded in the sound track.[22]

In summary, accounting should build mechanisms for feedback into the process and use the channel most appropriate for the message, the receiver, and the effects desired for the technical report. As with messages, the optimal channel is contingent upon the unique communication situation for which the report is created. This raises the question: What do we know about receivers and their patterns of information seeking?

Receivers

When analyzing a communication situation, one should consider factors about the audience such as their demographic and cultural background, prior attitudes, knowledge, behavioral patterns, and the social system or environment in which they will use the information. Generally, the more similar the receivers and the source are on these factors, the easier, and more effective the communication.

Audience Analysis

Knowledge about the receiver may be used to design more effective messages and deliver them via the most appropriate channel. Effective communication results when the information is specifically designed for the receiver. Consequently, accounting should rely heavily on empirical audience analysis. Accountants should investigate the intended, actual, and potential audiences prior to the production of documents. This analysis should determine the needs to be met by the planned materials. After the users' needs have been identified, the analysis of the potential audience should identify their demographic characteristics and level of expertise, along with the materials or people they currently use as information sources and their suggestions about the content and format for the new document. Feedback should be gathered from the intended audience about the report before presentation to ensure that it meets the actual audience's needs upon dissemination.

Behavioral accountants should also investigate patterns of information seeking by their clients and other users of business reports. The research concludes that people put little effort into information seeking and will use the sources that are most accessible. Information is sought because it is socially rewarding and can be discussed in the users' interpersonal network. Further, people rely less on formal sources, including the information technologies that require them to initiate information-seeking activities, than on what they learn in social conversations. This informal communication often takes place at lunch, coffee breaks, and professional gatherings such as conventions or seminars. These sorts of preferences can affect the way audiences use financial and business communications and may even determine whether a specific message reaches its intended audience at all. Therefore, accountants should devote greater attention to the patterns of social interaction and the use of informal communication channels by users of business information.

Network Analysis

The theoretical and empirical literature on communication networks is extensive and has been reviewed in great detail by E.M. Rogers and D.L. Kincaid.[23] Basically, descriptions of the communication structure of an organization are generated by examining the information flows among components of the system. The components may be individuals, small task groups, or entire formal organizations. Formal mathematical procedures exist to calculate descriptive indices that may be used to predict a number of social implications. Some network analysis methods provide a graphic description or sociogram of the communication structure and define network roles such as isolate, group member, liaison, and tree node. An example of a sociogram is presented in Figure 18-4.

The theoretical assumption underlying network analysis is that individuals' positions in an organization's communication structure determine their behaviors, attitudes, and knowledge. For example, the node labeled "isolate" in Figure 18-4 will probably not be knowledgeable about recent financial issues within the organization because that person has no contacts within the organization.

Innovative organizations must gather business information from the external environment. Boundary spanners (see Figure 18-4) serve this role. Their task depends on the nature of the organization's functions. For example, accounting is a service. Thus, accounting firms must have their members gather data about how to best meet their clients' needs. The greater the organization's task uncertainty, the greater its reliance upon external communication links. This raises the following questions: How is the information communicated to others internal to the organization? Are boundary spanners rewarded for going outside the organization for information? Are there gatekeepers or other bottlenecks that prevent the dissemination of this information to other members of the organization who need it to complete their jobs? Or, do boundary spanners perform the role of liaison by keeping abreast of recent developments and translating them into usable forms for the other members of the organization?

The optimal network structure varies with the functions that task groups perform. Generally, those groups involved with manifest productive tasks best perform their function when highly integrated. Those concerned with innovation require a great deal of boundary spanning and thus best perform

FIGURE 18-4
A Typical Network Analysis (Sociogram)

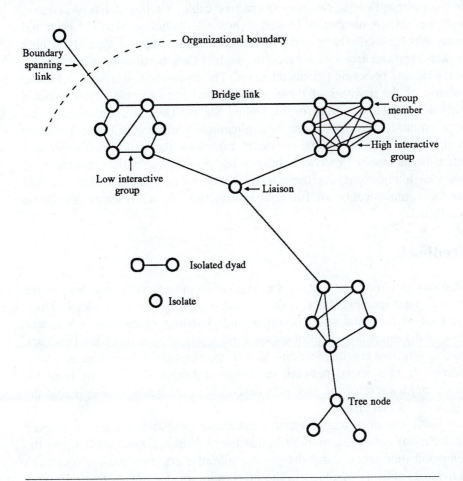

their function when loosely interconnected (see Figure 18-4). Accounting is primarily a service function. Functions of this sort must constantly span their boundaries to meet user needs. Generally, they function best when loosely integrated.

The role of the communicator is different when materials are developed for internal consumption than when the materials are to be disseminated into the environment. This raises a series of questions: Where do accountants fit into the communication structure of organizations? What role should they play in the structure? Indeed, this book suggests that they should be central rather than peripheral technical support staff. They should provide financial and management analysis for policy formulation and decisions in all phases of organizational activities.

One final area concerns the use of new communication technologies such as computer networks, two-way interactive cable, satellite delivery systems, and videotext. A number of brokerage houses—including Merrill Lynch and Paine Webber—now have computer-based decision support systems to help brokers keep and access client records, analyze their portfolios, and obtain up-to-the-minute prices and financial news. The research in this area is limited because of the newness of these technologies. For example, there is not a workable videotext system in the United States. Thus far, the research has been primarily descriptive and its implications unclear. But one only has to compare the current volume of shares traded on the major exchanges and international money flows with those of ten years ago to realize that there are financial implications. As these technologies become more widely adopted for the communication of financial information, future research should be conducted.

Feedback

Feedback is a message sent by the receiver to the source in response to the original message. Feedback makes possible the exchange of ideas. Thus, the goal of communication becomes understanding rather than a one-way flow or dissemination of information from a source to a receiver. Feedback ensures effective communication—that is, the comprehension of ideas among individuals in a social network or formal organization. Lack of feedback was a major cause of the problems described in the business dilemma at the beginning of this chapter.

G.A. Barnett[24] suggests that a cybernetic approach should be adopted for technical communication. It builds many feedback mechanisms into the communication process and changes the role of users from passive readers to individuals actively involved in the preparation of documents that will meet their needs. Feedback from users at the planning stage would help to determine the specific report's function, content, and treatment. Upon dissemination of the report, audiences should be solicited for feedback. Feedback to the following questions may be used to modify drafts of the document to improve its effectiveness:

1. How effectively does the report meet user needs? Was it understood?
2. Does the report meet the users' expectations?
3. How frequently is the report used, and for what purposes is it consulted?
4. Do users supplement the report by going to other sources?
5. Which other sources—documents and people—do users consult for the same information?

6. What additional information should the report contain?
7. What feedback can users offer on specific portions of the report?
8. What unanticipated feedback can users provide in response to open-ended questions?
9. What are the demographic and social characteristics of the actual users? Who is using the report?

If the discrepancy between the report's goals and its use is significant, modifications should be made to correct these problems. This process may be refined and repeated over time until the report meets the user's needs. In this way, the focus of communication shifts from a one-way flow concentrating on message production to the exchange of ideas between the accountant and the report's users. With this change of focus will come a change in the documents. They will be modular for easier modification as the need develops. They will be produced less expensively because they will not be viewed as permanent objects, but rather as the product of the most recent interaction between the user and the accountant. Finally, feedback may necessitate the development of computer-based financial materials because the production of permanent hard copy may not be appropriate or necessary. The user could access the financial information via a computer-based conference or electronic mail system and comment on the early drafts of the reports.

IMPLICATIONS

The context or environment in which communication occurs has important implications for accounting. The environment may produce "noise" that reduces the fidelity of information exchange. Noise is any signal or distraction that interferes with the reception of information. It is the ultimate limiter of communication and exists, if only in minuscule amounts, in all communication systems. Interference may result from a noisy channel, an unclear message, psychological factors with encoding or decoding, or any other aspect of the environment. When the disturbance is substantial, effective communication may be enhanced or recovered through increased redundancy.

Organizational Communication

Because the environments in which accounting information is produced and used are primarily formal organizations, it may be fruitful to examine communication in formal organizations. This is especially important for the managerial aspects of accounting. There has been considerable theorizing and empirical research in organizational communication, and it has been reviewed in great detail.[25] The basic notion underlying these theories is that formal organizations are information-processing systems. Indeed, the coordination of the activities of members of any organization is made possible only through communication. This communication must meet three major functions for an organization to grow and prosper:

1. *The operational, production or task-related function.* For example, IBM's operational goal is manufacturing and servicing computer equipment and General Motors' is manufacturing automobiles. Accounting firms perform the service of financial analysis and business reporting. Organizations must communicate technical information to their members to coordinate their behavior. This makes it possible to efficiently accomplish these goals.
2. *The socio-emotional or maintenance function.* Organizations must communicate human relations information to their employees to train them, indoctrinate them into the organizational culture, and provide information about company policies (health insurance and other benefits, hiring practices, rules for promotions, etc.).
3. *The adaptive or innovative function.* Organizations must communicate with their environment so that they can adapt to a changing world. Information must be gathered about competition, raw materials, labor, markets, general economic conditions, scientific and technical innovations, and the financial implications of these data. This makes it possible for organizations to grow and to accomplish future goals. These activities are usually performed at the periphery of the organization in research and development laboratories, marketing departments, and financial or strategic planning groups.

Thus, organizations must gather and disseminate information both internally and with the external environment. These external interactions may be with individuals or other organizations. Research has shown that organizational effectiveness is a function of the degree of both internal and external communication.

Information Load

Effective communication may also be hindered by distractions within the organization. One area that has received considerable attention is information load—both underload and overload. In overload situations, the receiver may not give enough attention to critical messages. The source may not take the time to prepare effective messages. Employees become stressed and job performance often suffers. In the dilemma at the beginning of the chapter, Anderson worked on the MEGA project at night—a sign that he may have been in an overload situation. There are a number of techniques that may be used to reduce information overload. Among them are queing (the planned putting-off of less important matters until the workload lightens), designing and assigning jobs with considerations for employees' information processing capacities, client self-service, and the use of management information or decision support systems.

In underload situations, the participants may be unaccustomed to dealing with information. They may even ignore it because the information is perceived as not being for them or they believe that someone else may take care of the problem. They may also become stressed and their self-concept may suffer.

Organizational communication research suggests that managers should pay special attention to information processes within their organization. With the adoption of office automation systems, data management, and computer networks, managers have the opportunity to design systems to ensure effective communication. How one does this is not obvious. The optimal organizational communication structure is contingent on the organization's goals, its tasks, and the rate of change (both technological and cultural) in the environment. The optimal design of any organization should match its information needs and processing system. Generally, the greater the environmental uncertainty (the difference between the information that is known and that which is needed), the greater the member integration that is required. However, this may not be true for boundary spanners (those individuals who gather information from the environment).

The Communication Audit

To analyze an organization's communication activities and to provide guidance in the design of communication structures, consultants generally use a procedure known as a communication audit.[26] The communication audit is used to determine the health of an organization's communication. Managing partners in accounting firms should use this technique to facilitate their effective management. Had an audit been performed at AF&W, the inadequacies of its communication activities could have been discovered and its practices altered. Anderson might have received all the information he needed and the MEGA account might have been retained.

The communication audit investigates three phases of communication activities: (1) the adequacy of information from organizational sources via particular channels about specific topics (content); (2) an organization's communication structure; and (3) its climate or the outcome of communication practices. Data about these areas are gathered using a variety of research methods, including questionnaires and open-ended personal interviews with the organization's members.

Adequacy of Information from Organizational Sources

In the first phase of a communication audit, employees are asked to report their frequency of interpersonal interaction with people at all levels in the organization, including co-workers, supervisors, middle management, and top management. Also, they report their frequency of use of mediated channels, in-house publications, letters, memos, electronic mail, and annual reports. Typically, the data collection only concerns topics that have been identified as important to that organization. This may include such things as feedback on job performance, organizational policies, human resources information, and financial information.

In addition to gathering data about the frequency of communication, the communication auditor gathers information about the perceived needed or desired level of communication for these sources, channels, and topics. Typically, the actual use is subtracted from the desired level to determine communication uncertainty. Where the discrepancies are great, management, with the help of a consultant, may intervene to improve the communication practices. For example, if employees' uncertainty about human resource issues is great, in-house seminars on these topics may be instituted. Uncertainty has been shown to be related to members' level of organizational satisfaction or the organizational climate. Further, past research has consistently demonstrated that people want more information from top management. This discrepancy shrinks as the source reaches the same level in the organization as the respondent. Also, people report that they use the "grapevine" more than they desire. These findings have led many organizations' top management to adopt the practice of communicating directly to subordinates at all levels of their organization. One major farm equipment manufacturer produces a five-minute, closed-circuit television news program that allows direct, one-way communication from top management to all employees about events relevant to the company. In this way, reliance on the rumor mill (grapevine) is lessened.

Finally, this section of the communication audit may include questions about the topics, sources, and channels' ease of access, accuracy, timeliness, and any other attributes that are deemed important by management or the consultant. These areas are generally discovered during pretest interviews with a cross-section of the organization. If problem areas are identified, organizational development techniques or communication training workshops may be employed to ameliorate the problem. A typical communication audit survey questionnaire is presented as Figure 18-5.

Communication Structure of the Organization

Network analysis is used in the second phase of a communication audit to describe the communication structure of an organization. Generally, a questionnaire listing all employees is distributed to every member of the organization. Recent audits have also included those individuals and organizations external to the organization with whom there is need for frequent contact. The organization's members simply indicate their frequency of inter-

Figure 18-5
FCB Communication Survey

INTRODUCTION

As you know, the State University of New York at Buffalo is currently conducting a study of First Community Bank's (FCB) communication system. Our goal is to use the results of this study to help develop a workable communication plan for the coming years.

As a part of this study, we are asking members of the Bank to complete this survey. We urge you to complete it as promptly as possible so that we may gain an adequate representation of the Bank's views on communication issues.

Upon completion, insert the survey in the provided envelope, seal it, and return to Kathy Mahoney, who will forward all surveys unopened to the State University of New York at Buffalo.

All of your responses will be treated in total confidence and nobody outside of the State University research team will see your individual responses. Individual responses will be summarized and grouped in order to help us form our conclusions.

Thank you in advance for your cooperation in this important project.

GENERAL INSTRUCTIONS

1. Please answer *all* questions honestly since each one is important for developing the best communication strategy for First Community Bank.
2. Don't give us your name (we want to preserve the anonymity of your responses).
3. A comment section has been provided at the end of the survey which gives you a chance to tell us your overall impressions on how we communicate at First Community Bank.
4. Place your answers directly on the questionnaire pages.
5. If there are any questions which do not apply to you, leave them blank.
6. Please return the completed questionnaire within five (5) business days.
7. This questionnaire is divided into seven (7) sections:

Section I	Some Information about You
Section II	Receiving Information from Others
Section III	Sending Information to Others
Section IV	Sources of Information
Section V	Organizational Communication Relationships
Section VI	Organizational Outcomes
Section VII	Comment Section

Figure 18-5
(continued)

8. All questions on this survey should be answered using a 100-point scale, where zero indicates "none," 50 indicates "an average amount," and 100 the "maximum possible." You may use any number between 0 and 100.

None	Average	Maximum
0	50	100

For example: If 50 is an average amount of information received, how much information do you currently receive about your job duties? If you feel you receive a greater that average amount of information, you should place an answer between 50 and 100 which accurately indicates how much information you receive.

There are no correct answers and you should use the number that is right *for you.*

Example: RECEIVING INFORMATION FROM OTHERS

TOPIC	How much I receive now	How dependable is it	How timely is it	How much I need
How well I am doing in my job	70	80	40	35
My job duties	84	53	88	82
Bank policies	62	70	64	58

9. The following defintions may be useful to you in answering the questions on the survey:

First Community Bank: Refers to the Buffalo Division.
Senior Management: Refers to Vice Presidents and above.
Middle Management: Refers to "Junior Officer level" positions, up to and including, Assistant Vice Presidents.

10. If there are any questions which you do not understand, please call: Kathy Mahoney (extension 5883). We appreciate your cooperation in this important survey. The results are confidential and in no way will be tied to you.

Figure 18-5
(continued)

Section I: SOME INFORMATION ABOUT YOU

Answers to question (1-7) will tell us a little about you and your position at First Community Bank. This will help us determine if there are any significant differnces of opinion among people with different lengths of service, organizational affiliation, geographic location, etc.

1. Do you work:

    a. Full time
    b. Part time

2. Do you work in:

    a. A branch
    b. A department
    c. Administration

3. How long have you worked for First Community Bank?

    a. Less than 1 year
    b. 1 to 5 years
    c. 6 to 10 years
    d. 11 to 15 years
    e. More than 15 years

4. How long have you held your present position?

    a. Less than 1 year
    b. 1 to 5 years
    c. 6 to 10 years
    d. 11 to 15 years
    e. More than 15 years

5. What is your position in the Bank?

    a. I don't supervise anyone
    b. First line supervisor
    c. Middle management
    d. Senior management
    e. Other (Please specify:_____)

Figure 18-5
(continued)

6. What is the last level you completed in school?

    a. Less than high school
    b. High school graduate
    c. Some college or technical training
    d. Completed college or technical school
    e. Graduate work

7. What is your age

    a. Under 20 years of age
    b. 21 to 30 years of age
    c. 31 to 40 years of age
    d. 41 to 50 years of age
    e. Over 50 years of age

Section II: RECEIVING INFORMATION FROM OTHERS

Instructions: Questions 8 through 20

You can receive information about various topics in the Bank. For each topic listed below give four separate scores. Write your response in the column that best indicates:

    a. How much information *are* you receiving on that topic?
    b. How dependable is the information you currently receive?
    c. How timely is the information when it gets to you?
    d. How much of the information do you need?

TOPIC	How much I receive now	How dependable is it	How timely is it	How much I need
8. How well I am doing in my job.	_____	_____	_____	_____
9. My job duties.	_____	_____	_____	_____
10. My immediate future in the Bank.	_____	_____	_____	_____
11. Bank policies.	_____	_____	_____	_____
12. Pay and benefits.	_____	_____	_____	_____

Figure 18-5
(continued)

TOPIC	How much I receive now	How dependable is it	How timely is it	How much I need
13. How technolgical changes affect my job.	_____	_____	_____	_____
14. How I am being judged.	_____	_____	_____	_____
15. How my job-related problems are being handled.	_____	_____	_____	_____
16. How Bank decisions are made that affect my job.	_____	_____	_____	_____
17. Promotion and career advancement opportunities in the Bank.	_____	_____	_____	_____
18. Important new product, service or program developments in the Bank.	_____	_____	_____	_____
19. How my job relates to the total operation of the Bank.	_____	_____	_____	_____
20. Specific problems faced by management.	_____	_____	_____	_____

Section III: SENDING INFORMATION TO OTHERS

Instructions: Questions 21 through 26

In addition to receiving information, there are many topics on which you can send information to others. For each topic listed, give two separate scores. Write your answers in the columns provided indicating:

    a.   How much information are you now sending on each topic?

    b.   How much information do you need to send on each topic?

Figure 18-5
(continued)

Remember, 50 indicates an average amount in each case.

TOPIC	How much I send now	How much I need to send
21. Reporting what I am doing in my job.	_____	_____
22. Reporting what I think my job requires me to do.	_____	_____
23. Reporting job-related problems.	_____	_____
24. Constructively criticizing my job and/or working conditions.	_____	_____
25. Requesting information necessary to do my job.	_____	_____
26. Asking for clearer work instructions.	_____	_____

Section IV: SOURCES OF INFORMATION

Instructions: Questions 27 through 49

You not only receive various kinds of information, you can also receive information from various sources within the First Community Bank. For each source listed below, write your answers in the columns provided to indicate:

a. The amount of information you are receiving from that source.
b. How dependable the information is that you currently receive from each source.
c. How timely the information is when it gets to you.
d. The amount of information you need to receive from that source (the amount you need from that source to do your job).

Sources of Information INSIDE the Bank

SOURCE	How much I receive now	How dependable is it	How timely is it	How much I need
27. Subordinates.	_____	_____	_____	_____
28. Co-workers in my own unit or department.	_____	_____	_____	_____

Figure 18-5
(continued)

SOURCE	How much I receive now	How dependable is it	How timely is it	How much I need
29. Individuals in *other* units/departments in the Bank.	_____	_____	_____	_____
30. Immediate supervisor.	_____	_____	_____	_____
31. Meetings.	_____	_____	_____	_____
32. Middle Management.	_____	_____	_____	_____
33. Senior Management.	_____	_____	_____	_____
34. The "grapevine".	_____	_____	_____	_____
35. Bulletin boards.	_____	_____	_____	_____
36. Memoranda or management reports.	_____	_____	_____	_____
37. Bank publications (for example: Newsletter or Weekly Bulletin).	_____	_____	_____	_____
38. Telephone.	_____	_____	_____	_____
39. The computer.	_____	_____	_____	_____
40. Mass media (newspapers, TV, radio).	_____	_____	_____	_____
41. Trade and business publications.	_____	_____	_____	_____
42. Vendors and suppliers.	_____	_____	_____	_____
43. Professional organizations and societies.	_____	_____	_____	_____
44. Contacts at other financial institutions.	_____	_____	_____	_____
45. Government agencies.	_____	_____	_____	_____
46. Community organizations.	_____	_____	_____	_____

Figure 18-5
(continued)

SOURCE	How much I receive now	How depend- able is it	How timely is it	How much I need
47. Customers.	_____	_____	_____	_____
48. Personal contacts (friends, relatives).	_____	_____	_____	_____
49. Seminars, work- shops and classes.	_____	_____	_____	_____

Section V: ORGANIZATIONAL COMMUNICATION RELATIONSHIPS

Instructions: Questions 50 through 54

A variety of communication relationships exists in organizations like the First Community Bank. Employees exchange messages regularly with supervisors, subordinates, co-workers, etc. Considering your communication relationships with the following sources in the Bank, please indicate the quality of each relationship.

If the item doesn't apply, do not answer. Remember, 50 represents an average amount.

Relationship	Quality of Relationship
50. Co-workers	_____
51. Subordinates (if applicable)	_____
52. Immediate supervisor	_____
53. Middle Management	_____
54. Senior Management	_____

Section VI: ORGANIZATIONAL OUTCOMES

Instructions: Questions 55 through 65

One of the most important "outcomes" of working in an organization is the amount of satisfaction you get from your job duties, co-workers, your supervisor, or the organization as a whole. Please indicate the degree of satisfaction with the following items.

Remember, 50 represents an average amount of satisfaction in each case.

Figure 18-5
(continued)

How satisfied I am

55. My present job duties.   _____

56. My overall job performance.   _____

57. My opportunity to "make a difference", to contribute
    to the overall success of the Bank.   _____

58. My opportunity to reach my own full potential in my
    present job.   _____

59. The Bank's overall communication efforts.   _____

60. The Bank as compared to other similar organizations.   _____

61. The Bank's overall efficiency of operation.   _____

62. The overall quality of the Bank's service.   _____

63. The Bank's achievement of its goals and objectives.   _____

63. My opportunity to define problems and find solutions
    in my job.   _____

64. My opportunity to make decisions that affect my job.   _____

Section VII: COMMENT SECTION

If there are any employee communication matters about which you would like to comment, please write them on this page. If you'd like to explain reasons for your answers to specific questions, please use this section and refer to the question number. Please do not sign your name.

_____

_____

_____

_____

_____

_____

_____

Thank you for your cooperation.

action with each of the listed individuals. Modifications of this procedure may exclude the listing of the employees, relying instead on unsolicited recall of past interaction or focusing on the interaction among task groups rather than individuals. These data are then computer analyzed to determine the organization's communication structure. This structure may then be compared to the formal organizational structure. Where discrepancies exist between the designed and actual structures, modifications can be made by adding or subtracting links as desired. For example, if an analysis of Figure 18-4 revealed the need for a link from the tree node to the high interaction group, an additional liaison could be employed to link those individuals. Manipulations of this sort are, however, a function of the organization's environmental contingencies, design, and strategic plan. A typical network analysis instrument is presented in Figure 18-6.

Outcome of Communication Practices

The final phase of the audit simply asks the employees about their level of satisfaction with a variety of the organization's communication practices. Additional information may be gathered as desired by the audited organization. For example, in the sample audit questionnaire (Figure 18-5), management was interested in the employees' knowledge about the company's businesses, an outcome of communication activities. As a result, a number of items were added. Additionally, demographic data are often gathered as part of the communication audit.

In summary, accountants should consider the environment in which the process takes place—generally, a formal organization. They should seek information about the users' positions in the organizational structure, their information load relative to their processing capabilities, the other information sources they use, and the other people they communicate with. These may be discovered using a communication audit. Accountants should consider the same aspects of their own environment. What are their positions in the communication structures? Do they receive all the information they need to complete assigned tasks? Ideally, they should serve the role of liaison, gathering information from the widest possible range of sources, processing it and communicating it in the most effective manner to those who need it to complete their tasks. In the future, the role of behavioral accountants will become one in which they will be recognized as liaisons.

DIAGNOSTIC REVIEW OF COMMUNICATION DILEMMA

The purpose of this section is to review the practices that the public accounting firm of AF&W should have used to prevent the loss of the MEGA account and

Figure 18-6

Directions:

As part of a study of Corporate Training & Development (CT & D), please complete the following questionnaire. Although individual's names are included here, and you will be asked to identify yourself, YOUR INDIVIDUAL RESPONSES WILL NOT BE MADE AVAILABLE TO ANYONE WITHIN FCB. You must be identified in order to make necessary connections in the network. The purpose of this questionnaire is to assess the communication activities within FCB.
In order to complete thise questionnaire, you should:

1. Find your name on the list and circle it.
2. **For each question**, indicate how often you communicte with each of the people listed in the left side of the questionnaire. (Choose any number that is representative of a TYPICAL month/week. It is unnecessary to fill in zeros.)
3. At the end of the name list you will find blank spaces. Please add individuals (and their title, location) or specific work groups that you communicate with during the time frame indicated in each question. Please note that you are being asked for individuals both within and outside FCB.

Special Notes:

* There are four distinct questions that you are being asked. Please note that the time frame for the first three questions is a typical **month**, while the last question asks about a typical **week**.
* Communication, as used in the questions, can be face-to-face, letters, memos, TOSS, phone conversations, meetings, etc.
* CT & D in the questions refers to the training function – Corporate Training & Development.
* A 100% response rate is necessary in order to make this questionnaire useful. Please return to Norman Eckert, Corporate Training & Development no later that APRIL 14th. If there are any questions, please contact Norman at extension 4860.

Figure 18-6
(continued)

Example:

	In a typical **month**, indicate how often you communicate with each of the following regarding innovative ideas and/or techniques.	In a typical **month**, indicate how often you communicate with each of the following about your client's or your department's goals.	In a typical **month**, indicate how often you communicate with each of the following about Corporate Training & Development goals.	In a typical **week**, indicate how often you share information with each of the following about any Corporate Training & Development or Bank related topic.
24 Mary Bailey	1		1	2
25 Meg Marlett		6	2	5
26 John Su	4	3	3	3

Figure 18-6
(continued)

	In a typical **month**, indicate how often you communicate with each of the following regarding innovative ideas and/or techniques.	In a typical **month**, indicate how often you communicate with each of the following about your client's or your department's goals.	In a typical **month**, indicate how often you communicate with each of the following about Corporate Training & Development goals.	In a typical **week**, indicate how often you share information with each of the following about any Corporate Training & Development or Bank related topic.
01 Cristina Escobar				
02 Terri Gitler				
03 Rosemary Kim				
04 John Maggio				
05 Bruce Bethell				
06 Melissa Madsen				
07 Marielle Brinkman				

Figure 18-6
(continued)

		In a typical **month**, indicate how often you communicate with each of the following regarding innovative ideas and/or techniques.	In a typical **month**, indicate how often you communicate with each of the following about your client's or your department's goals.	In a typical **month**, indicate how often you communicate with each of the following about Corporate Training & Development goals.	In a typical **week**, indicate how often you share information with each of the following about any Corporate Training & Development or Bank related topic.
08	Marilyn VanderLey				
09	Joe Skourup				
10	Christopher Herriot				
11	Peggy Delvalle				
12	Jennifer Yocum				
13	Peggy Gonzallez				
14	Kristin Dean-Grossmann				

Figure 18-6
(continued)

	In a typical **month**, indicate how often you communicate with each of the following regarding innovative ideas and/or techniques.	In a typical **month**, indicate how often you communicate with each of the following about your client's or your department's goals.	In a typical **month**, indicate how often you communicate with each of the following about Corporate Training & Development goals.	In a typical **week**, indicate how often you share information with each of the following about any Corporate Training & Development or Bank related topic.
15 Robert Hall				
16 Dean Dowdy				
17 Letty Johnson				
18 Laurie Sofka				
19 Richard Schnirring				
20 Patricia Young				
21 Amy McRae				
22 Barbara Jackson				

Figure 18-6
(continued)

Others – Please fill in Names and/or Functions
Within FCB

01 _____

02 _____

03 _____

04 _____

05 _____

Outside FCB

01 _____

02 _____

03 _____

Figure 18-6
(continued)

Comments (any remarks or problems you have concerning any area referred to above, CT & D in general, or this survey):

_____

_____

_____

_____

_____

_____

_____

_____

_____

Thank you for your cooperation.

the demise of David Anderson's promising career. These recommendations are based upon the material presented in this chapter.

1. Jones, Anderson's superior from corporate consulting, should have spoken with Anderson directly and followed up with a written memo. The conversation could have taken place over the telephone or in a face-to-face meeting. This is recommended because interpersonal communication allows for feedback. Further, redundancy across channels (verbal and written) generally improves the effectiveness of the communication. Jones should have taken the time to ask, "Are there any questions?" or, "Now David, how are we going to proceed?"

2. Anderson, recognizing the potential for error in the message, should have asked for a meeting with Jones to clarify the assignment. Further, he should have asked Jones for a liaison at MEGA and communicated directly with that individual rather than receiving all information through Jones. This would have reduced the distortion in the information from MEGA by reducing the number of possible sources of noise in the channel. It would also have eliminated the gatekeeper, Jones, and allowed for direct feedback from MEGA. In this way, the likelihood of MEGA receiving the information and analysis that they wanted would have increased.

3. Anderson should have talked with Smith, the AF&W local managing partner, about adjusting his workload. It was obvious that Anderson was in an information overload situation and could not effectively process all the relevant information. Smith should have let Anderson delay certain tasks until the MEGA project was completed.

4. Jones should have periodically followed up on Anderson's activities. A telephone call with the question, "What is going on with the MEGA project?" and "Do you have any questions about MEGA?" might have facilitated the successful completion of that project. Perhaps Jones did not follow up because she was also overloaded with business information that she could not process, thus reducing her effectiveness as a manager.

5. If Anderson had established a liaison at MEGA, he could have provided that person with a draft of the report and requested feedback. The following questions could have been asked: Did the report meet MEGA's needs? Was it clear? What additional information should it contain? Specifically, who will use this report? Adjustments could have been made in the report to meet the client's needs and objectives. This relationship would have insured that the local division manager at MEGA would have seen the report only when deemed appropriate by MEGA's corporate headquarters management.

6. The events surrounding the MEGA debacle were probably symptomatic of other, more serious communication problems within AF&W. This suggests that AF&W's management should have a consultant (either internal or external) conduct a communication audit. The quality of communication within the regional offices and the relations between these offices and the national corporate headquarters should be examined. Based upon the audit data, programs such as communication training or organizational develop-

ment could be instituted. Also, if major problems exist, redesigning AF&W through structural changes might also be undertaken. In these ways, AF&W could remain profitable by avoiding catastrophes like the loss of the MEGA account. Further, a communication audit could help the organization prepare itself for the environmental contingencies of the future.

SUMMARY AND CONCLUSIONS_____

This chapter has provided only a brief overview of communication theory and corresponding empirical research with applications for the accounting process. It excluded certain research areas that others might have discussed. Clearly, more theory from different perspectives would have been useful. Some implications have been stated as facts, but they should be viewed somewhat skeptically. Deductions made from theories generated for situations other than those to which they are applied may lead to erroneous conclusions. In this case, much of the communication theory cited was developed with persuasion rather than fidelity of information exchange as the central focus. Thus, future research is necessary to apply these and other theories specifically to behavioral accounting.

Finally, we live in a rapidly changing world characterized by new technologies and increased contact among many different societies, each with their own unique culture and language. Future research is needed to explore and define the role of the new communication technologies in the accounting process. Can they be designed to deal more effectively with the financial information needs and behavioral patterns of users? One important aspect of the design process is the effective communication of the information stored in the electronic data systems. Research is also needed on how intercultural communication affects or alters the communication processes of multinational organizations. How do accounting practices vary across cultures and how can common practices be established when two cultures come into contact?

REFERENCES_____

[1] Harold Lasswell, "The Structure and Function of Communication in Society," in *Communication of Ideas*, ed. L. Bryson (New York: Institute for Religious and Social Studies, 1948), 37-51.

[2] C. Shannon and W. Weaver, *The Mathematical Theory of Communication* (Urbana, Ill.: University of Illinois Press, 1949).

[3] David Berlo, *The Process of Communication* (New York: Holt, Rinehart and Winston, 1960).

[4] Bruce Westley and Malcolm MacLean, "A Conceptual Model for Communication Research," *Journalism Quarterly* 34 (1957): 35. Reprinted with permission.

[5] E.M. Rogers and D.L. Kincaid, *Communication Network: Towards a New Paradigm for Research* (New York: Free Press, 1981), 37-38.

[6] G. Siegel, *How Accounting Majors Perceive the Accounting Profession: A Multidimensional Scaling Approach,* Paper presented at the Midwest Meeting of the American Accounting Association, Chicago, March 1982.

[7] W.J. McGuire, "Persuasion, Resistance and Attitude Change," in *Handbook of Communication*, eds. I.S. Pool, F.W. Frey, W. Schramm, N. Maccoby and E.B. Parker (Chicago, Ill.: Rand McNally, 1973), 230.

[8] E.M. Rogers, *Communication of Innovations: A Cross-Cultural Approach*, 2d ed. (New York: Free Press, 1982).

[9] Berlo, *Ibid*.

[10] H.M. McLuhan, *Gutenberg Galaxy* (Toronto: University of Toronto Press, 1962) and *Understanding Media* (New York: McGraw-Hill, 1964).

[11] J. Woelfel and J. Saltiel, "Cognitive Processes as Motions in a Multidimensional Space," unpublished manuscript (East Lansing, Mich.: Michigan State University Department of Communication, 1974).

[12] McGuire, p. 295.

[13] G.R. Klare, "Reading Technical Writing: Some Observations," *Technical Communication* 24 (1977): 1-5.

[14] U.F. Andersson, "Methods of Measuring Communication Results," *Journal of Technical Writing and Communication* 1, (1971): 109-113.

[15] W. Schramm, "Channels and Audiences," in *Handbook of Communication*, eds. I.S. Pool, F.W. Frey, W. Schramm, N. Maccoby and E.B. Parker (Chicago, Ill.: Rand McNally, 1973), 116-140.

[16] McLuhan, *Gutenberg Galaxy*; and McLuhan, *Understanding Media* (New York: McGraw-Hill, 1964).

[17] M.E. McCombs and D.L. Shaw, "The Agenda-Setting Function of the Mass Media," *Public Opinion Quarterly* 36 (1972): 176-187.

[18] Rogers, *Communication of Innovations*, *Ibid*.

[19] J.T. Klapper, *The Effects of Mass Communication*, (New York: Free Press, 1960), p 109.

[20] S.H. Chaffee, "Mass Media Versus Interpersonal Channels: The Synthetic Competition" (Paper presented to the Speech Communication Association, Austin, Texas, November 1979).

[21] McLuhan, *Understanding Media*.

[22] F.R. Hartman, "Single and Multiple Channel Communication: A Review of Research and a Proposed Model," *AV Communication Review* 9 (1961): 241.

[23] Rogers and Kincaid, *Communication Networks*.

[24] G.A. Barnett, "Applications of Communication Theory and Cybernetics to Technical Communication," *Journal of Technical Writing and Communication* 9 (1979): 337-47.

[25] See, for example: G.M. Goldhaber, *Organizational Communication*, 3d ed. (Dubuque, Iowa: William C. Brown, 1983); R.V. Farace, P.R. Monge and H.M. Russell, *Communicating and Organizing* (Reading, Mass.: Addison-Wesley, 1977); E.M. Rogers and R. Agarwala-Rogers, *Communication in Organizations* (New York:

Free Press, 1976); G.M. Goldhaber and D.P. Rogers, *Auditing Organizational Communication Systems: The ICA Communication Audit* (Dubuque, Iowa: Kendall/Hunt, 1979).

DISCUSSION QUESTIONS

1. Based on the chapter how would you go about designing a communication system to guarantee "good" communication in Arnold, Fenner and Winston? What organizational factors would you consider? What communication factors? Why do you feel these factors are important?
2. You have just been hired by a "Big 8" accounting firm in the Human Resources Department to develop a training program for their partners and staff to help them communicate more effectively. Discuss the subject matter that you would include in the program.
3. Discuss the role of feedback in the accounting process. Are the mechanisms effective from an organizational perspective? Describe how you would alter these feedback mechanisms so as to increase their effectiveness.
4. Is the profession of accounting credible? From a communication perspective, discuss what you might do to increase the perceived credibility of accounting in general, and individual accountants in particular?
5. Which model of communication do you think can best be applied to accounting? Why?
6. Discuss the various types of messages accountants produce. How do they differ in content, organization, code, and treatment? Could any of these factors be changed to improve the effectiveness of these messages?
7. Organizations are making greater use of information technologies such as computer-based communication systems and decision support systems. How might the adoption of these communication channels affect the process of accounting?
8. Discuss how network analysis might be used to improve the communication within an accounting firm. What might the optimal communication structure of an accounting firm look like?
9. Discuss how tax laws might be altered to prevent accountants from experiencing periods of information overload and underload. How might queing theory be applied to smooth the work load of accountants?

CASE 18-1

The Company

XYZ Cosmetics Consolidated consists of three individual cosmetics companies—X, Y, and Z—each of which has its own line of cosmetics. Each of the three companies has its own accounting department, which is located at corporate headquarters in New York. XYZ Cosmetics Consolidated operates its manufacturing plant in a nearby suburb of New York. The plant manufactures cosmetics for all three companies of XYZ Cosmetics Consolidated and has its own accounting staff.

Bob Brown was recently hired as a corporate accountant for X Cosmetic Company. Brown was a recent college graduate and this was his first job. Theresa Jaron, the controller of X Cosmetics Company, hired Brown and was impressed with his grades in college. One of the first assignments Jaron gave Brown was to forecast ending inventory for the current quarter ending June 30. Jaron told Brown to start with the inventory at the beginning of the quarter, add forecasted production for the manufacturing plant, and subtract the cost of sales budgeted for the quarter to derive estimated ending inventory.

Brown was given the actual inventory at the beginning of the quarter and the forecasted sales for the quarter. Jaron then told Brown to call Mark Moore at the manufacturing plant to obtain the forecasted production data. Moore was recently hired as the accounting manager at the manufacturing plant.

The Dilemma

Brown called Moore and introduced himself as the new corporate accountant in New York. Brown then asked Moore for the forecasted production for the quarter. Moore gave Brown the forecasted production in sales dollars. Brown, being an intelligent accountant, reduced this production in sales dollars to production at cost by multiplying it by the prime cost percentage. Brown then computed the estimated ending inventory for X Cosmetic Company for the current quarter.

What Brown did not realize was that he was given forecasted production for XYZ Cosmetics Consolidated and not for just X Cosmetic Company. As a result, forecasted ending inventory was considerably higher than actual ending inventory. This also resulted in considerable differences in the forecasted and actual cash flow statements for the quarter ended June 30.

Required:

1. What were the communication problems in this situation? What could be done to improve the situation?
2. Draw a sociogram from the information in the case. What does this graphic reveal about the communication in the XYZ Cosmetics organization?

CHAPTER 19

Behavioral Dimensions of Income Taxes

by
W. Peter Salzarulo
Miami University
Oxford, Ohio

It is difficult to imagine a tax law that does not have some effect on human behavior. This effect is particularly important in a tax system based on self-assessment and voluntary compliance. These are major characteristics of the federal income tax in the United States. The overriding objective of tax legislation is to raise revenue, and the degree to which this objective is achieved depends on the motivational strength that the tax system instills in taxpayers to pay the correct amount of tax. The tax laws have also been used to influence human behavior in order to achieve various economic and social objectives. The basic psychological theories of motivational strength, which are examined in this chapter, can be used to analyze the effect of income tax laws on human behavior.

BUSINESS DILEMMA

The Bradford Lockbox Company

The Bradford Lockbox Company has been in business for over 50 years. It is one of a very few companies in the United States that manufactures post office lockboxes and other post office equipment. Its major customer has always been the U.S. government, but it also sells some of its products to universities, apartment complexes, businesses, and state and local governments.

All of the original stock in the company was owned by members of the Bradford family, but, in the last 15 years, the ownership of stock by family members has declined slightly. Currently, about 80 percent of the company's stock is still owned by ten family members. The remaining 20 percent of stock is owned by seven individuals who are employees or former employees of the company. The president and production supervisor are members of the Bradford family, but other executive positions are filled by people outside the family. The workforce contains a mix of skilled and unskilled employees. The company has a small foundry and equipment that is used to shape the metal products.

John Bradford, president of the company, is 55 years old and has spent the last 25 years working for the company. He became president upon the retirement of his father in 1965. Prior to that, he held a variety of engineering positions in the company. He owns approximately 20 percent of the company's stock.

Except for a rather dismal period in the late 1960s, the company has been profitable. During that period, because of the Vietnam War, the U.S. government curtailed the construction of new post offices, and sales plunged. Huge losses were encountered . . . and, for some time, the survival of the firm was in doubt. The company did survive, but several of its competitors were forced out of business at that time. When business returned to normal, Bradford was in an excellent position to substantially increase sales and profits. Currently, the company's large profits put it in the 34 percent tax bracket.

The president of the company and the other officers are highly compensated for their services. Their income from this employment places each of them in the 28 percent income tax bracket.

Although the company has been profitable for several years, it has a history of paying only a small dividend. In the past, many of the large shareholders were also employees of the company. Since their salaries were large, there was no need for the extra dividend income. Also, the company spent significant sums in the early 1970s to modernize the plant . . . and funds were generally unavailable for the payment of dividends.

Rita Parker, the company's tax specialist, has recently completed a draft of the company's federal income tax return for the previous year. The tax return shows that the company has incurred a large tax liability for the year. Parker is 28 years old and has been with the company for five years. She came to the company immediately after completing her master of taxation degree.

Parker took the tax return to George Long, the treasurer, so that he could review it. Long is 50 years old and has been employed by Bradford for ten years. Prior to joining the company, he was employed by a large national public accounting firm. He had been a partner in the audit area of the firm. He owns approximately 1 percent of the company's stock.

The Accumulated Earnings Tax

While Parker was in the treasurer's office, she told Long that the Bradford Lockbox Corporation might have a potential problem with the accumulated earnings tax. She explained that this tax is a penalty tax on corporations that have large earnings but pay little or no dividends to their shareholders. However, the tax is not imposed if there are sound business purposes for the accumulated earnings. The tax is aimed at those corporations that accumulate earnings for the purpose of defeating the "double tax" characteristics of the corporate form of business. Closely held corporations, such as Bradford, are particularly vulnerable to this tax.

In closely held corporations there is frequently a temptation to pay small dividends. This results from the fact that dividend income is fully taxable to the individual shareholders. Further, corporations are not entitled to a deduction for dividends paid. Therefore, the dividend income is taxed twice— once at the corporate level and again at the shareholder level. Where both the corporation and the shareholders are in high tax brackets, the combined tax can be substantial. There is an incentive to pay those individuals who are both employees and shareholders of the corporation a larger salary, since the salary payment is deductible. The amount of salary that can be paid must be kept within reasonable limits. The accumulated earnings tax imposes a tax rate of 27 1/2 percent on the first $100,000 of accumulated taxable income and 38 1/2 percent on amounts in excess of $100,000. This penalty tax is paid in addition to the regular federal income tax.

The accumulated earnings tax is assessed by the Internal Revenue Service. Corporations are not required to assess themselves for the tax. The Internal Revenue Service will normally discover the accumulated earnings problem during a tax audit.

The next week Bradford, Long, and Parker met to discuss the accumulated earnings problem. Parker listed the options that were available to the company. These included:

1. *The company can pay a dividend.* The tax will not be imposed if the corporation declares and pays a large enough dividend. The dividend can be paid after the year is completed, provided it is paid within 2 1/2 months after year-end.
2. *The company can attempt to justify the position that the earnings were accumulated to satisfy reasonable business needs.* Reasonable business needs include bona fide expansion of the business, replacement or modernization of equipment, retirement of debt, and other realistic business purposes. This would, of course, require that Bradford actually make plans to purchase new equipment or undertake another big project.
3. *The company can do nothing.* They could hope that this year's tax return will not be examined by the IRS or, if it is examined, that the issue of the accumulated earnings tax will not arise.

If the tax year had not already ended, other options would be available. For example, the corporation could have made the "S Corporation election" or increased certain discretionary expenditures like charitable contributions.

After the options were listed, Bradford spoke in favor of sitting tight and doing nothing. He mentioned that the extra cash could be very useful if the corporation would have to face another financial crisis of the kind that existed in the late 1960s. He also mentioned that a majority of the company's stock is owned by Bradford family members, almost all of whom are in the 28 percent income tax bracket. Therefore, an income tax would have to be paid on the dividend. Also, the company could always fight the IRS in court if the issue was discovered. Bradford stated that it was his understanding that the tax is imposed only on corporations that have accumulated earnings for the purpose of avoiding the tax on dividends. He felt that this subjective standard might make it easier for the company to win in court.

Parker argued in favor of paying a dividend large enough to eliminate any potential accumulated earnings tax problem. She remarked that a sufficient amount of cash was available to pay the large dividend. Also, the dividend would be helpful to some of the minority shareholders who were not members of the Bradford family. She also thought that the company was very vulnerable to the tax. If the controversy did reach court, Parker thought that the company would lose and incur substantial legal costs as well as the tax itself.

Long suggested that perhaps they should develop plans for expansion or purchase some new equipment. In the discussion that followed, Bradford reminded the others that they had previously forecasted little additional demand for their products over the next few years. Therefore, unless they wanted to diversify into other areas, there was no need for plant expansion. Also, Bradford commented that there had been little technological change in their industry since the major modernization effort of ten years ago. There was no real need for replacement of the existing equipment.

The meeting adjourned without any agreement on the best course of action. During the following week, the three individuals involved in the decision met again. Bradford had hoped that all three could agree on a common course of action. However, after the second meeting, there was still no consensus. Bradford threatened to do simply what he thought was proper. The other two asked him to reconsider his position because of the seriousness of the problem.

THE USE OF TAX LAWS TO INFLUENCE BEHAVIOR

Tax decisions are made by individuals. However, in the corporate environment, the individuals who make these decisions are sometimes constrained in their decision making by other corporate objectives. For example, favorable tax provisions may not be utilized because of the adverse effect on the income to be reported to shareholders. In some cases, if the provision is used for tax purposes, it must also be used for financial reporting purposes. Also, some corporations may have the policy of attempting to minimize tax disputes with the IRS because of legal fees, public image, or other reasons. This policy may cause the company to avoid some favorable but risky tax provisions. The tax decisions that individuals make will also be influenced by the various groups of which they are a part. Even though corporate policy and group dynamics are important determinants of tax decisions, the emphasis in this chapter is on individuals and the factors that motivate them.

The dilemma facing the officers of the Bradford Lockbox Company is typical of the kinds of situations that can arise when dealing with the federal income tax laws. Tax laws do affect human behavior. Most importantly, the tax laws attempt to motivate taxpayers to pay the proper amount of tax owed. Since the end of World War II, the tax laws in the United States have also been used to achieve economic and social objectives.

There is now a targeted jobs tax credit designed to encourage businesses to hire individuals from certain disadvantaged groups including economically disadvantaged ex-convicts, Vietnam-era veterans, and others. There is a research and experimentation credit designed to stimulate additional spending on research. There are special percentage depletion allowances designed to encourage the domestic development of important natural resources. There is a deduction available for charitable contributions that encourages public support for such organizations as churches, universities, libraries, hospitals, and museums. Investment in small business corporations is encouraged by a provision that permits investors to treat the first $50,000 of losses on their stock as an ordinary loss rather than the less favorable capital loss. There is even a credit designed to encourage the rehabilitation of certified historic structures.

Three major difficulties have arisen in regard to the provisions that were designed to achieve economic and social objectives. First, the provisions created a much more complex tax system. Second, these tax benefits were most frequently used by wealthy taxpayers, which causes other taxpayers to pay a disproportionate share of the tax burden. Third, investment decisions were often made on the basis of tax considerations rather than on the basis of economic fundamentals. These factors caused many taxpayers to feel that the tax system was unfair. Consequently, there was an increasing problem with taxpayers who found various illegal means to reduce their tax liability.

The Tax Reform Act of 1986 [1] was designed to alter the behavior of tax evasion by simplifying the revised tax law, instilling a sense of fairness, and encouraging growth. This was accomplished in large part by the repeal of a number of provisions meant to achieve various economic and social objectives. For example, the Tax Reform Act of 1986 repealed the investment tax credit and long-term capital gain deduction. The resulting increase in the tax base permitted the tax rates to be lowered.

PSYCHOLOGICAL THEORIES OF MOTIVATIONAL STRENGTH

There are many provisions in the tax laws intended to influence behavior. The success of these provisions depends on the degree of motivational strength that they instill in taxpayers. Obviously, Congress must be aware of the factors that influence motivational strength if the tax laws are to meet their objectives. In the corporate environment, it is also important to understand how the tax laws influence the motivational strength of those who make business decisions with tax implications. For example, a tax penalty may not create the same level of motivational strength for an employee as it would for one who would actually have to pay the penalty.

The problem of how best to motivate individuals by increasing their level of motivational strength is obviously of great significance in our society. Psychological research in this area is characterized by two major approaches. The first approach assumes that individuals are motivated by the expectation of some extrinsic reward such as money or promotion. The second approach assumes that individuals are motivated not by the value of extrinsic rewards, but by the satisfaction of internal needs for achievement. J.W. Atkinson's theory of motivational strength is typical of the theories in the latter approach and will be used as a frame of reference in studying the effect of the tax laws on human behavior. [2] This theory has been selected because of the emphasis that it places on an individual's motive or need for achievement. The other approach tends to ignore this factor. However, many psychologists believe that the two different approaches to the study of motivational strength are not contradictory, but rather compatible. They believe that both the value of the extrinsic reward and the intrinsic need for achievement play a role in determining the degree of motivational strength. For this reason, although Atkinson's theory is used here as the frame of reference for understanding motivational strength, the value of the extrinsic reward will also be considered.

ATKINSON'S THEORY OF MOTIVATIONAL STRENGTH

Atkinson has theorized that the strength of motivation to perform some task is a product of three factors: motive, expectancy, and incentive. Motivational strength, therefore, could be expressed as:

$$\text{Motivational strength} = f(\text{Motive} \times \text{Expectancy} \times \text{Incentive})$$

If the value of any of the three variables is zero, then there would be no motivational strength. This is true because the formula is multiplicative rather than additive. For example, if the expectancy of success is zero, there would be no effort to perform the task in spite of high values for motive and incentive. In other words, even though an individual may have an internal motivation to achieve and may place a high value on the incentive or reward, there will be no motivational strength if there is no probability that the reward can be achieved. The same would be true for zero values of motive or incentive. As will be explained later, there is a relationship between the value of expectancy and the value of the incentive. Each of the three factors that influence motivational strength will be examined in greater detail.

MOTIVE (NEED TO ACHIEVE)

Definition of Concept

The word "motive" in the motivational strength formula refers to the individual's need for achievement. According to the theory, individuals vary in the degree to which they find achievement to be a rewarding experience. The need for achievement seems to be acquired during an individual's younger years and is thought to be relatively stable. However, as will be discussed later, there is some evidence that the need for achievement can change over time.

Atkinson states that there are basically two different types of individuals. The first type needs achievement more than he or she fears failure. The second type fears failure more than he or she needs achievement. Both types are motivated by a desire to satisfy certain needs, but they will respond differently under the same conditions.

When given a choice, or in a constrained situation, individuals with a high need for achievement will seek intermediate risks. However, the individuals with a high motive to avoid failure, when given a choice, will seek tasks with extreme probabilities. That is, they will select tasks in which the probability of success is either very high or very low. They will choose the easier tasks because there is less probability of failure . . . or they will select the very difficult tasks because there is no stigma attached to failing at a very difficult task. But when these individuals are in a constrained situation— when they cannot select from among a number of tasks—they must decide whether to pursue the task or to avoid it. If they decide to perform the task, it is assumed that they will work hard so as to avoid failure.

The hypothesis concerning the relationship between need for achievement and risk-taking has been confirmed with remarkable consistency with many different populations, situations, and measuring instruments. In one study that tested the hypothesis,[3] a group was divided into those with high "fear of failure" and those with high "hope of success." It was found that the latter group chose tasks with a high probability of success. The "fear of failure" group chose tasks with a high probability of failure on the initial trials and also on the subsequent trials.

Influencing Factors

It was noted earlier that an individual's "motive" tends to be stable over time. However, studies have been conducted that sought to establish a link between success or failure and its effect on levels of aspiration. In one experiment, [4] an intelligence test was administered to a group of undergraduate students. After the test was graded, the students were informed that their score was either above or below the average for the class. The score that they were told they had attained was not necessarily their actual score. The students were then asked to estimate the score they hoped to achieve on a second, similar examination that was to be given. A high positive correlation was found between the reported score and the new, expected score. Therefore, it appears that past performance does have an effect on aspiration levels.

Aspiration levels have also been shown to affect future performance. One study [5] found a high positive correlation between the goals of individual students and their attained grades. That is, those students who had set higher goals performed better than those who had set lower goals. Those who had set higher goals did not necessarily reach the original goals, but they still performed better.

Other researchers have sought to establish a link between success or failure and future performance. For example, one experiment [6] manipulated conditions so that certain subjects would perform well on a set of initial trials and others would not. It was found that those subjects who performed well in the initial trials performed better than the other subjects in later, unmanipulated trials. A similar study [7] gave feedback on success or failure to male subjects who had run a specified distance. The feedback was presented with reference to past performance of either the individual or the group. Those who were told that they were doing well yielded optimum athletic performance in their subsequent running.

Some sociological evidence also suggests that the typical response to failure is a decrease in the aspiration level and the typical response to success is an increase in the aspiration level.

Many studies have examined the relationship between need for achievement or aspiration level and socioeconomic status. One such study [8] found that those in the lower classes showed a significantly lower need for achievement than did those in the middle or higher classes. Perhaps those in the lower classes had experienced failure and hence lowered their aspiration levels. Another possible explanation is that parents tend to instill in their children their own levels of aspiration. Even though an individual's "motive" or aspiration level may tend to be stable, there is some evidence that successful or unsuccessful experiences can affect it.

Impact upon Tax Decisions

An appreciation of the way people's motives or need for achievement affects their motivational strength can be important in understanding or perhaps influencing the way income tax decisions are made. Questions arise in taxation for which there are no definitive answers. Frequently, there are a number of possible solutions to a tax question. Each possible solution involves varying amounts of tax liability. Generally, the solutions that incur the smallest tax have the greatest degree of risk. The solutions that incur the largest tax would be relatively risk-free. Other solutions involve intermediate levels of taxation and risk. The objective in any tax decision is to reduce the tax liability to the lowest lawful level. However, extreme positions taken to achieve this objective run the risk that the income tax return will be audited by the Internal Revenue Service and the taxpayer's position overturned. Because of interest, penalties, legal fees, and other expenses, selecting the extreme position may ultimately prove very costly.

Individuals who make tax decisions may select different alternatives because of their different motives. For example, some individuals' need for achievement is greater than their fear of failure. These people will be more likely to select alternatives involving intermediate levels of taxation and intermediate risk. Alternatively, individuals whose fear of failure is greater than their need for achievement would be more likely to select one of the very safe positions. They may also select a solution involving a great deal of risk, since no stigma is attached to failing at a very difficult task.

DIAGNOSTIC REVIEW—MOTIVE

In the case of the Bradford Lockbox Company, the disagreement about the proper solution may be related to the different "achievement motives" of the individuals. In Atkinson's theory, the motive of the individual is related to an internal disposition for achievement. His concept of motive does not include external rewards, which will be examined later. Rita Parker wants to pay a large dividend to eliminate the potential accumulated earnings tax problem. This solution involves a large tax liability and no risk. Perhaps she made this choice because she has a great fear of failure that may have been instilled in her at an early age. Also, since she is not a member of the Bradford family, Parker may feel that her position would be jeopardized by a significant failure.

John Bradford has selected the solution that involves the greatest amount of risk. He wants to do nothing about the problem and hopes that the company will not be audited by the IRS. If the company's tax return is examined by the IRS, the accumulated earnings tax issue will likely arise and the company will have a very weak defense. This could result in a substantial tax liability. Bradford may have a fear of failure since he selected an option that involves one of the extreme solutions. His fear of failure could be based on several factors. His family has been successful in this business for over 50 years, and he may have been raised with the idea that he should not fail. Also, he may feel that his position as president is based more on his family relationship than his skills.

George Long has selected the option that involves an intermediate amount of risk. He has proposed that the company formulate plans for expansion in an attempt to justify the accumulation of earnings. He may have a preference for intermediate risks because his need for achievement may be greater than his fear of failure. This need for achievement could have been instilled in him at an early age and could have been enhanced by his past success as a partner in a large national public accounting firm.

EXPECTANCY (PROBABILITY OF SUCCESS)_____

Its Impact on Motivational Strength

The word "expectancy" in the motivational strength formula simply refers to the probability of success. In effect, the greater the probability of success, the greater the motivational strength. It is a relatively simple but important variable.

The importance of this variable can be seen in an article in the *Wall Street Journal* [9] about the impact of layoffs on employees who were still working. According to traditional management philosophy, those remaining on the job would be expected to work more diligently to avoid being laid off themselves. The reporter found that just the opposite was occurring. Morale was sagging and slowdowns were occurring more frequently. Many employees who had been good or even excellent workers before the layoffs were now very poor performers.

To generalize about the situation of these employees, it is assumed that some aspect of the layoffs affected their performance. It would appear that the most significant change was the uncertainty of future employment. Uncertainty can be defined as the inability to assign probabilities to different outcomes or a lesser probability that needs can be satisfied by a given or acceptable performance.

Even though the employees valued their jobs more highly than ever, their motivational strength was lower because they perceived the goal on continued employment as somewhat unrelated to their performance.

Diagnostic Review—Expectancy

In the area of taxation, Congress and the IRS should seriously consider the impact of expectancy on the motivational strength of taxpayers. Tax laws that attempt to influence human behavior can be effective only if they instill in taxpayers high levels of motivational strength. If taxpayers feel that the reward or punishment, regardless of how severe, will not actually be imposed, then there will be only low levels of motivational strength. The failure to attain the social and economic objectives that the tax laws were designed to achieve would likely result under these circumstances.

The accumulated earnings tax is an excellent example of a tax provision involving a great deal of uncertainty. This uncertainty is present because this penalty tax is based upon a very subjective standard, and the prohibited behavior is discovered only if the corporation is audited by the IRS.

Realistically, it is impossible to assign a probability to the likelihood that the Bradford Lockbox Corporation will be forced to pay the accumulated earnings tax if it does nothing. Each person, however, has assigned some level of probability to this in arriving at his or her preferred alternative. Under these circumstances, the range of probabilities among the officers could be quite broad. This could likely account for the difference of opinion among the officers. For example, John Bradford may feel that there is little likelihood that the tax will have to be paid even if the corporation does nothing. Therefore, he opts to do nothing because the penalty tax, in his opinion, will never have to be paid.

George Long and Rita Parker have selected alternatives that involve some cost to the corporation. They may feel that there is a high degree of probability that the tax will be imposed unless the corporation does something.

INCENTIVE

Intrinsic vs. Extrinsic Incentives

The incentive variable represents the attractiveness of a specific goal—the reward that is available for accomplishing a task. Atkinson's theory states that the greater the subjective value of the reward, the greater the amount of energy that should be exerted in seeking it. This direct relationship between the value of the reward and the motivational strength is sometimes referred to as incentive theory.

In Atkinson's theory, the incentive value of success is inversely related to the expectancy or probability of success. It is assumed that more pleasure, and thus a greater reward, is derived when one succeeds at a very difficult task. Conversely, one does not derive a great deal of pleasure or reward from succeeding at a simple task. Therefore, in Atkinson's theory, the incentive value of success is highly dependent on the probability of success. Tasks that have a high probability of success generally have low incentive values associated with them: tasks that have a low probability of success have high incentive values.

Atkinson's theory considers only the intrinsic value of the reward and totally ignores extrinsic rewards such as money. This could be considered a weakness in his theory, since others have emphasized the importance of extrinsic rewards. It is likely that both intrinsic and extrinsic rewards are important in determining individuals' motivational strength. There is no need for further discussion of Atkinson's intrinsic reward concept, since it is totally dependent on the expectancy of success. However, there is a need for a closer examination of some theories of extrinsic rewards.

Extrinsic Incentives

Most psychological theories recognize that human beings have certain needs. For an extrinsic reward to be valued by an individual, it should satisfy some human need. According to A.H. Maslow, [10] there is a hierarchy of needs ranging from the physiological needs to the self-actualization needs. In his theory, the most basic needs are the most important. Then, as each level of needs is satisfied, they become less important and are no longer motivators. The new motivators are the needs on the next higher level of the hierarchy. The needs, from the lowest to highest, are physiological, safety, love, esteem, and self-actualization. Although Maslow's theory is not new, it is among the most generally accepted theories of the needs that motivate people.

Certainly not all members of society or even of a single organization would be expected to be operating on the same level of needs. In most large organizations, one would expect to find some members who have not satisfied their needs for self-actualization. In a study of U.S. Army officers, [11] it was found that the greatest needs were those pertaining to self-actualization. Also, it was found that the higher the rank, the more satisfied the individual tended to be in terms of self-actualization. In a similar study of government employees [12] in the Veterans Administration, it was found that satisfaction with the job decreased from top to lower management levels. Once again, the areas of greatest dissatisfaction were autonomy and self-actualization.

From these studies, it appears that those in different levels of an organization tend to have different needs. Of course, even individuals in the same level of the organization could have different needs.

To instill in individuals a high level of motivational strength, it is necessary to discover what needs they are attempting to satisfy. After this has been determined, the reward that would satisfy these needs is offered to the individual as an incentive. It is assumed that the individual will perform the task in an effort to receive the reward.

This theory is deeply ingrained in current organizational practices. The officers of an organization determine which rewards are important to their employees and then offer these rewards to the employees to accomplish the necessary tasks of the organization. Empirical research in this area [13] has demonstrated that the amount of effort expended by people on the job was related to the perceived value of the reward that they could receive.

The incentives in taxation often take the form of a punishment. For example, there are penalties for failure to file tax returns, failure to pay the tax, failure to make estimated tax payments, and for the omission of income from the tax return.

There is a separate body of psychological literature dealing with punishment. The threat of punishment, rather than the punishment itself, is considered more important because, if one must resort to the actual punishment, the incentive value of the threat has not been successful. In addition, there is normally a cost associated with actually imposing the punishment. A threat can be defined as an intention to do something detrimental to the interests of another. The essence of a threat is a certain required behavior and a promise of an act detrimental to the individual if the required behavior is not performed.

One study [14] has suggested that the degree of compliance to a threat depends on the credibility of the threat and the magnitude of the promised punishment. The subjects were found to comply more often when they perceived the credibility or surety of the punishment to be high. As for the magnitude of the punishment, it was reported that the more severe the promised punishment, the more likely they were to comply.

Impact upon Tax Policy

Congress is limited in the type of extrinsic incentives that it can offer to increase taxpayers' motivational strength. The incentive can take the form of a reduction or deferral of a tax liability...or, alternatively, the incentive can take the form of a penalty or other addition to the tax liability. Based on the psychological theories, the greater the value of the extrinsic reward offered by the government, the greater the motivational strength on the part of taxpayers. However, in the case of extrinsic incentives that take the form of a reduction or a deferral of the tax liability, there is a cost to the government in the form of reduced tax collections. For example, the cost of lost revenues resulting from the deductibility of interest on home mortgages, which is in large part designed to stimulate the purchase of personal residences by making home ownership more affordable, amounts to billions of dollars each year. Congress must decide what cost it is willing to incur to achieve the desired behavior on the part of taxpayers. In the case of extrinsic incentives that take the form of a penalty or addition to the tax liability, there is no financial cost to the government in the form of lost tax revenues, but normally there is a cost associated with imposing the penalty. Based on the psychological theories, one would expect that a harsher penalty would instill a greater degree of motivational strength in taxpayers.

Diagnostic Review—Incentives

In the case of the Bradford Lockbox Company, the accumulated earnings tax represents an extrinsic incentive. However, most major decisions of this type are multidimensional. That is, there is more than one extrinsic incentive. Frequently these incentives are in conflict. For example, the managers of a publicly held corporation may be considering a switch to the LIFO inventory method. The tax law requires that if LIFO is used in computing taxable income, it must also be used in computing the net income that is reported to shareholders. The managers may want to switch to the LIFO method to reduce the firm's tax liability, but they may also be motivated *not* to make the change since it will lower the earnings that are reported to the shareholders.

John Bradford has decided not to take any action with respect to the potential accumulated earnings tax. He wants to maintain the large cash reserves that are currently available to the firm. The accumulated earnings tax probably does have incentive value for him. However, other incentives may be motivating him in the opposite direction. For example, Bradford was president when the corporation was on the verge of bankruptcy. He may be strongly motivated to keep the large cash reserves intact as a hedge against future economic difficulties. The potential tax penalty associated with his preference not to distribute a dividend or take other action may not be as strong as his incentive to maintain large cash reserves as a hedge against future unfavorable economic conditions.

Rita Parker and George Long are motivated to take some kind of action to avoid the accumulated earnings tax. Several extrinsic incentives may influence their decisions. However, the incentive value of the tax may be the strongest.

Another factor to be considered in this case is the relative value of the extrinsic incentive or, more specifically, the accumulated earnings tax. It would appear that tax rates of 27 1/2 percent on the first $100,000 of accumulated taxable income and 38 1/2 percent over $100,000, in addition to the regular corporate income tax, would represent a high level of incentive. However, the problem is that the potential additional tax would be imposed on the corporation and not on the three individuals who are confronted with the problem. The accumulated earnings tax might have only a low incentive value to the three individuals who must make the decisions on the proper course of action.

John Bradford might be able to identify more closely with the interests of the corporation because he is a large shareholder. Rita Parker, who is in favor of distributing a large dividend to avoid payment of the tax, would not personally incur the tax liability. The accumulated earnings tax might have little incentive value for her. However, one would expect that, if the company were forced to pay this tax, it would reflect unfavorably on Parker, the company's tax specialist. This may explain why she is in favor of a large dividend distribution.

SUMMARY AND CONCLUSIONS

The tax laws are being used in the United States to influence human behavior. They are designed to motivate taxpayers to pay the proper amount of tax owed. Additionally, they are used to motivate taxpayers to pursue certain activities in order to achieve various economic and social objectives. The success of these measures depends on the motivational strength that they instill in taxpayers.

In this chapter, an attempt has been made to identify some of the factors that influence an individual's level of motivational strength. In this respect, behavior was analyzed using Atkinson's theory of motivational strength, which emphasizes the importance of motive, expectancy, and incentive. The role of extrinsic incentives in determining the level of motivational strength was also examined.

It should be remembered that the theories examined in this chapter are only representative of the many theories of motivational strength. An analysis of all theories dealing with this topic is well beyond the scope of this book.

The emphasis in the chapter was on individuals and the factors that motivate them. However, it should be remembered that, in the corporate environment, the individual is only one part of the total organizational system. In other words, the kinds of decisions that a person makes will also be influenced by such factors as the formal organization and the informal organization. Decisions will also be influenced by the person's status, role, and the different groups of which he or she is a member.

REFERENCES

[1] Tax Reform Act of 1986 (P.L. 99-514), 99th Cong., 2d Sess. (1986).
[2] J.W. Atkinson, "Motivational Determinants of Risk-Taking Behavior." *A The-*

ory of Achievement Motivation, edited by J.W. Atkinson and N.T. Feather (New York: Wiley, 1966).

[3]J.G. Hancock and R.C. Teevan, "Fear of Failure and Risk Taking Behavior," *Journal of Personality* 32 (1964): 200–209.

[4]D. Koulack and P.D. Peterson, "Level of Aspiration: A Function of Anchor Distance and Direction," *Journal of Social Psychology* 77 (1969): 141–142.

[5]E.A. Locke and J.F. Bryan, "Grade Goals as Determinants of Academic Achievement," *Journal of General Psychology* 79 (1968): 217–218.

[6]N.T. Feather and M.R. Saville, "Effects of Amount of Prior Success and Failure on Expectations of Success and Subsequent Task Performance," *Journal of Personality and Social Psychology* 5 (1967): 226–232.

[7]H. Harari, "Levels of Aspiration and Athletic Performance," *Perceptual & Motor Skills* 28 (1969): 519–524.

[8]P.K. Shrivastava and M.L. Tiwari, "Socioeconomic Stratification of Need Achievement," *Psychological Studies* 12 (1967): 9–16.

[9]Amal Kumar Naj, "GM Now is Plagued with Drop in Morale as Payrolls Are Cut," *The Wall Street Journal* (May 26, 1987): 1.

[10]A.H. Maslow, *Motivation and Personality* (New York: Harper and Bros., 1954), chap. 3.

[11]P.V. Johnson and R.H. Marcum, "Perceived Deficiencies in Individual Need Fulfillment of Career Army Officers," *Journal of Applied Psychology* 52 (1968): 457–461.

[12]J.B. Rhinehart, et al., "Comparative Study of Need Satisfactions in Governmental and Business Hierarchies," *Journal of Applied Psychology* 53 (1969): 230–235.

[13]E.A. Lawler and L.W. Porter, "Antecedent Attitudes of Effective Managerial Performance, *Organizational Behavior and Human Performance* 2 (1967): 122–142.

[14]J. Horai and J.T. Tedeschi, "Effects of Credibility and Magnitude of Punishment on Compliance to Threats," *Journal of Personality and Social Psychology* 12 (1969): 164–169.

SUGGESTED READINGS

Conderacci, G., "Sagging Spirits," *The Wall Street Journal* (August 6, 1970): 1.

Feather, N.T., and M.R. Saville, "Effects of Amount of Prior Success and Failure on Expectations of Success and Subsequent Task Performance," *Journal of Personality and Social Psychology* 5 (1967): 226–232.

Hancock, J.G., and R.C. Teevan, "Fear of Failure and Risk Taking Behavior," *Journal of Personality* 32 (1964): 200– 209.

Harari, H., "Levels of Aspiration and Athletic Performance," *Perceptual & Motor Skills* 28 (1969): 519–524.

Horai, J., and J.T. Tedeschi, "Effects of Credibility and Magnitude of Punishment on Compliance to Threats," *Journal of Personality and Social Psychology* 12 (1969): 164–169.

Johnson, P.V., and R.H. Marcum, "Perceived Deficiencies in Individual Need Fulfillment of Career Army Officers," *Journal of Applied Psychology* 52 (1968): 457–461.

Koulack, D., and P.D. Peterson, "Level of Aspiration: A Function of Anchor Distance and Direction," *Journal of Social Psychology* 77 (1969): 141–142.

Lawler, E.A., and L.W. Porter, "Antecedent Attitudes of Effective Managerial Performance," *Organizational Behavior and Human Performance* 2 (1967): 122–142.

Locke, E.A., and J.F. Bryan, "Grade Goals as Determinants of Academic Achievement," *Journal of General Psychology* 79 (1968): 217–218.

Rhinehart, J.B., et al., "Comparative Study of Need Satisfactions in Governmental and Business Hierarchies," *Journal of Applied Psychology* 53 (1969): 230–235.

Shrivastava, P.K., and M.L. Tiwari, "Socioeconomic Stratification of Need Achievement," *Psychological Studies* 12 (1967): 9–16.

Weinstein, M.S., "Achievement Motivation and Risk Preference," *Journal of Personality and Social Psychology* 13 (1969): 153– 172.

Winterbottom, M.R., "The Relation of Need for Achievement to Learning Experiences in Independence and Mastery," in J.W. Atkinson, *Motives in Fantasy Action and Society* (New York: Van Nostrand, 1958).

CASE 19-1: THE GRIFFITH COMPANY————————

The controller of the Griffith Company has reviewed the federal income tax return for the year just ended. This is the first year that the new lower corporate tax rates that were introduced in the Tax Reform Act of 1986 were fully effective. The controller noted that the corporation's current total tax liability was larger than the tax liability before the reduction in corporate tax rates from 46 percent to 34 percent in spite of the fact that the business had been fairly stable over the past few years. The controller observed that tax reduction resulting from the lower tax rates had been more than offset by the loss of some special tax benefits. For example, the company had lost the benefit of the investment tax credit and the allowance method of accounting for bad debts. Both of these provisions had been repealed by the Tax Reform Act of 1986. Also, much of the new equipment that the company purchased had to be depreciated over longer lives.

Required:

1. The stated purpose of the Tax Reform Act of 1986 was to create a new tax system based on fairness, growth, and simplicity. How does the elimination of special tax benefits and the reduction of corporate tax rates as demonstrated in the Griffith Company case, help to achieve these objectives?

2. Do you think that the repeal of the investment tax credit and the generally longer lives for depreciable property used in business are compatible with the goal of creating a tax system that encourages growth? Explain.

3. How might the lower marginal tax rates of the Griffith Company and its individual shareholders affect management decisions in regard to charitable contributions, investment in new property and equipment, expansion, and dividend policy?

CASE 19-2: THE WAYNE CORPORATION_____

The Wayne Corporation, a publicly held company, has since its inception used the FIFO inventory method. Under this method, the corporation includes the cost of the oldest purchases of inventory in the figure for cost of goods sold. The tax manager has suggested to the president that the company change to the LIFO method of inventory valuation. Under this method, the cost of the most recent purchases of inventory is included in the cost of goods sold. The cost of the inventory items purchased by Wayne Corporation has steadily increased over time. The change to the LIFO method would result in a reduction of the company's tax liability since the most recent higher inventory costs are being deducted on the tax return.

The tax manager states that the IRS will grant permission to make the change provided that the company also adopts the LIFO inventory method for all financial reports. It is estimated that the effect of the change in inventory method will cause reported net income to show a slight decline for the current year instead of the small increase that was projected earlier. The president is fearful that the shareholders will think that the decline in profits is due to management incompetence.

Required:

1. Why does the IRS require that the LIFO inventory method also be used for reporting to shareholders if it is used for tax purposes?

2. How much incentive value does a reduction in the corporate tax liability have for a professional manager who owns none of the common stock of the employer company?

3. What can publicly held companies do to make the managers' interests compatible with the corporate interests?

CASE 19-3: THE STINSON COMPANY_____

The Stinson Company is engaged in the manufacture of personal computers. The company has previously reported annual profits of approximately

$6,000,000, but last year reported only $1,000,000 because of the highly competitive nature of the personal computer market. The marketing director of the company believes that sales have fallen because the engineers have been slow to improve its product through technological innovation. He argues that a major research effort is needed to enhance the capabilities of the company's computers. The president of the company would like to improve the product, but is fearful that the company lacks the financial resources to fund a major research effort in a time of declining sales. He feels that the company would need to spend an additional $500,000 this year on research to upgrade the product. He asks the treasurer to prepare an analysis of the after-tax cost associated with an additional research effort of $500,000.

The treasurer prepares a report that shows two major tax provisions dealing with research and experimentation costs. First, research costs can be expensed immediately. Second, a tax credit is available for research and experimentation costs. The credit is calculated by multiplying the increase in research costs by 20 percent. The increase in research costs is calculated by comparing the current research costs for the year to the average research costs for the three previous years. The company has incurred average research costs of $700,000 during the past three years.

The treasurer informs the president that if the company spends an additional $500,000 in research activities this year, the after-tax cost of the additional $500,000 will be only $230,000 due to tax savings of $270,000 that are associated with the project. The tax savings are composed of the following:

Tax Savings

An increase in deductible research expenses of $500,000 × 34 percent, which is the company's marginal income tax rate $170,000

The research and experimentation credit of $100,000, which is the increase in research costs of $500,000 × 20 percent 100,000

Total tax savings $270,000

Required:

1. What is the policy justification for the immediate expensing of research and experimentation costs?
2. What is the policy justification for the research and experimentation credit?
3. In the Stinson Company case, how will the tax effects influence the decision whether or not to undertake the major research project?

CASE 19-4: THE RICHMOND MANUFACTURING COMPANY_____

The Richmond Manufacturing Company purchased 100 acres of land about eight years ago as a future site for a new manufacturing facility. It was later determined by the board of directors that the site was not needed, and the company decided to donate the land to the county for use as a park. The company had paid $250,000 for the land, but assigned a fair market value of $1,500,000 in determining the deduction for tax purposes. However, the company's tax return was audited, and the IRS agent disallowed $300,000 of the charitable deduction, arguing that the fair market value of the land was only $1,200,000. An appeals conference with the Internal Revenue Service failed to resolve the dispute.

The corporate tax department consists of a manager and two tax specialists. The tax manager was interested in obtaining the opinions of both tax specialists in regard to the proper course of action. There are significant differences between the two top specialists in terms of education, age, and experience. One is 25 years old and joined the company two years ago after earning a master of taxation degree. The other tax specialist, who has been with the company for 30 years and is approaching retirement, earned a college degree in accounting ten years ago by attending school part-time in an evening program. The tax manager sent both tax specialists the identical note explaining the situation and asked for their opinion.

The alternatives available to the company are (1) to pay the additional tax and not litigate the dispute, (2) to pay the additional tax but sue for a refund in a U.S. District Court or the U.S. Claims Court, or (3) to refuse to pay the tax but plan on taking the case to the U.S. Tax Court.

Required:

1. Do you think the two tax specialists will make the same recommendation?
2. If different recommendations are made by the two specialists, what factors could account for the different recommendations?

CHAPTER 20

Human Resource Accounting: An Overview

by
Eric Flamholtz
Professor of Management
Graduate School of Management, UCLA

During the late 1960s, managers, behavioral scientists, financial analysts, and accountants became increasingly interested in the idea of accounting for people as organizational resources. Initially, the notion was to "put people on the balance sheet" because it was recognized that people are valuable resources and corporate financial reports are deficient if they do not reflect the status of human assets.[1] More recently, there has been a growing trend towards developing methods of accounting for human resources as managerial tools rather than for purposes of financial reporting. Some business organizations have already begun to develop systems of accounting for their human resources.[2]

This chapter is intended as an introduction to human resource accounting as a managerial tool.

BUSINESS DILEMMA

Excellent Electronics Company was formed in 1965 to develop and manufacture new types of electronic home entertainment products. Their first product was audio equipment. After 1975, video equipment was added to the firm's product line.

The firm's president, Sanford Harris, anticipated a growing market for the company's products because of the increased affluence of U.S. consumers and the dramatic increase in demand for consumer electronics such as calculators, microcomputers, and video equipment. From its inception in 1965 through 1980, the company experienced rapid growth. Sales in 1965 were $600,000 and in 1980 they exceeded $300 million.

During this period, the firm's work force increased to approximately 2,500, including 150 managers. Many of its workers were highly skilled and Harris felt that an effectively functioning "team" had been put together. As he stated:

> Our first fifteen years were quite successful. Not only our profitability increased, but we have developed a first-rate manage-

ment and work force. And after all, in addition to our reputation, people are our most valuable asset.

In January 1981, the company began to experience decreasing sales. For the year as a whole, forecasted sales were only $290 million, and the company was incurring increasing costs. In March, Harris expressed concern that profits would be significantly affected:

> If present trends continue for the rest of the year, we're really going to be hurting. We may, in fact, have to perform some surgery on the organization. We've got a lot of fixed costs in salaried personnel and we may have to lay off some of the work force and have the rest make up the slack. I hope we don't have to go that far.

By May 1981, business conditions had not improved, and Harris asked the company's controller, Carla Prizzi, to estimate the payroll savings from a layoff of 10 percent of the work force for periods of three, six, nine, and twelve weeks. The controller's estimate is shown in Table 20-1. The national sales manager estimated that seasonal sales would increase in twelve to fourteen weeks and most of the employees would be rehired at that time.

Before making a decision, Harris called a meeting of top management on May 12, 1981. The financial vice-president, Carter Roberts, agreed with the controller's estimates and felt that a layoff of nine weeks would substantially improve the firm's profit for the year. He stated:

> We need a layoff of nine weeks to save $1,050,000. That would make the bottom line look reasonable for the year.

However, the personnel manager, Jayne Barker, objected to the layoff decision. She argued that:

> A layoff will hurt us in the long run more than it will help us today. We've built a good organization, but a layoff will hurt morale. In addition, we will need these people by the end of

TABLE 20-1
Estimate of Payroll Savings from Layoff of 10 Percent of Work Force

Layoff Period (weeks)	Payroll Savings
3	$ 350,000
6	700,000
9	1,050,000
12	1,400,000

August. But by that time, some will have found jobs elsewhere and we won't be able to get them back. If we have to recruit, hire, and train replacements for many people who do not return, we will have substantial costs.

The president listened intently to the personnel manager's arguments, then turned to the controller: "What do you think about this, Carla?" The controller replied:

Well, it makes sense to me, but none of Jayne's arguments are backed by specifics. I *know* we can save $1,050,000 for a nine-week layoff—less of course, the costs Jayne has mentioned. But we don't know how much those costs would be. I suppose we will just have to factor them as an intangible into our final decision.

The president decided to postpone a decision until Barker could "put some numbers in her arguments." Barker was scheduled to report back to the executive committee on May 19.

The business dilemma faced by Excellent Electronics Company is one that is typical for many corporations in the United States. The key issue in the situation involves the cost and value of people to the organization. The solution to the dilemma involves the application of the concepts and methods of the field that has come to be called *human resource accounting* (HRA).

HUMAN RESOURCE ACCOUNTING: SIX BASIC QUESTIONS

This chapter presents the basic concepts and methods of human resource accounting. It deals with six basic questions:

1. What is "human resource accounting"?
2. What is the history of human resource accounting from 1960 to the present?
3. What is its role in managing people?
4. How can we account for human resources?
5. What are the practical applications of HRA?
6. What should an organization do to account for its human resources?

The chapter will conclude with a further discussion of the Excellent Electronics case to illustrate the application of HRA concepts.

CONCEPT OF HUMAN RESOURCE ACCOUNTING

Human resource accounting (HRA) has been defined by the American Accounting Association's Committee on Human Resource Accounting as "the process of identifying and measuring data about human resources and communicating this information to interested parties."[3]

In a literal sense, "human resource accounting" means accounting for people as an organizational resource. It involves measuring the costs incurred by business firms and other organizations to recruit, select, hire, train, and develop human assets. It involves measuring what it would cost to replace an organization's human resources. It also involves measuring the economic value of people to organizations. Thus, human resource accounting means measuring the investment made by organizations in people, the cost of replacing those people, and the value of people to the enterprise.

The term "human resource accounting" should not only be viewed literally, for it also has a figurative or symbolic meaning. It is not only a system of measuring the cost and value of people to organizations: it is also a way of thinking about the management of people. It suggests the need to think of people as valuable organizational resources—ones whose value may be appreciated or depleted as a result of the ways in which they are managed.

HISTORY OF HUMAN RESOURCE ACCOUNTING

The field of human resource accounting has been developing since the 1960s. The field is an outgrowth of the convergence of several independent but closely related streams of thought; it is also a response to the fundamental metamorphosis of the United States postindustrial economy into a service economy. All this has led to the increasing recognition that human capital or human assets are the distinctive feature of today's economy and a major part of today's organizational assets.

Growing Recognition of Importance of Human Assets

The United States is now experiencing a fundamental restructuring of its economy.[4] Specifically, the economy is in the process of a qualitative transformation from an industrial economy to a service-based economy, just as there was once a transformation from an agricultural economy to an industrial economy. This transformation, which began about at the end of World War II, has led to changes in the composition of the labor force not only in the sectors in which people are employed, but in the types and levels of skills demanded.

At present, we are rapidly becoming a knowledge-based economy and the services provided are becoming what can be described as high-technology services. These services are the product of considerable amounts of training and experience. Thus, the economy is increasingly comprised of white collar, technical, and professional personnel. The distinctive feature of the emerging economy is that there is an increasing emphasis upon human capital (the knowledge, skills, and experience of people) rather than physical capital. A related attribute is that the development of human capital is costly and requires significant investments both by individuals and the organizations that employ them.

Impetus for Development of Human Resource Accounting

Under agricultural and industrial economic structures, the extent of human capital was significantly less than it is today. The theories and methods of accounting did not treat either people or investments in people as assets (with the exception of slaves, who were viewed as property). However, with the increasing importance of human capital at the level of the economy as a whole, as well as at the level of the individual firm, a great deal of research has been designed to develop concepts and methods of accounting for people as assets. This field, described below, has come to be known as "human resource accounting" (HRA).

HRA is, at least in part, a recognition that people comprise human capital or human assets. The economic theory of human capital is based upon the concept that people possess skills, experience, and knowledge that are a form of capital, termed "human capital." Thus, Theodore Schultz, whose work on the economic theory of human capital has received the Nobel Prize, has stated, "laborers have become capitalists not from a diffusion of the ownership of corporation stocks as folklore would have it, but from the acquisition of knowledge and skills that have economic value."[5] In a review of the history of the development of the economic theory of human capital, Kiker indicated that the list of early economists who had recognized that human capital exists included Adam Smith, Petty, Say, Senior, Lists, Von Thunon, Roscher, Walras, and Fischer.[6] The two methods used by economists to measure the amounts of human capital were based upon cost-of-production and capitalized-earnings procedures.

Human resource accounting has also developed from a parallel tradition in personnel management known as the "human resources school," which is based upon the premise that people are valuable organizational resources and therefore should be managed as such. Personnel theorists such as Odiorne and organizational psychologists such as Likert have treated people as valuable organizational resources in their work.[7] For example, in his book, *The*

Human Organization: Its Management and Value, the late organizational theorist Rensis Likert states, "every aspect of a firm's activities is determined by the competence, motivation, and general effectiveness of its human organization."[8]

There is also support among some of the early accounting theorists for treating people as assets and accounting for their value, even before the nature of our economic structure changed and human capital increased in importance. For example, D.R. Scott noted, "A trained force of technical operatives is always a valuable asset."[9] Similarly, W.A. Paton has stated, "in a business enterprise a well-organized and loyal personnel may be a much more important asset than a stock of merchandise."[10]

In addition to academic theorists, practicing managers have for some time recognized the importance of human assets. For example, the 1966 annual report of Uniroyal stated: "our primary resource is people. We are essentially a collection of skills—the varied expertise of our 68,000 employees. . .Uniroyal has plants and has capital, but most of all, it has people."[11]

Taken together, these various streams of thought all led to the conclusion that organizations possess a valuable asset in the people who are in its employ, and that the people themselves are a form of capital—human capital. During the 1960s, this recognition led to both academic research and business development of concepts and methods of measuring the cost and value of people as organizational assets, or the field that is today known as human resource accounting.

Early Research in Human Resource Accounting

One of the earliest approaches for measuring and accounting for the value of human resources was developed by R.H. Hermanson, an academic accountant, as part of his Ph.D. dissertation. It was later published as a monograph in 1964 under the title "Accounting for Human Assets."[12] Hermanson's principal concern was that conventional financial statements fail to adequately reflect the financial position of a firm because they do not include human assets. Hermanson developed "the unpurchased goodwill method" to measure the value of human assets a firm has developed through the normal course of operations (recruiting, training, etc.) as opposed to those that have been purchased through one firm's acquisition of another.

In 1966, a group of researchers consisting of R.L. Brummet, E.G. Flamholtz, and W.C. Pyle began a program of research on human resource accounting at the University of Michigan.[13] This research was designed to develop concepts, models, and techniques of measuring and accounting for the cost and value of human assets. They also set out to develop possible applications for such measurements. This research led to a variety of theoretical concepts and models as well as applications of these approaches in actual organizations.

Under the direction of William C. Pyle, the R.G. Barry Corporation, headquartered in Columbus, Ohio, made the first reported attempt to develop a system of accounting for a firm's investment in people.[14] This system was intended for managerial rather than financial reporting purposes.

The first experimentation in an actual organization with the measurement of the value of human resources was done by Eric G. Flamholtz as the basis for his doctoral dissertation, "The Theory and Measurement of An Individual's Value to An Organization."[15] In his dissertation, Flamholtz developed a theoretical model for the measurement of an individual's value to an organization. This model was termed "The Stochastic Rewards Valuation Model." This model, which was later refined and published in an article in *The Accounting Review* as well as in Flamholtz's subsequent book, *Human Resource Accounting*, is described in the section on Measurement of Human Resource Cost and Value in this chapter.[16]

Subsequent Research on Human Resource Accounting

Since the early studies by Hermanson, Brummet, Flamholtz, and Pyle, there has been a considerable body of theoretical and empirical research to develop concepts, models, and methods of accounting for people as organizational assets. The field as a whole has come to be known as "human resource accounting." The state of the art of the field is described in an article published by E.G. Flamholtz in volume 1 of *Annual Accounting Reviews* in 1979.[17]

HUMAN RESOURCE ACCOUNTING'S MANAGERIAL ROLE

A major purpose of human resource accounting is to serve as a system for providing measurements of the cost and value of people to an organization. From a managerial perspective, human resource accounting is intended to help decision makers use a cost-value calculus—that is, an assessment of the costs and value involved in a decision.

Measurement of the cost and value of human resources are needed (1) to facilitate personnel planning and decision making by personnel management staff and (2) to enable top management to evaluate the effectiveness with which human resources have been developed, conserved, and utilized by lower levels of management (especially in large, decentralized companies). More specifically, management needs measurements of the cost and value of human resources to make decisions in all phases of the human resource management process: acquisition, development, allocation, conservation, utilization, evaluation, and rewards of human resources.

Acquisition of Human Resources

The acquisition of human resources involves recruiting, selecting, and hiring people to meet the organization's present and expected future manpower needs. The first step in human resource acquisition is to forecast manpower requirements; when they have been forecasted, management must translate its personnel needs into a "personnel acquisition budget." This is essentially a process of cost estimation.

Human resource accounting can be useful in budgeting personnel acquisition. It can provide measurements of the standard costs of recruiting, selecting, and hiring people, which can be used to prepare proposed manpower acquisition budgets.

Personnel selection is another process in which human resource accounting can play a role. In making selection decisions, managers need measurements of the economic value of alternative job candidates. A personnel manager, for example, faced with a choice among several attractive candidates for a job, would ideally like to choose the person possessing the greatest future value to the organization. However, measurements of the expected value of people are not presently available except in terms of nonmonetary surrogates such as scores on tests of "managerial potential." Thus, if monetary measurements of the expected value of people were available, personnel managers could use decision rules for employee selection designed to optimize the expected value of an organization's human resources.

Acquisition and Development Policy

By providing estimates of the current costs to acquire and develop people for various positions, human resource accounting can help management assess the trade-offs between the cost of recruitment from outside and development from within. Thus, it provides the economic information management needs to assist in formulating personnel acquisition and development policies.

Allocation of Human Resources

The allocation of human resources is the process of assigning people to various organizational roles and tasks. There are several, sometimes conflicting, objectives involved in allocation decisions. First, the task to be performed should be completed in the most efficient way. This may mean that management will allocate the "most qualified" person to a particular job. In addition, however, an organization's human resources must be developed, so management may wish to provide people with the opportunity to develop their skills thorough on-the-job learning. This suggests that the "most qualified" (experienced) person may not be assigned to a task. Third, management wants to allocate people to jobs that satisfy their needs. Ideally, then, management allocates people to jobs in a way that will optimize three variables: job productivity, human resource development, and individual satisfaction.

Human resource accounting can help quantify the variables involved in the allocation decision and express them in the common denominator of monetary units. This will help management understand the tradeoffs involved in allocation decisions and facilitate selection of the optimal course of action. For example, linear programming might be used to determine the optimal solution to the manpower allocation problem.

Conservation of Human Resources

Conservation of human resources is the process of maintaining the capabilities of people as individuals and the effectiveness of the human system developed by an organization. Failure to measure the extent to which human resources are being conserved in a division, plant, or department can be costly to an organization. In the short run, for example, a division manager may put pressure on people to temporarily increase their productivity or reduce costs, but may not measure the effects on employee motivation, attitudes, and labor relations. As a result, highly trained and skilled employees could become dissatisfied and leave an organization. The cost of replacing them may be substantial.

An organization must account for its human assets in order to prevent their depletion. Managers must be held accountable for conservation of the human resources allocated to them. Currently, the conservation of human resources is measured in terms of turnover rates. Measures of turnover, however, are inadequate indicators of human resource conservation for two reasons. First, they are historical and therefore unavailable to management until after turnover has occurred. Thus, they cannot be used as an early warning signal to suggest the need for special efforts at conservation. Second, turnover rates do not fully represent the economic impact of turnover, which is more realistically demonstrated by monetary measure.

Human resource accounting can assist management in conserving its human organization by providing an early warning system. It can measure and report social-psychological indicators of the condition of the human organization. Management can then anticipate trends in these variables prior to the actual occurrence of turnover or decreased productivity. Corrective actions can thus be taken before rather than after the fact.

Utilization of Human Resources

Human resource utilization is the process of using human services to achieve organizational objectives. Human resource accounting can help managers effectively and efficiently utilize human resources by providing a paradigm or conceptual framework for human resource utilization.

At present, the management of human resources in organizations is less effective than it might be because it lacks a unifying framework to guide it. Managers have neither a valid criterion to guide decisions affecting people nor a methodology for assessing the anticipated or actual consequences of such decisions. Clearly, the criteria of productivity and satisfaction have not been entirely helpful in coping with problems of managing people. Similarly, it is exceedingly difficult to measure productivity and satisfaction or to assess the rational tradeoffs a manager should be willing to make to increase one by decreasing the other. Therefore, it's not often possible to predict the economic consequences of alternative actions with respect to people.

The notion of "human resource value" provides one possible solution to these problems. It can serve as the *raison d'etre* of human resource management; it can simultaneously provide the goal and the criterion for the management of human resources. More specifically, the aim of human resource management can be viewed as the need to contribute to the value of the organization as a whole by optimizing the value of its human assets; the effectiveness criterion can be the measured change in the value of the organization's human resources.

If the aim of human resource management is seen as the optimization of human resource value, then task design, selection, role assignment, development, performance appraisal, and compensation are not merely a set of service functions to be performed. Instead, they are a set of available strategies that can be adopted to change the value of human assets and thus the value of the organization as a whole.

What does this mean for a manager? It means that the manager will have a theoretical framework to guide his thoughts, actions, and decisions in regard to people. The framework or paradigm posits that the ultimate guide to decision making involving people is the extent to which human resource value is optimized. It also means that the manager will receive measurements of the extent to which his ultimate objective is being achieved—that is, the degree to which the value of people to the organization is being optimized.

Evaluation and Reward of Human Resources

Human resource evaluation is the process of assessing the value of people to an organization. It involves measuring the productivity (performance) and promotability of people.

At present, human resources are typically evaluated by non-monetary methods. These methods, however, cannot be used in most of the human resource acquisition, development, allocation, and conservation problems and decisions cited above; monetary methods of human resource evaluation are needed instead.

Human resource accounting can be useful in the human resource evaluation process by developing valid and reliable methods of measuring the value of people to an organization. These methods will include both monetary and nonmonetary measurements. They will permit human resource management decisions to be made on a cost-value basis.

Human resource valuation will also have an impact on the administration of human resource reward systems. These systems are intended to motivate and reinforce the optimal performance of people in achieving organization objectives. "Rewards" include compensation, promotion, and symbolic "rewards" such as performance appraisals. Human resource valuation will permit organizational rewards to be administered in relation to a person's value to an organization. It will enable management, for example, to ultimately base compensation decisions on the value of people to a firm.

Human resource accounting can also be used to evaluate the efficiency of the personnel management function per se. It can help establish standard costs of acquiring and developing people and these standards can be compared with the actual costs the personnel department incurs in performing its acquisition and development functions. The variances (deviations) from standard may be analyzed to identify possible inefficiencies in the manpower acquisition and development process.

MEASUREMENT OF HUMAN RESOURCE COST AND VALUE

The prior discussion suggested how human resource accounting might be useful in managing people. This section briefly identifies and describes the concepts and methods that have been developed to actually account for the cost and value of human resources.[18]

Measuring Human Resource Costs

Three different concepts have been proposed for the measurement of human resource costs: original cost, replacement cost, and opportunity cost. "Original cost" is the actual, historical outlay incurred as an investment in resources. "Replacement cost" is the sacrifice (cost) that would have to be incurred today to replace an organization's resources. "Opportunity cost" is the maximum amount that resources could earn in an alternative use.

Original Cost

The original cost of human resources refers to the sacrifice that was actually incurred to acquire and develop people. This is analogous to the concept of original cost for other assets. For example, the original cost of plant and equipment is the cost incurred to acquire these resources.

The original cost of human resources typically includes costs of recruitment, selection, hiring, placement, orientation, and on-the-job training, as shown in Figure 20-1. Some of these items are direct costs while others are indirect costs. For example, costs of hiring and placement are direct costs while portions of the cost of a supervisor's time during training is an indirect cost.

Replacement Cost

The replacement cost of human resources refers to the sacrifice that would have to be incurred today to replace human resources presently employed. For example, if an individual were to leave an organization, costs would have to be incurred to recruit, select, and train a replacement.

The replacement cost of human resources typically includes the costs attributable to the turnover of a present employee as well as the costs of acquiring and developing a replacement, as shown in Figure 20-2. It includes both direct and indirect costs. Since replacement costs are intended for managerial uses, they should include opportunity as well as outlay cost components.

Opportunity Cost

The opportunity cost of human resources refers to the value of human resources in their most favorable alternative use. Although nominally a cost concept, this notion of human resource cost is closely related to the idea of human resource value. Hekimian and Jones, who proposed the concept, have suggested a system of competitive bidding to measure it.[19]

FIGURE 20-1
Model for Measurement of Original Human Resource Costs

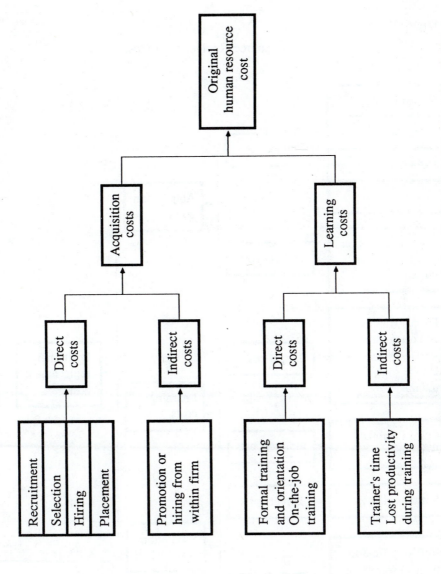

Source: Eric Flamholtz, *Human Resource Accounting* (San Francisco, Cal.: Jossey-Bass Publishers, 1985), 37.

FIGURE 20-2
Model for Measurement of Resource Replacement Costs

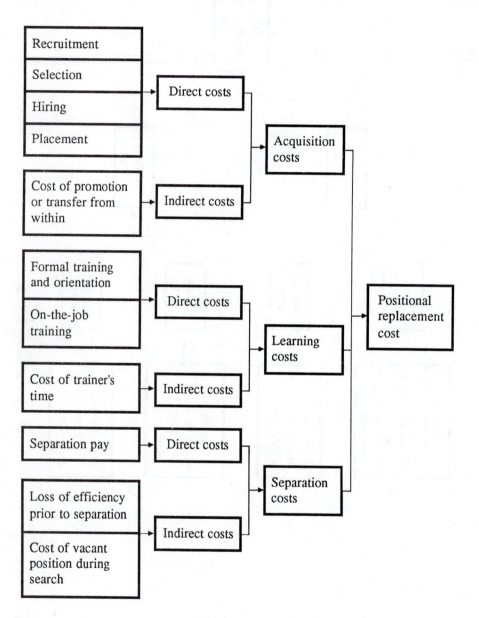

Source: Eric Flamholtz, *Human Resource Accounting* (San Francisco, Cal.: Jossey-Bass Publishers, 1985), 37.

Measuring Human Resource Value

The problems of accounting for human resource value are significantly different from those of measuring costs. The measurement of cost involves tracing costs and accumulating them. It is, to a great extent, a historical process. Value is oriented to the future, not to the past. It thus requires forecasts and is inherently uncertain.

The concept of "human value" is derived from general economic theory.[20] Like all resources, people possess value because they are capable of rendering future services. Thus, the value of human resources, like the value of other resources, may be defined as the present (discounted) worth of their expected future services. This concept of human resource value can be applied to individuals, groups, and the total human system.

In developing human resource accounting, both monetary and nonmonetary measures of the value of people have been proposed. Monetary measures are needed because money is the common denominator of business decisions. Nonmonetary measures are needed both because they are sometimes more appropriate than monetary measures and because they can serve as surrogates (proxies) when monetary measures are unavailable.

Nonmonetary Measurement of Human Value

Rensis Likert and David Bowers have formulated a model to explain the effectiveness of human systems and the organization as a whole.[21] They have suggested that the measurement of certain dimensions of a human organization (such as managerial leadership, organizational climate, and group process) by means of survey research techniques may be used to obtain estimated changes in the productive capability of an organization.

While Likert and Bowers have focused on groups, Flamholtz has attempted to develop a model explaining the determinants of an individual's value to an organization.[22] The model, shown in Figure 20-3, identified the economic, social, and psychological factors that determine a person's value to a firm. It is based on the premise that a person's value is a product of the attributes he brings to an organization (such as traits, skills, and motivation) and the characteristics of the organization itself (such as its structure, reward system, management style, and role descriptions).

Monetary Measurement of Human Value

Several methods for measuring the monetary value of human resources have been proposed. Some are intended to measure human value directly, while others are intended as surrogate or proxy measures.

Brummet, Flamholtz, and Pyle have suggested a direct approach to measuring a group's value.[23] Their method involves forecasting a firm's

FIGURE 20-3
Revised Model of the Determinants of an Individual's Value to a Formal Organization

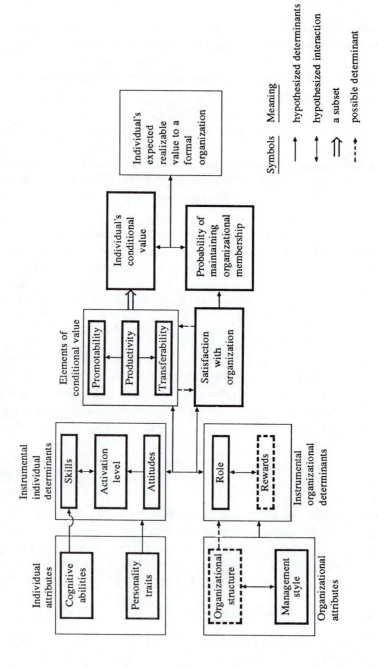

Source: Eric Flamholtz. "Assessing the Validity of a Theory of Human Resource Value: A Field Study," *Empirical Research in Accounting: Selected Studies, 1972,* supplement to vol. 10 of the *Journal of Accounting Research,* p. 257.

future earnings, discounting them to determine the firm's present value, and then allocating a portion to human resources based upon their relative contribution.

Flamholtz has focused on the problem of measuring an individual's value to an organization, which he has conceptualized as a "stochastic" process with rewards.[24] He has also presented a "stochastic rewards" model for the monetary valuation of individuals. The model, shown schematically in Figure 20-4, is based on the notion that a person is not valuable to an organization in the abstract, but in relation to the roles (services states) he is expected to occupy. Thus, a person is engaged in a process of movement among organizational service states through time. If the individual occupies a service state for a specified time period, the organization derives a given amount of services. Since the states that people will occupy in the future cannot be known with certainty, we must measure the mathematical expectation of a person's services. Thus, to measure an individual's value to an organization, we must: (1) estimate the time period during which the person is expected to render services to an organization; (2) identify the service states that the person may occupy; (3) measure the value derived by the organization if the

---

FIGURE 20-4

Three-Dimensional Representation of the Mobility Experiment as a Stochastic Process with Service Rewards

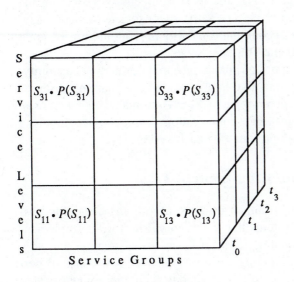

---

individual occupies the state for a specified time period; and (4) estimate the probability that a person will occupy each state at specified future times. The result is a direct measure of the person's expected value to an organization.

Hermanson has proposed two possible techniques for developing surrogate measures of the monetary value of "human resources": (1) the unpurchased goodwill method and (2) the adjusted present value method.[25] The former involves forecasting future earnings and allocating any excess above normal expected earnings for an industry to human resources. The approach is based on the premise that human resources are responsible for differences in earning among firms. The latter method is more accurately labeled "the adjusted discounted future wages method." It involves using the present value of the stream of future wage payments to people, adjusted by a performance efficiency factor, as a proxy measure of human resource value.

Lev and Schwartz have also proposed using discounted future compensation as a surrogate measure of human resource value.[26] They have suggested that their method can be aggregated to value groups and the total human organization.

A CONTINUUM OF HUMAN RESOURCE ACCOUNTING SYSTEMS

Different organizations require different degrees of human resource accounting capability. One firm may require only the most rudimentary system, while only the most advanced capability may be satisfactory for another company. Similarly, the human resource accounting capability appropriate for a firm at one stage may be quite inadequate at a later stage.

To illustrate the different types of human resource accounting capability, Table 20-2 presents a continuum of five human resource accounting systems. This table shows various functions of human resource management (human resource planning, decision making, conservation, etc.) and the human resource accounting capabilities provided by each system level.

Human Resource Accounting System I

An organization with a System I human resource accounting capability possesses most of the personnel systems that are *prerequisite* for the implementation of human resource accounting. System I consists of nominal but very elementary human resource accounting capability; that is, it consists of personnel systems that are aimed at the same functions of more sophisticated human resource accounting systems, but which lack the advanced capabilities.

This is the stage of most well-managed large and medium-sized corporations. Examples are numerous and probably include most, if not all, of the so-called "Fortune 500," the largest U.S. corporations.

Human Resource Accounting System II

In a System II organization, the human resource planning function incorporates estimates of costs of recruitment and training. Personnel costs are budgeted separately and not merely lumped in "General and Administrative" expenses. Personnel policy decisions are based on a cost-value calculus. For example, personnel selection decisions are based on such critieria as a person's expected value to the firm. Decision makers are more aware of the trade-offs between one person with a high expected conditional value and another with a high expected realizable value. In a System II organization, management not only has data on turnover rates, it also had data on the *cost* of turnover. Thus, turnover is expressed as a more meaningful common denominator. Attitudinal data, such as measures of satisfaction and perceived motivation, are available and they are used as leading indicators to forecast probable changes in turnover. Under System II, human resource evaluation is based on criteria of perceived value, which are obtained by alternation-ranking (totem pole) methods. The efficiency of the human resource management process is assessed and reports compare actual costs with historical costs of similar activities.

This system is thus based primarily upon accounting for the historical cost of human resources. Several organizations have engaged in experiments to develop this degree of human resource accounting capability. They include Honeywell-Bull, Elf Petroleum, AT&T, R.G. Barry Corporation, Touche Ross and Company, and Rank-Xerox.

Human Resource Accounting System III

Under System III, there is intermediate human resource accounting capability. Human resource planning incorporates replacement costs as well as original costs. Budgetary and policy decision making for human resources are subject to more systematic analysis. There is a formal system for budgeting recruitment, training, and the like. Personnel needs are planned as a formal part of overall corporate planning and not just on an ad-hoc basis. Policy decisions involving trade-offs between human resource variables are subjected to analyses. For example, the choice between recruitment of experienced workers versus hiring and training entry-level personnel is subjected to trade-off analysis. In System III, the replacement cost of turnover is measured and

TABLE 20-2
Human Resource Accounting Systems I–V

Human Resources Management Functions	System I Prerequisite Personnel System	System II Basic HRA System	System III Intermediate HRA System	System IV Advanced HRA System	System V Total HRA System
I. Human Resource Planning	Personnel skills inventory Replacement tables	Estimated costs of recruiting, training, etc.	Replacement costs	Standard and actual personnel costs Stochastic personnel mobility models Personnel simulations	Stochasic rewards valuation model Human resource value simulations
II. Human Resource Decision making: A. Budgetary	Personnel Costs included in "General and Administrative" expense	Personnel costs budgeted separately	Budgetary system for recruitment, training, etc. Budget replacement costs	Budget standard and actual costs Original and replacement costs	Human capital budgeting Budget ROI on human capital investment

B. Policy	Traditional selection, training, and placement methods	Value oriented selection decisions	Recruitment vs. training trade-off analyses	Personnel assignment optimization models	Value-based compensation
III. Human Resources Conservation: A. After-the-fact	Turnover rates	Turnover cost	Replacement cost	Opportunity cost	Human resource value depletion
B. Before-the-fact	N.A.	Attitudinal data	Expected turnover cost (replacement)	Expected opportunity costs; Human resource accountability	Expected conditional and realizable value depletion
IV. Human Resource Evaluation	Performance and potential ratings	Perceived value rankings	Psychometric predictions of potential value; Interval scaling of value	Measurements of economic value of groups	Measurement of economic value of individuals
V. Human Resource Management Efficiency Control	N.A.	Comparison of actual costs with historical costs	Comparison of budgeted and actual costs; Variance analysis	Comparison of actual costs against standard; Variance analysis	Interunit comparison of costs

Source: Flamhortz, Eric G., *Human Resource Accounting* (San Francisco: Jossey-Bass Publishers, Inc., 1985).

reported. Managers may be requested to explain controllable turnover. The human resource evaluation process is based on psychometric predictions of a person's potential; value is then assessed in nonmonetary terms using interval scaling methods. The efficiency of the overall human resource management process is based on a comparison of budgeted and actual personnel costs and explanations of variances are required.

In one firm, a U.S. insurance company, the data derived from a System III capability was used to evaluate the efficiency of personnel planning policies and practices. For example, there was a significant difference between standard personnel replacement costs and anticipated replacement costs. Upon investigation, these differences were traced to inadequate staffing practices.

In another organization, AT&T, an attempt is being made to measure the replacement cost of personnel to help control personnel turnover. Flanders reports that AT&T has developed a system of "human resource accountability" that is intended to:

> . . . increase managerial effectiveness in developing and retraining employees. It accomplishes this by treating employee-replacement costs (hiring, training, benefits, etc.) as if they were capital investment rather than operating expense, and holding managers directly accountable for those segments as the investment that fall within their area of responsibility.[27]

In another firm, a large multinational chemical company, the replacement cost of personnel is measured and used in personnel planning. Similarly, the executive vice-president of a large aerospace corporation once described how his firm had made faulty layoff decisions because of the failure to take into account replacement costs. He states that the decision would have been reversed if such costs had been recognized.

Human Resources Accounting System IV

An organization with a System IV capability has an advanced human resource accounting system. In such organizations, human resource planning is based on standard personnel costs. Stochastic models are used to forecast personnel mobility and predict future human resource needs. The computer is used to run human resource planning simulations: parameters in the models are varied so that sensitivity analyses can be performed. In the decision-making process, budgets are based on standard costs. Optimization models are used for personnel policy decisions. For example, personnel assignment may be based on optimization methods. Human resource conservation is assessed not only in terms of historical and replacement cost, but also in terms of the opportunity of human resources. The organization has an ongoing system of human resource accountability and one criterion used to evaluate managers is human resource conservation. The firm also has an ongoing turnover control program and it uses measures of expected opportunity cost of turnover as a basis for turnover control decisions. Under System IV, the organization accounts for the value of groups of people but not individuals. The efficiency of the human resource management process is evaluated by comparing actual costs against standard and there is a formal system for reporting and explaining variances.

System IV is based upon the use of opportunity costs. At present, no firms have developed such a capability, although a few have developed aspects of the system. For example, an office of Touche Ross & Company has used opportunity costs in accounting for its investment in people. Other firms, including a large multilocation corporation engaged in the manufacture and marketing of a wide variety of electrical products, have developed stochastic manpower mobility models. Such corporations have the present capability of adding opportunity costs to their models to convert them from quantitative to cost-value-based models. This would give them the ability to develop a System IV capability.

Human Resource Accounting System V

System V represents total human resource accounting capability. Human resource planning is based on a stochastic rewards valuation model and simulations of the effects of overall corporate plans on human resource value are performed. In the decision-making process, there is formal human capital budgeting. Return on investment is the criterion used to assess capital expenditures in human resources, just as it is used for other resources. Personnel policy decisions are based entirely on a person's expected value to the firm. Human resource conservation is controlled both before and after the fact. Ex ante, anticipated human resource depletion is measured in terms of expected conditional and realizable replacement costs. Turnover control programs are initiated when expected depletion is too high. The System V organization has a human resource accountability subsystem that charges managers with the opportunity cost of controllable human value depletion. They are expected to conserve human as well as physical and financial assets entrusted to them. The human resource evaluation process includes the measurement of the economic value of individuals per se as well as that of aggregates such as departments, plants, or divisions. Finally, the efficiency of the human resource management function is assessed not only by comparison of actual against standard costs, but also by comparison among comparable organizational units. In sum, System V represents maximal human resource accounting capability.

This system measures the economic value of people to a firm. It is extremely difficult to develop this capability because it has very stringent data requirements.

CONCLUSION AND DIAGNOSTIC REVIEW
OF BUSINESS DILEMMA_____

The purpose of this chapter was to introduce the topic of human resource accounting. We defined the concept of HRA, identified its role in the management of people in organizations, and described some methods of measuring human resource cost and value. We have also cited some examples of companies that are actually accounting for their human resources. Finally, we discussed the basic steps involved in developing a system of HRA and presented five levels of HRA systems.

From a managerial perspective, HRA has a dual purpose. It is a paradigm or way of thinking about the management of an organization's human resources; HRA emphasizes that people are valuable resources for the organization. It is also a system of providing management with the information needed to effectively and efficiently manage human resources.

The argument developed by Jayne Barker, the personnel manager of Excellent Electronics Company, falls into this perspective since she is weighing the short-term benefit of the nine-week layoff against the negative long-term impact. She is assessing the impact both on qualitative (morale) and quantitative (costs of rehiring, replacing, etc.) dimensions and she is determining the overall effect on the future earnings of the company.

During the week following the first meeting, Barker worked on a quantitative evaluation of her argument. She made the following assumptions, which were based on her previous experience rather than on a deep study because of the lack of time:

1. The greatest layoff period was twelve weeks because of the expected increase in seasonal demand in about twelve to fourteen weeks.
2. The cost of rehiring an employee is equal to one week's salary. This is the cost of getting the employee back up to normal productivity, but this is only a "guesstimate".
3. The cost of replacing one of the workers who did not return following the layoff is equal to half a year's salary. This is the cost of recruiting, selecting, and training a replacement.
4. The cost of decreased morale among employees not laid off was not considered.
5. Optimistic, most likely, and pessimistic estimates of the percentage of workers who would return after the layoff were also made. For purposes of aggregating the data, those estimates were a 10 percent chance of the optimistic condition occurring, an 80 percent chance for the most likely condition, and a 10 percent chance for the pessimistic condition.

On May 19, Barker presented her report:

> I have tried to estimate what it will cost us to start up operations again at the end of three, six, nine, and twelve weeks. I have

prepared estimates for "optimistic," "pessimistic," and "most likely" conditions as shown in my report.

See Tables 20-3, 20-4, and 20-5 for Barker's estimates.

These tables are based on estimates made by the personnel manager, Jayne Barker, from her previous experience. The lack of time explains the insufficient level of accuracy of the measurements. The key issue lies in the general paradigm that backed Barker's ideas: people are an organization's valuable resources and relevant information should be provided to efficiently manage human resources. The personnel manager tried to put this into practice in her report, which was intended to convince the firm's president, Sanford

---

TABLE 20-3

Estimated Cost of Retraining and Replacing Work Force After Layoff

Time period		Estimated percentage employees rehired	*Total retraining cost of rehires	†Total replacement cost of force lost	Total cost of layoff
	Opt.	95	$107,000	$ 139,500	$ 246,500
3 weeks	Most likely	80	$ 90,000	$ 558,000	$ 648,000
	Pess.	65	$ 73,000	$ 976,500	$1,049,500
	Opt.	90	$103,500	$ 279,000	$ 382,500
6 weeks	Most likely	75	$ 86,250	$ 697,500	$ 783,750
	Pess.	60	$ 69,000	$1,116,000	$1,185,000
	Opt.	85	$ 97,750	$ 418,500	$ 516,250
9 weeks	Most likely	70	$ 80,500	$ 837,000	$ 917,500
	Pess.	55	$ 63,250	$1,255,500	$1,318,750
	Opt.	80	$ 90,000	$ 558,000	$ 648,000
12 weeks	Most likely	65	$ 73,000	$ 976,500	$1,049,500
	Pess.	50	$ 57,500	$1,395,000	$1,452,500

*Assuming cost of retraining an employee is equal to one week's salary

†Assuming cost of replacing an employee is equal to one-half of a year's salary

TABLE 20-4

Calculation of Expected Cost of Rehiring and Replacing Work Force

Layoff period (weeks)	Optimistic		Most likely		Pessimistic		Expected cost
	Total cost	Prob.	Total cost	Prob.	Total cost	Prob.	
3	$246,500	.10	$ 648,000	.80	$1,049,500	.10	$ 648,000
6	$382,400	.10	$ 783,750	.80	$1,185,000	.10	$ 783,750
9	$516,250	.10	$ 917,500	.80	$1,318,750	.10	$ 917,500
12	$648,000	.10	$1,049,500	.80	$1,452,500	.10	$1,049,500

Harris, that alternative solutions could be found to the layoff procedure. The president, after having considered the information provided in Table 20-5, suggested reducing weekly work hours from 40 to 30 and cutting wages by about 20 percent since the expected net benefit of a layoff was not large enough to warrant implementing it.

This case illustrates the relevance of the HRA concept as a managerial tool. It also illustrates the difficulties of attempting to design methods to account for human resources. Although some progress on these problems has been made during the past decade, there is a great deal still to be done. Thus, this chapter should be viewed as a report on progress to date in developing human resource accounting.

TABLE 20-5

Comparison of Costs and Benefits of Layoff Decision

Period of layoff (weeks)	Estimated payroll savings	Estimated cost of rehiring and replacement	Net benefit (cost)
3	$ 350,000	$ 648,000	$(298,000)
6	$ 700,000	$ 783,750	$(83,750)
9	$1,050,000	$ 917,500	$ 132,500
12	$1,400,000	$1,049,500	$ 350,500

REFERENCES

[1] James C. Hekimian and Curtis H. Jones, "Put *People* on Your Balance Sheet," *Harvard Business Review* 45 (January–February 1967): 105–113.

[2] See Eric Flamholtz, *Human Resource Accounting* (San Francisco, Cal.: Jossey-Bass Publishers, 1985), especially chaps 4, 5, 9, 10, and 13.

[3] American Accounting Association Committee on Accounting for Human Resources, Report of the Committee on Human Resource Accounting, *The Accounting Review Supplement to Vol. XLVIII*, American Accounting Association 1973.

[4] For a discussion of the nature of this transformation, see Alvin Toffler, *The Third Wave*, Bantam Books, Inc., 1980. See also James Cook, "The Molting of America," *Forbes* (November 22, 1982): 161–167.

[5] Theodore Schultz, "Investment in Human Capital", *The American Economic Review* 51, no. 1 (March 1961): 3.

[6] B.F. Kiker, "The Historical Roots of the Concept of Human Capital," *Journal of Political Economy* (October 1968): 481–499.

[7] George S. Odiorne, *Personnel Policy: Issues and Practices*, (Columbus, Ohio: Charles E. Merrill Books, Inc., 1963); Rensis Likert, *New Patterns of Mangement*, (New York: McGraw-Hill Book Co., Inc., 1961).

[8] Rensis Likert, *The Human Organization: Its Management and Value*, (New York: McGraw-Hill Book Co., 1967).

[9] D.R. Scott, *Theory of Accounts*, Vol, I (New York: Henry Holt and Company, 1925), 258.

[10] William A. Paton, *Accounting Theory* (Chicago: Accounting Studies Press, 1962), 486–487.

[11] Uniroyal, Inc. *75th Annual Report—1966*, 1967, 10.

[12] Roger H. Hermanson, "Accounting for Human Assets," Occasional paper No. 14 (Bureau of Business and Economic Research, Graduate School of Business Administration, Michigan State University, East Lansing, Michigan, 1964).

[13] R.L. Brummet, E.G. Flamholtz, and W.C. Pyle, "Human Resource Measurement: A Challenge for Accountants", *The Accounting Review* (April 1968): 217–224.

[14] W.C. Pyle, "Accounting for Your People," *Innovation* no. 10, (1970): 46–54.

[15] Eric G. Flamholtz, "The Theory and Measurement of an Individual's Value to an Organization" (Unpublished Ph.D. dissertation, University of Michigan, 1969).

[16] See Flamholtz, *The Accounting Review, op. cit.* and Flamholtz, *Human Resource Accounting, op. cit.*

[17] Eric Flamholtz, "Human Resource Accounting: State of the Art and Future Prospects," *Annual Accounting Review* 1: 1979, 211–261.

[18] A thorough discussion of these methods is beyond the scope of this paper. See Flamholtz, *Human Resource Accounting, op. cit.*, especially Chapters 2, 5, 6, and 7.

[19] Hekimian and Jones, *op. cit.*

[20] See Irving Fisher, *The Nature of Capital and Income*, (London: Macmillan and Company, Ltd., 1927).

[21] Rensis Likert and David G. Bowers, "Improving the Accuracy of P/L Reports

by Estimating the Change in Dollar Value of the Human Organization", *Michigan Business Review* (March 1973): 15–24.

[22] Eric G. Flamholtz, "Assessing the Validity of a Theory of Human resource Value: A Field Study", *Empirical Research in Accounting: Selected Studies*, 1972, Supplement to vol. 10 of the *Journal of Accounting Research*, 257.

[23] R. Lee Brummet, Eric G. Flamholtz, and William C. Pyle, "Human Resource Measurement—A Challenge for Accountants", *The Accounting Review* (April 1968): 217–224.

[24] Eric Flamholtz, "A Model for Human Resource Valuation: A Stochastic Process with Service Rewards", *The Accounting Review* (April 1971): 253–267; and Flamholtz, *Human Resource Accounting*, 167–173.

[25] Roger H. Hermanson, *Accounting for Human Assets*, Occasional Paper No. 14 (East Lansing, Mich. Bureau of Business and Economic Research, Michigan State University, 1964).

[26] Baruch Lev and Aba Schwartz, "On the Use of the Economic Concept of Human Capital in Financial Statements", *The Accounting Review* (January 1971): 102–112.

[27] Harold Flanders, "The AT&T Company Manpower Laboratory, Circa 1971", *Academy of Management Proceedings*, 31st Annual Meeting (August 1971): 205–206.

DISCUSSION QUESTIONS

1. What types of strategic, managerial, and operational decisions would benefit from the consideration of human resource cost data? Human resource net present value data?
2. What types of behaviors and attitudes would be encouraged by measuring and reporting human resource accounting data?
3. Different organizations require different levels of investment in HRA systems. What are some of the determinants of the appropriate level of investment in such a system?
4. The HRA data presented by Jayne Barker to Sanford Harris at Excellent Electronics was enough to convince him of the long term negative consequences of a layoff even though the data were admittedly rough. How accurate must the data be to provide a useful perspective on decisions such as these?

CASE 20-1

The Company

James Electronics is an organization that manufactures electronic components for use in manufacturing communications, stereo, and television equipment. The firm started out as a family-owned electro-mechanical firm almost 45 years ago and had many government contracts during the war. The company has enjoyed profits that are considered very good for its industry.

Some of the employees have been with the company since it began. Many of the employees have encouraged relatives to seek employment at James. Twenty-five percent of James' employees have been with the company for twenty years or more. There was a great deal of mutual respect and loyalty between the company and the employees. James now employs 3,000 people and until two years ago, the company was managed like one very large family.

Five years ago, James was acquired by a very large organization. This organization had not made any major changes to James until two years ago, when the president of the company retired. At that time, the organization put one of its rising stars, Peter Mitchell, into the president's position.

Mitchell noted that the profits for James were very good when compared to other firms in the industry. Yet he felt that by making certain changes, he could increase profits. He knew that the parent organization would reward him with a big bonus and a prestigious promotion to the home office if he could improve profits significantly.

Many changes were instituted over the next several months. To reduce costs during the slow periods for the firm, Mitchell directed the supervisors to initiate some short-term layoffs. During the layoffs, some of the employees found other employment. Mitchell told the supervisors not to hire replacements, but to work the existing employees a little harder.

When he did this, some of the older supervisors became frustrated and took early retirement. When Mitchell found this out, he instituted an early retirement package. He knew that he could replace the $35,000 per year supervisors with fresh college graduates for $24,000 per year. To encourage early retirement, he looked for reasons to terminate some of the older employees when possible. In these cases, he saved some retirement benefit costs. In addition, many of the older employees became fearful that they were next, and some took early retirement even though they lost some of their benefits.

In one year, Mitchell had increased the profits of James by 30 percent over what the company had projected. Mitchell was given a very large bonus. Because the home office was so impressed with Mitchell's performance at James, they elected not to promote him to the home office, but to give him a large raise instead. If he could do all this in one year, they thought, just imagine how much he can accomplish in another.

The dilemma was discovered one year later when James reported its earnings information to the home office.

The Dilemma

At the meeting it was found that the company's profits had dropped dramatically and were *very* low for the industry. Expenses had increased drastically. Mitchell could not understand how this had happened when he had instituted all those cost-cutting measures that had worked so well the year before.

Mitchell went back to his office and called the controller, Deborah Ames. She told Mitchell that there were large expenses incurred to replace employees. These expenses included recruiting, training, and development costs. Turnover had increased significantly. Employee morale was down and it was going to require more than mere cost-cutting measures to improve the situation.

As a last resort, Mitchell asked Ames to do whatever she could to help the company (really him). He was given one more year to put James back on track. If he could not do it, he was out.

Required:

1. What caused the dramatic turnaround?
2. How could it have been prevented?
3. If you were in Ames's position, how would you proceed?

CASE 20-2

The Company

GFMC is a major food and beverage company in the world and is headquartered in White Plains, New York. GFMC has been around for over sixty years and has grown dramatically in the last five years. This growth is primarily from numerous major corporate acquisitions, but a small growth factor can be attributed to the introduction of new products that have been very successful.

As far as the industry goes, things are going extremely well for GFMC. Demand is at an all-time high for people who have a strong financial background at the plant level and can be used to headquarters' benefit.

Plant controllers are expected to hire a combination of three types of individuals. They are: (1) people who have MBAs and little or no experience; (2) people who have BBAs and little or no experience, but are willing to continue their education at GFMC's expense; and (3) experienced people who have an MBA or are willing to continue their education to earn an MBA.

The Chicago plant is the focal point of the beverage division, which is now "going places," thanks to the introduction of Nutra-sweet. The Chicago plant controller is expected to provide worthy candidates for promotion to New York from two to four years from the hiring date.

The Dilemma

There have been two controllers in the last six years at the Chicago plant. The controller has the final say as to whether or not candidates are hired.

During this six-year period, the company has hired at least 21 candidates who have had the potential to be promoted to New York. Also, an analyst exchange program takes place where a plant analyst goes to New York for a week while a corporate analyst comes to the plant to experience what each other's co-workers do. Normally, the plant analyst who goes to New York for the week is the next most likely candidate to be promoted to New York.

The status of these 21 candidates is:

- Two have been promoted to New York.
- One has been fired because of poor performance.
- Ten are still at the plant in various stages of "readiness" for New York.
- Eight have left GFMC for better career opportunities.
- Six of these eight candidates had gone to New York at some point in time. Note the poor showing of the Chicago controller—six of his eight most qualified New York candidates have left GFMC.

Some of the reasons the candidates have left are:

- Those who were hired with a BBA received the benefit of experience *and* full tuition reimbursement. Many left after they received their MBA's since they had no desire to transfer to New York.
- Those hired with MBAs usually received experience and then left. They, too, had no desire to be transferred to New York or the openings in New York were not worth the move to them.
- Most of the candidates who were hired with experience are still at the plant level and most signs show they will relocate to New York.

Other factors about the high turnover:

- All candidates are told at the time they are interviewed that they are expected to earn an MBA and that the possibility of transferring to New York is high. Before GFMC hires these people, the candidates agree to relocation at a later date.

- The candidates who were part of the analyst exchange program usually come back disappointed (i.e., too much "stuffiness" at headquarters).

Required:

1. What are some of the human resource costs involved in the high turnover at GFMC?
2. What can GFMC do differently to try to lower these costs?

CHAPTER 21

Social Accounting

by
Martin Freedman
Associate Professor, School of Management
State University of New York at Binghamton

DEFINITION AND SCOPE_____

Social accounting has been defined as "the ordering, measuring and analysis of the social and economic consequences of governmental and entrepreneurial behavior". Although social accounting focuses on both government and business behavior, we will concentrate on social accounting as it applies to business performance. In this respect, social accounting means identifying, measuring, and reporting on the relationship between business and its environment. The business environment includes natural resources, the community in which it operates, the people it employs, its customers, competitors, and other firms and groups with which it deals. The reporting process can be both internal and external.

Traditional accounting and economics models focus on the production and distribution of goods and services to society. Social accounting extends these models by incorporating the effects of the firm's activities on society. A paper mill, for example, not only produces pulp and paper products, but also solid waste and air and water pollution. On the other side of the ledger, the mill may contribute to the community by allowing employees time off for charitable work or by funding college scholarships for worthy students. Viewed from this perspective, social accounting can be seen as a useful approach for measuring and reporting a firm's contribution to the community.

Net profit has traditionally been considered the firm's contribution to society. Social accountants view this as too narrow a focus. They hold that to properly measure a firm's social contribution, both costs and profits should be included. As a case in point, profits may exist only because some social costs, such as water pollution, have not been included in the firm's calculation of profit.

BUSINESS DILEMMA_____

St. Clark Company, a manufacturer of pulp and paper products, has decided to use its property in Forest, Wisconsin to build a sulfite paper mill. The environment around Forest consists of rivers, lakes, and wilderness, all relatively free of pollution. Forest is a community of 20,000 independent and hardy people, many of whom are not sure if they want a paper mill nearby. The unemployment rate in Forest is 8 percent. Many of the unemployed are blue collar workers who lost their jobs when the local Ford plant shut down. These workers could be retrained and hired to work in the paper mill.

P. Bunyon, the mayor of Forest, has asked the company to present its plans to the town meeting next month. Angela Clark, the president of St. Clark, has asked Ron Money, the controller, to research the situation and present a convincing case for building the plant in Forest.

Mr. Money would like to fairly present the issue to the community because he believes that the community would benefit from the paper mill. He would like to include all the costs and benefits of building the plant, but he's not sure he can identify them or even measure the ones that he can identify.

What information should Mr. Money include in his report to the community, and how should it be presented? Will the citizens of Forest be "better off" if the paper mill is constructed? A knowledge of social accounting would help both Mr. Money and the community reach an acceptable decision.

HISTORICAL BACKGROUND

Social accounting is concerned with the identification and measurement of social benefits and social costs—concepts that are usually ignored by traditional accountants. To understand the development of social accounting, one must know how social benefits and costs have been treated in the past. For our purposes, social benefits and cost will be defined as negative and positive effects of economic development, industrialization, and technological change.

Social costs and benefits have always existed. Larry Ruff provides two examples of these phenomena:

> Spanish explorers landing in the sixteenth century noted that smoke from Indian campfires hung in the air of the Los Angeles basin, trapped by what is now called the inversion layer. Before the first century B.C., the drinking waters of Rome were being polluted.[1]

In the early 1900s, A.C. Pigou and other economists tried to include social benefits and costs in the neo-classical model of microeconomic theory. Despite their efforts, social benefits and costs were considered anomalies and were, for the most part, ignored by the majority of economists. Advances have been made, however, in the analysis, measurement, and presentation of social benefit and cost issues. Today, although outside of mainstream economic theory, environmental economics and natural resource management are viable subdisciplines within economics.

The basic accounting model (for both financial and managerial purposes) uses microeconomic theory to determine what to include or exclude from accounting calculations. Social benefits and costs, therefore, have been traditionally ignored by accounting theorists and practitioners.

Some of the mass movements of the 1960s, especially those dedicated to making government and business more responsive to society's needs, were responsible for focusing attention on social costs and benefits. Some examples follow.

The *civil rights movement,* which coalesced in the early 1960s and resulted in the passage of civil rights legislation in 1964, had a major impact on both government and business. Government was affected because voters included more people from minority groups, which made legislators more conscious of the needs of these new constituents. Furthermore, the federal government had to enforce the new laws and place itself in an adversarial position with state and local governments, especially in regard to school desegregation. Business was also affected because discrimination in hiring and promotion became illegal and affirmative action became a means of righting past wrongs.

The *women's movement* was analogous to the civil rights movement in the sense that it produced new voting pressures on government and new hiring and promotion procedures in the workplace. Because women are included in affirmative action enforcement of civil rights laws, they have been making inroads in business similar to those of minority groups.

The 1960s also saw the growth of the *environmental movement* as more people became aware of the effects of industrialization on the quality of air, water, and land. Federal and state legislation was passed to protect these natural resources and control the disposal of toxic wastes. The laws set standards for pollution emissions and imposed fines for violating them. Businesses were asked to control pollution emissions and to work with federal and state officials to develop and implement pollution reduction plans.

Consumers became more assertive in the 1960s, which resulted in the *consumer rights movements.* Spurred on by Ralph Nader and other activists, consumer groups attempted to make businesses and their products more responsive to consumers' needs. Attempts were made to have dangerous or unhealthy products rendered less harmful or taken off the market. *Caveat emptor* ("let the buyer beware") was no longer considered to be normal business practice. Numerous books on product safety and quality helped to encourage consumer rights and protection legislation.

Although there was no movement associated with the passage of *occupational safety and health* (OSHA) legislation in the early 1970s, the event had a significant impact on business. Workers' compensation laws had existed for many years, but were not effective in eliminating unsafe and unhealthy working conditions. With the passage of occupational safety and health legislation, businesses failing to meet certain standards could be fined or shut down until they complied.

By passing laws in these areas, the government forced individuals and businesses to become more responsive to social needs. Although enforcement of these laws tends to be weak, the fact that they exist and carry penalties encourages compliance. One negative result, however, has been the creation of massive bureaucracies and a mountain of paperwork.

Corporate Response

Prior to the 1960s, several companies had been considered "good citizens." They earned this reputation by producing quality products, treating workers with respect, contributing to the community, or helping the needy. Since the 1960s, many other companies not previously noted for their sensitivity to social needs became more socially responsive. Management may have realized that their firms were part of the community: that for the company to survive, the community must be a healthy place to live and work and that people need the financial security to buy the company's products. Also, being responsive to social needs was good public relations and would probably be profitable in the long run.

On the other hand, many companies and industrial associations fought to change the new federal regulations or tried to undermine them through non-compliance. In these cases, management may have felt that some of the regulations (e.g., environmental protection laws and OSHA) would have negative economic effects on their companies because the costs of compliance were not worth the benefits.

Overall, corporate acceptance of social responsibility has run a wide gamut, ranging from non-compliance with laws at one extreme to having standards higher than those required by law at the other extreme. Many firms exhibit good corporate citizenship in areas where there are no laws.

The degree of social responsibility that a corporation accepts requires an active decision. Management must decide how much pollution to emit and how much to clean up, who to hire, how much to improve working conditions, and how much to contribute to the opera. If management endorses social responsibility solely for the sake of short-run profits, it is unlikely that a company would go beyond complying with the law. Managerial philosophy is a key factor in determining a business' relationship with its community.

Response of the Accounting Profession

Although accounting academicians and practitioners had discussed how their profession could contribute to corporate social responsibility prior to the movements of the 1960s, major progress in this area was made from the late 1960s to the middle 1970s. With the passage of legislation establishing government social programs (such as Headstart and CETA), some accountants felt that they should apply their expertise to determine the programs' effectiveness.[2] Furthermore, someone needed to measure corporate responsiveness to the concerns voiced in the 1960s. Thus was born social accounting.

In the late 1960s and early 1970s many people noted the need for corporate social accounting. Robert Beyer, then managing partner of Touche Ross in New York, wrote:

> Restrictions on the use of "free" air and water are also matters of social accounting. Society is now examining costs that have always existed. Costs in terms of life and death, damaged buildings and art works, fouled beaches, ruined foliage, and all other noxious effects of pollution. The only difference is that these costs are being transferred to the extent that is feasible—from the community at large to those who cause them and benefit from them.[3]

Other articles written in this period focused on who would use social accounting data if it could be generated. What groups would use social accounting data as aids in decision making? Some authors suggested that certain investors such as church groups or universities would be interested in socially responsible companies. Others believed that social accounting data would be used by employees, community leaders, and government regulatory agencies.

In summary, the early social accounting literature stated that accountants are needed to generate data on corporate responsibility and that constituencies (other than the firm) exist that would be interested in this data. This early literature was not concerned with identifying, measuring, and reporting social data.

Subsequently, the literature developed a theoretical framework for social accounting, including reporting schemes and actual social audits. These activities will be described later in the chapter. However, the reader should be aware that despite major work in identifying and reporting social accounting data, the field is still in its infancy. Social accounting is not universally accepted as a field by academicians or practitioners, and not everyone believes that firms should be generating social accounting data. Much is still being written to justify social accounting's existence. It is therefore difficult to progress because for every two steps forward, the field must take a step backward to explain itself again.

ACCOUNTING FOR SOCIAL COSTS AND BENEFITS

The basis for much of the theory of social accounting comes from A.C. Pigou's 1948 analysis of social costs and benefits.[4] A.C. Pigou was a neo classical economist who introduced the notion of social costs and benefits to microeconomics in 1920. His critical point was that Pareto-optimality (the point in welfare economics where it is impossible to increase one person's welfare without decreasing the welfare of someone else) cannot be achieved as long as the social net product and private net product are unequal. Basically, Pigou's argument was this: A producer creates a product from which he accrues certain private benefits (which accountants term revenues). However, it is possible that society as a whole receives a benefit from the product that is even greater. For example, the smell outside a bakery or from a coffee roasting mill are social benefits. Similarly, the fact that someone is willing to pay more for a product than the producer is charging indicates a social benefit exists. Pigou termed all benefits of making a product—regardless of who received them—social benefits. The difference between social benefits and private benefits (called "unappropriated social benefits") can be divided into external economies (such as the smell from a bakery) and the consumer surplus element (the difference between the price consumers actually pay and what they are willing to pay).

A similar analysis can be made concerning costs. To Pigou, social costs consisted of all costs of making a product, regardless of who pays them. Costs paid by the producer are called private costs. The divergence between social costs and private costs (called "uncompensated social costs") can be caused by many factors. A firm that pollutes is putting a cost on society, but is not reimbursing society for that cost. This is called an external diseconomy. A situation in which a worker incurs an occupational disease for which the worker is not fully compensated can be labeled an exploitation of a factor of production.

According to Pigou, Pareto-optimality can only be achieved if marginal social benefits equal marginal social costs. The difference between Pigou's model and the traditional economic model—in which marginal revenue equals marginal cost—stems from the divergence between social and private benefits and social and private costs. If the net divergence between the two sets of costs and benefits were zero, then there would be no difference between Pigovian and traditional economic theory. There is no reason to expect that to happen.

Nevertheless, economists have treated the divergences as minor anomalies to be ignored in the basic microeconomic model.

Thus, when accountants measure private benefits (revenues) and private costs (expenses) and ignore everything else, they are being consistent with traditional economic theory. The movement toward social accounting has, for the most part, consisted of trying to include uncompensated social costs and unappropriated social benefits into the accounting model.

Theory for Social Accounting

Based on Pigou's analysis and the notion of a "social contract," K.V. Ramanathan[5] developed a theoretical framework for accounting for social costs and benefits. In Ramanathan's view, the corporation possesses an implied contract to provide net social benefits to society. Net benefits are the differences between a firm's contribution to society and the detriments it causes to society. Although he uses different language, what Ramanathan is basically saying, using Pigou's terms, is that social benefits should exceed social costs and corporations should therefore make a net contribution to society. He believes that accountants should be measuring the historical net contribution (analogous to a balance sheet) and annual net contribution of an entity to society.

There are two major problems with Ramanathan's approach. First, in order to determine net contributions to society, some type of value system has to be posited. How does the entity determine what is a contribution or a detriment to society? One person's nectar could be another person's poison. Some detriments such as pollution are universally disliked and their inclusion in an accounting statement is relatively easy to justify. However, the evaluation of other items may depend on the beliefs of management. For example, discrimination is considered a detriment, but solving the problem with quota systems may be considered a benefit by some people and a detriment by others. An argument can be made that for the sake of consistency, firms should either attempt to develop a social contribution statement based on the values of management or else have outsiders do a social audit (social audits will be discussed in another section of this chapter).

The second major problem concerns measurement. It is difficult to quantify a number of the items that would be included in a statement of net contributions to society. This causes a problem that will be discussed next.

Measurement

One of the major reasons for the slow progress of social accounting has been the difficulty in measuring contributions and detriments. This is a three-step process:

1. Determining what constitutes a social cost and benefit
2. Attempting to quantify all relevant items
3. Placing a dollar value on the final amount

Determining Social Costs and Benefits

Deciding what is a social cost and benefit is not a trivial problem. It involves not only a precise definition of social cost and benefit, but an understanding of various value systems. Pigovians would define uncompensated social costs as external diseconomies and exploitation of the factors of production. To put this definition into operational terms, it might be easier to define uncompensated social costs as all the detriments that humans suffer as a result of economic activities for which they are not fully compensated. For example, the air pollution from a paper mill having a harmful effect on the health of the people living near the mill would be a detriment. One problem that the St. Clark Company (from the example at the beginning of the chapter) will have is convincing the people of Forest that the environment, and therefore the people in Forest, will not be adversely affected by the mill. Unappropriated social benefits would be all benefits from economic activities that have accrued to people but are not fully paid for.

Obviously, a society's value system is a critical determinant of social benefits and costs. Assuming that we can overcome the value problem by using some type of community standards, our next problem is identifying specific detriments and contributions. A number of schemes for categorizing events that cause social costs and benefits to arise have been discussed in the literature. In a study of social disclosures made by large public companies, Ernst & Ernst (1978) found the disclosures were related to eight subjects: (1) environment, (2) energy, (3) fair business practice, (4) human resources, (5) community involvement, (7) products, (8) "other." A number of researchers have utilized the Ernst & Ernst model in analyzing social disclosures, but it has not yet formed a basis for an overall reporting model.

Another way to identify the origins of social costs and benefits is to examine an individual firm's production and distribution process to identify detriments and contributions and determine how they occur. If we examine one part of the production and distribution process—the point at which products are made—we may discover negative by-products being created in tandem with useful items. It is at this point in the production process that social costs such as air or water pollution are especially likely to arise, leading to uncompensated negative effects on humans.

Quantification of the Costs and Benefits

Once the activities that give rise to social costs and benefits are determined and particular detriments or contributions are identified, the effects on people can be calculated. These can be categorized as either direct or indirect. A direct effect, for example, would be black lung disease caused by inhalation of coal dust while working in a coal mine. An indirect effect would be water pollution that dirtied a stream and killed its fish. The pollution may result in a loss of a potential food source (fish), loss for recreational opportunities (fishing, swimming, boating) and negative aesthetic consequences. To measure the true detriment, the loss that people suffer as a result of these events would have to be calculated.

Although this calculation can be done in some instances, it often is difficult to do more than provide a rough estimate or a surrogate measure. In the next section we will use an example of asbestos in the workplace to show how detriments may be calculated. We will follow it with a discussion of the use of surrogate measures.

To measure a detriment, we need information about the key variables of time and effects.

Time.   Some events that produce social cost take several years to cause an effect. In the case of asbestos exposure, at a given level of dust, a worker must work about 8 years to contract asbestosis (a crippling and often fatal disease). Furthermore, it may take many years after initial exposure for people to actually be affected by the detriment. This is true whether we are discussing the effects of pollution, the misallocation of resources, occupational diseases, or numerous other events. The period of time between initial exposure to the event causing a detriment and the manifestation of an adverse impact is called the "gestation" period. In terms of measurement, it is crucial to determine the length of this period. Long-term effects should be weighted differently than short-term effects.

Effects.   People can be impacted economically, physically, psychologically and socially by various detriments. To measure the social cost it is necessary to identify these losses and quantify them.

Once these tasks have been accomplished, an attempt can be made to quantify the loss from society's perspective.

To continue with the asbestos example: asbestos workers may contract one of three crippling and often fatal diseases. In one study, 50 percent of all asbestos workers contracted one of these diseases. The detriment therefore, is the effect of the costs of contracting an asbestos-related disease less any compensation to the worker from the firm. The costs may be classified as economic loss, physical loss, psychological loss, or social loss.

Economic costs.   These costs are composed of uncompensated medical and hospital bills, lost productivity, and an income loss suffered by the worker. Obviously, double counting of the loss of income and productivity must be avoided. Furthermore, all of these expenses will occur anywhere from twenty to forty years after initial exposure to the asbestos dust, and therefore have to be discounted at an appropriate interest rate to the present.

Physical Loss. Workers contracting an asbestos-related disease will suffer from shortness of breath and the possibility of premature death. Calculating the value of human life or health is difficult to do, but often is attempted in traditional cost-benefit analysis. These losses, too, must be discounted to take the long gestation period into account.

Psychological Loss. Although many psychological maladies can occur from contracting an asbestos-related disease, we will discuss only one. The worker may feel inadequate and become despondent from: (1) losing the income-producing role in the family; (2) being unable to perform physical activity; and (3) knowing that death may be imminent. These losses are also difficult to quantify and must be discounted at an appropriate interest rate.

Social Loss. Within the worker's family, role changes may occur as a result of the disease. The family may be so traumatized that it breaks up. Numerous other negative social consequences are possible. The present value of all these effects must somehow be calculated.

The total detriment from working with asbestos would be the total of all these detriments for all workers multiplied by the probability of a worker contracting an asbestos-related disease. Obviously, this is not an easy calculation. Since it is so difficult, a number of surrogate measures have been used. For example, in the case of asbestos, the cost of cleaning an asbestos mill, including capital expenditures for new machinery and equipment, is sometimes used. The resulting figure will probably bear no relationship to the true cost of the detriment, but at least it is measurable. In the case of water or air pollution, the costs of cleaning up a body of water or of installing pollution control devices are often used.

To summarize, the difficulty of measuring the true detriment or contribution of an activity often leads us to measure what is easy to quantify and to use that number as a substitute for the true cost or benefit. Unfortunately, this calculation may not be related to the true costs, so decisions based upon it may be suboptimal. Developing better measures using both monetary and nonmonetary means of quantification is critical for the advancement of social accounting.

REPORTING OF SOCIAL PERFORMANCE

A social accounting framework has not yet been fully developed and there are serious measurement problems concerning costs and benefits. Even so, a number of authors have advocated that firms report their social accounting performance both internally and externally. Various reporting approaches have been discussed in the social accounting literature. They include social auditing, separate social reports, and social disclosure in annual reports. Each of these approaches will be discussed in this section.

Social Auditing

A social audit measures and reports the economic, social, and environmental impacts of socially oriented programs and regular company operations. There are several ways to do this. One successful strategy begins by developing an inventory of activities that have had social impacts. Although production of such an inventory sounds simple, in reality it can be quite difficult. One suggested tactic is to ask the firm's managers to make up a list of activities with social consequences. After the list is produced, the social auditor then tries to assess and measure the impacts.

Social audits benefit companies by making managers aware of the social consequences of some of their actions. This may be accomplished even if impacts cannot be quantified. Also, such audits can cause managers to try to improve their performance in social areas by developing social performance plans and performance measures based on such plans.

A social audit is similar to a financial audit in that it attempts to independently analyze a firm and assess performance. A major difference exists, however, regarding what is being analyzed. In a social audit, the auditor is examining the operations to assess a firm's social performance instead of its financial performance. It has therefore been suggested that accountants are not qualified to do such an audit on their own, but that a team of social scientists (including accountants) should be used to measure and attest to the social performance of the firm.[6]

After a social audit has been completed, the firm must decide whether to make it available to the public. Most firms consider the social audit an internal document and keep its results confidential. Some firms issue a special report highlighting its positive contributions to its constituencies, but ignoring negative effects.

ABT Associates has been one of the exceptions to this rule. For some time, this company has done social audits and made them publicly available without suffering negative repercussions. Each year, ABT has used different social auditing techniques. In 1973, for example, it surveyed its constituents to determine their social concerns, then based the relevant line items in its social report on the results of the survey. Furthermore, in each social report, ABT monetizes all line items. The ABT Associates model has not been adopted by other firms, even though it seems to have caused the company no problems.

Social Reports

Separate external reports describing the firm's relationship with the community have been issued by many U.S. and foreign firms. The U.S. firms issuing these reports include Norton Company, First National Bank of Minneapolis, and First Pennsylvania Bank. Companies' usual practice, however, is to disclose social information in the annual report to shareholders. Alternative reporting formats for presenting these social reports have been proposed by both academicians and practitioners.[7]

In this section, we will examine two theoretical approaches to developing a social report (those of Linowes and Estes) and one actual social report (First National Bank of Minneapolis), before discussing disclosures made in annual reports and developments abroad.

David Linowes developed the Socio-Economic Operating Statement for use as a basis for reporting social accounting information. Linowes divides his statement into three categories: (1) Relations with people; (2) Relations with the environment; and (3) Relations with product. In each category, he lists voluntary contributions by the firm and then subtracts from them any detriments caused by the company's activities. Linowes monetizes everything in the statement and arrives at a final balance, which he calls total socio-economic net actions for the year. In Linowes' statement, all contributions and detriments must be computed monetarily—something that we have seen is quite difficult to do. Linowes' approach has not been adopted by any firm.[8]

Ralph Estes developed a model that utilizes the Pigovian perspective on social benefits and social costs. He calculates social benefits as all contributions to society stemming from the firm's operations (e.g., employment provided, donations, taxes, environmental improvements.) Social costs include all the costs of operating the firm (e.g., raw materials purchased, loans, environmental damage, work-related injuries and illnesses). Social costs are subtracted from social benefits to arrive at a net benefit or cost. Estes considers his model a conceptual statement that can be used internally by management in assessing the firm's net benefit to society. Here, too, many of the items in the model are difficult to measure. For those that can be measured, several approaches are available and provide a wide range of results.[9]

First Minneapolis Bank has issued social reports since 1972. Its 1977 report, entitled "The Internal Social-Environmental Report," was typical and consisted of two sections: Community Investment Assets and Employee Investment Assets. For most line items in both sections, the bank disclosed its 1977 plan, its actual 1977 performance, and its 1978 plan. Line items include housing improvement loans, foundation contributions, energy conservation, career development, compensation, and health. Because the report has no overall structure analogous to either Linowes' or Estes' model, it ignores numerous other bank activities that have a social impact. Since most of the line items reflect positive bank performance, this creates an apparent bias towards benefits. For example, although employee turnover is a major problem for banks, it is not discussed. The bank's statement is voluntary, though, and it does provide more information on social activities than most institutions make available.

Disclosure in Annual Reports

Many firms issue annual reports to shareholders containing some items of social information. Ernst & Ernst did an annual survey of social disclosures made by the top 500 industrial firms in their annual reports from 1971 to 1978. It was discovered that in general, the number of firms disclosing social information and the amount of disclosure steadily increased. About 90 percent of the firms included in the 1978 report made some form of social disclosure. Since most social information disclosed by firms in annual reports is voluntary and selective, however, it can be argued that it is of questionable value and that one cannot assess the social performance of any U.S. firm based on its annual report.

Developments Abroad

European firms have taken the lead in disclosure of social information in both special reports and annual reports. A number of firms, including the Swiss firm Migros and the Fortia Group of Sweden, have issued extensive social reports. France passed a law requiring firms with large numbers of employees to report on items of employee relations. Involved in these reports are chapters on (1) employment, (2) salaries and social changes, (3) hygiene and job security, (4) other working conditions, (5) training, (6) industrial relations, and (7) other relevant social arrangements.

The European reporting model that has been adopted by a number of firms is the one developed and utilized by Deutsche Shell (German Shell Oil Company). Similar to the reports of companies from France, Deutsche Shell's report emphasizes the firm's relationship with its employees. However, it also provides information about a number of other areas dealing with corporate social responsibility.

Deutsche Shell's report contains some unusual items. In addition to the typical financial statements, there are social accounts and value added statements, both concerned with the firm's contribution to society. The social accounts statement reports on company activities impacting on the firm's important constituents, including employees, investors, the community, and the firm itself (in the sense of capital maintenance). Basically, the social accounts statement is a more extensive view of various line items already reported in the firm's other financial statements. By emphasizing the relationship of the firm to its constituents, however, Deutsche Shell's annual report adds a new dimension to financial reporting.

The value added statement is intended to describe the value increment that the firm contributes to society by producing its product or service. One part of the statement describes sources of value to the firm, including sales revenue, changes in inventory, and self-constructed assets. Another part explains how the value is distributed to the firm's constituents. Similar to the social accounts statement, the firm takes various line items from the other statements and recasts them into a value added statement.

The Deutsche Shell annual report also includes a description of the firm's goals, some of which go beyond the concern for profit and market share. These include considerations of employees' interest and regard for public concerns. The goals are divided into subgoals and activities undertaken to achieve them are discussed.

There is no comparison between the social information disclosed by Deutsche Shell and other European firms and such disclosures by American firms in their annual reports. European firms are seriously trying to use annual reports as a vehicle for disclosing some social information, but U.S. firms have not made this commitment. American firms interested in disclosing meaningful social information in their annual reports might consider using Deutsche Shell's example as a starting point.

CURRENT RESEARCH

Research in social accounting has been fairly extensive and has focused on numerous subjects ranging from development of a theoretical framework to surveying potential users of social accounting data. Current academic research, however, is primarily concerned with the usefulness of social accounting data for investors. Critics consider this current fad myopic, but it can be justified by the need to convince "mainstream" accountants of the utility of social accounting data. If it can be shown that investors will use this data as part of their information set in making investment decisions, this would be a strong justification for generating and disseminating social accounting information.

Studies concerning the usefulness of social information to investors can be divided into two main areas: (1) surveys of potential investors, and (2) empirical tests of the market effects of social accounting disclosure. Investor surveys have not produced any conclusive statement regarding the need for social accounting information. Some investors seem interested in certain aspects of social accounting information, but others are not.

Studies on the stock market reaction to disclosure of social information suggest that investors adjust expectations due to disclosure of social accounting information. No clear conclusions have emerged from research on the relationships between social performance, economic performance and social disclosure.

Research still needs to be done in the areas just discussed and in other aspects of social accounting such as determining the potential users of social accounting information (other than investors). A theoretical framework continuing in the vein of Ramanathan's (1976) pioneering work must be developed. Reporting formats should be placed into practice, and Bauer's work in social auditing should be extended.

From the standpoint of making major progress in social accounting, the most critical outstanding problem area probably is that of measurement. Theoretical, empirical and pragmatic research needs to be done on this subject. As long as people believe that social accounting attempts to describe phenomena that, for the most part cannot be measured, it will not be taken seriously as a discipline.

Diagnostic Review

We are now ready to help Mr. Money with his problem concerning the building of a paper mill in Forest, Wisconsin. Mr. Money should first make a list of all the contributions and detriments that the paper mill will provide to the citizens of Forest. He might survey the potential constituents informally as to what impacts they expect, or use a social reporting model (e.g., Estes' model) as a guide in developing the list. He will find that some of the items on the list (e.g., employment provided, taxes) are quantifiable, and some are not.

Although it may appear risky to list detriments, excluding them would be riskier. All businesses incur detriments, and it is in everybody's best interests to know the true implications of having a paper mill in town. Furthermore, because the decision as to how much pollution to emit, or how safe to make the workplace, are active management decisions, Mr. Money therefore should be able to present his firm's managerial philosophy concerning these and other detriments. Some amount of pollution is expected from pulp and paper production, and Mr. Money should disclose this expected amount and try to quantify its effects, if possible. If the effects cannot be quantified, they should at least be described.

What Mr. Money must remember is that as long as the mill's contributions exceed detriments, he will be able to sell the idea to the town. People want jobs and towns usually want increased business, so he has a potentially receptive audience. If he omits social accounting data, however, the argument in favor of the mill becomes more nebulous. People like a fair presentation that includes the quantification of both benefits and costs, to the fullest extent possible, that will lead to the best decision for all.

REFERENCES

[1] Larry Ruff, "Economic Common Sense of Pollution," in *Economics of the Environment*, R. and N. Dorfman (eds.) (New York: W.W. Norton & Co., 1972).

[2] See, for example, D. Linowes, "An Approach to Socio-Economic Accounting," *The Conference Board* (November 1972).

[3] Robert Beyer, "Pilots of Social Progress," *Management Accounting* (July 1972): 14.

[4] A.C. Pigou, *The Economics of Welfare*, 4th ed. (London: MacMillan and Co., 1948).

[5] K.V. Ramanathan, "Toward a Theory of Corporate Social Accounting," *The Accounting Review* (July 1976): 516–528.

[6] D. Linowes, "Socio-Economic Accounting," *The Journal of Accountancy* (November 1968): 37–42.

[7] In the United States, these include:
S. Dilley and J. Weygandt, "Measuring Social Responsibility: An Empirical Test," *The Journal of Accountancy* (September 1973): 62–70; R.W. Estes, "A Comprehensive Social Reporting Model," *The Federal Accountant* (December 1974): 9–19; Linowes, "An Approach to Socio-Economic Accounting"; and L. Seidler, "Dollar Values in the Social Income Statement," in *Social Accounting: Theory Issues and Cases*, L.J. and L.L. Seidler ed. (Los Angeles, Cal.: Melville Publishing Co., 1975).

[8] Linowes, "An Approach to Socio-Economic Accounting."

[9] Estes, "A Comprehensive Social Reporting Model."

[10] This case was developed based on a business law lecture given in March 1986 by Father McKalen of Loyola University of Chicago.

SUGGESTED READINGS

ABT Associates, Inc., Annual Report and Social Audit, 1973.

Anderson, J.C. and A.W. Frankle, "Voluntary Social Reporting: An Iso-Beta Portfolio Analysis," *The Accounting Review* (July 1980), pp. 467-79.

Bauer, R. and D. Fenn, Jr., "The Corporate Social Audit (New York: Russell Sage Foundation, 1972).

Buzby, S.L. and H. Falk, "A Survey of the Interest in Social Responsibility Information by Mutual Funds," Accounting, Organizations and Society (1978), pp. 191–201.

————, "Demand for Social Responsibility Information by University Investors," *The Accounting Review* (January 1979), pp. 23-27.

Ernst & Ernst, *Social Responsibility Disclosures* (Cleveland: Ernst & Ernst, 1971–1978).

Freedman, M. and A.J. Stagliano, "A Taxonomic Approach to Defining Industrial Social Costs, *Advances in Accounting,* vol. 2, 1984.

Ingram, R.W., "An Investigation of the Information Content of (Certain) Social Responsibility Disclosures," *Journal of Accounting Research,* (Autumn 1978): 270–285.

Jaggi, B., "An Analysis of Corporate Social Reporting in Germany," *International Journal of Accounting Education and Research,* 15, no. 2, 1979.

Jaggi, B., and M. Freedman, "An Analysis of the Information Content of Pollution Disclosures," *The Financial Review* (September 1982) 142–152.

Longstreth, B. and H.D. Rosenbloom, *Corporate Social Responsibility and the Institutional Investors* (New York: Praeger Publishers, 1973).

Mobley, S.C., "The Challenges of Socio-Economic Accounting," *The Accounting Review* (October 1970) 762–768.

Most, K., "Corporate Social Reporting 'Model' Report by Deutsche Shell," *The Accountant* (February 10, 1977)., pp. 164-167.

Pearce, D.W. and S.G. Sturney, "Private and Social Costs and Benefits: A Note on Terminology," *The Economic Journal* (March 1966), pp. 152-8.

Schreuder, H. "Facts and Speculations on Corporate Social Reporting in France, Germany and Holland," Working Paper, Economic and Social Institute of the Free University of Amsterdam, Amsterdam, 1978.

Shane, P.B. and B.H. Spicer, "Market Response to Environmental Information Produced Outside the Firm," *The Accounting Review* (July 1983), pp. 521-538.

Ullmann, A.A., "Data in Search of a Theory," *Academy of Management Review* (July 1985), pp. 450-557.

DISCUSSION QUESTIONS————————————————

1. What constitutes the business environment? How does it relate to social accounting?
2. What is the difference between social accounting and traditional accounting? What are some concepts used in social accounting but ignored by traditional accountants?
3. Distinguish between social costs and private costs. What parts do these play in social accounting?
4. What are two major problems encountered in using Ramanathan's framework for accounting for social costs and benefits?
5. What are the steps involved in the measurement of contributions and detriments? What is involved in the determination of social cost and benefit?
6. What are some key variables that must be taken into consideration when measuring a detriment? Why are these important?
7. How are costs quantified in the measurement of a detriment? How is this figure related to the true cost of the detriment?

8. What are some approaches used by companies to report their social performance? What kind of information is disclosed in these reports?

9. What is the most critical problem that is halting the progress in social accounting? How can this be overcome?

CASE 21-1[10]

The Company

Premier Beverage Company (PBC) is the industry leader for both carbonated soft drinks and alcoholic beverages (primarily beer). PBC has held this distinction for over forty years and is known for its promotional push to the consumers every spring/summer—so much so that most of PBC's competitors use PBC's lead to plan their promotions.

A major portion of PBC's sales and profits come from the aluminum can division for both soft drinks and beer. The theme for the soft drink division is to show younger children and teenagers/young adults playing hard and giving their "all" (at sports functions, outdoor work, etc.) The reward shown in the ads is an ice-cold can of PBC's soda. The theme for the beer division is very similar. This focus is on young to middle-aged adults who work and play hard, therefore deserving a PBC beer.

The Dilemma

The Consumer Protection Agency (CPA) has received so many calls and complaints centered around aluminum cans that it has formed a separate division to handle these cases. These complaints can be grouped into two main categories: (1) complaints about unsightly litter and (2) complaints about safety issues brought about by these littered cans.

This division of the CPA has decided to put most of its efforts into forcing PBC to be socially accountable for the litter and the safety risks their cans create (primarily children being cut by the flip-tops, hurting themselves with the cans, etc.).

The CPA is going after PBC for a variety of reasons:

1. Since PBC is the industry leader and since PBC's competition works from PBC's lead, a victory against PBC will almost assure compliance by other companies in the industry.

2. PBC could best communicate to consumers the damages of littering and the benefits of putting trash where it belongs.

3. The CPA's records show that the complaints they have received involving PBC's products are proportionally greater than PBC's sales over the last four years.

Required:

1. Theoretically speaking, should PBC (and other companies in the soft drink and beer industries) be held socially accountable for the unsightliness and/or the safety issue involving the aluminum cans?
2. For argument's sake, let's assume PBC loses. What can/should PBC do to possibly reduce some of the social costs associated with the can division of the company?
3. What are some possible ways to "account for the costs" associated with these aluminum cans?

CASE 21-2

The Company

The city of Waterloo is located on the southeastern coast of the United States. The homes in the older downtown section of Waterloo were built in the early 1800s.

In 1966, Michael Mazey founded the Historic Waterloo Foundation. The goals of the foundation are to preserve and maintain historic downtown Waterloo. The foundation got professional estimates of the tourist potential and a professional inventory of approximately 700 noteworthy buildings. The results of these estimates convinced the foundation members that they should restore as much of downtown Waterloo as possible. The foundation borrowed money, had members cosign notes, established a historic fund, and established a line of credit so that they could buy and restore buildings.

By 1976, most of downtown Waterloo was transformed from a city eyesore to a main tourist attraction. The city's tourism revenue tripled over the decade. Many members of the Historic Waterloo Foundation, as well as many of Waterloo's elite, moved into the houses of the downtown district.

The Dilemma

Of the 700 buildings that the foundation sought to restore, at least half were occupied by low-income families. When these homes were sold to the Foundation for restoration purposes, the occupants were faced with a dilemma. If the families could qualify for federal rent subsidies, they could afford the rent required by the foundation. (The foundation justified the higher rents with the costs of restoration.) If the families did not qualify for a rent subsidy, they were forced to find housing elsewhere. Approximately 60 percent of the low-income families qualified for federal assistance while 140 families, or 40 percent, did not qualify for a rent subsidy and were subsequently displaced from their homes.

Required:

1. How can the displacement of these low-income families be measured against the additional revenues generated by the restored downtown area?

2. Now that downtown Waterloo attracts high-income residents, the local small businesses have been upgraded. The low-income residents can no longer shop in their own neighborhood because they cannot afford designer boutiques and exclusive restaurants. How can this inconvenience be measured?

CASE 21-3

The Company

The company is a fairly large life insurance company located on the near north side of a major city. Over the 50 years the company has been in existence, it has been located in the same area, although it has expanded.

Over the years, the company has played a very vital role in the community—mainly in community development and rehabilitation. Although the area itself has been in decline for quite a few years, the company has been instrumental in keeping it afloat. The company sponsored neighboring church events and school programs, kept merchants afloat with the business the employees brought in, and kept most of the neighborhood employed. For its own expansion efforts, the company would buy out stores about to close, rehabilitate them, and use them for office space.

The Dilemma

Approximately five years after the president and founder died, upper management decided that it was time to, once again, consider moving out of the area. They were considering moving to a more professional looking, more marketable area (the company was in the midst of being sold) in the suburbs where the company owned a tract of land.

This move would not only destroy the community, but would also leave most of the approximately 300 clerical employees jobless. This would mean having to replace all of those people. It would also require constructing a new building on that land and selling—perhaps with some difficulty—the property already owned on the near north side. Another major obstacle was the community itself, which was trying to fight the move all the way.

Required:

1. What are the social costs and benefits of the relocation?
2. Is such a move justifiable from a cost-benefit standpoint?

CASE 21-4_____

The Company

A medium-sized, multidivisional organization allowed its plant managers a high degree of latitude in establishing company- sponsored programs. Certain fringe benefits such as health and life insurance and a pension plan were standard throughout the company, but at that point, all similarity among the divisions ended. In addition, it was company policy that the cost of all such programs be borne by that division.

The Dilemma

Plant manager A was very concerned about his workforce and the impact a layoff would have on his community. Demand for his division's product was slipping and he was predicting that layoffs may be in the offing. With the cooperation of local groups and trade schools, he began to offer after-hours instruction to his workforce to help them hone old skills and develop new ones. His intentions were simple: If no layoffs occurred, his workforce would be better trained and more loyal to the company for its efforts; if layoffs occurred, his workforce would be better able to locate other positions and could also be more willing to return, if recalled, to a company that demonstrated concern for its workforce.

The economic slowdown was not only affecting Division A, but the company at large. Increasingly stronger pressures were being brought to bear on each division manager to strengthen the bottom line. Home office management wanted these "excessive" fringe benefit costs brought under control.

Required:

1. As plant manager A, write a report to the division manager justifying your educational programs and requesting permission for their continuance.